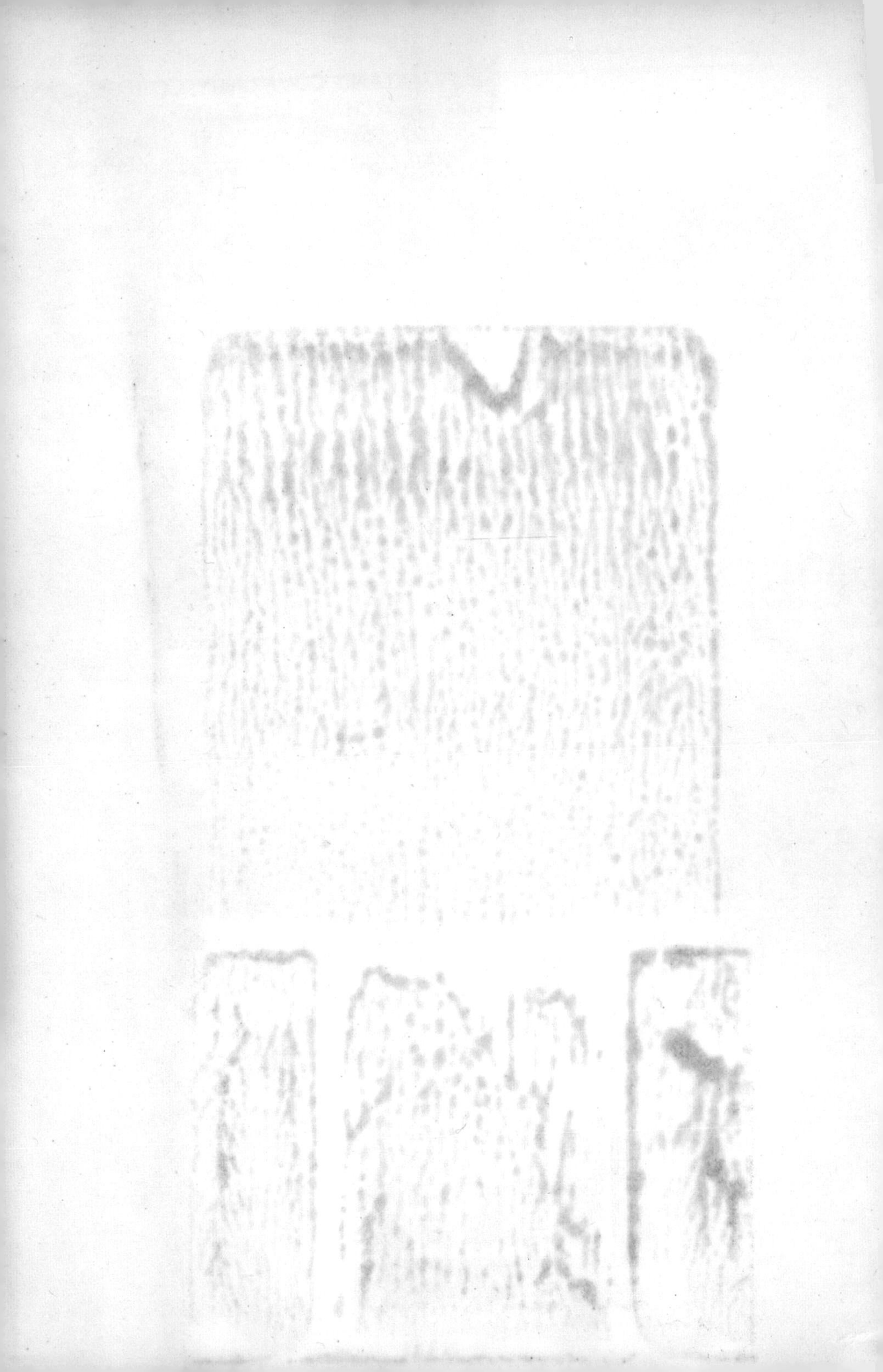

William G. McLoughlin, Jr., is Professor of History at Brown University. He received his A.M. and his Ph.D. in American Civilization from Harvard University, where he became Assistant Dean of the Graduate School of Arts and Sciences. Dr. McLoughlin studied at London University under a Fulbright Scholarship, gathering material on the revivals of Moody and Sankey in England and Scotland. He is also the author of *Billy Graham: Revivalist in a Secular Age,* published by The Ronald Press Company.

MODERN REVIVALISM

Charles Grandison Finney to Billy Graham

William G. McLoughlin, Jr.
ASSISTANT PROFESSOR OF HISTORY
BROWN UNIVERSITY

THE RONALD PRESS COMPANY • NEW YORK

2-VR

Library of Congress Catalog Card Number: 58–12959

PRINTED IN THE UNITED STATES OF AMERICA

To

Virginia

To

Virginia

Preface

History has not dealt fairly with American revivals. Their chroniclers, intent upon the colorful or the bizarre, have created a false stereotype. Their real meaning and drama have been lost in exaggerations of their eccentricities. It is a mistake to think that all revivals are orgies of mass hysteria and all revivalists are grim or theatrical prophets of hellfire and damnation. If that is all there were to revivals, they might well be dismissed as quaint or picturesque sidelights of American life. But they have been far more than that.

On the other hand, those clerical eulogists who have portrayed revivals as the most epic-making events in American history have been equally misleading. It is true that, over the years, revivals have been for a great many Americans the most important and far-reaching events in their lives. They have not only brought the individual face-to-face with the eternal questions of his nature and destiny, but they have compelled him to re-examine his personal obligations toward his family, his church, his community, and his country. They have changed men, and by changing men they have endeavored to change the world. But the world is not so easy to change.

This book is concerned with religious revivalism in the United States since 1825. It attempts to explain the part which revivalism has played, and is playing today, in the social, intellectual, and religious life of America. The aim has been, in describing the development of modern revivalism and the men who devoted their lives to it, to look below the surface phenomenon in an effort to discover why revivals have constantly recurred, what their effects have been, and what they meant not only to those directly concerned but to all Americans. If the revivals of the past century and a quarter have not always been the crucial factors in the course of American history that their devout exponents claimed, they have nevertheless been more significant than the social historians have yet acknowledged.

I would like first to acknowledge the kindness and generosity of those who not only gave me access to original papers and manuscripts, but who also offered me their hospitality and personal assistance. In this regard I am particularly indebted to Mrs. Mary R. Moody, Mrs. Emma Moody Powell, the Reverend and Mrs. Walt Holcomb, and to the late Mrs. Helen A. Sunday. Thanks are also due for crucial financial assistance received at various stages in the preparation of this book from Harvard University in the form of a traveling fellowship and from the American Philosophical Society in the form of a research grant. A Fulbright Scholarship from the United States Department of State made possible essential research abroad. The friendly advice of Dr. Robert Greaves of Bedford College, London University, and of Mrs. Frances Kelley of the Presbyterian Church Library in London was of great help during my research in the United Kingdom. The staffs of a score of libraries, great and small, have invariably proved courteous and efficient, and I wish especially to express my gratitude to the staffs of the Brown, Harvard, and Oberlin College libraries for services above and beyond the call of duty.

Once again I wish to acknowledge my indebtedness to Oscar Handlin for his wise and generous counsel. My parents gave considerable direct as well as indirect help to my labors. I have tried in the dedication of this volume to express a small measure of my deep gratitude to Virginia Ward McLoughlin for patience, understanding, and judicious critical assistance at every stage of the long way.

William G. McLoughlin, Jr.

Providence, Rhode Island
January, 1959

Contents

CHAPTER | PAGE
1 "The Church Has Been Almost Revolutionized" . 3
2 "The Laws of Mind" and "The Right Use of Means" 65
3 "Those Expert and Practical Itinerant Tacticians" 122
4 "The Right Man at the Right Hour" 166
5 "Old-Fashioned Revival with the Modern Improvements" 217
6 "The Golden Rule . . . Up to a Certain Point" . 282
7 "The American Type of Christianity" and "This Godless Social Service Nonsense" 347
8 "Christianity and Patriotism Are Synonymous" . 400
9 "Specialists in the Engineering of Mass Consent" . 455
Epilogue: "Diligent in Business" 523
Note on the Sources 531
Index 537

MODERN REVIVALISM

CHAPTER 1

"The Church Has Been Almost Revolutionized"

Perhaps the most surprising thing about revivals in America is not that they have occurred so frequently but that they have occurred so seldom. As the term is generally used, there do not appear to have been more than four or five periods of about ten years each during the three hundred years of American history when the American people as a whole have shown a demonstrably burning concern over their spiritual welfare.

The second surprising thing about religious revivals in America is that even when they have occurred and have seemed most pervasive and profound they have produced so few tangible or lasting results. Revivals in Europe, as the Reformation, the Counter-Reformation, and the Puritan movement surely were, have induced far-reaching social, political, and even economic changes. But the historian of revivalism in America is hard put to measure the effects of what are usually called revivals except in terms of increased church membership or sporadic moral reform movements.

There are, of course, certain obvious ways to account for these facts. The infrequency of revivals in America during the first two centuries after 1607 was certainly due in large part to the theological belief that revivals were divine miracles outside the power of man to institute or control. And the lack of tangible results in the social order has undoubtedly been related to the predominantly sectarian element in American

Protestantism which has from the beginning maintained a clearcut distinction between church and state. European revival movements have often been conscious rebellions against very concrete social and political privileges accorded to a state church. Hence they could not help but result in tangible changes in the social structure, either for better or worse, to the would-be reformers. But in America the zealous Christian has had little to strike against except the internal lethargy among his own group of believers or the alleged decadence of national morality. Revivalism has been perforce pre-eminently spiritual and there is a tendency to see it as little more than an internalized ecclesiastical phenomenon—a domestic broil in the house of faith.

And yet these explanations do not get at the heart of the problem. The nature of American civilization has so exacerbated the search for meaning and security which all men crave that something more is required to account for the limited and ephemeral quality of revivalism. America has been settled by people who fled from persecution, poverty, and hopelessness in the Old World to seek a better life in the New. Even the irreligious or nonreligious immigrants have been infused with the belief that America was, or could be, a new Eden. And yet this expectancy has never been fully realized. The nation's practices have never conformed to its ideals. Certainly to the pietistic Christians who made up a high proportion of the early settlers, political self-government and self-reliant prosperity have seemed as much a snare as a blessing. The expectancy of a New Jerusalem has been tinged with an anxious fear that the nation's preoccupation with material success might bring sudden judgment instead. Even the moderately religious American has continually been torn between his chauvinistic pride and his belief in Christian brotherhood, between his personal self-satisfaction and his sense of Christian humility, between the profit motive in economic competition and the altruism of Christian selflessness, between the comforts of his own high standard of living and the Christian concern for a suffering world.

These tensions have been considerably heightened by the constant atomization of American society. As a rootless nation of middle-class parvenus and self-conscious nouveaux riches, America has become increasingly restless in its industrial, urban, and suburban environment. The virtues of a free and socially mobile society have produced a gnawing sense of insecurity. Even ceaseless activity in work and leisure cannot effectively repress the desire for certainty in a country where the social structure is so fluid, where all institutions (including the family and the church) are so unstable, and where even in making the simplest decisions it is necessary to weigh the probabilities of mercurial public opinion.

Obviously the potential for revivalism has always been great in America, in fact, increasingly great. Yet neither the churches nor the revivalists have been able to make the most of it.

A more complex theory underlies the infrequency and short-lived nature of American revivalism, as it is commonly portrayed, than the theory that revivals were miracles and the fact that America has had no established national church. Fundamentally there are two reasons. One is the fact that even though church and state are technically separate the pietistic fervor of the earliest and subsequent waves of Protestant immigrants has in effect been nationalized by the irresistible tendency to equate the millennial hope of Christianity with the progress and destiny of America. The other is that in the course of time the pietistic spirit became secularized by embracing too many aspects of the eighteenth-century rationalists' enlightened faith in a brave new utopian world based on human reason and constructed by science. The pursuit of an earthly utopia destroyed the asceticism and the otherworldliness of pietism and channeled the nation's moral fervor into perennial movements for social and political reform. As the sects grew into thriving "denominations," their religious leaders became sanctifiers of national progress, and, at the same time, progress itself became embued with a moralistic quality. On the one hand John Calvin's ethic of thrift, sobriety, industry, and piety for the glory of God merged into Benjamin Franklin's success myth for the pursuit of happiness. On the other, every political election, social reform movement, and war in which Americans engaged became itself a revivalistic crusade infused with all the pietistic zeal of the war of Good against Evil.

This amalgamation of the sacred and the secular did not

come suddenly or consciously, but by 1835, as Alexis de Tocqueville perceived, it was virtually complete. The Protestant churches had lost their sectarian character and thrown in their lot with the American democratic faith. From that time on, evangelicalism became a national religion (on a voluntary basis) wedded to the individualistic ideals of Whiggism in politics and laissez-faire in economics. The churches, like the government, were reduced to the roles of umpire and samaritan in the battle for success. The average minister, whether he preached from Franklin's favorite text, "Seest thou a man diligent in business? He shall stand before kings," or from the slightly more pious text, "Seek ye first the kingdom of God and his righteousness and all these things shall be added unto you," was in either case expounding a cultural ethic. In such a situation it becomes necessary to ask why there were any revivals at all and whether those movements which have been called revivals were anything more than ritualistic reaffirmations of the tribal faith in the American dream. There was certainly an irresistible urge on the part of the leaders of every revival from 1735 to 1955 to explain the descent of the Holy Spirit into the temporal world as an indication of Jehovah's personal concern for the redemption of America in order that it might fulfill its predestined (and of course glorious) role in the divine scheme of things.

The rationalist and the skeptic had another deceptively facile explanation of mass revivalism. Individual conversions were self-induced psychological or emotional adjustments of personality conflicts. Small-scale revivals in a church or group of churches were caused by means of hypnotic manipulations and crowd psychology (consciously or unconsciously employed) by a charismatic, spell-binding preacher. Nationwide revival movements were waves of mass hysteria generated by economic, political, or social stresses which baffled and thwarted the average man. What the pietist saw as the return to health of the ailing churches, the rationalist diagnosed as the delirium of a sick social order. Both explanations were obscurantist.

Revivalism is susceptible of no simple explanation. There is no meaningful correlation, for example, between the great national awakenings in America and the great periods of political or economic crisis. Neither wars, nor depressions, nor critical elections have produced revivals. In fact, they have more often brought about a decline in religious enthusiasm. Nor is the personality, talent, or organizing ability of a revivalist a primary factor in inaugurating a revival, although it may be important in giving it expression. If great preachers and crowd psychologists could produce revivals, the life spans of a handful of revival leaders from Solomon Stoddard to Billy Graham were sufficiently long to have kept the nation in a constant state of excitement since the 1680's.

Since revivalists alone cannot manufacture revivals and since social crises do not automatically produce them, their explanation must lie in a particular combination of men and events. It becomes evident upon examination that a concatenation of four general circumstances has produced the matrix out of which each great national revival has been generated. The first of these is a grave theological reorientation within the churches (a process invariably connected with a general intellectual reorientation in American society at large). The second is an ecclesiastical conflict associated with this reorientation and in which personalities play a large part. Third is a particularly grave sense of social and spiritual cleavage both within the churches and between the churches and the world which flows from the welling up of pietistic dissatisfaction with the prevailing order. Finally there must be a feeling on the part of those outside the churches that Christianity has a particular relevance to their contemporary situation both individually and corporately.

These four developments can be summed up as the reexamination and redefinition of the nation's social and intellectual values which must take place from time to time in order to maintain a balance between tradition and change. Without such periodic reorientations and reformulations of the cultural ethos, a civilization inevitably dries up and disintegrates. The religious aspects of such transitional periods in American history have been rightly called "great awakenings." The term "revival," however (which has come to be applied to any series of spontaneous or organized meetings which produce religious conversions whether they occur in one church, a dozen churches, or in hundreds of churches under the leadership of a spectacular itinerant evangelist), does not have the same significance. Revivals and revivalism are a part of all great awakenings, but not all revivals constitute awakenings.

To put the matter more concretely, it is demonstrable that over the three hundred years since its founding, America has really had only four great awakenings, one of which is now in progress. But each of them has been national in scope and each of them has lasted about a generation. Roughly speaking the first of these extended from 1725 to 1750; the second from 1795 to 1835; the third from 1875 to 1915, and the fourth from 1945 to, perhaps, 1970. In each of these periods a theological and ecclesiastical reorientation coincided with an intellectual and social reorientation in such a way as to awaken a new interest in the Christian ethos which underlies American civilization. And in each case the awakening has produced significant alterations in the definition of that ethos and its relationship to American life.

The first great national awakening took a somewhat different form in the different sections of the colonies, but historians have agreed that it was unified. In New England, the Middle Colonies, and the South it represented the first open conflict between the pietistic spirit and the eighteenth-century enlightenment. Pietism, in its sectarian form, emphasizes the priesthood of all believers and, by elevating the laity at the expense of the clergy, it favors the congregational polity over the episcopalian. In its liturgy and theology it stresses the emotional, devotional, and ascetic qualities of religion in preferance to the intellectual, the ritualistic, and the ethical. The pietists of the first great awakening in America phrased their theological message in Calvinistic terms, but it was neither the sixteenth-century Calvinism of Geneva nor the seventeenth-century Calvinism of the Puritans. It was an evangelical Calvinism of which George Whitefield (rather than Jonathan Edwards) is rightly taken to be the prime exemplar. And it was Whitefield's itinerant revivalism which united the southern, middle and New England colonies both in theology and revival technique. Whitefield also led the battle against those church systems which were fast slipping into a sterile legalism and an arid rationalism (as the Reformed churches on the continent and the Anglican, Presbyterian, and Congregational churches both in England and America were doing). His own refusal to honor the liturgical and ecclesiastical regulations of his Anglican superiors symbolized the beginning of an anti-clerical revolution which broke the back of the established church system in New England and helped the churches of the middle and southern colonies to cut their ecclesiastical ties to the state-churches in England, Scotland, Holland, and the German states. In this respect the first awakening was a symptom of the acculturation of the immigrant churches, an ecclesiastical declaration of independence from the Old World. But more important, to paraphrase Tocqueville, it brought into being a new system of religion for a New World, a religion that was sectarian and (comparatively) democratic in polity, puritanical in morality, and pietistically evangelical in theology.

But old systems die slowly and religious fervor burns quickly. One generation and one awakening did not suffice to complete the revolution. In New England the semi-established system lingered even when the New Lights gained control of it, and in the middle and southern colonies the New Side Presbyterians, the German and Dutch Reformed churches, and the Methodists compromised their victory by maintaining the Old World ecclesiasticism on a slightly less formal basis. Among many of the better educated, and not a few of the uneducated, neo-Calvinism failed completely, and deism temporarily gained a foothold from the Vermont frontier to Unitarian Boston and from Transylvania to nominally Anglican Virginia. Social pretensions separated the lower from the better orders in the churches and a learned clergy still dominated an uneducated laity. Most important, the theology of the first awakening failed to complete the reorientation from Calvinism to evangelicalism which was implicit in the preaching of the revivalists.

The second great national awakening, which began in the camp meetings of Kentucky and Tennessee, therefore had to wage part of the same battle over again. But there was no doubt that the awakening from 1795 to 1835 was as much of a piece as the various phases of the first awakening. This was evident not only in the steady advance of theology from neo-Calvinism to outright Arminianism but also in the steady revision of the concept and purpose of the ministerial office from that of pastor to that of soul-winner. The intellectual and social reorientation which historians have traced in the ages of Jeffersonian and Jacksonian democracy clearly paralleled these ecclesiastical and theological transitions. From the first camp meetings through the Cumberland schisms, the disestablishment of Congregationalism, the formulation of the New Haven theology, and the revivals of the burnt-over district, to the anticlimactic schism of Old School and New School in 1837, the line runs without a break. The pattern of emerging evangelicalism and the formation of a national religion and a revivalistic clergy are traced below in some detail.

Of the three phases of the third great awakening following the Civil War, it is only necessary to state here that the revivalism of Dwight L. Moody and Billy Sunday was merely one aspect of the theological revolution which produced liberal Protestantism, the social gospel movement, and the Federal Council of Churches. Moody's revivals in the 1870's were the opening and half-unconscious battle of the modernist-fundamentalist schism. Theistic evolution, progressive orthodoxy, "the new theology," and the higher criticism were significant elements in the same reorientation. By 1915, the modernists were assuming control of the denominations and the seminaries while the fundamentalists rallied vainly around the revivalism of Billy Sunday. The ecclesiastical fireworks of the 1920's, like the schism of 1837, were pure anticlimax.

It is too early to date clearly the fourth great awakening. But certainly it was well under way in 1945 when neo-orthodoxy and neo-fundamentalism began seriously to challenge the prevailing ideology of liberal Protestantism. Whether Billy Graham's revivalism is a climactic phase of this awakening or the opening of a new phase in the reorientation, it is apparent that he did not start it and that he will not finish it. The revolution is far broader than his work encompasses. Moreover, the history of revivalism indicates that mass meetings of the sort conducted by Graham have played a steadily decreasing role in America's religious awakenings. In the first awakening the role of the revivalists was of primary importance. In the second it was central but not dominant. In the third and fourth it was almost peripheral to the deeper issues at stake.

It was in the second great awakening that "modern revivalism" began, and modern revivalism (or professional mass evangelism) seriously altered the position of the revival preacher as a significant leader in the life of American Protestantism. The reasons for this constitute the bulk of the discussion which follows. And the natural starting point of such a discussion is the career of Charles Grandison Finney, who, in the years 1825–1835, created modern revivalism. He did so for the better advancement of the pietistic ideals of evangelical Protestantism. He built not wisely but too well.

When Charles Grandison Finney left his law office in 1821 to devote his life to saving souls, he inaugurated a new era in American revivalism. He not only developed new techniques for promoting conversions and a new style for pulpit oratory, but he transformed the whole philosophy and process of evangelism. In certain respects he must share his contribution with the doctrinal innovations of Nathaniel W. Taylor and the entrepreneurial skills of Lyman Beecher, but it is not to either of these men that professional evangelism traces its origin. They cleared the ground for modern revivalism, but Finney laid the foundation.

The essence of the old revival tradition can be seen in Jonathan Edwards' almost incredulous wonderment in 1735 at the "surprising work of God" which brought about "the conversion of many hundred souls in Northampton" in the opening phase of the First Great Awakening.[1] Exactly one hundred years later Charles Finney wrote quite matter of factly after the stirring awakenings in which he had participated from 1825 to 1835 that a revival "is not a miracle, or dependent on a miracle in any sense. It is a purely philosophical result of the right use of the constituted means."[2] The difference between Edwards and Finney is essentially the difference between the medieval and the modern temper. One saw God as the center of the universe, the other saw man. One believed that revivals were "prayed down" and the other that they were "worked up."

[1] See Sidney E. Mead, "Denominationalism: The Shape of Protestantism in America," *Church History,* XXIII (December, 1954), 307. For further discussion of the difference between Finney and Edwards on this point see chap. 2, note 37.

[2] Charles G. Finney, *Lectures on Revivals* (New York, 1835), p. 12.

The Calvinistic, or neo-Calvinistic, theology of Edwards and the other leading figures of the first great awakening not only maintained the old theocentric concept of the universe but also the doctrine that salvation was granted to the elect only by the arbitrary and sovereign grace of God. But the boost which the American and French Revolutions gave to the rationalistic ideals of the Enlightenment, particularly to the belief in the dignity of man and the benevolence of nature and of nature's God, seriously undermined the hold of the pessimistic doctrines of Calvinism upon the average American. In the opening phase of the second great awakening, associated primarily with the boisterous camp meetings of Kentucky and Tennessee from 1795 to 1810, the optimistic free-will theology of Methodist Arminianism was preached side by side with the Calvinistic predestination of the Presbyterians and Baptists. Yet these camp meeting exhorters were so intent upon saving souls that they were not particular about the fine points of theology and the two views began to run together. Moreover, though the intense emotionalism of the camp meetings masked the fact, it was evident after 1800 that the element of surprise was fast disappearing from revivalism. In its place appeared the carefully organized and pragmatically contrived techniques which Finney was to consolidate into modern mass evangelism.[3]

The second phase of the second awakening, from 1810 to 1825, saw Calvinism undermined in a far more subtle way by the learned theological speculations of Timothy Dwight, Lyman Beecher, and Nathaniel W. Taylor, who carefully reinterpreted the old dogma to suit the new intellectual climate. These years also saw the final breakdown of the established church system in New England, a fact which greatly heightened the interest of the Congregational clergy in the promotion of a more modern type of revivalism.

Finney's career and writings in the years 1825 to 1835 constituted the third and final phase of the second great awakening. He helped to knock the last props from under the old

[3] For descriptions of how camp meeting revivalism become a carefully organized means of recruiting church members among the Methodists see Charles A. Johnson, *Frontier Camp Meeting* (Dallas, 1955) and Elizabeth K. Nottingham, *Methodism and the Frontier* (New York, 1941). In this and the succeeding chapter I am concerned with similar developments among the Congregationalists and Presbyterians.

Calvinist system and to establish in its place the Arminianized Calvinism called evangelicalism. In the process he firmly established a coherent rationale for the new tradition of worked-up revivals and securely harnessed the spontaneous, ecclesiastically schismatic force of frontier revivalism to the institutionalized church system in America's rapidly expanding western towns and eastern cities. His work did much to stabilize and unify American evangelical Protestantism and to transform it into a national religion without destroying its zeal for soul winning or its independent denominationalism. He provided a simple, almost mechanical, outlet for Protestantism's pietistic fervor and an efficient method for its growth and renewal. But by institutionalizing revivalism he also helped, quite unwittingly and contrary to his intentions, to push evangelical Protestantism toward those inherent weaknesses of any national religion: a propensity for empty formalism, bland uniformity, social conformity, and political conservatism.[4]

Finney's contemporaries, however, were slow to recognize the important part which he was playing in the reorientation of the nation's religious thought and practice. In the 1820's, Lyman Beecher and Nathaniel W. Taylor were considered the leading figures in the attempt "to introduce a radically new system of religion" called the New Haven Theology or "the New Divinity" into the closely affiliated and nationally predominant Presbyterian and Congregational churches.[5] When the rash and rustic young Finney appeared on the scene in 1825, Beecher and Taylor did not consider him a particularly useful ally in their strenuous, but cautiously waged, revolution against "hyper-Calvinism." In fact, they disapproved of Finney's work in its initial stages and apprehensively tried to dissociate themselves from him.[6]

[4] For a brief general statement of the developments in American Protestantism of which I take Finney to be the culmination, see Sidney E. Mead, "The Rise of the Evangelical Conception of the Ministry in America, 1607–1850," in *The Ministry in Historical Perspective,* eds. H. R. Niebuhr and D. D. Williams, (New York, 1956), pp. 207–49.

[5] Quoted from *Biblical Repertory and Theological Review* (Presbyterian, Philadelphia), n.s. IV (April, 1832), 301.

[6] For the best analysis of the work of Taylor and Beecher in developing and spreading "the New Divinity" (sometimes called Taylorism or Beecherism) see Sidney E. Mead, *Nathaniel W. Taylor* (Chicago, 1942).

By 1835, however, the conservative opponents of Beecher and Taylor were identifying Finney as the man who "takes the lead in the prevalent system of disorganization" in the churches.[7] In that year he was also recognized as an equal member of the revolutionary triumvirate by Beecher himself when Beecher, on trial for his theological life before the Synod of Cincinnati, told the assembled judicatory that he had heard more truth from Finney than from any other man in the same space of time: "I have felt the beatings of his great, warm heart before God." [8]

By 1838 many felt that Finney's role in the religious reorientation of the period had been primary. "Mr. Finney of all others," said the editor of conservative Congregationalist *Literary and Theological Review,* "has taught the New-Haven theology in its greatest purity and has ventured to push its principles to their legitimate results." [9] "Who is not aware," asked this editor in an article discussing Finney's revivals, "that the Church has been almost revolutionized within four or five years by means of such excitements?" As an opponent of the revolution, the editor was not merely lamenting the emotional excesses of revivalism and the "false converts" which he claimed it produced in such vast numbers. The problem went deeper than that. There are now, he said, "two parties" within the churches "who, with opposing sentiments on fundamental points can never be united," and "We see the most conclusive evidence that there is a settled policy to make these excitements an engine for party purposes." [10]

[7] *Literary and Theological Review* (Congregationalist, Andover, Massachusetts), II (December, 1835), 705.

[8] "The Trial of Dr. Beecher for Heresy," *The Christian Examiner and General Review* (Unitarian, Boston), XIX (September, 1835), 116 ff. See also *Biblical Repertory and Theological Review,* n.s. VII (October, 1835), 659 n.

[9] *Literary and Theological Review,* V (March, 1838), 70 n. Due allowance ought to be made for the editor's desire to tar the New Haven school with the brush of western revival extremism, but the statement was not without truth. The editor was Charles D. Pigeon.

[10] "Thoughts on the New-Haven Theology," *ibid.,* 158. Two years before this, the Rev. Leonard Woods, then editor of the *Literary and Theological Review* and Professor of Theology at Andover Theological Seminary, wrote to the Rev. W. S. Plumer on February 8, 1836, denouncing the "notions" which are peculiar to Dr. Taylor and Mr. Finney" and stating his belief that "there is a perfect understanding among those in every part of the country who are opposed to Calvinism and that they are acting in concert" to overthrow it. Quoted

The editor referred to the growing discord among New England Congregationalists and to the violent schism which had taken place in the Presbyterian church in 1837. In this schism, which divided the Presbyterians, the most prominent denomination in the nation, into two almost equal parts, the conservatives not only exscinded four-ninths of the churches and ministers, but they also abrogated the Plan of Union which for thirty-six years had coordinated the religious activities of the Congregationalists and the Presbyterians. The anti-new divinity, or "Old-School," Presbyterians and the anti-new divinity, or Hopkinsian, Congregationalists felt that excision and abrogation were forced upon them as the last line of defense against a "dark conspiracy" to subvert the Calvinistic purity of their churches. Finney's role in this "plot" was considered central if not dominating.[11] That an uneducated backwoods preacher, unheard of in 1825, should within a decade have become nationally recognized as one of the foremost religious forces of his time indicated, however, that far more was afoot than a mere party feud within the Presbyterian and Congregational churches.

Charles Grandison Finney was born in Warren, Connecticut, in 1792. Two years later his family joined that sizeable portion of Americans, and especially of New Englanders, who were moving westward. Finney spent his boyhood in Oneida County in central New York and his adolescence on the shore of Lake Ontario. From 1808 to 1812 he taught in a district school, and then his family sent him back east to complete his education. Finney claimed that after completing two years at a Connecticut academy he was dissuaded from entering Yale by his tutor who told him that he was bright enough to educate himself in less time and at less expense.[12]

---

in E. H. Gillett, *History of the Presbyterian Church in the U.S.A.* (Philadelphia, 1864), Vol. II, p. 458.

[11] In writing his personal account of the history of the schism of 1837, Samuel J. Baird devoted a chapter to Finney's role. The chapter opened with the words, "The Reverend Charles G. Finney was the first preacher who adequately attempted to employ the theology of New Haven in its practical relation." Samuel J. Baird, *A History of the New School* (Philadelphia, 1868), p. 217.

[12] The primary source for biographical facts is Finney's *Memoirs* (New York, 1876). Necessary corrections and additions are contained in George F. Wright, *Charles Grandison Finney* (New York, 1891); Robert S. Fletcher, *A History of*

From 1814 to 1816 he taught school in New Jersey and then, at his parents' request, returned home. In 1818 he entered the law office of Judge Benjamin Wright in Adams, New York, a small town sixty-five miles northwest of Utica. Here he successfully completed his study for the bar and began to practice as "Squire" Wright's assistant. At the time of his conversion, he was well on the way to a profitable legal career.

Finney's story of his conversion experience is one of the classics of American religious folklore. Though he had attended church regularly while at school in Connecticut and though he had led the choir and faithfully attended the Presbyterian church services and prayer meetings in Adams for three years, Finney later claimed that he was "almost as ignorant of religion as a heathen" until he began to study Mosaic law in connection with his legal work. Finally one Sunday night in the fall of 1821, the repeated prayers of his fiancee and the insistent solicitations of his pastor and church friends compelled him, he said, to try to "settle the question of my soul's salvation at once." [13]

For three days he struggled with his conscience, wondering whether he had committed the unpardonable sin and overwhelmed with the feeling that if he were suddenly to die he would immediately "sink down to hell." On Wednesday evening, October 10, after a morning spent on his knees in prayer in the woods, he was sitting alone in "Squire" Wright's darkened law office earnestly seeking for spiritual guidance when all at once, he said, "My heart seemed to be liquid fire within me. All my feelings seemed to rise and flow out. . . ." The room suddenly appeared brilliantly lighted, and "it seemed as if I met the Lord Jesus Christ face to face." Finney fell on his knees in tears before the vision, poured out his confession of faith, and "received a mighty baptism of the Holy Ghost" which "like a wave of electricity going through and through me . . . seemed to come in waves of liquid love."

The next morning Finney made his famous statement to a deacon of his church for whom he was to plead a case that day: "Deacon, I have a retainer from the Lord Jesus Christ to plead

Oberlin College, 2 vols. (Oberlin, Ohio, 1943); and Whitney R. Cross, *The Burned-over District* (Ithaca, New York, 1950).

[13] Finney's account of this conversion is contained in his *Memoirs,* pp. 12 ff.

his cause and I cannot plead yours." And thereupon, said Finney, "I . . . sallied forth from the office to converse with those I should meet about their souls" convinced "that God wanted me to preach the Gospel." At the age of twenty-nine, Finney abandoned his legal career to devote the remaining years of his life to revivalism and theology.

Finney was six feet two inches tall, slim, blond, blue-eyed, and handsome. His piercing eyes stared out from their deep sockets with frightening intensity, and when he spoke from the pulpit, guilt-ridden auditors quailed and fainted under his gaze. But his smile was quick, his lips full and firm, his features mobile and yet austere. There were heavy lines between his brows which deepened with age and his strong nose grew more hawk-like, but his poise and self-assurance never altered. In the years of his greatest popularity, from 1825 to 1835, his face was smooth shaven, but in the 1840's he succumbed to the fashion for frizzled side-whiskers and in old age he grew a short but full white beard.

Finney's compelling appearance was re-enforced by a marvelous stage presence, a mellow, wide-ranging voice, and a dramatic talent that made him one of the best pulpit actors of his day. He put his whole body into his preaching and in his early years writhed, gesticulated, and groaned so in the pulpit that unfriendly observers thought him coarse, crazy, or hypocritical.[14] Most of his auditors, however, especially in western New York, found him solemn, "pungent," inspiring, and usually overpowering. For a decade he was the most sought-after preacher in the United States, and thereafter until the day of his death in 1875, he was considered the national dean of evangelists.

There was a mystical element in Finney's make-up which explained to those who knew him many of his later eccentricities. In the weeks after his conversion he practiced excessive fasting and spent whole days in concentrated prayer "without ceasing." He startled some of his friends by describing his visions of bright light, like that which "prostrated Paul on his way to Damascus." Obtaining little sympathy or encouragement on this score from his "surprised" and "incredulous" confidants, Finney said, "I soon learned to keep quiet in regard

14 See the descriptions by contemporaries quoted in Fletcher, *Oberlin*, Vol. I, p. 16.

to these divine manifestations." Until his death, however, he retained the feeling of intimacy with the supernatural. He firmly believed that God, the Holy Spirit, Christ, and the Devil were concrete personalities fighting for or against him in his daily battle for souls. Sometimes the Devil would try to kill him by frightening his normally tame horse. At other times God would let loose an "awful stroke of divine indignation" and kill one of his opponents.[15] Finney usually succeeded in making this daily spiritual warfare as real to his listeners as it was to him.

His first task as a potential revivalist in 1821 was to learn something about the Bible and the theology of his church. Finney, like most New England Congregationalists in western New York, had attended a Presbyterian church because, through the Plan of Union of 1801, the two denominations had virtually amalgamated in the West. Although under the plan the Congregational system was permissible, most settlers felt that Presbyterian polity was better suited to frontier conditions. The intermingling of New England and Scotch or Scotch-Irish Calvinism in what came to be called "Presbygational" or "Plan of Union" churches was the root of much of the difficulty which Finney was to encounter later. But in 1821 it never occurred to him to do otherwise than prepare himself to be a Presbyterian minister. In order to learn enough theology to pass an examination before the local presbytery, he studied for two years with his pastor, the Rev. George Gale, who had learned his Calvinism at Princeton Seminary. While studying, Finney also preached in the vicinity and converted many of his friends and neighbors. With Gale's help he succeeded in obtaining a license to preach from the St. Lawrence Presbytery on December 30, 1823. Six months later he passed the ordination examination, and a year later he was admitted to membership in the Oneida Presbytery.[16]

At his ordination Finney was required to affirm his belief in the Westminster Confession of Faith. This statement of Calvinism had been the creedal basis of both Presbyterian and

[15] Finney, *Memoirs,* pp. 34–5, 228, 166.

[16] Finney is vague on these dates in his *Memoirs,* but see P. H. Fowler, *Historical Sketch of Presbyterianism within the Bounds of the Synod of Central New York* (Utica, 1877), p. 258.

Congregational churches since its promulgation in 1647. It was largely on the basis of this unity of creed that the two denominations had merged on the frontier in 1801. In theory Finney's orthodoxy depended upon his rigid adherence to this creed. But as everyone knew, various theologians had been reinterpreting the Confession ever since its adoption. When Finney began to preach in 1824 there were at least half a dozen ways of interpreting it, all of which claimed to be within the bounds of orthodoxy. The New England theologians in particular had offered widely variant views of the Confession over the years and the lack of a central hierarchy or ecclesiastical judicatory within Congregationalism which could judge and expel heretics had permitted this latitudinarian process to go unchecked. New England men designated their orthodoxy not by reference to the Confession but by reference to one or another of their esteemed local interpreters of Calvinism. They quibbled endlessly over whether Jonathan Edwards, Samuel Hopkins, Joseph Bellamy, Nathaniel Emmons, or Timothy Dwight was more correct in his interpretation of abstruse points of Calvinist doctrine. The doctrines had not, of course, seemed abstruse when New England was founded, but they became increasingly so thereafter.

Unfortunately for the cause of orthodoxy, in 1824 neither Finney nor most other ordinary New Englanders east or west of the Alleghenies understood all the subtleties of these reinterpretations. What was more important, they were beginning to wonder whether any of them made sense. Hopkinsianism was the most widely accepted version of Calvinism among New Englanders at that time, and Finney once summed up its "two great points" as they "were understood to be" by the average churchgoer in western New York: "that man ought to be willing to be damned for the glory of God and that God was the author of sin." [17]

[17] Finney, *Memoirs,* p. 241. This was of course a grossly inadequate view of Hopkinsianism. Finney always exaggerated the "hyper-Calvinism" of his opponents. Most Hopkinsians had given up the doctrine of a limited atonement for the concept of a general atonement and many of them were willing and anxious to promote revivalism provided it was clearly stipulated that sinners must have a new principle infused by the Holy Spirit before they could be regenerated. Finney's own theological views contained more of Hopkins's ideas than he ever acknowledged. See below, chapter 2.

The Presbyterians, whose intellectual and ecclesiastical life centered in the region around Princeton and Philadelphia, did not particularly care for the Hopkinsian view of Calvinism either as it was in fact or as it was commonly understood to be.[18] They claimed to have stayed much closer to the literal meaning of the Westminster Confession than the New Englanders because in their church the presbyteries, synods, and General Assembly could, and did, try for heresy any persons suspected of deviating from the standards. The nub of the quarrel which was to arise over Finney's views and those of the new divinity or New Haven theology after 1824 lay in the fact that the Presbygationalists of the West were not as strict in their Calvinism as the Presbyterians of the middle and southern states, and they were fast drifting away from the Hopkinsianism of New England. But it is doubtful whether many of the churchgoers who called themselves Presbyterians in 1824 understood the intricacies of the Westminster Confession any better than the Congregationalists understood Hopkinsianism. Finney summarized what he and the average Westerner took to be the orthodox Presbyterian view of Calvinism this way: it maintained that all men "are justly sentenced and exposed to eternal damnation for Adam's sin" and are "by natural generation . . . wholly sinful" so that they are "totally unable to perform any act acceptable to God"; but because Christ came to earth "as an embodiment of all the sins and guilt of the elect" and "fully discharged" their "debt" by his death, the elect "are saved" if they will "repent" and believe; the act of salvation or "regeneration" of the elect consisted "in a change of nature" effected by "the influence of the Holy Spirit" and this influence was "physical and not moral." [19]

The end result of both New England Hopkinsianism and Princetonian Calvinism, as far as Finney and the inhabitants of western New York were concerned, was that God demanded obedience to his laws by all men even though all men were so depraved that only the miraculous act of conversion by the Holy Ghost could make it possible for them to obey. And those who

[18] For a discussion of the quarrels within the Presbyterian Church over Hopkinsian errors in the years 1810–1817 see Gillett, *History of Presbyterian Church,* Vol. II, pp. 213–30.

[19] Finney, *Memoirs,* pp. 57–59.

were not among the predestined elect would never be regenerated by the Holy Spirit and hence were doomed to hell. Most pious New Englanders nourished the secret hope that they were among those whom God had arbitrarily elected to be saved, and they expected some day to feel the power of the Holy Spirit descending upon them to implement their regeneration. But they were told by their ministers that there was nothing they could do to bring this event to pass except to repent and pray and wait. Meanwhile they lived in daily fear that if they suddenly met with death through sickness or accident they would certainly go to hell. Some New England theologians, like Nathaniel Emmons, went so far as to say that because unregenerate men did not know whether they were among the elect or not they should not even pray for salvation, for if they were among the reprobate their prayers were really a mockery and a blasphemy.

A popular jingle of Finney's day summed up the average man's jaundiced view of the frustrating and apparently contradictory tenets of Calvinism regarding man's part in conversion:

> You can and you can't;
> You will and you won't;
> You're damned if you do,
> And damned if you don't.[20]

Nevertheless this anxiety-ridden theology was accepted as the faith of their fathers and New Englanders were reluctant to give it up. When the first generation of Yankee settlers came west to New York and Ohio after 1790, they carried their faith with them and passed it on to their children in the same school primers containing the Shorter Westminster Catechism which they had used back east.

The second generation, to which Finney belonged, attained manhood in a more settled, prosperous, and confident atmosphere than their parents had faced. Their faith in man's ability to solve life's problems by himself, and their growing optimism about the future, made the pessimistic religion which their parents had found strangely satisfying seem singularly unattractive and unreasonable. They therefore listened boldly

[20] For variant versions of this rhyme see Charles G. Finney, *Sermons on Various Subjects* (New York, 1835), p. 71, and *Biblical Repertory and Theological Review,* n.s. VII (July, 1835), 516.

to the rationalistic arguments of deists and skeptics or to the more sanguine theologies of Universalism and Methodism and found in them much that "made sense." [21] When Americans began to require, as they did after 1800, that theology justify itself before the common sense of the average man, the mysterious and miraculous qualities of religion were on the way out. Respect for tradition and for clerical authority tended to slow down this process in the East, and the exciting, inexplicable hysteria of the camp meetings served to maintain something of the awesomeness of religion among the less well-educated settlers of the Southwest. But the Yankees of western New York and Ohio were neither so tradition bound as the easterners nor so ignorant as the southerners.

The camp meeting revivalism of the Methodists, Campbellites, Stoneites, Cumberland Presbyterians, and Baptists which swept the southwestern frontier after 1798 did not spread northward into New York and Ohio with anything like its original force. In part this can be accounted for by the more unsettled condition of the northern frontier before 1824 and in part by the determined opposition of the Presbyterian and Congregational ministers to both the theology and the emotionalism of the camp meetings. But equally important was the respect for learning and for social position which the New Englanders retained even on the frontier. The western Yankees were not without snobbery and their failure to be as impressed with camp meeting preachers as the southerners can be attributed in part to the lingering social prejudice of New England Congregationalists who equated all other sects (except the Presbyterian) with the lower classes, the ignorant, and the unstable.[22]

Finney, for example, usually designated all Methodist, Bap-

[21] Typical of many complaints by conservative Calvinists against the religious innovations demanded by the younger generation of Finney's day was that of the Rev. Daniel Dana of Newburyport, Massachusetts, who wrote in 1832 in opposition to Finney's revivalism, "Does not a disposition prevail to depart from the simplicity of gospel truth; to fritter away its substance; to soften down its harsher lineaments and to give it a form and features less offensive to the fastidious taste of the age? Do not many . . . make reason the final umpire in matters of religion? . . . While the enterprising spirit of the age is accomplishing such wonders in art, and even in science, numbers seem to anticipate corresponding improvements in theology." In William B. Sprague, *Lectures on Revivals of Religion* (Albany, 1832), appendix, pp. 17–18.

[22] For a detailed discussion of the New England heritage of western New York see Cross, *Burned-over District, passim.*

tist, Campbellite, and other non-Presbyterian preachers in the West as "ignorant exhorters." In his *Memoirs* he described the amusement with which the people in his home town in New York listened to itinerant preachers: "The people would return from the meeting and spend a considerable time in irrepressible laughter at the strange mistakes which had been made and the absurdities which had been advanced." [23]

Most young men who grew up in western New York in Finney's day went to church or attended religious meetings when they were available, but like Finney they attended from a sense of duty or for social intercourse. Unable to believe the teaching of their catechism or of their preachers and unwilling to accept the camp meeting religion of the lowly Methodists and Baptists, they lived in doubt and anxiety. Like Finney, most of them suffered the guilt pangs of disobedient children while their mothers, wives, or sweethearts prayed nightly for their souls.

Finney seems to have effected his conversion, when the pressures got too great, by a combination of determined will power and a mystical strain of mind. The force of the experience pushed him into the ministry, and he finally had to come to terms with the creed of Calvinism. Though it hardly seems possible, Finney later claimed that at the time he was licensed to preach he had not read the Westminster Confession. He affirmed his belief in it, he said, assuming that it was merely a summary of what he had been studying with George Gale.[24]

Shortly thereafter Finney obtained a copy of the Confession and was shocked to find that it categorically defended the most rigid interpretation of Calvinism as it was portrayed *in terrorem* by the Universalists and deists. What was even worse, he found that the Biblical text proofs quoted in the Confession did not to his mind sustain it at all. "I was absolutely ashamed of it," he wrote. "I could not feel any respect for a document that would undertake to impose on mankind such dogmas as those,

[23] Finney, *Memoirs,* pp. 4–5.

[24] There were apparently some presbyteries in western New York which, in their effort to overcome the shortage of ministers, took very lightly the affirmation of the Westminster Confession by licentiates in this period. But this does not explain why a Princeton graduate like George Gale would omit any study of it in preparing a candidate for the ministry. See Gillett, *History of Presbyterian Church,* Vol. II, pp. 467, 482.

sustained for the most part by passages of Scripture that were totally irrelevant and not in a single instance sustained by passages which, in a court of law, would have been considered at all conclusive." [25]

He went to Gale for proof of the creed and found that Gale had no proof that would be sustained in a court of law. Gale told him that he would have to stop trying to have his "intelligence satisfied" and rely upon "the opinions of great and good men" and the authority of the church for the truth of the creed. Finney rebelled: "I could not be honest in doing it," he wrote. "I could not respect myself. . . ."

His own conversion experience justified his belief in God. Now he turned to the inspired word of God and the use of his God-given intelligence to find out for himself what the true doctrines of the Bible were. With the typical American combination of sectarian piety and eighteenth-century rationalism he explained, "I had nowhere to go but directly to the Bible and the philosophy or workings of my own mind." Never doubting that the Bible contained the revealed word of God, he assumed, with the self-reliant optimism of his age, that "Reason was given us for the very purpose of enabling us to justify the ways of God" to man. As he puzzled over the Bible, he said, "I gradually formed views of my own . . . which appeared to me to be unequivocally taught in the Bible." These views, however, were not the accepted views of Calvinism in any of its varieties. How was he to prove the truth of his interpretation and the falsity of the Westminster Confession to men like Gale and Gale's church members? They would not yield simply to his assertions. In such ultimate questions, the proof lay, as John Locke in 1690 and the American patriots of 1776 had declared in regard to political rebellion, in the appeal to heaven. God would indicate in the results which followed such an appeal whether or not its advocates were in the right.

The day came when Finney had to rescue Gale from the inadequacy of the strict Calvinism he had learned at Princeton and to put his own views to the ultimate test. It occurred while Finney was still living in Adams in 1824. A Universalist minister came to town and began to "promulge his objection-

[25] For Finney's discussion of his early theological development as discussed below, see his *Memoirs,* pp. 42 ff.

able doctrines" regarding universal salvation and the nonexistence of hell. His arguments against the inconsistencies of the Westminster Confession were so forceful that the people "seemed to be shaken in their minds." Gale was too ill at the time to combat his influence in open debate, and he requested Finney to do so. Finney told him, "Mr. Gale, I cannot do it without contradicting your views on that subject and setting them all aside. With your views . . . he cannot be answered." In desperation Gale gave Finney permission to go ahead and say what he pleased: "It will never do to let the thing remain as it is."

With considerable relish Finney related in his *Memoirs* how he confuted the Universalist first by abandoning the untenable ground of the Westminster Confession in regard to passive regeneration and the predestination of the elect, and then by proving that while Christ died to remove the burden of original sin from all men, nevertheless his death did not automatically grant salvation to all men. Christ's death, said Finney, merely rendered it possible for God "to proclaim a universal amnesty inviting all men to repent, to believe in Christ, and to accept salvation." Since every man was free to accept, it was only justice for God to punish by eternal damnation any man so wicked as willfully to reject this benevolent amnesty. The Universalist was right, said Finney, in pointing out the inconsistencies in Calvinism, but he was wrong in denying the existence of and necessity for hell. It was common sense that God was good and that men often were not. By reconciling the Bible with this very reasonable argument, Finney carried the crowd with him, for it was implicitly acknowledged by all parties in the debate that God's will was reconcilable with human reason. The discredited Universalist left town, and George Gale was left to mull over the wreck that Finney had made of his creed.

But Gale was a man of his age. Though he was not moved by Finney's intelligence, he was by his practical results. Finney had saved the faith of the church members, and in addition his argument brought new converts into the church who might have become Universalists. Here, said Finney, was "the evidence that the Spirit of God had blessed my views of the atonement." Heaven had made its judgment, though as so often happened in a democracy, the voice of God sounded very much like the voice of the people. Gale soon abandoned his "crippling" Calvinistic views for those of Finney, and it was not many years before all of western New York followed suit.

Finney was successful in spreading this "new divinity" because he knew the mind of the frontier Yankee, because his own doubts were their doubts, and his own common sense view was their common sense view. He once said that the people of western New York were, theologically speaking, in a state of "betweenity" in the decade 1825–1835.[26] "Many good men" were "halting and doubting whether they should reject" the dogma of Calvinism as preached in the Presbyterian and Congregational churches or not. Many had already plunged into infidelity as a result of "this wonderful theological fiction." It was from this betweenity that Finney set out to rescue not only the inhabitants of western New York but the Calvinists and infidels of the whole United States.

On March 17, 1824, three months after he was licensed to preach, Finney was appointed by the Female Missionary Society of the Western District of the State of New York "a Missionary to labor in the Northern parts of the County of Jefferson and such other destitute places in the vicinity as his discretion shall dictate. . . ."[27] The pious women who made up the society paid Finney a salary of six hundred dollars a year. He worked as their missionary for two years and then joined a band of itinerant preachers called the Oneida Evangelical Association. This association was made up of licensed and ordained Presbyterian evangelists and several theological students, all of whom agreed to pool any compensation or gifts they might receive for their services and to pay themselves each a fixed salary out of the net proceeds. The group included a number of men who were later to achieve fame or notoriety in western New York, such as Jedidiah Burchard, Horatio N. Foote, Daniel Nash, Herman Norton, Nathaniel Smith, Augustus Littlejohn, and Luther Myrick.[28] By 1826 Finney was one of the leading evan-

26 Finney, *Sermons on Various Subjects,* p. 80.

27 The letter of appointment from the society is among the Finney Papers in the Oberlin College Library, Oberlin, Ohio (hereinafter referred to as OCL).

28 Cross, *Burned-over District,* p. 187.

gelists in the Oneida region, and it is probable that he turned over to the association far more than the six hundred dollars a year which they paid him back as his salary for the next few years. In 1828 the president of the association wrote to Finney, "The society I consider under your patronage more than you under ours." [29]

Finney rose from local to national fame in the years 1825 to 1827 when he conducted spectacular revivals in the towns of Western, Rome, Utica, Auburn, and Troy. Prior to 1825 he had been highly successful in such small villages as Evans Mills, Antwerp, Perch River, Brownsville, LeRayville, Rutland, Gouverneur, and Dekalb, but it was not until his revival in the town of Western in September, 1825, that eastern newspapers began to carry reprints from the upstate New York papers about him and to publish eyewitness reports. From the outset of his career, his manner, methods, and theology were subjects of violent controversy. According to one report, Finney told an audience in Western, "Your prayers are so very cold they do not rise more than six feet high; you must strive hard and struggle —you must groan, you must agonize, why you must pray till your nose bleeds, or it will not avail. If you do not do better I must soon shake my garments against you and clear out and be gone. I would not have you think that I will *stay here* and go *to hell* along with the rest of you." Another report called him a "zealous fanatic" and said that he "publicly declared not long since that he was one of the Brigadier Generals of Jesus Christ with a special commission from the court of heaven to preach the gospel, and all that did not believe him would be eternally damned." [30] But these were statements by Universalists. A more friendly account of his work in Rome in April, 1826, stated, "A Mr. Finney came to help the pastor. . . . After he came the Spirit of God was shed down with such power that nothing seemed able to resist it. . . . The revival was remarkable for its solemnity and deep heart-searching." [31]

In addition to the newspaper reports, various interested parties were soon publishing small tracts attacking or defend-

[29] A. B. Johnson to Finney, April 15, 1828, Finney Papers, OCL.
[30] *Gospel Advocate* (Buffalo, New York), January 13, 1826, pp. 3, 5.
[31] Quoted from the *Boston Telegraph* in Wright, *Finney*, p. 58.

ing Finney's work. A Unitarian named Ephraim Perkins denounced his hellfire and damnation preaching because it "frightens the feeble-minded" and arouses the excitable until they "lose their sober sense and self command." Perkins' description of Finney's preaching in Utica was, despite obvious prejudice, probably a fairly accurate account of his early style: You "raise your voice, lift high your hand, bend forward your trunk, fasten your staring eyes upon the auditors, declare that they know it to be God's truth that they stand upon the brink of hell's gaping pit of fire and brimstone, and bending your body and bringing your clenched fist half way from the pulpit to the broad aisle, denounce *instant and eternal damnation* upon them unless they repent forthwith." [32]

Finney's friends in the Presbytery of Oneida issued a defense of his work in which they denied Perkins' charges and concluded with a ringing cry directed against those "enemies of the cross of Christ" who opposed revivals. In declaring that "a mighty battle is yet to be fought" between the friends and foes of revivals, Finney's friends spoke more truly than they realized." [33]

Probably the most damning account of Finney's work in these early revivals came from a man named Brockway who was a member of the church in which Finney conducted a revival in Troy in the winter of 1826–1827. Brockway claimed that the pastor of the church, Nathaniel S. S. Beman, had invited Finney in order to draw attention from his own coming trial before the local presbytery for un-Christian conduct. According to Brockway, Beman told a member of his church that "if a successful revival could be matured under his auspices it would place him beyond the reach of censure." The importance of this charge lay in the fact that Beman was eventually to earn the title of "the War-horse of the New School" and to be chosen Moderator of the Presbyterian General Assembly in 1831. Brockway also charged Finney with "shaking his fist" in the face of a woman who was a member of Beman's church because she said that Calvinism taught her that she must wait for the influence of the Holy Spirit before she could repent: "You lie!"

32 Quoted in the *Christian Examiner and Theological Review,* IV (May–June, 1827), 248.

33 *Ibid.,* 264–65.

Finney shouted; "You can repent and be converted immediately." [34]

Finney made no defense against these various charges. It seemed evident to him that revival preaching must be vehement and perhaps even vituperative in order to rouse his hearers out of their complacency. In his *Memoirs* he frankly described how in the town of Antwerp in 1824, "The Lord let me loose upon them in a wonderful manner" and "the congregation began to fall from their seats in every direction and cry for mercy. . . . The whole congregation were either on their knees or prostrate." And in the town of Rome, in 1825, "Convictions were so deep and universal that we would sometimes go into a house and find some in a kneeling posture and some prostrate on the floor. Some bathing the temples of their friends with camphor, and rubbing them to keep them from fainting and, as they feared, from dying." In the town of Auburn, "In the middle of my discourse, I observed a person fall from his seat near the broad aisle who cried out in a most terrific manner. . . . When I told the congregation who it was they all knew him . . . and it produced tears and sobs in every part of the house." At Stephentown, Finney preached on "God Is Love" and "a man of strong nerves and of considerable prominence . . . fell and writhed in agony for a few moments; but he afterwards became still and nearly motionless, but entirely helpless." He had to be carried home, but "He was very soon converted." [35]

If Finney's methods seemed extravagant, those of his imitators worried even the most ardent supporters of the new revival movement. George Gale wrote to Finney in March, 1827, that the Oneida Presbytery had recently decided "with respect to females praying in the presence of men and praying for individuals by name" that such practices ought to be confined to "social circles" and not used in public meetings. According to Gale the presbytery felt that it had to take a stand on these and other new measures coming into vogue in western New York in order that "some of our Evangelist[s] might be kept in proper

[34] *Ibid.*, 247. See also Wright, *Finney*, p. 127, and J. Brockway, *Delineation of the Characteristic Features of a Revival of Religion in Troy in 1826 and 1827* (Troy, New York, 1827).

[35] Finney, *Memoirs*, pp. 103, 198, 230. See also the MS of the *Memoirs*, p. 316, in the Finney Papers, OCL.

bounds. Smith an[d] Myrick you know have been a little latitudinarian with respect to these." A week after Gale's letter, Finney's friend, the Rev. John Frost of Whitesborough, admitted his distaste for some of the excesses of the movement: "Br. N. Smith needs a curb bit and there is danger that two or three rash spirits may abuse your things. He is for having no limits fixed to females praying nor praying for persons by name. . . . I have no doubt that a degree of censoriousness has prevailed that needs to be checked." [36] Some of the evangelists thought it their duty to invade parishes where local ministers opposed them and to denounce such men as "cold," "dead," "lukewarm," or "enemies to God and revivals." One church elder wrote to a friend in New England, "I have been fairly skinned by the denunciations of these men and have ceased to oppose them to get rid of their noise. But I warn you not to introduce their spirit into your church or society." [37]

The disorder became so great in western New York that the opponents of Finney and his corevivalists decided in the fall of 1826 that they must have help from the New England leaders of Congregationalism in order to put a stop to it before it destroyed the stability and good name of the churches. It was natural that the two men to whom the antirevivalists should turn were Lyman Beecher and Asahel Nettleton. These men, if any, had the respect not only of the ministers but of the church people generally. It was believed that if they would but raise their voices in protest, the revivalists would either have to cease their rash new measures and their emotional preaching or else the church people would turn against them and refuse to listen. During the course of the debate between the easterners and the westerners, however, social and political overtones crept into the theological discussion which illustrated how far out of touch with the spirit of the West the New England leaders were.

Lyman Beecher was to American churchgoers of the Jacksonian era what his son, Henry Ward Beecher, was to the

[36] George Gale to Finney, March 14, 1827; John Frost to Finney, March 22, 1827, Finney Papers, OCL.

[37] *Letters of the Rev. Dr. Beecher and Rev. Mr. Nettleton on the "New Measures" in Conducting Revivals of Religion* (New York, 1828), p. 12. See also pp. 71–72 for instances in which "new measure" revivalists tried to get ministerial opponents dismissed from their pastorates.

churchgoers of the succeeding generation: the outstanding pastor and church leader on popular questions in the nation. As a prime mover in the crusades against dueling, intemperance, lotteries, Sabbath-breaking, deism, disestablishmentarianism, "Popery," and a dozen other "moral" problems of the day, he managed to stay constantly in the public eye from the year 1804 when he was only twenty-nine until well into the 1840's. He accomplished this by an adroit use of publicity, a talent for popular oratory, a trenchant pen, magnificent skill as an organizer, and a positive genius for seizing upon one issue after another which could be invested with the aura of a holy war against sin. In 1826 this wiry, energetic, plain-looking little man was at the peak of his fame, and he had just left his parish in Litchfield, Connecticut, near New Haven, to go to Boston where he could better lead the fight against the latest Satanic menace, Unitarianism.

As a student of Timothy Dwight at Yale and a close friend and collaborator of Nathaniel W. Taylor, Beecher had slowly abandoned his belief in the more rigid interpretations of Calvinism preached by Jonathan Edwards and his pupil, Samuel Hopkins. In a sermon entitled "The Faith Once Delivered to the Saints" published in 1823, Beecher had stated that "men are free agents, in the possession of such faculties, and placed in such circumstances as render it practicable for them to do whatever God requires." This was taken by many as an assertion of the sinner's ability to convert himself and thus an abandonment of the Calvinistic doctrine that a sinner could only be converted by direct aid from the Holy Spirit.[38] Beecher, however, denied any such implication, and maintained that he was still an orthodox Calvinist even though he did not agree at all points with Hopkinsianism. When Nathaniel Taylor, who had espoused similar views from his post in Yale seminary, was attacked in 1825 for departing from the Calvinist theory of original sin, Beecher said, "I have regarded him as adopting one of the half dozen ways in which orthodox men explain and defend that difficult doctrine." [39] Beecher managed to qualify his own views of free will so carefully and to express them so

[38] Lyman Beecher, *Autobiography, Correspondence, Etc. of Lyman Beecher*, ed. Charles Beecher (New York, 1865), Vol. I, p. 554.

[39] *Ibid.*, Vol. II, p. 25.

circumspectly that he was able to keep a foot in both camps of the great controversy for years. He was finally cornered not on any of his own statements but because he refused to dissociate himself from Taylor and Finney who were not so able nor so willing to indulge in sophistry.

Asahel Nettleton was a quiet, thin man who for years after graduating from Yale in 1809 nursed a constantly frustrated ambition to become a foreign missionary. Poor health finally forced him to abandon the idea. He was licensed to preach in 1811, and for the next eleven years he conducted a series of emotionally restrained but very successful revivals at the invitation of various pastors throughout Connecticut and in parts of Massachusetts and New York. In 1817 he was ordained as an evangelist by the South Consociation of Litchfield, Connecticut. Theologically Nettleton was a Hopkinsian Calvinist and as such he belonged to the old revival tradition. To him a revival was a miraculous act of divine grace. According to his intimate friend and biographer, Bennet Tyler, "Dr. Nettleton never held out to churches the idea that they could 'get up a revival,' or that they could have a revival at any time. . . ."[40] He believed that a revival occurred when God, for reasons of his own, suddenly decided to send the Holy Spirit into a church or a community to regenerate twenty or two hundred souls within a brief space of time. A revival was a heavenly "shower of blessings" over which a revivalist had no more control than the farmer had control over a shower of rain.

According to Nettleton, the revivalist's only duty was to instruct sinners in the truth of the gospel and to urge them to repent and to pray in the hope that God had predestined them for salvation. If so, God would in his own good time transform their wicked hearts. Meanwhile no action of will or feeling on the part of the sinner would be of any use. Nettleton never countenanced excitement of any sort. Whenever anyone showed signs of becoming overwrought at his meetings, Nettleton would tell them to go home and pray. If someone fainted or became hysterical before he could stop them, he would, according to Tyler, request a physician "to attend to the case."

[40] Bennet Tyler, *Memoir of the Life and Character of Rev. Asahel Nettleton, D.D.* (Hartford 1844), p. 210. See also William B. Sprague, *Annals of the American Pulpit* (New York, 1857), Vol. II, pp. 542 ff.

Between 1811 and 1826, as his friendship with Beecher and Taylor grew more intimate, Nettleton cautiously advanced from a strict Hopkinsian Calvinism toward a belief in some measure of free will which might assist sinners to effect their conversion. In 1823 he wrote to Beecher approving of his sermon "Faith Once Delivered to the Saints" and said, "I believe it to be a matter of fact that you and I are *really* a different kind of Calvinists" from the Hopkinsians and "that we do preach moral obligation and dependence different from many of our old divines—that in some things the Calvinism of Connecticut or New England has undergone an important change." [41] For Beecher to win over to the new divinity this paragon of New England Congregationalism was, or would have been, a major triumph. But after hearing Finney's views and noting Beecher's reaction to them, Nettleton was to have some serious second thoughts about the direction which New England Calvinism was taking under the leadership of Beecher and Taylor.

In the fall of 1826 Nettleton reacted to the calls for help from his ministerial friends in western New York with considerable feeling, but without much tact. It seemed to him that the new measures and emotional excesses which Finney was using to promote revivalism were a direct affront to his own success with the old measures. Recalling the excesses of James Davenport, whose half-insane ravings had virtually put an end to the First Great Awakening in the 1740's, Nettleton wrote in regard to Finney's activities: "Whoever has made himself acquainted with the state of things in New England near the close of the revival days of Whitefield and Edwards cannot but weep over its likeness to the present." [42] The more Nettleton heard about Finney and his cohorts the more irascible and petty he became until everyone recognized that he saw Finney as Davenport *redivivus* to his own Edwards.

In December, 1826, Nettleton went to Albany to spy out the land and while he was there he wrote a long letter to Finney's friend, the Rev. Samuel C. Aiken of Utica, in which he complained bitterly about Finney's revival methods. During the month of January Nettleton either read or sent copies of this indictment to twenty Presbyterian ministers in New York State in

[41] Quoted in Beecher, *Autobiography,* Vol. II, p. 25.
[42] *Letters of the Rev. Dr. Beecher and Rev. Mr. Nettleton,* p. 13.

order to warn them against the movement and to make clear his own distaste for it. "The evil is running in all directions," he said. "Those ministers and Christians who have heretofore been most and longest acquainted with revivals are most alarmed at the spirit which has grown out of the revivals of the West. . . . the great contest is among the professors of religion—a civil war in Zion—a domestic broil in the household of faith. The friends of brother Finney are certainly doing him and the cause of Christ great mischief. They seem more anxious to convert ministers and Christians to their peculiarities than to convert souls to Christ." Nettleton listed some of the "new measures" which he said were at the root of the trouble: "The practice of praying for people by name" which has become "an engine of public slander"; the "desperate attempt to introduce the practice of females praying with males"; the invasion of towns without invitations from the local pastors; the attacks upon ministers who oppose revivals and the attempt to "skin" them or "break them down"; over-familiarity with the deity in prayer, "This talking to God as a man talks to his neighbour . . . telling the Lord a long story about A. or B. and apparently with no other intent than to produce a kind of stage effect"; the use of language which borders on "profanity" and blasphemy; and in general the introduction of a very "disorganizing spirit" into the churches. Nettleton indicated something of his own pique when he declared that "My plans have been laid to visit many towns and cities [in the West] and have been wholly defeated by these students of divinity [who imitate Finney] thus running before me." [43]

Finney was preaching in Aiken's church in December, 1826, when Nettleton's letter arrived, and as Nettleton no doubt expected, he was shown the letter. But instead of replying in kind, Finney delivered a sermon on the text, "How can two walk together except they be agreed?" in which he not only defended the right of revivalists to arouse the attention of a dormant church by means of exciting new measures but also the right of awakened church members to "shake off" their pastor if he opposed the revival. Leaning upon Jonathan Edwards' *Treatise Concerning Religious Affections* and *Thoughts on the Revival of Religion in New England* which he had just

[43] *Ibid.*, pp. 11, 1–18 *passim*, 17, 35.

been reading, Finney said that it was often necessary in revivals to appeal to the emotions or "religious affections," especially when the regular ministry was "at ease in Zion" and preaching only dull, formal sermons not calculated to arouse any concern for salvation. And in conclusion he noted, "It is the natural effect of some revivals to stir up *wrong feelings in wrong hearts.*" Nettleton, refusing to admit that Edwards would countenance Finney's methods or exegesis, took the sermon as a personal rebuke. He decided that Finney and his friends were trying to arouse the lower orders against their betters. Thereafter Nettleton referred to the western revivalists as "the raga-muffins" and "the irregulars" and to their followers as "the *ignobile vulgus*" and "the insurgents." [44]

Finding his own influence too weak to quell the Finney uprising, Nettleton wrote to urge Beecher to lend the weight of his name to save the honor of decency, order, and respectable revivalism. Beecher cautiously sounded out Leonard Woods, Ebenezer Porter, Moses Stuart, and some of the other learned ministers in Connecticut and Massachusetts and then wrote to Finney's friends Nathaniel Beman and John Frost expressing his opinion that the western revivals exhibited a "severe and repelling mode of preaching," used "harsh and provoking epithets" which were "a violation of civilized decorum and Christian courtesy," encouraged "the delirious exultation of spiritual pride," and produced "a self sufficient and daring state of mind which is reckless of consequences and incorrigible to argument or advice." [45] He listed the same objections to the new measures that Nettleton made and, like Nettleton, he also seemed to think that the lower orders were getting out of hand in the rising tide of Jacksonian democracy: "We are on the confines of universal misrule and moral desolation and no time

[44] Finney's sermon was first published in Philadelphia in March, 1827, after he had repeated it several times. It is included in his *Sermons on Important Subjects* (New York, 1836, published by John S. Taylor) under the title "Christion Affinity," pp. 186 ff. For Nettleton's rebuttal see *Letters of the Rev. Dr. Beecher and Rev. Mr. Nettleton,* pp. 15, 22 ff., and Tyler, *Nettleton,* pp. 252 ff. See also Beecher, *Autobiography,* Vol. II, pp. 89-108, Finney, *Memoirs,* pp. 190-92, 202 ff., and Mead, *Taylor,* pp. 200 ff. for the interplay between Finney and the New Englanders at this time. Unfortunately, Edwards could be quoted with some accuracy by both Finney and Nettleton, for while he had defended most aspects of the revival excitement in the 1740's he had also deplored its excesses.

[45] *Letters of the Rev. Dr. Beecher and Rev. Mr. Nettleton,* p. 80.

is to be lost in forestalling and holding public sentiment correctly before the mass shall be put in motion by fierce winds before which nothing can stand. . . ." Beecher particularly deplored the view of democratic Western revivalists "that all men, because sinners, are therefore to be treated alike by ministers of the gospel without respect to age or station in society." This attitude was especially dangerous, said Beecher, in regard to persons in authority "in republican governments where public opinion is the only law," for if "those who rule over men" were treated the same as the average man, "a levelling of all distinctions of society" would result and this "would be the sure presage of anarchy and absolute destruction." Beecher compared the levelling aspect of the western revival to the mob rule which prevailed in France during the Revolution. He did not call the western revivalists "ragamuffins" but he said that their converts would probably be "impudent young men . . . poured out as from the hives of the North to obliterate civilization and roll back the wheels of time to semi-barbarism." And in another letter he called for "the entire demolition of these new measures" and the "deserved reprehension" of "such men as Finney." [46]

Somehow one of Beecher's letters attacking Finney found its way into print early in 1827 and there was an instant reaction. "Had it come from an obscure minister," said one man who admired both Finney and Beecher, "I should have set him down as an enemy of revivals." [47] But while some rallied to defend Finney, others recoiled. George Gale wrote to Finney in March, 1827, that several who had formerly been friendly toward him were now turning against him from fear of "the great gun at Boston." [48]

At this point Nathaniel Beman, whose trial in Albany was still in the offing, decided that only a face-to-face conference between representatives from East and West could iron out their growing mistrust and antagonism. Beecher took this as a sign that the westerners were ready to listen to reason and persuaded eight of his colleagues to meet with an equal number of Fin-

[46] *Ibid.*, pp. 89, 98. *Christian Examiner and Theological Review,* IV (May–June, 1827), p. 265; *Biblical Repertory and Theological Review,* n.s. IV (October, 1832), 481; *ibid.*, n.s. VII (October, 1835), 659 n.

[47] Beecher, *Autobiography,* Vol. II, p. 98.

[48] George Gale to Finney, March 4, 1827, Finney Papers, OCL.

ney's friends at the town of New Lebanon, New York, just across the border from Massachusetts. The convention lasted from July 18 to July 27, 1827, but it succeeded only in making matters worse.

In the light of future events the New Lebanon Convention could have been a major move in the strategy of the religious revolution which Beecher and Finney were separately waging.[49] If Beecher had only had the perspicacity to see that Finney was not simply a fanatical upstart but the embodiment of a deep and widespread religious discontent that could no longer be held back, he might have conciliated Finney instead of merely antagonizing him. As it was, the convention devoted itself to futile bickering over the superficial question of "new measures" and ignored the more basic problems of theological interpretations and ecclesiastical politics.

In his letter to Beman attacking Finney's revival movement, Beecher had noted as one of its greatest potential evils the possibility "that it will prevent the great evangelical assimilation which is forming in the United States." [50] By "the great evangelical assimilation" Beecher primarily had in mind the continued harmony of the various wings of Congregationalism within New England and the strengthening of its ties with the Presbyterians to the south. But he also had a secondary and more grandiose plan which called for the gradual unification of all the major Protestant denominations in the nation around this core of Presbygationalism. The details of this ecumenical movement were not worked out in Beecher's mind though they later took shape in the formation of the Evangelical Alliance in 1846.[51] In 1827 he was still concerned with solidifying the

[49] See Mead, *Taylor,* pp. 200–210 for a concise summary of the issues at stake in the New Lebanon Convention from the viewpoint of Beecher and Taylor.

[50] *Letters of the Rev. Dr. Beecher and Rev. Mr. Nettleton,* p. 98. For a more extended statement of Beecher's attitude toward evangelical assimilation see his letter to Ebenezer Porter in his *Autobiography,* Vol. II, p. 167 ff.

[51] Samuel J. Baird, a leader of the Old School Presbyterians, wrote in 1868 regarding the assimilating activities of Beecher and his friends, "the authors of the policy dazzled their imaginations with visions of a national church as comprehensive in its embrace as the ambitious 'national [benevolent] societies' by which it was to be developed. . . . The churches of New England, the Presbyterian Church, the Reformed Dutch, the Scotch, German and Associate Reformed—these all were to be included. And not these alone. Prospects undefined and boundless opened to the imaginations of the patrons of these schemes." Baird, *History of the New School,* p. 369. Steps toward uniting the Dutch Re-

Hopkinsian and other New England factions behind the new divinity, a task which he hoped to achieve by means of carefully worded reinterpretations of doctrine combined with vigorous revivalism. By adjusting his doctrinal interpretations to suit the changing spirit of the age, Beecher believed that he could make them attractive enough to the populace to produce a continuous wave of new conversions and additions to the churches. These would attest to the divine approbation of his views should the more strict Calvinists, either Hopkinsians or Presbyterians, challenge his orthodoxy.

This was of course the very method Finney had employed in refuting Gale's Calvinism, except that Finney was far too brash in his outright denunciation of the Westminster Confession. Beecher clearly saw that direct frontal assaults upon Calvinism could only lead to schism rather than to harmony. He asserted that if the ministers of New England had been asked point blank in 1827 whether they stood for the new theology of Taylor or the old theology of Jonathan Edwards and Samuel Hopkins, three-fourths of them would have chosen the old.[52] And if three-fourths of the Hopkinsians would have made such a choice, it was obvious that virtually all of the Presbyterians to the south would have preferred the Westminster Confession to Finney's new theology. Beecher was convinced therefore at the time of the New Lebanon Convention that the subtle reorientation in Calvinism at which he and Taylor had been working for over fifteen years could only be achieved by continuing to play down doctrinal disputes and to play up revival crusades directed, if necessary, against Unitarians, deists, Universalists, Roman Catholics, or any other obvious enemies of the faith. In order to do this it was essential to maintain the good repute of revivalism. If fanaticism, vituperation, hysteria, or ecclesiastical disorder of any sort became associated with it, the Hopkinsians and Presbyterians would react against it just as they had against the camp meetings of the Campbellites and Stoneites. Hence Finney had to be dealt with before he rocked the boat too far and spoiled not only the unity

---

formed and Associate Reformed Presbyterian churches to the Plan of Union had already been taken in the early 1820's. See Gillett, *History of the Presbyterian Church,* Vol. II, pp. 231–36.

52 Beecher, *Autobiography,* Vol. II, pp. 163, 180.

of Presbygationalism but the eventual evangelical assimilation of all Protestantism under the banner of Beecherism. The plan was worthy of Beecher's genius but for once his skill as a leader failed him and the failure was crucial.

Short of taking Finney into his confidence, Beecher could not have hoped to achieve anything at New Lebanon. His task was impossibly difficult. He not only had to take a sufficiently strong stand against the westerners to pacify Nettleton and the conservative Hopkinsians, but he also had to avoid giving too much satisfaction to the Unitarians and other opponents of revivalism by exposing to the public this "domestic broil in the household of faith." Also at stake was the friendship between the westerners and the easterners, but Beecher thought that his own high standing and the traditional ties of New Yorkers with New England would stand the strain of his rebuking a bunch of impudent boys.

For nine days Beecher and his eight colleagues debated fruitlessly with Finney and his eight colleagues at New Lebanon over the alleged excesses of the revival and the validity of the new measures. The westerners shrewdly countered the complaints of the easterners by denouncing not only the dead formality of the churches prior to the revival, but also the unwarranted interference by outsiders into their local affairs upon unsubstantiated charges made by "enemies of revivals." When the convention adjourned *sine die* on July 27, neither side could claim a victory so both sides did. Nettleton was the most disappointed by the outcome because he had fully expected the westerners to be roundly denounced, forced to admit their errors, and made to mend their ways. When the westerners came out of the fray undiminished in any way, he began to lose faith in Beecher's leadership. From that day on Nettleton withdrew little by little from his allegiance to the new divinity and within five years he was helping to lead the schism within New England Congregationalism which Beecher had worked so hard to avoid.

The Unitarians in Boston were so convinced that Beecher had played into their hands that they published the complete minutes of the convention the next month with the wry comment that though it made "melancholy" reading it was "a most instructive display of the state of religious character in a portion of our community." Beecher's famous remark to Finney made at the conclusion of the convention, that he knew Finney was planning to come into Connecticut and Boston like "a streak of fire" and that he would fight Finney "every inch of the way to Boston and then I'll fight you there," was so hollow that four years later he ate his own words and personally invited Finney to Boston.[53]

But a great deal was to happen between July, 1827, and Finney's arrival in Boston in August, 1831. Beecher claimed that by 1831 Finney had modified his methods and become reasonable. Finney claimed that Beecher realized the mistake he had made in 1827 and was trying to make up for it. What actually happened was that the doctrinal fireworks that had lain unnoticed under the convention table began to explode one by one in New England and the Middle Atlantic states as Finneyism and Beecherism matched claims for the leadership of the new divinity and the great plan of evangelical assimilation. By 1831 Finney had proven himself as important a figure in the revolution as Beecher, and when he could no longer be ignored, Beecher reluctantly rose to the occasion and joined those he could not beat.

The display which the New Lebanon Convention made in the journals and newspapers of the day pushed Finney into a far more prominent position than before. In the fall of 1827 Finney was itching for bigger game than the small towns and cities of the West. Since early that spring he had been receiving invitations to hold revivals in the big cities of the East and he was tempted to try his strength. Now that he had stood up to "the great gun at Boston" he felt more confident than ever that he was the instrument of a higher power. On April 20, 1827, he had received a letter from the Rev. James Patterson of Philadelphia saying, "It is my powerful desire that you would visit this great and wicked city . . . tho' there are many here who still look aghast at revivals yet latterly [they] don't talk so freely against them. To oppose them openly might be unpopular." [54] Finney had obviously been tempted by this and

[53] *Ibid.*, Vol. II, p. 101. For the complete minutes of the convention see *Christian Examiner and Theological Review*, IV (July–August, 1827), 357 ff.

[54] James Patterson to Finney, April 20, 1827. Finney Papers, OCL. For Patterson's revivalistic activities and New School outlook see Sprague, *Annals of the American Pulpit*, Vol. IV, p. 427.

similar letters so flattering to his prowess. But when he broached the matter of going east to his friends they advised against it. Theodore Weld wrote to him, "You expressed in your last letter the belief that those eastern cities would fall speedily. . . . Don't be in too great haste to get hold of the cities. . . . Kindle *back fires* . . . over the interiors; the while you are engaged there the cities are preparing fast—when ripe —at the favorable nick of time—give the word—rally your forces and in the twinkling of an eye make a plunge—and they are a wreck." [55] And George Gale cautioned him in New Lebanon: You say "You want a wider field" and speak of "going east" to Boston. But if you do "you would have to sustain the weight of the contest with the Unitarians and instead of receiving aid from those who ought to aid you [you] would probably find them throwing obstacles in your way. Let Doct. Beecher . . . fight it out. The Presbyterian Ch. furnishes an ample field. . . . You will have to fight here, but it will be a different warfare. . . . Many in New York and in Philadelphia, as well as others south will be your warm friends and supporters." [56]

It was evident from these letters that Finney and his friends were interested in more than saving souls. They were out to reform the Presbyterian church. To do this they planned to employ revivalism as both a means and an end. It was to be the means of proving the validity of their new theology of free will and free grace, and its end was to instill the spiritual fervor of frontier pietism into the lukewarm churches in order to reform both them and the world. Or, put another way, Finney planned to cut the ground out from under the dead hand of hyper-Calvinist exponents of the Westminster Confession by inaugurating a concerted "low Church" movement within Presbyterianism.[57] The great question was whether he, as the recognized leader of the movement, should concentrate his efforts in the West or in the East. In the fall of 1827 Finney made the fateful decision to go east.

His reason given for this in his *Memoirs* was simply that he had received pressing invitations from eastern ministers and

[55] Theodore Weld to Finney, March 19, 1827, Finney Papers, OCL.

[56] George Gale to Finney, September 6, 1827, Finney Papers, OCL.

[57] For reference to Finney's movement as "low Church" see *Letters of Theodore Weld, Angelina Grimke Weld, and Sarah Grimke, 1822–1844,* eds. Gilbert H. Barnes and Dwight L. Dumond (New York, 1934), Vol. I, p. 91.

laymen which could not be ignored. Probably of equal importance, however, was a growing sense of mission and of power which impelled him to forsake the easier arena of the West, in which he had already achieved success, in order to carry the war into the enemy's camp.

Whether he actually used the term or not, Finney doubtless did think of himself in these years as "the Brigadier General of Jesus Christ" and he marshaled the ebullient, self-confident "revival men" of the West for a great crusade. Under his generalship revivalism became more an engine of war than Beecher had ever meant it to be. Finney began his assault upon the eastern ramparts of sin and desiccant Calvinism by accepting an invitation from the Rev. E. W. Gilbert to conduct revival services in his church in Wilmington, Delaware. But he was somewhat shocked to discover upon arrival in Wilmington in November, 1827, that Gilbert was far from being a true "new measure" revival preacher. "I soon found," Finney wrote, "that his teaching had placed the church in a position that rendered it impossible to promote a revival among them till their views could be corrected. . . . They had the oldest of the old-school views of doctrine; and consequently their theory was that God would convert sinners in his own time. . . . It was plain that nothing could be done unless Mr. Gilbert's views could be changed." Finney at once proceeded to renovate the antiquated theology of his host just as he had renovated that of his pastor, George Gale. Gilbert was so eager to have a revival that he willingly capitulated. When his parishioners challenged his about-face by saying to him that if what Finney preached was correct "Then you have never preached the Gospel," Gilbert replied, "Well, I am sorry to say I never have." [58] Finney may have exaggerated this story in his *Memoirs* but contemporary evidence indicates that his preaching, and particularly the results which it achieved in terms of conversions, persuaded a great many ministers that Calvinism was dead.

Having successfully demonstrated his skill in Wilmington, Finney advanced to Philadelphia, the dead center of Presbyterianism in the United States. The most conservative and stalwart leaders of the denomination were located there and the

[58] Finney, *Memoirs,* pp. 234–38.

First Presbyterian Church of Philadelphia was the scene of the annual General Assemblies of the denomination at which all fundamental decisions were made. Finney began his preaching in James Patterson's church on the outskirts of the city, but soon he was invited to speak in several of the leading pulpits downtown, including those of Dr. James P. Wilson, pastor of the First Church, and Dr. Thomas H. Skinner, two of the most influential ministers in the denomination. As one friend of Finney's wrote to him from New York in February, 1828, "Dr. Wilson having taken you into his pulpit it has almost petrified opposition here. He has more weight here than perhaps any Minister in the Presbyterian Church." [59] But Finney's initial success was temporarily halted when other Presbyterian ministers in the city who were not so broad-minded as Wilson and Skinner heard what he was preaching and how he was conducting his meetings. By the middle of March opposition had become so strong within the city that he ran back to Patterson's church to preach for a few weeks. E. W. Gilbert wrote to him there, "I don't understand your motives in the matter. Are you so afraid of opposition? . . . Satan will never let go such a stronghold without a mighty resistance. It is his metropolis—his headquarters—the citadel of his power so far as the Pres. chh is concerned. . . . What did you mean by retiring as soon as the great guns began to load?" [60]

Though Finney soon regained his confidence and returned to preach in the largest German Reformed church in the city, he wrote to Weld at the end of March calling Philadelphia an "AntiRevival city." And he added significantly, "I am told that by some of the ministers the people are warned against the false doctrine which is getting into the city and forbidden to go after strange ministers." These hostile ministers, said Finney, made no distinction between the radical new revivalists of western New York and the conservative New England revivalists like Nettleton. "I hear nothing here recently about the distinction contended for at the East [New England] between old and new measures. The fact is, that here we are all hereticks, Alias

[59] David L. Dodge to Finney, February 25, 1828, Finney Papers, OCL. Wilson and Skinner were leaders of the moderate wing of the Presbyterian Church which dominated the denomination from the time of the Plan of Union until shortly after Finney's visit to Philadelphia.

[60] F. W. Gilbert to Finney, March 14, 1828, Finney Papers, OCL.

Hopkintonians, who don't sit quietly down in a corner of the Triangle and wait God's time."[61]

The term "Triangle" referred to a series of pamphlets written in 1816–17 by the New England Hopkinsian, Samuel Whelpley, as an attack upon the hyper-Calvinism of Princeton and Philadelphia Presbyterianism. Whelpley, following the modifications made by Samuel Hopkins, held that the Presbyterians enclosed the unsaved in a triangle of fatalism by their strict interpretation of the three doctrines of original sin, a limited atonement, and the inability of the sinner to do anything to save his own soul. Finney found it amusing that in Philadelphia he was considered a Hopkinsian when for the past five years he had been vigorously attacking the Hopkinsians of western New York. But he was unable, or unwilling, to see that Hopkinsianism, for all its rigidity, was a liberalization of strict Calvinism. As far as he was concerned, Hopkinsians held virtually the same doctrines that Whelpley attacked and Finney applied the terms "hyper-Calvinist" or "Triangular" to Hopkinsians as well as to Princetonians and Philadelphians. Finney seemed totally unaware that Lyman Beecher was doing his best to coax the New England Hopkinsians into the new divinity camp. Because Beecher's attack upon Finney had included statements which seemed to condemn the doctrine of sudden conversion, and because Beecher's eastern colleagues at New Lebanon (men like Caleb J. Tenney, Heman Humphrey, Justin Edwards, Joel Hawes, and Nettleton himself) were generally considered to be Hopkinsians, Finney at this time lumped all New Englanders with Philadelphians and Princetonians as enemies of revivalism.

Beecher recognized the danger to his plan of gradual assimilation in Finney's assault upon Philadelphia, and he considered it an attempt on Finney's part to replace his own subtle leadership in the revolution by extending eastward the crude tactics of the western revivals. "In the spring of 1828," Beecher wrote in his *Autobiography,* "I found out that Mr. Finney's friends were laying their plans to make an impression on the General Assembly. . . ." So he went to Philadelphia to stop them. He believed that he prevented the Finneyites from installing

[61] Finney to Theodore Weld, March 27, 1828, in *Letters of Theodore Weld,* Vol. I, p. 10.

one of their men, perhaps Nathaniel Beman, in the pulpit of Dr. Skinner who had just retired. But while Beecher was in Philadelphia he signed an agreement with Finney and his friends in which both sides promised to cease publishing attacks upon each other. As Beecher explained to the disgruntled Nettleton, who was not consulted about this agreement, to continue the controversy with Finney over new measures "would tend to keep up a party in the Church who, identified with their leader, might in self-defense be embodied to defend him and might introduce a controversy in the Presbyterian Church. . . ." This was the first step in Beecher's attempt to conciliate Finney, and as he admitted to Nettleton, he took it because if the fight continued much longer it "might be dangerous to oppose him." [62] Nevertheless it was becoming obvious that Beecher could not continue much longer to play on all sides at once. The harder Finney pushed for reinterpretation of Presbyterian orthodoxy, the more difficult Beecher's position became within Congregationalism.

The New England aspect of the new divinity movement reached a turning point in September, 1828, when Nathaniel Taylor published in his *Concio ad Clerum* sermon in New Haven a new and more clear-cut expression of his (and Beecher's) views on free will. The struggle within Presbyterianism reached its first crisis in Philadelphia in 1829 when the Rev. Albert Barnes, a Princeton graduate, publicly endorsed Taylor's views in his sermon "The Way of Salvation." In 1830, the members of the Rev. James Wilson's First Church in Philadelphia invited Barnes to succeed their retiring pastor. This brought the theological heresy of the new divinity right into the citadel of the Presbyterian church and the conservatives reacted violently.

Just how blind the Middle Atlantic Presbyterians had been to the possibility that Finney's revivalism in Philadelphia in 1828 was the Trojan horse in their midst was reflected in Finney's remark that they had taken no interest in the distinction made at New Lebanon between new and old measures. They thought him to be merely a crude western exponent of Hopkinsianism, and while they did not like Hopkinsians they had learned to put up with them. When Taylor and Barnes en-

[62] Beecher, *Autobiography*, Vol. II, pp. 105–6.

dorsed the doctrines of free will, however, it suddenly dawned upon the Presbyterians that New England Congregationalists were split into two camps and that Finney's "new measures" were not simply a matter of revival procedure but a matter of doctrine which put him in the camp of the liberalizers. As the *Biblical Repertory and Theological Review,* the official journal of Princeton and Philadelphia Calvinism, announced with naive wonder a few years later, "it was a matter of surprise to many when the conjunction took place between the coarse, bustling fanaticism of the New Measures and the refined intellectual abstractions of the New Divinity." And then to pile error upon folly, the journal claimed that Taylor and Beecher had concocted their New Divinity in 1828 as a theological justification of Finney's methods: "The new measures, we believe, were in full action before the theology of New Haven shed its light upon the world." [63] This was surely a left-handed tribute to the subtlety with which the men from Yale had advanced their views since 1812.

In the spring of 1828, however, Finney seems to have been almost as ignorant as the Presbyterians of the coming conjunction between his western movement and the Beecher-Taylor movement. The peace treaty he signed with Beecher in May of that year made so little impression upon him that in later years he denied ever having seen it. Until 1830 he continued to view Beecher and Taylor more as enemies to modern revivals than as the men whose theology and experimentation since 1812 had helped to clear the ground for him in the East. The only comment in Finney's correspondence on Taylor's *Concio ad Clerum* came from a New York admirer, David L. Dodge, who was later to give Finney considerable financial support. Dodge wrote on September 17, 1828, to Finney, "Dr. Taylor, I understand, has come out with his particular views . . . so as to be understood and many of the ablest divines are alarmed. . . ." Dodge went on to say that he was glad that these matters would at last get a thorough airing "because speculative men" had distorted the Bible in their efforts to combat "Arminianism." [64] Dodge's view seemed to indicate

[63] *Biblical Repertory and Theological Review,* n.s. VII (October, 1835), 656–57. For confirmation of the fact that Taylor was preaching free will long before Finney was converted see Mead, *Taylor,* pp. 113 ff.

[64] David L. Dodge to Finney, September 17, 1828, Finney Papers, OCL.

that, at this time, Finney and his friends considered Taylor's fight in New England simply another theological imbroglio such as "speculative men" often became involved in but which really did little to advance revivals.

Hopkinsians in New England, however, men like Nettleton, Nathan Perkins, Caleb Tenney, Bennett Tyler, Joseph Harvey, Nathaniel Hewitt, Ebenezer Porter, and Leonard Woods, looked upon Taylor's sermon as rank heresy. When the conservative Calvinists in the Philadelphia presbytery, led by Ashbel Green (formerly president of Princeton) brought Albert Barnes to trial in 1830 for endorsing Taylorism, the New England Hopkinsians applauded. Only then did Finney realize where his true course lay and throw his weight behind Beecher and Taylor.

Finney's part in the Barnes controversy, and in Philadelphia generally, was catalytic rather than direct. His most ardent admirers in that city seem to have been among the more radical and unstable elements of the church, particularly among the laity. As Dodge wrote to Finney from New York, in March, 1828, it was rumored that in Philadelphia "the best informed christians were displeased with you but a zealous, unstable class are making a party in your favour that will probably throw the churches into convulsion and disorder." [65] Finney's own excited state of mind while in Philadelphia can be seen in the letter he wrote to Weld that same month lamenting, "The churches here are in a dreadful state. This city inste[a]d of being the 'radiating point,' the 'mainspring and rallying point [for Christian] enterprise of the Presbyterian church,' is almost solid darkness; [she reeks o]f corruption and in her putrid embrace, she holds the country north and south, locked up in her loathesome horrid death." He concluded with a warning, "I am in a land where many would entangle me in talk. Be careful what you do with my letters." [66]

The crux of the problem as Finney and his zealous friends in Philadelphia saw it in 1828 was the shortage of "revival men" to awaken and reform that putrid metropolis. "O how much I want your help," Finney wrote to Weld, "and that of

[65] David L. Dodge to Finney, March 18, 1827, Finney Papers, OCL.

[66] Finney to Theodore Weld, March 27, 1828, *Letters of Theodore Weld,* Vol. I, p. 11.

20 others who understand revivals. There is hardly *any one* [here] or in this region who can help [me]. . . ." It was a typical aftermath of Finney's revivals that two years after he left the city the church in which he had done most of his preaching, the Race Street German Reformed Church, dismissed its pastor and tried to persuade Finney to take his place because "the congregation are longing for the time when they shall have revival preaching again." [67]

But more important than this squabble was the First Presbyterian Church's choice of Barnes less than a year after it had been aroused by Finney's revival preaching. As Patterson wrote to Finney, "Dr. Wilson's people have called Rev. Mr. Barnes of Morristown, N. J. Dr. Green, Dr. Ely, and Mr. Potts, it is said, don't like that he should come into this Presbytery because of his New Divinity. He is a revival man, and it is said he is a very devoted man . . . I think he will be an acquisition to the cause of revivals in this city." [68] When Barnes came he was promptly accused of heresy by Green. The moderates and revival men in the city combined to sustain Barnes. Green appealed to the synod. The synod sustained Green in 1831 and the Barnes faction appealed to the General Assembly. Finneyites and Beecherites worked strenuously to see that this ultimate court of appeal was packed in favor of new divinity men.[69]

Contrary to Patterson's information, Dr. Ezra Stiles Ely, editor of the *Philadelphian,* a prominent Presbyterian journal, took Barnes's side in the struggle. His assistant editor, S. B. Ludlow, reported the situation to Finney in January, 1830: "The High Church Regency (Dr. G[reen] etc.) have . . . now resolved to publish a paper of their own to regulate the faith and practice of the denomination in the United States and to make them conform to the *standards* [i.e., the Westminster Con-

[67] *Ibid.,* and Caspar Schaeffer to Finney, April 6, 1830, Finney Papers, OCL.

[68] James Patterson to Finney, March 26, 1830, Finney Papers, OCL.

[69] The Barnes controversy in Philadelphia had roots which went back to the New-Side Old-Side schism during the First Great Awakening. The same factions had quarreled in 1816–17 over Whelpley's attack on "Triangularism." As the New Haven theology became more prevalent after 1828 the conservatives stiffened their resistance and finally forced the moderates to take sides for or against the wing of the church which followed the views of Taylor, Beecher, Barnes, Duffield, Beman, *et al.* See Gillett, *History of the Presbyterian Church,* Vol. II, pp. 465 ff.

fession]. So you and all *heretics* like you who sit in the darkness may soon expect a great light." Ludlow then went on to plead with Finney to help find some new subscribers for the *Philadelphian* in its hour of need: ". . . you once told me, if the paper would *come to the point,* that the friends at the west would lend us their shoulders to move the wheels." [70] The paper had now come to the point. It was ready to climb on the revival band wagon and sound the trumpet. The conjunction between the new measure men of the West and the new divinity men of the East was under way.

A year later, in February, 1831, another friend wrote to Finney that Philadelphia "is beginning to wake up." Ely, Livingston, and Skinner, who had given Finney only lukewarm support, were now holding prayer meetings to get up a revival. "There is a vastly different feeling here now on the subject of revivals to what there was when you were here, the seed sown has been generating and the Barnes controversy has drawn a line and given an impulse to the cause of evangelical sentiments. I believe that your ministry would meet with far less opposition here now than formerly and I hope the door will be open for your return ere long." [71] Finney did not return to Philadelphia, but after the Barnes heresy case was settled in Barnes's favor by the General Assembly of 1831 (which had been successfully packed by new divinity men and moderated by Nathaniel Beman) Finney had the satisfaction of knowing that his backfires had begun the wreckage of Philadelphia. Even before the Assembly met, the Barnes dissension had split the Philadelphia presbytery so irrevocably that Patterson, Gilbert, Ely, and eleven other liberals and moderates had petitioned the General Assembly to be allowed to split off and form a second presbytery of Philadelphia. Finney's friends happily referred to this as a "revival presbytery" and the General Assembly of 1831 granted it the right to exist over the loud protests of the conservatives.[72]

70 S. B. Ludlow to Finney, January 30, 1831, Finney Papers, OCL.

71 Caspar Schaeffer to Finney, February 20, 1831, Finney Papers, OCL.

72 *Ibid.* For the quarrel over the establishment of the Second Presbytery on the basis of "elective affinity," which played a prominent part in provoking the schism of 1837, see Baird, *History of the New School,* pp. 392 ff., and Gillett, *History of the Presbyterian Church,* Vol. II, pp. 467 ff. Patterson is said to have openly admitted that the purpose of forming the Second Presbytery was to en-

From Philadelphia Finney passed on to rally the revival forces in New York City. During the year he was in Philadelphia (1828–29) sowing these seeds of rebellion, he was under constant pressure from a group of new measure laymen in New York to come to their aid. The steps which led him to New York offered a revealing picture of how and why the revival theology and mechanisms of the frontier filtered into the urban centers of the East. Because the pastors of New York had close ties with New England, they recognized earlier than the Philadelphians that the western revival measures had divisive theological undercurrents. A few New York ministers who might have welcomed Finney were frightened by the opposition which he aroused in New England in 1827. Beecher's influence was strongly felt among the transplanted Yankees who were later to make up the core of Finney's support in that city. And Nettleton had had the tactical shrewdness to beat Finney to New York and sound the alarm against him before he could be heard there himself.

But Finney was not without influential friends. Judge Jonas Platt and his son Zephaniah had moved to New York City shortly after feeling the magnetic power of Finney's preaching in Utica in 1826. In New York they quickly became friends of Anson G. Phelps, David and William Dodge, Lewis and Arthur Tappan, and other Yankee-born merchants and businessmen who formed a coterie of New England pietists in the city. The Platts and Phelpses belonged to the well-known Brick Presbyterian Church whose pastor, Gardiner Spring, had been invited by Beecher to join him against Finney at the New Lebanon Convention. As a conservative Hopkinsian, Spring would certainly have enjoyed bridling Finney, but he had been unable to attend. Samuel H. Cox, who was pastor of the Laight Street Presbyterian Church attended by the Tappans and Dodges, likewise distrusted Finney.[73] The

able the liberals to license and ordain new divinity candidates for the ministry whom the old presbytery would never have consented to license. See Baird, *op. cit.*, p. 400.

[73] Spring and Cox were, like Wilson and Skinner of Philadelphia, members of the moderate wing of Presbyterianism. Cox vacillated in his attitude toward the new divinity but eventually sided with the New School in the schism. Spring was consistently cool toward the new views and in 1837 sided with the Old School. In his autobiography Spring wrote, "I had no predilection for Mr. Finney nor for his doctrines. . . . I did not unite in the request to Mr. Finney

laymen of the city therefore took the first steps toward bringing Finney to New York. They arranged a meeting in mid-December, 1827, in Anson Phelps's home at which Finney and various of his upstate friends, including Aiken, Beman, and Weld, met with several of the New York pastors to discuss the matter. Through prayer and talk the prejudices against Finney were somewhat modified.[74]

A few days after the meeting, when Finney had returned to his revival labors in Wilmington, David Dodge wrote to him saying that Spring had now dropped his violent opposition though he still refused to come out definitely in Finney's favor: "I believe at least four ministers in our Presbytery would give you not only the right hand of fellowship but open their pulpits to you if they could be satisfied you would not introduce some things that has [*sic*] been such an occasion of handle to opposers." Dodge admitted, however, that Nettleton's recent visit to New York had stirred up much opposition even though Nettleton had ultimately made himself somewhat obnoxious by his continual harping upon the dangers of Finneyism.[75]

A few weeks later Anson G. Phelps wrote to Finney, "we shall expect to see you soon in our Stupid, Poluted, and Perishing City." Zephaniah Platt wrote in March, 1928, "Our New York churches are generally in a cold stupid state but I am happy to tell you that there is a very general change of sentiment here in regard to yourself and the Western Revivals. . . . [the] tumult of prejudice which Mr. N[ettleton] had excited" is disappearing among "men who not long ago would have voted you a room in the Lunatic Asylum." [76] Finney's backers thought it might help to gain support for Finney if New York-

---

to visit our city, but I greatly desired that this divisive spirit might be healed. . . . It seemed to me due to Mr. Finney that he *should be heard*. . . ." However, Spring's general hostility to the new revivalism was obvious. "Revivals are always spurious," he said, "when they are got up by man's device and not *brought down* by the Spirit of God." Gardiner Spring, *Personal Reminiscences of the Life and Times of Gardiner Spring* (New York, 1866), Vol. I, pp. 217–18, 225–26.

[74] See Fletcher's *Oberlin*, Vol. I, pp. 25–28.

[75] David L. Dodge to Finney, December 18, 1827, Finney Papers, OCL. In the eyes of Finney's supporters the most telling fact against Nettleton was that his revival preaching in New York and vicinity had failed to produce any converts.

[76] See A. G. Phelps to Finney, January 7, 1828; Zephaniah Platt to Finney, March 10, 1828, Finney Papers, OCL.

ers could hear a sample of his preaching, so in August, arrangements were made to have him supply Samuel Cox's pulpit for four weeks while Cox was away on vacation. This annoyed Cox, who claimed he was not asked about it, and it did not succeed in overcoming the hesitation of the other ministers.[77]

Finney returned to his work in Philadelphia and vicinity while the exasperated laymen of New York gave up trying to win over the clergy and made plans to organize a revival meeting on their own. Anson G. Phelps rented a vacant church on Vandevanter Street and after further correspondence Finney came there in the fall of 1829 for a prolonged assault on the city. He preached in the Vandevanter Street church for three months with the help of his friends Beman and Dirck Lansing. Then Phelps purchased outright a former Universalist church on Prince Street near Broadway where Finney continued to hold meetings until mid-summer of 1830. A sufficient number of converts were made at these meetings to form a church devoted to Finney's principles. The leaders in organizing the church were the Tappan brothers and James C. Bliss. The church was included in the New York presbytery, but because the Tappans were anxious to reach the poor in the city, the native-born poor who had come from the countryside and needed to be protected from the city's evils, no charge was made for pew rent and the church became known as the First Free Presbyterian Church. The Rev. Joel Parker, a staunch revival man from Rochester, became the first pastor. Meanwhile Herman G. Norton, a former Oneida Association evangelist, had been installed in another revival church in the city. Both men owed their appointments to Finney's preaching as well as to his direct recommendation.

This first attempt to awaken New York City was not a great success in terms of converting the Presbyterian pastors to the new divinity or the new measures. But it did see the founding of a newspaper in New York friendly to Finney. The *New York Evangelist* was launched in March, 1830, with funds advanced by Judge Platt. Two years later the Tappan brothers took over the task of subsidizing it. It became the voice of

[77] See Lewis Tappan to Finney, September 25, 1828. Photostat of letter is in the Lewis Tappan Papers, Library of Congress.

Finneyism throughout the country and provided an eastern mouthpiece which the new measure men sorely needed.

The first New York campaign also had long range results in terms of Finney's friendship with the Tappan brothers. The financial aid of these wealthy New York merchants was of vital importance to the future of the revival movement. They also lent their devoted personal support to struggling new revival churches in the city by constantly changing their membership (and hence their wealth and prestige) from one to another of them as fast as they were founded in the wake of Finney's revival. The Tappans were also leaders in the various charitable and benevolent societies which were busily trying to reform America in the 1830's, and they brought Finney a host of new allies from these enterprises as well as enlisting his followers in them. Finney claimed that it was indirectly through him that Lewis Tappan became converted from Unitarianism to the "support of orthodox [evangelical] views and revivals of religion" in 1825–1826.[78]

The Tappans had at first sided with Beecher and Nettleton, and it was not until 1829 that they actively began to support Finney. For a time they impartially helped both Beecher and Finney, but in 1835 they gave up Beecher entirely. In later years when Finney sent the manuscript of his *Memoirs* to Lewis Tappan for perusal and pointed out that in it he had taken issue with some statements that Beecher had made in his *Autobiography,* Tappan wrote to him in a letter which spoke volumes about the whole Finney-Beecher controversy: "I put no confidence in Dr. B's statements so far as they differ from yours. . . . He was a trimmer and had less respect to means than to ends. I thought everything of him until I met you. You had system and he jerks. He had some qualities superior to yours. Notwithstanding this he did not always follow his convictions of duty. He believed in the doctrine of expediency to a criminal excess I thought. Of course, his fence was in Virginia fashion, while yours was on a straight line." [79]

After a summer vacation in 1830, Finney was planning to return to New York City to follow up his initial inroads when,

[78] See Finney, *Memoirs,* p. 282.

[79] Lewis Tappan to Finney, June 10, 1868, Lewis Tappan Papers, Library of Congress.

through one of his unaccountable mystical impulses, he decided at the last minute to accept an invitation to hold revival meetings in Rochester instead. (The invitation was tendered by Josiah Bissell, an ardent supporter of Finneyism and a lay elder of the church which Joel Parker had recently left to become pastor of the First Free Presbyterian Church in New York City.) It proved to have been a wise decision, for the Rochester revival of 1830–31 was the most successful and widely publicized of Finney's career. It was the first city-wide campaign that deserves to be compared to the urban revivals of the post-Civil War era. In conducting it Finney made full use of the theories and practices of modern revivalism which he bequeathed to all professional evangelists for the succeeding century and a quarter. Here for the first time in a city he had the full cooperation of all the Presbyterians, lay and clerical, and here also the other denominations, although not directly associated with him, cooperated with the movement. From the outset of Finney's career his preaching had been nondenominational in character. In the interests of promoting revivalism he purposely stressed a broad evangelical approach and avoided sectarian differences. (As he shrewdly explained to Lewis Tappan on another occasion, "The true Philosophy of promoting and consummating an excitement and publick action upon any subject is to confine the publick mind to *a point*. . . . Revivals of religion afford almost endless illustration of this. Introduce Baptism, Election, or any other doctrine that does not bear on the question of immediate acceptance of Christ and you either Kill or retard the work." [80])

In addition to the nonsectarian aspect of his preaching in Rochester, it was also of major importance to modern revivalism that in this campaign Finney first made temperance reform an integral part of conversion.[81] Of course, Rochester was a western city and a small one compared to Philadelphia or New York. Its population was about 10,000. But nonetheless the whole affair was a striking performance and it did more to advance the causes of the new divinity and evangelical assimilation than all of Finney's previous efforts.

[80] Finney to Lewis Tappan, April 30, 1836, Finney Papers, OCL.

[81] For a discriminating analysis of Finney's Rochester revival in relation to the social temper of the city in 1830 see Cross, *Burned-over District*, pp. 152 ff.

Contemporaries were particularly struck by how radically the Rochester revival differed from the boisterous meetings of Finney's early career. His methods and manner had matured considerably during his three years in the East. In Rochester he proved himself a master of the respectable, efficient, carefully organized revivalism of the future. Finney's friends were not altogether pleased by his new urbanity. Theodore Weld sensed a change for the worse coming over Finney's preaching as early as the spring of 1828. He wrote to him in Philadelphia, "I have clearly discerned that *revivals* have become with you a sort of trade, to be worked at so many hours every day and then laid aside. . . . Do you not find yourself running into *formality,* a round of formality in the management of revivals? . . . The machinery all moves on, every wheel and spring and chord in its place; but isn't the *main spring* waxing weaker?" [82] And while Finney was in New York in 1829 his friend Moses Gillet wrote from Rome fearing that his popularity in the East might go to his head: "you may be surrounded by men of wealth and distinction whose attention and flattery may not be the most favorable to prayer and humble dependence on God." George Gale added his warning when he told Finney early in 1830 that some of his friends were saying about him, "Is there not danger of his turning into an intellectualist?" [83] Future revivalists were to meet the same criticism from their early supporters when they made the inevitable adjustments which went with success and respectability. Somehow evangelists seemed to lose their "unction" when they became "citified."

The accounts of Finney's preaching in Rochester fully substantiated this suspicion. Finney was no longer the heedless enthusiast whose holy vehemence cut sinners off the benches by the score in the backwoods towns of Rome, Antwerp, Auburn, and Stephentown. An eyewitness in Rochester described him as "A tall, grave-looking man, dressed in an unclerical suit of gray. . . . Light hair covered his forehead; his eyes were of a sparkling blue, and his pose and movement dignified. I listened. It did not sound like preaching, but like

[82] Theodore Weld to Finney, April 22, 1828, *Letters of Theodore Weld,* Vol. I, p. 15.

[83] Moses Gillet to Finney, October 26, 1829; George Gale to Finney, January 21, 1830, Finney Papers, OCL.

a lawyer arguing a case before a court and jury. . . . The discourse was a chain of logic, brightened by felicity of illustration and enforced by urgent appeals from a voice of great compass and melody." [84] "Logic," "felicity," gravity, and dignity all added up to city preaching, but it was still revival preaching. Finney had not lost the sense of urgency in his message nor the compelling magnetism of his burning eyes.

Finney admitted, however, with ill-concealed pride, that he appealed to an entirely different type of audience in Rochester from that in earlier days. "It was soon seen," he wrote, "that the Lord was aiming at the conversion of the highest classes of society" in the city. "My meetings soon became thronged with . . . lawyers, physicians, merchants, and indeed all the most intelligent people. . . . The great majority of the leading men and women in the city were converts . . . the most influential people. . . ." [85] Though he recorded that these "prominent people" often wept and sighed in personal conversations with him about their souls, none of them cried out in the meetings, none fell in the aisles or writhed in agony on the floor or had to be carried out in a coma. Revivalism was becoming with Finney not only a trade but a respectable trade. It had to do so if it was to acquire and maintain the support of persons influential enough to carry through the revolution within the churches.

The "highest classes of society" in Rochester, however, were not like the sophisticated set in Philadelphia or Boston. They were more like the Yankee merchant pietists who had backed Finney in New York. Few of them were well educated or had any long-established position through ancestry or hereditary wealth. In this new commercial center on the Erie Canal most of the better people were simple sons and daughters of farmers who had emigrated westward from the poorer rural sections of New England at the turn of the century and who had made good. They were well-to-do but not so sophisticated as to deny their religious heritage. When Finney gravely asked them to come forward "to certain seats which I requested to be vacated" in the front of the church "and offer themselves to God," among the first to walk up the aisle was "a prominent lady and several

[84] Henry B. Stanton, quoted in Fletcher, *Oberlin,* Vol. I, p. 18.
[85] Finney, *Memoirs,* pp. 289, 293, 297.

others of her acquaintance" who belonged to the best "circle of society." The wealth and social position of this circle was so new that they almost felt guilty about it or fearful that it might suddenly be taken from them because they did not deserve it. By constantly assailing the sins of pride, social climbing, and the perils of laying up treasure on earth, Finney touched the nouveaux riches at their most tender point. Moreover, since Finney was preaching a new divinity, he urged even regular church members to come forward to the "anxious seats" and make a profession of faith. Church membership was no sign of regeneration, especially membership obtained under the auspices of hyper-Calvinists trained in eastern seminaries. A new conversion experience under true revival preaching was the only sure ground for salvation.[86]

The principal activities, or "machinery" as Weld called it, of the Rochester revival were Finney's preaching (three times on Sunday and three nights a week from September 10, 1830, to March 6, 1831), daily prayer meetings, the use of the anxious seat, frequent "enquiry meetings" for personal conversations with the anxious, and as a grand finale, a five-day Protracted Meeting at which Finney was assisted by eight or nine pastors and revivalists in conducting meetings from sunrise to midnight while all business activity came to a halt. Although the statistics of conversions were wildly exaggerated in the enthusiastic reports of the religious press as well as in the statements of ministers and laymen who participated, the best estimates fix the number of new church members in Rochester's three Presbyterian churches at about 350.[87] There was no estimate of the increase among the Methodists and Baptists though they also benefited. It was the reconsecration or reconversion of old church members which filled the anxious seats and the inquiry meetings. The revival spread far beyond Rochester as revivalists and pastors who visited the city carried its enthusiasm and message back to the surrounding towns. A wave of revivals broke out from New England to Ohio as the new divinity suddenly caught hold and the new measures proved an effective method for advancing them. Five years later Finney claimed that 100,000 persons had been added to the churches

86 Finney's theology and social message are discussed more fully in chap. 2.
87 See Fletcher, *Oberlin*, Vol. I, pp. 19–24.

in 1831 as a result of the spark ignited in Rochester. Presbyterian statistics more realistically record 60,000 new members between 1830 and 1833 over the whole nation.[88] Hyper-Calvinists might complain that most of the revival converts were hypocrites or self-deceived persons whose statements of faith were superficially obtained under pressure, but the days of cautious conversion were over. Between 1800 and 1835 the proportion of Protestant church members to national population grew from 7 per cent to 12½ per cent primarily as a result of revivalism and growing evangelical unity. Finney merely capped the climax of the second great awakening and solidified the new approach.

When the Rochester revival ended Finney was a man to be reckoned with both east and west. His influence was prodigious among the younger and more radical young men in the churches and particularly among the self-made Yankee businessmen. His correspondence contained letters asking advice on every conceivable aspect of church life. He was asked to recommend good strong revival ministers to fill important posts; he was asked to suggest revivalists to hold campaigns in cities to which he could not come; his advice was sought on the founding of new theological seminaries to train revival men and on rejuvenating old periodicals or starting new ones to support revival measures. Scores of calls for his services came from pastors and laymen across the country.

Finney was particularly anxious to promote the work in New York City which he had left unfinished. With the storm over Barnes in full force in Philadelphia in the spring of 1831 and with Taylor and Beecher battling for the new divinity in New Haven and Boston, Finney was hopeful that New York would soon be ripe for a concerted rallying of the forces. In October, 1830, eight of the ministers in New York who sympathized with the new measures or who were moderate Hopkinsians received permission from the Synod to establish a

88 For Finney's claim see his letter to Weld, July 21, 1836, *Letters of Theodore Weld,* Vol. I, p. 318. For other statistics see Herman C. Weber, *Presbyterian Statistics Through One Hundred Years, 1826–1836* (pub. by The General Council, Presbyterian Church in the U.S.A., 1927); Robert Baird, *The State and Prospects of Religion in America* (London, 1855), *passim;* Charles C. Cole, Jr., *The Social Ideas of the Northern Evangelists 1826–1860* (New York, 1954), pp. 13, 76–77.

Third Presbytery in the city and Finney's friends were fast making this into another "revival presbytery."[89] Lewis Tappan gave Finney a frank account of affairs in the city two weeks after the close of the Rochester revival which disclosed the mixture of pietistic fervor and cool calculation which characterized the urban phase of the anti-Calvinist revival movement. "The ministers generally do not much like your coming and will not probably invite you to preach in their pulpits. You would be cordially received I think by Messrs Norton, Leavitt, Parker, Austin, Dickinson, Baldwin, and Ludlow [the *avant-garde* revival nucleus]. The tide of feeling is too strong in the churches of Messrs Cox, Patton, Spring, Mason, Mathews, Snodgrass, Woodbridge, and White [the moderate Hopkinsians] for the ministers to *oppose* you. Influential laymen in the above churches and nearly all those who attend the morning prayer meeting will rejoice in your being here. A stream would flow that unless the ministers went with it would leave them high and dry. I fear no *schism* on account of your coming . . . and if there *is* a schism it must be all on the side of those who wish to go on in the old, dull, quiet way." Tappan concluded by urging Finney to come and erect "a battering Ram with which to assail the satanic ramparts in this City." In Tappan's mind these ramparts were associated more with the Calvinist-dominated ecclesiastical system than with the worldly dens of vice and corruption.[90]

Finney, however, was wiser than he had been in 1827. Experience had taught him that a revival undertaken in the face of strong clerical opposition in a large city was an almost hopeless task.[91] It was for this same reason that he had recently turned down invitations from revival men in Hartford and

[89] When the Third Presbytery of New York was formed officially on January 4, 1831, it contained thirteen ministers, almost all of whom eventually sided with the New School in 1838 although not all of them were friendly to Finney in 1831. See S. D. Alexander, *The Presbytery of New York 1738 to 1888* (New York, 1888), p. 101.

[90] Lewis Tappan to Finney, March 18, 1831, Finney Papers, OCL.

[91] See letter of Mathew LaRue Perrine to Gardiner Spring, April 9, 1831, in which Perrine says that Finney "does not wish to come [to New York] against the feelings of his brethren in the ministry" but which warns, "Attempts, Brother Spring, will be made to get Mr. Finney to visit New York. Many are engaged in it and will not be turned from their purpose. Can you not consistently express your approbation?" Spring, *Reminiscences,* Vol. I, pp. 223–25.

New Haven, though he must have felt flattered to have been invited to Taylor's bailiwick by ministers like Leonard Bacon, Timothy Dwight, Jr., Samuel Merwin, and C. A. Boardman.[92] He decided to let the situation in New York ripen a little longer and to make a bid for support in Boston by way of Providence.

He had received in May, 1831, an invitation from the Committee of Supply of the Union Orthodox (Congregational) Church in Boston to fill the pulpit in August during the absence of the pastor, the Rev. Samuel Green. Some of Finney's New York friends considered it a miracle that any church in Boston would open its doors to him, but Finney seemed to feel that he could get more support if he were cautious. In order to reconnoitre the situation he accepted an invitation from Josiah Chapin and his pastor to preach for a short time in Providence in July, 1831. As he suspected, he had scarcely been there a week when he received a letter from Lyman Beecher with an enclosure from Catharine Beecher explaining their stand in regard to his coming to Boston. Beecher, in his best Virginia-fence fashion, explained that he and his friends did not feel that Boston was "the best point of entrance for you into New England nor the *present* the best time. . . ." Beecher protested that he had no prejudices about "past differences of opinions about measures" for "with very little difference and that now on points of discretion unessential, you and I are as much, perhaps even more, *one* than almost any two men whom God has pleased to render conspicuous in his church." But certain "local and peculiar and, if we succeed, temporary Reasons" made the present time injudicious. True to his vision of ultimate evangelical assimilation, Beecher said he lamented "any division . . . in that great body of Evangelical men who seem to be called by heaven to lift the standard of revivals . . ." but nevertheless there were still obstacles that prevented Finney's coming to Boston.

Catharine Beecher explained these obstacles in more detail: "There is a large community here of literary, fastidious, pow-

[92] See Timothy Dwight [Jr.] to Finney, March [?], 1831, and Samuel Merwin *et al.* to Finney, April 12, 1831, Finney Papers, OCL. While these letters of invitation to New Haven made no reservations about Finney's doctrines they did express some hesitancy about his measures and preaching style which may have caused Finney to decline.

erful, and influential men, earnestly enlisted against revivals. . . . There is also a set of timid though good men who are already trembling for the present bold measures and whom it is very important to hold in one united body." Because of these men, Catharine went on, her father had been obliged to trim "all that is exceptionable in manner of language or modes of conducting religious instructions" from his methods. Of course, if Finney came to Boston, the Beechers would support him, but surely he would realize the difficult position that would put the revival leaders in; ". . . as you would not wish to cause them trouble . . ." Catharine concluded, "Hartford or New Haven would be a better location for you than Boston." Perhaps, some day, she said, wistfully, Finney and her father could be "fellow laborers *in the West.*" [93]

In other words, Beecher was still worried about the Hopkinsians and the Unitarians, and he did not trust Finney. A letter from Green's committee of supply put the matter more frankly. It said that when the question of inviting Finney had been placed before a meeting of the Boston ministers and laity the ministers felt "that your manner of presenting the truth is such that the minds of the Unitarians (we mean men of influence and education who would be attracted to hear you preach . . .) would be still more prejudiced against it; an evil which they have been laboring for years to remove. . . ." The ministers voted down the recommendation of "twenty deacons, or other influential members of the churches" to invite Finney, but the laymen of Green's church told him to ignore the opposition of the faint-hearted and come anyway.[94]

Finney was now in a position to force Beecher's hand. He wrote to the committee that he felt that he must abide by the decision made by the ministers. "I have been extensively supposed by New England ministers to be a kind of interloper crowding myself in here and there when I was not wanted. Dr. Beecher himself has viewed me in this light and accused me of floating upon the tide of popularity and laying ministers under a moral necessity of falling in with me and in my hear-

[93] Lyman Beecher and Catharine Beecher to Finney, August 2, 1831, Finney Papers, OCL.

[94] Committee of Supply of Union Church to Finney, August 2, 1831, Finney Papers, OCL. For Beecher's account of this see *Christian Examiner and General Review,* XIX (September, 1835), 124–25.

ing solemnly pledged himself to use his influence to oppose me if I came to New England." Finney made it quite clear that in his own mind "my views in regard to doctrine and revivals of religion are not that I know of materially changed," thereby implying that if anyone was to change it would have to be Beecher. "I have always felt," he concluded, "and do now believe that Dr. Beecher has been but very imperfectly acquainted with my views and practices." [95]

Upon receipt of this letter the influential laymen of Boston evidently appealed to Beecher to change his mind. Whether they threatened to move without him, as the laymen of New York had done, or whether they merely accused him of letting a personal grudge hinder the revival cause, Beecher decided that he must find a way either to yield gracefully or to obtain more substantial ammunition against Finney.[96] Beecher's way out of the dilemma was to send the Rev. Benjamin B. Wisner, pastor of Boston's Old South Church, to Providence to sit in, surreptitiously, on Finney's meetings in order to see whether or not Finney had changed and how much havoc he might wreak if he were to come to Boston. Wisner went, and after hearing three sermons, he was so impressed that instead of remaining incognito he introduced himself to Finney saying, "I came here a heresy hunter but here is my hand and my heart is with you." He promised to return to Boston and do his best to bring Finney there.[97]

On August 15 a letter was sent to the committee of Green's church signed by Beecher, Wisner, J. H. Fairchild, and G. W. Blagden on behalf of the Boston Congregational ministers' association: "During the last week one of our members [Wisner] has been providentially thrown in with Mr. Finney in conducting a four day's meeting and the beginning of a revival in Providence and has had full and free communications with Mr. Finney. The results have been communicated to us, and we

95 Finney to John Starkweather, August 8, 1831, Finney Papers, OCL.

96 Beecher's continued opposition was made more awkward by the fact that the religious journal which he edited, *The Spirit of the Pilgrims,* had that very month begun to publish a series of articles praising the new wave of revivalism in the West which had commenced under Finney's leadership at Rochester (an editorial decision which he must have made before he knew of the invitation to Finney by Green's church).

97 P. C. Headley, *Evangelists in the Church* (Boston, 1875), p. 164.

are happy to say that the difficulties and grounds of hesitation we felt are entirely removed." Finney was thus able to come to Boston not as the vacation supply of Green's church but, at the request of the Congregational ministers' association of Boston, "as a general labourer among the Evangelical churches in this city."[98] Though he preached principally in Park Street Church (in which Edward Beecher was acting as stated supply) he also held meetings in other churches in the city, including Lyman Beecher's.

Finney stayed in Boston for seven months, from August, 1831, to April, 1832. Beecher said patronizingly in his *Autobiography* that "he did very well," but Finney was not enthusiastic in his report of the work: "There seemed to be a peculiar type of religion there, not exhibiting that freedom and strength of faith which I had been in the habit of seeing in New York." He found that his "searching sermons" were "not at all palatable to the Christians of Boston" and "the attendance at Park Street Church became less and less." When he inquired why the church people seemed to dislike his preaching it turned out that they, like their ministers, were afraid of what the Unitarians would think of them if they showed too much enthusiasm. Finney wrote disparagingly in the manuscript of his *Memoirs* that Beecher evidently set "a very low" standard of spiritual zeal for membership in his church.[99] It was a perennial complaint of the rural pietist against the city pastor.

Beecher's fears that Finney would not be quite right for Boston were not entirely based on prejudice. Not only were the Unitarians on the lookout for any slip which might give them a handle, but the controversy between the Hopkinsians and the leaders of the New Haven theology was reaching a new crescendo at that very moment as a result of the great controversy between Nathaniel Taylor and Bennett Tyler. Finney was not familiar with the bitterness of New England theological quarrels nor with the pettiness with which minor deviations were, in times of stress, picked up and magnified by the

98 Lyman Beecher *et al.* to Committee of Supply of Union Church, August 15, 1831, Finney Papers, OCL.

99 Finney, *Memoirs,* pp. 313 ff., and MS of the *Memoirs,* p. 635. Finney Papers, OCL. Finney claimed that after their initial hesitancy the people of Boston warmed up to his preaching and that his revival was a success.

polemicists in the various religious journals which battened on controversy. Beecher might well have been jittery in 1831 as he saw his fond hopes for evangelical unity drifting over the dam.

Beecher's worst fears about Finney's coming to Boston were realized when, toward the end of October, Finney preached a sermon in Park Street Church entitled "Sinners Bound to Change Their Own Hearts." A Hopkinsian conservative named Asa Rand, who edited a religious journal in Boston called the *Volunteer,* was at the meeting. He took notes on the sermon and shortly after burst into print with a violent attack upon its "sentiments which we deem *subversive of the Gospel.*" It was clear that Rand was using Finney's sermon as a club with which to beat Beecher and Taylor, for the title of his pamphlet was *The New Divinity Tried.*

Beecher was upset. Wisner, who felt personally responsible for Finney's presence in Boston, published a reply to "Mr. Rand's strictures." Beecher reviewed Rand's article and Wisner's answer in the *Spirit of the Pilgrims.* The Princetonians lent their support to Rand in the *Biblical Repertory and Theological Review.* Finney simply kept on preaching and let his conversions attest to the validity of his views.

At last it was evident that a conjunction between the most radical features of western revivalism and the New Haven theology had taken place. Beecher and Wisner tried to express some qualifications in their defense of Finney, but they could no longer repudiate him or his measures. The issue which had been avoided at New Lebanon at last came home to roost in Beecher's own backyard. He had been trying for years to make Taylor's abstruse views seem orthodox. From now on he had the much more difficult task of making Finney's flat assertions seem so. The controversy which ensued from 1831 to 1837 made the issue of modern revivalism central in what had formerly been merely a speculative debate. In the process it destroyed Beecher's grand design to reform Calvinism from within for God, for country, and for Yale.

CHAPTER 2

"The Laws of Mind" and "The Right Use of Means"

Finney had escaped theological assault prior to 1831 primarily because he had never published any of his views (with the exception of his brief and nondoctrinal rebuttal to Nettleton). When Finney finally did publish two volumes of sermons and lectures in 1835, the *Biblical Repertory and Theological Review* of Princeton rejoiced that "the public can now learn what the new system is from the exposition of one of its chief promoters." Professor Albert B. Dod, who wrote the review, went on to say, "We have never had any doubt what would be the decision of the public mind respecting the new divinity and new-measure system of our day if its distinctive features could be brought out in the light and exposed to general observation." [1] The decision would be that it was heresy.

But what was heresy in that generation turned out to be orthodoxy in the next. By 1870 the Old School Presbyterians had joined hands with the New School and the democratically defined interpretation of orthodoxy proved victorious. In fact, by 1840, the evangelical views of Finney and Beecher and Taylor were held by the ministers of almost every nonliturgical denomination except the Old School Presbyterians, a few die-hard

[1] *Biblical Repertory and Theological Review* (Philadelphia), n.s. VII (July, 1835), 482. For discussion of this review, see below.

Hopkinsians, and the hard-shelled Baptists.[2] It was the same evangelicalism for which Barton W. Stone and Alexander Campbell had been forced out of the Presbyterian church in the first decade of the century, but the Princetonians were quite correct in seeing Finney as "one of its chief promoters." Finney's revivalism broke the dam maintained by "The Traditions of the Elders" (the title of one of his most pungent sermons) and transformed "the new system" from a minority to a majority religion. By mid-century it was in fact the national religion of the United States.

The sermon which the Rev. Asa Rand exposed to the light and heat of debate in the fall of 1831 was the first sermon included in Finney's first published volume, *Sermons on Various Subjects* (copyrighted in 1834) and the key to his theology. Rand had undoubtedly sat in Park Street Church night after night listening to Finney for the express purpose of evaluating his orthodoxy. He pounced upon "Sinners Bound to Change Their Own Hearts" with the infallible instinct of the heresy hunter. To him it seemed obvious that no man who held the views contained in this sermon could claim to believe in the Calvinism of the Westminster Confession. And yet Finney, unlike Stone and Campbell, had not repudiated Presbyterianism nor the Westminster Confession when he began to preach free will: "I could receive it," he said of the Confession, ". . . as containing the substance of Christian doctrine" even though "I could not put the same construction [on its statements] that was put on them at Princeton." [3]

Finney considered himself orthodox according to the standards of reason and experience and he did not feel that any other standards were necessary or valid: "The fact is, unless [a minister] can preach the Gospel as an experience . . . his speculations and theories will come far short of preaching the Gospel." [4] This pietistic concern for personal faith coupled with the implicit reproach against a learned, speculative min-

[2] Even the liturgical denominations, such as the Episcopalian and Lutheran, were markedly influenced by evangelicalism in the nineteenth century. See Sidney E. Mead, "The Rise of the Evangelical Conception of the Ministry (1607–1850)," in *The Ministry in Historical Perspective,* eds. H. R. Niebuhr and D. D. Williams (New York, 1956), p. 223.

[3] C. G. Finney, *Memoirs* (New York, 1876), p. 239.

[4] *Ibid.,* p. 56.

istry epitomized the whole evangelical movement. After 1835 churchgoers and ministers alike dropped their preoccupation with theology and based their religion on "experience." "Experience religion" or "heart religion" as opposed to "head religion" was the essence of modern revivalism from its outset despite Finney's (and Beecher's) Lockean claims regarding the reasonableness of Christianity.

When Finney first began to reason with sinners, his starting point was his own experience plus as much theology as common sense could make out of the Bible. He found that the doctrines which seemed to be most deeply imbedded in the religious thought of western New York, and in the eastern churches as well, were "physical depravity, consequent inability, and constitutional regeneration." It annoyed him intensely that men and women who were aroused by his preaching to a state of extreme anxiety over the sinful condition of their hearts nevertheless told him that they were born constitutionally wicked, that they could not overcome this wickedness by themselves, and that they were therefore prayerfully waiting and hoping that God would soon send the Holy Ghost to regenerate them and seal their election, if indeed they were among the elect. This attitude Finney called "cannot-ism" and it was primarily against "cannot-ism" that his "New Heart" sermon was directed.

Unlike Beecher and Taylor, who were more subtly attacking the same attitude in New England,[5] Finney did not try laboriously to construct a new speculative theory which would preserve the letter of Calvinism while redefining its spirit. The formula which Taylor concocted to save Calvinism ("Certainty with power to the contrary" [6]) was too abstruse for Finney and his auditors. To them Taylorism (or Beecherism) was just one more statement of "You can and you can't." Better to abandon Calvinism altogether than to save it at the expense of common sense. The beauty of Finney's sermon (which Rand failed to appreciate) was that it combined reason and emotion, faith in the Bible and faith in human intelligence, belief in the benevolence of God and belief in the perfectibility of man.

[5] For Beecher's opposition to the "fatalism" and "doctrine of dependence" which produced cannot-ism, see Lyman Beecher, *Autobiography, Correspondence, Etc.*, ed. Charles Beecher (New York, 1865), Vol. II, p. 187.

[6] See Sidney E. Mead, *Nathaniel W. Taylor* (Chicago, 1942), pp. 189–90.

In addition, Finney adroitly reconciled religion with the growing faith of Americans in science by justifying his revival methods in terms of human psychology, or, as he called it, "the laws of mind."

Taking his text from Ezekiel 18:31, "Make you a new heart and a new spirit, for why will ye die," he began by asking whether or not it was "reasonable" of God "to require the performance of the duty" of making a new heart and a new spirit "when at the same time he knows we have not power to obey; and that if ever the work is done, he must himself do the very thing which he requires of us?" [7] Here Finney reduced the whole complex system of the Westminster Confession to the simplicity of a yes-or-no question. What was more, he put the question in such a way that there could be no doubt of the answer which any "reasonable" man would give. The sermon went on to demonstrate how unreasonable the Calvinists (Princetonian or Hopkinsian) were to think God would be so "evidently unjust" or inconsistent as to require men to do what they could not do. If learned theologians had not confused the issue, anyone who used his common sense would see that God's words meant exactly what they said. They were a reasonable request to perform a reasonable task. "As therefore, God requires men to make to themselves a new heart on pain of eternal death, it is the strongest possible evidence that they are able to do it."

In the process of proving this, Finney assumed that God worked according to fixed laws of psychology. Appealing to the American penchant for practical scientific explanations, he put religion squarely on the side of progress: "although the Bible was not given to teach us mental philosophy, yet we may rest assured that all its declarations are in accordance with the true philosophy of mind." Like everyone else in 1831, Finney had a mechanistic concept of "the laws of mind" and he claimed elsewhere that they were "in some respects analogous to the law of gravitation in the material universe." [8] A large part of the confusion in theology, he maintained, was the result of the deplorable ignorance of Luther and Calvin concerning the

[7] This and the subsequent quotations from the "New Heart" sermon are taken from C. G. Finney, *Sermons on Various Subjects* (New York, 1835), pp. 3–28.

[8] *Ibid*, p. 58.

science of the mind. Their "reformation was but partial" because they used "the systems of mental philosophy that still prevailed" in those old days. As a result, they "introduced embarrassments and contradiction, mystery and absurdity into the gospel" which has "to the present day clogged the chariot wheels of [God's] mercy." [9]

The "New Heart" sermon demonstrated by means of the modern system of mental philosophy the absurdity of the three Calvinistic dogmas which clogged the chariot wheels of Finney's nineteenth-century reformation of the Reformation. It was a reformation based upon a strange mixture of the two prevailing patterns of contemporary philosophy, the religious psychology of the Scottish Common Sense school and the self-reliant intuitionism of the American transcendental school, though Finney probably was not aware of his debt to either. In his sermon Finney asked whether it was sensible to construe God's command to make a new heart so as to mean "that we are to bring to pass any constitutional change in ourselves?" Was it not absurd that "some persons speak of a change of heart as something miraculous—something in which the sinner is to be entirely passive, and for which he is to wait in the use of means, as he would wait for a surgical operation or an electric shock"?

The gist of Finney's arguments against a "constitutional change" was that such a change was "unnecessary" because there was nothing physically wrong with the human heart in the first place. Far from being born morally corrupt and unable ever to act rightly, he said, man "has the understanding to perceive and weigh; he has conscience to decide upon the nature of moral opposites; he has the power and liberty of choice." The heart, or soul, of man was not depraved by Adam's sin but prejudiced by self-interest and ignorance. It did not need a supernatural electrical shock, but a humanly engineered reorientation. To alter the heart the preacher merely had to jar it out of its prejudice for evil. "I understand a change of heart, as the term is used here, to be just what we mean by a change of mind. . . ."

Because in American democracy all the complex problems of freedom and power were reduced to voting for, or against,

[9] *Ibid.*, p. 60.

one of two candidates, Finney applied the political metaphor to religion: "the world is divided into two great political parties; the difference between them is that one party choose Satan as the god of this world. . . . The other party choose Jehovah for their governor." Conversion was the decision to vote for Jehovah and to support his administration. It did not "imply a constitutional alteration of the powers of the body any more than a change of mind in regard to the form of administration of human government." In this metaphor, God proposed and man disposed. Instead of his electing men to heaven, they elected him to rule the world. Revival preaching, therefore, amounted to a kind of campaign oratory for Jehovah's party.

One of the promises of the revivalistic campaign orator was to insist that under God's administration everyone would be happier. "God has established a government and proposed by the exhibition of his own character to produce the greatest practical amount of happiness in the universe." For a sinner to have a change of heart was for him "to prefer supremely the glory of his sovereign and the good of the public to his own separate interest." Or, "In other words, a change from selfishness to benevolence." [10] Finney refused to believe those sinners who told him that the motives tempting them to selfishness and iniquity were stronger than those which would lead them to prefer "the infinitely greater good" of God's kingdom. Wickedness was "an obstinate choice of sin" and, Finney asked, "Is it not as easy to choose right as wrong?" He exalted man's free will to virtual omnipotence when he said that to resist choosing right "When the Son of God approaches you, gathering motives from heaven, earth, and hell, and pours them in a focal blaze upon" the mind is "to exert such a giant strength, I had almost said the strength of Omnipotence." [11] Contrary to Calvinism, grace was not only resistible, but the depraved exerted omnipotence in refusing to transform themselves.

Nevertheless Finney did not want to reduce God to the role of a frustrated parent capable only of punishing his recalcitrant children. True, the sinner alone had the responsibility for accepting or resisting the grace of God, but he could not reform

[10] *Ibid.*, pp. 11, 7. For the relationship between this idea of conversion and that of Samuel Hopkins, and for its implications regarding social reform, see below, pp. 102 ff.

[11] *Ibid.*, p. 14.

himself without some external help. Finney devoted the major part of the "New Heart" sermon to explaining the respective roles of the "four different agencies" which were active in the conversion of a sinner. He did this by means of his famous illustration about the daydreamer walking along the bank of Niagara Falls: "Suppose yourself to be standing on the bank of the Falls of Niagara. As you stand upon the verge of the precipice, you behold a man lost in deep reverie, approaching its verge, unconscious of his danger. He approaches nearer, until he actually lifts his foot to take the final step that shall plunge him in destruction. At this moment you lift your warning voice above the roar of the foaming waters and cry out, *Stop*. The voice pierces his ear and breaks the charm that binds him; he turns instantly upon his heel, all pale and aghast, quivering from the verge of death."

The man in the reverie, said Finney, was the careless sinner on his way to hell. The observer who shouted to him was the revival preacher or soul-winning Christian. And the word "Stop" was "the word of life," the truth of the gospel. (And, incidentally, the paleness and quivering were the unavoidable emotional excitement that accompanied such a crisis experience.) Now the agency of the sinner in turning himself, and the agencies of the preacher and the Word were clear enough, but where was the agency of God or the Holy Spirit? Finney claimed that there were two ways in which God's agency was at work in this instance. In the first place his agency was "a providential one." If God in his providence had not placed the observer at the right spot at the right time, the careless daydreamer would have plunged to his death. Surely it was an act of God, Finney wrote elsewhere, that "sometimes sends a minister along just at the time he is wanted," and surely it often happened that sinners were "awakened by some providential circumstances, as sickness, a thunderstorm, pestilence, death in the family, disappointment or the like. . . ." [12]

The second way God's agency worked was more important. Providential acts might awaken a sinner, but they seldom were sufficient of themselves to make him change his heart. "In the conversion of a sinner there is something more than the provi-

[12] Charles G. Finney, *Lectures on Revivals of Religion* (New York, 1835), pp. 15, 149.

dence of God employed; for here not only does the providence of God so order it that the preacher cries, *Stop,* but the Spirit of God forces the truth home upon him with such tremendous power as to induce him to turn." In other words, the preacher and the Spirit worked hand in hand, for it was "through the living voice of the preacher [that] the Spirit cries *Stop.*"

Later in the sermon Finney compared the work of the Spirit upon the mind to that of a lawyer upon a jury and said that "the strivings of the Spirit of God with men is not a physical scuffling but a debate; a strife not of body with body but of mind with mind . . . in the action and reaction of vehement argumentation." The Spirit was an expert in the laws of the mind, a psychologist far more skilled than the preacher. The Spirit of God "knows perfectly" the state of the sinner's mind and "understands all the reasons that have led him" to hold out. Only the Spirit was able to combat those unspoken arguments by which the sinner justifies his resistance to God.

Finney admitted, however, that in the end "The particular manner in which the Spirit of God carries on his debates and strivings with the mind is what, in this life, we shall probably never know. Nor is it important that we should," because "Every Christian knows that in some way the truth was kept before his mind and made to bear and press upon him, and hedge him in until he was constrained to yield. These are matters of experience." The appeal to experience was the last resort in the face of the ultimate mystery. It bolstered the pietistic view that no one could understand religion who had not experienced conversion. But Finney never quite asserted that. He insisted that religion could be made comprehensible.

Yet the harder he labored to make it comprehensible the farther the agency of the Holy Spirit receded into the background and the more the voice of the preacher advanced to the foreground. "You see," he said at the conclusion of the "New Heart" sermon, "it is most reasonable to expect sinners, if they are converted at all, to be converted under the voice of the living preacher. . . ." His final remarks in the sermon were therefore addressed to the preacher: "he who deals with souls should study well the laws of the mind" because only a man thoroughly skilled in the workings of the human mind can "adapt his manner and his matter to the state and circumstances" of each new situation. The scientific or pragmatic approach was, he claimed, as valid in religion as in nature. The basic fallacy of Calvinism was that it taught that "there is no philosophical connection between means and ends in the conversion of sinners." This resulted in the foolish idea that sinners must "sit and quietly wait for some invisible hand to be stretched down from heaven and perform some surgical operation, infuse some new principle, or implant some constitutional taste; *after* which they suppose they shall be *able* to obey God." As long as Calvinists, of whatever variety, expounded their "metaphysical subtleties, absurd exhibitions of the variety of the sovereignty of God, inability, physical regeneration, and constitutional depravity" the average man would "dismiss the subject" of religion as "altogether incomprehensible," and rightly so.

The sermon ended with the call for sinners to obey God's reasonable command and make their own new hearts at once. The sense of urgency was emphasized by the injunction which was henceforth a *sine qua non* of all revival preaching, "Another moment's delay and it may be too late forever."

It is not difficult to see why a conservative Hopkinsian like Asa Rand would denounce the "New Heart" sermon's derogatory caricature of his beliefs. It is also not difficult to see why Rand welcomed such a blunt, frontal assault, for here at last all the heresies which the Calvinists had suspected in the new divinity were stated so openly that no one could miss them. Nor did Rand fail to see that by attacking Finney in Boston he would be able at the same time to attack Beecher and all those who had invited Finney there. Rand pointed out that these views of Finney's which he believed "to be unscriptural and dangerous" were "somewhat prevalent in orthodox congregations at the present time." They were, he said, "subversive of the Gospel." [13]

Finney was not particularly upset by Rand's accusations, but Beecher and Wisner and the other ministers supporting the revival were deeply offended. They insisted that they were as faithful Calvinists as any, and Wisner began his review of

[13] Asa Rand, *The New Divinity Tried* (Boston, 1832), p. 13. This pamphlet is a slightly revised reprint of the article Rand had printed in the *Volunteer* in November, 1831.

Rand's strictures on Finney by pointing out that "other orthodox Congregational ministers in the city are implicated" in Rand's wild cries of heresy and Arminianism. By carefully defining and redefining Finney's terminology, Wisner proceeded to show that his views could easily be made to square with one or another of the various interpretations of Calvinism which had been advanced since the time of Edwards. With great ingenuity he managed to quote Edwards, Hopkins, Emmons, Bellamy, Leonard Woods, and even Calvin and Augustine in defense of Finney. Finney, he asserted, "agrees with Augustine, Calvin, President Edwards, Dr. Hopkins, Dr. Woods, and the great majority of orthodox divines in New England . . ." on the basic point that "moral character is to be ascribed to voluntary exercises alone."[14] The only criticism which Wisner would allow of the sermon was that "Mr. F. holds that the Spirit in converting men does not move them 'by a direct and immediate act' but 'presents motives by means of the truth' and so 'persuades' them and they yield to his persuasion." This was the central issue at stake and Wisner admitted siding with Rand when he said he believed that the Spirit's operation "is by an immediate influence on the mind" and not simply by persuasion. Nevertheless, Wisner concluded by flatly maintaining that Finney was orthodox "in doctrine even if not in the philosophical manner of explaining doctrine."[15]

Beecher expressed his approval of Wisner's rebuttal to Rand and said it was regrettable that Rand had tried "to render Mr. F. an object of suspicion" and "to divide and distract the Orthodox community" over the sermon.[16] Most of the novelties "charged upon Mr. F. disappear upon a right explanation of terms," Beecher insisted. He agreed with Wisner, however, that Finney's view that the Spirit merely acts by persuasion

[14] Quoted in the review of Rand's and Wisner's pamphlets in *The Spirit of the Pilgrims* (Boston), V (March, 1832), 167.

[15] Finney in his *Memoirs* did not consider that he and Wisner were in agreement about Calvinism despite Wisner's good intentions in defending him. Wisner "was not then prepared to take the ground against President Edwards, and the general orthodox view of New England that the Spirit's agency was not physical but moral." *Memoirs,* p. 317.

[16] It seems a fair assumption that under the delicate circumstances it was Beecher who reviewed the pamphlets of Rand and Wisner in the *Spirit of the Pilgrims,* V (March, 1832), 161 ff.

rather than by "a special and direct influence . . . upon the mind" was not in agreement with his own view of the matter, yet he saw no reason to classify Finney with the Arminians. Beecher put a bold face on the situation by concluding his review of Rand's attack: "In the controversy the parties on both sides are decided believers of the Orthodox faith—in the strict technical sense of the term *equally* Orthodox; as they agree in maintaining the great and essential doctrines of the gospel and differ only in their modes of stating and explaining some of these doctrines."

This was too much for the Calvinists of Princeton. The month after Beecher's irenical mist settled over Boston, the *Biblical Repertory and Theological Review* issued its defense of Rand, excusing his publication of Finney's sermon abstract without Finney's permission on the ground that "there may be cases in which the evil produced by a popular preacher constantly presenting erroneous views in his discourses is so serious that the usual etiquette of literary proceedings should be sacrificed. . . ." The Princetonians felt that Wisner's defense of Finney was far more to be condemned than Rand's strictures because "instead of clearly and frankly stating the distinguishing principles" of the new and old divinity, it was "an anxious attorney-like mincing of matters; a claiming to agree with everybody." [17]

The effect of the quarrel upon Finney's friends and followers was evident from some of the letters which he received at the time. A layman from Auburn, New York, wrote him praising the sermon for its *"simplicity, beauty,* and *plainness* of evangelical doctrine" and said that its views "are not only founded on the principles of common sense but that they are the very *perfection of common sense."* [18] Another friend complained that Wisner's defense of Finney had not been vigorous and forthright enough: "great men not infrequently get into fogs, and it seems to me there is a particle of mist about Dr.

[17] *Biblical Repertory and Theological Review,* n.s. VII (April, 1832), 278 ff. The review was written by Charles Hodge.

[18] T. Spencer to Finney, February 22, 1832, Finney Papers, OCL. Since the sermon does not appear to have been published until 1835, Spencer either received a manuscript copy from Finney or merely commented upon the pamphlets and reviews which quoted it.

W."[19] Joshua Leavitt, editor of the *New York Evangelist,* whom Finney consulted about publishing the sermon, warned him against using the term "moral suasion" in discussing the agency of the Holy Spirit. But Leavitt went on to reveal much about the theological outlook of Finney's supporters when he said, "You know one half the good men do not know but that all doctrine is alike, if only seasoned with a little 'pious talk,' and that falsehood will do just as well as truth to convert the world." The subscribers to the *New York Evangelist* "are all the while ringing in my ears about too much doctrinal discussion" in its columns.[20]

What the readers of Leavitt's paper wanted, and what Finney's preaching provided, was a nondenominational theology based on a simple, literal interpretation of the Bible. They wanted a theology which could be grasped, believed in, and expressed by the average man no matter how little schooling he had had. Above all, they wanted a theology which was in harmony with the optimistic spirit of the times. Lewis Tappan did not even want to call it a theology: we have "too much 'theology' in the church now and too little of the Gospel" he said in 1831. He wanted "ardent and practical men," not theologians and controversialists.[21] In working toward "the great evangelical assimilation," Finney was more than willing to satisfy supporters like Tappan. He continually attacked sectarian creeds and dogmas which, he said, encumbered the truth and divided men on nonessential points. His sermons contained frequent references to "the fundamental truths," "the substance of the gospel," and "the cardinal doctrines of Christianity which are enhanced in the experience of every true convert." "No church on earth," he said in 1835, "has a right to

19 S. H. Mann to Finney, March 9, 1832, Finney Papers, OCL. Throughout the Finney Papers there are frequent sarcastic references by Finney's friends to "learned Doctors of divinity" and "D.D.'s" which indicate the pietistic impatience with a learned ministry.

20 Joshua Leavitt to Finney, February 26, 1832, Finney Papers, OCL. Leavitt also said that the subscribers did not like him to attack the Methodists for their Arminianism in the *New York Evangelist.* "Let the Methodists alone," they told him.

21 Lewis Tappan to Theodore Weld, October 25, 1831, *Letters of Theodore Dwight Weld, Angelina Grimke Weld, and Sarah Grimke, 1822–1844,* ed. G. H. Barnes and D. L. Dumond (New York, 1934), Vol. I, p. 52.

impose its extended confession on a young convert who admits the fundamentals of religion." [22]

"Those great fundamental points" which were to be the basis of evangelical unity for the next century were, according to Finney, "the divine authority of the scriptures, the necessity of the influences of the Holy Spirit, the divinity of Christ, the doctrine of total [but "voluntary"] depravity and [total "voluntary"] regeneration, the necessity of the atonement ["equal to the wants of all mankind"], justification by faith, and the eternal punishment of the wicked." But even this was an over-complicated way of explaining the truth. Finney considered it a perfectly proper and complete statement of faith if a convert, after a conversion experience, could honestly say, "I love the Lord Jesus Christ and wish to obey his command." [23]

The controversy over Finney's "New Heart" sermon henceforth committed Beecher to defending Finney just as he had defended Taylor. It also drew the Hopkinsians further away from Beecher and Taylor and closer to the Presbyterians of Princeton and Philadelphia.[24] The growing split in New England was evident in several ways. The same issue of the *Spirit of the Pilgrims* which contained Beecher's defense of Finney in March, 1832, also contained a letter from Taylor defending himself to Joel Hawes of Hartford against charges "that I am unsound in the faith" and denying that he believed in conversion by "moral suasion." Five years before, Hawes had gone to New Lebanon with Beecher to rebuke Finney; now he was rebuking Taylor. Shortly after Taylor justified himself to Hawes, Leonard Woods, whom Beecher had consulted about the New Lebanon meeting but who did not attend it, published an article which Finney took to be a direct attack on the "New Heart" sermon.[25] In April, 1832, Heman Humphrey of Am-

[22] Finney, *Sermons on Various Subjects,* pp. 54, 78; Finney, *Lectures on Revivals,* pp. 148, 364–65. This was a direct assault upon the common practice in Presbyterian and Congregational churches of requiring all applicants for church membership to affirm their belief in the tenets of the Westminster Confession. For an illustration of this practice, see William B. Sprague, *Lectures on Revivals of Religion* (Albany, 1832), appendix, p. 54.

[23] Finney, *Lectures on Revivals,* pp. 364–65. See also Finney, *Memoirs,* p. 134 for a statement of "the fundamentals."

[24] For proof of this, see the sympathetic review of Sprague's *Lectures on Revivals* in *Biblical Repertory and Theological Review,* n.s. IV (October, 1832), 455 ff., esp. 487.

[25] Finney, *Memoirs,* p. 317.

herst, another of Beecher's allies at New Lebanon, joined Ashbel Green of Philadelphia and nineteen other ministers, including Edward D. Griffin, Joel Hawes, and Noah Porter, to provide a prolific rebuttal to new measure revivalism in the appendix to William Sprague's *Lectures on Revivals* (for which Leonard Woods wrote the introduction). Sprague had specifically designed the book and solicited the letters for its appendix in order "to distinguish between a genuine revival and a spurious excitement."[26] It was also in 1832 that plans were first set on foot by Nettleton, Caleb J. Tenney (another New Lebanon ally), Bennett Tyler, Nathan Perkins, and a score of other Hopkinsians to found a new theological seminary in East Windsor, Connecticut, to preserve the ancient faith from the heresies of Yale.

In short, the schism within the ranks of the New England Calvinists was virtually completed by the time Finney left Boston. By the spring of 1832 the lines were also drawn in the coming conflict within Presbyterianism. During the course of the controversy from 1832 to 1837, the Presbyterians tried both Lyman Beecher and his son, Edward, for heresy, Finney left the Presbyterian church in disgust, and the wave of revivalism which Finney had helped to inaugurate in 1825 ground slowly to a halt.

When Finney concluded his revival in Boston in April, he was tired and somewhat discouraged. The revival had not been particularly successful and although he had received invitations from many other places he did not know where to go next. Joel Parker informed him that a Second Free Presbyterian Church had been organized in New York and asked whether Finney would come and be its pastor. At the same time Theodore Weld began to press him to come west to Cincinnati where some conservative Presbyterians were trying to prosecute Finney's old friend and coworker from Rochester, Asa Mahan, for new divinity heresy. The Presbytery of Cincinnati was fast becoming the center of new divinity activity in the West just as the Second Presbytery of Philadelphia and the Third Presbytery of New York were new divinity centers in the East. The old conflict in Finney's mind between rallying his

26 Sprague, *Revivals,* preface, p. v.

forces in the East or in the West returned again in even more dramatic form as Weld and Lewis Tappan posed the respective arguments. "I suppose," Weld wrote to him in February, 1832, "you will still reiterate the old assertion that in *New York* especially you can sway the West thro the hundreds of business men who resort thither from here." But these visitors were "but a drop in the bucket" of the great population of the West, and besides they could not be "Finneyized" simply by hearing him once or twice amid the bustle of the city. "You can never move this vast valley by working the lever in Boston, New York, or Philadelphia." And since the Ohio and Mississippi Valley was "to be the battle field of the world," it was essential that Finney come there. "You could command audiences of thousands. Their camp meetings all over this region would afford you immeasurably greater field of effort than you have ever occupied." Weld concluded by warning him, "Here Satan's seat is. A mighty effort must be made to dislodge him *soon* or the West is undone." [27]

Tappan's letter two weeks later countered Weld by reminding Finney that he himself had warned "about the danger of too many men abandoning the east." Weld had forgotten, said Tappan, that "measures adopted here thrill the nation" because of the awe with which people look upon "the mighty power of a multitudinous city." New York was the heart of the nation and "This city must be converted or the nation is lost. Do what may be done elsewhere, and leave this city the headquarters of Satan, and the nation is not saved. . . ." [28]

With Satan's headquarters established both east and west, Finney chose to go to New York. Weighing heavily in his decision was the news that Lewis Tappan had bought and remodelled the Chatham Street Theater to house the Second Free Presbyterian Church. When Finney first heard about the purchase of a theater as a revival center, he agreed with Tappan about "the *sensation*" it would cause. But he expressed some qualms about the propriety of the move: "Is not the location too filthy for decent people to go there?" he asked. Tappan

[27] Weld to Finney, February 28, 1832, *Letters of Theodore Weld,* Vol. I, pp. 66–68.

[28] Lewis Tappan to Finney, March 16, 1832, Lewis Tappan Papers, Library of Congress.

said that it was not. Finney then remarked that it was "contiguous to Dr. Spring, Mr. Rice," and other well-known Presbyterian pastors. To which Tappan replied tersely, "Would it be murdering souls to draw away half of Dr. Spring's congregation?"

Tappan took a leaf from Finney's revival tactics and theories: "By taking this theatre and appropriating it for a church the whole city will talk of it, wonder, inquire, and visit it. We then have secured the attention of a vast multitude, and the measures subsequently taken will be made known to them. . . . It will have the effect [that] storming a redoubt, or taking cannon and turning them upon the enemy has in an army. The time seems to have come to take bold and decided measures. Have you lost your courage? Have you become 'prudent'?"

Finney knew the advantage of bold and decided measures to excite attention, but he still wondered whether "decent people would go there permanently." Tappan said that they would, though perhaps they would not be "such xians as some of the fastidious deacons, etc. of Boston who think there must be 'pomp and circumstance' connected with a church and nothing out of the way to offend the polite, formal, etc." would prefer. Tappan also pointed out that he was willing to pay $3000 for renovating the theater and to help sustain the rent of $2000 a year, and that Finney's salary would be $1500. The theater, he said, would hold 2500 to 3000 persons and "There is a dwelling house contiguous to the theatre *for the minister*" which Tappan would provide $700 to furnish. Finney raised a last query about his desire to do some revival preaching in other places from time to time, and Tappan answered, "The brethren w^{d} consent to your ranging 2 months in hot weather I presume." [29]

So Finney went from Boston directly to New York to become the pastor of the Chatham Street Chapel (the Second Free Presbyterian Church) and a member of the Third Presbytery. He had been an itinerant revivalist for over ten years, since the day of his conversion in 1821. His revival days were by no means ended, for he continued to spend part of each year in

[29] Lewis Tappan to Finney, March 16, 1832, Lewis Tappan Papers, Library of Congress.

such activity for the rest of his life, including two trips to England to hold meetings. But he was never again to devote himself wholly to revivalism, nor did any of his later meetings match his early success.

A few months after Finney began his pastorate in New York an event occurred which dramatically highlighted the shifting complexion of the fight for the new divinity. Lyman Beecher decided to give up the attempt to save Boston from the Unitarians and New England Congregationalism from a schism. He accepted a long-standing offer to go west to Cincinnati to become President and Professor of Theology at Lane Seminary. In a sense he was going out to substitute for Finney whose repeated refusals to heed the Macedonian cries of Weld and Mahan from that city had convinced them to look elsewhere. Lane was a new divinity Presbyterian seminary to train revival men. Asa Mahan had accepted a position as trustee in the fall of 1831 as part of his attempt to wrest the city and the Ohio Valley from the Scotch-Irish hyper-Calvinists who had crept into the region from the South. The money behind the seminary came from New England and western Yankees, and the Tappan brothers were among its principal supporters. The choice of Beecher for president marked a further step in the unity of the western and New England wings of the revival movement. Because Lane was a Presbyterian seminary, Beecher had to be "Presbyterianized" in order to take the job. But he was not sure that the conservatives in the Presbytery of Cincinnati would accept him. He therefore applied for admission to the Third Presbytery of New York from which he could easily transfer to the Presbytery of Cincinnati. Finney and his friends controlled this presbytery but they were willing to forget the New Lebanon convention. They certified that Beecher was orthodox in his interpretation of the Westminster Confession and could be accepted into the Presbyterian ranks. The Rev. Gardiner Spring, however, whom Beecher had considered an ally at the time of the New Lebanon convention, opposed this action by the Third Presbytery and refused to admit Beecher's orthodoxy. In fact, Spring was so provoked by what he considered Beecher's capitulation to the new views that when Beecher was admitted to the presbytery Spring protested to the

Synod of New York in a vain attempt to keep Beecher from contaminating the Presbyterian church.[30]

The last stage in Finney's career began in 1835 when, after three fruitful years in New York, he went west to become Professor of Theology (and later President) of Oberlin Collegiate Institute. Here he carried out the work which Beecher bungled so badly at Lane. Beecher's innate conservatism had reacted against the rising tide of abolition which engulfed the Midwest in general and revival men in particular after the founding of the American Anti-Slavery Society in 1833. When Beecher sided with the Lane trustees in prohibiting the students from discussing abolition in August, 1834, ninety-three out of the one hundred students, led by Theodore Weld, left the seminary in protest. The Tappans were furious. They had both become ardent in the antislavery cause, which in their minds was one of the most important aspects of the revival movement to reform the country. "The Lane rebels," those students who had resigned, were the cream of the revival crop, most of them in their late twenties and early thirties, like Weld, and all of them devoted to the causes of benevolent reform and new measure preaching. It was to save these future leaders that the Tappans, Mahan, and Weld persuaded Finney to give up his New York pastorate in 1835 and assume in a new form the leadership of the cause he had promoted for so long.[31]

Finney's interest in abolition was hesitant and vacillating but his interest in educating a new set of revival men to replace the inefficient and lukewarm graduates of eastern seminaries had always been strong. In 1827 he assisted George Gale in founding the Oneida Academy for this purpose. In 1831 he helped Gilbert Morgan's Rochester Institute for Practical Education, and he was instrumental in the founding of the Troy and Albany School of Theology in 1833. Concerning the latter he and Beman had written to Weld in 1832, "We have determined, if the Lord will, to build a new school" in Troy based upon "low Church, new measure, manual labor" principles. "We intend to strike a blow and a heavy one too" for the re-

[30] See Robert S. Fletcher, *A History of Oberlin College* (Oberlin, Ohio, 1943), Vol. I, p. 53; Beecher, *Autobiography,* Vol. II, p. 284; Samuel J. Baird, *History of the New School* (Philadelphia, 1868), p. 468.

[31] See Gilbert H. Barnes, *The Anti-Slavery Impulse* (New York, 1933), pp. 64 ff., and Fletcher, *Oberlin,* pp. 142 ff.

vival cause. "If you want to see ministers made of the right stamp, lend a hand in this enterprise." [32]

Finney had had no hand in the founding of Oberlin in 1834, but the man who carried the main burden of it, the Rev. John J. Shipherd, was a new measure man whom Finney had asked to accept a pastorate at Stephentown, New York, after his revival there in 1827. In accepting the offer to go to Oberlin, Finney explained to two of the Lane rebels, "I see and have long seen that without a new race of ministers we can not possibly go much further." [33] To the creation of this new race he devoted the remainder of his life and during the vacations at Oberlin he conducted revivals himself.

On the eve of his departure for Oberlin, Finney published the most significant single work of his career, the *Lectures on Revivals of Religion.* Its influence upon revivalism and the profession of evangelism during the next century was immense. It was in reviewing this book (and simultaneously his *Sermons on Various Subjects*) in 1835 that the Presbyterians of Princeton acknowledged Finney to be "one of the chief promoters" of "the new system" of religion and demanded that he admit his heresies and "leave our church" at once.[34]

Finney's doctrinal heresies had been under attack ever since Rand's article in 1831, but what annoyed the Princetonians in the *Lectures on Revivals* was Finney's open denunciation of the ecclesiastical polity of the church. Finney not only denounced the General Assembly's report on the revivals of 1831 (which had damned them with faint praise), but he specifically attacked the ecclesiastical trials directed against the new school leaders, Beman, Barnes, and George Duffield: "These things in the Presbyterian church, their contentions and janglings are so ridiculous, so wicked, so outrageous, that no doubt there

[32] Finney and N. S. S. Beman to Weld, November 30, 1832, *Letters of Theodore Weld,* Vol. I, p. 91.

[33] Finney to H. B. Stanton and George Whipple, January 18, 1835, Finney Papers, OCL.

[34] *Biblical Repertory and Theological Review,* n.s. VII (July–October, 1835), 482, 474. Finney did leave the Presbyterian church in March, 1836, when he gave up his pastorate of the Second Free Presbyterian Church to become pastor of the Congregational Broadway Tabernacle, a position which he held simultaneously with his professorship at Oberlin until 1837. See also Susan H. Ward, *The History of the Broadway Tabernacle* (New York, 1901), pp. 27 ff.; Finney, *Memoirs,* p. 325.

is a jubilee in hell every year about the time of the meeting of the General Assembly." [35]

But the lasting importance of the *Lectures on Revivals* lay not in its strictures on Presbyterian ecclesiasticism nor in its doctrines, but in its careful delineation of the means and measures for promoting revivals. The Princeton reviewer, Professor Dod, was not far wrong when he said that through Finney's "experiments" with "the efficacy of different measures . . . the house of God becomes transformed into a kind of laboratory." The twenty-two lectures constituted a professional handbook of revival techniques which represented the quintessence of thirteen years of extensive preaching experience and shrewd observation. The treatment of such subjects as "How to Promote a Revival," "How to Preach the Gospel," "Means to be Used with Sinners," and "What a Revival of Religion Is" provided the definitive statement of techniques and criteria for modern revivalism. Few revivalists since have failed to quote Finney's defense of new measures in combatting the enemies of revivals in their own day.

The *Lectures on Revivals* purported to be based as soundly upon scientific laws as any book of physics or engineering. In his "New Heart" sermon Finney had briefly indicated the laws of mind which governed the conversion of individual sinners. In this book he explained the laws of cause and effect which governed the successful promotion of mass revivalism. "God has connected means with ends through all the departments of his government—in nature and in grace." Consequently, "promoting a revival of religion," like preaching to individual sinners, ought "to be judged by the ordinary rules of cause and effect." Revivalism was as much a science as bridge building. It was in the first lecture of this book that Finney asserted with the finality of a physicist defining a law of leverage that a revival "is a purely philosophical result of the right use of the constitutional means," and by philosophical he meant scientific.[36]

[35] Finney, *Lectures on Revivals,* pp. 268–69.

[36] *Ibid.,* pp. 17, 13, 12. Finney's book was not the first to discuss the theory and practice of revivalism but it was the most popular and the most clear-cut in its defense of *modern* revivalism. It is apparent that Finney borrowed some ideas from Calvin Colton's *History and Character of American Revivals* (see especially pp. 63–64, 204–20, in the second edition of Colton's book [London,

Finney went even farther: "The connection between the right use of means for a revival and a revival is as philosophically sure as between the right use of means to raise grain and a crop of wheat. I believe, in fact, it is more certain and that there are fewer instances of failure." In this sense "philosophical" meant virtually "inevitable." He specifically refuted the old view of Jonathan Edwards that revivals were miracles which ministers "had no more agency in producing than they had in producing thunder or a storm of hail or an earthquake." This, said Finney, was as "absurd" as to believe that men had to wait upon God for conversion. If men could change their own hearts they could also promote revivals.

In his explanation of conversion according to the laws of mind, he had made a slight obeisance to the agency of the Holy Spirit. Now he did his best to leave God some part in the production of revivals by saying, "But means will not produce a revival, we all know, without the blessing of God." However, this brief acknowledgment of the supernatural element in revivals was buried beneath such a mass of scientific certitude in the other direction that it was forgotten. Men were, for all practical purposes, as omnipotent in this sphere as in effecting or rejecting their own conversions.[37]

The basic laws of the mind were not dealt with at great length in the *Lectures on Revivals,* but a knowledge of them

1832] for parallels) just as he did from Edwards, but Finney went far beyond all his predecessors. Colton became an Episcopalian in 1836 and repudiated his endorsement of revivalism. See Calvin Colton, *Thoughts on the Religious State of the Country* (New York, 1836), p. 14.

37 Finney, *Lectures on Revivals,* pp. 29, 18, 12. It is true that Edwards said that ministers "should use their utmost endeavors to promote" a revival and that he advocated "the use of proper means and endeavors" in this promotion. But by "promote" Edwards meant "to improve" something that was already under way. He did not mean, as Finney did, "to initiate" or "to institute." Edwards insisted that the revival of 1740 was "the work of God and not the work of man. Its beginning has not been of man's power or device and its being carried on depends not on our strength or wisdom." And he pointedly cautioned ministers and churches that in their eagerness for revival they "should not show a hasty spirit" and should not "as it were *stir up, and awake Christ,* before his time." "Christ has an appointed time for thus awakening out of sleep and his people ought to wait upon him and not, in an impatient fit, stir him up before his time." Jonathan Edwards, *Thoughts on the Revival of Religion in New England,* in *Works,* 4 vols., Worcester edition (8th ed., New York, 1843), Vol. III, pp. 333, 408. For an analysis by a contemporary of the differences between Edwardsean revivals and the revivals of 1810–1835 see Calvin Colton, *History and Character of American Revivals,* pp. 2–15, 130 ff.

was assumed. That they were hopelessly crude and mechanical by twentieth-century standards was unimportant. The lectures dealt primarily with the concrete means of arousing attention and the specific techniques of pressing home the truth which Finney had found to work in practice. As a later practitioner of Finney's methods was to say, "theory has got to go into the scrap heap when it comes to experience." [38] The significant fact for the history of modern revivalism was not that Finney's psychological theories were crude but that both he and his followers believed it to be the legitimate function of a revivalist to utilize the laws of mind in order to engineer individuals and crowds into making a choice which was ostensibly based upon free will.

The relationship between the laws of the mind and the laws of revivals was of course fundamental. It was, in modern terms, the relationship between clinical psychology and social psychology. One of the laws of mental philosophy which Finney had discovered, or recovered from earlier speculative error, was that almost every conversion took place in two distinct steps or stages: that of being awakened and that of being convicted. This was of prime importance in promoting revivals. An awakened sinner was one whose "ears are open . . . ready to hear on the subject of religion with attention and seriousness and some feeling." A sinner "under conviction" was able "to understand something of the extent of God's law and sees and feels his guilty state and knows what his remedy is." Ordinarily the state of conviction was tantamount to conversion, for as soon as a sinner understood God's law and felt his own guilt, he would recognize his duty and submit.[39]

The significance of the distinction between the two stages was that during the first the revivalist was to address himself to the "animal feelings" or the natural affections, while during the second he addressed the spiritual or religious affections.[40]

[38] William A. Sunday, quoted in the Boston *Herald,* November 14, 1916, p. 3. For Sunday's quotations (without credit) from Finney's *Lectures on Revivals,* see William T. Ellis, *Billy Sunday, the Man and His Message* (Philadelphia, 1936), pp. 292–98.

[39] Finney, *Lectures on Revivals,* pp. 149–51. Finney did not invent the terms "awakened" and "convicted," of course, but he redefined them to fit his own theory of psychology.

[40] Here again Finney was drawing upon Jonathan Edwards' *Treatise Concerning Religious Affections.*

Those who objected to revivalists' arousing the animal emotions of sinners forgot, said Finney, that "God has found it necessary to take advantage of the excitability there is in mankind to produce powerful excitements among them before he can lead them to obey. Men are so sluggish, there are so many things to lead their minds off from religion and to oppose the influence of the gospel that it is necessary to raise an excitement among them till the tide rises so high as to sweep away the opposing obstacles." [41]

Here was the perfect excuse for all the theatrics which a revivalist cared to exploit. Finney was quite explicit about the kind of excitement he had in mind to start a revival: "What do the politicians do? They get up meetings, circulate handbills and pamphlets, blaze away in the newspapers, send coaches all over town with handbills . . . all to gain attention to their cause and elect their candidate." Extending the political metaphor of his "New Heart" sermon, he said "The object of the ministry is to get all the people to feel that the devil has no right to rule this world but that they ought all to give themselves to God and vote in the Lord Jesus Christ as the governor of the Universe." A minister who wished to work up a revival should show the same wisdom as the politicians and use "the appropriate means to the end." [42] The most important means which Finney described were precisely those new measures which Nettleton and Beecher had tried to condemn at New Lebanon. He was particularly insistent on the need for a new style of preaching and on the utility of protracted meetings, anxious meetings, and the anxious seat.

Finney believed that "The great end for which the Christian ministry was appointed is to glorify God in the salvation of souls" and therefore that "all ministers should be revival ministers and all preaching should be revival preaching." Preaching was good if it won souls and bad if it did not.[43] To be practical, said Finney, revival preaching had to attract attention. To do this it had to be exciting. It also had to suit the tastes of the age, to reach the understanding of "the common people," and to produce an active response on the part of the

[41] Finney, *Lectures on Revivals,* p. 9.
[42] *Ibid.,* p. 167.
[43] *Ibid.,* pp. 161, 203.

auditor. These have doubtless always been the bases of popular pietistic preaching but Finney endeavored to make them the bases of all preaching. He wanted Presbyterian pastors in Philadelphia, New York, and Boston to preach like Methodist circuit riders and Baptist exhorters. "We must have exciting, powerful preaching or the devil will have the people, except what the Methodists can save," he said. Few Presbyterian ministers in recent years "have gathered so large assemblies or won so many souls" as the Methodists, he said, simply because they failed to see that "The character of the age is changed." Instead of conforming to the new age, the Presbyterians still "retain the same stiff, dry, prosing style of preaching that answered half a century ago." What was needed was a "plain, pointed, and simple but warm and animated mode of preaching." Ministers educated at eastern seminaries were taught to write out their sermons and to make them "literary essays" or doctrinal dissertations in which the artificial rhetoric of classical antiquity replaced the natural eloquence that came from burning conviction.[44]

"They used to complain, " Finney said in his *Memoirs* in reference to college-educated ministers, "that I let down the dignity of the pulpit; that I was a disgrace to the ministerial profession; that I talked like a lawyer at the bar; that I talked to the people in a colloquial manner; that I said 'you' instead of preaching about sin and sinners and saying 'they,' that I said 'hell' and with such an emphasis as often to shock the people." Seminary graduates illustrated their sermons by references to ancient history; he illustrated his ideas "by references to the common affairs of men" and "among farmers and mechanics and other classes of men I borrowed my illustrations from their various occupations . . . I addressed them in the language of the common people." Preaching should be "conversational" and should arouse interest by anecdotes "real or supposed." If the learned carped, "he tells stories," or he is simply a "storytelling" minister, let them remember that "that is the way Jesus preached. And it is the only way to preach."[45]

One of Finney's great objections to written sermons was that

[44] *Ibid.*, pp. 253, 252, 184.
[45] Finney, *Memoirs*, pp. 83, 81; Finney, *Lectures on Revivals*, p. 194.

they impeded not only the natural flow of thought but also the natural flow of emotions and the use of gestures. "Gestures are of more importance than is generally supposed. Mere words will never express the full meaning of the gospel." Later evangelists could turn to Finney for justification of almost any sort of pulpit gymnastics. He specifically said that a minister must do what the actor does, "so throw himself into the spirit and meaning of the writer as to adopt his sentiments . . . embody them, throw them out upon the audience as a living reality. . . . If by 'theatrical' be meant the strongest possible representation of the sentiments expressed, then the more theatrical a sermon is the better." Those who cry out that this is letting down "the dignity of the pulpit" ought to remember that while they are preaching "sanctimonious starch" the "theatres will be thronged every night" for "the common-sense people *will be* entertained. . . ."[46]

But entertaining anecdotes and theatrics were not enough. In order to change men from selfishness to benevolence, from complacency to conviction, it was often necessary to threaten or even to frighten them. Finney thought of sinners as intensely wicked and disobedient children who must see "the rod uplifted" before they would submit. "If you are willing to do your duty when you are shown what it is, fears and terrors and great excitement of mind are wholly unnecessary." But since most sinners were not willing to do their duty, Finney let the rod fall: "Look, look, see the millions of wretches biting and gnawing their tongues as they lift their scalding heads from the burning lake [of hell]. . . . Hear them groan amidst the fiery billows as they lash and lash and lash their burning shores."[47] To those in Finney's audience who sincerely believed in hell, as most of them did, listening to his sermons was a nerve-wracking experience. This was true even after he became too respectable to cut people off their seats and send them writhing onto the floor. Professor Edwards A. Park of Andover Theological Seminary recalled distinctly fifty-eight years afterward a sermon he heard Finney preach in 1831 which so upset him and

[46] Finney, *Lectures on Revivals,* pp. 196, 204.

[47] Finney, *Sermons on Various Subjects,* p. 31; quoted in J. Brockway, *Delineation of the Characteristic Features of a Revival in Troy in 1826–27* (Troy, New York, 1827), p. 40.

those next to him that the board on which they were sitting "actually shook beneath us." [48]

This was not the type of preaching which Beecher and Taylor used. Beecher described his own style in Boston as "affectionate exhortation" applied "mildly and kindly" and "divested of obnoxious terms." The Taylorites who invited Finney to New Haven in 1831 pointed out that "All our addresses to sinners have been as much as possible in the spirit of kindness. Here let us add, is our prejudice in regard to you—the fear that your preaching is somewhat in the severe threatening type, that which terrifies and overwhelms rather than that which melts and subdues." [49] In this respect Finney's revivalism looked back toward Jonathan Edwards rather than forward toward Dwight L. Moody. For all his exaltation of human reason and free will Finney still believed in a stern God of justice rather than a tender God of love. In spite of God's benevolence and man's common sense the human heart was still desperately wicked and the human will desperately perverse. Consequently the task of the minister was primarily to subdue the sinner, "to strip him of his excuses, answer his cavils, humble his pride, and break his heart." The revival preacher must "pour in the truth, put in the probe, break up the old foundation, and . . . use the word of God like a fire and a hammer."

To the sensitive observer this often seemed to amount to sadistic browbeating.[50] "I once saw a woman under distress of mind," said Finney, "who had been well nigh driven to despair for months. . . . She was emaciated and worn out with agony. The minister [Finney] set his eye upon her and poured in the truth upon her mind and rebuked her in a most pointed manner. The woman who was with her interrupted, she thought it cruel and said, 'O, do comfort her, she is so distressed, don't trouble her any more, she cannot bear it.' He turned and rebuked *her* and sent her away and then poured in the truth upon the anxious sinner like fire. . . ." In this case Finney suc-

[48] Quoted in George F. Wright, *Charles Grandison Finney* (Boston, 1891), p. 74.

[49] Beecher, *Autobiography*, Vol. I, pp. 542–43; Samuel Merwin, C. A. Boardman, Leonard Bacon to Finney, April 12, 1831, Finney Papers, OCL.

[50] For an interesting discussion of Finney's psychological techniques in terms of the modern concept of "brain-washing," see William Sargant, *Battle for the Mind* (New York, 1957), pp. 140–43.

ceeded in converting the girl and she "went home full of joy." But in other cases, when such overwrought persons went insane, Finney concluded that the sinner had simply "made himself deranged by resisting" the Spirit.[51]

Yet he was no advocate of emotionalism for its own sake. In his *Lectures on Revivals* Finney was careful to emphasize the necessity for the revivalist to keep careful control over his meetings. He quoted the Biblical injunction, "Let all things be done decently and in good order." Forgetting his own early lapses in this regard, he condemned the "recklessness of some individuals" whose "fanaticism" and "rash zeal" had "spread a pall over the churches for years" after the great revivals of Edwards and Whitefield.[52] In addition to losing control of their meetings and causing dissension among the churches, overzealous and fanatical revivalists, like James Davenport or the ignorant camp meeting exhorters among the Methodists and Baptists at the turn of the century, were to be blamed for their failure to comprehend the true laws of mind and the right use of means. It was all very well to excite individuals in order to "awaken" them, but a very different approach was necessary to get them from that state to a state of conviction. The ignorant revivalists stopped at arousing the animal emotions instead of proceeding on to appeal to the religious affections.

As Finney pointed out in part two of his "New Heart" sermon, "You cannot change your heart by an attempt to force yourself into a certain state of feeling." Too many sinners, and too many revivalists, "seem to think that all religion consists in highly excited emotions or feelings." A revivalist who preached that a man could be converted simply by directing his attention to his *feelings* toward God failed to see that this "is just as absurd as it would be for a man to shut his eyes on the lamp, and try to turn his eyes inward to find out whether there was any image painted on the retina." Of course a man could not see the light by looking inward, he must look outward. The same laws applied to the religious affections as to sight or sound or touch: "Our moral feelings are as much an object of consciousness as our senses." The revivalist who was trying to get an

51 Finney, *Sermons on Various Subjects,* p. 27; Finney, *Lectures on Revivals,* pp. 349, 313.

52 Finney, *Lectures on Revivals,* pp. 250, 255.

awakened sinner under conviction must direct the sinner's attention away from his inward feelings of fear and guilt and toward those outward truths of the gospel which would arouse in him the desire to obey God. The proper objects or motives (for Finney considered objects to be motivating forces) upon which a preacher should fix the attention of his listeners in order to stir their religious affections were "either the reasonableness, fitness, and propriety of [the] Maker's claims," "the hatefulness of sin, or the stability of [God's] truth." In order to establish these objects firmly in the sinner's mind the revivalist must preach like a lawyer addressing a jury, not like a rabble-rouser stirring up a mob. A good sermon did not reduce sinners to madness or hysteria nor the impotence of a fainting fit. It produced a profoundly moving yet perfectly reasonable decision to serve God rather than Satan.[53]

According to Finney the only thing more effective in converting sinners than a good sermon based on these sound oratorical and psychological principles was a series of such sermons. Hence he advocated the use of "Protracted Meetings." "The design" of a protracted meeting, he said, was "to devote a series of days to religious services in order to make a more powerful impression of divine things upon the minds of the people." [54] In the eighteenth century, when revivals had been considered miraculous events, no special measures, except fasting and prayer, were employed to induce them. They occurred under the regular Sunday and mid-week services of the pastor. Itinerant evangelists were frowned upon and no attempt was made to arouse the people by special preaching or meetings. Even Nettleton's revivals from 1811 to 1822 included no extended series of meetings night after night. Nettleton usually shared the pulpit alternately with the pastor who invited his services and at most the two of them preached on Sunday, Wednesday, and Friday.

The practice of "Protracted Meetings" grew out of the three- and four-day camp meetings on the southwestern frontier during the Second Great Awakening. These in turn were an outgrowth of the Quarterly Sacramental meetings which could

[53] Finney, *Sermons on Various Subjects,* pp. 32, 37–38; Finney, *Lectures on Revivals,* p. 35.

[54] Finney, *Lectures on Revivals,* p. 242.

be traced back to the rural areas of Scotland in the seventeenth century and to the Quarterly Conferences of the Methodists in England in the eighteenth century.[55] The difference between the four-day camp meetings and the four-day protracted meeting was that protracted meetings were held in towns and villages rather than on the outer edges of the frontier. They were directed by the regular ministers of the town, who conducted the services in their own churches and not outdoors under the trees. Usually for a protracted meeting ministers sought the aid of two or three neighboring pastors and occasionally of an itinerant evangelist or home missionary whom they trusted. The principal purpose of these meetings was to arouse a new interest in religion among church members and to get a revival started within the churches which would attract non-church members. Like the four-day camp meetings, protracted meetings consisted at first of a continuous series of meetings for preaching, prayer, and talking with the anxious from sunrise to midnight with time out only to eat and sleep. When the churches in a town began a protracted meeting, pious businessmen and shopkeepers closed their stores, wives dropped their household duties, farmers left their fields, and everybody concentrated on the task of saving souls, first their own, then their children's and neighbors'. Finney said in discussing such meetings that Christian businessmen ought to be "willing to lock up their stores for six months if it is necessary to carry on a revival" but normally the protracted phase of any revival constituted either the first or last four days of what was usually called a revival.

Between 1800 and 1825 protracted meetings were used occasionally in western New York and gradually spread eastward and into New England, though the practice was stoutly resisted by most Presbyterian and Congregational ministers during this period because they believed them fanatical and disorderly. Finney's justification of them was typical of his outlook. "Their novelty excites and fixes attention. Their being continued from day to day served to enlighten the mind and has a philosophical tendency to issue in conversions." [56] But though he and his

[55] See Charles A. Johnson, *The Frontier Camp Meeting* (Dallas, Texas, 1955), 28 ff., and James H. Hotchkin, *History of the Purchase and Settlement of Western New York* (New York, 1848), pp. 161–69.

[56] Finney, *Lectures on Revivals,* pp. 242–45.

fellow Oneida evangelists used them regularly in western New York and Ohio after 1825, he found that they had to be modified somewhat for use in large cities. Here it was impossible to expect all business to come to a stop and even Christian businessmen could hardly be expected to close down for four days in the face of the bitter competition from non-Christians. Hence the practice grew up of conducting revival meetings in the evenings and protracting them night after night over a three- or four-week period. In the spring of 1833, for example, Finney preached for twenty consecutive nights in the Chatham Street Chapel, while during the day Christians went about their regular business.

Finney also altered the practice of having a number of different pastors or evangelists alternately conduct the services. He believed that the evangelist or pastor concerned should conduct all the services. "Suppose a person who was sick should call in a different physician every day," he said in illustration. The physician "would not know what the symptoms had been nor what was the course of the disease or the treatment nor what remedies had been tried nor what the patient could bear. Why he would certainly kill the patient." His lectures were full of examples of revivals which had been killed by the inept practices of ministers unskilled in the science of revivalism. The future of revivalism was given a precarious turn by this justification for letting the visiting specialist become the center of attention and the directing force in all aspects of a revival. Eventually protracted meetings in their original form fell out of use as the system of employing an outside revival preacher to conduct two or three weeks of nightly meetings was adopted. After 1835 the generic term "revival meeting" was applied indiscriminately to all such efforts. During the years 1825–1835, however, the protracted meeting was one of the most controversial issues between the new divinity men and the Calvinists. Not only did the Calvinists associate it with the emotionalism of the frontier camp meetings and of Finney's early western revivals, but they also objected to the fact that anxious meetings and the anxious seat were an integral part of all protracted meetings.

As Finney said, the ultimate design of any revival was to make men "ACT" or to "push matters to an issue." The anxious seat and the anxious meeting constituted the hand-to-hand combat which followed the heavy cannonading of the revival sermon. Finney described the anxious seat as "the appointment of some particular seat in the place of meeting [usually the front benches or pews] where the anxious may come and be addressed particularly and be made the subject of prayers and sometimes conversed with individually." Anxious meetings for more prolonged conversations with those who had not been convinced while sitting in the anxious seat were usually arranged outside the place of meeting, in the parish house or the basement of some church or even in a private home. Finney was convinced from his own experience that the use of anxious seats and anxious meetings was "undoubtedly philosophical and according to the laws of mind." They not only helped to break "the chains of pride" but they forced a definite commitment "to be on the Lord's side" from persons who might otherwise hold back.[57] He rightly pointed out that pastoral visits to converse with the anxious individually or in groups had been used by Nettleton as well as by Jonathan Edwards. But while the anxious meeting had a long tradition behind it, the anxious seat was a comparatively new measure which went back no farther than the use of the "Mourner's Bench" at the Methodist camp meetings.

There were two objections to the anxious seat, one on grounds of social and ecclesiastical propriety and the other in terms of theology. The first was typified by Albert Dod in his review of the *Lectures on Revivals.* When a sinner answered the call to come forward and sit in the anxious seat after a particularly moving sermon, said Dod, "The divine truth which was but now occupying his mind is forced away, while he revolves the questions, shall I go or not. Who else will go? What will they say of me?" Furthermore, it "involves the capital error that no sinner who is truly awakened can refrain from obeying the call to the anxious seat. It assumes that to go to the anxious seat is 'to do something for Christ' and that it is impossible for him who refuses to go to be a Christian." [58] In other words, the anxious bench was considered by many critics

57 *Ibid.*, pp. 242, 246–49.

58 *Biblical Repertory and Theological Review,* n.s. VII (October, 1835), 642–43; see also pp. 638–47.

to be simply a means of exerting social pressure upon individuals, a device for holding them up to the praise of friends and neighbors if they went forward, or to calumny if they did not. It forced awakened sinners to take into consideration factors which were entirely outside the realm of their spiritual relationship with God, said the critics. It produced hypocritical and self-satisfied "Christians" and admitted to church membership persons who went forward from false motives. Finney, like most later revivalists, denied these charges. In his day few American churchgoers were so hardened or sophisticated as to dare the vengeance of God by going forward to the anxious bench just to please their friends or to avoid scorn. Yet in comparing the anxious seat to the rite of baptism Finney unconsciously predicted how easily this new practice of committal might become formalized into a ritual.

The second objection to the anxious seat concerned the theological implications of forcing sinners to choose at once whether they would accept or reject Christ. As Finney said, the purpose of dealing individually with the anxious was "to lead them immediately to Christ." To this Dod remarked, "It will be at once seen how this measure plays into the rest of the system" of the new divinity. Finney demanded immediate "submission" because he believed that the individual was free to save himself and that waiting for God's help was simply avoiding a decision and hence rejecting God's freely offered grace. This was the theological aspect of the westerners' new measures which Beecher had failed to face openly at New Lebanon. That Beecher was aware of these implications, however, was evident from his letter to N. S. S. Beman in January, 1827, in which he condemned the new measures because they led to "the hasty recognition of persons as converted" and the "assuming without sufficient evidence that persons are unconverted." [59] Despite his belief in free will, Beecher followed the teaching of his mentor, Timothy Dwight, in maintaining that while conversion itself was "instantaneous" the process leading up to conversion might be long and agonizing. Harriet Beecher Stowe said that the practice followed by her father during his Boston pastorate from 1826 to 1832 was not to demand immedi-

[59] *Letters of the Rev. Dr. Beecher and Rev. Mr. Nettleton on the "New Measures" in Conducting Revivals of Religion* (New York, 1828), pp. 83–84.

ate submission by awakened sinners but to tell them to "go to some solitary place . . . and pray," "open your Bible and read a chapter," "break off all outward and known sins, put yourself in the way of all religious influences, and I will venture to say you cannot pursue this course a fortnight, a week, without finding a new and blessed life dawning within you." In 1829, Beecher wrote to his daughter Catharine, who was struggling through the agony of a particularly long, drawn out conversion, "I do not suppose that we are bound, or that it is best, to rely chiefly on peremptory demands of immediate submission. . . ." [60]

Finney, of course, believed just the opposite. He attacked those who told anxious sinners that their conversion would eventually come about if they would "read their Bibles, keep clear of vain company, use the means of grace, and pray for a new heart." This advice, said Finney, was "just such as would please the devil" because it allowed the sinner to put off an immediate decision.[61]

Between Finney and Beecher the objection to the anxious seat eventually boiled down to a matter of taste, for Beecher was willing to admit that immediate conversions were possible while Finney was ready to make the anxious seat and anxious meetings as respectable a process as possible. Moreover, the use of this test of faith had a practical purpose in revivalism as a symbol of commitment to the evangelical fundamentals. Because it was a comparatively new practice, it had none of the controversial or sectarian connotations which made baptism, for example, an unacceptable test of faith in interdenominational religious services. Although the Methodists had used the anxious seat most persistently it had never been strictly limited to that denomination. Once its association with the emotionalism of camp meetings was overcome it proved of great practical value to revivalists and after 1835 it was an indispensable fixture of modern revivals. The conservative Hopkinsians and

[60] Beecher, *Autobiography,* Vol. II, pp. 116–17, 208. In the revivals conducted by Nettleton from 1811 to 1822, all converts had to undergo a period of probation lasting from two to twelve months before they were considered safe for church membership. Nettleton's converts seldom were bold enough to say they were saved. They simply "indulged a hope" that they were. See Sprague, *Revivals,* appendix, p. 54.

[61] Finney, *Sermons on Various Subjects,* p. 25.

Old School Presbyterians never did become reconciled to the anxious bench in its original form but later revivalists made modifications which seemed more palatable.[62] What Dod failed to see or admit in criticizing Finney on this score was that the Calvinist system of conversion with its prescriptions of long and agonizing prayer and "waiting upon God" had itself become such a formalized ritual as to produce hypocrisy and superficiality of a different kind. Many Calvinists measured a man's piety by the number of months he spent "agonizing" before he found salvation. A quick and certain conversion was to them a sign of ignorance and bad breeding. The well-bred person took a decent length of time before he expressed demurely his hope that he was among the elect. It was as much in reaction to this desiccated religious temper as in deference to the laws of mind that Finney justified his use of new measures.

In addition to protracted meetings, anxious meetings, and the anxious seat, Finney also devoted space in his handbook to such important matters as the necessity for clerical cooperation in revivalism and the value of organizing prayer groups in order to "cultivate Christian confidence" in the success of a forthcoming revival. But for some reason Finney did not include in his lectures on revivals some of the techniques which he had employed to promote his revival meetings at the Chatham Street Chapel. For example, he carefully "trained" the members of his church in New York to "go out in the highways and hedges to bring people to hear preaching." "When we wished to give notice of any extra meetings, little slips of paper, on which was printed an invitation to attend the services, would be carried from house to house in every direction" by both men and women of the congregation. By this method of advertising "the house could be filled any evening in the week."

Once the house was filled, Finney instructed his band of trained personal workers, or soul winners, to "scatter themselves over the whole house and to keep their eyes open in regard to any that were seriously affected under the preaching." Whenever they found such persons, they tried "to detain them after preaching for conversation and prayer." "Special inquiry rooms" were located in the building where the anxious or awak-

[62] For the system preferred by New England conservatives in 1832 see Sprague, *Revivals,* p. 147 and appendix, p. 38.

ened could be taken. "In this way conversion of a great many souls was secured."[63]

Another extremely important aspect of revival meetings which Finney failed to discuss in his lectures was the use of music to give the audience a sense of participation and to put them in the proper frame of mind. The frontier camp meetings had strongly emphasized congregational singing, but the Presbyterian and Congregational churches were slow to abandon the old psalms and the stolid hymns of Isaac Watts. Finney did his best to promote good choir singing and to introduce more modern music into his meetings. His friend Joshua Leavitt was one of the first of a long line of evangelistic workers who hoped to make money out of publishing popular song books for revival meetings. In 1830 he wrote to Finney in Rochester that he was sending him some copies of a hymnbook he had just compiled called *The Christian Lyre #1,* containing "the favorite tunes and hymns of the various denominations" especially designed "to aid in revivals of religion." "If you approve the work," Leavitt wrote, "allow me to request of you the favor to aid its circulation, particularly in your own place. If you and some other friends would raise a few dollars and procure 50 or 100 of No. 1 and scatter them in your prayer meetings the work would be introduced at once and with very little expense."[64] When Finney came to New York in 1832 he brought with him as his musical assistant a man named Thomas Hastings of Utica. Hastings compiled several songbooks, taught and wrote music, directed Finney's choir, and composed the melody for "Rock of Ages." A student of the more famous hymn writer, Lowell Mason, Hastings set a precedent for future "choristers" and musical "co-evangelists."[65]

All of these aspects of revival technique used by Finney became part of modern revivalism. If few of the "new measures" were entirely original with Finney, nevertheless he did modify them and amalgamate them into a completely new approach to revivals, an approach which later revivalists adapted to the

[63] Finney, *Memoirs,* pp. 321–22.

[64] Joshua Leavitt to Finney, November 15, 1830, Finney Papers, OCL. This compilation replaced Nettleton's *Village Hymns* and Simeon Jocelyn's *Zion's Harp* as the foremost revival hymnbook in the pre-Civil War era. It went into over twenty-six editions.

[65] See Fletcher, *Oberlin,* Vol. I, pp. 14, 32; Vol. II, p. 784.

changing times but never basically altered. Whether later evangelists turned to his *Lectures on Revivals* or his *Memoirs* for the rationale of these methods, they found that his basic validation was the pragmatic one tested by his own results. "When the blessing evidently follows the introduction of the measure itself, the proof is unanswerable that the measure is wise." "Success" in terms of the number of converts is, he said, "a safe criterion." And he challenged those who opposed his new measures, "Show me the fruits of your ministry and if they so far exceed mine as to give me evidence that you have found a more excellent way, I will adopt your views." [66] In subsequent years the cry, "But he gets results," was to vindicate the extravagances of more than one professional revivalist.

However, Finney's fame and success rested upon more than his experimental and pseudoscientific rationale for new measures. His theology had a message for this world as well as the next, and it was a message which fitted perfectly the ebullient optimism of the 1830's. Lyman Beecher, who had for years been a leading figure in the religious reform movements of the East, sensed in 1827 that there was a radical element in the western revivals which went deeper than the use of new measures. Beecher's fears of "anarchy," "barbarism," "impudent young men," and "a levelling of all distinctions of society" seemed to him to have been justified by the rebellious spirit of the Lane students in 1834. The reform aspect of Beecher's preaching was theocratic in temper while Finney's was democratic. Beecher, who deplored the overthrow of the Standing Order in Connecticut, strove for church harmony and "evangelical assimilation" in order to maintain the clerical domination of the social order which had been traditional in colonial New England. But the social outlook implicit in Finney's theology was the Christian counterpart of Jacksonian democracy.

When Finney found that in order to overthrow the Calvinistic "traditions of the elders" he not only would have to dispense with the theology of the Westminster Confession but also with the ecclesiastical structure of Presbyterianism and Presbygationalism, he did not hesitate to do so. And when he discovered that Beecher, like the hyper-Calvinists, took a cautious attitude toward social reform on the grounds that radicalism in

[66] Finney, *Memoirs,* p. 83; Finney, *Lectures on Revivals,* pp. 175, 178.

this area was as destructive of good order as radicalism in theology and ecclesiasticism, Finney considered that Beecher was temporizing with sin. Yet Finney himself refused to follow the social implications of his views to their logical conclusions. In the mid-1830's his converts, friends, and students found him guilty of a similar temporizing, and to their minds, Finney lacked the justification which Beecher's more pessimistic view of human nature provided. Finney's tendency to draw back from social action may have been the result of an innate Yankee conservatism, of his professional training in the law, or a sense of personal insecurity which was apparent throughout his career, but in his own mind he acted always out of the higher impulse to be true to "the cause of Christ" above all else.

The theological roots of the social reform element in Finney's preaching lay in his instinctive belief that God was benevolent and man was reasonable. His faith in progress and ultimate perfectibility stemmed from the prevailing concept of a divinely ordered universe with which man was capable of putting himself in harmony by means of the intelligent use of his faculties. Just as God had disclosed the true laws of mind to modern philosophers and the laws of physics and chemistry to modern scientists, so He was gradually disclosing all of His moral truths about human behavior and conduct in terms comprehensible to the common people. The fundamental laws of society, politics, economics, and morality were all becoming more evident from day to day and soon their relationship to God's divine government would be patent to all. Once they were understood by all, Finney had no doubt they would be lived up to by all, at least by all who truly professed to be Christians.[67]

This concept of a gradual or progressive revelation of God's will complemented three other theological doctrines current among evangelicals of the day which were central to Finney's preaching and which had obvious social overtones. These were the doctrine of disinterested benevolence, the concept of per-

[67] This reliance on "farther light" in the application of God's revealed will to man's historical development was characteristic of New England theology from the days of the Puritans. It in no way implied that Finney doubted the plenary inspiration of the Bible. For a discussion of Finney's views on plenary inspiration, see Wright, *Finney,* pp. 185–88. For Beecher's belief in "farther light," see his *Autobiography,* Vol. I, pp. 129.

fectionism or sanctification, and the doctrine of millennialism. Although he never acknowledged it, Finney adopted the idea of disinterested benevolence from his archenemies the Hopkinsians, and Samuel Hopkins got it directly from Jonathan Edwards. Hopkins formulated the concept of disinterested benevolence as a complement to the sombre Calvinistic doctrine of God's arbitrary sovereignty. Like Edwards, he used the term "Being in general" as a synonym for God and maintained that the "true holiness" of the Christian "consists in disinterested, benevolent affection" toward God, or Being in general. But Hopkins went beyond Edwards when he claimed that "The law of God leads us to consider holiness as consisting in universal, disinterested good will, considered in all its genuine exercises and fruits and acted out in all its branches toward God and our neighbor." Once Hopkins began to stress love for his neighbors as a definition of love for "Being in general," he easily passed on to such statements as "true benevolence always seeks the greatest good of the whole" and said that the law of God commanded men to act "for the sake of the glory of God and the greatest good of mankind." [68]

Hopkins made these statements in 1773. By Finney's day the phrase "the greatest good of mankind" was receiving more attention as a criterion in theology and philosophy than "the glory of God." Although Finney's discussions of disinterested benevolence often seemed to be mere paraphrases of Hopkins, it was clear from their tone that he had abandoned the Calvinistic emphasis on divine sovereignty. For him, as for most Americans in the age of Jackson, men worked for the glory of God when they engaged in "the pursuit of happiness." "Disinterested benevolence" became strangely similar to "enlightened self-interest." Finney made explicit the utilitarian implications of Hopkins' doctrine, but it was a pietistic form of utilitarianism.

"Look at the utility of benevolence," said Finney in the second part of his "New Heart" sermon. "It is a matter of human consciousness that the mind is so constituted that benevolent

[68] Samuel Hopkins, *An Inquiry into the Nature of True Holiness* (Newport, Rhode Island, 1773), pp. 41, 57, 68, 71. There is a good discussion of Hopkins' theology in Joseph Haroutunian, *Piety Versus Moralism* (New York, 1932); see esp. pp. 82 ff.

affections are the source of happiness; and malevolent ones the source of misery." Because "benevolence is good will, or willing good to the object of it" it follows that "If we desire the happiness of others, their happiness will increase our own, according to the strength of our desire." In other words, the more vigorously a man pursued do-goodism, the more he tasted "the cup of every man's happiness." And inasmuch as "God's happiness consists in his benevolence," therefore do-goodism, by advancing the happiness of the universe in general, advanced the will of God. On this basis it was natural for Finney to say of young converts, "They should set out with a determination to aim at being useful in the highest degree" and "if they can see an opportunity where they can do more good, they must embrace it whatever may be the sacrifice to themselves." [69] In the light of these statements it is not surprising that many of Finney's converts engaged in the manifold reform movements of the day with the dedicated, and often self-righteous, zeal of persons assured that they were serving the Lord.

The doctrine of perfectionism (or sanctification or holiness or entire consecration, as it was variously called by Finney) reenforced the doctrine of benevolence, for only a perfectly holy person could hope to know exactly what God's will was and could live up to its demands. Having said, in the "New Heart" sermon, that the test of a true Christian was that he would "prefer the glory of God and the interest of his kingdom to his own selfish interest" Finney went on to explain that "sanctification" consisted in the "strength, stability, firmness and perpetuity" of this preference. "The perfect control of this preference over all the moral movements of the mind brings a man back to where Adam was previous to the fall and constitutes perfect holiness." Finney believed that this state of Adam-like perfection could be attained through "the special influence of the Spirit" and in the years after 1836 he developed this idea along the lines of John Wesley's sanctification. He believed that all Christians could be brought to the ultimate stage of perfection on earth by means of a second "baptism of the Holy

[69] Finney, *Sermons on Various Subjects*, p. 43. Finney, *Lectures on Revivals*, p. 375. Since earlier sermons are not available (other than the "New Heart" sermon) it is not certain when Finney first adopted the doctrine of disinterested benevolence, but all indications are that it was soon after his ordination.

Ghost" or a "second blessing" which would constitute an "assurance of faith" beyond that of the ordinary Christian.[70] All converts, he said in his *Lectures on Revivals,* "should aim at being holy and not rest satisfied till they are as perfect as God." On the strength of his maxim that "obligation and ability are commensurate" Finney inevitably had to maintain that it was possible for men to obey the command "Be ye therefore perfect even as your Father which is in heaven is perfect." After 1836 he became preoccupied with this doctrine and when he came to write his *Systematic Theology* in 1846, he asserted that those who are truly converted "habitually live without sin and fall into sin only at intervals so few and far between that, in strong language, it may be said in truth they do not sin." [71]

This radical theology led to his being abandoned by most of his former Presbyterian and Congregational colleagues and caused many to associate his "Oberlin Perfectionism" with the "antinomian" or "free love" perfectionism of John Humphrey Noyes and the Oneida community. In view of the fact that the eccentric Noyes had been a student of Nathaniel Taylor at Yale and specifically stated that Oneida perfectionism grew out of the new divinity, Lyman Beecher had to be particularly vehement in his repudiation of all perfectionists, including Finney. This did not help Beecher much with the Hopkinsians and Old School Presbyterians, however, for they were convinced that the evils of perfectionism were the inevitable and logical results of new school theology and they went out of their way to lump Beecher with Finney and Finney with Noyes. Finney, of course, was no more sympathetic with Noyes's views than Beecher and insisted that perfectionism as he defined it did not mean that converted men, even after sanctification, were entitled to follow their impulses and dispense with the ordinary

70 In 1837 he advised all his New York church members to read Wesley's *Plain Account of Christian Perfection* which he called "an admirable book." See C. G. Finney, *Lectures to Professing Christians* (Oberlin, 1880), pp. 358–59; see also the letter to him from William Green, Jr., December 6, 1837, Finney Papers, OCL. For Finney's personal experience with the second blessing, see his *Memoirs,* pp. 373 ff.

71 Finney, *Sermons on Various Subjects,* pp. 7, 12, 5; Finney, *Lectures on Revivals,* p. 374; C. G. Finney, *Lectures on Systematic Theology* (Oberlin, 1878); ed. J. H. Fairchild, pp. 317–18.

rules of morality.[72] To Finney the doctrine of perfectionism meant that the sanctified Christian could learn to restrain his evil impulses and to perform his obligations in "perfect obedience to the law of God."

The doctrine of millennialism constituted the social equivalent of individual benevolence and perfection. Finney, like most of his contemporaries, including Beecher and Taylor, believed that through the spread of Christianity the world itself was gradually working toward a state of perfection. Eventually there would be a period of one thousand years of universal peace and plenty which would lay the basis for the return of Christ and the ultimate establishment of God's kingdom on earth. Because of the widespread interest in revivalism in the nineteenth century and because of the great strides which the United States was making toward freedom, prosperity, piety, morality, and the pursuit of happiness for all its citizens, most evangelical ministers of the day agreed with Finney that the millennium spoken of in the Bible was to begin in America and that it would probably begin within a very short time. In his *Lectures on Revivals,* for example, Finney stated, "If the church will do her duty, the millenium [*sic*] may come in this country in three years." [73] However, he had no use for the premillennial theory of William Miller, the New York Baptist farmer who toured the country in the years 1833 to 1843 preaching that the millennium would not begin until after the

[72] For Finney's perfectionism after 1835, see *Memoirs,* pp. 339 ff.; *Systematic Theology* (London, 1851), pp. 568 ff.; and C. G. Finney, *Lectures to Professing Christians,* pp. 341 ff.; C. G. Finney, *Sermons on Important Subjects* (New York, 1836), *passim;* Joseph I. Foot, "An Inquiry Respecting the Theological Origin of Perfectionism and Its Correlative Branches of Fanaticism," and "The Influence of Pelagianism on the Theological Course of Rev. C. G. Finney Developed in His Sermons and Lectures," *Literary and Theological Review* (New York), III (March, 1836), 19 ff., and V (March, 1838), 38 ff. For Noyes's perfectionism, see G. W. Jones, *Religious Experience of John Humphrey Noyes* (New York, 1923), *passim.* For Beecher's opposition to Finney after 1836, see Finney, *Memoirs,* pp. 344–45.

[73] Finney, *Lectures on Revivals,* p. 282. For similar views on the relationship between American progress and revivalism, see Colton, *History and Character of American Revivals,* pp. 31, 164, and Lyman Beecher quoted in Barnes, *Antislavery Impulse,* p. 7. For Jonathan Edwards' millennial views see his *Thoughts on the Revival of Religion* (1740) in *Works,* 4 vols., Worcester edition (8th ed., New York, 1843), Vol. III, p. 334.

Day of Judgment and predicting that Christ would return to judge the world in the year 1843. "I have examined Mr. Miller's theory," Finney wrote in April, 1843, "and am persuaded that what he expects to come after the judgment will come before it. Read the sixty-fifth chapter of Isaiah. The Prophet there speaks of the advancement to be made as the creation of a new heaven and a new earth." [74] Finney and his colleagues at Oberlin thought Miller was utterly mistaken to believe that the world was getting worse and worse instead of better and better. How could he fail to see the great progress in morality that had come with the new interest in revival activity and the reform movements against duelling, lotteries, intemperance, and infidelity? "Are these evidences of the world's growing worse and worse? The world is not growing worse, but better . . ." said an editorial in the *Oberlin Evangelist* in October, 1843.[75] One of the most significant differences between Finney's message and that of almost every post-Civil War evangelist was that they adopted Miller's pessimistic premillennialism rather than Finney's optimistic postmillennialism. They did not set any date for the Second Coming as Miller had, but they expected it imminently. The postmillennialists of the post-Civil War era were the social gospelers and the social darwinian modernists, not the revivalists.

Finney's doctrines of benevolence, perfectionism, and postmillennialism added up to his conclusion that because true Christians "supremely value the highest good of Being, they will and must take a deep interest in whatever is promotive of that end. Hence their spirit is necessarily that of the reformer. To the universal reformation of the world they stand committed." [76] In the face of Finney's apparently overwhelming commitment to universal reformation, individual and collec-

[74] *Oberlin Evangelist,* V (April 12, 1843), 58.

[75] *Ibid.,* V (October 25, 1843), 173. There were many different concepts of what the millennial system was to be. Miller visualized it as the personal rulership of Christ over the earth; Beecher saw the millennium as a theocratic system similar to the Bible Commonwealth of seventeenth-century Massachusetts. Society might, in Beecher's eyes, attain a kind of perfection under the guidance of the churches and clergy, but human nature would never be perfectible on earth. Finney's millennium consisted of a mixture of Christianized direct democracy and perfectionist anarchy. See C. G. Finney, *Lectures on Systematic Theology,* ed. George Redford (London, 1851), pp. 361–62.

[76] Finney, *Lectures on Systematic Theology* (London, 1851), p. 450.

tive, it seems strange that he should have been so cautious and conservative in politics, economics, and the burning social issue of the day, abolition.

But for all his faith in man and in God's benevolent utilitarianism, when it came down to the practical problem of how much of his time a Christian should allot to working for immediate political or social reforms and how much to ultimate spiritual ends, Finney insisted on putting first things first. Saving souls was more important than winning votes. Promoting revivals was more important than promoting new legislation. Man's fate in the next world was more important than his fate in this. According to Finney the practical reformation of this world in terms of social action, however desirable in theory, usually tended in fact to produce constant quarreling and disorder instead of universal harmony. Even worse, since no two reformers ever agreed, these activities often turned Christian against Christian and thus disturbed that great evangelical assimilation which was of primary importance for the promotion of revivals. Faced with the fact that man-made plans for dealing with the complex temporal problems of the day were imperfect and divisive, Finney drew back from the concrete application of his principles to social reform. Instead he took the higher ground that it was impossible to make a better world until the individuals in it were reformed. Despite the heavy emphasis he laid on free will, Finney was not a Pelagian. He believed at bottom that an act of God or the Holy Spirit was necessary to change the human heart and guide it to perfection. His optimism lay not so much in his faith in man as in his faith that God's transcendent power over the world, the flesh, and the devil was readily available to man. Hence soul winning, not social reform, was the one great end to which Christians should devote their energies. "No man is truly converted who does not live to save others. Every truly converted man turns from selfishness to benevolence and benevolence surely leads him to do all he can to save the souls of his fellowman." [77] Because Finney thought of sin primarily in terms of individual morality he was convinced that economic and political injustices as well as those discriminatory social institutions,

[77] C. G. Finney, *Sermons on Gospel Themes,* ed. Henry Cowles (Oberlin, Ohio, 1876), p. 344.

conventions, and prejudices which lie at the heart of a culture could be easily altered by means of revivalism.

The best illustration of this was Finney's ambivalent attitude on the question of slavery. It was significant of his lack of social consciousness that he did not begin to consider the relationship between Christianity and slavery until twelve years after his conversion. Even then he did not come to adopt anti-slavery views on his own initiative. His interest was drawn to the movement not through his doctrine of disinterested benevolence nor by his personal study of the Bible, but by the arguments and activities of his friends Theodore Weld, Joshua Leavitt, and the Tappans. These men in turn were inspired not by any social message explicit or implicit in Finney's theology but by the example of the British anti-slavery movement and the publications of William Lloyd Garrison.[78] Once aroused to work for immediate emancipation in the winter of 1832–33, they made plans to organize an American antislavery society and urged Finney to join them. The first available evidence of Finney's having taken a stand on the question was a letter signed by him, the Tappans, Weld, and several others which appeared in the *Emancipator* on June 25, 1833. The letter was an attack upon the American Colonization Society for its failure to take a bold stand in favor of immediate abolition.[79]

Some time later Finney explained his tardy adoption of the abolition cause on the ground that the sin of slavery was one of God's gradual revelations of moral truth. "The time was when this subject was not before the public mind but recently the subject has come up for discussion and the providence of God has brought it distinctly before the eyes of all men. Light is now shed on this subject. . . . Facts are exhibited and principles established . . . and it is demanded of [the churches] 'IS THIS SIN?' " After 1833 Finney had no doubt that the churches must answer that it was SIN. It was so because it

[78] See Fletcher, *Oberlin,* Vol. I, p. 144; Lewis Tappan, *Arthur Tappan* (London, 1870), p. 128; Barnes, *Anti-Slavery Impulse,* pp. 33 ff. and 212, note 10. It seems to me that Barnes exaggerates the importance of Finney's preaching and personal influence in the antislavery movement. Finney's own statement that he adopted antislavery views before he accepted his pastorate in New York City must be discounted. There is no evidence to confirm it. See Finney, *Memoirs,* p. 324.

[79] See Barnes, *Anti-Slavery Impulse,* p. 217, note 20.

was selfish. It was robbing another human being "of himself —his body—his soul—his time and his earnings to promote the interest of his master." [80]

In the first months after Finney made up his mind to join his friends in attacking the sin of slavery, he took part in the formation of the New York Anti-Slavery Society, attended meetings to publicize abolition, and, in December, 1833, banned "slaveholders and all concerned in the traffic" from communion in his New York church.[81] But when violent opposition to abolition in the form of mob riots took place in the summer of 1834, Finney's ardor for the movement cooled. In November, 1834, he wrote to his wife from New York, "I don't believe that it would do to say too much about abolition here in publick." And when Joshua Leavitt forgot Finney's "prudent" admonitions that same year and lost subscribers by devoting too much space to antislavery propaganda in the *New York Evangelist,* Finney came to his rescue by writing his lectures on revivals specifically for publication in the paper in order to divert public attention from the issue.[82]

In one of these lectures Finney took pains to say about abolition, "Nothing is more calculated to injure religion and to injure the slaves themselves than for Christians to get into an angry controversy on the subject. . . . The subject of slavery is a subject upon which Christians, praying men, need not and must not differ. . . . Great care should be taken to avoid a censorious spirit on both sides. . . . A denunciatory spirit, impeaching each other's motives, is unchristian and calculated to grieve the Spirit of God and to put down revivals." He was willing, he said, that "temperate and judicious" tracts on the subject should be disseminated and "prayerfully examined," but he went on, "I do not mean by this that the attention of the church should be so absorbed by this as to neglect the main question of saving souls. . . . I do not mean that such premature movements on this subject should be made as to astound the Christian community and involve them in a broil." [83]

[80] Finney, *Lectures on Revivals,* pp. 265–66; Finney, *Lectures On Systematic Theology* (London, 1851), p. 369.

[81] Finney, *Lectures on Revivals,* p. 277.

[82] Finney to his wife, November 24, 1834, Finney Papers, OCL. Finney, *Memoirs,* p. 329.

[83] Finney, *Lectures on Revivals,* pp. 275–76.

In 1836, the year after Finney went to Oberlin, Lewis Tappan recorded in his diary his opinion that Finney was "unsound on the slavery question" and doing great "injury to the anti-slavery cause." So strongly did Tappan resent what he considered Finney's "cowardly" approach to the question that he threatened for a time to cut off his support of Oberlin.[84]

There were several reasons why the Tappans lost faith in Finney's devotion to the cause. In the first place they thought it inconsistent with the ideals of Christianity that Finney declined to treat Negroes as equals. In spite of their opposition, Finney had refused to abolish the segregated seating of Negroes in the Chatham Street Chapel and in February, 1836, he opposed the election of a Negro as a trustee of the proposed new Free Presbyterian Church on Chapel Street.[85] Even at Oberlin Finney wanted Negro students to sit separately from whites.[86] Finney believed, like most northerners, that there was a difference between freeing the slaves and treating Negroes as social equals. As he wrote to Lewis Tappan's brother in April, 1836, "You err in supposing that the principles of Abolition and Amalgamation are identical. . . . Abolition is a question of flagrant and unblushing wrong. A direct and outrageous violation of fundamental right. The other is a question of prejudice that does not necessarily deprive any man of any positive right. . . . I admit that the distinction on account of color and some peculiarities of physical organization is a silly and often a wicked *prejudice.* I say often because I do not believe that it is always a wicked prejudice. A man may certainly from *constitutional taste* feel unwilling to mar[r]y a colored woman or have a daughter mar[r]y a colored man and yet be a devoted friend of the colored people." [87]

But it was not simply Finney's defense of "constitutional taste" that made Lewis and Arthur Tappan accuse him of cowardice in the cause. During the year 1835 Finney became less active in antislavery activities and even refused to pray or preach on the subject. (In fact, he never in his life devoted

84 Lewis Tappan, Diary MS, entries for April 24, 1836; May 5, 1836; pp. 42, 48, Lewis Tappan Papers, Library of Congress.

85 *Ibid.*, entry of February 25, 1836, pp. 2–5.

86 See Weld to Lewis Tappan, October 24, 1836, *Letters of Theodore Weld*, Vol. I, pp. 327–28.

87 Finney to Arthur Tappan, April 30, 1836, Finney Papers, OCL.

a sermon to an attack upon slavery.) Theodore Weld admitted to Lewis Tappan in November, 1835, that Finney "has thought, felt, said, and done less on the subject than he should have done." [88] By 1836 Finney was openly undermining the abolition movement because he found that some of the students at Oberlin were more interested in freeing the slaves than in preaching revivalism. One of the Lane rebels wrote to Weld in August, 1836, that Finney "poured out his soul before us in agony in view of our continuing in the abolition field—said that his great inducement to come to Oberlin was to educate the young men from Lane Seminary (our class)—that the revival part of the church were looking anxiously for us to enter upon the work of Evangelists, and would be exceedingly grieved if we did not—that we would accomplish the abolition work much sooner by promoting revivals . . . that the only hope of the country, the church, the oppressor and the slave was in *wide spread revivals*." [89]

Finney had written in the same vein to Weld a month earlier: "We are in our present course going fast into a civil war," he said. "How can we save our country and affect [*sic*] the speedy abolition of slavery?" His answer was to avoid direct action for the indirect way: "If abolition can be made an append[a]ge of a general revival all is well. I fear no other form of carrying this question will save our country or the liberty or soul of the slave." [90] The historian of Oberlin College noted that it was Finney's single-minded devotion to soul-winning which caused the college to contribute "so few abolitionist lecturers after 1837." [91]

It is important to note, however, that Finney's emphasis on revivalism rather than abolitionism did not stem from the same premillennial pessimism which caused later evangelists to withdraw from worldly activity and leave social reform up to supernatural interposition via the Second Coming. Finney was so excessively optimistic that he said in 1836 that revivalism could

[88] Weld to Lewis Tappan, November 17, 1835, *Letters of Theodore Weld*, Vol. I, p. 242.

[89] James A. Thome to Weld, August 9, 1836, *Letters of Theodore Weld*, Vol. I, pp. 327–38.

[90] Finney to Weld, July 21, 1836, *Letters of Theodore Weld*, Vol. I, pp. 318–19.

[91] Fletcher, *Oberlin*, Vol. I, p. 252.

peacefully spread abolition across "the whole land in 2 years." If only, he pleaded with Weld in 1836, "the publick mind can be engrossed with the subject of salvation and make abolition an appendage, just as we made temperance an appendage of revival in Rochester" the whole problem would be solved. "Then 100,000 were converted in one year, every one of which was a temperance man. The same w'd be the case in abolition." [92]

While Weld believed that Finney had not done "his duty" on behalf of abolition, he sympathetically defended Finney in a revealing letter to Lewis Tappan in 1835: "The truth is Finney has always been in revivals of religion. It is his great business, aim, and absorbing passion to promote them. He has never had hardly anything to do with Bible, Tract, missionary, Education, Temperance, moral, reform, and anti-slavery societies." Just as Weld had abandoned all his interest in other reforms from the conviction that "revivals, Moral Reform, etc. etc. must & [will] remain nearly stationery until the Temple is cleansed" of slavery, so "Finney feels about revivals of religion and the promotion of the church ministry in doctrines and measures. . . ." [93] Finney believed that all other reforms must remain subsidiary to revivalism: "I did not," Finney said of abolition in his *Memoirs,* "turn aside to make it a hobby or divert the attention of the people from the work of converting souls." [94]

[92] Finney to Weld, July 21, 1836, *Letters of Theodore Weld,* Vol. I, pp. 318–19.

[93] Weld to Lewis Tappan, November 17, 1835, *Letters of Theodore Weld,* Vol. I, p. 243.

[94] Finney, *Memoirs,* p. 324. Finney seems to have abandoned his "judicious" approach toward abolition after 1839 and to have adopted an increasingly militant outlook. This may have resulted from the fact that the Southern Presbyterians made it perfectly evident in the schism of 1837 that they were not going to permit their people to be converted either to Finney's new divinity or to abolition. (See C. Bruce Stieger, "Abolitionism and the Presbyterian Schism of 1837–38," *Mississippi Valley Historical Review,* XXXVI [December, 1949] 391 ff.) In 1839 Finney advocated the formation of an antislavery political party; in 1846 he opposed the war with Mexico; in 1850 he denounced the Fugitive Slave Act and assisted in the Underground Railway, and in 1851 he took Garrisonian ground by suggesting "the dismemberment of our hypocritical union" if necessary. "To adopt the maxim 'Our union even with perpetual slavery,'" he said in 1851, "is an abomination so execrable as not to be named by a just mind without indignation." In 1860 he considered Lincoln too lenient toward slavery and in 1864 he favored Benjamin F. Butler for President. After the Civil War Finney was a staunch advocate of harsh Reconstruction. This jump from judicious restraint to violent action is the inevitable result of

Finney's attitude on contemporary problems of political economy exhibited the same preference for reform by conversion, by testimony, and by example. His economic theory was a strange combination of altruistic utilitarianism, the Protestant ethic, and the medieval ideal of a Christian society. He had no use for the popular new doctrines of Manchester liberalism with their emphasis on self-interest instead of disinterested benevolence. For him, society had the static quality of an agrarian economy rather than the mobility of an industrial one. If a man was poor it was not the result of his personal sinfulness or his lack of push but simply that this was the station in life to which he had been ordained by providence. The poor man, he said, if he is a Christian, will be "submissive and happy in his poverty." He will not "complain and be envious at others who are not poor." "He will allow the judge his ermine, the king his robes of state, and the merchant his capital, and the husbandman his fields and his flocks, and will see the reasonableness and propriety of all this." [95] Although Finney praised all the virtues of the Protestant ethic, thrift, hard work, honesty, sobriety, and piety, there was little in his sermons which resembled the Horatio Alger success myth. Hard work in a calling did not necessarily raise a man from his appointed rank in society. Thrift and diligence built a man's character and "idleness" he said, "is a snare to the soul," but "The only possible use of making money for the glory of God is to use it for the conversion and sanctification of sinners." [96]

Far from endorsing the incipient industrial revolution in America, Finney went out of his way to attack it. In a discussion of "the credit system" on which modern capitalism is based, he condemned the whole process by preaching on the text from Romans 13:8, "Owe no man anything." The "prevailing system of doing business on borrowed capital," he said, was "worse than useless" for the text applied "not only to individuals but to corporations and nations." Supporters of

---

frustrated perfectionism. It has typified much of American life and thought. See Charles C. Cole, *The Social Ideas of the Northern Evangelists 1826–1860* (New York, 1954), pp. 209–11, 219; Fletcher, *Oberlin,* Vol. I, pp. 387, 396–98; and Finney, *Lectures on Systematic Theology* (London, 1851), pp. 368–69.

95 Finney, *Lectures on Systematic Theology* (London, 1851), pp. 467–68.

96 Finney, *Sermons on Important Subjects* (New York, 1836, published by John S. Taylor), pp. 216, 264.

Andrew Jackson's attack upon the national debt and the national bank no doubt applauded these sentiments. But Finney went even farther. He denied the farmer the right to borrow against his future crop: "The consumers of merchandise instead of anticipating their yearly crops and yearly income and running in debt with the expectation of paying for these . . . [should] take a little pains to reverse the order of things and be a year beforehand, paying down for what they purchase and having the income each year beforehand so as to contract no debts." If the farmers who went west had reversed the prevailing order of things as Finney suggested, it would have been a long time before the frontier was settled.[97]

Finney admitted that he was considered "rash" (meaning old-fashioned) for saying this, but he insisted that "the whole credit system if not absolutely sinful is nevertheless so highly dangerous that no Christian should embark on it." He lamented the fact that "It has come to pass that a man may not only be considered a respectable citizen but a respectable member of the Church who suffers himself to be in debt. . . ." And like John Cotton of the Massachusetts Bay Colony, he had little use for the economic theory that a businessman might justly charge what the traffic would bear. "One maxim runs through the whole" of business, he said, in 1837, "to 'buy as cheap as you can and sell as dear as you can, to look out for number one' and to do always as far as the rules of honesty will allow, all that will advance your own interests, let what will become of the interest of others." To accept this view of business, "that everyone should take care of himself, purchase as low and sell as high as he can; take advantage of the state of the market, the scarcity of articles in which he deals" was to conform to the selfish principles of Satan. "Christians are by no means to conform to the business maxims of the world." Like Cotton he spoke of "the just price" and denounced rich men who, "greedy of filthy lucre," ground the faces of the poor. And, like the social gospelers at the close of the nineteenth century, he urged the businessman to ask himself "What was the spirit Jesus Christ exemplified on earth?" and to practice that "spirit of self-denial, of benevolence, of sacrificing himself to do good to others" that typified Jesus. The worldly

[97] This sermon is in the *Oberlin Evangelist,* II (July 31, 1839), 129.

minded, said Finney, "will screw down a poor man who is doing a little piece of work for them to the lowest penny. If they are dealing on a large scale, very likely they will be liberal and fair, because it is to their advantage. But if it is a person they care not about, a laborer or a mechanic or a servant, they will grind him down to the last fraction, no matter what it is really worth; and they actually pretend to make conscience of it, that they cannot possibly give any more." [98]

Finney had no patience with businessmen who told him that if they did not do business as other men did, on "false" principles, they would not be able to compete with their rivals. This was nonsense: "Only make it your invariable rule to do right and do business upon principle and you can control the market." If all Christian businessmen acted on right principles, "The Christians would soon do the business of the world," and this would show "the power of the church to regulate the commerce of the world." [99] Whether he was discussing relations among businessmen, between businessmen and employees, or between businessmen and the public, Finney offered only the same solution for the ethical problems of the system of laissez faire capitalism arising in the United States that he did for the evils of slavery: i.e., the personal reformation of the individual malefactor. His economic ethic was based on the face-to-face commercial system of the storekeeper, the small shop, the farmer and the hired hand, the merchant who knew all his clerks and customers by name. "Take the case of two servants, one devoted to his master's interests, and other having no conscience or concern but to secure his wages. Go to one, and he throws into the shade all personal considerations and enlists with heart and soul in achieving the object [desired by his master]. The other will not act unless you present some selfish motive; unless you say, 'Do so, and I will raise your wages or set you up in business.'" Business was to Finney a matter of personal relationship, man-to-man bargaining and trading. On this level it was perhaps relevant to talk about economics in terms of brotherly love and honest weights and measures. "A man who will cheat and defraud his neighbor does not love him

98 Finney, *Lectures to Professing Christians,* pp. 130–31, 183; Finney, *Sermons on Important Subjects,* p. 263; Finney, *Lectures on Revivals,* pp. 408, 100.
99 Finney, *Lectures on Revivals,* p. 138.

as he does himself." "God listens to every bargain and every lie" that a merchant may "tell behind his counter." But Finney was blind to the incipient dangers of industrialism in the broader social sense which contemporaries like Orestes Brownson, Theodore Parker, Robert Owen, Henry Thoreau, and Herman Melville protested against. His view of factory life was taken from a visit made to the Oriskany Woolen Mill near Utica in 1826 where the owner, finding that Finney was eager to conduct a revival meeting, gave orders to "Stop the mill and let the people attend to religion; for it is more important that our souls should be saved than that this factory run.[100] According to Finney's paternalistic outlook, no employer who cared so much for the spiritual welfare of his employees would ever be guilty of overworking or underpaying them. Religion taught man brotherly love and love would solve all problems of social and economic conflict. If a man made his clerks attend church regularly, as the Tappans did, then he was fulfilling his Christian obligation as an employer.

Finney's dislike for the selfish profit motive of capitalism led him to warn businessmen against using their profits "to enlarge their capital and their business" when the money might be put to better use in advancing revival and missionary activities. But he was cautious in answering those devout perfectionists who asked, "should every man give up all his capital and means at once of promoting the cause of Christ?" by selling out his business and giving the money to Christian work? He warned such extremists, "This might not be Christian economy. A man's capital, if it be not larger than is necessary for the wisest transaction of business is to be considered in the light of tools with which he serves God and his generation." [101] Through this portal, so casually left ajar in the stronghold of stewardship, drove the whole caravan of pious nineteenth-century business moguls.

The political didactics in Finney's sermons exhibited the same emphasis on personal morality, the same tendency to with-

[100] Finney, *Lectures to Professing Christians,* p. 29; Finney, *Sermons on Important Subjects,* p. 258; Finney, *Lectures on Revivals,* p. 408; Finney, *Memoirs,* p. 184. Even in 1874, Finney was unable to see any need for a law to enforce the eight hour day in industry. See Charles C. Cole, *The Social Ideas of the Northern Evangelists* (New York, 1954), p. 188.

[101] Finney, *Sermons on Important Subjects,* p. 268.

draw from making decisions on complex questions and to treat all problems in terms of pietism and perfectionism. "Christians must vote for honest men," he said in 1835. "Instead of voting for a man because he belongs to their party, Bank or Anti-Bank, Jackson or Anti-Jackson, they must find out whether he is honest and upright and fit to be trusted." Once let it be known that Christians would refuse to vote "bad men into office" and all parties would be eager "to put up honest men as candidates." He did not say on what grounds a Christian should choose between honest candidates of different parties, for presumably it would not matter which party were in power if all candidates were honest. To a perfectionist any sanctified administrator would be able to solve the problems of society simply by applying Christian principles of love and benevolence. Finney's faith in the moral omnicompetence of the Christian was the evangelical equivalent of Jackson's faith in the political omnicompetence of the average man. But Finney left the Christian voter up in the air when it came to deciding between two somewhat dishonest candidates. If there were no "strictly honest" men on the ticket he declared that the Christian should not vote, even though he would thereby leave government in the hands of the wicked. Many men have "erred," he wrote in 1839, by voting for a party "instead of voting universally for good men or refusing to vote altogether." [102]

Finney was obviously a short-sighted and fumbling guide in the realms of political, economic, and social reform, but in the realm of personal moral reform he was in his element. Here he walked sure-footedly over the most difficult terrain and had no difficulty whatever in applying his general religious principles in the most detailed and concrete fashion to all the problems of social custom and behavior. He was even able to assimilate into his theology such avant-garde refinements on human physi-

[102] Finney, *Lectures on Revivals,* p. 274; Finney, *Lectures to Professing Christians,* pp. 141–43. 151; *Oberlin Evangelist* (April 24, 1839), p. 73. Though Finney does not seem to have expressed his views on Jackson, he probably agreed with Lewis Tappan that he was "a very unfit man to be at the head of the Government"; see Cole, *Northern Evangelists,* p. 140. William E. Dodge, a staunch supporter of Finney in New York, seems to have reflected the general attitude inculcated by Finney's political principles. Though an antislavery Whig, Dodge did not believe that honest men should have anything to do with politics. See Richard Lowitt, *A Merchant Prince of the Nineteenth Century: William E. Dodge* (New York, 1954), p. 202.

ology as hydropathy, phrenology, vegetarianism, and the dietetic reforms of Sylvester Graham, the inventor of the Graham cracker. During 1840–41, for example, at the height of the fad over Grahamism, Finney and his colleagues on the faculty at Oberlin compelled the students who ate at the college dining hall to do without meat, tea, coffee, and pastries on the ground that they were harmful to the health. To Finney, as to most New Englanders, self-gratification and the use of bodily stimulants were *ipso facto* sinful. All true reformers, he believed, deserved the respect of their fellow men if they "are honestly endeavoring to reform mankind and denying their appetites." One of the strongest counts against the "antinomian perfectionism" of John Noyes and the other experimentalists in free love was the obvious fact that they were encouraging rather than thwarting their bodily appetites. They forgot Finney's maxim that "a self-indulgent Christian is a contradiction."

Finney called upon all true Christians to abandon forthwith any "habit of character" which might injure the health "that precious gift of God" or "sear the conscience." Among such self-indulgent habits he listed "smoking, chewing or snuffing tobacco, using injurious stimulants of any kind, high and unwholesome living, extravagant dressing or equipage, retiring late at night and rising late in the morning, eating too much or between meals." His students at Oberlin had to listen to lectures on "the duty of keeping their nails clean and their clothes dry, of sitting straight in their chairs when in company without tipping back on two legs," and all the other tortuous refinements of proper midwestern Victorianism.[103]

In formulating this refined code of Christian manners which he believed to be in harmony with the will of God, Finney reflected his own frontier upbringing and New England heritage. A large part of the code originated in a distrust of the diversions of city life, a horror of the refinements of "Society," and an inbred aversion to luxury, recreation, and the fine arts. Dancing, gambling, drinking, card playing, and theater-going were only slightly less heinous than adultery and murder. "Take care how you dress," he told women in his audience. "What is that on your head? What does that gaudy ribbon and those

[103] Finney, *Lectures on Systematic Theology* (Oberlin, 1878), pp. 312–16; Wright, *Finney*, p. 169.

ornaments upon your dress say to everyone that meets you? It makes the impression that you wish to be thought pretty. Take care! You might just as well write on your clothes, 'NO TRUTH IN RELIGION.' It says, 'GIVE ME DRESS, GIVE ME FASHION, GIVE ME FLATTERY, AND I AM HAPPY.' " Hell, he said, holds a jubilee and heaven puts on mourning when women "bow to the goddess of fashion, fill their ears with ornaments, and their fingers with rings . . . put feathers in their hats and clasps upon their arms, lace themselves up till they can hardly breathe." [104]

Preaching in New York in 1835 he said, "It is easy to see why revivals do not prevail in a great city." It was due to the fashionable life of the high society circle. "What a calamity to be in such circles!" he told an audience undoubtedly made up of country people like himself who had only recently come to the city. "See how crazy those are who are scrambling to get up to these circles, enlarging their houses, changing their style of living, furniture, etc. It is like climbing up [the] masthead to be thrown off into the ocean. To enjoy God you must come down, not go up there. God is not there, among all the starch and flattery of hell." God was down among the respectable common people who might secretly envy the rich and the fashionable but who knew in their hearts that virtue was its own reward. Not even charity balls whose profits went to the poor could reconcile Finney to the sins of dancing, "the dissipation and surfeiting and temptations connected with them. . . . strange charity to eat and drink and dance and when they have rioted and feasted until they can enjoy it no longer, they deal out to the poor the crumbs that have fallen from the table." [105]

Just as plain and simple living was more wholesome and godly so ignorance of the intellectual frivolities which were associated with a knowledge of literature and classical languages was a benefit rather than a hindrance to true Christians. The trouble with most eastern colleges was that "the student spends four years in college at *classical* studies and no God in them." When they graduate these "learned students may understand their *hic, haec, hoc,* very well and may laugh at the humble Christian and call him ignorant although he may know how to

[104] Finney, *Lectures on Revivals,* pp. 141–42.
[105] *Ibid.,* pp. 142, 112, 215.

win more souls than five hundred of them." Like most American pietists Finney believed that "a good education is indeed a great good, but if not sanctified, it is all the more odious to God." English literature was as worthless as the study of pagan languages: "I cannot believe that a person who has ever known the love of God can relish a secular novel." A man's character was revealed by the books he kept: "Let me visit your chamber, your parlor, or wherever you keep your books. What is here? Byron, Scott, Shakespeare, and a host of triflers and blasphemers of God. . . ." [106]

The only aspect of education that seemed to him free from contamination was science. Paley's proof of God from the design of the universe had yet to be shattered by the discoveries of Darwin, Freud, and Einstein. Finney was confident that science and the revealed word of God could always be reconciled: "Acquaint yourselves as far as possible with books on natural science," he urged his students. "Examine works on anatomy, physiology, natural, mental and moral philosophy and such books as will make you thoroughly acquainted with the structure and laws of the universe; for all these things declare the wonderful works of God." [107]

This faith in the harmonious relationship between nature and the supernatural was central to Finney's philosophy and theology. Calvinism had grimly maintained that the gap between man and God was unbridgeable no matter how much men learned about the laws of the universe. Finney spoke with the exuberant self-reliance of his age when he refused to believe that men must remain passive in the most vital of all human concerns, the salvation of their souls. Like those other spokesmen of the 1830's and '40's, Jackson, Emerson, Whitman, Bryant, he insisted that man was meant to be the master of his own fate. It was for this that God endowed man with reason, conscience, and common sense so that he might, through increasing knowledge of the natural world, discern and act in accord with the laws of the spiritual world.

In preaching the vision of American progress and human perfectibility, Finney, like Beecher and Taylor, consciously re-

[106] *Ibid.*, pp. 203, 177. Finney, *Sermons on Gospel Themes,* p. 358. *Oberlin Evangelist,* I (December 4, 1839), 193; and (April 24, 1839), 73; IV (August 17, 1842), 131.

[107] *Oberlin Evangelist,* IV (August 17, 1842), 131.

worked Christian orthodoxy to suit the times. Deism, which flourished briefly at the turn of the century, was bound to fail in America despite its rationalism and optimism because it rejected too much of the Christian tradition. The new divinity managed a more subtle amalgamation of science and religion which maintained all the rationalism of deism and all the emotionalism of Christianity. Evangelical ministers in agreeing upon a few fundamentals of doctrine sought the same kind of synthesis in the realm of faith that scientists sought in the realm of nature. Finney's scientific rationale for revivalism was a unique contribution to the development of American Protestantism precisely because it blended reason and faith so neatly. His unprovable assumptions were buttressed pragmatically in terms of experience and results. By utilizing Finney's principles, Americans thought they could effect the nation's Christian liberty just as quickly as they had effected its political liberty. The promotion of revivalism was to be the final development in the rising glory of America. Through this device for harnessing the divine to the human, it seemed to Finney and his contemporaries that American ingenuity and the clear insight of free men in a new world had solved the last problem in the way of achieving the millennium.

The breath-taking scope of this vision, the sincerity and earnestness with which Finney's fellow evangelical Christians worked for its fulfilment and believed in its imminence, was both praiseworthy and hopelessly ingenuous. When the vision failed to materialize, however, the spirit went out of revivalism. It became as mechanical and formal as the Calvinistic tradition which it had helped to overthrow. Finney played a major part in the collapse of Calvinism but in the end his efforts to perfect mankind through the creation of a new race of revival ministers failed. Instead of making evangelists out of all preachers in order to hasten the millennium, Finney's efforts served primarily to establish a new profession of specialists in the laws of mind and the right use of means whose principal goal was the recruitment of new church members.

CHAPTER 3

"Those Expert and Practical Itinerant Tacticians"

The second great awakening was at an end by the time Finney left New York City for Oberlin in 1835. The reorientation in theology and ecclesiasticism was complete and the age of Jackson was shortly to give way to the reaction of 1840. The Presbyterian schism of 1837 was a last resort of the Old School but in the end it went for naught. Calvinism was dead and evangelical Protestantism was oiled and geared to coast complacently for a generation or more.

In the forty years after 1835 itinerant evangelism became a respected profession. Its task was not, however, to stir up pietistic fervor or millennial hope but to perform the routine function of maintaining a steady rate of church growth. The skill with which it accomplished this gave a new status to what had formerly been a race of outcasts. In the eighteenth century peripatetic preachers, responsible to no one but themselves, had been viewed askance by the regular clergy of all denominations, but especially by the Presbyterians and Congregationalists. The vulgar emotionalism and fanatical attacks upon the learned but "unconverted" ministry in which most itinerants indulged during the first great awakening aroused bitter and lasting clerical antagonism toward them. Similar excesses by roving camp meeting exhorters during the second great awakening did nothing to lessen this prejudice. The conservative itinerant revivalism practised by Nettleton in New England for the fifteen years preceding Finney's arrival on the scene paved the way for a more tolerant attitude as did the new theology forged by Taylor and Beecher. But it was not until Finney's successful career both in the West and in the East that a new climate for itinerant preachers emerged. Behind Finney's success lay several less obvious factors, however, which provided the real impetus toward a re-evaluation of itinerancy. One of these was the problem posed by the expanding frontier. Another was the general acceptance of the theory that revival preachers constituted a special branch of the ministry. And the third was the growing theological unity among all Protestant denominations.

As eastern church members dispersed westward, it became impossible to provide a learned ministry to fill the urgent demands for pastors in the rising new towns and villages. Congregationalist and Presbyterian leaders in the East perforce let down their standards after 1800 and permitted the Plan of Union presbyteries and associations in New York, Ohio, and elsewhere to license young men who seemed to have the calling for the ministry even though their theological education was as flimsy as Finney's. The western presbyteries needed little encouragement to do this. Some of them went even farther. In order to make the ministry more attractive to young men like Finney who found Calvinism contrary to common sense, the more liberal Presbygational presbyteries adopted "abbreviated Confessions" which required licentiates to assent only to the fundamentals of the faith instead of to the Westminster Confession *in toto*.[1] After 1825 new school presbyteries began to license evangelists or home missionaries who, instead of being assigned to preach in thinly populated, unchurched areas, were specifically assigned to areas where the churches were supplied by conservative pastors who refused to preach the new divinity or to utilize the new measures.[2]

Once the idea of itinerant revivalism was accepted by Presbyterians and Congregationalists in the West, it was not long before uses for it were found in the East. One of the most important aspects of Finney's career was his influence in making the tenets and practices of frontier revivalism seem

1 See Samuel J. Baird, *A History of the New School* (Philadelphia, 1868), p. 340.

2 E. H. Gillett, *History of the Presbyterian Church in the U.S.A.* (Philadelphia, 1864), Vol. II, pp. 336 ff., 482 ff.

respectable in the larger cities both in the West and in the East. By theory and practice he proved that revivals were man-made, and from this it followed that certain men naturally possessed greater talents for revivalism than others. For the good of the evangelical faith and the spread of the gospel, therefore, it came to be accepted by 1835 that such skillful men should be allowed greater freedom, not only in style and methods, but in the scope of their work. In fact, itinerant revivalists were encouraged by Finney, and gradually by the clergy as a whole, to offer their services wherever they thought they were needed. Ample proof that the concept of modern revivalism was gaining ground even among conservative ministers in the early 1830's was provided in William Sprague's *Lectures on Revivals of Religion.*

Although one of Sprague's avowed purposes in publishing this work in 1832 was to offset Finney's new measure revivalism, his book clearly reflected the growing preoccupation among ministers of all evangelical denominations with the importance of "promoting revivals." Twenty leading ministers of six different denominations wrote letters for the appendix of Sprague's book, stressing the churches' duty to encourage revivals. Except for a hesitation over the use of certain measures, like the anxious seat, praying for persons by name, all-night prayer meetings, and females praying in mixed public meetings, the difference between the Spragueites and the Finneyites was not as great as each supposed. Both groups believed that soul winning was the primary purpose of the clergy, both agreed that there were certain "means" which men could use in effecting conversions, both believed in a core of "fundamental truths" underlying all doctrinal differences, both agreed that God worked through "human instruments" in promoting revivals, both believed in interdenominational cooperation wherever possible, both shared the same social and moral code, and both believed that revivalism in the United States was currently reaching a climactic peak of efficiency which would soon usher in the millennium. Sprague himself was even willing to condone the use of protracted meetings if they were carefully regulated.[3] Although differences in emphasis upon free will,

[3] Perhaps the key sentence in Sprague's book was this: "God has not limited his people in their efforts to advance his cause to what may properly be called

animal excitement, and a lukewarm learned ministry placed the followers of Sprague in the opposite camp from the followers of Finney when the schism came in 1837, nevertheless Sprague's volume demonstrated that the old tradition of miraculous, "prayed-down" revivals was virtually dead. As for the question of interdenominational unity, Sprague declared "where is the man who would not consider it comparatively a light matter whether an individual should join one particular communion or some other provided he gave evidence of being a real disciple of Christ?" Presbyterians admitted, he said, "that our neighbors around us hold the fundamental truths of the gospel and are walking in the way to heaven." [4] Despite the bitterness caused by the schism, the differences in emphasis between Sprague and Finney were glossed over by the end of the 1840's in order that the churches might get on with their main task of evangelizing the world. Even in growing frontier towns where competition for new church members was most bitter, ministers who would unite on nothing else would usually cooperate in a revival meeting. In these years, revivalists paid particular heed to Finney's advice and example regarding the necessity for avoiding controversial issues in conducting their business.

But a hard core of ultraconservatives, who harbored the ancient prejudice against itinerancy and who coupled a devotion to the old revival tradition with a bitter dislike for Beecherism and Finneyism, provided a running fire of criticism of the new evangelical system almost up to the Civil War. These critics pointed out with remarkable clarity the damaging effect which institutionalized professional revivalism was to have upon American Protestantism over the next century and a quarter. Typical of their outlook was an article by the Rev. William Mitchell which appeared in 1835 in the *Literary and Theological Review* of Andover Seminary. It was entitled, "An Inquiry into the Utility of Modern Evangelists and Their Methods." In it Mitchell discussed with alarm the transforma-

divine institutions: he permits them to adopt means to a certain extent *of their own devising. . . .*" W. B. Sprague, *Lectures on Revivals of Religion* (Albany, 1832), p. 117. Note also the sympathetic review of Sprague's book by John Breckenridge in *Biblical Repertory and Theological Review,* n.s. VII (October, 1832), 455 ff.

[4] Sprague, *Revivals,* p. 58.

tion which had taken place in evangelism during the preceding decade. "The term *Evangelist* as denoting a distinct grade of office has lost its original meaning," he began. Formerly it meant one who "received a temporary appointment to preach" in "destitute places" and who "gathered churches among the heathen." Such evangelists "were not employed either as promoters or conductors of revivals in the churches over which the Holy Ghost had appointed overseers." Now, he lamented, all that had changed. Today "the main question is whether the labours of those who now bear the name of Evangelists are, on the whole, either necessary or beneficial to the churches supplied with regular pastors." [5]

In his discussion of modern evangelists, Mitchell admitted that "Such men as Wesley, Whitefield, the elder Tennent and a few others of recent date [like Nettleton] may have been needed to rouse the slumbering churches," but these men were "extraordinary instruments" raised up by God. What Mitchell and other conservative churchmen objected to was not evangelism itself but to "Evangelists as organized into a distinct, permanent body," evangelists who claimed that "their only commission so far as it is to come from this world must be the favourable opinion of a Christian community," and who employed all sorts of "machinery" not "sanctioned by the word of God" on the ground that "the *end* will sanctify the *means*."

Nettleton, or men like him, said Mitchell, "carefully preserved the unity of the churches and strengthened the hands of pastors by their cooperation and by yielding them in all things their place as the constitutional guardians of the flock." But under the modern system of revivals "the chief *management* has been either assumed by the Evangelist, or of necessity yielded to him; and he performs, in his own irresponsible way, almost all the services. He has his own measures, proclaims the number of converts, accomplishes their speedy admission to the church, and assigns, for the time being, a subordinate place to the pastor in the care of his own flock."

Mitchell concluded his article by declaring his strong doubts as to "the expediency of committing the churches at all to the spiritual guidance of an Evangelist. He is under the pressure of

[5] William Mitchell, "An Inquiry into the Utility of Modern Evangelists," *Literary and Theological Review,* II (September, 1835), 494 ff.

constant excitement. He is followed by a throng of admiring hearers, is subject to little responsibility, and probably receives a greater compensation for his services than three ordinary pastors." The problem had assumed such proportions by 1835 that Mitchell warned, "The present system of Evangelism has become well nigh a hierarchy with its lords spiritual," and if continued, "we may soon count upon the dissolution of the pastoral office." Had he said "diminution" he would have been more accurate.

Most conservatives held Finney and his rash young imitators personally responsible for this, yet Finney had not planned it that way. He discountenanced the idea of spasmodic revival activity[6] and, far from wanting to create a new hierarchy of professional evangelists "organized into a distinct, permanent body," his avowed ambition was to train up a new race of pastors, all of whom would be perpetually preaching revivalistically. One reason for the miscarriage of his ideal and for his being made the scapegoat of the conservatives was that in abandoning the destitute West in order to rout hyper-Calvinism out of the "polluted and perverted" East he deliberately set an example for others who were eager to undermine or alter the influence of the regular clergy. In addition, by the theological and scientific justification which he offered for his revivals Finney, more than anyone else, inculcated the notion that special knowledge and special skills beyond those of the ordinary pastor were needed to promote revivals and to guarantee results. And moreover, Finney apparently did not, in all simplicity, see that the excitement, the adulation of the crowds, or even the greater financial compensation of city revivalism might become, for less dedicated men, an end in itself.

There was ample justification for the qualms which conservative ministers like Mitchell expressed regarding the trend to professionalize evangelism. Within two years after the New Lebanon convention in 1827 a writer in Nathaniel Taylor's *Quarterly Christian Spectator* attacked the "repeated" demands by prominent laymen in Connecticut for the creation of "a corps of Evangelists to be employed for life exclusively amidst revivals of religion." The result of such an innovation, said the writer, would be to spread the belief among churchgoers

[6] C. G. Finney, *Lectures on Revivals* (New York, 1835), p. 246.

"that their own ministers are incompetent" to deal with revivals. The assumption would grow that the pastor "may be trusted to toil on with the parochial duties in times of spiritual coldness, but it will soon be thought hazardous, if not impious, to trust him without counsel and assistance" from an expert evangelist in times of awakening.[7]

This article was less critical of the laymen who made the proposal than of the Congregational Associations and occasional councils whose duty it was to license candidates for the ministry. These "ordaining authorities," said the writer, were to blame for the rise of itinerant professional evangelists because they were too eager to ordain young men as evangelists instead of merely licensing them to preach. No one questioned the right of such bodies to ordain evangelists but this right had been exercised too indiscriminately of late. In the past a seminary student or otherwise properly trained young man who felt the call to preach was licensed by the association of ministers in his area, but he was not ordained until such time as he was called to be the pastor of a church. If a man were ordained as an evangelist, it was only "for some particular enterprise or station" in the home or foreign mission field. But now that revival preaching was all the rage, church associations and councils were ordaining young men as evangelists by the score. They were thereby creating, in effect, a new rank in the ministry and killing off the old rank of the licentiate. Since the ordained evangelist could administer the ordinances of baptism, marriage, and communion while a licentiate could not, naturally all young candidates for the ministry preferred to be made evangelists. As ordained evangelists they attained all the privileges and authority of the ministry with none of its responsibilities. Many men so ordained would, said the article, never settle down but would prefer to roam about continually conducting revival meetings and disrupting the regular life of the churches. It was

[7] "Review on the Employment of Evangelists in Our Older Settlements," *Quarterly Christian Spectator,* I (September, 1829), 425 ff. It is significant that when a committee was appointed by the General Association of Connecticut in 1820 to discuss the advisability of forming "an order of evangelists" to assist pastors in promoting revivals, Nettleton opposed it so vehemently that the matter was dropped. See Bennet Tyler, *Memoir of the Life and Character of Rev. Asahel Nettleton, D. D.* (Hartford, 1844), pp. 60–61.

well known that evangelists were not noted for their amenability to ecclesiastical authority. Yet some who advocated that the churches establish "a corps of Evangelists" had "even gone so far as to call on volunteers to go forth . . . without ordination to labor according to their own judgment. . . ."

Similar alarm over the rise of a new ministerial rank was expressed by the official organ of Princeton Presbyterianism in 1831. "We believe . . . that the influence of the ministry is in danger of being counteracted by the prevalence of some wrong views on the subject of evangelism," said the review of a book on *The Christian Ministry*. "It is becoming a popular notion, and we already see it to some extent reduced to practice, that there should be a set of men trained up for the special purpose of conducting revivals of religion; and that wherever there is a revival, they should be invited to labour; and that for the time being the stated pastor should feel himself to be nothing more than a curate." Many presbyteries were abetting this practice by their habit of ordaining men, as Finney had been ordained, as evangelists. The reviewer did not mention Finney, and even expressed belief that there were cases where evangelists were necessary and useful, "but we object to their being regarded as a distinct set of men with somewhat higher power than other ministers. . . ." [8]

Two prominent British Congregationalists who visited the United States in 1834 wrote a book on the state of the American churches in which they noted certain unhealthy tendencies growing out of the new emphasis on revivalism. They were shocked to find that "some churches send for a 'revival minister,' get up a round of special meetings and exciting measures, with the deliberate purpose of introducing a state of religious feelings which is to continue only while the revival lasts, and to consider the departure of the preacher a signal for cessation of labour and a collapse of feeling." The new criteria of religious fervor were quantitative, to be measured by the number of days a revival lasted and by the number of conversions obtained. "Already a seven days' meeting has a sound of reputation about it which is denied to one of three or four days." And protracted meetings were now being extended for as long

[8] *Biblical Repertory and Theological Review,* n.s. III (October, 1831), 466 ff.

as forty days in some places with a consequent state of complete exhaustion at their conclusion.[9]

As for the evangelists whom the British visitors saw and heard about, their conclusion was that "Rash measures attract rash men." The measures were of course Finney's new measures with which the Britishers had no sympathy. And the evangelists were "A number of young and raw men, previously unknown to the ministry and without pastoral experience" who "have chosen this shorter method to ministerial efficiency. They have announced themselves as the revival preachers and have chosen to itinerate over the church, unsettling everything and settling nothing." Because their continued popularity was dependent upon their ability to produce results, the rashness and statistical measurement in soul winning grew worse and worse. The British concluded that the result of the new revival movement had been "most disastrous" for the American churches.

The efforts of most religious conservatives in the 1830's to blame either "the complicated system of which 'New Measures' is merely the technical name" or to blame the church authorities for catering to the public demand for novelty and excitement overlooked a more basic cause for the revival enthusiasm of Finney's day. Lyman Beecher seems to have been one of the few men who saw beyond the narrow ecclesiastical and doctrinal horizon of the controversy to find the reason for Finneyism and "ultraism" in the social and cultural changes taking place in the United States. However, Beecher saw these changes as dangers which the proper sort of revivalism ought to check or control rather than encourage. In an article which Beecher printed in the *Spirit of the Pilgrims* in September, 1831, (and with which he certainly agreed if he did not actually write it) some of the "appalling" dangers of the day which made the right kind of revivals a necessary security measure against democratic anarchy were listed: "our vast extent of territory, our numerous and increasing population," "the fury of sectional jealousy and hate," power-thirsty politicians, "the corrupting influence of pre-eminent national prosperity," atheism,

[9] Quotations are from the review of Andrew Reed and James Matheson, *A Narrative of the Visit to the American Church by the Deputation from the Congregational Union of England and Wales* (New York, 1835) in *Biblical Repertory and Theological Review,* n.s. VII (October, 1835), 598 ff.

"religious party strife," "the intrigues of Catholic Europe," "the increase of intellectual power" among the common people, and "the universality of suffrage." Certainly these were among the major aspects of social ferment which helped to produce and stimulate revivalism. But to Beecher's conservative mind revivals were meant to act as a check upon these forces, and the article concluded by praising the churches as the inculcators of Christian humility, submissiveness, and self-restraint, which alone could subdue this democratic "ocean of unstable mind." [10] The title of the article was "The Necessity of Revivals to the Perpetuity of Our Civil and Religious Institutions." It was prophetic of the tone of post-Civil War revivalism, but it was not an attitude which characterized the revivalism inspired by Finney.

Beecher was undoubtedly correct in relating Finney's revivalism to the turbulent forces of Jacksonian democracy. Just as Jacksonian democrats tried to wrest the federal government from the aristocrats and the monopolists and place it in the hands of the common man so Finney and his colleagues sought to overthrow what they considered the ecclesiastical tyranny of the learned eastern hierarchy in the churches and re-establish the priesthood of all believers. Like all pietistic movements, the second great awakening had strong anticlerical tendencies. In addition, revivalism in this period was both a symptom of social change and a means of social change. In the hands of Western revival leaders it was a tool by which pious Americans sought to build the New Jerusalem in "God's country." Unfortunately revivalism of this sort did not measure up to Beecher's specifications, for it unleashed rather than restrained the frothy ocean of unstable mind. It took religion out of the hands of the educated, conservative clergy and put it into the hands of unstable upstarts. It broke down the distinction between social classes, put the laity on an equal plane with the clergy, encouraged equality of the sexes, and pursued in a wild and fantastic way all manner of social reforms. The pietistic radicalism which lay at the heart of rural

[10] "The Necessity of Revivals of Religion to the Perpetuity of Our Civil and Religious Institutions," *Spirit of the Pilgrims,* IV (September, 1831), 467–68. Beecher's most explicit attack upon Jacksonian radicalism was contained in his *Lectures on Political Atheism,* written in 1852. See Lyman Beecher, *Works* (Boston, 1852), Vol. I.

and frontier revivalism had to be shorn of its primitive fervor and naive idealism before it could win the support of the eastern leaders of Protestantism. The process by which revivalism was tamed and harnessed to the institutional structure of the churches was not entirely managed by its conservative opponents. Finney himself began to have qualms about new measure revivalism after he moved east. Many of the itinerant evangelists who claimed to be following in his footsteps seemed as rash to him as he had formerly seemed to Beecher. After 1827 Finney began to dissociate himself from what he considered the extravagant methods of itinerant western evangelists like Daniel Nash, Nathaniel Smith, John Ingersoll, Luther Myrick, Augustus Littlejohn, Horatio N. Foote, James Boyle, and Jedidiah Burchard. But Finney's refusal to endorse these men stemmed as much from their own extremism as from his growing cautiousness. Of this particular group of revivalists all but two abandoned or were forced out of the ministry by 1845. Three became involved in the "free love" experiments of the radical perfectionists and one was unfrocked for adultery. Theodore Weld reported in 1844 that "Within the last four years not less than thirty ministers of evangelical denominations have been guilty of the most flagrant licentiousness" and been removed from the ministry.[11] And Asa Mahan reported in his autobiography that out of all the evangelists of the 1830's who were inspired by Finney, "I cannot recall a single man, brother Finney and Father Nash excepted, who did not after a few years lose his unction and become equally disqualified for the office of evangelist and pastor." [12]

Father Nash, who collaborated with Finney in the years 1824–27, was honest at heart.[13] But he did not see anything wrong with offering "agonizing" prayers "with his utmost earnestness lying upon his belly." Nor did he think it bizarre to

[11] Weld to Lewis Tappan, February 6, 1844, *Letters of Theodore Weld, Angelina Grimke Weld, and Sarah Grimke,* eds. G. H. Barnes and D. L. Dumond (New York, 1934), Vol. II, p. 994.

[12] Asa Mahan, *Autobiography* (London, 1882), p. 229.

[13] For brief biographical sketches of some of the figures mentioned below see P. H. Fowler, *Historical Sketch of Presbyterianism within the Bounds of the Synod of Central New York* (Utica, 1877), and P. C. Headley, *Evangelists in the Church* (Boston, 1875). See also W. R. Cross, *The Burned-over District* (Ithaca, New York, 1950), pp. 173 ff., where the democratic aspects of western revivalism are discussed in some detail.

take part in revival meetings with a double black veil over his face, like the minister in Hawthorne's short story, on the ground that his eyes were infected and could not stand the bright sunlight.[14]

Augustus Littlejohn was described by one eyewitness who was generally friendly toward new measure revivalists as "a mad enthusiast," "grossly unsound in doctrine, boisterous in manner" and a man whose sermons were characterized by "coarseness, vulgarity, and abuse." He was expelled from the ministry in 1841 for seducing various of his female admirers much to the chagrin of his wife.[15]

Jedidiah Burchard, for whom Finney expressed great admiration in 1829, was considered "totally unsafe" by him four years later. A contemporary account described him as " 'Theatrical' in the highest possible degree. He frequently struck his hands together making a loud report. Every nerve and muscle was called into requisition" in his preaching and as soon as he entered the pulpit, the church "at once became a *theatre*." In 1833 he conducted a thirty-three-day protracted meeting in Auburn, New York. Once he told an audience in Burlington, Vermont, "I felt the Holy Spirit come right down, rush! rush! rush! into my soul." His wife conducted meetings for mothers and children and they both took down the names of all converts in a book and bragged about their statistical success from town to town. "I expect to live to see the day when I shall see three thousand souls converted in a day," he boasted. When Finney returned to Rochester in 1842 for a revival among the upper classes, he found Burchard excitedly stirring up the lower classes.[16]

One of Finney's most ardent admirers and the man who claimed to be the true heir of his method in western New York after 1827 was Luther Myrick. Myrick and Burchard occasionally conducted revivals together with startling results. "It was

[14] *A Calm Review of the Spirit, Means, and Incidents of the Late "Oneida Revival"* (Utica, 1827), p. 16 n. Finney, *Memoirs,* p. 70.

[15] James H. Hotchkin, *A History of the Purchase and Settlement of Western New York* (New York, 1848), p. 171. Cross, *The Burned-over District,* p. 194.

[16] Finney to Weld, March 30, 1829, *Letters of Theodore Weld,* Vol. I, p. 24; J. Hopkins to Finney, July 29, 1833, Finney Papers, Oberlin College Library; Headley, *Evangelists in the Church,* p. 278; Jedidiah Burchard, *Sermons, Addresses and Exhortations* (Burlington, Vermont, 1836), pp. 118, 49; Finney, *Memoirs,* p. 358.

as much as we could do [to] stand brother Burchard with his excentricities [*sic*]," wrote a friend in Auburn to Finney in 1833, "but for apparent conceit and magnifying by every means *important I* he was by no means as offensive as Brother Myrick." [17] Myrick's career provided a prime example of the difficulty Finney was under as the acknowledged leader of the new measure revivalists and of the extremes to which Finney's views could be carried. One of Finney's correspondents accused Myrick of denying "every doctrine which distinguishes the Presbyterian Chh from the Methodist"; of "Entering congregations and holding protracted meetings without the consent of either Pastor or Church"; of "Irreverent praying" such as " 'God smite the Devil, God smite the whited sepulchre. Jesus Christ come down here and attend to these hardened cases' accompanied by loud resounding, smiting fists and groaning, jumping, leaping, stamping, etc."; of "Profane language such as you are black as hell, The Devil is in you, Hell hardened, God provoking," and of calling ministers who did not cooperate with him "the children of the Devil, Drone bees in God's hive too cussed lazy to work. . . ." [18]

Finney's friend in Auburn warned him in 1833 that Myrick was "putting in with some of the perfectionists" of the most radical sort and that "There is [in progress] a . . . deliberate attempt by men of the Old School to make the publick believe that New School [New Haven theology] and Phinneyism and Myrickism are all alike." Another correspondent added, "Br. Myrick is sailing under your colors and using your name in such a way as to appear to agree with you . . . he says you and he agree. I have told him you *do not.* We are in trouble." [19]

Myrick, who apparently was not a close friend of Finney, had been ordained as an evangelist by the Oneida Presbytery in 1827. But in 1833 the presbytery put him on trial for heresy, for promoting disorder in the churches, and for "publick lying in the papers." Myrick wrote to Finney that "a combination" had been formed by his enemies among both the new and old school ministers "to put down Myrickism." He pleaded that his only heresy was preaching the very doctrines which Finney

[17] J. Hopkins to Finney, July 15, 1833, Finney Papers, OCL.

[18] The Rev. Mr. Corning of Otsico, New York, to Deacon Town (?) of Auburn, enclosed in a letter from Myrick to Finney, July 15, 1833, Finney Papers, OCL.

[19] J. Hopkins and T. Spencer to Finney, July 15, 1833, Finney Papers, OCL.

had preached. "O this Tyranny," he wailed. "This is evidently done to destroy my influence." Then he virtually pleaded guilty to at least one of the charges against him by suggesting to Finney that the only solution for the "oppressive" ecclesiasticism of the Presbyterian church was to secede from it and form a new "union of churches [of] the various denominations" based on the fundamentals.[20]

When Finney advised Myrick to be more restrained and to confess his errors to the presbytery and repent, Myrick was shocked. "You have assumed the very position that Nettleton did. And I would fain seize upon the sword you seem to have laid aside." The truth was, said Myrick, that Finney had "come down on a level" with his old opponents who "say you are now about right." "You are like Samson with his locks shorn. O this popularity!" When Finney cautioned him about seceding from Presbyterianism, Myrick quoted Finney's sermon "Can Two Walk Together Except They Be Agreed" and remarked, "You recognize as Christians [the] Baptists and unite in labours with them, but are they not really and sentimentally opposed to the presbyterian chh? . . . your present theory is directly opposed to the doctrine of your printed sermon." [21]

Myrick was suspended from the Oneida Presbytery in 1834 and set in motion his abortive scheme to organize an interdenominational church. There was more than a little truth to his argument that revivalism was incompatible with denominationalism just as there was considerable truth to his opinion that Finney had become more conservative and respectable over the years. If, as Finney proclaimed, the Westminster Confession of Faith was a hindrance to revivalism and only the fundamentals were important, Myrick was right in crying out against all creeds, "Down with them," "fasten the eye on the one great object (Viz. the salvation of souls)." Myrickism was simply Finneyism pushed further than Finney cared to push it in 1833. Yet three years later Finney himself left the Presbyterian church to become a Congregationalist largely because, like Myrick, he disliked its creed and its ecclesiastical tyranny.[22] And in 1836

[20] Myrick to Finney, July 15, 1833, Finney Papers, OCL.

[21] Myrick to Finney, October 1, 1834, Finney Papers, OCL.

[22] See Cross, *Burned-over District,* p. 280; Myrick to Finney, October 1, 1834, Finney Papers, OCL; Finney, *Memoirs,* pp. 324–35; Robert S. Fletcher, *History of Oberlin College* (Oberlin, Ohio, 1943), Vol. I, p. 22.

Finney also publicly espoused perfectionism. Finney's "Oberlin perfectionism" excluded him from playing the role within the church system which he deserved, but after 1827 his efforts were always on the side of good order. Yet while he did his best to make revivalism a respectable and integral part of the church system Finney never ceased to believe in the pietistic ideal of the unity of all Christian believers.

Because Finney did, as Myrick said, unite in labors with members of other denominations, his influence on itinerant evangelism extended beyond the Presbyterian and Congregational churches. The interdenominational aspect of the revival movement was evident in the changes which took place in the Baptist churches during the 1830's. The Baptists, like the Congregationalists, had no fixed creed and no ecclesiastical hierarchy, but the majority of them in 1830 were, in theory at least, confirmed Calvinists. Baptist revivalists, like Jacob Knapp and Jabez Swan, who brought Finney's theology and methods into their denomination after 1830, had to fight the same battle he did against "hyper-Calvinism" and the fear of "new measures." "A general impression among the Baptists prevailed," wrote Swan, "that there were set times for God to work in pouring salvation upon communities and that any attempt at awaking and trying to break up fallow ground was getting ahead of God." Baptists told Knapp that "When God wanted to convict or convert a sinner he knew where to find him and how to do it without the intervention of human effort, and in his own 'good time' he would, in his own way, bring his elect into the fold." Both Swan and Knapp gave Finney the credit for teaching the Baptists "to discern the connection between 'the means and end' " in religion.[23] The rapidity with which Calvinism was overthrown among the Baptists after 1830 and the differences in tone between Finney's revivalism and that of Swan and Knapp indicated that, among the less well-educated and poorer churchgoers who comprised the Baptist denomination, the new divinity and new measures struck an even more vibrant chord than among Presbyterians and Congregationalists.

[23] Jabez Swan, *The Evangelist, or Life and Labors of Rev. Jabez S. Swan,* ed. F. Denison (Waterford, Conn., 1873), pp. 101, 181; Jacob Knapp, *Autobiography of Elder Jacob Knapp* (New York, 1868), pp. 38–39, 62.

Jabez Swan brought a friendly, folksy tone into revivalism which became more typical of the profession than the fire and brimstone of Presbyterian evangelism. Jacob Knapp added elements of a less savory nature: commercialism, flamboyance, and publicity-seeking notoriety which characterized the worst aspects of the profession. Their careers, which extended from the 1830's to the 1870's, spanned the transition from sporadic popular evangelism to its formal institutionalization. They themselves helped to reduce modern revivalism to a sterile convention.

Swan worked his way through Hamilton Literary and Theological Institute and was ordained in 1827. During his pastorates in Stonington, Connecticut, (1827–1830) and Norwich, New York, (1830–1838) he devoted more time to assisting neighboring churches in revivals than in preaching to his own parishioners. Soon after 1830 he acquired a reputation as "the chief protracted meeting engineer of the Chenango Valley." During his revivals in Owego, Nye, Auburn, Wellport, Stonington, Mystic, New London, Albany, and elsewhere, he made liberal use of the anxious seat and aroused at first a great deal of antagonism among his Baptist colleagues for his use of new measures and his attacks upon Calvinism. "The ungodly reviled and mocked the whole thing," he said of one of his first protracted meetings. "But God rolled a tide of divine influence like the ground swell of the Atlantic which no earthly power could successfully resist" and soon the opposition from "high-geared" and "double-extra Calvinists" died down.[24]

Swan was a tall, gaunt man with twinkling eyes and a sense of humor. "I could never preach in a new suit of clothes," he said, "till I had worn them through a rain storm." He was utterly devoted to the task of saving souls and his persistence overcame all but the most determined opposition. He held his first four-day protracted meeting in 1832. By 1838 he was holding twelve-week meetings with preaching twice a day and three times on Sunday. Though not so emotional as camp meeting exhorters, Swan aroused his full share of animal excitement in faintings, shriekings, and groanings. On one occasion he wrought himself up as well as the crowd and finally fell pros-

[24] Swan, *Autobiography*, pp. 90, 96.

trate in the pulpit where he claimed to have had a vision of the promised land.[25] Although he never felt himself particularly limited as an itinerant by the fact that he was the pastor of a church, he decided after 1841 to devote himself entirely to evangelism and gave up pastorates except during occasional respites.

Occasionally Methodist, Congregational, and New School Presbyterian churches cooperated in Swan's revivals, but because he believed that baptism by immersion "in the liquid grave" was an essential seal of conversion, this generally alienated other denominations. The rite of baptism, however, added a spectacle to his proceedings which Swan made the most of. He often marched his hymn-singing converts in long lines from the church to the river, immersed them, and marched them back again while gawking throngs lined the way. More than once he conducted this ceremony at midnight and justified the noisy parade on the ground that slumbering sinners needed to be awakened.

Swan's revivalism contained all the characteristics of modern revivalism including even some instances of faith healing, though he effected cures by prayer rather than by laying on of hands. In his autobiography he recorded several stories of cripples who were restored to health in answer to his prayers.[26] All-night prayer meetings were a regular feature of all his revivals and so were days of fasting and abstention from all worldly activity. Like Finney he was an ardent advocate of temperance and no man was considered truly converted at his meetings who did not at the same time sign the temperance pledge. In 1842 he worked strenuously for a law prohibiting the sale of liquor in Connecticut. Parades to advertise temperance and Sunday school rallies were as regular in his meetings as the baptizings.

When his son left home to enter Hamilton Seminary, Swan put his hand on his shoulder and said, "Charlie, gird on the sword of the Lord against rum, hell, and Universalism." Like all revivalists Swan found it handy to have a number of concrete enemies of Satan against whom to direct attention. Universalists, deists, Unitarians, and Masons had been prime en-

25 *Ibid.*, p. 197.
26 *Ibid.*, pp. 106, 295.

emies in Finney's early days. Swan added Swedenborgians, German pantheists, Mormons, and Odd Fellows, with now and then a brickbat at Roman Catholicism. He was a stout advocate of abolition and made several speeches on behalf of Fremont's candidacy in 1856.

Yet Swan always considered himself a Jeffersonian Democrat even when he voted for the Republican party. It was the slavery Democrats who were the "new-fangled democrats, recreant to the faith. You may take all these perverts from the faith—these renegade democrats—locofocos, true blue—here in New London country, and put them into the hands of a steam doctor, and steam them three weeks and then bleed them and you would not get genuine democratic blood enough out of the whole batch to dot an *i*." [27] This type of preaching might have been controversial had it been done in the larger cities in a nonsectarian meeting, but among the rural Baptists of New York Swan was on safe ground.

Swan's reputation for arousing "the power of sacred mirth" in his meetings was a habit Finney had almost fallen into until Nathaniel Beman warned him against "the indulgence of anythink like *wit* in the pulpit." [28] Swan evidently found it too useful to abandon. He spoke of a hardened sinner as "a perfect iron-clad and copper-fastened individual. . . . Arrows of gospel truth would rattle upon his shield like shot on the scales of an alligator." He referred to dancing as "kick-ups of the Devil," and called the Universalist church "the Fire Insurance Company" because as far as he was concerned all its members were assured of a place in hell. But he reserved his most scathing sarcasm for those "miserable specimens of whiskey-pickled humanity" who supported the liquor trade.

Rum-sellers were "fit only to be hung, though not from any decent tree. They ought to be hung in the night, in a swamp, from a pepperidge" tree. In a mock dialogue with a group of whiskey-sellers who complained that the temperance movement would ruin their business, Swan said, "I commend to you the honorable and useful profession of poultry raising. And to expedite the business, relieving the fowls from a waste of their time in the process of incubation and to avoid the expense of

[27] *Ibid.*, p. 437.
[28] Beman to Finney, October 23, 1829, Finney Papers, OCL.

the new French system of employing steam and hot-air, I suggest that you liberally furnish the posterior sections of your pantaloons with tar and feathers and devote yourselves to hatching hens' eggs." [29]

He applied this same humor to his renditions of Bible stories. Telling the story of the whale that swallowed Jonah, he said, "The great fish splashed, foamed, and pitched up and down, here and there, and everywhere, to get rid of his burden. At length, growing more and more sick, as well he might, he made for the shore and vomited the nauseous dose out of his mouth." And in explaining the story of Peter's catching the fish which contained the tribute money in its mouth, he said, "How the silver coin came to be there, I don't know, but I guess God drowned some stingy old miser and sent that fish to pick his pocket." [30]

Swan's sermons blended humor and pathos in a continuous string of anecdotes from his own career. His homespun style followed a simple pattern which later revivalists easily turned into a formula. He carried Finney's story-telling principle to an extreme, and frequently moved his audiences to tears with tales of dying children who managed by their prayers to convert their parents or some other hardened sinners. Though he warned of hellfire awaiting the persistent rebel against God, he was more anxious to tell the sinner to "Go to Jesus for everything. . . . Let him be your friend and companion. . . ." This note of sentimental supplication entered revival preaching toward the middle of the century and soon replaced hellfire preaching altogether. Swan seems to have employed more of it than his colleague, Jacob Knapp.

Knapp, who graduated from Hamilton two years before Swan and who began itinerant evangelism in 1833 after a pastorate in Watertown, New York, was almost as well known as Finney by 1840. He claimed to have conducted 150 separate revivals and to have converted 100,000 persons by 1874, the year he died. His heavy debt to Finney was evident in his famous sermon on "The New Birth" which was simply a paraphrase of Finney's "New Heart" sermon.[31] He boasted that he

[29] Swan, *Autobiography,* pp. 163, 147, 149, 153, 434, 436.
[30] *Ibid.,* pp. 405, 410.
[31] See Knapp, *Autobiography,* pp. 323 ff.

once baptized sixty people in thirty minutes and claimed that his labors "resulted in the conversion of more during a given number of years than all the conversions reported by our missionaries in the home field."

Because he liked the crowds and the higher compensation, Knapp preached in cities in preference to rural towns. Between 1835 and 1842 he conducted meetings in Utica, Ithaca, Rochester, Albany, Brooklyn, New York, Baltimore, Washington, New Haven, Hartford, Providence, and Boston. In most cases he worked exclusively with the Baptist churches because, like Swan, he believed that baptism was an essential part of conversion. He was seldom able, however, to win the cooperation of all the Baptists in any city. He called his opponents "old fogies" and "hyper-Calvinists" but it seems likely that many of them merely opposed his vulgarity and exhibitionism. Contemporary reports even from friendly sources invariably referred to his "lack of good taste" in the pulpit. The Rev. R. W. Cushman, pastor of the important Bowdoin Square Baptist Church in Boston, wrote of him in 1846, "I could not, I say, approve of inviting a man to my pulpit who never could be satisfied without a storm and who was known to resort to dramatic exhibitions—to eccentricities of expression, voice, and manners—to assault on the usage of the churches and on the reputation of ministers—to public personal attacks on private character—for the purpose of raising one." [32] Knapp habitually asked his supporters to provide information regarding the personal habits and beliefs of prominent local citizens in order to cause a sensation by attacking them by name in his sermons. His vituperation led to his being mobbed in Boston, Rochester, and New Haven and the police had to be called out to protect him.

Knapp fancied himself as a special commissioner to clean up gambling dens, and in Rochester and New Haven he attacked from the pulpit individuals whom he said owned or promoted iniquitous card and billiard rooms. He seemed to welcome the attacks upon him which resulted from these exposures because he believed that God was on his side. In his autobiography he recounted how the Lord twice sent thunder and light-

[32] R. W. Cushman, *A Calm Review of the Measures Employed in the Religious Awakening in Boston in 1842* (Boston, 1846), p. 16.

ning to break up mobs which stormed his meetings. Twice he was indicted for libel and in Providence he was convicted and fined one hundred dollars for slandering a woman. As he explained it, "A good brother gave me some information which I repeated from the pulpit concerning a woman in that city which further investigation proved to be incorrect to the extent that they [*sic*] related to her husband instead of herself." [33]

Like Swan, he made Universalists and rum-sellers the principal butts of his abuse, and like Swan he was an abolitionist. He spoke out against slavery in Baltimore, Washington, Richmond, and Louisville, and for his pains he was forced to leave the last two cities without completing his revivals. He insisted that "Christianity is a radical principle. A Bible Christian cannot be a conservative," but except for abolition his radicalism consisted principally of attacks upon dancing, novel reading, gambling, and drinking. He also arranged public bonfires at which his followers destroyed all the novels and other vicious books which they could lay their hands on.

Knapp's chief claim to fame in the history of modern revivalism was that he was the first new measure evangelist to be publicly accused of making money from his preaching. At the peak of his career, between 1839 and 1842, he made over $2000 a year at a time when the average pastor did not make one-quarter as much. His revivals in New York, New Haven, and Boston brought him between $1000 and $1300 each for seven or eight weeks' work. Once when asked to extend a revival an extra two weeks he demanded a flat fee of $200. By 1842 he owned $15,000 worth of property in his hometown of Hamilton, New York. But these facts alone would not have been held against him. What annoyed people was the way he went about getting the money. Since he was dependent upon free-will offerings he made his appeals directly to his audiences and purposely misrepresented his financial status in order to make people feel sorry for him.

Various members of the church at which he preached in New Haven in 1841 stated that "When the contribution for himself was about to be taken up" Knapp gave everyone the impression "that he was a poor man wholly dependent on the compensation that he received for his labors as an evangelist for the sup-

[33] Knapp, *Autobiography*, p. 123.

port of himself and his family." The audience was "moved to tears" when he said that his wife was ill from want of the necessities of life. He told them it would be a great relief "could he be assured that his family were all comfortable—he had often to fear that . . . his family at home were in want." The pastor of the New Haven church made a pathetic plea for a generous free-will offering for Knapp, and he received over one thousand dollars. In New Bedford "his appearing in a white vest in the pulpit and intimating that he had no other thin one of a dark color and inquiring whether or not it would be noticed" led everyone to assume that he was poverty stricken.[34]

Another of Knapp's methods for obtaining a large offering was to instruct pastors to "request persons to write [him] notes expressive of their feelings, enclosing their personal contribution." He said that "people will do more when they give in this manner, with their names [signed] than when they put into an open box." A local church member who helped to open the letters Knapp received from donors in New Haven, said that Knapp never even looked at the "expressive" notes but merely took the cash accompanying them. Furthermore, he had the temerity to complain to pastors in one city about the poor compensation he had received for his work in preceding cities.

The rumors and charges against him reached such proportions in 1842 that Knapp decided to try to clear his reputation. He persuaded a group of his friends to form a committee to examine and refute the charges. It took them two years to deliberate and then they did not exactly deny the charges in their decision but merely said that there was "nothing in the case which ought to interrupt Elder Knapp's connection with the church of his labors as a minister of the gospel." Unfortunately, however, the committee could not agree to give a statement exonerating Knapp to the public. Knapp then took his case to the Baptist church in Hamilton of which he was a member and asked the church to give him an "exculpatory" endorsement. This tactic backfired when the church's investigating committee reported adversely. Knapp only succeeded in

[34] For the details of Knapp's financial affairs and the committees which investigated them, see Charles Burchard, *A Statement of Facts in Relation to the Case of Jacob Knapp* (New York, 1846), and R. Jeffrey, introductory essay to Knapp, *Autobiography*, pp. xxi ff.

extricating himself by appealing passionately to the church members to repudiate the report of the committee and give him a vote of confidence. This they did, but Knapp never succeeded in quieting the suspicions against him. For the remaining thirty years of his life he conducted revivals in the western and Middle Atlantic states and seldom ventured into New England. He learned by hard experience that the notoriety which came from controversial preaching in the cities was no help to revivalism.

By 1842 there were scores of imitators of Knapp, Swan, Burchard, Myrick, and Finney practicing revivalism all over the country. Few of them achieved the fame of these men. Most of them itinerated in the small towns and rural villages rather than the cities. They were clearly recognized as "revivalists by profession" but they were not professional in the modern sense of the word. Most of them were self-taught, "Spirit-inspired" men who operated in what was an age-old folk tradition. They were not exactly radicals or prophets but neither were they hirelings or salesmen. They went their own ways. The common people heard them gladly because they were commoners. Their refusal to be the servants of an ecclesiastical system or to conform to authority sets them apart from the greater part of the succeeding practitioners of the profession. Because of their independent attitude there continued to be a certain amount of friction between them and the more conservative ministers.

This conservative opposition which manifested itself against Finney in the 1820's and against new measure revivalists in the early 1830's was re-enforced by a general slump in religious enthusiasm throughout the country after the climactic year of 1831–32. The slump was caused in part by the reaction from the excesses of the movement, in part by the growing schism within Presbyterianism which the moderates tried to avoid by playing down new measure revivalism, in part by the wearing off of the novelty of protracted meetings, and finally by the growth of reform activities (notably antislavery) which drained off religious energies. Revival excitement had burned feverishly in one area of the country or another since early in the century. After thirty years of it there was bound to be a let-down. Those in a state of "betweenity" had been won; many of the deists and skeptics of Revolutionary days who were driven into an uneasy infidelity in revulsion from the rigid dogma of Calvinism had returned to the fold. The growth of the churches from 1830 onward proceeded more gradually.

Proof of the declension in the rate of growth was manifest even in the pages of the *New York Evangelist,* which had a vested interest in keeping up revival excitement. In a review of religious activities which had taken place during the year 1832, the editor noted, "Revivals of religion have not been as numerous or as powerful, particularly in the Northern and Middle States, as they were the preceding year." In December, 1834, the editor noted that revival interest had steadily declined since 1831, and asked querulously, "Have the American churches abandoned revivals?" And by August, 1836, the editor confessed that "there is at the present time a general declension prevailing *in all* the churches."[35]

The official statistics of the Presbyterian church which began to be published in 1826 revealed the rapid increases in membership for the years 1826–31, followed by an equally precipitous decline after the peak year 1831–32. The accuracy of specific figures may be questioned, but their general trend is probably correct. In the five years following 1826, the church membership increase averaged 11,000 per year. For the year 1832 alone it increased by 35,000. But in the succeeding five years the accessions by faith declined at an accelerating rate to an average of only 2200 a year. Between 1834 and 1836 the churches actually suffered a net loss of over 27,000 members.[36]

Albert Dod, in reviewing Finney's *Lectures on Revivals* in 1835, neatly turned Finney's own criterion of success against him: "The time was when an argument of this nature might have been plausibly maintained," said Dod, probably looking at the figures for 1826–31. "But it is too late now for Mr. Finney's appeal in defense of his measures to the number of converts made by them [or] to the flourishing state of religion in

[35] *New York Evangelist,* January 5, 1833, p. 2; December 6, 1834, p. 194; August 6, 1836, p. 126.

[36] Herman C. Weber, *Presbyterian Statistics 1826–1926* (General Council of the Presbyterian Church in the U.S.A., 1927), pp. 10 ff. Part of the decline in Presbyterianism after 1831 was due to the rapid withdrawal of Presbygational churches from Presbyterianism to Congregationalism and hence does not represent a loss of church members in over-all terms. See Gillett, *History of the Presbyterian Church,* Vol. II, p. 449.

the western part of New York. . . . It is now generally understood that the numerous converts of the new measures have been in most cases like the morning cloud and the early dew. In some places not a half, a fifth, or even a tenth part of them remain." [37]

Lyman Beecher sensed the temporary disappointment over revivalism in 1836 and immediately tried to make capital out of it. In a vain attempt to placate both the Old School Presbyterians and the Hopkinsians of New England, Beecher offered a package proposal to the General Associations of the Congregational churches of Connecticut and Massachusetts. At their annual sessions in June, 1836, he proposed, and succeeded in pushing through, a set of resolutions which not only kept out abolition agents and all other speakers for benevolent enterprises but also barred itinerant evangelists from the pulpits of New England. "Dr. Beecher spoke with feeling," said a report of his speech to the Massachusetts ministers, "on the subject of getting ISMS into the church over the heads of the ministers. There is ultraism not simply on the subject of slavery. Agents to promote moral reform are also claiming a *right* to be heard. Revivalists too are going about seeking whom they may devour. . . ." A week earlier he had taken even stronger ground against revivalists in speaking to the Connecticut General Association: "Dr. Beecher began by saying he wished to confess his sin. Formerly he thought it a fine thing to have evangelists to move among the churches to assist settled pastors. But he was wrong. The duty of evangelists is to go into destitute places and there gather up and build churches. They have no place among settled pastors. Their labor among them is full of disaster." [38]

Beecher's speeches were seconded by diatribes from conservative Hopkinsians like Heman Humphrey who blasted "modern itinerant evangelists" as "the greatest improvement on the high pressure system of which I have ever heard." Both General Associations resolved that henceforth itinerant agents, lecturers, and revivalists were not to be permitted in any church without "the consent of the pastors and regular ecclesiastical bodies." They specifically deplored "The existence in the

[37] *Biblical Repertory and Theological Review,* n.s. VII (October, 1835), 660.
[38] *New York Evangelist,* July 9, 1836, p. 110; July 16, 1836, p. 114.

churches of an order of itinerating evangelists devoted to the business of excitement and to the promotion of revivals. . . ." After reporting these proceedings, Joshua Leavitt, the editor of the *New York Evangelist,* spoke for the revival men when he asked imploringly in an editorial, "Are revivals to be given up?" [39]

His lament was premature and Beecher's attempt to placate the Old School was unsuccessful. Princeton continued to hold Beecher and Taylor as responsible for revival extravagances as Finney. Six years later the *Biblical Repertory and Theological Review* published an article on "The Influence of the New Divinity on Religion" which devoted considerable space to an attack upon "those expert and practical itinerant tacticians who claim to be revival preachers *eminenter.*" [40]

The unkindest blow of all to the revival cause came in the fall of 1836 when Finney himself seemed to acknowledge the failure of his work. He declared in a lecture which was published in the *New York Evangelist* that of all the converts of the revivals of the preceding ten years "the great body of them are a disgrace to religion. Of what use would it be to have a thousand members added to the Church to be just such as are now in it." When this remark was quoted against him Finney explained that he did not mean that those revivals were necessarily spurious or worthless, but merely that those converted were, in later years, "a disgrace to religion on account of the low standard of their piety." In terms of his new perfectionist beliefs this may not have seemed to him a damaging admission, but it was enough to convince many of his opponents that he, like Beecher, had confessed his sins. He admitted also that his new emphasis on entire sanctification and holiness after 1836 was due to his recognizing that revivalism was inadequate to train Christians properly: "My stay at every place was too short to accomplish much in the work of leading converts to manhood in religion. The same has been true of my brethren who have been evangelists." Why he did not think that the regular pastors were equal to the task of training Christians he did not say.

Finney stated in 1839 that he had turned to the doctrine of

[39] *Ibid.,* August 8, 1836, p. 126.

[40] *Biblical Repertory and Theological Review,* n.s. XIV (January, 1842), p. 20.

sanctification because, after ten years as a revivalist, "I was fully convinced that converts would die—that the standard of piety would never be elevated—that revivals would become more and more superficial and finally cease unless something effectual was done to elevate the standard of holiness in the church." [41] Comparatively few evangelists, however, followed Finney into the realm of outright perfectionism, and as they tried to overcome the declension in church growth many of them did become increasingly superficial. Critics were correct who said that it was "a grand point with all modern revivalists to explain away religious experience into a mere purpose, resolution, or determination to live and act religiously." [42] As time went on, revival conversions became spur-of-the-moment decisions lacking in depth or meaning. The process of walking forward to sit in the anxious seat, instead of being an act of profound spiritual travail, became a stereotyped and forced ritual. One critical observer declared by 1842, the anxious seat "is the essence of formalism and hypocrisy"; it was one of those "outward rites and observances" which "are exalted so as to be deemed influential in procuring divine favor." Revivalists might say that they employed the anxious seat merely as a divinely constituted means of breaking the sinner's pride and that it was not true that "taking the anxious seat" constituted or was synonymous with conversion, but others saw it as a mere "external ceremony" which was often easier to participate in than to avoid: "When men of the world are unexpectedly surprised into a dilemma, one horn of which is to go along with a bewildered and excited concourse of people, and the other to be set down in the black list as sinners of extraordinary hardihood and desperation, very few have the nerve and courage to choose the latter." [43]

When accused of producing spurious conversions by means of new measures like the anxious seat instead of waiting God's time in prayer, revivalists retorted "that in this age the world moves by steam and unless we accept some more improved, rapid method of converting it, it will run away from us." In

[41] Finney's 1836 remark is quoted in *Literary and Theological Review,* V (March, 1838), 66 n.; his later remarks are in *Oberlin Evangelist,* January 30, 1839, pp. 25–26.

[42] *Biblical Repertory and Theological Review,* XIV (January, 1842), 19.

[43] *Ibid.,* 19, 23, 28–30.

these circumstances, they said, "if any choose to travel in ox-carts or scows they can, but we prefer a steamboat or a locomotive." A Princeton conservative, noting the declension in church membership in 1835 in spite of all the fuss and roar of revivalism, remarked, "If we may judge from the report, the locomotive has exploded and left the heavy train attached to it hopelessly at a stand." [44]

It was easier, however, to point out the follies and extravagances of the new measures than to put a stop to revivalism. Even during the worst years of the declension the itinerant evangelists continued to find welcome listeners and cooperative pastors. The cure for the religious slump was thought by all but the ultraconservatives to be more revivalism, not less. There was no possibility of turning back to the Calvinistic view of religion. The revival locomotive might explode now and then but the principle on which it operated was known and if the old model could not keep up a sufficient head of steam it was only a matter of hitching up a newer model built on slightly more modern design.

The more thoughtful churchmen found themselves in a quandary as painful as the "betweenity" from which Finney had rescued them. They had given up the Old School views, but they saw only too plainly that modern revivalism had just as many pitfalls. They admitted that men could make their own new hearts but they disliked the means which Finney had evolved to persuade them to do it. If Finney's theology was correct then there was no choice but feast or famine in religion. The church must either be in a constant state of agitated enthusiasm or in a state of exhausted lethargy.

From this dilemma a new concept of evangelical religion began to emerge which sought to restore the dignity of the pastor and the importance of the institutional life of the churches. By the end of the century it provided the basis for a more far-reaching schism in American Protestantism than that which Finney had helped to produce in 1837. The most influential and the earliest spokesman for this new theological rationale was Horace Bushnell. Although his views were not generally adopted until the decline of revivalism in the twentieth century, his voice was first raised against revivalism in the

[44] *Ibid.*, 44, and VII (October. 1835), 614.

year 1838. In an unsigned article entitled "The Spiritual Economy of Revivals of Religion" which was published in Nathaniel W. Taylor's *Quarterly Christian Spectator,* the young Bushnell broached the question of "Christian Nurture" as the alternative to revivalism. These views were later influential in the loosely connected movements for Progressive Orthodoxy, for the Social Gospel, for Liberal Protestantism or "Modernism," which flourished after the Civil War.

Having graduated from Yale Seminary in 1827, Bushnell was in the fifth year of his twenty-one-year pastorate at the North Congregational Church in Hartford when his article appeared. Superficially the article seemed to be merely one of dozens appearing at the time lamenting the evils of revivalism and pleading for a more cautious approach to the task of soul winning. It was not, on the surface, an outright attack on revivalism, for Bushnell stated that his purpose was "to establish a higher and more solid confidence in revivals." But he added that he wanted "at the same time to secure to the cause of evangelical religion a more natural, satisfactory, and happy as well as a more constant movement." [45] In 1851, when he was in the midst of fighting off a trial for heresy for expounding views which he said he had hoped would reconcile Congregationalism and Unitarianism, he took part in inviting Finney to come to Hartford to conduct a revival. This triple reconciliation outdid even the assimilation envisioned by Beecher.

Nevertheless, the weight of Bushnell's new emphasis ran counter to the essential doctrines and methods of Finney and the professional evangelists. In regard to revivalism Bushnell wrote in 1838 that "a capital mistake is that of supposing that we ought to have a revival, so-called, or the exact mood of a revival at all times." Finney and most of the evangelical clergy after 1840 held that ideally revivalism should be the normal state of the churches. Bushnell also disagreed with "the saying constantly repeated and without qualification, that it is the great business of the gospel and of christian effort to convert men, has about as much error as truth in it. . . ." While Finney was willing after 1836 to admit Bushnell's argument that conversion "is the beginning of the work" of making a true

[45] (Horace Bushnell) "The Spiritual Economy of Revivals of Religion," *Quarterly Christian Spectator,* X (February, 1838), 131–147.

Christian, he certainly did not accept Bushnell's theory that "there is a more efficacious way" of winning souls than revivalism. Nor did he concur with Bushnell that "religion has as deep an interest in the proper conduct of times of non-revival as in these periods of glowing excitement. For many religious purposes, and those not the least important, a revival is less advantageous than other times."

Bushnell judiciously chose his words so as not to offend those who believed in the value of revivals, but underneath he was presenting an almost diametrically antithetical approach to Christian evangelism. This approach was summed up succinctly in his discourses on Christian nurture published nine years later in which he defended the principle "That the child is to grow up a Christian and never know himself as being otherwise." The germ of this idea, with its implicit disapproval of the extraordinary crisis conversion which was basic to revivalism, was contained in the 1838 article. Here he spoke of the duty of the minister to show parents "the manner in which children may be trained up in the nurture of the Lord" so that conversion would "come to pass naturally or emerge as a natural crisis of the ordinary." This, he said, could be accomplished by utilizing periods of "non-revival" to inculcate "a sense of character" through the example "of Christ's life and manners." In this way both pastor and parents "provide for a higher class of attainments, a more constant growth towards God, and favor the preparation of a new order of christians." This was "the more efficacious way." "What we complain of and resist," he said, "is the artificial firework, the extraordinary jump and stir, supposed to be requisite" to true religion. "The christian warfare is not all battle."

Bushnell did not directly assail the doctrines of the new divinity nor did he assail Calvinism. Insofar as this first essay expounded any doctrine it was what he called the doctrine of "God's omnipresence" by which he meant that it was wrong to think of the Holy Spirit as being present only during the times of revival. He also said that since "we can conceive of no place above God's works or outside of them where the divine nature resides" men are therefore "obliged to think of God as an in-resident in his works." "He is in all things . . . by presence or power, design, and feeling, moving in all, advancing in all towards his great appointed ends." And "the most ready illustration of this subject is the soul residing in the body." Bushnell never denied the possibility of, nor, indeed, the necessity for, some sort of supernatural conversion experience. And Beecher-like, he qualified all these statements and refined them so as not to be accused of transcendentalism, or of stating that all men were, as the Unitarians claimed, born with a touch of divinity in them which could be educated into Christ-like living. But it was not surprising that the *New York Evangelist* in later years accused him of being a pantheist, that the Old School called him naturalistic and hence Pelagian, and that post-Civil War Darwinians claimed him as a forerunner of "theistic evolution."[46]

In Bushnell the alternative to revivalism was provided, but it was many years before the average evangelical pastor grasped what he was driving at. Meanwhile itinerant professional evangelism continued to be the central force in the expanding religious life of the nation despite the declension of the 1830's and the continued opposition of the conservatives.

In the 1840's Finney conducted revivals in Providence, Boston, Rochester, Cleveland, Cincinnati, and Detroit during his winter vacations from Oberlin. In the 1850's he held meetings in New York, Brooklyn, Hartford, Syracuse, Boston, and Charlestown. He also made two extended tours of various cities in the British Isles in 1849–51 and 1858–60 which included revivals in London, Birmingham, Boston, Manchester, Edinburgh, and Aberdeen. Not until the Civil War broke out did he retire completely from itineracy and even then he promoted revivals annually at Oberlin until his death in 1875. Jabez Swan conducted half a dozen or more revivals every year from 1840 until the 1870's. Though he was active principally in the smaller towns of Connecticut and New York, he was a central attraction from time to time in Albany, New London, Hartford, Willimantic, and Providence. Jacob Knapp left New England after his contretemps in 1844–45, but during the next twenty-five years he and his wife conducted meetings in Chi-

[46] For the ambivalent attitude of the Princeton Presbyterians toward Bushnell, see the review of his *Discourses on Christian Nurture* in *Biblical Repertory and Theological Review,* XIX (October, 1847), 502–39.

cago, St. Louis, Louisville, Middletown, Canton (Ohio), Philadelphia, Newark, Elizabeth, Trenton, and Wilmington.

The religious journals contained repeated references to revivals promoted in the 1840's and 1850's by such respectable itinerant evangelists as Daniel Baker, Edward N. Kirk, Orson G. Parker, Samuel G. Orton, James Gallaher, John N. Maffitt, Arthur Granger, Emerson Andrews, Elder Simmons, Thomas S. Sheardown, A. C. Kingsley, Lewis Raymond, and James Caughey. All the major denominations contributed men to the ranks of the new profession. These names represented only a small proportion of those who made a career of evangelism between 1830 and 1860. Countless others undertook revival work for a year or two between pastorates or obtained leaves of absence from their churches to engage in it.[47]

This first generation, Finney's generation, of modern revivalism was succeeded by a new crop of itinerants who carried the profession down to the last quarter of the century and who came to be associated with the second great nineteenth-century revival leader, Dwight L. Moody. Among the more prominent of Moody's immediate predecessors were William Taylor, Absalom B. Earle, Edward Payson Hammond, Mrs. Maggie Van Cott, Henry Varley, Henry Moorehouse, and George C. Needham. The last three were British and after 1865 a constant exchange of American and British professional evangelists added a cosmopolitan flavor to what had previously been a provincial institution.[48]

The careers of Earle, Hammond, and Van Cott were of importance less for what they contributed to the theory of revivalism than because of the manner in which they stereotyped and ritualized its management. They were good itinerant tacticians, but they were also good organizers and administrators.

[47] For an able discussion of revivalism in the 1840–1860 period, see Timothy L. Smith, *Revivalism and Social Reform in Mid-Nineteenth Century America* (New York, 1957).

[48] Brief biographical accounts of Taylor and of the other evangelists mentioned below can be found in the *New Schaff-Herzog Encyclopedia of Religious Knowledge,* S. M. Jackson, ed., 11 vols (New York, 1911); in W. F. P. Noble, *A Century of Gospel Work* (Philadelphia, 1877); in P. C. Headley, *Evangelists in the Church* (Boston, 1875); in Frank G. Beardsley, *History of American Revivals* (New York, 1912); on Taylor see also *Christian Advocate* (Methodist Episcopal, New York), August 5, 1875, p. 245; August 19, 1875, p. 261.

They took the first fatal steps into the realm of efficient and often meretricious manipulation.

A. B. Earle gave up a Baptist pastorate in 1856 and itinerated through New England and New York for ten years. Then he went west in 1866 and toured the cities and mining towns of California, Oregon, and Nevada. In 1868 he returned to his home in Newton, Massachusetts, to write an account of his career. He continued to preach in eastern cities until late in the 1870's. Because he played down denominational differences (including baptism) and always tried to obtain the cooperation of all evangelical denominations, he came to be known as "the union evangelist." But he was not alone in this. After 1850 the term "union meeting" became synonymous with revival meeting. In San Francisco in 1866 Earle rented a hall which held 3000 persons for his five weeks of meetings though he normally preached in churches. He admitted that his invitations to conduct revivals often came "from church members longing to see their pastors more in earnest in the work of saving souls" but he did not engage in Finney's early techniques of "blistering" pastoral opponents. His most famous sermon was entitled "The Unpardonable Sin," which he claimed in 1869 had already converted 5000 persons. The unpardonable sin was saying "No, no, no to the offers of mercy until you are a sinner let alone or given up by the Holy Spirit." He called upon those who wished to be prayed for or who cherished a desire "to serve God" to rise in their seats and then to come forward to the anxious benches or the inquiry room, but his preaching was more anecdotal than vehement. He employed sentiment and entreaty rather than argument or doctrine: "Is there not some loved one now pointing down from heaven and saying to you, Give your heart to Jesus?" Or, "Are you loving some earthly object more than Jesus? God may sever that tie—may take away your little Mary or Willie or some dear friend. Will you not come to Jesus without such a warning?" A San Francisco newspaper account of his meetings stated that there was "no excitement, nor endeavour to create excitement." By 1876 he had acquired a coworker who sang solos and directed the choirs at his meetings but he probably adopted this idea from Moody's success with Ira D. Sankey.

Like Knapp, Earle took his compensation in free-will offerings "enclosed in envelopes with a note from the donor." [49]

Some insight into the new tone which revivalism began to take after the middle of the century can be obtained from the printed card which Earle passed out to each person who "came forward" at his meetings. On one side the card contained a list of the "Ten Evidences of Conversion: For Young Christians," and on the other side were ten questions of "Self-Examination for Older Christians." The ten evidences of conversion were:

1. A full surrender of the will to God.
2. The removal of a burden of sin, gradually or suddenly.
3. A new feeling of love to Christians and to Jesus.
4. A new relish for the Word of God.
5. Pleasure in secret prayer, at least at times.
6. Sin, or sinful thoughts, will cause pain.
7. Desire and efforts for the salvation of others.
8. A desire to obey Christ in his commands and ordinances.
9. Deep humility and self-abasement.
10. A growing desire to be holy and like Christ.

The list was followed by the question in boldface: "Are you a Christian? If not, why?" The self-examination for older Christians was summed up in the tenth question, "Am I sweetly resting in Christ, by faith, now?" [50] Moody and his successors were to carry this sentimental evangelicalism to new heights.

Edward Payson Hammond was known as "The Children's Evangelist." A graduate of Williams College, he attended Union Theological Seminary in New York in 1858–59 and then spent two years preaching in England and Scotland where, it was claimed, his preaching helped to promote "social peace" between the upper and "lower strata of society." In 1861 he returned to the United States, obtained a Master of Arts degree from Williams, and was ordained by the New York Presbytery. In the 1860's and 1870's he conducted large-scale meetings in Rochester, Newark, Chicago, Boston, Detroit, Philadelphia, St. Louis, Washington, Baltimore, and San Francisco. Among the influential businessmen who assisted him in these

[49] A. B. Earle, *Bringing in the Sheaves* (Boston, 1869), pp. 185, 130, 84–85, 291; *Buffalo Commercial Advertiser*, April 8, 1876, p. 3, and April 22, 1876, p. 3.

[50] Earle, *Bringing in the Sheaves,* pp. 226–27.

years were Mathias W. Baldwin, founder of the Baldwin Locomotive Works, and George H. Stuart, the Philadelphia merchant-banker who was to play so large a part in the career of D. L. Moody.[51] An observer in San Francisco wrote that Hammond "was not restrained by any of the conventionalities of the pulpit . . . he was full of nervous activity and variety, at one moment stirring to laughter and the next, perhaps, uttering with bated breath some threatening of God's word which sent terror into every hearer. He stopped sometimes in the very midst of his sermon to give out a verse or a hymn. . . ." This "lively, dramatic style" and "unconventional freedom and naturalness proved a wonderful attraction." But not to everyone. His revivals, said one critical observer, "seldom present an attractive appearance. There will seem to be too much engineering in them and too much bustle." [52]

Hammond was one of the first evangelists to enjoy getting his name in the newspapers. He boasted to a reporter that in St. Louis he had been invited by "Madame" Stillman to conduct meetings in her *"maison de joie"* where he converted fifteen out of the seventeen "inmates." [53] He was also one of the first evangelists to hold meetings for men only and for women only, thereby gaining a prurient notoriety. In San Francisco he attracted attention for his meetings by riding through the streets on a white pony followed by a wagon with an organ and organist playing gospel hymns. He compiled his own hymnbook for use in his meetings, and his choirs in some cities numbered three hundred. By 1875 his meetings were so large that the Committee on Arrangements in Oakland, California, had to construct a special "tent pavilion" capable of holding 4500. A souvenir volume commemorating his eight-week revival in San Francisco was published.

One of the more important new techniques introduced by Hammond was his practice of asking every person who came

[51] George H. Stuart, *The Life of George H. Stuart,* ed. R. E. Thompson (Philadelphia, 1890), p. 113 n.

[52] See P. C. Headley, ed., *The Harvest of the Holy Spirit Illustrated in the Evangelistic Labors of Rev. Edward Payson Hammond* (Boston, 1862); *E. P. Hammond's Eight Weeks in San Francisco* (San Francisco, 1875); and P. H. Fowler, *Historical Sketch of Presbyterianism within the Bounds of the Synod of Central New York* (Utica, 1877), p. 278.

[53] *Washington Evening Star,* February 15, 1876, p. 4.

forward to the anxious seat or inquiry room to sign a "Covenant Card." The card stated, "I, the undersigned, hope I have found Jesus to be my precious Saviour; and I promise, with His help, to live as his loving child and faithful servant all my life." [54] The card was kept by the signer but the convert's name was recorded in a special book. Hammond, like Burchard and Knapp, was always ready to report to the press the total number of converts or "covenanters" at any particular moment in one of his revivals. He claimed to have converted 2,000 in San Francisco and 1,900 in Washington, D.C., but over half in both places were children under sixteen.

Children's meetings, which had originated with Mrs. Jedidiah Burchard in the 1820's, became his specialty. His success with children was indicative of the fact that the Sunday school movement of this era was not designed to promote Bushnell's theory of Christian nurture but to prepare children for the decisive moment when they would experience conversion.[55] Hammond published several volumes on the subject of converting children, in one of which he claimed to have the approval of Horace Bushnell for his work.[56] Descriptions of his meetings tell of scores of sobbing eight- and nine-year-olds crying, "Oh, dear. I'm lost! I'm lost! and I can't find Jesus! I have never loved Jesus at all!" Or, "Oh! I feel that I have been a great sinner not to love that dear, dear Saviour who died on the cross for me."[57] The following dialogue between Hammond and a six-year-old reportedly took place during his revival in San Francisco in March, 1875. Hammond called the child out of the audience and interrogated him on the platform:

> How old are you, my boy?
> Six, sir.
> Have you signed the covenant card?

[54] This use of a covenant card to certify individual conversions appears to mark the inglorious decay of the church covenants signed by seventeenth-century Puritans. It was symbolic of the religious individualism of nineteenth-century evangelism.

[55] According to the *Annual Report* of the Sunday School Union in 1857, "Sunday school instruction must be regarded as only a means to an end *and that end the conversion of the soul. . . .*" See Addie G. Wardle, *History of the Sunday School Movement in the Methodist Episcopal Church* (New York, 1918), p. 108.

[56] E. P. Hammond, *The Conversion of Children* (New York, 1878), pp. 30–31.

[57] *Ibid.*, pp. 131, 17.

Yes, sir.
Do you love Jesus?
Yes, sir.
Why do you love him, dear?
Because he first loved me.
Were you a great sinner, pet?
Yes, sir.
And you felt very sorry for your sins?
Yes, sir.
What sins did you commit?
Sir?
What did you do that was so wicked?
I forget, sir.
You see, dear children that the little boy could not remember all of his sins, but by his intelligent answers showed that he fully understood the great plan of life.[58]

Maggie Van Cott, "the first lady licensed to preach in the Methodist Episcopal Church in the United States," was the daughter of John Jacob Astor's real estate manager, William K. Newton. She started church work in 1866 after the death of her husband. For two years she worked as a home missionary among the unchurched in "Five Points," the slum district of New York City. Her success in this work brought invitations to hold special services in various churches in other parts of New York state. She decided to make a vocation of preaching and in 1869 was licensed by the church. In 1869–70 she toured the Methodist churches in New England; in 1870 she was in Wisconsin; in 1871 in Connecticut; in 1873 in Nebraska and San Francisco; 1874, Nevada and New Orleans; 1875, Pennsylvania, New Jersey, and New York.[59]

During her first year as a "lady preacher" she delivered 335 sermons, added 500 new church members, travelled 3,000 miles, and received $735.35 in free-will offerings. In many cities she obtained the cooperation of other churches in addition to the Methodist. To attract crowds she advertised special meetings for Mothers, for Old Veterans, and for Children. She also specialized in Praise Meetings, Silent Meetings, and "Love Feasts." At the conclusion of each revival she organized Prayer Bands of converts and church members to keep up the revival spirit.

[58] *The Liberal Christian* (New York), March 27, 1875, p. 3.
[59] *Mrs. Maggie Van Cott* (New York, 1883); and Noble, *Century of Gospel Work,* p. 450.

Mrs. Van Cott was described as "a stout lady with a rosy, pleasant face which looks out with exceedingly good nature from beneath two matronly rows of black, glossy curls." She said that only "one half of those who came to the altar in response to her exhortation became members of the Methodist Church," but she claimed that three-quarters of those who did join became "good working Christians." A description of one of her children's meetings told of her walking among twenty-five or thirty kneeling youngsters (seven to fourteen years old) holding "a large fan of Ostrich feathers" with which she fanned herself while "calling grace down passionately." "Altogether it was a curious group," wrote a reporter: "Widow Van Cott, stout and buxom, moving among the children, with face flushed and voice husky from the vigor of her exhortations, waving her great fan which fancy might have transformed into some angelic wing—though not appertaining to the Widow Van Cott herself who is too material a figure for any such decoration—placing a hand upon the head of each kneeling child in turn and calling down special blessings thereupon; the children on their knees and interpolating shrill 'Amens' as the exhortation progresses and the pastor in the background with deep set eyes closed in fervent tightness and hands clasped together and striking upon the pulpit as he cries out after Mrs. Van Cott portions of her exhortation." [60]

The three British itinerants, Varley, Moorehouse, and Needham, were lay preachers affiliated with the Plymouth Brethren. Like the "California Street Preacher," William Taylor, they were in the old folk tradition. They specialized in Bible readings. When giving a Bible reading, as Needham described it, the preacher offered "First a Scripture and its explanation; then an illustration . . . then an anecdote of his own or another's experience to confirm the truth, and finally, an appeal or exhortation." [61] All three men came from lower-class backgrounds in Britain and their style and methods closely resembled those of the Salvation Army. They all consciously directed their efforts toward reaching the urban poor. Moorehouse and Needham toured the United States in the late

[60] Quoted in *Washington Evening Star,* February 5, 1876, p. 7.

[61] George C. Needham, *Recollections of Henry Moorehouse* (Chicago, 1881), p. 8.

1860's; Varley did not arrive until the 1870's. Varley was described by a Unitarian journal as speaking in an "emphatic, rough and ready manner calculated to impress people whose minds are not over-sensitive," but he was popular enough in New York to fill Barnum's Hippodrome for several weeks in the spring of 1875. He was later pointed to as "the John the Baptist who had prepared the people for the coming of Moody and Sankey." [62] Moorehouse and Needham generally preached only in the more pietistic revival churches in the cities, including Moody's church in Chicago. William Taylor was an American Methodist itinerant who made his reputation holding meetings on street corners preaching salvation to the "Forty-niners" in California. The real fame of these four men came after 1875 through their association with Moody. They were important because they represented the continuation of the pure form of primitive itineracy which has never died out. At times, however, it has almost been absorbed into the more professional branch of the calling.

By 1875 almost all opposition to professional revivalism had died out, and the annual revival meeting conducted by an itinerant specialist was such an integral part of evangelical church life in America that the editor of a religious journal stated, "The usage, now almost universal in our churches, of holding such services during the winter months has made that season the harvest time of the churches. . . ." Not only did the church members join in these services, said the editor, but "the unconverted also look forward to these seasons, expecting in them to be brought to Christ." The editor also noted that every church "wants the good name of having a revival—it wants it to fill empty pews and empty contribution boxes." [63] This editor happened to be a Methodist but the same attitude prevailed among all denominations. For better or for worse the system which the conservatives of the 1830's so greatly feared had become institutionalized.

In most evangelical churches, both urban and rural, the revivalist was looked upon as a kind of spiritual masseur employed once a year to tone up the body religious. When he

[62] *Liberal Christian,* March 20, 1875, p. 3; *New York Times,* October 26, 1875, p. 206.

[63] *Christian Advocate,* March 23, 1876, p. 92; February 18, 1876, p. 49.

arrived the church was placed in his hands for a thorough overhauling. For a fortnight or so he became the central figure in the religious community and the pastor merely an assistant. As a result of his preaching, church members expected to be whipped back into shape themselves and then to go out and round up those who had strayed from the path since the preceding revival. Sunday school pupils who had grown old enough to become full-fledged members of the flock were urged forward to the anxious seat to go through the *rite du passage*. The novelty and excitement of the revival meeting were also designed to attract nonchurchgoers who might attend from curiosity and then be caught up in the carefully manipulated enthusiasm. The pastor often had ulterior motives: "It is a matter of common observation," wrote one authority on revivals in 1867, "that never is it so easy to induce a church to make large contributions for a benevolent object, never so easy to pay off a debt, to improve a Sunday school, to contribute to missions, to furnish support for indigent students, to endow colleges, or to do any other work of active and sacrificing service for the cause of Christ, as it is in the full tide of a religious revival." [64]

Although a decade or two of sectarian rivalry after 1830, especially in the growing communities of the West, made interdenominational revivals difficult at first, the more prominent evangelists often succeeded in uniting Presbyterian, Congregational, Baptist, Methodist, and related evangelical churches in their efforts to awaken a whole town or city at once. The "Bible Christianity" based on "the fundamentals" which Finney and Beecher and all subsequent evangelists espoused provided a basis for union meetings which were offensive to no sect. Only external differences such as the mode of baptism, the requirements for membership, or ecclesiastical polity distinguished the various denominations after mid-century. The most striking symbol of the breakdown of the old creedal differences and the abandonment of Calvinism was the reunion of the Old and New School Presbyterians in 1870 on the basis of a latitudinarian approach to the Westminster Confession. According to this settlement every Presbyterian was left to make his own interpretation of the church's creed just about as he

[64] R. Jeffrey, introduction to Knapp, *Autobiography*, p. xi.

chose, and most ministers chose to accept the New School views.

But long before 1870 there were "Old School" Presbyterian evangelists such as George J. Mingins, Arthur Granger, and Daniel Baker, whose revivalism was indistinguishable from Finney's or Knapp's.[65] Baker, who was called "the Whitefield of the South," began to itinerate as a revivalist early in the 1830's and while he claimed to be a strict Calvinist he engaged in protracted meetings and used the anxious seat with as much enthusiasm as any new measure man. His only distinguishable Old School characteristic was his unwillingness to attack slavery. In fact, he declared, "I verily believe that the relation of master and slave was recognized in the Bible and that ecclesiastical bodies have no right to legislate upon the subject." [66] This led to his being driven out of some towns in the North just as all northern evangelists who preached antislavery views were driven out of southern towns. But the process of revivalism was not to be stopped by such peripheral questions as slavery. The Biblical uncertainty about the status of the negro proved an uncomfortable problem at times, but most professional evangelists either ignored the issue or adopted the attitude of their section of the country and then confined their activities to that section. The slavery issue did distract some attention from revivalism from 1835 to 1860, but it did not put an end to the profession either north or south. After the Civil War even this barrier ceased to distinguish the prevailing evangelical conformity throughout the nation.

Some traced the harmonious spirit of the churches in the latter part of the century to the effects of the great "Prayer Meeting Revival" of 1857–58. The Rev. John F. Hurst described this revival as "the third general revival in the history of the country" but said that it was "very different" from the First Great Awakening of 1731–42 and the Second Great Awakening of 1792–1808. "In the preaching there was no new stress on the leading doctrines of revelation. There were no prominent evangelists who seemed to be the chief agents in bringing about the extraordinary displays of divine power. But there

[65] For the ordination of Mingins, see Stuart, *Autobiography,* p. 109. For accounts of Baker's use of new measures, see *New York Evangelist,* January 5, 1833, p. 1, and February 23, 1833, p. 31.

[66] P. C. Headley, *Evangelists in the Church,* p. 204. See also William M. Baker, *The Life and Labors of the Rev. Daniel Baker, D.D.* (Philadelphia, 1858).

was a singular union, never before approached in the history of American Christianity, of the principal religious bodies in prayer and conference. . . . Clergymen and Christian laymen who had always stood aloof were brought together for the first time, as participants in the great work of common interest and enjoyment. These beautiful relations," said Hurst, writing in 1876, "have never been interrupted." [67]

The religious excitement of 1857–58 scarcely deserved to be called the Third Great Awakening. As everyone recognized at the time, it developed out of the financial panic of 1857. Ministers considered it highly commendable that "those who were losing treasure on earth" should flock into prayer meetings after the crash in order "to lay up treasures in heaven." [68] The mass-circulating, penny daily newspapers, just becoming a prominent feature of American life, particularly the *New York Herald* and the *New York Tribune,* were quick to feature stories of the scramble from this-worldly to other-worldly activity among the men of property. James Gordon Bennett and Horace Greeley competed for circulation by playing up the movement. Downtown churches in New York opened their doors during the noon lunch hour for union prayer meetings and displayed signs calling the harassed businessmen to seek divine help for their problems. Newly completed telegraph lines which linked the nation as never before flashed the latest news of bankruptcy and prayer meetings from New York to the cities of the North and West and they too turned to prayer. It became the practice for businessmen in one city to wire businessmen in another acquainting them with the progress of their prayer meetings. For this purpose the telegraph company generously allowed messages to be sent free of charge at certain specified hours.

Finney, who was holding meetings in Boston in the winter of 1857–58, thought it "peculiarly interesting" that this movement was carried on "through lay influence, so much as almost to throw the ministers into the shade," but he could find no

[67] *Christian Advocate,* August 24, 1876, p. 216.

[68] Lyman H. Atwater, "Revivals of the Century," *Presbyterian Quarterly and Princeton Review,* XLVIII (October, 1876), 716; see also Talbot W. Chalmers, *The Noon Prayer Meetings of the North Dutch Church* (New York, 1858); Smith, *Revivalism and Social Reform,* pp. 63 ff.; W. F. P. Noble, *A Century of Gospel Work* (Philadelphia, 1876), pp. 417–42.

reason to criticize it.[69] Asa Mahan seems to have been one of the few clergymen who disliked it. He called it "a very melancholy contrast" to the revivals of 1830–31 because "speaking to sinners did not appear to be welcome" and the "preaching was not characterized for the most part by fervency of spirit.[70] Apparently a great many worried people joined a church during the height of the excitement, but it was not primarily a revival designed to win new church members. On the whole it seems to have been a very respectable affair in which attending prayer meetings became the thing to do for the season. It was the last instance, perhaps the only instance (outside of seventeenth-century New England), in which Americans sought divine help in the midst of economic difficulties.

If its consequences seemed important later, it was because the episode coincided with the steady trend toward evangelical unity. An article in the *Bibliotheca Sacra and Biblical Repository,* the official organ of Andover Seminary, discussed in 1859 the difference between the prayer meeting revival and the revivals of 1740, 1800, and 1830. The tone of the article disclosed the vast change that had come over the theological atmosphere of New England within thirty years, for Andover had previously been the headquarters of conservative Hopkinsianism. Now, under the leadership of a new generation, it offered a blanket endorsement of any and all revivalism. The article stated: "We should not condemn or undervalue one or another style of revival because it does not square with our preconceived notions"; we must remember that "there are diversities of operations" and "it is the same God that worketh all in all." [71]

It was in this tolerant mood that the various revival styles of A. B. Earle, E. P. Hammond, the Widow Van Cott, and Henry Varley were taken in stride by so many churchmen, lay and clerical, in the years preceding Moody's appearance. But the significant fact about Dwight L. Moody was that in the face of such bland complacency he managed to give revivalism a new meaning and a new vigor. In the early 1870's he razed the

69 Finney, *Memoirs,* p. 242.

70 Mahan, *Autobiography,* p. 22.

71 A. P. Marvin, "Three Eras of Revivals in the United States," *Bibliotheca Sacra and Biblical Repository,* XVI (April, 1859), 299.

ramshackle revival structure which had been thrown together over Finney's sturdy foundations and built the imposing edifice which constituted modern revivalism as it was to be known for the next seventy-five years. If the professional revivalists who came between Finney and Moody were simply "practical tacticians," Moody, like Finney, was a creative institutional architect.

CHAPTER 4

"The Right Man at the Right Hour"

Charles Finney made revivalism a profession, but Dwight L. Moody made it a big business. "The Hippodrome work," said an observer of Moody's revival in New York in 1876, "is a vast business enterprise, organized and conducted by business men, who put their money into it on business principles, for the purpose of saving souls." [1] Although periodic revivals in individual churches or groups of churches had become a fixture of evangelical Protestantism by 1875, it was not until Moody applied the techniques of corporate business enterprise to evangelism that it became possible to promote city-wide interdenominational revivals at will. Finney had established the theory of modern revivalism, but with the inadequate facilities and divisive theological atmosphere of his day he did little more than experiment in the urban application of it. His greatest success was achieved in towns and cities with less than 10,000 population. Moody's reputation was based upon his ability to galvanize the religious element of cities whose population was in the millions. "Water runs down hill," Moody said at the outset of his evangelistic career, "and the highest hills are the great cities. If we can stir them, we shall stir the whole nation." [2]

[1] William Hoyt Coleman, quoted in William R. Moody, *The Life of Dwight L. Moody,* "The Official Authorized Edition" (New York, 1900), p. 281.
[2] William R. Moody, *D. L. Moody* (New York, 1930), p. 249.

In adapting modern revivalism to the urban metropolis of the 1870's, Moody was an innovator of great ability and foresight. But, like Finney, his pietistic concern with soul winning seriously limited his view of theology and of the churches' role in society. The most striking feature of Moody's outlook, and of all modern revivalism in the years between the Civil War and the First World War, was its conservatism. Finney and his colleagues had been radicals, not only in their theological and ecclesiastical views but in their attitude toward social change. In some respects they were even in advance of their times. But Moody and his successors were out of step with their times and resisted the changes taking place around them. Finney was an optimist, a post-millennialist, who saw no conflict between science and religion and who firmly believed that progress, in all its forms, was divinely directed toward the perfection of the world. Moody was an uncompromising premillennialist and in many respects a pessimist who believed that most of what went under the name of progress in his day was Satanically inspired and directed against the laws of God. Fifty years after Moody's death, when all Americans began to lose faith in progress, there were many who looked back to Moody as a prophet. But in his own day the conservative outlook in religion and society for which he stood was deplored even by many who admired him most and who fully sympathized with the Christian spirit which motivated his work.[3]

Moody has often been grouped with Jonathan Edwards and Charles Finney as the central or instigating figure of a great national revival movement. But, like theirs, his revivals were simply one expression of a broad social and theological reorientation which extended far beyond the efforts of any individual. As the first and foremost of a group of prominent pro-

[3] A good example of this was the evaluation of Moody's career by the Rev. George Adam Smith (later Sir George Adam Smith), the prominent Scottish theologian, who was closely associated with Moody's revivals for many years and a respected personal friend. Writing specifically of Moody's impact on the religious life of Britain in the last quarter of the century, Smith stated, "the evangelical movement which Messrs. Moody and Sankey did so much to reinforce has required every iota of the influence of science to teach it tolerance, accuracy, and fearlessness of fact, and all the strength of the Socialist movement to reawaken within it that sense of civic and economic duty by which the older evangelicalism" was distinguished. George Adam Smith, *The Life of Henry Drummond* (New York, 1898), p. 100.

fessional revivalists who conducted city-wide mass evangelistic campaigns across the United States (and abroad) in the years 1875–1915, Moody represented only one aspect of what may properly be called America's third great awakening. The various social, economic, and political forces which brought about the significant reorientation of American life in this period are well known: It was during this era that the country shifted from an agrarian to an industrial economy, from a rural to an urban-centered population, from an anticolonial to an imperialistic nation, from a relatively homogeneous to a polygenetic people, and from a system of relative laissez-faire to the first stages of governmental social control. The massive influx of millions of immigrants whose cultural and religious outlook was so different from the prevailing culture, brought into new focus the traditions of American life and compelled a redefinition of them. At the same time the social distinctions between social classes became more clearly defined and those who called themselves "the people" began to differentiate themselves from those whom they called "big business" or "the idle rich" on the one hand and those whom they referred to as "labor" or "the masses" on the other. These profound changes and the shocks that accompanied them registered most heavily upon those country-bred, evangelically oriented, intellectually unsophisticated, and sentimentally insecure individuals who made up the bulk of the nation's churchgoers. It was from this group that the professional revivalists received their most fervent support.

The theological and ecclesiastical reorientation of this era has been less fully examined, but its main features are clear enough. In theology the concepts known as progressive orthodoxy, theistic evolution, the higher criticism, the social gospel, have been often described. Together they formed what was called in its day "the new theology." Later it acquired the title "liberal Protestantism." The opponents of this movement, the Old School as it were, were at first called conservative evangelicals, or simply "conservatives." As the lines of battle hardened in the twentieth century, the two groups derisively dubbed each other "modernists" and "fundamentalists." Although the last skirmish in this struggle was not fought until the twenties, the reorientation was complete by 1915. As in the past, the New School won out.

The foremost ecclesiastical change in this third great awakening was the ecumenical movement which, in the United States, was the logical outcome of the steady drift toward evangelical assimilation since 1800. The movement consummated in the formation of the Federal Council of Churches of Christ in 1908. It was a distinctive feature of the Federal Council, and one which linked it to the theological reorientation of the period, that it had as one of its principal purposes the reestablishment of Protestantism as a social and political force in the nation. According to the pietistic opponents of the Council, it represented a backward step toward ecclesiastical tyranny and a closer relationship between church and state. On the part of its proponents, however, it was a justifiable advance over the extreme individualism of nineteenth-century evangelicalism and a reassertion of the divine mission of the body of Christ to act in unison for the establishment of His kingdom on earth.

Moody's most successful revivals occurred in the decade from 1873 to 1883 before the full import of these changes was recognized and given expression, but he lived long enough to become aware of their ramifications. At the time of his death in 1899 he was trying desperately to reconcile the warring factions within evangelicalism by means of the same arguments which Finney had used to try to soothe over the squabble among Christians regarding abolition. Since both factions hoped to avoid schism, it appeared for a time as though revivalism might succeed in sublimating the differences. But it did not.

If Moody and Finney were at all alike as professional revivalists, and they did have much in common, it was primarily because they shared the pietistic concern for soul winning and the perfectionist belief that a truly converted Christian was free from sin and all its temptations. Finney rallied youthful idealists and aggressive businessmen against the dead hand of Calvinism and ecclesiasticism in the name of national progress toward the millennium. Moody roused the same two groups for a return to individual piety in the face of increasing secularism and engrossment with material gain; his premillennialism stressed the weakness of unaided human endeavor and the need to concentrate upon Christian humility. Both Finney and Moody called for selfless sacrifice and devotion to high ideals of Christian duty. Both inveighed against religious formalism and intellectual aridity. But it was significant that the outstanding converts of Finney's revivals worked to free the American Negro from chattel slavery while Moody's most promising converts went off to Africa and Asia to save the benighted heathen from spiritual enslavement. Moody was aware of the grave domestic problems of the day, particularly the plight of the lower classes in Britain and America, but he, like Finney, chose "the indirect way" to alleviate conditions. The social outlook of the two revivalists fully agreed in this respect: they both believed that society could only be reformed by the moral and spiritual regeneration of individuals and that all political, social, and economic reform must be an appendage of revivals.

Dwight Lyman Moody was born in Northfield, Massachusetts, in 1837.[4] He was the son of a ne'er-do-well brick and stone mason who was addicted to drink and who left his wife penniless with seven children and a heavily mortgaged farm when he died suddenly in 1841. Twins were born to the widow a month after his death. Friends urged her to place some of the children, the oldest of whom was thirteen, in the homes of relatives and neighbors and to give up the farm, but she refused. With the help of her two brothers, who paid off the mortgage, she managed to hold on to the place and to bring up all nine of her children on their labors and the produce of two acres.

Young Moody, like his brothers and sisters, was baptized

[4] For biographical data on Moody, see the two editions (1900 and 1930) of his biography by his son William R. Moody; the biography by Paul Moody, *My Father* (Boston, 1938); Gamaliel Bradford, *D. L. Moody: A Worker in Souls* (New York, 1928); A. W. Williams, *Life and Work of Dwight L. Moody* (Philadelphia, 1900); W. H. Daniels, *D. L. Moody and His Work* (Hartford, 1876); W. H. Daniels, *Moody, His Words, Work, and Workers* (New York, 1877). A typed manuscript entitled "Moody of Northfield" by Elmer W. Powell written in 1940 contains a good deal of original biographical data on Moody which has not been published; this typescript is in the library of Crozer Theological Seminary, Chester, Pennsylvania. See also Wilbur M. Smith, *An Annotated Bibliography of D. L. Moody* (Chicago, 1948). I have supplemented the information in these volumes with material in the Moody Papers owned by Mrs. Emma Moody Powell (East Northfield, Massachusetts) and the Moodyana Collection of the Moody Bible Institution (Chicago, Illinois) as well as by conversations with various descendants and friends of Moody, especially Mrs. William R. Moody, Mrs. Emma Moody Powell, and Mr. William R. Barbour.

into the Unitarian church of his parents and attended its services regularly. He had little time for schooling, however, and even in Northfield's one-room schoolhouse he never got past the seventh grade. His labor in the fields gave him a sturdy constitution which later stood him in good stead. When his older brother ran away from the drudgery at home in 1843 to seek his fortune in the world, the event seems to have imbedded the sorrow of praying mothers and wandering sons indelibly on his mind. It was an experience he shared with a large portion of Americans in the nineteenth century.

Generally speaking his boyhood was that of the normal rural New Englander. His mother later remembered that he always dominated his playmates in their games and that he had a curious habit of repairing to the attic of his home to engage in mock addresses to imaginary crowds. These were speeches, however, not sermons, for he took no particular interest in religion. At seventeen he persuaded his mother that he could be of greater financial assistance if he were to use his talents in the big city and he left home for Boston. Unable to find employment on his own, he sought out his uncle, Samuel Socrates Holton, and took a job as clerk in Holton's shoe store on Court Street near Scollay Square.

His uncle placed three prerequisites on hiring him. He had to agree to live in a boardinghouse selected by his uncle; he could not drink, gamble, or enter any place disapproved by his mother; and he had to attend his uncle's church without fail. It was a Congregational church and its pastor was the Rev. Edward N. Kirk, formerly of the Fourth Presbyterian Church in Albany. Kirk had been educated at Princeton, but he became an ardent new measure man in 1829 and welcomed Finney to his Albany pulpit. From 1833 to 1837 he aided Nathaniel S. S. Beman in conducting the Troy and Albany School of Theology to train up revival itinerants. From 1839 to 1842 Kirk was himself engaged in itinerant evangelism and was highly successful at it. But after being called to the Mt. Vernon Congregational Church in Boston in 1842 he threw in his lot with Lyman Beecher and repudiated both Finney's perfectionism and his antislavery views. When Moody began attending his church in 1854, Kirk was preaching the vague mixture of Calvinism and free will which characterized conservative New School Presbyterianism after 1837.[5]

The hard-working young Moody went to sleep regularly under the influence of Kirk's polished sermons. However, Moody joined Mt. Vernon Church's Sunday school, and it was through his Sunday school teacher that he at last decided to make a new heart, abandon Unitarianism, and join his uncle's church. His conversion experience was not at all like the profound emotional crisis through which Finney passed. It occurred on April 21, 1855, during working hours at the shoe store when his Sunday school teacher came in and had a heart to heart talk with him. At that time, as Moody told the examining committee of the Mt. Vernon Church when he applied for membership a month later, he first "became anxious about himself. Saw himself a sinner," repented and "purposed to give up sin." But the examining board was startled when, in reply to their question, "What has Christ done for you and for us all that especially entitles Him to our love and obedience?," Moody failed to give the standard reply, "He died for our sins." Instead, Moody said awkwardly, "I think He has done a great deal for us all, but I don't know of anything He has done in particular." The board decided that despite his good intentions Moody did not give sufficient evidence of conversion to be admitted to the church. Three members of the church were appointed to provide him with further spiritual guidance and instruction and it was not until March, 1856, that he was permitted to join the church.[6]

Moody continued working at his uncle's store until September, 1856, and then went west to Chicago to get out from under his uncle's rigorous eye and niggardly wages. He obtained a job at once in Charles E. Wiswall's boot and shoe store at $30 a

[5] See David O. Mears, *Life of Edward Norris Kirk* (Boston, 1877). Kirk became so hostile to Finney that in 1857 he refused to cooperate in a movement to invite Finney to Boston. Kirk to Finney, March 1, 1858, Finney Papers, OCL.

[6] Elias Nason, *The Lives of the Eminent American Evangelists Dwight Lyman Moody and Ira David Sankey* (Boston, 1877), p. 48. I am indebted to James Findlay, Jr., for information confirming the date of Moody's conversion over which there has been considerable confusion. See also W. R. Moody, *Moody* (1930), pp. 33–34; W. R. Moody, *Moody* (1900), pp. 43–44; Wilbur M. Smith, *Annotated Bibliography of D. L. Moody*, p. xx; and Elmer W. Powell, "Moody of Northfield," pp. 74 ff.

week. Soon he was caught up in the excitement of the booming city, which at that time numbered less than 85,000 but which within a few decades became one of the largest cities in the nation. "I can make more money here in a week than I could in Boston in a month," he wrote to his brother in Northfield.[7] He presented his letter of membership from Mt. Vernon Church to the Plymouth Congregational Church in Chicago and was soon actively engaged in its activities. His frank, impetuous personality, his ambition to get ahead in the world, his quick mind and untiring energy guaranteed him a rapid rise to success in the new metropolis.

In 1858 he took a new and better job with another boot and shoe firm. "I have a good position and I mean to work my cards to make it better," he wrote home in the language of the card sharp. He was now making money enough to try his hand at investing it. "If I get a hundred dollars I lay it right into land and at the rate it has increased I can make twenty-five per cent on my money." In the cash-hungry city, Moody boasted of making short-term loans which brought him 17 per cent interest *per day*. It was his ambition at that time to make $100,000. Within five years after his arrival his income was over $5000 a year and he had $7000 in the bank.[8]

At first he was not entirely happy. "How lonely it feels to be off in a city like this," he wrote, "for it is so wicked. The stores are all open on the Sabbath." But when his employer gave him the task of collecting bills from delinquent rural storekeepers who were going or had gone broke in the aftermath of the panic of 1857 he entered into it with great zest. "I am collecting for a house in Chicago. I like it better than anything I have ever done. It is nothing but excitement all the time." The hardships wrought by the depression did not seem to trouble him though he attended prayer meetings regularly during the Great Prayer Meeting Revival. "I find the better I live the more enjoyment I have and the more I think of God and His love the less I think of this world's troubles."[9]

The mixture of hard work, piety, thrift, business shrewdness, and love of excitement which marked his letters in this

[7] W. R. Moody, *Moody* (1930), p. 39.
[8] *Ibid.*, pp. 39, 67.
[9] *Ibid.*, pp. 37–39, 42.

period remained permanent characteristics of his personality. In Chicago, Moody threw himself into church work with the same enthusiasm that he demonstrated in his business career. He joined the newly formed YMCA. He spoke up so often and so volubly at prayer meetings that he was asked to refrain from taking part. He tried to teach Sunday school but was considered too ignorant of the Bible to be of any use so he devoted himself to rounding up pupils for others to teach. He spent part of his income, like a good Christian steward, to rent four extra pews in Plymouth Church which he filled with strangers whom he personally invited to attend. He gave out tracts in the poorer sections of the city and generally engaged in religious activity not only in his own church but in the First Methodist Church, where he met the wealthy dry goods merchant, John V. Farwell, and at the First Baptist Church, where he met Fleming H. Revell, whose sister he later married. Idleness, whether on the Sabbath or during vacations always seemed sinful to Moody. "How I do pity people who hang about these summer resorts doing nothing! My! it would send me crazy." [10]

In the fall of 1858 Moody decided to start a Sunday school of his own for the children of "the Sands," the Chicago slum area. He rented a former saloon on Michigan Avenue where he and two friends began to teach and convert the local ragamuffins. Moody was so successful at rounding up Sunday school scholars that he soon wrote to his brother, "I think I have got the best school there is in the west. Anyway, it is the largest this side of New York." [11] It became so large that he was able to persuade the mayor of Chicago to give him the hall over the city's North Market for his meetings, rent free. Well-to-do businessmen like Cyrus McCormick, George Armour, John V. Farwell, and Isaac H. Burch, whom he met through his church and YMCA work, gave him financial assistance in this "missionary" activity. Soon he had close to one thousand pupils and decided to erect a building for them. Estimating that it would cost $10,000, he printed "stock certificates" in the name of the North Market Hall Sabbath School Association and sold forty thousand shares at twenty-five cents each, telling investors that for dividends they should apply at

[10] W. R. Moody, *Moody* (1900), p. 55.
[11] W. R. Moody, *Moody* (1930), p. 49.

the Sabbath School any Sunday morning to see the scholars at work. This type of business push in religious activity appealed to many influential citizens and Moody was soon a prominent figure in Chicago's evangelical circle.

In 1860, after what he called "the hardest struggle I ever had in my life," Moody decided to give up his business ambitions and devote himself entirely to religion. He had seven thousand dollars in the bank on which he figured he could live for seven years. After that he would let the Lord provide. For the next twelve years he worked night and day in a wide variety of religious endeavors in and around Chicago. He became a leading organizer for the national Sunday school movement and helped to establish "the Illinois system" in various states. He rose to be President of the Chicago YMCA at the age of twenty-eight and served in that capacity from 1866 to 1869. In 1862 he became an agent for the City Relief Society. During the Civil War he played an active part in the United States Christian Commission, erecting prayer tents in the army camps and nursing the sick and wounded in the army hospitals. He continued his work among the slum children of Chicago and began to hold evening meetings for their parents or any other unchurched adults whom he could persuade to attend. He conducted street corner evangelistic services, distributed tracts, and made a vow to let no day pass without asking at least one stranger, "Are you a Christian?" in the hope of winning a new convert. Many people in Chicago called him "Crazy" Moody for his fanatic devotion to his calling, but his hardheaded, efficient management of every task he undertook soon won him the respect and admiration of church leaders all over the country.

Moody was a short man whose stocky build soon turned to adiposity. But his energetic drive, his quick step, and his brisk habits of speech and thought belied his heaviness. His homely face was friendly but assertive. His square head rested on a short bull neck and the heavy black beard which he adopted in the 1860's made this neck seem even shorter. His manner was brusque, often pugnacious, but his quick anger was equally quick to dissolve in tears. He bullied his way into friendships but proved so warm-hearted and generous that few resented his blunt manners. For all his aggressiveness he was always ready to acknowledge his own limitations and his mistakes, and for this he was unstintingly loved and admired by those who knew him best.

In 1864, Moody founded the Illinois Street Church which later became the Chicago Avenue Church and before his death was known simply as Moody Church. He started it at the request of some of those slum dwellers and parents of his Sunday school pupils whom he had converted in his city missionary work. They were unwilling to join the regular uptown churches and Moody agreed to act as their pastor even though he had no theological training and no intention of seeking ordination. But he was founding no new sect. The Moody Church was one of the first in a long line of independent fundamentalist tabernacles and storefront churches which were founded on nondenominational lines as a protest against the increasing formality and sophistication of the regular churches. Moody and his followers drew up their own articles of faith, consisting simply of Biblical texts strung together to spell out the doctrines of the trinity, the infallibility of Scripture, the sinfulness of man, the substitutionary atonement of Christ, the availability of salvation to all men, and the practice of communion. Moody performed all the rites of the church, except that of marriage, from 1864 to 1866.[12] Financial support came from the same wealthy men who supported Moody's other religious enterprises and who provided his income when his savings ran out. Although Moody persuaded the church to obtain a regular pastor after 1866, he always remained its guiding force.

Moody was not gaited for the sedentary life of a pastor. His forte was the ability to manage people, and it found expression in organizing meetings, raising funds, directing conventions, and goading sinners and churchgoers into fervent religious activity. Standing outside Farwell Hall, the Chicago YMCA building erected through his soliciting ability, Moody would recruit congregations for the noon prayer meetings in the 1860's by accosting passers-by with the question, "Are you

[12] *Ibid.*, p. 99. For the articles of the church, see W. H. Daniels, *D. L. Moody*, pp. 108 ff. Moody's church was undoubtedly influenced by the beliefs of the Plymouth Brethren with which Moody was greatly impressed at this time. See Elmer W. Powell, "Moody of Northfield," p. 137.

for Jesus?" Whether they answered yes or no, Moody insisted that their attendance at the meeting was imperative and pushed them into the building. When a crowd was obtained he often went in and led the meeting himself. After prayers, Bible reading, and a hymn, he would single out newcomers by calling from the platform, "You, brother, over there by the first window, don't you love the Lord?" "That red-haired man on the back seat, are you a Christian?" Weak or negative answers brought him storming down the aisle with the question, "Do you want to be saved, now?" And the startled man was down on his knees beside Moody and other YMCA members before he had time to object.[13]

In connection with his YMCA and Sunday school work, Moody made three brief trips to the British Isles in 1867, 1870, and 1872 to attend international religious conventions, to examine British organizational methods in religious work, and to meet such influential evangelical leaders as Charles Haddon Spurgeon, George Williams, George Mueller, Newman Hall, R. C. Morgan, and the Earl of Shaftesbury. He had also become interested in the literalistic and nondenominational lay evangelism of the Plymouth Brethren and visited some of their conferences in Dublin. Because of his friendship with leading American evangelicals like Cyrus McCormick, George H. Stuart, John Wanamaker, and William E. Dodge, Moody was able to make himself known in Britain and was asked to speak at various meetings and churches in London, Edinburgh, Birmingham, and Dublin.

In 1872, the Rev. William Pennefeather, founder of the Mildmay Christian Conferences, asked Moody if he would consider coming to England in the near future to conduct a series of evangelistic meetings. This invitation was seconded by two philanthropic laymen, Henry Bewley of Dublin and Cuthbert Bainbridge of Newcastle, who offered to help sustain the expenses of such a venture. Under ordinary circumstances Moody would have turned this offer down, but the disastrous Chicago fire of October, 1871, had temporarily brought his work there to a standstill. It had destroyed his home, his church, his Sunday school, and his YMCA, and though he had at once set about raising funds to rebuild them all, the con-

[13] W. H. Daniels, *Moody, His Words,* pp. 35–47.

struction process was slow. He decided that he could spare six months for evangelism in England, and the decision proved to be as great a turning point in his life as his decision to give up making money.

The trip to Britain also had a profound influence upon the subsequent course of modern revivalism. The system which Moody worked out in Britain and the factors which made him successful there were in large measure the same as those which were to shape the course of revivalism in the United States during the next half century.

Evangelistic preaching was not entirely new to Moody in 1873. Most of his prayer meetings, outdoor preaching, and pastoral work was primarily devoted to soul winning. In 1866 his friend, George H. Stuart, had persuaded him to conduct revival meetings in Philadelphia. Two years later Moody joined Henry Moorehouse, whom he had met in Dublin in 1867, conducting a series of seventy-two one-night evangelistic meetings in various cities of the Midwest. In the winter of 1872 he conducted revival meetings in the Rev. Theodore Cuyler's church in Brooklyn. But he never considered revival preaching more than a sideline.

Having decided in 1873 to take up revivalism more seriously, Moody had a stroke of genius when he concluded that he should employ a hymn singer as a coworker for the English tour. Although Moody was absolutely tone deaf, he recognized the psychological value of singing in religious work. First he tried to hire Philip Phillips, who had previously travelled around England giving concerts of "sacred song" and who was well known as a hymn writer and soloist on both sides of the Atlantic. When Phillips refused, he asked Philip Paul Bliss, who was second only to Phillips in this field. Bliss also declined. He then fell back upon a man whom he had heard singing at a YMCA convention in Indianapolis in 1870 and whom he had hired to direct the musical aspects of the Chicago Avenue Church, Ira David Sankey. He agreed to pay Sankey $100 a month for the tour.

There was nothing particularly novel about Moody's having received an invitation to conduct revival meetings in England. Finney's tours in 1849–50 and 1858–60 had set the pattern for international evangelistic cooperation and evangelists like

Moorehouse, Needham, Taylor, and Varley had carried it on. These tours were haphazard affairs, however, with the evangelist crossing the ocean at the invitation of one or two friends and the promise of financial support from a well-to-do layman. If he was popular and obtained conversions in suitable numbers, he received invitations from other pastors after he arrived and went from city to city preaching for a month in one church or six weeks in another and occasionally hiring a hall or speaking in a YMCA lecture room until either his funds, his energy, or his invitations ran out. Then he returned home.

Moody and Sankey arrived unnoticed in Liverpool in June, 1873. When they left from that same city to return to the United States in August, 1875, they were world famous. In 1873 they could scarcely obtain a hearing; two years later they were courted by the most prominent churchmen in Britain and America and the evangelical leaders of the largest cities in both countries begged for their services. Moody deserved credit for making the most of the opportunities which opened before him, but much of his success was due, as the Earl of Shaftesbury said at the time, to the fact that Moody was "the right man at the right hour." [14]

Shaftesbury's reasons for thinking this were motivated by his evangelical Tory conservatism, but he represented a fairly typical attitude among Moody's supporters. According to Shaftesbury, Moody came "at the time when the masses are lying in indifference and are nevertheless impressible." The assumption of course was that Moody and Sankey would impress the masses with the views which the Earl thought best for them. Shaftesbury was a vigorous opponent of the Reform Act of 1867, which doubled the electorate of England. He opposed it, he said, because he did not think the masses were ready for the privilege of voting. He also opposed the Ballot Act of 1873, which for the first time enabled an Englishman to vote by secret ballot. Shaftesbury had worked hard for the alleviation of some of the worst abuses of the English factory system, but he did so from a sense of *noblesse oblige* and Christian charity, not from any sense of the rights of labor. He believed that reform ought to be paternalistically managed from the top

14 Edwin Hodder, *The Life and Work of the Seventh Earl of Shaftesbury*, 3 vols. (London, 1886), Vol. III, p. 358.

down and introduced gradually under the leadership of the upper classes. He emphasized duties, not rights, in his thinking. If the poor man did his duty in obedience, humility, sobriety, and piety, then the rich and well-born would take care of him. But to give the poor and ignorant the political power to effect their own reforms was, in Shaftesbury's eyes, to invite communism, anarchy, and mob rule. Like Lyman Beecher, he saw revivalism as a means of deflecting and checking the "ocean of unstable mind" and the "levelling of all distinctions of society" which would result from granting the poor the rights of political democracy, especially in a time of serious economic maladjustment.

Shaftesbury thought that Moody's form of urban evangelism would help to impress the Christian virtues of meekness, patience, and self-restraint upon the newly enfranchised working class of Britain who were, fortunately, as yet indifferent to the erroneous doctrines of socialism and unaware of their new power. Speaking in Parliament in 1870 against that section of the Education Act which would exclude the Bible from the schools, Shaftesbury had said, "We have now come to a period in the history of our country when there has just been granted to the people almost universal suffrage. Is this a time to take from the mass of the population in whom all power will henceforth reside, that principle of internal self-control without which there can be no freedom? . . . Is this a time to take from the mass of the people the checks and restraints of religion?" [15]

Nevertheless, Karl Marx's collaborator, Friedrich Engels, was oversimplifying, as usual, when he maintained that the British bourgeois, "not content with his own native religious machinery . . . appealed to Brother Jonathan, the greatest organizer in existence of religion as a trade, and imported from America revivalism, Moody and Sankey and the like" to keep the masses drugged with the opiate of religion.[16] Engels was wrong not only in implying that Moody's revivalism was useful in "the evangelization of the lower orders" but also in implying

[15] *Ibid.*, Vol. III, p. 265.

[16] Friedrich Engels, introduction to the English translation of *Socialism, Utopian and Scientific* (New York, 1935), p. 24. Engels wrote the introduction for the London edition in 1892.

that it was primarily employed as a subterfuge to "put down" the working class. Reaching "the masses" was one element in nineteenth-century professional evangelism, but there were other elements equally patent in uniting British and American church leaders, lay and clerical, behind Moody. There was, for example, the problem of maintaining and strengthening Protestant unity in the face of internal dissensions aroused by science and the higher criticism. There was the problem of forming a united front against the growing intellectual disdain for the supernatural among educated people, against the outright agnosticism and secularism of a large body of nonchurchgoers, as well as against the new vigor of Roman Catholicism in the two countries. There was the simple but powerful missionary urge to spread the true faith among unbelievers and to live up to the ideals of charity, stewardship, and brotherly love which were central to Christianity no matter how variously interpreted and applied. The revivalism of Moody, and of the professional evangelists who followed him, favored the most conservative side in contemporary issues, it is true, but this scarcely justified Engels in reducing revivalism to a bourgeois plot.

Moody's projected tour of Britain almost collapsed at its beginning when he found that between the time the invitation had been extended to him and the time of his arrival two of his sponsors, Pennefeather and Bainbridge, had died. Since no prior arrangements had been made for him he was fortunate in receiving an invitation from a YMCA acquaintance to conduct some meetings in York, and he went there to preach first. His friend, Richard Cope Morgan, editor of a nondenominational weekly published in London called *The Christian,* informed interested persons through his columns that they could obtain Moody's services by writing to him at York. Moody preached and Sankey sang for five weeks in York where two Wesleyan Methodist chapels, a Baptist chapel, and a Congregationalist chapel shared their services. The Rev. F. B. Meyer, who later became a popular evangelical leader, was their principal supporter there. From York they went to Sunderland for five weeks at the invitation of Moody's friend, the Rev. Arthur A. Rees, an open communion Baptist who had acquired a reputation for his sensational evangelical preaching and for his attacks on "the red-tapists of religion." [17] Four weeks later they moved on to Newcastle, where for the first time a Presbyterian church cooperated with them. "We have not done much in York and Sunderland," said Moody, "because the ministers opposed us; but we are going to stay in Newcastle till we make an impression and live down the prejudices of good people who do not understand us." [18]

The objections came from Anglicans and from the more respectable middle-class dissenters who disliked the fact that Moody was a lay preacher and who felt that his unconventional style, like Sankey's solo singing, was out of place in religious services. But the less formal evangelicals of the lower middle class were highly pleased by Moody's strenuous manner, his Yankee dialect, his simple Bible readings, and by the novel revival measures which he introduced to keep up the interest and excitement of the meetings. Although he did not use the anxious seat, he did hold "after meetings" or "inquiry meetings" for the anxious. Many considered this an innovation though revivalists in England had used inquiry meetings since Finney's first visit. Moody's energetically conducted noon prayer meetings and his special services for merchants, for mechanics, for young converts, to which persons were admitted by ticket, aroused considerable attention.

Sankey's gospel songs proved to be so popular that R. C. Morgan, who was also a partner in the publishing firm of Morgan and Scott, published a cheap edition of them in September, 1873. During the next few years the Sankey hymnbook became a sensational best-seller. Out of Moody's first meetings in northern England, however, very little came except a renewed spirit among those already devoted to the evangelical cause. Two or three hundred in all were claimed as converts in York, Sunderland, and Newcastle, but "the great majority of those who professed to have been converted," wrote an early Moody biographer, "were those who had known the Scriptures from infancy, and had been regular attendants at the house of God." [19] But this fact was not generally bruited at the time, and by November, 1873, *The Christian* began to tell its avid

[17] *The Christian* (London), August 21, 1873, p. 11.
[18] W. H. Daniels, *D. L. Moody,* p. 254.
[19] *Ibid.,* p. 257.

evangelical readers that a new wave of revivalism similar to that of 1859–60 was about to sweep the British Isles.

The British revival of 1859–60 played an important part in preparing the way for Moody and Sankey. It had been stimulated, if not inaugurated, by reports of the Prayer Meeting Revival in the United States. Beginning in Northern Ireland among the pious, rural, and uneducated Scotch-Irish Presbyterians, it was significant for Moody's work more by way of contrast than of similarity, for it was accompanied in most places by the same type of hysteria and prostrations which characterized the American camp meetings of the Second Great Awakening.[20] The religious and secular press picked up the reports of these exciting manifestations of hysteria almost as soon as they started in 1859, and ministers and laymen from all over the British Isles converged upon Ulster to share in "the showers of blessings." From Ulster they returned to Wales, Scotland, and England "to extend the blessing." The Anglican and Presbyterian churches soon dissociated themselves from the movement, but it stirred up the dissenting sects for several years. It was particularly marked by the rash of itinerant lay evangelists who wandered through the countryside, visiting fairs and racing meetings, and invading the cities on market days to exhort and harangue the crowds on street corners and in open lots. Most of these lay evangelists returned to their homes after the revival died down, but several dozen of them continued to make a living at the profession, and the more successful were still active in various parts of the United Kingdom when Moody arrived. *The Christian,* which was founded in 1859 as *The Revival* with the express purpose of promoting the movement, devoted much of its space to the reports of the activities of these itinerant preachers and to the various conferences of Christian workers which were held annually after 1860 in Aberdeen, Mildmay, Perth, and Dublin to discuss evangelistic activity. The Conference of Christian Workers which met quarterly in London was "in reality an association of evangelists." [21] Moorehouse and Varley were prominent in this group, along with

[20] For a broad but generally uncritical treatment of this movement, see J. Edwin Orr, *The Second Evangelical Awakening in Britain* (London, 1949). Also useful on the relationship between this revival and Moody's work in Britain is George E. Morgan, *R. Cope Morgan* (London, 1909), *passim.*

[21] P. C. Headley, *Evangelists in the Church* (Boston, 1875), p. 406.

men like Joshua Poole, Lord Radstock, W. H. M. Hay Aitken, Reginald Radcliffe, William Booth, W. P. Lockhart, J. Denham Smith, John Hambleton, H. Grattan Guinness, Stevenson Blackwood, Gordon Forlong, J. Thain Davidson, J. Laidlaw, Baptist Noel, Duncan Mathews, Ned Wright, A. N. Somerville, Gawin Kirkham, Harrison Ord, Richard Weaver, and Brownlow North.

These evangelists, almost all of them laymen, received financial assistance from the same evangelical businessmen and members of the nobility and lesser nobility who were to assist Moody. Among them were the Earl of Shaftesbury, Earl Cairns, James C. White (later Lord Overtoun), the Earl of Kintore, Arthur Kinnaird (later Lord Kinnaird), Lord Polwarth, the Duchess of Gordon, the Countess of Effingham, James E. Matheson, Hugh Matheson, Quintin Hogg, and a group of minor figures like Finney's host, Potto Brown, and Moody's friends, Bewley and Bainbridge. The ordained ministers of all denominations were seriously divided over the value of lay evangelism, but even among the established churches of England, Ireland, and Scotland there were clergymen like Bishop Moule, Bishop Chavasse, the Bishop of Ripon, Bishop Waldegrave, and the Dean of Carlisle who were sympathetic to this movement toward professional revivalism.[22]

The constant theme of the British evangelical revivalists and lay leaders in their speeches at Christian conferences and in their letters to evangelical journals was the need for united action among Protestant evangelists in order to meet the various religious crises of the day. Their particular complaints in the 1860's were against Darwinism, "Popery," rationalism, establishmentarianism, and political radicalism. Finney had noted in his visits to England that "sectarian lines are much more distinctly drawn and the members of the different churches keep more closely within their lines than in this country." [23] But these lines were fast breaking down even while Finney was there and an observer of Moody's work in Newcastle wrote in

[22] An indication of the extent to which revivalism had entered the Church of England were the Pre-Lent Preaching Missions in London in 1869 and 1874 in which many Anglican churches took part aided by such professional evangelists as W. H. M. Hay Aitken, Reginald Radcliffe, and J. W. Bonham. See *ibid.*, pp. 380 ff.

[23] C. G. Finney, *Memoirs* (New York, 1876), p. 470.

1873, "Denominational lines have been in a great measure obliterated. Ministers of the various sects have assembled in crowds under the banner of one God. . . . Efforts for ecclesiastical unity that had extended over years have been crowned with success in a day." [24] Moody undoubtedly reaped the benefit of fifteen years of interdenominational revival activity which grew out of the awakening of 1859–60.

The Rev. David Lowe, who had brought Moody to Newcastle, made a suggestion, probably conceived by Moody, to advance the cause of interdenominational unity under the revivalistic banner of Moody and Sankey. He wrote to the editor of *The Christian* in November, 1873, "I find that where I have been all the ministers are with me heart and hand if they have seen *The Christian* and that reports of what is going on are stirring up ministers and churches." He proposed that a fund of £2000 be raised at once to send a three-month subscription to *The Christian* to every one of the 40,000 ministers in the United Kingdom. R. C. Morgan printed the letter and cordially endorsed the idea "not only because it would add an important and influential element to our circulation, but because, humanly speaking, there would be no more effectual way of extending the gracious work at present in progress among us." [25] Two weeks later *The Christian* commenced sending issues to 1000 ministers of Scotland. By January 1, 1874, the £2000 had been raised and *The Christian* was reaching every minister in the British Isles with its astonishing reports of "the wonderful work of God" which was flowing from the labors of Messrs. Moody and Sankey.

Publicity was helpful, but it could not of itself have produced or sustained the revival which was so ardently desired by the evangelistic element in the churches. The success of Moody and Sankey in Britain came about through the efforts of the pastors of Edinburgh who, in the first fine careless rapture of united effort, threw themselves wholeheartedly behind Moody's work for eight weeks in December and January of 1873–74. Although 82 per cent of the churchgoing population of Scotland was Presbyterian, that denomination had for thirty years

[24] Quoted from the Newcastle *Chronicle* in W. R. Moody, *Moody* (1930), p. 151.

[25] *The Christian,* November 27, 1873, p. 14.

been split into three warring factions: the established Church of Scotland (which had 1254 churches in 1870), the Free Church of Scotland (with 873 churches), and the United Presbyterian Church (with 600 churches).[26] By competitive building throughout every town and village in Scotland, these denominations had succeeded in establishing many more churches than could profitably be used. Moreover, although they had all managed to keep up a steady rate of growth, they were not successfully meeting the needs of the urban poor. Their churches were more numerous and grew faster in the well-to-do suburban parts of the cities than in the slums. In the decade 1861–1871, the number of persons in Glasgow who belonged to no church increased from 110,000 to 120,000 out of a population of 516,000. In Edinburgh, 50,000 out of the city's 200,000 population were not church members. Yet there were 220 churches in Glasgow and 120 in Edinburgh which, according to one estimate, were capable of seating the entire adult populations of those cities. "Taking Scotland as a whole," said a prominent Presbyterian pastor in 1873, "it [is] over-churched and over-ministered" and yet "the first cardinal point in theory and practice with the Scottish Churches [is] never to think of one another except for purposes of opposition . . . instead of contending with one another there should be an agreement and a division of the land. . . ."[27]

There were two reasons why the much needed unity between the Presbyterian churches was being delayed. The first was the question of disestablishment and the second, the question of permitting a more Arminian or evangelical interpretation of the Westminster Confession of Faith to which all three denominations adhered. Moody's arrival in Scotland in the winter of 1873 was intimately related to the settlement of both of these problems. The United Presbyterians generally favored disestablishing the state church and they had also taken an evangelical attitude toward the Confession. Since 1843 they were theologically in the position that the New School Presbyterians of the United States had been in during the early 1830's, claiming to be good Presbyterians yet advocating free will and

[26] Robert Wallace, "Church Tendencies in Scotland," in *Recess Studies,* ed. Sir Alexander Grant (Edinburgh, 1870), pp. 187 ff.

[27] Archibald Charteris in Edinburgh *Courant,* November 24, 1873, p. 3.

free grace. A majority of the Free Church of Scotland were also leaning toward this evangelical interpretation of doctrine, and they also favored disestablishing the state church. Since 1863 a movement had been on foot to unite the Free Church and the United Presbyterian Church in order to strengthen the attack upon the established church. However, a strong minority of conservative (Calvinistic) ministers within the Free Church wanted to rejoin the Church of Scotland, from which the Free Church had split in 1843 on a technical point of ecclesiastical polity. These Free Church conservatives opposed any union with the United Presbyterians, whom they considered "heretical" because of their evangelical attitude toward the Westminster Confession (the Free Church conservatives closed their eyes to the evangelicalism within their own denomination). Their opposition to the union of the Free Church and the United Presbyterian Church was so vehement that they openly threatened a schism if the union movement was consummated. The established Church of Scotland in turn was split between those who wanted to liberalize the interpretation of the Confession and to modernize the liturgy and those who wished to adhere as strictly as possible to tradition. Of course no one with the Church of Scotland favored the movement for disestablishment and all its clergy would have welcomed unity with the other two denominations provided agreement could be made in terms of theology and liturgy so as to absorb the schismatics within the established system.

The bitter animosity over these issues between and within all three denominations had inevitably led to an outbreak of ecclesiastical trials and virulent charges of heresy and disorder during the ten years preceding Moody's visit. One of the more prominent liberals to be charged with heresy in the Church of Scotland was the Rev. Dr. Robert Wallace of Edinburgh. He was tried in October, 1873, for having been so bold as to take up with the higher criticism and to express some doubts about the literal infallibility of the Bible. Though he was exonerated, he resigned from the ministry in disgust shortly after his trial, convinced that the attempt to hold fast to the old dogma of Calvinism would alienate from the church the most serious and intelligent members of the younger generation. "Religious thought" in Scotland, he said, "may be said to be moving away from external authority towards self-reliance; from an objective towards a subjective standard of truth. Here, as elsewhere throughout the world, the empire of private judgment is steadily pressing forward its boundaries. This exhibits itself in a very widespread loosening of opinion, in the growth of a questioning and doubting spirit . . . the decrees of the Church, the definition of the Standards and Articles, the infallibility of the letter of Scripture itself are not what they were." The church must give up its narrow literalism and its rigid adherence to seventeenth-century dogma or face a steady decrease in respect and influence.[28] The conservatives were more than half fearful that Wallace spoke the truth.

The uneasiness and emotional tension among the Scottish clergy in the year 1873 were evident in the speech of the Rev. Alexander Duff, the renowned old missionary to India, at the Free Church's General Assembly which took place in Edinburgh in May. This speech pointed up many of the issues which Moody's revival was to capitalize upon six months later in the attempt to resolve the churches' dilemma. Duff was a moderate on the questions of liberalizing the Confession and disestablishing the state church. In the interest of Christian unity he had at first actively promoted the movement toward union between his denomination and the United Presbyterians, but as the tension mounted over the years he became more circumspect. To his mind another schism in the Presbyterian ranks would be a catastrophe. He had been elected Moderator in 1873 in order to soothe over the friction which had developed between the Calvinistic conservatives and the evangelicals within the Free Church. His keynote address was directed toward the major problem facing the Assembly that year, the final vote on whether or not to consummate the union with the United Presbyterian Church. After ten years of debate the climax was at hand. Those in favor of the union had a sufficient majority to effect it, but many moderates, like Duff, were uneasy over the threats of secession which the conservatives had stubbornly repeated.

[28] Wallace, "Church Tendencies . . ." *loc. cit.*, p. 202. For Wallace's trial and exoneration see Edinburgh *Courant*, August 8, 1873, p. 7 and October 10, 1873, p. 3. At about the same time the Rev. William Knight of Edinburgh, who was under discipline for heresy in the Free Church, also resigned from the ministry. See Edinburgh *Courant*, October 24, 1873, p. 7.

The theme of Duff's keynote address therefore was "mutual brotherly forbearance," and the message he urged upon the assembled brethren was that they must unite in a fight against their common enemies instead of against each other. And who were the enemies of the church? According to Duff's impassioned address they included the atheists who sprang out of the French Revolution, the German rationalists, the British skeptical philosophers, the devotees of the new "physical and mechanical sciences." They were those who supported the rise of "ritualism" in the Church of England and the return of Jesuitism and Popery to England under Cardinals Newman and Manning. He pointed fearfully to the pernicious literature "provided for the masses" by the Sunday papers and vulgar journals in which "orthodoxy is not only placed at a discount but positively discouraged." He called for the repeal of the Contagious Diseases Act, which, he said, by requiring physical examinations for prostitutes, virtually legalized this iniquitous traffic. He shivered at the increase in drunkenness, in luxurious living, in financial speculation, in fraud, in the adulteration of food, in the worship of money, and in the "spirit of lawless insubordination, wilful independence, and contempt of authority" among the working class as manifested in the rise of "Radicalism and Communism" and in "the epidemic rupture between employers and employed in every department of mining, trading, and manufacturing industry—all, all tending to inaugurate the reign of universal anarchy and misrule and threatening to unhinge, if not dissolve, the entire fabric of society." [29] It was enough to make the blood of the assembled delegates run cold.

In his peroration Duff turned to the sober-faced clergy and laity and asked woefully, "What have we ever done in our individual or collective capacity to stem or arrest or hurl back the prodigious rush and torrent of the mighty flood of error and unbelief and abounding wickedness" that prevails?

His appeal succeeded. The majority of Free Church delegates voted to postpone the decision to amalgamate with the United Presbyterians (a postponement that lasted twenty-seven

[29] This address was printed in a Special Extra Edition of *The Christian* in May, 1873, and is bound in the back of the 1873 volume of that journal in the British Museum.

years) and to close ranks in the face of the grave emergency facing the forces of righteousness. Delegates of all theological shades joined hands with one another in voting to hold a series of conferences to inquire into the "spiritual destitution" among the masses and to seek new methods of winning them to orthodox Christianity.

The conciliatory evangelical leader of the Church of Scotland, the Rev. Archibald Charteris, Professor of Biblical Literature at the University of Edinburgh, offered a somewhat different solution to reconcile the warring factions within his church. In a lecture to his students delivered ten days before Moody reached Edinburgh, Charteris declared that "There is fast, very fast, coming upon us a conflict for the very essentials of the faith." He warned the conservatives that "we feel the burden of the unnecessary minuteness of the creeds." His solution for preserving the faith while doing away with the minuteness of creeds was to produce an abbreviated confession consisting of the "essentials" or the fundamentals. He stated, "Creeds designed for general acceptance ought to be confined to statements of the main doctrines of the faith of Christ." [30] This was of course the view of Beecher, Finney, Moody, and all modern revivalists who sought evangelical unity. But the dogma enshrined in these "main doctrines" proved to be even more rigid than the subtleties of the Westminster Confession. This became evident within a year after Moody left Great Britain when Charteris led the famous heresy hunt which drove Professor William Robertson Smith from his post in the Free Church College of Aberdeen for disputing the inerrancy of Scripture. Since Charteris did not belong to Smith's denomination he could only raise the hue and cry over Smith's scholarly publications, but Moody's revivalism had so effectively united the defenders of "the essentials" in all denominations that the work of driving Smith out of the Free Church could be safely left up to Moody's supporters within that denomination, men like Horatius and Andrew Bonar, Alexander Moody Stuart, Sir Henry W. Moncrieff, and Professor Robert Rainy.

Into this sea of theological and ecclesiastical troubles in November, 1873, walked Moody and Sankey, two innocents abroad. Those who later reported their success and wrote their biog-

30 Edinburgh *Courant,* November 13, 1873, p. 7.

raphies never ceased to marvel at the miracle they wrought in Edinburgh. That two uneducated American laymen should lead a revival among the learned doctors of the Scottish Presbyterian churches and should win acceptance for their Yankee innovations in "conservative, tradition-loving Scotland" could be attributed only to supernatural influence. Yet nothing could have been more logical than that amid all the tension and the cries of peace where there was no peace, the diversionary activity of a restrained but exciting revival was the very thing to let off steam. If the revival could only avoid doctrinal quarrels and emotional excesses, if it could claim to reach the masses, if it welcomed cooperation in winning souls from men of all shades of evangelical belief, then it was the perfect antidote to incipient ecclesiastical epilepsy and decline. Moreover, in the muddy waters of the revival movement ecclesiastical politicians were able to realign their forces, form new alliances, and redefine the issues which had become brittle with oversharpening.

The Rev. John Kelman, an evangelical Free Church pastor of Leith (a suburb of Edinburgh), made a careful personal investigation of Moody's work in Newcastle early in November and then returned to organize his friends to extend an invitation to the Americans to preach in Edinburgh. There were ten or twelve revival enthusiasts whom he could count on, among them the Rev. W. G. Blaikie, Professor of Apologetics and of Ecclesiastical and Pastoral Theology at the Free Church New College. It was in Blaikie's home that Moody stayed during his visit. Blaikie was described in the Edinburgh *Daily Review* as "one of those men who keep their eyes and ears open. . . . He is of the modern school in the best sense that while radically and pervasively Evangelical, he is alive to the importance of taking note of the forms and phases of religious life of the age. . . ." What this meant was evident in Blaikie's book, *For the Work of the Ministry,* which was published that fall. Blaikie believed, "We live in evil times. Vice, unbelief, and worldliness are threatening the extinction of evangelical religion and the Church must bestir itself if it is not to go down with the tide." He urged all ministers to adopt more "winsome" and "earnest" methods of preaching and of conducting their services in order to reach "the sunken masses." No man,

Blaikie wrote, should be ordained who had not been converted and who did not believe that the Bible was "the written Word of God" from cover to cover. Like Charteris, he believed in reducing the Westminster Confession to the fundamentals, "the great central truths," in the interest of unity and evangelism.[31]

Blaikie and Kelman and Charteris organized a committee of ten or twelve pastors and laymen in Edinburgh (Alexander Duff joined them later) to start a daily prayer meeting to pray for a revival and to spread as much favorable information as they could about Moody's Newcastle meetings. After canvassing their friends they felt they had sufficient support to extend an invitation to Moody, who accepted at once. Moody and Sankey arrived in Edinburgh on November 23 and Moody conducted the noon prayer meeting attended by 1200 persons the next day in Queen Street Hall. "Several hymns were sung by the audience accompanied by Mr. Sankey on the American organ" reported the Edinburgh *Daily Review*. "Mr. Moody gave a few remarks on the power of prayer and said he wished the meetings to be free social meetings, and he would be obliged if anyone who pleased would take part. Previous to the revival in 1859 [Moody declared] the prayer meetings in America were all of a stereotype, but now the stiffness and formality was broken up and anyone could rise up in the meetings and give his experience." Moody said he hoped that the same informality would prevail at the prayer meeting through the next weeks.

That night Moody conducted the first evangelistic meeting of the revival in the Rev. J. H. Wilson's Barclay Church. About 2000 persons attended. The ministerial committee sat on the platform in front of the pulpit. Moody said that "he did not come to them with any new story; he had nothing to tell them but the old story. When the news of the gospel was presented to some folks they looked as if they had received their death warrant; but it was the best news that ever fell on the ears of man. . . . Mr. Moody then urged on his audi-

[31] See the review of Blaikie's book in the Edinburgh *Daily Review,* December 1, 1873, p. 5, and William G. Blaikie, *For the Work of the Ministry* (London, 1873), pp. 18, 27, 78, 342. It is significant that the three American ministers Blaikie singled out for praise in his book were Henry Ward Beecher, T. DeWitt Talmage, and Theodore L. Cuyler, all of whom knew and worked with Moody. See p. 74.

ence the necessity of availing themselves of the means of salvation of the human race. After the benediction had been pronounced, Mr. Moody held another meeting in the classroom where he was consulted by nearly thirty persons" who were anxious about their souls.[32]

This stress on the old orthodoxy, or the fundamentals of the old orthodoxy, plus the new emphasis on informality and on the singing of "human hymns" to an organ as opposed to the singing of the Psalms without accompaniment were the most salient characteristics of the revival which followed. It was a judicious and perfectly timed blend of the old and the new. Soon the Edinburgh papers were praising the "touching pathos" of Sankey's singing which came "from the heart" and unquestionably was "the means of winning many souls for Christ." Sankey's use of the organ was justified on the ground that it was needed to "maintain the pitch" and besides, "the American organ is 'only a little one.' " Moody's sermons were admired because "in simple, vigorous, and telling language he holds up before men the truth as it is in Jesus and makes most earnest and powerful appeals to heart and conscience."

Of particular importance was the fact that "There is very little excitement" in the meetings. "There is no extravagance" of the sort which marred the revival of 1859. "The effect of the service is seen in the manifest impression produced in the audience." The Edinburgh *Daily Review* noted after the first two weeks that ministers "who at first had difficulties and stood somewhat aloof are finding their difficulties melting away by personal contact with the work. . . . It is truly delightful to witness the unbroken unity and brotherly love that prevails. . . . Denominational differences are for the time lost sight of. . . . It seems as if a winter of wonderful blessing were lying before Edinburgh and Leith." [33]

Charteris wrote to one of his more conservative friends, "Do try to attend Moody's and Sankey's meeting tomorrow. . . . I heard nothing and saw nothing you would not approve of." [34]

32 Edinburgh *Daily Review,* November 25, 1873, p. 2.

33 *Ibid.,* December 8, 1873, p. 3.

34 W. R. Moody, *Moody* (1930), pp. 165–66. Charteris also felt it necessary to point out to his friends "There is no Plymouthism" in Moody's revivals. Not only was Plymouthism associated with the disorderly revivalism of 1859, but its origins and tenets were antiecclesiastical.

The Rev. Andrew Thomson, one of the original committee, wrote a letter which was published widely in the press defending the inquiry meetings: "I witnessed no excesses in the inquiry rooms but there was often deep and melting solemnity, sometimes the sob of sorrow and the whispered prayer of contrition or gratitude." He also insisted that "There was nothing of novelty in the doctrine which Mr. Moody proclaims. It is the old gospel—old, yet always fresh and young . . . in which the substitution of Christ is placed in the center." [35] The Rev. Horatius Bonar admonished those who were unhappy over Moody's "Yankee vulgarisms" and lack of ordination: ". . . confronted as we are with the augmenting mass of human evil, we must fight or go down before it. . . . Let us not be too scrupulous of the appearance of the vessel in which we adminster the medicine if we are satisfied that it is for the healing of the world." [36]

One after another of the leading clergy of Edinburgh added their assent to the movement. Behind and before them came such lay leaders as Arthur Kinnaird, Lord Polwarth, Hugh Rose, James M. Balfour, the Earl of Cavan, and George F. Barbour. With each prominent addition to Moody's platform of dignitaries a half-dozen of the younger and less consequential pastors climbed on the bandwagon. "How anxious some of our ecclesiastics are to patronize anything and everything that may help to bolster up their self-importance and love of rule" wrote one antagonist of Moody's work. "Our Scottish Churches are losing all their strength and manliness by succumbing to the dictation of self-constituted leaders who are supported by a clique of moneyed elders and followed by the younger clergy like a flock of sheep. If many of our Presbyters are 'priests writ large,' the bulk of our ministers are curates *writ small*." [37] But the opposition was soon a minority and its protests went unheard in the atmosphere of mingled awe and holy enthusiasm which soon pervaded the city.

Moody preached and conducted the whole movement with his usual skill and aplomb. By the time the revival was in its third week he had arranged for two evangelistic services to be held simultaneously each evening at 7 P.M. For a time he was

[35] Edinburgh *Daily Review*, December 10, 1873, p. 7.
[36] *Ibid.*, January 2, 1874, p. 8.
[37] Glasgow *Herald*, April 4, 1874, p. 4.

assisted in this by a British lay preacher, Reginald Radcliffe, who since 1859 had become known as "the gentleman evangelist." When Radcliffe proved unsatisfactory Moody assigned the other meeting to one or another of the more "winsome" Edinburgh pastors. Moody also organized a series of meetings for young men at 9 P.M. each evening. He arranged to be present with Sankey at four different evangelistic meetings in four different churches each Sunday. He continued to conduct the daily noon prayer meetings. He devoted every Monday night to a young converts' meeting. In the fourth week he started giving afternoon Bible readings at three P.M. twice a week and added a 9 A.M. service on Sundays for Sabbath School and Bible Class teachers. He was indefatigable, but he received able assistance from young Scottish divinity students such as Henry Drummond and James Stalker as well as from the Edinburgh pastors and laymen.

Among his most sensational and highly publicized meetings were three which he conducted in the Edinburgh Corn Exchange near the Grassmarket slum district in an effort to reach "the poorer parts of the community" who seldom appeared at his regular meetings. These slum services were said to have converted thousands. The first week in January was also a special feature of the meetings for it was designated the "Week of Prayer for Scotland" and the Edinburgh pastors signed a request which was sent to all the ministers in the country asking them to hold simultaneous daily prayer meetings in their churches to ask divine aid for the spreading of the revival throughout the United Kingdom.

Moody soon was receiving requests for his services from all over Scotland, England, and Ireland. He accepted those from the largest cities and sent some of his Edinburgh assistants to the others. On January 14, 1874, he conducted a Christian Convention in Edinburgh to which all ministers and interested laymen of Scotland were invited. At this convention he led discussions on how to reach the masses, how to conduct prayer meetings, and how to deal with anxious souls. He held his last meeting in Edinburgh on January 20, spent two weeks in Dundee, and then moved to Glasgow for two months of meetings which followed the same pattern as those in Edinburgh. Religious journals were now filling columns with reports of the great work in progress in Scotland. Evangelical clergymen everywhere were excited by the thought that if conservative, learned, tradition-loving old Edinburgh had been stirred to its depths by a revival there was hope for other cities as well. Moody and Sankey decided to extend their stay in the British Isles indefinitely. After eight weeks in Glasgow they moved on to Belfast, Dublin, Manchester, Sheffield, Birmingham, Liverpool, and finally concluded their two-year triumphal tour with five months of revival meetings in London.

The London meetings were a mammoth affair. Plans had been under way for them since January, 1874, when a group of London laymen led by R. C. Morgan and the prominent banker, Hugh M. Matheson, had gone to Edinburgh to persuade Moody to come there. He arrived on March 9, 1875, and began five weeks of preaching in Agricultural Hall in the northern part of the city. Then he moved to the east side, where a frame building covered with corrugated iron and capable of seating 9000 was specially constructed for him. He preached in this Bow Road Hall for four weeks. The Rev. William Taylor, "the California street preacher," carried on the preaching at Agricultural Hall for five weeks after Moody moved on, and when Moody went from Bow Road Hall to the Royal Haymarket Opera House on the west side of the city, Henry Varley and W. H. M. Hay Aitken moved into the Bow Road Hall. Moody often spoke twice each evening at this stage of the revival, shuttling back and forth between the Opera House and the Bow Road Hall. In the south of London, he spoke for several weeks in the Victoria Theatre and then a special tabernacle for 8000 was constructed on Camberwell Green. Here Moody finished his five months of preaching in the largest city in the world.

A great deal of Moody's success in England was due to the curiosity aroused by the publicity he received in Scotland. But there were other factors. Lord Shaftesbury's remarks pointed to the churches' growing concern for evangelizing the newly enfranchised lower class in order to avoid political radicalism in a period of economic crisis. English ministers were as worried as the Scottish over the increasing secularism among all classes. Quarrels over ritualism, church rates, public education, and disestablishment had kept the dissenters and Anglicans at odds for several decades and there were many ministers on both sides who thought that Moody's revivals would sublimate antagonisms and cause evangelicals of all denominations to join hands against such mutual enemies as socialism, popery, atheism, evolution, and the higher criticism.

Moody's tour from Edinburgh to London had not gone unopposed, however. In Glasgow the city's leading daily paper questioned editorially whether the meetings were not "only a theatrical exhibition" with the "new feature" of "the 'starring system'." Other critics deplored the "miserable flunkeyism" of the Glasgow clergy and laity who raised the evangelists "almost to the apostolic stature," called them "God's messengers" and allowed themselves to be ordered about, if not actually "superseded," by these "religious drill sergeants" whose "sensational humbug" and "trashy hymns" were making a "travesty of religion." "Why," demanded one outraged conservative, "should two American laymen be permitted to override Presbyterian order with their pretentious Yankee tomfooleries?" What Moody's supporters praised as his forthright and resolute assurance and sincere convictions, his critics in Glasgow denounced as "religious quackery" spoken in a tone of *"ipse dixit"* "like the infallible Pope, but with a rudeness and an arrogance which the Papal potentate seldom displays." [38]

In Dublin, Moody and Sankey were satirized in a music hall by two comedians and ridiculed in a journal called *Public Opinion* by the young George Bernard Shaw. In Liverpool, they were hooted at in the streets. At the opening of the London meetings the jeering mob surrounding Agricultural Hall was deplored by one Moody admirer because "Oaths, jests, slang and mockery were all let loose together, but not one serious face, not one thoughtful countenance, not an idea of God's judgment or of eternity in all the vast changing multitude." [39]

More serious opposition came from conservative Anglicans. The Archbishop of Canterbury issued a statement that "evil

[38] *Ibid.*, March 14, 1874, p. 3; March 26, p. 7; April 2, p. 7; April 4, p. 6; April 7, p. 6; April 9, p. 5; April 14, pp. 3, 6; April 21, p. 7.

[39] *Christian Advocate* (Methodist, New York), March 25, 1875, p. 73; Hesketh Pearson, *GBS, A Postscript* (New York, 1950), pp. 128–29 (Among other things Shaw said, "Mr. Moody's orations were characterized by an excess of vehement assertion and a total absence of logic. . . ."); London *Times*, February 18, 1875, p. 11; W. R. Moody, *Moody* (1930), p. 215.

may arise" from the revival meetings: "I cannot think that the delicate and difficult duty of thus ministering to anxious souls ought to be entrusted to any who have neither been set apart by the church for this especial office nor have given proof of such spiritual insight as may in certain cases be held to take the place of this particular call to cure souls." [40] The London *Times* spoke for upper-class Victorian opinion when it admired Moody's "simple," "honest," and "earnest" efforts to raise the masses to thoughts of "something higher," but lamented the fact that in the doctrines preached, the "truths" of the Christian religion "are narrowed and hardened." Furthermore, the *Times* went on, Moody's sermons were "often, it must be owned, a little vulgar," for "he speaks of deep and mysterious problems as he would of buying so many pieces of cotton." [41] *Vanity Fair* printed two scabrous cartoons of the revivalists in its "Men of the Day" series by "Spy" and described Moody as "a shrewd, commonplace person, absolutely without culture, utterly without literary education," who made conversion "a vague process" which only amounted "to the reception by the convert of shadowy symbols." [42]

When the Countess of Gainsborough tried to persuade Queen Victoria to attend one of Moody's meetings, the Queen replied, "though I am sure they are very good and sincere people, it is not the *sort* of religious performance which I like. This sensational style of excitement like the Revivals [of 1859] is not the religion which *can last,* and is not, I think, wholesome for the mind or heart, though there may be some instances where it does good." [43]

Queen Victoria's comment was not publicly known, but even if it had been it could hardly have overshadowed the immense amount of favorable publicity which filled both the religious and secular press after the initial success in Scotland. Even the American newspapers began to comment on the meetings. What newspaper could resist the urge to play up the story of two humble Americans stirring the heart and soul of the British Empire? The fact that Moody reserved the first gallery of the

[40] London *Times,* May 25, 1875, p. 11.

[41] *Ibid.,* March 16, 1875, p. 9; March 19, p. 8; March 26, p. 5.

[42] *Vanity Fair,* XIII (April 3, 1875), 187. Spy was the pseudonym of Leslie Ward.

[43] W. R. Moody, *Moody* (1930), p. 213.

Royal Opera House for the nobility and that this tier was filled day after day with the peers of the realm profoundly impressed the American public. The conjunction of American simplicity and vigor with British tradition and culture was a common theme not only of contemporary novels and plays but of the popular magazines and Sunday society pages. Moody's meetings were attended by such prominent figures as the Princess of Wales, the Lord Chancellor, the Duke of Marlborough, the Duchess of Sutherland, the Countess of Gainsborough, the Earl of Shaftesbury, and the recently defeated Prime Minister, William E. Gladstone. An unexpected stroke of publicity favored Moody during the London visit when he accepted an invitation to speak at Eton. Several patrons of this stronghold of high-church Anglicanism were so upset at the thought of exposing the future leaders of the empire to Moody's "performances" that the matter was brought to the attention of Parliament and touched off a brief debate in the House of Lords.[44]

When Moody and Sankey left England in August, 1875, almost every account of their tour claimed that the United Kingdom had experienced a revival which not only stirred the churches but reached into all levels of society from the peerage to the slums. The three aspects of the movement which were most frequently praised were Moody's success in "reaching the masses," the new interdenominational unity resulting from coordinated efforts, and the inauguration of more informal, lively, and popular methods of conducting religious services. These were certainly the aims which Moody and his followers had in mind and which they constantly reiterated throughout. It was not long, however, before it became apparent that wishful thinking played a larger part in assessing the results of the revival than sober judgment.

The claims for Moody's work were so inflated that even some of his most ardent friends and admirers became embarrassed and tried to qualify them. "A certain class of minds," wrote one such friend, became so inflamed by "the general excitement" as to lose "all sense of facts, and to corrupt their consciences for accuracy." [45] But Moody's friends were not the only ones at fault, for even the London *Times* claimed that he

[44] London *Times,* June 21, 1875, p. 9; June 22, p. 9.
[45] George Adam Smith, *Drummond,* p. 99.

"reaches the poor" and "the lower strata of London of our towns generally." The reports of Moody's success in the American press were as exaggerated as any published by Moody's admirers in Britain. The New York *Herald* said that "never during the century had there been such a religious awakening among the dry bones there since the days of Wesley and Whitefield." Moody and Sankey "have aroused the stagnant and formal religion that was spreading itself" over Europe and "like the apostles of old, have turned the world upside down. . . ." [46]

Although Moody's work was considered to have been phenomenally successful everywhere in the British Isles, it was generally agreed that he had achieved his best results in Edinburgh and Glasgow. (About 3000 conversions in each of these cities was the most common estimate.) Horatius Bonar spoke in typical fashion of the Edinburgh results when he said, "The spiritual influence (contagion some call it) has struck into every rank and circle"; "This movement has not only reached the great houses in Moray Place and the west end of town, but has penetrated to the lowest depths of iniquity in the Cowgate, Cannongate, and Grassmarket." [47]

Church membership statistics, though notoriously unreliable, give some indications of the trends in church growth in Scotland in this period. They indicate that Moody's impact was slight and that his meetings barely scratched the surface of the unchurched. The United Presbyterian Church kept the most complete records at the time. Statistics are available for its churches in Edinburgh and Glasgow for the ten years from 1868 to 1878. They indicate that in Edinburgh in the five years preceding Moody's arrival that denomination was losing an average of 74 members per year, while in the five years following 1873 the denomination increased by an average of 359 members per year. These figures, however, scarcely mark any great upsurge in the religious life of this most evangelical of the three major denominations. The sixty-odd United Presby-

[46] London *Times*, April 3, 1875, p. 8; July 16, p. 4; The *Herald* is quoted in W. R. Moody, *Moody* (1930), p. 244.

[47] For estimates of conversions see Glasgow *Herald*, February 9, 1874, p. 4, Chicago *Weekly Tribune*, October 4, 1876, p. 7, and *Narrative of Messrs. Moody's and Sankey's Labours in Scotland and Ireland Compiled from the* British Evangelist *and* The Christian (New York, 1875), pp. 30–31, 45, 50. For Bonar's remarks see Edinburgh *Daily Review*, January 2, 1874, p. 8; January 4, p. 3.

terian churches in Edinburgh averaged a gain of about six members each per year from 1873 to 1878 and the denominational total in that city increased only from 26,028 to 27,852. Still Moody could be credited with reversing an inauspicious trend.

The United Presbyterian Church in Glasgow had been gaining an average of 951 members per year from 1868 to 1873. This jumped to an average of 1261 a year from 1873 to 1878. The total membership increased from 39,707 in 1873 to 46,010 in 1878. But once again, the numerical increase for each of the 85 or so United Presbyterian congregations in Glasgow rose only from 11 new members per year in the five years before Moody's revival to 15 new members per year in the five years following it. This hardly indicated an overwhelming return to religion on the part of the unchurched.[48]

A report published in 1888 comparing the growth of the three major Presbyterian denominations in Scotland to the growth of the Scottish population for the ten years from 1873 to 1883 showed that whatever boost Moody may have given to the churches was not sufficient to keep their growth proportionate to that of the population. During that decade the population of Scotland increased by 11.2 per cent. The communicants in the United Presbyterian Church increased by only 4.7 per cent. The communicants in the Free Church increased by 9.3 per cent. Those in the established Church of Scotland, which was the least cordial of the three to Moody's work, increased by 18.1 per cent. The average for the three denominations was 10.7 per cent or .5 per cent less than the rate of population growth. It was significant also that this report pointed out that the United Presbyterian and Free Church increases, unlike those of the Church of Scotland, took place almost entirely in the suburbs and better class neighborhoods of the large cities.[49]

That the urban churches of Scotland were, on the whole, in just as serious a plight after Moody's meetings as before seems unquestionable. In 1879 one of the elders of the Free Church

48 These statistics are taken from the *United Presbyterian Church: Reports Presented by the Home Secretary to the Synod,* published in Edinburgh from 1874 to 1878, Robert S. Scott, Home Secretary, compiler.

49 See James Rankin, *A Handbook of the Church of Scotland,* 4th ed. (Edinburgh, 1888), pp. 374–75.

in Glasgow made an analysis of the position of his denomination in that city "from a commercial and practical point of view." He quoted facts and figures to show that almost all of the 70 Free Church buildings in Glasgow were "less than half filled" each Sunday, and indicated that it would be only sensible and economical to dispense with the 22 weakest of these and consolidate the churchgoers into the remainder. When his paper was read to the assembled elders of the Glasgow Free Churches, several of them took deep offense and insisted that it was not right to consider religion from the commercial point of view. "Some of the objectors said that if we had an outpouring of the Spirit, our churches would soon be filled." To this the author of the report replied, "Undoubtedly we had such a blessing when Mr. Moodie [*sic*] was here lately, the results of which, however great in other directions, have not manifested themselves in filling our half-empty churches." What was more, the author claimed that the Free Church, which had been by far the most prominent in support of Moody, was in a worse plight in Glasgow than either the United Presbyterian or the Church of Scotland.[50]

More significant than these statistics, however, were some of the comments written later, or which went unnoticed at the time, regarding the class of persons who were seen at the meetings or who joined the churches afterward. Moody's son and official biographer reported of Moody's meetings in the south and east of London which were supposed to be especially designed to reach the slum dwellers, "Many came from other parts of London and Moody was disappointed in finding that the class in attendance was more respectable than he had anticipated."[51] George Adam Smith wrote that "Among the large numbers who were certified as adhering to the Mission, there was a proportion of the comfortable class who spent their leisure in running from meeting to meeting" in London and elsewhere.[52]

Moody himself was reported in the newspapers as saying in London, "It's time for Christians to stop coming here and crowding into the best seats. It's time for 'em to go out among

[50] *The Position of the Free Church of Scotland in Glasgow and Suburbs from a Commercial and Practical Point of View* (Glasgow, 1877).

[51] W. R. Moody, *Moody* (1930), p. 221.

[52] George Adam Smith, *Drummond*, p. 98.

these sailors and drunkards and bring them in. . . ." And when crowds from Agricultural Hall followed him to the east side, wrote one early biographer, Moody looked down at the "too amiable" and "too well dressed" assemblage and realized "that he was failing to attract a suitable proportion of the poor and wicked into his meeting." "I see too many Christian people here," Moody told his Bow Road Hall audience one night, "I know you. A great many of you were at my meetings in Islington. You are converted already. Now, I want you to get up and go out and leave room for the hundreds of those sinners who are waiting outside for a chance to come in and hear the Gospel." [53] But those waiting outside were exactly like those sitting inside. The Rev. Charles Edginton, rector of the Anglican parish in which Bow Road Hall was located, wrote to the London *Times* that whenever he attended the meetings there he "saw but very few of the working class." He doubted whether Moody had any effect at all upon "the masses" and described the congregations as consisting of "ordinary church and chapel goers, clergymen, dissenting ministers, and visitors from the country who were attracted by the novelty" of the meetings.[54]

One of the principal proofs offered by those who claimed that Moody did reach the masses was a report by Horatius Bonar of one of Moody's meetings for men only at the Edinburgh Corn Exchange near the Grassmarket slums. The meeting on December 28, 1873, was attended by 6000 persons, and at its conclusion Moody asked all those who wished to have further conversation with him about their souls to follow him from the Corn Exchange to the Free Church Assembly Hall in the upper part of town. According to Bonar, "Six hundred of the Grassmarket men streamed up from the Corn Exchange and into the Assembly Hall and falling on their knees gave themselves to God." Bonar of course assumed that the 600 men were from the ranks of the poor and wicked, the dregs of Edinburgh society.[55] But another minister who assisted at these meetings took issue with Bonar's statement. "What a pity that Christians should exaggerate like that and give the enemy cause

[53] See W. R. Moody, *Moody* (1930), p. 224; W. H. Daniels, *D. L. Moody*, p. 366.

[54] London *Times*, June 22, 1875, p. 8.

[55] Edinburgh *Daily Review*, January 2, 1874, p. 8.

to ask incredulously, Where were your 600 Corn Exchange converts when the converts' farewell meeting was held? . . . A similar band of men, 400 strong, came up from the Corn Exchange on a subsequent Sunday evening, and filled the body of the Assembly Hall; and to an outsider and onlooker they would have appeared to be 400 anxious inquirers, but on being tested at the close (as was done) they were found to be mostly Christian men—many of them helpers in the work; and it turned out that there was not a score of anxious souls amongst them." As far as this observer was concerned, Bonar's claim was "preposterous." The 600 men whom he had seen were merely the Christian workers who had marched to the slums to see Moody reach the poor and then marched back again to assert anew their dedication to religion.[56]

Moody was also credited with having been particularly effective in reaching respectable young men and women who were drifting into infidelity and atheism. But one minister describing the "anxious" young ladies in the inquiry rooms in Edinburgh said, "I could judge from their Bibles that were well marked, that they were not careless persons, but probably Christians who would not like to commit themselves by saying they were 'saved.' . . ." [57] A report in *The Christian* by the Rev. George Wilson shortly after Moody left Edinburgh stated, "Here again we have to point out that the majority of young men impressed, and to all appearances gathered in, were intelligent, well-educated, and some of them highly cultivated. It was no rare thing to find a young man in the inquiry room with his Greek Testament upon his knee waiting to be spoken to about his own misery and the way of salvation. . . ." [58] Their misery was not that they were drifting away from the church but that they had been striving too hard to get close to it. Moody provided them with just the excitement and fervor they needed to feel that at last they had obtained the faith they had so long sought.

Four months after Moody left Edinburgh and several weeks after he had left Glasgow, a little-publicized report was made by the Committee on Religion and Morals of the Free Church.

[56] *Narrative of Messrs. Moody's and Sankey's Labours,* p. 31.
[57] *Ibid.,* p. 17.
[58] *The Christian,* January 29, 1875, p. 3.

It summarized a detailed investigation of the effects of the revival in both Edinburgh and Glasgow by saying, "The blessing has fallen chiefly on those who may be called the church-going portion of the community and on the youth of both sexes under instruction. . . . As to any check given to open immorality and wickedness little can be said. The movement has not reached much beyond the outwardly decent church-going part of the community, and therefore little effect has been produced on the masses among whom ignorance and open wickedness abound and abide. From the large towns especially it is reported that notwithstanding the numerous crowded meetings and the impression made on many, the masses have not been reached, and there is no perceptible change in their moral condition." [59] Even Horatius Bonar eventually admitted that "the great meetings in the capital of Scotland were not attended by the 'masses' but by the better orders of people." "This work has been not so much among the profane and godless as among the children of godly parents." [60]

But all of these negative aspects of the meetings were ignored in the excitement. This was largely because of the very favorable reports of a few of the more energetic and hard working pastors who had been prime movers in the revival in their cities and who had gathered forty or fifty new members into their already popular churches and increased their Sunday schools and Bible classes proportionately. These were the ministers who preceded or followed Moody from city to city giving talks on the great work he had done for their churches. These were also the ministers who wrote long letters to the religious journals telling other pastors how they too could reap a rich harvest of souls by cooperating with Moody. The Rev. J. H. Wilson, who with John Kelman had been among the first to ask Moody to come to Edinburgh, reported to the readers of *The Christian* in 1874 that he had admitted eighty new members to his church shortly after Moody left the city. But when writing his autobiography twenty years later Wilson added, "most of them [were] previously connected with the congregation and comparatively few [were] from outside." [61] They were, in other

[59] Quoted in the Edinburgh *Daily Review,* May 23, 1874, p. 6.

[60] *The Christian,* February 6, 1874, p. 16; April 23, p. 11.

[61] *Ibid.,* April 30, 1874, p. 4; J. H. Wilson, *These Forty Years* (Edinburgh, 1894), p. 18.

words, regular churchgoers already. Ministers who read or heard the reports of these pastors at the time, however, convinced themselves that if Moody came to their city he would add fifty to one hundred new members to every congregation. Their disillusionment was typified in a letter of the Rev. A. G. Gowan, pastor of the East End Tabernacle of London, written three months after Moody had concluded his London meetings: "Up to the present time we have received into fellowship thirty-six who attribute their conversion to the services of the Bow Road Hall. About one half of these were not in the habit of attending any place of worship regularly prior to the opening of the Hall. Viewed in one light it were worth while to put up the Hall if *only for them,* but I cannot refrain from saying that thus far the results have greatly disappointed me." [62] If Gowan was disappointed with thirty-six new members, how much more so were the vast majority of the cooperating ministers who received scarcely any additions. Even Newman Hall, one of the most prominent members of the dissenting clergy in London and a staunch supporter of Moody, wrote in 1881, "I hailed that visit [in 1875], took part in it, assisted in the 'inquiry room' and occasionally preached in connection with it. Some of the services were held very near 'Surrey Chapel'; yet out of a membership of one thousand three hundred we have not three who were the fruits of that mission." [63]

But the desire of churchmen in Britain to reach the masses and add great numbers to their communicants' rolls was not the only reason for the eagerness with which Moody was endorsed, nor was it the only measure of his success or failure. Many considered Moody's influence in modernizing the religious procedures of the churches equally important. Moody's methods, said one Scottish clergyman early in 1874, "have led many of us to feel the need of changing somewhat our modes of

[62] A copy of Gowan's letter dated London, November 3, 1875, is among the Moody Papers in the possession of Mrs. Emma Moody Powell of East Northfield, Massachusetts.

[63] Newman Hall, "Revivals," *Christian Monthly and Family Treasury* (London), August, 1881. Hall's article was answered by David MacLaren in the November issue of the same magazine, but even in defending Moody MacLaren had to admit that "there were very few congregations which received large additions to their communicants' roll as the result of the mission." Copies of these articles are among the Moody papers owned by Mrs. Emma Moody Powell, East Northfield, Massachusetts.

operation and of seeking to improve our stereotyped Sabbath services as well as our week day meetings. The people will demand this at our hands all over the country. . . ." Another minister reported that by May, 1874, "New methods of conducting meetings are already finding favor. Some may be in danger of surrendering hastily their individuality and adopting modes of speech and action foreign to them." [64]

There is no doubt that by encouraging members to take a more active part in prayer meetings and in soul winning Moody instilled a new pietistic spirit into the life of many churches. But this new spirit had a double edge, for it inevitably became involved in questions of ecclesiastical order and theological orthodoxy. It was one thing to enliven the church services by introducing hymns to an organ accompaniment and by encouraging lay participation in church services and evangelistic activities. It was quite another thing to challenge the traditional authority of the churches and the clergy. Moody encouraged the former and tried to discourage the latter, but as the whole course of European and American history had demonstrated, there was inherent in evangelical pietism a highly radical potential which it was not entirely in Moody's power to control. Finney's career had recently demonstrated this anew, and to some extent Moody's revivalism in Scotland contained the same elements of revolt against Presbyterian ecclesiasticism and hyper-Calvinism that Finney's had. Only Moody was not Finney, Scotland was not America, and the 1870's were not the 1820's. In the highly charged atmosphere of Scottish theological controversy in 1873, Moody might have produced the spark for a general explosion, but he deliberately dampened it, and the majority of the ministers who supported him had the tactical diplomacy to follow Lyman Beecher's example and bend with the wind. As a result, the evangelical leaders of the Scottish churches managed to keep a firm control over anticlerical tendencies among the laity and over heretical tendencies among the ministry.

In spite of his efforts to avoid controversy, Moody made remarks which were critical of the prevailing state of the churches: "Christianity is dying of respectability," he said.

[64] Edinburgh *Daily Review,* January 12, 1874, p. 5; *The Christian,* May 28, 1874, p. 6.

"Most of the sermons in Scotland are a hundred feet over the heads" of the people, and "I would rather have zeal without knowledge than knowledge without zeal."[65] Such observations inevitably aroused a certain amount of antagonism between anticlericals and hyperclericals. The former defended Moody; the latter attacked him. A heated exchange of letters in the Glasgow *Herald* during the revival there revealed very clearly the issues involved. The first letter, signed "A Clergyman," sounded almost exactly like the attacks of the Hopkinsians and Princetonians upon Finney. It began by deploring "the position in the churches which the American brethren have come to occupy. Virtually and for the time being they have superseded the pastors in this city." It went on to deprecate the fact that "Night by night in one of the city churches, the young men meet together to strengthen and encourage each other and to receive their instructions and their marching orders from the leaders whom they delight to recognize. And I suppose we shall soon have a well-organized band of unordained and unauthorized preachers going forth on their evangelistic crusade without the slightest misgiving in regard to their calling . . . it is clear that we are on the very eve of the introducing of grave disorders." The results, said this Scottish Nettleton, might well be "schism" and "the loosening of bonds between ministers and people," or at least a state of mind in which "the ordinances of the Church are of small account and ministers of no account at all." "The life born of such excitement will have great difficulty in surviving in the cold atmosphere of our work-a-day world. Is there no danger of so identifying Christian life with prayer meetings and evangelistic meetings and meetings of associations for the conversion of young men as to conclude that these are its highest fruits? How are we to let down from the fever heat of these meetings to the quiet, old-fashioned manifestations of the Christian life such as faithfulness in business, brotherly kindness, gentleness, goodness, meekness, respect for constituted authority, and reverence for those who are over us in the Lord?"[66]

[65] *The Christian,* April 23, 1874, p. 6; *North British Advertiser* (Glasgow) April 18, 1874, p. 4.

[66] Glasgow *Herald,* February 27, 1874, p. 4.

This letter was answered with striking candor by "A Free Church Layman" in the next issue of the paper. "So far as mere churchism is concerned," he began, "those evils pointed out by 'A Clergyman' may possibly follow. But churchism is not Christianity and I have no hesitation in saying that in Scotland we have too long submitted to accept of such clerical doctrine. . . . The Christian people of Scotland have failed to exercise the inherent rights of members of the Christian Church . . . and I hail the present movement as one well fitted to correct many evils which have sprung up unchecked within all our Churches. . . . Nothing that has ever happened in Scotland is so well calculated to teach our clergy the evils of a moribund Church system. I for one hold that the Christian people have a mission and their rallying around those honoured evangelists . . . ought to humble those who assume to themselves a position in the Christian Church such as may be confused with mere ordination without the accompanying evidence of the spiritual call. . . . A blessed day it will be throughout Christendom to get rid forever of all forms of clerical supremacy. . . ." This sentiment was backed up in succeeding letters by other laymen who hailed "the loosening of the bonds of ministerial authority which have too long perverted the spirit of the gospel" and proclaimed "We are all a royal priesthood." [67]

This anticlericalism was intimately connected with the prevailing dissatisfaction with the Westminster Confession and a growing anti-Calvinism in Scotland. Moody had not been in Edinburgh a month before a letter appeared in one of the daily newspapers declaring, "Scotch preaching has for fifty years been little else but a reiteration of doctrines which to me, at least, are unintelligible . . . the whole ingenuity of our preachers has been to convince us that we are the subject of God's wrath and that it is only by believing in a complex theological puzzle . . . that we can gain God's favor and forgiveness." This writer rejoiced, he said, that at last "two strangers [have] come amongst us and sing and recite the declaration of God's goodness and forgiveness." They "believe in God's love" as "the foundation of all Christian strength and health and happiness." Now

[67] *Ibid.*, February 28, 1874, p. 3; March 3, p. 7.

the educated clergy should give up "that complex system they have learned in the theological hall and which has made Christianity a lifeless and meaningless puzzle." [68] The optimistic sentimentalism of Victorian Britain, the middle-class belief in progress and common sense, had produced, as Robert Wallace noted, the same revolt among Scottish churchgoers against the traditions of the elders that the self-reliant optimism of Jacksonian democracy had produced among middle-class churchgoers in America a generation earlier.

Had Moody wished he could have fanned this flame into a holocaust, but he had no such desire. His revivalism was designed to save the church system, not to overthrow it. Moody's evangelical supporters, who were "modern in the best sense," used the pietistic fervor generated by the revival to thwart the die-hard Calvinists on the one hand and the liberals on the other. Like Lyman Beecher, they recognized that the time was ripe for a renovation of the old ecclesiastical system and dogma, and rather than let matters get out of hand they capitulated to the point of ignoring the Westminster Confession and emphasizing a simple orthodoxy based upon the fundamentals. They then directed the pietistic zeal of those awakened by the revival into the familiar moral crusades against intemperance, gambling, prostitution, popery, atheism, and, above all, theological liberalism. Like Beecher also, they preferred not to quarrel directly with the conservatives in their ranks. They hoped to outflank them and gradually convert them to the new doctrinal emphasis in the name of evangelical unity and evangelism.

One of the more ironic sidelights of the revival in Scotland was the fact that the clergymen who invited Moody to Glasgow refused to permit any members of the Evangelical Union, an offshoot from Presbyterianism, to participate officially in the movement because this denomination had frankly abandoned the Westminster Confession as a test of orthodoxy. Moody's supporters pretended not to countenance the open advocacy of free will and free grace. To do so might have turned their conservative colleagues against them and against the revival.[69]

68 *The Scotsman* (Edinburgh) December 18, 1873, p. 6.

69 Part of the irony of this refusal to cooperate with the Evangelical Union was that when Finney had come to Edinburgh and Aberdeen in 1859 he had preached entirely in the churches of that denomination although his theology

Moody probably was unaware of this aspect of the movement and he must have caused his evangelical friends the same kind of anxiety at times that Finney caused Beecher in Boston.

Moody's worst blunder was his failure to make allowance for the deepseated conservatism of the rural Presbyterians of the Scottish Highlands. In Glasgow a report of one of his meetings described him as saying that "From what he had heard there appeared to be two kinds of theology in Scotland—a thing which he could not understand—they had a theology for the Highlands and a theology for the Lowlands, and the theology of the former, as indicated to him by a Highlander, seemed to be that it would take six months before a man could be saved. Why a man might be dead and damned before that. He would rather take the theology of the Bible than any Highland or Lowland theology, for it taught that a man could be saved now—'Now is the accepted time, now is the day of salvation!' There needed to be no weeping and singing and groaning, but just a free and instant acceptance of Christ. . . ." [70] This was coming perilously close to Arminianism. But by relying wholly on the literal words of the Bible, Moody saved himself much of the difficulty that Finney faced in trying to formulate a systematic theology.

In Edinburgh Moody said that "one troubled old woman" had come to him in the inquiry room and said "that she wanted to be saved but did not know if she was elected." Salvation, said Moody, "had nothing more to do with election than with the laws of China." [71] All who mentioned the doctrine of election were referred to Acts 13:39: "By Him all that believe are justified from all things from which ye could not be justified by the law of Moses." This usually astonished the more simple-minded of the Highlanders and others who had been brought up on the Shorter Catechism. "Is that all? Have I only to believe it?" they asked. "Yes," they were told. "Then I do believe!" "Then God says you are justified from all

---

was much closer to Calvinism than Moody's. Finney admitted, however, that he did not agree with the views of the Evangelical Unionists in regard to election and faith and he was unhappy over the fact that because he spoke under their auspices he could not get the cooperation of the other Presbyterian denominations. Finney, *Memoirs,* pp. 455–58.

[70] Glasgow *Herald,* March 2, 1874, p. 4.

[71] Edinburgh *Daily Review,* January 8, 1874, p. 3.

things." [72] The more sophisticated conservatives preferred not to argue over the niceties of Scriptural interpretation as long as Moody was saving souls, and Moody's evangelical friends blandly denied that they found anything contrary to the Westminster Confession in Moody's preaching.

The Rev. William Arnot, for example, one of Moody's ardent Free Church supporters in Edinburgh, maintained that there was no conflict between Calvinism and Moodyism. He told a group of English Presbyterians that the revival "did not change our creed at all." But then he went on to say, as if he were not contradicting the common interpretation of the Confession in regard to the limited atonement, "there is one notion that seems to have been changed and overturned; formerly, for the most part, in Scotland, we were of the persuasion that Christ came to receive the saints, but now we have become convinced that 'this Man receiveth sinners.' " [73] The Rev. George Craig, a pastor of the Evangelical Union, regarded such explanations as mere sophistry. He believed that the revival would make it obvious to all that the Westminster Confession had been abandoned by those Presbyterians who supported Moody: "The republican indifference to forms displayed in this movement, and the call to large audiences to make up their minds to be saved there and then . . . is certain to set young men thinking. . . . May not the comparison of the free offers [of salvation] from the pulpit with the words of the Confession of Faith . . . have something to do with the loss of respect" many are showing toward religion? [74]

A Unitarian observer in Glasgow noted even more satirically, "It is high time for the believers in the Standards to come to their rescue. Chapter iii of the Confession of Faith says plainly enough that some men and angels are 'pre-ordained to everlasting death' and that the number of these 'is so certain and definite that it cannot be either increased or diminished.' And yet here we are watching stairheads, waylaying even strangers in the streets, frightening girls and young men out of their wits with fear of hell, and all in order to rescue souls and

72 *Narrative of Messrs. Moody's and Sankey's Labours,* p. 12.

73 *The Christian,* May 28, 1874, p. 7.

74 Glasgow *Herald,* February 28, 1874, p. 3. See also Craig's letter in the same, March 7, 1874, p. 3.

'pluck them as brands from the burning.' It may be all proper and necessary but in the meantime Calvinism is in abeyance and the Standards are hauled down. Theologically this country seems to be in a wonderful muddle. What would the Westminster divines think if they could see George Gilfallen and Mr. Kidston, Dr. Caird and Dr. Begg, Dr. Tulloch and Dr. Jameson accepting the same standards and all of them accepting the aid of Moody and Sankey?" [75]

But there was a good reason why the moderate and the conservative Presbyterians, the evangelicals and the hyper-Calvinists, preferred to pretend that there was no conflict between the Westminster Confession and what Moody called "the old gospel truths" (or "Bible Christianity," or "the essentials"). It was the same reason which caused the question of disestablishment to fall into the background after 1875. This was the fear of the liberals within the church. The liberals were those who believed that both Calvinism and Moodyism were in conflict with the latest scientific and scholarly research. They believed that a literal interpretation of the Bible, whether it led to the Westminster Confession or an orthodoxy of the fundamentals, was equally out of step with the times and a hindrance to the cause of Christian faith.

That Moody had no use for these liberals was clear from the dogmatic manner in which he stated his belief in the literal infallibility of the Bible on every occasion. He devoted an entire Bible lecture in Edinburgh to the subject, "The Scripture Cannot Be Broken." In this address he said, "If there was one portion of the Scripture untrue, the whole of it went for nothing." Moody went on, said the report of this lecture, "to 'make the Bible prove itself that it is true.' He condemned the unbelief of men who go digging up from the bowels of the earth old carcasses and trying to make them testify against God. He thought it the work of the devil." His proof of the infallibility of Scripture was simple. "He proceeded to point to the prophecies that occur in the Old Testament and to their fulfillment as recorded in later portions of the same or in the new. He dwelt particularly on those that foretold the coming of the Saviour." [76]

[75] *Ibid.*, March 7, 1874, p. 3.
[76] Edinburgh *Daily Review*, January 10, 1874, p. 3.

One liberal retorted to this assault, "The revivalists . . . shut their eyes to the beauty of the world, to the progress of mankind, to the revelations of science. . . ." A university student who went to hear Moody's sermon on "The Blood" came away appalled by the anti-intellectualism expressed in it: "Mr. Moody has spoken and all the results of modern science, critical and experimental, must be blotted out. . . . Men must not ask questions but believe as Mr. Moody tells them. . . . Our professors must be cashiered as dangerous men, the universities must be dedicated to universal ignorance . . . civilization must be rolled back 2000 years. Mr. Moody . . . has swallowed Jonah and his whale and we must do the same." [77]

That Moody's revivals helped to produce a major realignment in the religious life of Scotland was evident by the speeches made during the Christian Convention which he called in Glasgow at the conclusion of his meetings there. Principal Patrick Fairbairn of the Glasgow Free Church College began by telling the assembled lay and pastoral delegates how glad he was to see that the doctrines which were the basis of the revival were the old fashioned scriptural doctrines which they all loved so well: "They are not . . . the doctrines of what are called the advanced things of our day." Fairbairn then launched into an attack on those modernized versions of theology by which Christianity was "turned into a philosophy . . . adapted to some cultured minds." His speech was followed by that of the Rev. R. T. Jeffrey who declared that "It was time the Church should know and act on the principle that every Christian was a commissioned evangelist. . . ." The Rev. Mr. Hurditch said that "What was wanted in these days was 'button-hole theology'—the theology that took hold of a man and going straight to the point asked him 'Have you found Christ?'" These remarks were vigorously applauded by the 2000 churchmen who had come to Glasgow from all over the British Isles to learn the secret of Moody's success. They particularly applauded a paper by Archibald Charteris in which he said that "From this movement we have learned that union is strength. Our petty aims, our sectarian divisions, our con-

[77] Glasgow *Herald,* March 20, 1874, p. 6; March 31, p. 7.

gregationalism, our denominationalism had been falling away that we might be united in prayer and work."[78]

The new interdenominational unity in Britain, however, might more accurately have been described as the unity of all the evangelical conservatives against all the liberals. Moody was the right man at the right hour for those who opposed "the advanced things of the day" and who preferred to divert attention from the difficult religious and social problems in order to concentrate upon personal regeneration. But he was not the right man for the future prosperity of British religious life as a whole. The pyrrhic victory which Moody's friends won in ousting Robertson Smith from his professorship because he was too liberal was the beginning of a long decline in the prestige and support of evangelical Protestantism in Britain. When Moody returned to England and Scotland in 1881 for what was planned as a second triumphal tour, his failure to arouse the interest or enthusiasm of the public was attributed by one of his sons directly to the "change over the whole Church in Great Britain" which resulted from "the famous heresy trial of Robertson Smith" and its aftermath.[79]

This aftermath was described by one Scottish historian as "a division between scholarship and religion in the very life-blood of the Church." After the success of the fundamentalists against Smith, "The more cultured and thoughtful laymen" of Scotland "ceased to be interested" in religion. The churches fell into the hands of "new lay magnates" who were "men of large purses and small minds" and "who had all been more or less infected with the new brand of religiosity that had been brought from America by Moody and Sankey and whose avowed purpose was to convert the Free Church into a permanent evangelistic mission."[80] This was not entirely correct, for a few

[78] *Ibid.*, April 17, 1874, p. 7. Moody's revivals in Scotland undoubtedly deserved credit as a catalytic agency in the modifications of the Westminster Confession formally voted by the United Presbyterian Church in 1879, the Free Church in 1892, and the Church of Scotland in 1910 (the Church of Scotland had ceased to require licentiates to subscribe to all details of the Westminster Confession in 1889). See G. D. Henderson, *The Claims of the Church of Scotland* (London, 1951), p. 50.

[79] Paul Moody, *My Father*, p. 180.

[80] Donald Carswell, *Brother Scots* (London, 1927), p. 119. For a similar view see George Adam Smith, *Drummond*, p. 99.

men like Henry Drummond and George Adam Smith, who had been influenced by Moody, stood up for Robertson Smith and remained interested and active in the life of the churches and even in Moody's type of evangelism. But such influence as Drummond and George Adam Smith exerted upon the younger and more thoughtful minds of Britain was largely the result of their adopting views of religion which were very similar to those of Robertson Smith.

Moody himself was only indirectly to blame. He was not interested in playing church politics nor in heresy trials. He was not as bigoted as he sometimes sounded. For him the important outcome of his meetings in Britain was the recognition that he had found a new vocation. After 1875 he gave less attention to his YMCA work, his Chicago Church, his Sunday school conventions. He had taken up the mantle of Finney as America's foremost revivalist. His campaigns in British cities acquainted him with the problems of uniting the churches and reaching the unchurched. They demonstrated that, with the proper means and management, urban mass evangelism was a feasible enterprise. It took planning, organization, publicity, vast sums of money, a host of workers, skillful executive direction—in short, all the techniques and facilities of any big business. In 1875 Moody was as surely the rising young tycoon of the revival trade as Andrew Carnegie was of the steel trade or John D. Rockefeller of oil. America welcomed him home on precisely those terms.

CHAPTER 5

"Old-Fashioned Revival with the Modern Improvements"

When Moody and Sankey stepped off the ocean liner in New York on August 14, 1875, they were met by a flock of reporters and a dozen prominent churchmen representing the enthusiastic interest of thousands of curious and admiring countrymen. The reporters wanted to hear of their past success and present opinions. The church committees wanted to engage their services for future revivals. Some cities had already obtained general commitments from Moody in London. During the next two months, while Moody rested at his mother's home in Northfield, committees representing the pastors and laymen of the largest cities in the nation waited upon him and jockeyed for the honor of a high priority on his proposed itinerary.

To all such invitations Moody set two conditions. The first was "that there must be unity of opinion in Evangelical churches" to support the revival in any city seeking his help. The second was that no time limit should be set on the duration of the revival.[1] Upon this latter condition, however, he soon had to compromise. At first Moody told all applicants, "I don't know where the first meetings will be held. I am waiting to see where I am led." He was certain that it was best to start in the largest cities, but he wanted to be sure that he would have the cooperation and assistance which he knew was essential to such a vast business enterprise.

[1] *New York Times,* September 16, 1875, p. 2; September 26, p. 12.

The zealous invitation proffered on behalf of the Brooklyn community by his old friend, the Rev. Theodore Cuyler, finally persuaded Moody that this city was the most ripe for an awakening. As Moody put it, "the feeling is stronger in Brooklyn than elsewhere."[2] He agreed to start there on October 31, 1875, and Cuyler commenced the preparations early in October. This decision greatly upset the delegations from New York, Philadelphia, Boston, and Chicago, some of which had been dickering with Moody since the start of the London meetings. The Philadelphia group, led by John Wanamaker, George H. Stuart, and W. P. Breed, frankly told Moody that unless he held his meetings in Philadelphia that autumn the revival would be a failure because the Centennial Exposition celebrating the Declaration of Independence was scheduled to begin there in January, 1876. This, said the Philadelphia churchmen, would provide too great a counterattraction to the revival for Moody to overcome. Besides, Philadelphia had already lined up two hundred ministers behind the movement and had started work on a tabernacle in which to hold the meetings.[3]

This note of urgency impressed Moody. He wrote to Cuyler at once and telegraphed to the Philadelphia committee, "I have asked Brooklyn to let me off. I will commence in Philadelphia on October 31, God willing." But the Brooklyn committee refused to let him off. His only alternative was to limit the Brooklyn revival to three weeks and commence in Philadelphia on November 21.[4] William E. Dodge, chairman of the committee which wanted Moody to hold his American debut in New York, was unhappy about this. Dodge, the son of David L. Dodge, had been on hand in New York in 1827 when his father and his father-in-law, Anson G. Phelps, had invited Finney to that city. Trying to carry on the family tradition, he brought pressure on Moody to set an early terminal date for the Philadelphia meetings so that the New York revival could get under way by February, 1876. This put the Chicago committee off until late in 1876. Boston, Baltimore, Cleveland, St. Louis, and San Francisco had to wait even longer.

2 *Christian Advocate* (Methodist-Episcopal, New York), October 14, 1875, p. 325.

3 *New York Times*, October 5, 1875, p. 12; October 9, p. 1; October 12, p. 5.

4 *Ibid.*, October 12, 1875, p. 5; *Christian Advocate*, October 21, 1875, p. 333.

The reasons for this eager solicitation of Moody were similar to those which had made him the man of the hour in Britain. "There never was a time when a higher sense of the value of moral and Christian obligations was so necessary as it is now," wrote the New York *Tribune*. The corruptions of the Grant administration, the Tweed Ring exposure, the financial manipulations of Jay Gould, Jim Fisk, and various railroad barons were proof that "our politics are sordid and corrupt" and "our business principles are wanting in businessmen." [5] Many also believed that a "religious spirit" had been "lately aroused" in America as a result of "the general trade and business depression. . . ." [6]

The *New York Times*, which had ridiculed Moody and Sankey while they were in London, calling them "vulgar," "coarse," and ignorant fanatics, completely reversed itself shortly after their return. It now hailed them as a potential counterforce to secularism and "indifferentism." "In an age when the teachers of infidelity are so numerous and so active," said the *Times*, "the exertions of these two gentlemen to bring home to what is called the common mind the truths of Christianity deserve the warmest sympathy and encouragement." [7] A Methodist journal in Baltimore thought Moody's greatest asset was his ability to give the lie to those "sons of Belial," "the Tyndalls, the Huxley's and other scientists of the day to whom all eyes were directed. . . ." Surely it was providential, said this journal, that Moody appeared in England just at this hour so that "These proud sons of science . . . were swept away and hid in oblivion by a poor, unlettered evangelist. . . ." [8]

One remarkable aspect of the widespread endorsement of Moody and Sankey was the extent to which it pervaded the secular as well as the religious press. Finney seldom received attention from the secular newspapers of his day, nor were there four hundred religious journals in the country then looking for copy. It was also remarkable that endorsements of Moody cut across all denominational lines and all types of ministers from Phillips Brooks to T. DeWitt Talmage, from James McCosh

[5] Quoted in W. R. Moody, *D. L. Moody* (New York, 1930), p. 254.

[6] *Ibid.*, p. 254.

[7] *New York Times*, July 5, 1875, p. 1; February 12, 1876, quoted in W. R. Moody, *Moody* (1930), p. 265.

[8] *The Southern Review* (Methodist, Baltimore), XIX (January, 1875), 192.

to Henry Ward Beecher. Moody was praised by those who were soon to be labelled social gospelers, like Stephen H. Tyng, Jr., Henry Codman Potter, Lyman Abbott, and R. Heber Newton, as well as by those who were to fight some of the early battles of fundamentalism, like Charles Hodge, A. J. Gordon, A. T. Pierson, and A. C. Dixon. Only the Roman Catholics, Unitarians, and Universalists remained aloof or critical. No one knew exactly what Moody's denominational background was and none cared. It did not even seem to matter that he and Sankey were not ordained. In fact, many considered this an advantage.

In an article on "Evangelists and Lay-Exhorters," published in the *Presbyterian Quarterly and Princeton Review* (the successor to the *Biblical Repertory and Theological Review* which had so abused Finney) the Rev. J. M. P. Ott, like Lord Shaftesbury, called Moody "the right man in the right place." Ott asserted that although Moody was a layman, "We believe that Mr. Moody . . . is constructively ordained to the work of an evangelist by the general consent of the holy Catholic Church" and that "there is just as truly the authority of ordination in his ministry as ever there was in the ministry of John Calvin and John Knox." Since Edinburgh and Glasgow had given Moody their imprimatur, Ott continued, "Presbyterians ought to be very well satisfied with Messrs. Moody and Sankey. They are more than satisfied; they rejoice in their work and thank God for giving such workmen to the church and the world." [9] Modern revivalism received its ultimate seal of approval in America when Princeton's President, James McCosh, together with Professor Charles Hodge, personally persuaded Moody to sandwich a week of meetings for the Princeton students in between his Philadelphia and New York revivals in 1876.

A large part of this wholehearted interdenominational support for Moody was the result of a growing sense of urgency felt in America, as in Britain, over the problem of "the unchurched masses" in the cities. As American home missionary activity began to shift its emphasis from the frontier to the city, Moody's methods seemed to offer a quick and easy system to meet the new need. The religious climate and facilities of the

[9] J. M. P. Ott, "Evangelists and Lay Exhorters," *Presbyterian Quarterly and Princeton Review,* XLIX (April, 1877), 305–6.

1870's made possible revivalistic endeavors far beyond Finney's dreams. Growing interdenominational unity, the general acceptance of modern revivalism, the rise of lay influence, improved methods of communications and transportation, the multiplication of inexpensive newspapers and magazines, and the increased literacy provided the general means for promoting and coordinating urban mass evangelism on a large scale. Moody may never have read Finney's *Lectures on Revivals,* but its principles were common knowledge by 1875, and his revivals were promoted throughout according to Finney's experimental laws of the mind and the right use of means. An editorial in the *Nation* aptly remarked of Moody's New York meetings in 1876, "The Moody and Sankey services are an old-fashioned revival with the modern improvements." [10]

In 1879 Professor George P. Fisher of Yale Seminary said of Moody's work that in observing "The machinery of revivals . . . one is sometimes reminded of the arts and devices of the political campaign." [11] But most observers compared Moody's efficient methods to those of big business. The *Unitarian Review,* for example, which criticized Moody's "somewhat coarse and commercial conception of Christianity," nevertheless stated of his Boston revival in 1877, "The thorough organization and clear business sense in this movement are to be admired." [12]

Moody's lay and clerical friends in each city usually took the first steps in arranging for a revival. They approached the leading evangelical pastors and citizens of their city and persuaded them to sign an invitation to Moody pledging their cooperative support. Moody was once asked what a church should do if its trustees opposed revivalism. Like Finney, he answered, "Pray the opposition out of the trustees or the trustees out of office, being very sure to put converted men in their places." [13] While individual support was being collected privately among ministers and laymen likely to add prestige to the movement, interested clergymen rose in their ministerial or denomina-

[10] *The Nation* (New York), XXII (March 9, 1876), 156–57. The editorial was written by A. G. Sedgwick.

[11] George P. Fisher, "Recent Evangelistic Movements," *The New Englander,* XXXVIII (January, 1879), 40.

[12] "Mr. Moody at the Tabernacle," *Unitarian Review* (Boston), IV (March, 1877), 315–19.

[13] *Christian Advocate,* May 4, 1876, p. 139.

tional associations to urge resolutions pledging the full cooperation of the group to Moody should he come. When a sufficiently widespread desire for a revival had been expressed, a special delegation of the most influential churchmen wrote or visited Moody, obtained his acceptance, and fixed an opening date for the meetings.

An executive committee of fifteen or twenty prominent ministers and laymen took charge of the preparatory work. They appointed chairmen for various subcommittees, each charged with a specific task: a finance committee to raise and expend the funds, a prayer committee to select a place for the noon prayer meetings in a downtown church and to put the rank and file to work to pray for the success of the meetings, a home visitation committee, a committee to select and train ushers and choir members, and usually committees for charitable work, temperance, Bible study, and ticket arrangement. One of the more important committees was the publicity committee. "A generous part" of $40,000 was spent for posters and newspaper announcements in the Philadelphia revival.[14] When objections were raised to the use of commercial advertising in connection with religious work, Moody remarked, "Some ministers think it undignified to advertise their services. It is a good deal more undignified to preach to empty pews, I think." [15]

Prominent businessmen always headed the finance and executive committees. The chairmen of the other committees were usually ministers. The workers in the committees were local church members and the staff of the YMCA, for in this era the YMCA considered promoting revivals a more important aspect of its work than providing recreation for its members. Choir members were chosen from the local church choirs. Usually 600 to 1000 persons were selected and then were divided into two or three groups which sang on alternate evenings at the meetings. They were taught Sankey's gospel songs and trained to start any hymn with an introduction of only a single chord on the organ. The ushers, numbering from 100 to 200, were cleancut, churchgoing young men who eagerly sought the privilege of wearing a red or blue ribbon and carrying a tall wooden pole, called a "wand," which were their badges

[14] W. R. Moody, *Moody* (1930), p. 256.
[15] *Ibid.*, p. 420.

of office. They were instructed in how to handle unruly crowds politely, how to care for fainting women, and how to silence crying children. In Philadelphia, John Wanamaker, a member of Moody's executive committee, required all the salesmen in his store to act as ushers.[16] The "personal workers" in the inquiry rooms were more carefully selected, usually from among the deacons, elders, Sunday school superintendents, and Sunday school teachers. They were trained by one of the pastors in the correct method of dealing with the anxious, a procedure which consisted primarily of learning which texts in the Bible could be quoted to answer various types of spiritual doubt or objections to immediate salvation. All this preparation took weeks of work in advance of Moody's arrival.

Of especial importance in each city were the site, size, and facilities of the hall in which the meetings were to be held. Except in Scotland, where the predominance of Presbyterianism obviated the problem, Moody preferred in his early years as an evangelist not to hold his meetings in churches. He did so first because this might have led to charges of sectarianism and second because none of the churches were large enough. The Brooklyn committee renovated an indoor skating rink to hold 6000 persons, and the local street car company laid extra tracks up to it. In Philadelphia John Wanamaker donated the use of a former railroad freight depot which he had recently purchased to convert into a store. Wanamaker supervised and paid for the renovations enabling it to seat 11,000. He was accused by some critics of using Moody's meetings as a means of advertising the new store. P. T. Barnums' Hippodrome at Madison Avenue and 26th Street was selected by the New York executive committee. It was divided into two halls, one holding 6500 and the other 4000 for overflow meetings. No convenient building was available in Boston so the revival committee there raised funds to build a brick "tabernacle" in the Back Bay area capable of seating 6000 with standing room for 1000. The Chicago tabernacle held 6000 to 8000 and was designed and built by John V. Farwell, who shrewdly gave it a basement and two-story wall of permanent construction so that after the meetings he could convert it into a "first-class wholesale business house."

[16] H. A. Gibbons, *John Wanamaker* (New York, 1926), Vol. I, p. 133.

All of these "tabernacles" were arranged to provide adequate space for inquiry rooms within easy access of the main meeting room. The interiors of the buildings were decorated with signs bearing Biblical texts, such as "Now Is the Appointed Time." In Chicago the words "God Is Love" were formed by gas lights above the platform. The platform in each was constructed to hold not only the hundreds of choir singers but also a large number of ministers, committee members, and local dignitaries who gave the proceedings a tone of respectability and authority as well as providing an interesting spectacle. Of the 11,000 seats in the Philadelphia tabernacle 1,304 were on the platform.

In the center of the platform a small projection with a low railing around it held Moody's lectern and Bible. Nearby was the cabinet organ on which Sankey accompanied the choir and his own solos. Accommodations for the newspaper reporters was provided on the platform. Wanamaker supervised the installation of an elaborate speaking-tube and telegraphic network in the Philadelphia building which enabled Moody to give signals to ushers, doorkeepers, and other personnel from a switchboard panel near his lectern.[17]

The vastness of these undertakings required sums of money far beyond the ordinary budgets of the churches themselves. Only the generous cooperation of wealthy men could float such

[17] For details of the Philadelphia meetings, see L. A. Loetscher, "Presbyterianism and Revivalism in Philadelphia since 1875," *Pennsylvania Magazine of History and Biography*, LXVIII (January, 1944), 56 ff. The care with which Moody watched over these preparations was illustrated by a letter he wrote to Wanamaker in 1896 in answer to an invitation to return to Philadelphia for another revival:

East Northfield
October 9, [1896]

My dear Wanamaker—

Nearly a quarter of a century ago I left your city with what I called and thought a good work behind me, and not until last Saturday have I had what I call a good invitation to go back. I have had a good many for some one church but nothing that would lay hold of the city as a city. Now I would like to know all about the Hall and where it is and if the people could get to it without any trouble and can 6000 be heard or can they hear my voice and can I have a committee of business men like what I had in 1875. I think I would be inclined to look over the field if there is a fair chance.

(signed) D L. Moody

A copy of this letter is in the personal files of John Wanamaker, which are located in the Wanamaker Store in Philadelphia.

enterprises. Consequently the laymen tended to take the most prominent part on Moody's committees. Few ministers could fail to join a movement led by Cyrus McCormick and George Armour in Chicago, Jay Cooke and John Wanamaker in Philadelphia, Cornelius Vanderbilt II and J. P. Morgan in New York, Amos A. Lawrence and Joseph Story in Boston.[18] These men did not consider the expense of the revivals exorbitant. The London meetings cost over $140,000; the Chicago meetings, $70,000; the Boston meetings, $42,000; the Philadelphia meetings, $50,000; the New York meetings, over $30,000. The average expenses per week in a big city were more than $5000.[19]

In most cities itemized accounts of these expenses, duly audited, were published by the finance committees at the conclusion of the meetings. Invariably the tabernacle constituted the principal expense. The Boston building cost $32,000; the Chicago tabernacle, $21,000; the Hippodrome, $10,000 to renovate plus $1500 per week for rent for ten weeks and $4000 for chairs; John Wanamaker renovated the Philadelphia "Depot Church" at a cost of $20,000 out of his own pocket.[20] The itemized account of the Boston expenses explained the various expenditures involved.

[18] Also prominent in support of Moody in Philadelphia were A. J. Drexel, George W. Childs, John R. Whitney, George H. Stuart. For a more complete list of Moody's New York supporters, see below. His backers in Chicago can be seen from the list of those who contributed to the expenses of the revival and to support the YMCA (solicited by Moody as part of his campaign in that city): A. M. Billings, $5000; J. V. Farwell, $5000; R. C. Morgan (of London), $2500; Henry Field, $2500; George Armour, $2500; H. J. Welling, $2500; T. W. Harvey, $1000; W. A. Fuller, $1000; D. A. Hale, $1000; C. H. McCormick, $1000; J. M. Adams, $1000; William Blair, $1000; H. C. Durand, $1000; Mark Skinner, $1000; Gammon and Deering, Inc., $1000; John Crerar, $1000; Daniel Jones, $1000; Charles P. Kellogg, $1000; Elbridge G. Keith, $1000; C. M. Henderson, $1000; Philander Smith, $4000 (in real estate); O. S. A. Sprague, $500; J. F. Armour, $500; J. and E. Buckingham, $500; D. K. Pearson, $500. Chicago *Daily Tribune,* January 17, 1877, p. 10.

[19] See *New York Times,* September 5, 1875, p. 5; January 22, 1876, p. 1; Chicago *Daily Tribune,* January 17, 1877, p. 10; Boston *Transcript,* January 22, 1877, p. 3; April 11, 1877, p. 5; London *Times,* August 21, 1875, p. 1; W. R. Moody, *Moody* (1930), p. 256. The audited expense account of the Philadelphia revival totalled $29,538, but this did not include the $20,000 which Wanamaker spent to renovate the railroad depot.

[20] See *The Independent,* October 12, 1876, p. 12; F. G. Bearsley, *History of American Revivals* (New York, 1912), p. 271; Elias Nason, *The Lives of the Eminent American Evangelists Dwight Lyman Moody and Ira David Sankey* (Boston, 1877), p. 143.

Rent of land	$ 2,500.00
Entire cost of building	32,000.00
Coal and gas (for heat and light)	1,000.00
Advertising, printing, postage	2,500.00
Hire of halls	850.00
Running expenses for 14 weeks	1,200.00
Extras and incidentals	600.00
Total	$42,250.00 [*sic*] [21]

The money to meet these expenses came for the most part from private donations, though local corporations sometimes gave. A large amount of the money was subscribed in advance and was called a "Guaranty Fund" by the finance committee. In New York the interested laymen signed a joint promissory note stipulating their contributions:

We hereby agree to pay J. Pierpont Morgan, Treasurer, at such times as may be needed, the sums set opposite our respective names as a private 'GUARANTY FUND' to defray the expenses of the religious meetings to be held in New York by Mr. Moody and Mr. Sankey under the terms of the circular of November 30, 1875 with the understanding that any excess of the general subscription is to be returned to us *pro rata* in proportion to the amount we have advanced:

W. E. Dodge	$1000	James Lenox	$ 500
Morris K. Jesup	1000	Anson Phelps Stokes	500
S. I. Prime	500	Alfred C. Post	100
Nathan Bishop	500	Alexander McL. Andrew	500
H. M. and S. B. Schieffelin	500	John Taylor Johnston	100
J. C. Havemeyer	500	John E. Parsons	250
C. C. Colgate	500	R. L. and A. Stuart	1000
W. E. Dodge, Jr.	1000	C. Vanderbilt	1000
D. Willis James	1000	James Stuart	500
Adrien Iselin	500	John Aitken	500
Stewart Brown	500	Fred K. Marquand	500
J. Crosby Brown	500	Bowler Colgate	250
		Eliot S. Shephard	250 [22]

Three weeks after the meetings had started in New York, a notice appeared in the *New York Times* which read, "The expenses of these meetings are large and must be defrayed by private subscription. Contributions can be sent to J. Pierpont Morgan, Esq., No. 23 Wall Street." [23] A similar but somewhat

21 Boston *Evening Transcript,* April 11, 1877, p. 5.

22 A copy of this agreement is on exhibition at the Moody Museum in East Northfield, Massachusetts.

23 *New York Times,* February 28, 1876, p. 5.

more explanatory notice appeared in the Boston *Evening Transcript* during the course of the revival there:

> Previous to the coming of Messrs. Moody and Sankey a comparatively small number of persons were ready to give largely to the prospective expenses. When, however, a sum was secured which the committee felt justified them in going forward, the necessary building was erected in the fullest confidence that the time would come during the progress of the meetings when numbers would be glad to show their gratitude to God for his mercies and blessings to themselves and their friends.

This notice stated that $21,500 was still needed to meet the expenses. "Those who wish to share in this great work" were invited to send "a subscription" to the treasurer of the committee, D. E. Snow.[24]

Another method of raising money was to hold a special dedication ceremony at the tabernacle prior to the revival to which admittance was by special invitation only. Printed on the invitation was the statement, "The person using this ticket is expected to make a freewill offering to the Lord of not less than one dollar toward meeting the expense of this sacred enterprise; or more as God may have given ability." If each member present at the Boston dedication gave three dollars, a member of the committee announced, no further appeals for money would be needed. But of the 8000 envelopes passed out only 2,961 were returned (553 empty) with a total of $2,390.68.[25]

Moody was always proud of advertising that "No Collection" was taken at any of his services, but in Boston the failure of the private subscriptions to meet the deficit forced him to go back on his promise. On the first day of the collections, $7,283.25 was received, $5000 of which came from the noon prayer meeting for downtown businessmen. That night a group of Boston businessmen met at Meionaon Hall and pledged themselves to meet any deficit that still remained.[26]

Still another way in which money was raised was to sell the materials used in building or renovating the meeting halls after

24 Boston *Evening Transcript,* April 11, 1877, p. 5. Among the members of the Boston finance committee who signed this notice were E. R. Mudge, A. J. Gordon, Phillips Brooks, Russell Sturgis, Jr., Joseph Story, and Amos A. Lawrence. For a similar notice for the Philadelphia meetings see W. R. Moody, *Moody* (1930), p. 260.

25 Boston *Evening Transcript,* January 22, 1877, p. 1; January 26, 1877, p. 22; Boston *Daily Advertiser,* January 29, 1877, p. 1.

26 Boston *Evening Transcript,* April 27, 1877, p. 2.

the revival. A notice in the Philadelphia newspapers announcing the need for an additional $9000 to meet the expenses said, "At the close of the meetings the flooring and other lumber fittings, and also the furniture will be sold at public auction for the account of this fund.'" An account of this auction in the Washington *Evening Star* noted that a sofa and chair used by Moody and Sankey in their "retiring room" at the tabernacle "brought prices far above their value." Then "the towels used by the evangelists were taken up. Mr. Shaw handled them in a reverential manner, announcing the great importance attached to them as relics and asked someone to start them. '50¢' cried one of the auditors. '$1' said another. Two, three, four, and finally five dollars apiece was bid for the two used by Mr. Moody and knocked down to a Mr. Johnstone. 'Now,' said the auctioneer, 'I have the towels used by Mr. Sankey. . . .'" Mr. Shaw also managed to auction off the Bible rest, the crimson plush on the pulpit, and the chairs the evangelists had sat upon on the platform.[27]

In several cities, however, there were still deficits facing the committees when the revivals concluded. In Liverpool, England, there was a reported deficit of $8000 and the London audited account showed a deficit of £158 10s.[28] These were doubtless made up by members of the committees. Apparently there were no deficits in the American revivals, but the strain of meeting the expenses had a great deal to do with Moody's decision after 1878 not to use the tabernacle system for his meetings but to speak in the churches. Nevertheless he had set a pattern which later evangelists were to follow regardless of the expense.

With the question of finances bulking so large in his revivals, Moody had to take special care that his own remuneration should not become a matter of public suspicion. The finance committees always stated in their accounts that "There is no expense for the services of the Evangelists." Moody had been embarrassed in Britain by accusations that he and Sankey were agents for American portable organs and Bagster Bibles. His wife described his annoyance when an Edinburgh newspaper

27 Washington *Evening Star,* February 12, 1876, p. 6.

28 *Liberal Christian* (New York), July 3, 1875, p. 12; *New York Times,* September 5, 1875, p. 5.

mentioned the questions of his payment there: "I think on that account," she wrote, "if they give him a present here he will have it sent to the church. It will show them that he is not after their money and do the church good in these hard times." [29]

But the question of finances became even more unpleasant when the Sankey hymnbook, which Moody had persuaded the firm of Morgan and Scott to publish, became such an astounding success. Moody and Sankey accepted the royalties from the early editions of the books for a year or so, but on January 1, 1875, Moody made an agreement with the publisher that all the royalties for the following eight months should be turned over to the London committee to help them defray the expenses of the revival there. Approximately $25,000 accumulated between January 1 and the time Moody left England, but the committee, having met its expenses by subscription, declined to accept it. Moody used the money to pay for the completion of his new church building in Chicago. But still the royalties poured in. Finally Moody decided to set up a trust fund to be administered by his three friends, Farwell, Dodge, and Stuart, which would thereafter receive all the royalties. Of course, the trustees spent the money just as Moody told them to, but neither Moody nor Sankey ever received a penny of it. From 1875 to 1885 the trust dispersed $357,338.64, mostly to YMCA's and other "religious and educational institutions." After 1885 the trust was closed and the income transferred to support the schools which Moody established in Northfield, Massachusetts.[30]

The only fund-raising which Moody engaged in himself at his revivals was for the sake of worthy causes. In London he solicited $200,000 for "an evangelistic building in the West End." In New York, Philadelphia, Chicago, and Boston he raised pledges at his meetings for the YMCA's buildings. The sums raised or pledged in each city respectively were $150,000, $125,000, $85,000, and $50,000.[31]

[29] W. R. Moody, *Moody* (1930), p. 162.

[30] *Ibid.*, pp. 211, 200 ff.

[31] *New York Times*, August 12, 1875, p. 1; January 22, 1876, p. 1; *Christian Advocate*, April 20, 1875, p. 125; Boston *Daily Advertiser*, April 26, 1877, p. 4; W. R. Moody, *Moody* (1930), p. 271; W. H. Daniels, *Moody, His Words, Work, and Workers* (New York, 1877), pp. 53, 55, 60.

Though no publicity was ever given to it, Moody and Sankey did receive honorariums in each city raised privately by the executive or finance committee and handed to the evangelists in an envelope on their departure. The sums were never disclosed but they were sufficient to enable Moody to live securely on the twelve-acre farm he purchased next to his mother's home in Northfield, where he indulged his tastes as a gentleman farmer to his heart's content. At his death he left an estate consisting of this farm, five hundred dollars, and a "modest provision for his wife." [32]

The preparatory work for a revival, apart from the raising of the guarantee fund, was not always efficiently managed by the volunteer church workers, but upon Moody's arrival the movement picked up momentum. "My gift is to get things in motion," he once said. "As he stood on the platform," wrote Lyman Abbott, "he looked like a businessman, he dressed like a businessman; he took the meeting in hand as a businessman would." [33] He was only five feet six inches tall, weighed 280 pounds, and had developed a sizeable paunch by 1875. The Boston *Herald* described him as "stout, short-necked, full-bearded, with a rather unprepossessing head." But it praised his "Common sense, business-like habits, earnestness and tenderness" which "combine in him with a certain shrewdness, wit, and readiness of adaptation not often found among preachers." [34]

Because it was Moody's aim to supplement the work of the churches rather than to center all attention upon himself, he made every effort to schedule the many meetings connected with the revival so as not to interfere with the regular church services.[35] The proceedings for each of his major campaigns

[32] W. R. Moody, *Moody* (1930), p. 468. Paul Moody in his biography of his father describes Moody's experiments on his farm with sheep, bees, peacocks, pheasants, swans, turkeys, pigs, geese, dairying, fruit orchards, and truck farming. He also tells of the equanimity with which Moody bought dozens of custom-made shoes and ties and purchased oriental rugs and oil paintings in bulk. See *My Father* (Boston, 1938), *passim*. See also Moody's letters to his brother George, who acted as manager of the farm, in the Moody Papers owned by Mrs. Emma Moody Powell, East Northfield, Massachusetts.

[33] Lyman Abbott, *Silhouettes of My Contemporaries* (New York, 1921), p. 200.

[34] Boston *Herald*, September 14, 1875, p. 6.

[35] Moody was so devoted to helping the organized churches that he refused to associate with the Salvation Army after a talk with William Booth convinced

followed the same pattern: three meetings were held daily, a morning Inspiration Service at 8 A.M., a noon prayer meeting, and the main preaching service at 7 or 7:30 each evening. There were no meetings on Saturdays, which were Moody's day of rest. On Sundays he preached in the tabernacle at 4 P.M. and 9 P.M. When possible he organized nightly meetings for young men at some church near the tabernacle which he addressed after the evening service. He also held daily meetings for women at the tabernacle following the noon prayer meeting. Ostensibly the purpose of the noon prayer meetings were "to bring the business men under religious influences at the noon hour." Usually there were as many women present as men.

These prayer meetings were one of the most popular features of Moody's revivals, and as he conducted them they were a new departure in revival technique. They began with a hymn and a brief Bible reading and exposition; after that they were opened for requests for prayer and for "testimony." The prayer requests were generally received in writing in advance and were read by Moody from the platform. At one meeting in the New York revival Moody received requests for prayers in behalf of twelve churches, eleven families, and five Sunday schools, for fourteen husbands by their wives, for two drunkards, four infidels, a saloon keeper, a young gambler, and a lady "slave to opium"; for the temperance cause in Ohio, for an infidel editor by his mother, and for twenty-nine individuals who were anxious about their own souls.[36] Often Moody read touching letters accompanying these prayer requests or related some incident appropriate to them illustrating the power of prayer. After the list was read other requests were accepted from the floor. Then Moody led the assemblage in praying for divine help in the fulfillment of these worthy supplications. It was a satisfying way for the pious to spend a lunch hour.

Prayer meetings were given variety by setting aside one each week for reports on "What the Lord is doing" to further the revival. Ministers from local churches told of the number of conversions in their congregations and letters were read from

---

him that the Army was in effect a new denomination. W. R. Moody, *Moody* (1930), pp. 287–88.

36 *New York Times,* November 20, 1876, p. 2.

praying pastors in nearby towns. Individuals who had been saved gave their testimony, usually emphasizing how wicked and miserable they were before and how serene and happy they were now. Each Friday the noon prayer meeting was devoted to Temperance. These were by far the most popular. Reformed drunkards like Charles Sawyer, Carl Irland, and J. H. Shorey followed Moody from city to city to tell of their tragic lives of sin and their sudden redemption by faith. "It was difficult to conceive that what these men said was true," wrote one reporter, "and still more difficult to imagine them as they represented themselves to have been in their past days of degradation." Shorey claimed to have been "the greatest drunkard in New York" for thirty years, yet he was "a fine, honest, frank, manly-looking" fellow. The stories told by these converts "brought tears to the eyes of many present." [37] Such performances were the evangelical churchgoers' substitutes for the drama and catharsis of the theater.

But the main attraction of the revivals was the big meeting in the tabernacle each evening. The crowds, the hymnbook and photograph vendors, the singing, the general hubbub and excitement encouraged many to come to the warm, friendly meetings for a free evening of entertainment which bordered on the secular and yet which was good for the soul. For many regular churchgoers the meetings were social occasions for meeting friends and brightening drab lives. Moody wisely insisted that the advertisements for his meetings be placed on the amusement pages of the newspapers. These advertisements carried Moody's sermon topics for the coming week, and when popular ones were announced such as his famous "Sowing and Reaping," or his sermons on Heaven and Hell, the crowds were exceptionally large.

Special meetings were popular. Children's meetings put Moody in the same camp with E. P. Hammond, and like Hammond he maintained "there is no child too young to be brought to Jesus." Temperance meetings at the tabernacle featured talks by Frances Willard of the WCTU, John B. Gough, and Francis Murphy, as well as by Moody's standard prayer meeting performers. Moody had no use, however, for the signing of temperance pledges. He insisted that only conversion could

[37] Boston *Evening Transcript,* February 3, 1877, p. 4.

save a man from drink. It was his narrowness on this point that forced Frances Willard to break her association with him. He wanted her to concentrate on saving souls, not on the activities of the WCTU, and he ordered her not to appear on any platform with a Unitarian even if it were for the temperance cause.[38]

Occasionally special meetings were held at the tabernacle for businessmen or for the unemployed. The Sunday afternoon meetings were primarily for women and Sunday evenings primarily for men. When Moody received a letter from a prostitute in Chicago who accused him of pandering to society women in his meetings, he promptly set aside a meeting for "Fallen Women." He also went to police headquarters and got the addresses of all the brothels in the city in order that the society women might visit "these places" and try "to lead these poor girls to Christ." [39]

However, these special meetings were not necessary to fill the tabernacle. Moody seldom spoke to less than a packed house in the early years of his career. "The real attraction," according to the London *Times,* was the singing. Moody once said, "The people come to hear Sankey sing and then I catch them in the gospel net." Although Finney's employment of Thomas Hastings in his New York church was similar, Moody was probably the first itinerant evangelist to employ a professional soloist to accompany him from place to place. After 1875 this practice became universal among revivalists.

Ira Sankey's suavity, tact, and bland good looks provided a valuable complement to Moody's gruff and rugged personality. Sankey's mutton-chop whiskers were trimmed in the height of fashion and his carefully fitted frock coat was tailored to disguise his bulging form. He always introduced a solo with a short talk concerning its origin or message and generally prayed briefly that it might enter someone's heart and be the means of bringing him to Christ. In later years people complained that

[38] Ray Strachey, *Frances Willard* (New York, 1913), p. 217. When the WCTU began to advocate woman suffrage as a step toward prohibition laws, Moody declared this "a master stroke of the devil" because it distracted attention from soul winning. Quoted in Gamaliel Bradford, *D. L. Moody: A Worker in Souls* (New York, 1928), p. 220. For Moody's belief that conversion was the only effective cure for intemperance, see Moody, *"To All People,"* pp. 136–37.

[39] W. H. Daniels, *Moody, His Words* (New York, 1877), pp. 441–42.

Sankey talked too much in introducing his solos and there was a general feeling that he had grown vain and pompous with age, but in the 1870's he was thought by many to be the equal of Moody as an evangelist. He often took part in the personal work in the inquiry rooms. It was the custom to advertise Moody's meetings with the slogan, "Mr. Moody will preach the gospel and Mr. Sankey will sing the gospel."

Sankey never had any musical training and had never sung professionally before he met Moody, but he had a sweet, lyrical voice with a natural plaintiveness that transcended its lack of precision. One professional critic described his voice as "a powerful baritone of small compass. He touches E flat with considerable difficulty and even E strains his voice. He sings only from the chest register and his intonation is far from perfect. But he makes up for all these deficiencies by his grand delivery and clear enunciation of the words." [40]

There were three types of singing at the meetings: solos by Sankey, ensembles by the choir, and congregational singing by the audience. The most important quality of all the hymns was their simplicity of thought, words, and melody. English critics called them "music hall" songs. The *Nation* noted that the hymns, "while written to religious words, are made attractive by many secular contrivances. . . . Determine the pleasure you get from a circus quickstep, a negro minstrel sentimental ballad, a college chorus, and a hymn all in one and you have some gauge of the variety and contrast." [41] Sankey wrote the music for several hymns but almost never the words. He was primarily a singer and compiler. Most of the songs he made famous were written by Philip Phillips, P. P. Bliss, George C. Stebbins, and James McGranahan, all of whom later became associate editors of the numerous editions of Sankey's *Sacred Songs and Solos* and his *Gospel Hymns*. What made Sankey famous was his association with Moody and Moody's willingness to incorporate this type of music into evangelistic meetings. At first Sankey was occasionally embarrassed by the fact that audiences broke into applause after his solos. Moody quickly put a stop to that sacrilege.

40 Edward F. Rimbault, "A Few Words on the Music of Messrs. Moody and Sankey," *Leisure Hour,* XXXIV (1875), 476.

41 *The Nation,* XXII (March 9, 1876), 156.

Most of the songs in Sankey's hymnbooks were suitable for congregational singing, but the sacred solos which "filled the great hall with sobbing" and left audiences "bathed in tears" were of such a delicate nature as to be suited only for the single voice of the singing evangelist. The most famous of these was "The Ninety and Nine," a story of the one lost sheep whom Christ brought home to the fold. One of the solos which Moody liked best was "Jesus of Nazareth Passeth By," a narrative ballad summarizing in six verses the meaning of Christ's life. It concluded, "But if you still His call refuse . . . 'Too late! too late!' will be the cry—'Jesus of Nazareth *has passed by.*' "

Some of these solos were so bathetic that Moody compelled Sankey to omit them from later editions. For example, the song "Room Among the Angels" told about a little girl named Mary whose mother had once cruelly struck her for being in the way. Shortly after when Mary lay dying she said, "I was always in your way, mother—you had no room for little Mary. And shall I be in the angels' way?"

When the dewy light was fading,
  And the sky in beauty smiled,
Came a whisper, like an echo,
  From a pale and dying child;
"Mother, in the golden region,
  With its pearly gates so fair,
Up among the happy angels,
  Is there room for Mary there?

"When my baby-sister calls me,
  And you hear my voice no more,
When she plays among the roses
  By our little cottage door,
Never chide her when you're angry—
  Do it kindly and in love,
That you both may dwell with Mary
  In that sunny land above." [42]

An even more pathetic one called "Scatter Seeds of Kindness" warned mothers who disliked dirty finger marks,

[42] *Sacred Songs and Solos (Words Only) Sung by Ira D. Sankey at Gospel Meetings* (London, 1874), p. 8. This paperbound edition which sold for two pence is one of the earliest still extant. A copy is in the British Museum.

If we knew the baby fingers
Pressed against the window pane
Would be cold and stiff tomorrow,
Never trouble us again,
Would the bright eye of our darling
Catch the frown upon our brow?
Would the prints of rosy fingers
Vex us then as they do now? [43]

Moody's audiences always enjoyed a good cry. The song "Where Is My Wandering Boy Tonight?" struck a responsive chord in many a parental bosom. However, even the most sympathetic audiences must have winced at the song about "Little Willie" written by P. P. Bliss:

"I should like to die," said Willie, "if my papa could die too;
But he says he isn't ready 'cause he has so much to do;
And my little sister, Nellie, says that I must surely die,
And that she and mamma, then she stopp'd, because it made her cry.

"But she told me, I remember, once while sitting on her knee;
That the angels never weary watching over her and me;
And that if we're good (and mamma told me just the same before),
They will let us into heaven when they see us at the door.

"There will be none but the holy—I shall know no more of sin;
There I'll see mamma and Nellie, for I know He'll let them in;
But I'll have to tell the angel, when I meet him at the door,
That he must excuse my papa, 'cause he couldn't leave the store." [44]

Probably the tunes which the whole congregation could sing were more popular in the long run than these narrative solos. A great many of the congregational hymns were doctrinal in character, telling of God's merciful salvation, free for all. Sankey had no qualms about taking old hymns, even those by Isaac Watts, and revising their Calvinistic theology to fit the more Arminian temper of Moody's meetings. But whether by Watts or some contemporary "religious poet," like the blind Fanny Crosby, these doctrinal hymns reiterated Moody's sermon messages with even greater simplicity:

43 *Ibid.*, p. 14.

44 *Sacred Songs and Solos with Standard Hymns Combined, Compiled and Sung by Ira D. Sankey* (London, n.d.) No. 415. This early edition, probably published about 1875, is available in the Harris Collection, Brown University Library, Providence, Rhode Island.

Free from the law, oh, happy condition!
Jesus hath bled, and *there* is remission!
Cursed by the law, and bruised by the fall;
Grace hath redeemed us, once for all.

or,

That gate ajar stands free for all
Who seek through it salvation:
The rich and poor, the great and small,
Of every tribe and nation.[45]

Others dealt with the joys of heaven and the solace of knowing that it would eventually be the lot of all Christians. These included "Sweet Bye and Bye," "We Are Waiting by the River," "Beulah Land," and "One More Day's Work for Jesus, One Less of Life for Me."

Perhaps the most typical hymns, however, were those dealing with the peace and contentment of the close personal relationship with Jesus which came with conversion:

Go tell it to Jesus,
He knoweth thy grief;
Go tell it to Jesus,
He'll send thee relief;
Go gather the sunshine
He sheds on the way;
He'll lighten the burden—
Go, weary one, pray.

Many hymns were concerned primarily with hope and consolation:

In some way or other the Lord will provide,
It may not be *my* way,
It may not be *thy* way,
And yet in His *own* way,
"The Lord will provide." [46]

But the hymns which startled the critics of Moody's revivalism were the hearty, cheerful, march-like songs describing the victory of the Christian life, such as "Hold the Fort," "Only an Armor Bearer," "Pull for the Shore," and "Dare to Be a Daniel." These were the tunes that sounded like college cheers

[45] *Sacred Songs and Solos (Words Only)* (London, 1874), pp. 2, 11.
[46] *Ibid.*, pp. 7, 22.

and circus quicksteps. "Hold the Fort" was based on an incident that occurred in the Civil War during Sherman's march through Georgia, but its words were evangelistic:

> "Hold the fort, for I am coming,"
>   Jesus signals still;
> Wave the answer back to heaven,
>   "By thy grace we will." [47]

Moody's favorite in this category was the spirited exhortation to all Christians to stand up and be counted:

> Dare to be a Daniel! Dare to stand alone!
> Dare to have a purpose firm! Dare to make it known!
>
> Many giants great and tall
>   Stalking through the land,
> Headlong to the earth would fall
>   If met by Daniel's Band!
>
> Hold the gospel banner high!
>   On to victory grand!
> Satan and his host defy,
>   And shout for Daniel's Band! [48]

It is difficult to imagine J. P. Morgan or Phillips Brooks singing these verses, but they did. This was not far from the sort of song which had roused Methodist camp meetings to such a pitch of excitement seventy-five years earlier. But Moody knew how to keep the emotions they stimulated within bounds. Reporters told of groups returning from Moody's meetings singing these songs on the streets or in the trolleys, but there were no reports of shouting, handclapping, or gyrating in the aisles of Moody's tabernacles. The simple, catchy tunes, the sentimental or inspiring words helped to mold a crowd of strangers into a warm, responsive unit, but there was nothing really spontaneous about Moody's carefully controlled and manipulated meetings.

The most clear-cut example of the manipulatory power of song was the use to which it was put at the conclusion of each sermon. Moody, having made his usual plea for those who were willing to be saved to rise in their seats and then to come forward to the inquiry rooms, would motion to Sankey; Sankey

[47] *Ibid.*, p. 3.
[48] *Ibid.*, p. 10.

would gently sound a chord on the organ, and the choir would sing "Softly and tenderly, Jesus is calling," or "Only trust him, only trust him, he will save you now," as the penitents walked down the aisles. These songs were called "invitation hymns" and were specifically written for the purpose of coaxing people out of their seats and into the inquiry rooms. They pleaded with the sinner, hypnotically tugging him forward by repeating over and over again the words "come," "trust," "now" as he debated with his conscience. It was a vastly different atmosphere from Finney's righteous warning to take the anxious seat.

Yet notwithstanding the London *Times*'s comment and Moody's tribute to Sankey's drawing power, the people who came to Moody's meetings were enthralled just as much by Moody's sermons as by Sankey's hymns. In the first place Moody could be just as sentimental as Sankey. "Ah," said one minister, "it is that tender weeping power in dear Mr. Moody that is so overwhelming." And another noted, "Perhaps the most striking feature [of his style] is his tenderness. He weeps and his audience weeps with him. Standing beside him in the pulpit . . . I have heard the sound of his weeping as he pled with God for perishing men, while in the intervening pauses I could distinctly hear the weeping of the people." [49] Finney occasionally spoke of converts whose "sensibility gushed forth" under his pleading, but Moody raised the use of mass pathos to a fine art. That the gruff and business-like Moody could weep as easily as a woman was considered by the mass of his audience a gratifying assurance of his "sensibility" in that sentimental age.

Moody demonstrated his tenderness by an inexhaustible supply of heart-rending anecdotes about the softening influence of conversion upon drunkards, thieves, and prodigal sons. Even British audiences were moved by his "touching" narratives" of "the wounded of the Federal Army" whom he had nursed during the Civil War. Typical of these was the one about the dying soldier "in our late war" who "lay on his cot" in an army hospital while a nurse read him a letter from his mother. The letter to her dying son contained a plea that he

[49] *Narrative of Messrs. Moody's and Sankey's Labours in Scotland and Ireland, compiled from the* British Evangelist *and the* Christian (New York, 1875), p. 13. John MacPherson, *Revivals and Revival Work: A Record of the Labours of D. L. Moody and Ira D. Sankey* (London, 1875), p. 54.

might turn to Christ before it was too late, and quoted the text "Him that cometh unto Me, I will in no wise cast out." As the nurse finished the letter the soldier said, "Did mother put that in the letter?" "Yes," said the nurse. "And does the Bible say it?" "Yes," said the nurse. "And if mother says it and the Bible says it, it must be true," said the soldier. "And, dear friends," Moody concluded, "he believed and received Christ" and thus died a happy and a saved man.[50]

Sickness and death were the principal themes of such anecdotes and these always found a misty-eyed response. Moody was a superb story-teller. "He will take them with him to some affecting deathbed and his tone will show how profoundly his own heart is touched by what is happening there. The vein of pathos comes out tenderly and beautifully. He seems as if he were lying on the ground and pleading with his hearers to come to Christ." [51] The number of dying sons, redeemed profligates, praying mothers, sick children, and long-suffering wives who paraded through his sermons sometimes made Christianity seem a lugubrious business at best. He was accused of downright cruelty by some critics for telling audiences of weeping women that they would never join their children in heaven unless they immediately became converted themselves. "Lift your eyes heavenward tonight, mothers; you have loved children that have gone before you; they will be at the marriage supper of the Lamb . . . will you be missing?" [52]

Despite the preponderance of sentimentality in his sermons, observers also reported "a remarkable naturalness, a want of all approach to affectation or sanctimoniousness, and even a play of humor which spurts out sometimes in his most serious addresses." The rapidity with which he jerked his audiences from tears to laughter to solemnity and anxiety was the essence of his pulpit technique. "His straight-forward, slap-dash style gives a fascinating air of reality to all he says, while his humor, capital hits, vivid and homely illustrations and now and again his deep feeling seldom fail to rivet the attention of his hearers." Attention was also riveted by what one critic in Edinburgh called "a slight want of reverence in treating of holy subjects such as

[50] D. L. Moody, *"To All People"* (New York, 1877), pp. 156–57.

[51] Edinburgh *Daily Review,* January 6, 1873, p. 3.

[52] *Liberal Christian,* December 11, 1875, p. 3; W. H. Daniels, *Moody, His Words* (New York, 1877), p. 446.

I remarked in the speeches of the Rev. Henry Ward Beecher when he was in Scotland. Some friends ought to hint to Mr. Moody the propriety of not inventing dialogues between a saint or a sinner and his Creator which may for the moment impart some dramatic form to the appeals but which is objectionable." [53]

But American audiences, more used to the Beecher style, were not so easily shocked. Moreover, it was one of Moody's conscious purposes to make his meetings as unlike the regular church services as he could without resorting to outright secularization. It was because the average church service was so dull and formal that Moody adopted his dramatic style. Moody was not as harsh in his criticism of the churches as Finney because so few of them opposed him, but like Finney he felt that they obviously needed to be jacked up or they would not have been so eager for his services. "We want the ministers quickened," he told his Boston audience on the opening night in that city. He said he did not fear the rising tide of infidelity "half so much as I do this dead, cold, formalism that has come into the Church of God." The Boston *Evening Transcript* commented upon this pietistic upbraiding of the churches that supported him, "There is something half droll and half pathetic in the way in which he so pointedly signifies even to the ministers grouped around him and to the elect of the communions, that he is going to do something which they ought to have done but which they have failed to do." [54] Like all professional revivalists Moody saw himself as a rejuvenator of dead churches.

With shrewdness and yet with sincerity, Moody capitalized upon his own lack of education and training. "Oh, I'm sick and tired of this essay preaching; I'm nauseated with this 'silver-tongued oratory' preaching. I like to hear preachers and not windmills." His sermons were made up of short, simple sentences, colloquial rhythms and idioms, blunt, almost earthy, forthrightness, and a lively sense of rustic humor. "I hate to come to a new place," he would confide to a first-night crowd. "It takes a week or so to get down to work. The people say,

[53] Edinburgh *Daily Review,* January 6, 1873, p. 3; *Narrative of Messrs. Moody and Sankey,* p. 48; *Dumfries and Galloway Courier,* December 23, 1873, p. 4.

[54] Boston *Evening Transcript,* January 29, 1877, pp. 2, 3; February 3, 1877, p. 4. See also Moody, *"To All People,"* pp. 17–18, where he attacks the "lukewarmness and unbelief in the Church of God."

'May, ain't that a big choir! Ain't they a lot of ministers! This is going to be a big work!' We must get our eyes off of these things. Everyone is going to be disappointed in these meetings if he ain't quickened himself." [55] This was Finney's formula for a new style of preaching, but as Finney recognized, it was also the age-old formula of the street preacher, political orator, and the popular entertainer. Moody, like Finney, knew his audience and he had the all-important knack of making them feel that he was one of them.

Moody's opening sermon in Brooklyn in 1875 showed how effective his dramatic style could be in waking up a crowd. He began the meeting by reading the Biblical report of the land flowing with milk and honey. Then stepping away from his lectern and leaning familiarly over the low railing, he peered into a face picked from the center of the audience and remarked quizzically, "A strange kind of report that, ain't it? I never heard of such a report as that being made to Congress. Did you?" Using a few brisk motions with his arms and speaking at the rate of 220 words per minute, he portrayed the battle of Jericho in vigorous language, hardly glancing at the notes held in the center of his Bible with an elastic band. When he came to describe Joshua's army marching around the walls of Jericho blowing their horns, he paused. Turning to point at the phalanx of Brooklyn divines sitting in dignified attention on the platform behind him, he asked the audience, "How would Dr. Talmage and Dr. Budington and Bishop Potter look marching in single file, blowing ram's horns?" The audience burst into laughter.

As he concluded this standard opening sermon on "Gideon's Army," he applied his theme to the present by declaring that in order to "take the land" in Brooklyn "we have got to bid farewell to the world—stop parties and festivals and lectures." A chorus of "Amens" came from the ministers behind him. Moody picked it up. "Dr. Budington, are you ready?" he called. The learned doctor shouted back, "Yes!" "Dr. Cuyler, are you ready?" "Yes." "Mr. Stuart of Philadelphia, are you ready?" "All ready." At this there were more cries of "Amen" and someone in the audience yelled, "Hurrah!" Moody beamed

[55] W. R. Moody, *Moody* (1930), p. 533; New York *World*, February 8, 1876, p. 8.

with satisfaction. "Thank God," he said, "for these manifestations of His spirit." [56]

This type of audience participation, even though it never got out of hand, was considered undignified by some ministers, but it was stimulating and refreshing to the average churchgoer. Conservatives were even more annoyed, and audiences even more pleased, by Moody's modernized versions of Biblical stories. In condemning the sectarian attitude of many church people, he retold the story of the Good Samaritan in dialogue:

> Suppose a Methodist had been down there trying to get that poor fellow on to his beast and wasn't quite strong enough to lift him up, and a Presbyterian had come along and the Methodist says, "Help me get him on the beast."
>
> "What are you going to do with him? What church is he going to join," asks the Presbyterian.
>
> "I haven't thought of that," says the Methodist; "I am going to save him first."
>
> "I won't do it. I shan't help him till I know what church he is going to join."
>
> An Episcopal brother comes along and wants to know if he has been confirmed.
>
> "We haven't got time to talk about that," says the Good Samaritan, "Let us save him."
>
> "What inn are you going to take him to?" asks another. "A Congregationalist, Methodist, Baptist, or Episcopal Inn?"
>
> Isn't that the spirit of our age? [57]

It was significant that a Methodist was the hero of the piece and the more upper-class Episcopalians, Presbyterians, and Congregationalists were cast in the roles of villains, or at least, of stuffed shirts.

His sermon on David and Goliath was even more dramatic: "Moody, in his vivid realization of this scene, performed as if he would throw off his coat and rush out to make Goliath's life a burden to him." [58] And in describing Christ's interrogation

[56] *New York Times,* October 25, 1875, pp. 1, 2.

[57] W. H. Daniels, *Moody, His Words* (New York, 1877), pp. 213–14. Moody's opposition to sectarianism and his desire for the establishment of a universal church of true evangelical Christians was sometimes expressed more vehemently: "The different denominations that exist in the Christian church are the work of the Devil" and "issued from the infernal pit," he said once. Glasgow *Herald,* April 14, 1874, p. 6.

[58] New York *World,* February 6, 1876, p. 8.

before Pilate he made the audience feel as though they were spectators sitting in court at a contemporary murder trial.[59]

Moody was often described as preaching like "a jury lawyer trying to get a verdict" or "a salesman trying to sell a bill of goods" but there was no comparison between his sermons and the "relentless legal arguments" of Finney. He did not write sermons, he evolved them. He would take a theme like Grace, Repentance, Faith, or Heaven and using Cruden's concordance and a topical text-book go through the Bible noting all the times the word was mentioned. Then he would try to string all the verses together into some meaningful order. He kept his sermon notes in large manila envelopes labelled with the titles and into these he slipped poems, stories, newspaper clippings, or scribbled notes from time to time until he had amassed sufficient material for a sermon. The result was a hodgepodge of illustrations and texts all reiterating one simple idea over and over again. His notes for a sermon on "Heaven" contained such references as,

> Heaven is a place . . . I Kings 8–30 . . .
> Jesus is there
> Angels. . . .
> Man dide [*sic*] worth a 1,000,000

The notes for the sermon "Is Anything Too Hard?" read:

> There was a time when I thought I would liked to had lived in the days of the Prophets. But I have got over that. . . .
> New York = Babylon
> Child Rolling Whop [*sic*]. . . .
> Astronomers tell us 80,000,000 other Suns. . . .[60]

But regardless of their construction, these sermons succeeded in bringing streams of tearful and serious men and women into Moody's inquiry rooms.

One of Moody's important modifications of Finney's revivalism was his abandonment of the anxious bench. "No unconverted individual need hesitate to attend the Moody meetings

[59] See the description in Edinburgh *Daily Review,* January 7, 1874, p. 3.

[60] Several dozen of Moody's sermon notes were preserved by his son and are now in the possession of Mrs. W. R. Moody, East Northfield, Massachusetts. These quotations are taken from them.

for fear of being made conspicuous or uncomfortable," wrote a Boston reporter who did not realize that professional evangelism had long before become respectable, "for the old-time revival methods are not being employed by the Northfield evangelist. There is no impassioned exhortation to repentance, no fervid appeals to the wicked to be saved, and no hallelujah shouting."[61] Occasionally some person would break out with too many "Amens" or "hallelujahs" but Moody would cool him off by saying, "Never mind, my friend, I can do all the hollering." If the person persisted, Moody would halt his sermon and ask the audience to sing a hymn while the ushers removed the disturber. "We distinctly discountenanced any hysterical excitement, confusion, or noise," said Sankey.[62] The days were long gone when Baptists and Methodists, let alone Congregationalists, Presbyterians, and Episcopalians, considered hysteria a manifestation of the Spirit and a certain sign of conversion. Whenever someone in his audience fainted Moody would say calmly, "Some one has fainted, but it is nothing. In large congregations like these it would not be strange to have four or five faint at each service. It is nothing remarkable. Satan wants to attract your attention in this way. But now never mind; let us go on, with our attention upon the sermon."[63] Moody could easily have produced hysteria had he wished, but like Finney, he recognized that this was not the way to win the cooperation of urban ministers nor the most effective way to produce new church members.

Moody did, however, think it proper and useful to ask those in the audience who were anxious for their souls, or who wished to be prayed for, to stand. "If a man is to be saved, he must take up his cross, and it is sometimes a great cross for a person to confess his anxiety before others. Many are blest in the very act of rising." This was daring to be a Daniel, daring to take a stand. It was precisely what Finney believed made the anxious bench an appropriately constituted use of means. But coming forward to sit in the anxious bench was quite a different matter from coming forward to enter the comparative privacy of an

[61] Boston *Herald,* January 6, 1897, p. 6.

[62] Boston *Daily Advertiser,* February 9, 1877, p. 4; *Christian Advocate,* August 26, 1875, p. 265; W. R. Moody, *Moody* (1930), p. 224.

[63] Moody, *"To All People,"* p. 306.

inquiry room. The act of coming forward might require some effort, might even be embarrassing, but it was far easier than sitting before the entire congregation while the evangelist poured in the truth or put in the probe until submission was compelled or refused for all to see.

Moody did not exactly say so, but one important reason for using inquiry rooms in his revivals was that fewer and fewer people understood the theology of conversion. "In my own experience," he said, "I find that where one person has been converted under the sermon, a hundred have been converted in the inquiry room." [64] They had to have it explained to them more fully than he could do in his sermons, although his sermons were certainly simple enough. He was once confronted by a woman in the inquiry room who said, "I want you to know that I do not believe in your theology," and he answered, "My theology! I didn't know I had any. I wish you would tell me what my theology is." [65] To Moody, theology meant creeds and dogma and he would have none of them. The closest he ever came to stating a theology was when he was asked in New York what doctrines were best for revival preaching. "Why, the good old doctrines of our fathers: Man is fallen; Christ comes to seek, redeem, and save him." [66] These were the doctrines which he spoke of as "the Christian fundamentals" and he claimed that the gospel could be reduced to the "three R's": "Ruin by sin, Redemption by Christ, and Regeneration by the Holy Ghost." [67] Finney wrote a book of almost one thousand pages to explain how his systematic theology differed from Calvinism. Moody simply stated, "I am an Arminian up to the Cross; after the Cross, a Calvinist." [68] But by 1875 the terms Arminian and Calvinist had become so blurred that this explained nothing.

The amorphous state of theology in the 1870's was exemplified not only by the readiness with which the Scottish Presbyterians accepted Moody, but also by a statement in the *Princeton Review* that Moody's "preaching and tone" were

[64] *New York Times,* March 30, 1876, p. 8

[65] *Life and Sermons of Dwight L. Moody* (New York, 1900, pub. J. S. Ogilvie), p. 191.

[66] *New York Times,* March 31, 1876, p. 8.

[67] W. H. Daniels, *Moody, His Words* (New York, 1877), p. 256.

[68] W. R. Moody, *Moody* (1930), p. 437.

"singularly scriptural and sound." [69] Yet it was hardly orthodox Calvinism for Moody to ridicule those who "come out to meetings and wait through the meeting for something to strike" them. Regeneration, he said, was not a thunderbolt from heaven; grace was not irresistible. "There is such thing as a man going on rejecting and rejecting the Spirit of God" and becoming "hardened" by this process until God could no longer help him.[70] This was the very same view of man's omnipotence for which Hopkinsians and Presbyterians had denounced Finney forty years earlier.

Moody once remarked that until 1868 he had preached Calvinism but after hearing Henry Moorehouse preach seven successive sermons one week on the text "For God so loved the world . . ." he changed his mind. "I used to preach that God was behind the sinner with a double-edged sword ready to hew him down. I have got done with that. I preach now that God is behind him with love, and he is running away from the God of Love." [71] Or as he phrased it more fetchingly for an English audience in 1875, the sinner was like a "poor beggar" fleeing madly across London Bridge with the Prince of Wales in hot pursuit waving a bag of gold and shouting, "Oh, beggar, here is a bag of gold." [72]

The central and all-inclusive fact of Christian theology for Moody was that sinful men could all obtain eternal life simply by believing that Christ died for their sins. If men did not "accept Christ" they would certainly spend eternity in hell. What Finney described as making a new heart, Moody called repenting and turning from sin. His fundamental text was

[69] L. H. Atwater, "Revivals of the Century," *Presbyterian Quarterly and Princeton Review,* XLIX (October, 1876), 716–17. This same article finds Finney's revivals more objectionable for their new measures than for their theology.

[70] D. L. Moody, *The Great Redemption* (New York, 1888), pp. 377, 209. I have quoted extensively from this edition of Moody's sermons, which are those he delivered in Cleveland, Ohio, in the fall of 1879. However, the same or similar quotations can be found in almost any other edition of Moody's revival sermons. He used the same sermons over and over and made no significant changes in them or in his theology between 1873 and his death in 1899.

[71] W. R. Moody, *Moody* (1930), pp. 119–20. Henry Moorehouse belonged to the Plymouth Brethren, a denomination in which Moody was interested long before 1868, so it seems unlikely that his theology changed very radically in that year though he may have slightly shifted his emphasis. For Moody's interest in the Brethren see *ibid.,* p. 101.

[72] W. H. Daniels, *D. L. Moody and His Work* (Hartford, 1876), p. 385.

Acts 17:30, God "commandeth all men everywhere to repent," which he explained much as Finney explained, "Make you a new heart:" "You say you can't repent? When God commands anything He gives you the power to obey," said Moody.[73] "We are free agents. God allows us to choose." The doctrines of innate depravity and predestined election were nonsense. When a man said "I am so constituted I can't believe," Moody told him, "Men can believe if they will. It is not because men cannot believe; it is because they will not believe." And he offered the same refutation of "cannot-ism" that Finney did: "Do you think God would command us to do something we could not do and then punish us eternally for not doing it? . . . Away with such a doctrine as that! He would be an unjust God. . . ." [74]

Like Finney, Moody often called repentance or conversion "a change of mind" and compared it to a soldier's doing a "right about face" or a businessman's getting off a train going in the wrong direction and getting on one going in the right direction. He also compared it to a voter's decision to change his party: "If you belonged to a party and you were thoroughly convinced tonight that you were in the wrong party, do you tell me you could not change tonight and join the other party and go out to the polls and go to work tomorrow and be on the other side of the question?" Revivalism was still electioneering for God's party. For the voter it was a very simple choice. "There is no neutrality about this matter. We are either for God or against him." The choice "is a fair, square, practical thing, isn't it?" Moody asked. His sermons, like Finney's, concluded with the same call for immediate decision: "Where will you spend eternity?" But Moody always put it on a more sentimental plane than Finney: "Will you spend it in the mansion He has gone to prepare for you, with that sainted godly mother, with that praying godly wife? Will you spend it with that lovely child that has gone on high?" [75]

Moody was also as equivocal as Finney about the part played in conversion by the Holy Spirit. In one sermon he stated that God "has done everything that he could toward your salvation. You need not wait for God to do anything more." But in an-

[73] *New York Times,* October 28, 1875, p. 8.

[74] Moody, *Great Redemption,* pp. 284, 314, 94.

[75] *Ibid.,* pp. 88–89, 92, 109, 213, 284.

other sermon he declared that sinners "are dead in sin until the Holy Ghost brings them into life. . . ."[76] Moody certainly agreed with Finney, however, that revivals were not miraculous events sent from heaven and uncontrollable by man. He told a convention of ministers, "A great many people seem to think that revivals come like famines and like hurricanes and that they have nothing to do with it. . . . Now I firmly believe it is in our power to have a new interest in the church. . . ."[77]

Yet Moody insisted that the Holy Spirit was a necessary agent in conversion. If he sometimes seemed to contradict Finney, as when he said, "When I was born of God I got a new principle planted in me" he did not mean by this that any physical change took place in his soul or heart. He meant only that the Spirit gave a man "new power" or new moral strength, "the power to love my enemies" and the "power to serve God." Moody was so convinced that this new power could save a man from sin that his statement about being a Calvinist "after the cross" probably meant that he believed the old doctrine of the perseverance of the saints. At any rate it led to his belief in "the second blessing" which was a form of sanctification or perfectionism very similar to Finney's, although Moody preferred to think of it as an "annointment for service." Even those who had been saved, said Moody, still needed to be "baptized by the Holy Ghost so that they shall have the power."[78] The persistent strain of optimism that gleamed through his basically pessimistic message stemmed from this confirmed faith that with God all things are possible, that nothing is too hard for the truly converted man.[79] If a man relied upon God, Moody believed that he could conquer all problems.

But despite these similarities to Finney in theology, the general tone of Moody's revivalism was very different. Essentially it was the difference between emphasizing the justice of God's

[76] See John T. Walsh, *Moody versus Christ and His Apostles* (St. Louis, 1880), p. 63, for an attack upon Moody in the name of orthodoxy.

[77] Moody, *Great Redemption,* p. 439.

[78] *Ibid.,* pp. 172, 377, 396. W. R. Moody, *Moody* (1930), p. 130, quotes Moody's personal experience with the second blessing; compare this with Finney's experiences described in his *Memoirs* (New York, 1876), pp. 341, 376 ff.

[79] "All things are possible with God. It is an easy matter for God to save souls in Boston, it is an easy matter to save all the drunkards in Boston, to call back all the wandering prodigals all over the country." Moody, *"To All People,"* p. 115.

moral government and emphasizing the mercy of God's love. Finney, in order to combat Calvinism's "cannot-ism," emphasized the fact that God always worked according to certain fixed laws which were not only knowable to man but which were commensurate with man's ability to obey.[80] Moody reduced Christianity to a sentimental personal relationship with a personal God. Christianity "is not a dogma; it is not a creed; it is not doctrine; it is not feeling; it is not an impression; but it is a person." Since God the Father was too awesome a figure for the ordinary man to establish a personal relationship with, Moody placed his emphasis on Jesus, the Son, "the God-man," the Lamb, the Shepherd, the tender, kind, and gentle friend. "The gospel is this: that Christ has come to meet your need. There is not a need that you feel in your heart today but that Christ can meet if you let Him. God sent Him here to meet man's need." Or, "I might go on to speak of him as a shepherd. I have known him now upwards of twenty years as a shepherd. He has carried my burdens for me. Oh, it is so sweet to know that you have one to whom you can go and tell your sorrows! You can roll your burdens at his feet. Blessed privilege we have, dear friends, to go to Him with our burdens and our sorrows. . . . Think of Christ as a burden-bearer!" [81]

By burdens Moody usually meant the burdens of sin, but the term could also be interpreted to mean such worldly afflictions as pain, sorrow, poverty, sickness, a prodigal son, or loneliness. Moody made a conscious attempt to make his hearers identify themselves with Jesus: "It seemed to just pain the heart of the Son of God when he was down here, to find so few people that wanted Him. . . . I would like to ask this congregation, did you ever have this feeling come over you that no one wanted you? I had it once. I remember, when I left my mother and

[80] See Albert Dod's criticism of Finney for his failure to preach repentance: "The great duty which he [Finney] urges upon the sinner is unconditional submission to God. It is submission to God as the creator and ruler of the world —the God of providence rather than of grace. Now it will at once occur to every reader of the Bible that this is not the duty which the sacred writers most frequently urge upon the sinner. They called upon men to repent, and believe in the Lord Jesus Christ." If Dod is here expounding Calvinism, as he claimed to be, then, perhaps, Moody was nearer to Calvinist orthodoxy than Finney. *Biblical Repertory and Princeton Review,* VII (July, 1835), 511.

[81] Moody, *Great Redemption,* pp. 377, 316, 65.

went off to Boston. . . . Oh! my friend, is there room for Him in your heart?" [82]

Having established this sense of personal identification, Moody then led his listeners to the point of repentance by appealing to their sense of horror and guilt. His famous sermon on "The Blood," said one auditor, concluded with "a vivid description of the scenes and events of the last hours of Christ, so life-like as to be absolutely painful . . . the scourging, the crown of thorns, the mockery . . . the nailing of his blessed body to the cross, his death cry. . . ." [83] Then Moody turned to the audience and asked, "My friends, what will you do with the precious blood tonight? Will you trample it under your feet and send back an insulting message to God that you don't care for His Son, or for the blood that flowed from Calvary?" [84] In the era of Victorian gentility, Moody found it more effective to portray concrete scenes of suffering on earth rather than generalized pictures of suffering in hell. The martyrdom of Stephen and the whippings of Paul were portrayed as vividly as the sufferings of Christ. Sometimes the exaggerated horror became unintentionally ludicrous, as in the story of the drowning man trying to climb into an overcrowded lifeboat: "They begged him to let go, but he would not. . . . A man took a sword and cut off the man's hand, and the man swam up a second time, and he laid hold of that boat with his left hand and they cut off the left hand; and with both hands cut off he swam up to that boat and seized it with his teeth. It touched their hearts. They could not cut his head off and they drew him into the boat." [85] In all of these scenes each member of the audience was made to feel that he shared the experience either as victim or perpetrator or both.

The point of the lifeboat anecdote was to describe how important eternal life was and how desperately every man should seek to save his own. Moody claimed that he did not try to frighten people into repentance with stories of hell and judgment. He did not, he said, try to "alarm" his audiences or get them "wrought up." Yet the rapid alternation of heartrending

[82] *Ibid.,* pp. 131–32.
[83] W. H. Daniels, *Moody, His Words* (New York, 1877), p. 311.
[84] W. H. Daniels, *D. L. Moody* (Hartford, 1876), p. 432.
[85] Moody, *Great Redemption,* pp. 346, 360.

and bloody scenes was perfectly adapted to build up the type of tension which only a walk down the aisle and a personal confession in the inquiry room could exorcise, especially when Moody emphasized the peace, the joy, the contentment which followed conversion: "How sweet our life will be, how pure our conscience will be, if God has forgiven everything, if we have brought everything to light and turned from our sins. . . ." [86]

Though Moody spoke of doing everything for the glory of God, his sermons usually centered on the value of salvation to the individual. There was none of Finney's or Hopkins' appeal to disinterested benevolence, no assumption that the public good might be superior in value to the private welfare. Being a friend of Jesus solved a man's personal problems and once a man was right with God he was right with the world. If Moody disliked frightening men about hellfire, he saw nothing wrong with offering them the rewards of heaven. "If Jehovah should send Gabriel down here to say to any one in this building that you might have any one thing you asked for. . . . You would not ask for money. If there was only one thing to ask for, you would ask for eternal life. It is a great thing to live forever." This personal reward was enhanced by the mental picture he drew of walking through the streets of heaven with departed loved ones, the saints, the apostles, and even with the members of the Trinity. Heaven became a private club and Moody more than once compared salvation to joining the Masons.[87]

There were even more tangible bribes offered to the individual. Obedience to God brought not only peace and contentment, it brought prosperity. Looking about him at the wealthy men who sat on the platform at his meetings, the Dodges, McCormicks, and Wanamakers, Moody noted that they were all devout church members, all "born again" Christians. He noted also that few if any of the poor in the slums of Chicago, London, or New York attended church. Many of his wealthy backers had once been poor boys, but few of the nonchurchgoing slum dwellers showed any signs of getting rich. The conclusion seemed self-evident. "It is a wonderful fact that men and women saved by the blood of Jesus rarely remain subjects of

[86] *Ibid.*, pp. 86, 99.
[87] *Ibid.*, p. 361; W. R. Moody, *Moody* (1930), p. 438.

charity, but rise at once to comfort and respectability." [88] Moody radiated optimism when he contemplated the effect of true conversion upon a poor man: "I don't see how a man can follow Christ and not be successful." And "I never saw the man who put Christ first in his life that wasn't successful." [89]

If someone pointed to a rich man who was not converted, Moody said that that man was first of all a fool, second he was probably suffering or would shortly suffer from some secret sorrow or misfortune, and third, he was doomed, like Dives, to spend eternity in hell. Like Finney, Moody devoted a great deal of his efforts to the nouveaux riches whose sudden prosperity rested uneasily upon their pietistic consciences. He was particularly anxious to show businessmen "the sagacity" of caring for their soul's welfare as well as their business profits: "if a man neglects his business and leaves it to itself he will soon become a bankrupt. If a man neglects his health he will become an invalid. It is just as true that if a man neglects his soul he will be lost." To the businessman, Moody preached salvation as a kind of spiritual insurance. Why "take such a chance?" he asked, "supposing that there is one chance out of a million that there is no chance of repentance after the grave. Can you afford to take even that chance?" [90] But religion had its earthly rewards as well. "I pray you businessmen, be warned by the life of this worldly-minded man," he said in his sermon on Lot; "If you are a member of the church and are getting rich and increasing in goods, don't forget the words of the Lord which says, 'Seek ye first the kingdom of God and his righteousness and all these things shall be added unto you.' " [91] In Moody's sermons, religious individualism blended perfectly with rugged individualism.

If a man claimed to be saved but still had not risen to comfort and prosperity, he probably had not been truly converted: "There are a great many professing Christians who never get on intimate terms with God and so they never amount to much." [92]

[88] W. R. Moody, *Moody* (1930), p. 171.

[89] Boston *Daily Advertiser*, February 12, 1877, p. 4; A. W. Williams, *D. L. Moody* (Philadelphia, 1900), p. 324.

[90] W. H. Daniels, *Moody, His Words* (New York, 1877), p. 195; Moody, *"To All People,"* p. 314.

[91] W. H. Daniels, *Moody, His Words* (New York, 1877), p. 121.

[92] *Ibid.*, p. 66.

If Moody were shown a man who had undoubtedly been converted and was intimate with God but was nevertheless still poor, he resorted to the text, "Whom the Lord loveth he chasteneth." Moody sensed no inconsistency in telling those who, though duly converted, lived and were bound to die in hardship and poverty, that "God gives us a little adversity here, a little prosperity there and works all for our good" although "we are not able to read the problem now or to see just why we are afflicted."[93] Those who, despite their best efforts, were disillustioned with the American dream of success found solace in Moody's words. Some even felt that the blame lay not in the system but in themselves.

Speaking in New York City in 1876, where 50,000 men were out of work because of the depression, Moody remarked, "I know there is great misery and suffering in this great city, but what is the cause of most of it? Why the sufferers have become lost from the Shepherd's care. When they are close to Him, under His protection, they are always provided for." If a man lost his job, he should look upon it as a judgment of God for his sins. "If you had a son who wouldn't obey you, you would not expect him to prosper, and you wouldn't be anxious that he should because prosperity in wickedness would be an injury to him." Moody was convinced that by and large poverty was the result of personal sin. "I believe today one reason why so many men's ways are hedged up, and they do not prosper is because they have dishonored their parents" or broken some other commandment. Sometimes, as in his own life, poverty was simply the result of not being a converted Christian: "The whole of my early life was one long struggle with poverty; but I have no doubt it was God's way of bringing me to himself. And since I began to seek first the kingdom of God, I have never wanted for anything." [94]

The wickedness of the unemployed and the poverty stricken was demonstrated by the continued sales of liquor and tobacco even during the depression: "I do not believe we would have these hard times if it had not been for sin and iniquity. Look at the money that is drank up! The money that is spent for

[93] Moody, *"To All People,"* p. 333.

[94] *New York Times,* February 19, 1876, p. 8; W. H. Daniels, *Moody, His Words* (New York, 1877), pp. 430, 431; Moody, *Great Redemption,* p. 160.

tobacco! That is ruining men—ruining their constitutions. We live in a land flowing with milk and honey. God has blessed this nation; yet men complain of hard times." [95] Moody was fond of quoting a saying which may have been true enough in rural New England, but which hardly answered in the industrial slums of the cities: "Rags are the emblems of the drunkard's child." Since converted men never drank, ragged children were *ipso facto* being raised by sinners.

The other prevailing sin of the poor was laziness. Laziness, like drunkenness, was automatically cured by conversion. "I will tell you that laziness does not belong to Christ's Kingdom. I don't believe a man would have a lazy hair in his head if he was converted to the Lord Jesus Christ." Speaking in Boston in 1877 at a meeting in the tabernacle for converted drunkards who were out of work, Moody told them, "Get something to do. If it is for fifteen hours a day, all the better, for while you are at work Satan does not have so much chance to tempt you. If you cannot earn more than a dollar a week, earn that. That is better than nothing and you can pray to God for more." He was convinced that in this land of milk and honey men who were willing to work would always reach the top: "They will make room for you." His sermon to the unemployed took on a Horatio Alger glow:

> Work faithfully for three dollars a week, it won't be long before you have six dollars and then you will get ten dollars, and then twelve dollars a week. You want to get these employers always under an obligation to you. You must be such true men and be so helpful to your employers that they cannot get along without you and then you will work up and your employer will increase your wages. If a man works in the interest of his employer, he will be sure to keep him and treat him well. . . .

The man who could not get ahead on his own initiative and self-reliance was not worth helping. "Work your way up to the top of the ladder and you will like to stay up there; but if you are lifted up there by somebody, you will be all the time tumbling back." [96]

[95] Moody, *Great Redemption,* pp. 355–56.

[96] Moody, *"To All People,"* pp. 450–51, 489–90, 491, 494, 488. It should be said, however, that in his later sermons Moody also held employers responsible for being loyal to their employees: "We treat our servants just about as we treat our sewing machines," he said in 1894. "If they do their work well, all right; but if they don't, we kick them out." He called the New York department store

Since there were 48,000 persons applying for poor relief in Boston while Moody was making this sermon, Moody also suggested, "If you cannot get work in the city, strike out into the country." "It is not degrading to go out and hoe and shovel in the field," he told those who were out of jobs. "It is noble, I think." How the poor farmers of New England were to absorb this vast army of unemployed he did not explain.[97]

Inasmuch as poverty could in most cases be cured by conversion, Moody proclaimed that it was the highest duty of a Christian to "visit the homes of the poor and wicked and tell them how the Son of God came into the world to seek the fallen and those who were lost." [98] Finney had proclaimed that all true Christians would devote themselves to the reformation of the world, and although he had inconsistently tried to make all social reform an appendage of revivals, his social outlook was considerably broader than Moody's. Moody did say, "It is not enough to give alms; personal service is necessary," but he made it quite clear that by personal service he meant simply personal soul winning. Whenever he was asked what type of work young converts should take up for the church, he suggested first that they "visit the sick or go around and distribute tracts and invite people to come to church." [99] He urged "young ladies" of "leisure" to visit the "homes of the masses" and preach the gospel and sing hymns to them. "Talk of being sickened at the sight of the world's degradation," he said in 1874, the blackest sight of all was to see Christians in the cities, living in the midst of the unchurched masses, "rubbing shoulders with them every day upon the streets and never so much as lifting a finger to warn them of death and eternity and judgment to come." [100]

Moody was as inconsistent as Finney in shifting the blame for the nation's ills now upon individual sinners and now upon the divine order of things. But as a premillennialist he lacked

---

owner, A. T. Stewart, "supremely selfish" because "One of his clerks got sick and couldn't come to the store for two or three or ten weeks; his wages were cut right off" because Stewart felt "he wasn't responsible" for helping the clerk. *Moody's Latest Sermons* (Providence, Rhode Island, 1894), p. 54.

[97] Moody, *"To All People,"* p. 491.

[98] Boston *Evening Transcript,* January 30, 1877, p. 2.

[99] Moody, *Great Redemption,* p. 475.

[100] W. R. Moody, *The Life of Dwight L. Moody* (Chicago, 1900), p. 217.

Finney's buoyant hope that the millennium was just around the corner and that a little more effort on revivalism and moral reform would usher it in. Moody believed that until Christ returned none of the basic problems of the world could be solved. In his sermons on the imminent Second Coming, he discouraged those efforts toward reform which were the distinguishing mark of the social gospel movement after 1890. Moody was optimistic about the destiny of all true Christians and even about the destiny of his country, but he was not at all sanguine about the future of the world or of the human race. "Talk about men improving so very fast," he snorted, "I would like to see them." [101] It was almost as though he adopted a pessimistic attitude just to spite the advocates of theistic evolution and social Darwinism. "I look upon this world as a wrecked vessel," he said. "God has given me a lifeboat and said to me, 'Moody, save all you can.' " [102]

Here Moody not only parted company with the optimism of Finney and the social Darwinians, but he parted company with a good many of the ministers who sat on his platform and nodded agreement with his Poor Richard parables and his Horatio Alger anecdotes. This doctrine of premillennialism was to become one of the test points between modernists and fundamentalists in the days ahead. Its popularity among post-Civil War evangelists was the result of an increasingly pessimistic view of life on the part of those intellectually unsophisticated and socially insecure individuals who made up the hard core of urban revival audiences. The growing complexity of modern life and the breakdown of traditional beliefs and values made these people far less certain about the progressive improvement of American society than their parents and grandparents had been. To these fearful and perplexed folk, the miraculous cataclysm of the Second Coming offered a far more reassuring hope than the impious and confusing doctrines of Herbert Spencer and the theistic evolutionists.

Moody probably adopted premillennialism quite unthinkingly in the 1850's along with many other interpretations of the Bible which he learned from the Plymouth Brethren. As a pietistic sect of the disinherited, the Brethren found social

[101] Boston *Evening Transcript,* February 17, 1877, p. 2.

[102] W. H. Daniels, *Moody, His Words* (New York, 1877), pp. 475–76.

consolation in the doctrine of Christ's speedy return. Moody utilized the doctrine as a convenient handle against the theological liberals who challenged either his revivalism or his social views. When confronted with the postmillennial argument he asked stubbornly, "Where do you get it. I can't find it. The word of God nowhere tells me to watch and wait for the coming of the millennium, but for the coming of the Lord. I don't find any place where God says the world is to grow better and better, and that Christ is to have a spiritual reign on earth of a thousand years. I find that the earth is to grow worse and worse and that at length there is going to be a separation" of the saved from the unsaved at Christ's return.[103] On that day the liberals and the worldly would get their come-uppance and the saving remnant their crowns of glory.

There were also certain practical values to the premillennial theory for revivalism. "I don't know of anything," said Moody, "that will take the men of this world out of their bonds and stocks quicker than [the thought] that our Lord is coming again."[104] And what could be more dramatic as a stimulus to immediate conversion than the warning, "The trump of God may be sounded, for anything we know, before I finish this sermon."[105]

It was not surprising, however, that Moody found "certain wealthy and fashionable churches" where "this doctrine is not preached or believed."[106] Businessmen did not take kindly to the thought of losing their stocks and bonds. Persons whose status had risen with their incomes did not see the virtue of believing that the world was getting worse and worse. It hardly made sense to those prosperous British and American businessmen who had steadily worked their way up the ladder of success for Moody to insist that mankind was a failure, "the antediluvian world was a failure, the Jewish world was a failure, man has been a failure everywhere. . . ." Nor was it really consistent with Moody's view of America as that "blessed nation" "flowing with milk and honey" in which anyone could

[103] *Ibid.*, p. 474.
[104] Moody, *"To All People,"* p. 510.
[105] W. H. Daniels, *Moody, His Words* (New York, 1877), p. 472.
[106] *Ibid.*, p. 475.

rise to the top. Of course, Moody meant "failure" in terms of sin and not in terms of social position, scientific discovery, or material profits. But to doubt progress in any form in the nineteenth century was to run counter to the American democratic faith. Moody's well-to-do evangelical supporters may have paid lip service to this doctrine but it was among the unsuccessful that it elicited the most enthusiastic response. Moody never succeeded in reconciling his own successful career with his belief in Christian humility and so he constantly vacillated between annoyance and sympathy for those who failed to get ahead. "God does not propose to reward his children here," he said in this sympathetic mood. "He is to reward them up yonder. We are to work here." Finney thought men would build the New Jerusalem on earth. Moody said "We are travelling to the New Jerusalem" which is in the next world. "If we don't find everything down here just as we want it, we shall be satisfied there." Moody did not think men could do much to make the world as they wanted it, but he told the poor to take heart: "There is a better day for us my friends" and "we are enduring the tribulation until He come." Then "You will have a seat at His right hand" for then the last shall be first. "I pity those men who are building those fine mansions" on earth for they forget that "you may have the wealth of the world, but you can't take a penny with you." [107]

The combination of consolation and reward, prosperity and eternal life, which constituted the heart of Moody's message appealed to millions just as surely as Sankey's songs and solos. The promise of the inquiry room was a simple, quick, and certain end to all anxiety and guilt and a promise of success, if not in this world, then certainly in the next, and perhaps both. To those who criticized him, either for his lack of logic or his business-like machinery or his maudlin hymns and stories or his vulgarity and slang, Moody had only one answer, "It doesn't matter how you get a man to God provided you get him there." [108]

As the anxious filed into the inquiry room after one of his

[107] Moody, *Great Redemption,* pp. 344, 356; Moody, *"To All People,"* pp. 265, 513; W. H. Daniels, *Moody, His Words* (New York, 1877), p. 478.

[108] Boston *Daily Advertiser,* February 3, 1877, p. 4.

sermons, they were seated in rows of chairs while the trained personal workers sat beside them or ranged themselves along the walls, Bibles in hand, waiting for Moody to begin the meeting. Moody entered briskly, marched to the front of the room, climbed up on a chair so that everyone could see him, and read briefly from the Bible some passage about the freedom of salvation for all who believed. Then he made a short, forceful exposition of the text, insisting upon the necessity for immediate surrender to Christ. He asked all who wished to find God "to get on their knees until the thing was settled." All the inquirers knelt. Moody then asked them to repeat after him, "Lord, what wilt thou have me do?" If he did not get a hearty response, he would make them repeat it again.[109]

Then he gave the signal for the personal work to begin. For half an hour or more he and his coworkers went from person to person, asking them why they were not Christians, what doubts kept them from immediately accepting the terms of salvation. If the doubts were due to ignorance of the meaning of the terms of salvation, appropriate texts from the Bible were read to the kneeling sinner and his assent to their truth demanded. If there were doubts of personal worthiness or general hesitancy, questions were asked regarding possible secret sins such as the love of worldly things or some past un-Christian act.

Moody never tried to reason with sinners. "The voice of reason is the voice of the devil," he said.[110] You must seek God "with your heart, not with your head." When a man came to him and said, "I don't believe anything I can't reason out," Moody threw up his hands: "If a man takes that ground he might as well throw away the whole Bible and go over to atheism at one leap." Most of the persons who approached salvation from this viewpoint were, in Moody's eyes, not really in earnest. They were trying to cover up for some secret sin: "The longer I live the more I am convinced that the reason men do not come to Christ is because they do not want to give up sin. That is the trouble. It is not their intellectual difficulties . . . it is some darling sin they are holding on to. They are not willing to give up the harlot; they are not willing

[109] Boston *Evening Transcript,* February 7, 1877, p. 2.
[110] Quoted in Gamaliel Bradford, *Moody,* p. 63.

to give up gambling, they are not willing to give up drinking. . . ." [111]

Sometimes the interrogation by unskilled and overzealous personal workers into a young inquirer's "darling sins" led to embarrassment and resentment. One angry Boston mother wrote a letter of protest to the *Evening Transcript* stating, "The *inquiry rooms* of the Tabernacle I know to have been used by men for conversations of anything but a religious nature with young girls." [112]

Moody's conversations with inquirers were little more than *ad hominem* arguments, a sort of spiritual browbeating. Moody would begin by asking, "My friend, what is your difficulty?" Most persons would answer that they were searching for God but did not know how to find Him. "Do you believe you are a sinner?" "Yes, I know that." "Christ is able to save you," and a dozen texts were produced to prove it. If the man said, "I cannot believe it," Moody challenged, "Who?" "Well, I cannot believe." "Who cannot you believe—God? It is a pretty serious charge not to believe God." Moody then quoted more of God's words until the sinner either gave in and said "I see it now. I see it," and was considered converted, or else was temporarily abandoned as a very hardened case.[113]

Moody realized that different methods had to be used with different types of inquirers. If "they talk about sin in a light flippant way, why it is best not to give them the consolation of the gospel; it is best to give them the law." In dealing with infidels, get "down on your knees and pray with them and convert them to God. A good many infidels have been converted, but not by argument." All questions of doctrine were dismissed as irrelevant in the inquiry room, but such Christian ideals as forgiveness, meekness, restitution, and humility were insisted upon. One woman was told in the inquiry room that what was blocking her conversion was her refusal to forgive her worst enemy. "There is one woman I never will forgive," she said. Moody told her that God would never forgive her then. "The last I heard of her," said Moody, "she had gone

111 Moody, *Great Redemption*, pp. 359, 141, 104.

112 Boston *Evening Transcript*, April 13, 1877, p. 6.

113 This dialogue is a composite of several such encounters as described by Moody in the Edinburgh *Daily Review*, January 8, 1874, p. 3, and Moody, *Great Redemption*, pp. 445, 466.

out of her mind, and some infidels say religion drove her out of her mind, but it was the want of it, that is what it was." [114]

At the other extreme the conversion process became so simple that the regenerate usually described it as "I felt very bad and then I felt very good." [115] By emphasizing the moral aspects of the Christian life, Moody reduced conversion for many churchgoers to the simple act of confessing belief in the fundamentals and promising to give up wine, tobacco, dancing, theater-going, card-playing, novel reading, or, in short, resolving to live according to the same moral code which Finney and rural Americans had always defined as Christian. "If we want anything, we want a revival of right living," said Moody. "God wants downright uprightness." [116] The inquiry room produced some dramatic conversions, of course, such as those by avowed atheists, drunkards, and thieves, for Moody maintained that a man could be "vile as hell itself one moment and saved the next." But these cases were rare even in his wide experience. For the most part all that happened in the inquiry room was that pious people became more pious.

When Moody concluded an inquiry meeting either he or some other worker was ready to announce to the press the number who had been saved that night.[117] If a reporter could not get an estimate from one of the workers he took a guess at the figures himself. In any case the public was always given to believe that the Spirit of God was nightly at work in Moody's tabernacles and that souls were being saved in great quantities.

The total number of conversions made in each revival was never more than a rough estimate. No two reporters ever had the same count, and Moody at first kept no statistical records. Yet it was significant of the changing temper of revivalism and of the general recognition that it was a business undertaking that such statistics were considered an essential part of measuring the efficiency of any series of meetings. Moody expressed

[114] Boston *Evening Transcript,* February 16, 1877, p. 3; Moody, *"To All People,"* pp. 175, 124. See also the article "Crazed by Religion" in the *New York Times,* April 14, 1876, p. 10.

[115] *New York Times,* November 16, 1875, p. 1.

[116] Moody, *Great Redemption,* p. 98.

[117] See for example the description of an inquiry meeting in Boston in which "Mr. Moody announced fifty" as having reached a state of hope while one of his assistants "announced" the conversion of various individuals. Boston *Evening Transcript,* February 7, 1877, p. 2.

annoyance at this, but it could hardly have been avoided, and most laymen and clergymen who took part in the revivals reveled in the statistical side of the enterprise. The following estimates were offered for the total conversions in Moody's early revivals:

		Low Estimate	High Estimate
Edinburgh	eight weeks	1500	7000
Glasgow	six weeks	3200	3500
London	twenty-two weeks	3000	7000
Brooklyn	four weeks	1000	2000
Philadelphia	ten weeks	3500	12,000
New York	ten weeks	3500	8000
Chicago	sixteen weeks	2500	10,000 [118]

The low estimates came from the most reliable sources. Although the reporter for the Philadelphia *Sun* estimated 12,000 conversions in that city, the *New York Times* noted that only 3500 persons appeared at the meeting held for those converted during the Philadelphia revival.[119] In Chicago, where converts were asked to sign a book with their names and addresses, 6000 "registered" as "converted or reclaimed." It was typical of the confusion that the Chicago *Tribune* reported "About 2500 have been converted, between 6000 and 8000 have been seriously impressed." [120] Whether the terms "impressed" and "reclaimed" were synonymous was not clear, and in either case it left the question of new converts as doubtful as the question of how many new members joined the churches. Some critics accused Moody of padding the statistics: The "revivalists were not satisfied with their record on high; they wanted a record in the newspaper." [121] But the blame lay less with Moody than

118 *The Christian* (London), February 26, 1874, p. 8; May 28, 1874, p. 6; *Christian Advocate,* July 8, 1875, p. 1; February 10, 1876, p. 45; November 11, 1875, p. 356; April 27, 1876, p. 133; *New York Times,* February 5, 1876, p. 1; Boston *Daily Advertiser,* January 27, 1877, p. 1; W. H. Daniels, *Moody, His Words* (New York, 1877), pp. 50, 53, 55; George Adam Smith, *Henry Drummond* (New York, 1898), p. 60; F. G. Beardsley, *History of American Revivals* (New York, 1912), p. 268–70; A. W. Williams, *Moody,* pp. 184, 206–7; Elias Nason, *Moody and Sankey,* p. 203. See also Chapter 4, note 47, *infra.*

119 *Liberal Christian,* May 6, 1876, p. 5; *New York Times,* February 5, 1876, p. 1.

120 Chicago *Daily Tribune,* January 17, 1877, p. 10; W. H. Daniels, *Moody, His Words* (New York, 1877), p. 60; Boston *Daily Advertiser,* January 27, 1877, p. 1.

121 Quoted in the *Christian Advocate,* December 14, 1876, p. 397.

with reporters who wanted bigger headlines and with ambitious clergymen who wanted more publicity.

In later years Moody used "decision cards" to remedy the confusion and to meet the demands of pastors that better provision be made for following up conversions. These decision cards were issued beforehand to the personal workers who were told to take down the names, addresses, and place of worship of all inquirers. The use of these cards marked a major innovation in modern revivalism, but they played little part in Moody's major campaigns.[122]

Moody's supporters always maintained that the estimates of converts published in the newspapers were too low. They claimed that many persons were converted outside the inquiry rooms whose decisions were never recorded. In London and Boston, for example, Moody divided the city into small districts and organized squads of consecrated Christians to visit the homes in each district. The *New York Times* described this type of home visitation as "a sort of guerilla warfare" in which "a cloud of sharp shooters was deputed to push themselves uninvited, or without any inquiry as to whether their visits were agreeable, into private families where they bully and insult those who are caught in their interviews." [123] The visits of some of these "sharp shooters" to the homes of proper Bostonians on Beacon Hill and Back Bay where Unitarianism held the fort produced irate letters to the Boston *Evening Transcript*. The letter writers resented being asked "Are you a Christian? Where do you attend church? Have you been to the tabernacle?" One writer suggested that the visitation squad "would be serving their Lord *much* more acceptably" if "they would visit some of our poor families" instead of "calling upon families who are supposed to be able to decide for themselves where they will go to church." [124]

[122] One of these cards and a copy of the form letter issued to all personal workers during Moody's revival in Portsmouth, England, in 1882, is among the Moody Papers in the possession of Mrs. Emma Moody Powell, East Northfield, Massachusetts. The importance of this innovation is discussed *infra,* chap. 6.

[123] *New York Times,* February 5, 1876, p. 1. See also *Liberal Christian,* May 6, 1876, p. 5.

[124] Boston *Evening Transcript,* April 9, 1877, p. 6.

Those who sought to enhance Moody's reputation by statistics often quoted the impressive attendance totals estimated at 2,400,000 in London, 1,500,000 in New York, and 1,050,000 in Philadelphia. But such figures did not allow for the fact that the same persons attended night after night. "It seems that those interested in this movement," wrote a Boston reporter, "have settled down to a regular attendance, and the congregation is assuming that similarity and distinctiveness which is observed in all religious bodies." [125] And as in Britain, Moody repeatedly had to scold, "It's time for Christians to stop coming here and crowding into the best seats." On several occasions when Moody asked all those in the audience who were Christians to stand, reporters stated that "almost the entire audience rose." [126]

The over-all effect of Moody's revivals in the United States was just about the same as that in Scotland and England. He boosted the morale of the regular churchgoers, but he did not reach the masses and he did not add appreciably to the numerical growth of the churches. An analysis made of his influence upon the Presbyterian churches in Philadelphia revealed that his work was less effective there than in Edinburgh or Glasgow. In the five years preceding Moody's Philadelphia revival of 1876–77 the Philadelphia presbytery received an average of 679 new members per year. In 1876 the figure jumped to 1492; in 1877 it was 709. For the next four years it declined steadily until it reached only 396 for the year 1881. Even including the two revival years, the average additions to the Presbyterian churches of Philadelphia for the ten years from 1876 to 1885 amounted to only 652 per year—26 per year less than the average annual increase for the five years preceding the awakening. That this slump was not to be blamed upon the removal of the city churches into the suburbs or any other factor making for a long range decline was evidenced by the return to an average increase of 764 per year in the five years after 1886. The Presbyterians of Philadelphia held Moody directly to blame for their "change for the worse" after his coming. Since the Presbyterians were among the most

[125] *Ibid.*, February 15, 1877, p. 3.
[126] W. H. Daniels, *Moody, His Words* (New York, 1877), p. 287.

prominent and active supporters of Moody's work in Philadelphia they had a fair right to complain.[127]

A similar study was made of Moody's impact upon the churches of New England as a result of his Boston revival in 1877 and a series of smaller revivals the following winter in Burlington, Montpelier, Concord, Manchester, Providence, Springfield, Hartford, and New Haven. The average gains for Congregational, Baptist, Methodist, and Episcopal churches in New England for the five years preceding 1877 totalled 12,112 per year. During the year 1877 these four denominations gained 21,075. But in the five year following the revival they averaged only 10,374 new members per year, a decrease of 1,738 from the pre-revival average. Even if the additions of the year 1877 were added in,the average increase for the six years 1877–1882 inclusive was only 12,155, an increase of 43 over the pre-revival average for all New England. What was more, the Congregational churches of Massachusetts gained a total of only 16,035 new members for the six years 1877–1882 as compared with a total gain of 16,521 new members in the five previous years. In other words, the effect of Moody's revivals in Boston, and Springfield, Massachusetts, was adverse to the growth of Congregationalism in that state.[128]

Contemporary comment on Moody's spiritual influence varied widely. The *New York Times* said immediately after the revival there, "The work accomplished in this city for private and public morals will live. The drunken have become sober, the vicious virtuous, the wordly and self-seeking unselfish, the ignoble noble, the impure pure. . . ." But the Boston *Evening Transcript* declared the revival in Boston "a failure" because Moody's "type of religion . . . has not secured the confidence of the community." "Mr. Moody's efforts," said the *Transcript,* "have been wholly futile outside the range of the so-called evangelical churches." A Philadelphia pastor did not even think the revival in his city had been good for the evangelical church members. "It was like feeding people upon pheasants and champagne for several weeks. After the revival-

127 See L. A. Loetscher, "Presbyterian Revivals in Philadelphia Since 1875," *Pennsylvania Magazine of History and Biography,* LXVIII (January, 1944), 66–67.

128 See Samuel W. Dike, "A Study of New England Revivals," *American Journal of Sociology,* XV (November, 1909), 361–78.

ist left it was hard to bring the people back to roast beef and cold water." [129]

But again, as in Britain, the greatest disappointment was expressed over Moody's failure to reach those referred to variously as "the unchurched," "the poor and the wicked," "the neglected classes," "the working class," and "the criminal class." Moody's supporters, particularly the more well-to-do of them, considered themselves benevolent patrons of the poor and underprivileged. Like Shaftesbury, they sincerely wished to help the workingman to rise to respectability and prosperity, but they insisted that he do this according to the "tried and true" principles of the Protestant ethic. If the poor man heeded Moody's sermons and became pious, industrious, thrifty, sober, and honest he would automatically better his condition. But if he chose to use the threats of strikes, boycotts, and union activities to take by force what he could not gain by merit, he was a criminal. The former was the American way of getting ahead; the latter came to be considered un-American. Since a high percentage of the unskilled workingmen were foreign-born, and were either Roman Catholics, Jews, or nonchurchgoers, it seemed logical to many of Moody's supporters to conclude that Americanization and evangelization were synonymous.[130] The home missionary movement from 1870 onward was consciously motivated by the idea that to evangelize was to Americanize, and Moody's revivalism was part of this city missionary activity. Finney's urban revivals had also been partly directed toward reaching the unchurched poor, but in his day these unfortunates were looked upon simply as lost souls. In Moody's day they were more than a challenge to Christian endeavor, they were considered a danger to national security.[131]

[129] *New York Times,* March 24, 1876, p. 4. Boston *Evening Transcript,* April 28, 1877, p. 6; quoted in the *Christian Advocate,* December 14, 1876, p. 397.

[130] In 1870, William E. Dodge denounced Roman Catholic attempts to obtain public tax money for their parochial schools not only by arguing for the separation of church and state but also by defending the public schools as the place where "the true type of American character" could be formed. Richard Lowitt, *A Merchant Prince in the Nineteenth Century: William E. Dodge* (New York, 1954), p. 345.

[131] John V. Farwell exhibited typical evangelical zeal for Americanization and fear of the foreign-born in an introduction he wrote for a book published by Moody's brother-in-law, Fleming H. Revell, entitled, *The Secret of Success,* in

This line of thought was amply demonstrated in an article entitled "Our Unevangelized Masses" which appeared in the Methodist *Christian Advocate* in August, 1875, a few days after Moody returned from Britain. The unevangelized masses, said the article, live "chiefly in our cities"; they are "mostly, not wholly, foreigners or the children of foreigners. . . . Large proportions of them are Romanists having no higher concepts of real Christianity than millions of pagans who never heard of its existence. . . . Many are skeptics. . . . Multitudes are indifferentists. . . . All these classes make up a corrupt, and corrupting, mass of humanity." These "lost multitudes" were "making mightier and mightier those bad forces which are corrupting morals and leading with unerring certainty even to the ultimate overthrow of our political institutions." [132]

Earlier that same year the same journal had printed an article entitled "The Workingman and His Foes" which showed that these unevangelized masses threatened American economic institutions as well. "In order to gain relief from the alleged wrongs of unjust employers," said the writer in reference to the growth of trade unions, the workingman "has been unwise enough to betake himself to leagues. And here he has subjected himself to an outrageous despotism. . . . It is from the leagues that the strikes of late years have sprung. . . . The Church has been too inactive a spectator of this great issue. . . . John the Baptist set a good example of the preaching in this direction when he advised the Roman soldiers, 'Be content with your wages.' . . . The principles of the Gospel must be applied to the muscular labor of the world. For in the words of an eminent writer, 'Where the laws of God are obeyed and Christian morals prevail, there is also reciprocity of confidence and good-will; the workmen and their families are comfortable and contented and the proprietors prosperous.' " [133]

1889: "for many years Europe has used America for a dumping ground into which she has cast her moral and political refuse," he said. So far America had made good citizens of most of this "wretched materials. I am reminded of the terrible earnestness of our purpose to do this as revealed in the execution of the Chicago anarchists. The significance of that tragic event lay in the determination to make these men an example to all those who refused to adopt the lofty standard of American citizenship." John T. Dale, *The Secret of Success* (New York, 1889), p. vii.

[132] *Christian Advocate,* August 19, 1875, p. 257.

[133] *Ibid.,* March 4, 1875, p. 68.

A great many church and lay leaders who agreed with the views expressed in these articles welcomed Moody as a force for order and stability.[134] Many of Moody's more insecure supporters sublimated their dislike for those just below them in the social scale by praying that Moody would save their souls. There was no doubt that Moody too saw a threat to the traditional American way of life in the lack of religion among the unchurched. He told a revival audience in Cleveland in 1879, "Let this country go over to infidelity; what would become of the nation. It was not a great many years ago that, in a convention in Lyons, in France, they voted that the Bible was a fiction . . . and it was not very long before blood flowed very freely in France. And you let atheism and pantheism and deism and infidelity go stalking through this land and property won't be safe." [135] Four years later he gave an address to a convention of Christian workers, ministers, and laymen in Chicago in which he described the nonchurchgoing working men of England as "hard-hearted and hard-headed men" who "gather in their shops on Sunday, or some place else, and talk communism or infidelity." He warned that "we are drifting in the same way in this country." It was essential to convert "the lower classes of people here in Chicago" before it was too late. "I say to the rich men of Chicago, their money will not be worth much if communism and infidelity sweep the land." [136] And later, in the wake of the Paris Commune, the Haymarket Riot, the increasing number and violence of strikes, the rise of the Knights of Labor, and the Communist International, Moody wrote to some of the leading businessmen of Chicago, "there can be no better investment for the capitalists of Chicago than to put the saving salt of the Gospel into these dark homes and desperate centers from which come forth the criminals" and those who increasingly support "the desecration of

[134] John Wanamaker offered the following explanation for his admiration of Moody's revivalism as it affected Philadelphia in 1876–77: "I give this testimony as a businessman in the witness box and bearing testimony to the truth. Hundreds of men converted, out of work, and wandering about the streets have been kept in the way they chose when they embraced the religion of Jesus Christ." Quoted in Grover C. Loud, *Evangelized America* (New York, 1928), p. 217.

[135] Moody, *The Great Redemption,* p. 147.

[136] Quoted in Wilbur M. Smith, *An Annotated Bibliography of D. L. Moody* (Chicago, 1948), p. 79.

the Sabbath." [137] By the end of the nineteenth century, there were some ministers in almost every denomination who were anxious to side with labor in its just grievances against capital, but Moody instructed all of his ministerial supporters in 1897, "Don't let Sunday be given up to talking on topics you don't understand such as capital and labor." [138]

Apart from his endorsement of the six-day week, there was little in Moody's sermons to appeal to the workingman. His message was directed toward the rural-born American, the farm boy who possessed at least a knowledge of reading, writing, and arithmetic, who was thoroughly imbued with the spirit and methods of the success myth, and who, if he were a pious evangelical church member, could easily get a white-collar job in the front office where he might put his employer under obligation to him by his push, tact, and industry. But the majority of the "lost multitudes" who made up the working class did not even speak "good English" and never saw their employers. Even the British working men who did speak English were kept out of the white-collar jobs and the chance to work up in the firm by a rigid class discrimination which made their lot just as difficult as that of the American foreign-born workers.[139]

It soon became apparent to Moody's more observant supporters, and to Moody himself, that he was no more successful in reaching the masses in the United States than he had been in Britain. In Boston the newspapers reported that his audiences were made up of "the better class of people." In New York the *Nation* said "The audience at the Hippodrome is not in any way noticeable except from the absence of the very poor." In Brooklyn "many came in carriages. It was not an assembly derived from the poor and ignorant classes." Even the *Christian Advocate,* which ardently supported Moody's

137 Fund-raising form letter dated March 15, 1889, in the files of the Moodyana Collection at the Moody Bible Institute, Chicago, Illinois.

138 Boston *Herald,* January 8, 1897, p. 10.

139 It is true that many of the leaders of the British labor movement came from pious evangelical homes where they may have sung Sankey's hymns as children, but it would be difficult to show that they were in any way influenced by Moody's social message in their work for the British Labour Party. And in America, Samuel Gompers stated in 1894 that the evangelical denominations had done less for the laboring man than the Ethical Societies, the Unitarians, the Non-believers and the Roman Catholics. See Henry F. May, *The Protestant Churches and Industrial America* (New York, 1949), p. 221.

revivals, admitted that in Brooklyn "the unwashed masses are not touched by the morning meetings." And though the editor maintained that there were "more of them" at the evening meetings he described the evening crowd as being generally "well-dressed." A policeman guarding the doors of the Brooklyn tabernacle was seen "thrusting off by main force a poor scalawag, dirty, and ill-clad—a rough—with harsh words, 'Get out of here; away with you.' " The poor seemed out of place at Moody's meetings and the police consequently thought it their duty to keep them out. These were gatherings for the better sort.[140]

Partly for this reason, partly because of the expense, and partly because he, like Finney, found the effect of mass revivalism too ephemeral, Moody varied his approach to evangelism after 1878. Instead of ten-to-sixteen-week campaigns held in centrally located tabernacles, Moody tried staying six months or more in a city and preaching almost entirely in churches. In the winter of 1878–79 he divided Baltimore into four districts, picked the largest evangelical church in each, and conducted six to eight weeks of meetings in each district. Then after a brief revival in Cleveland, in October–November, 1879, he rented a house in St. Louis and stayed there for half a year preaching a month in each of six different churches located in six different parts of the city. In 1880–81 he preached in San Francisco and other Pacific coast towns, chiefly under the auspices of the YMCA.

None of these revivals was particularly successful. The lack of a central tabernacle decreased the expenses but it also diffused the interest. Newspaper publicity flagged as the meetings dragged on month after month. Moody realized that by speaking in churches he seriously limited his audiences, for the unchurched masses were much less likely to come to a church than a tabernacle. But he justified the new approach on the ground that if he could only "quicken" the church members and set them to work as individual soul winners he might have a more lasting and far-reaching effect in the long run. In this his hopes failed to materialize.

140 Boston *Daily Advertiser,* January 30, 1877, p. 4; *New York Times,* October 25, 1875, p. 4; the *Nation,* XXII (March 9, 1876), 156; *Christian Advocate,* November 11, 1875, p. 354.

He continued to hold revival meetings throughout the United States and Britain until his death, but he and those who supported him abandoned any hope of inaugurating a "tidal wave of revival" which would transform the country.[141] Moody came to believe that dedicated "Christian workers" were the only means of continuously reaching the unchurched. After 1880 he concentrated on the problem of educating a corps of such workers, much as Finney concentrated in training up a new race of ministers at Oberlin. In 1879 Moody founded Northfield Seminary for girls and in 1881 Mt. Hermon school for boys, both designed to give a "Christian education" based on the Bible to young people "in the humbler walks of life." Although only a small proportion of these students actually became fulltime Christian workers, Moody encouraged them all to work at "bringing souls to Christ" in whatever careers they chose.[142] In 1886 he inaugurated a series of summer College Students' Conferences in Northfield in order to inspire educated young men to take up careers in Christian work. The Student Volunteers Movement for foreign mission work grew out of these conferences and adopted as its motto, "The evangelization of the world in this generation." Many talented young men were inspired by Moody to carry the gospel to the heathen as a result of these conferences.

But more important for the future of modern revivalism than these efforts was the founding of the Moody Bible Institute in Chicago. Started in 1886 as the Chicago Evangelization Society, this school became one of the fountainheads for training professional evangelists although this was not its primary purpose. "One great purpose we have in view in the Bible Institute," said Moody, "is to raise up men and women who will be willing to lay their lives alongside of the laboring class and the poor and bring the gospel to bear upon their lives." Moody wrote to a friend in 1889 that through this institute, "I am trying to work out the greatest problem of this century," and as he said elsewhere, "The greatest subject before the people to-

[141] For examples of some of Moody's later failures as a revivalist, see Frederick M. Davenport, *Primitive Traits in Religious Revivals* (New York, 1905), p. 208; Charles Stelzle, "Passing of the Evangelist," *The Presbyterian Tribune,* June 27, 1935, pp. 9–10; *The Congregationalist,* April 29, 1897, pp. 598–99.

[142] W. R. Moody, *Moody* (1930), pp. 305 ff.

day [is] what should be done with and for the workingman?" [143] His answer was, "Save their souls." The Bible Institute was designed to make men and women "familiar with aggressive methods" of Christian work so that they could act as "pastors assistants, city missionaries, general missionaries, Sunday school missionaries, evangelists, Bible readers, superintendents of institutions, and in various other fields of Christian labor at home and abroad." [144] Moody called these Christian workers "gap men" or "irregulars," "men who will go out and do work that the educated ministers can't do: get in among the people and identify themselves with the people." [145]

Realizing that some might take the founding of the Institute as an attack upon the regular ministry and upon established seminaries, he insisted, "I am not seeking to make any short cut to the ministry." But he also noted that in the seminaries "Ministers are often educated away from the people." The Bible Institute was to train "lay workers" taken from the ranks of the people in the art of soul winning and then send them back to evangelize the masses in language they could understand.[146]

At a meeting to raise funds for buildings for the Institute in 1889, J. V. Farwell donated $100,000; Cyrus McCormick (Jr.), $25,000; Robert Scott, $20,000; T. W. Harvey, $10,000; Elbridge G. Keith, $10,000; Marshal Field, $10,000; and L. Z. Leiter, $10,000.[147] The first classes were held in Moody's Chicago church and in the YMCA, but by 1890 five buildings had been bought or erected. The Rev. Reuben A. Torrey was made its first superintendent. By the year of Moody's death the Institute had graduated 1,153 students from its two-year training course. Most of them were engaged in city mis-

[143] D. L. Moody to D. W. Whittle, Northfield, May 24, 1889. This letter is among the Moody Papers owned by Mrs. Emma Moody Powell, East Northfield, Massachusetts. The other quotation is in W. M. Smith, *Moody Bibliography,* pp. 75–76.

[144] A. W. Williams, *Moody,* p. 293.

[145] *A College of Colleges,* ed. T. J. Shanks (Chicago, 1887), pp. 212–13.

[146] Moody, quoted in W. M. Smith, *Moody Bibliography,* pp. 75, 79.

[147] D. L. Moody to D. W. Whittle, Northfield, May, 1889. In the Moody Papers owned by Mrs. Emma Moody Powell, East Northfield, Massachusetts. It was for this meeting that the letter quoted above to the capitalists of Chicago was probably sent. Previous donations to the Institute, including $100,000 by the younger Cyrus McCormick, are mentioned in W. M. Smith, *Moody Bibliography,* pp. 75–76.

sionary and evangelistic work.[148] Moody probably agreed with the Earl of Shaftesbury, who said in 1876 that if London did not have its 400 city missionaries supported by evangelical churchgoers to preach to the poor, it would have to employ 40,000 more policemen to keep the city in order.[149] At the time of Moody's death the Chicago Bible Institute was referring to itself as "The West Point of Christian Service" and twenty-one years later, during the height of the "Red Scare" in 1920, the Institute ran a two-page advertisement appealing for funds in a religious journal in which it described itself as "The Answer to Labor Unrest" where "'agitators' for righteousness" were trained to combat the "agitators of class hatred and revolutionary radicalism" abroad in the land.[150]

The Chicago Bible Institute and the Northfield Schools and conferences were Moody's ultimate answers to the religious problems of his day. Ten years after his death, however, the trustees of the Northfield Schools and the trustees of the Bible Institute quarrelled. Northfield went modernist and the Bible Institute went fundamentalist. Both claimed to be carrying on in the spirit of Moody, but the schism which he had worked so hard to avoid was inevitable.[151]

When Moody first began his revivalism in the mid-1870's, American churchmen were just beginning to worry over the impact of Darwinism. Some who supported Moody's revivals, like Henry Ward Beecher and Lyman Abbott, were among the first to reconcile evolution and theology and start down the road to modernism. But a large proportion of Moody's most ardent backers rejected it entirely from the outset and accepted Charles Hodge's conclusion that Darwinism was atheism. Moody himself, of course, rejected evolution, but when he found that many of the men whom he admired and respected most as Christians, men "out and out for Christ," accepted some aspects of it, he refused to reject them. He found it advantageous to

148 W. R. Moody, *Moody* (1900), pp. 343–44.

149 Quoted in the *Christian Advocate,* February 3, 1876, p. 37.

150 *Watchman-Examiner* (Baptist, New York), July 15, 1920, pp. 904–5.

151 Indicative of how liberal and respectable the Northfield schools had become by the 1950's was the fact that they declined to ask Billy Graham, who claimed to be following in Moody's footsteps, to speak on their campus when he came to visit the school. They feared that the parents of their students would think the schools too revivalistically inclined. (Conversations with Mrs. Emma Moody Powell and Mrs. W. R. Moody, June 7, 1956.)

invite some of these moderate "liberals," or "liberal conservatives," to his summer conferences so that college students who were troubled by the threat posed to their faith by science could be reassured. The men whom he invited to reassure them, Henry Drummond, S. Parkes Cadman, James A. Broadus, and George Adam Smith, were so staunchly evangelical that to them evolution and soul winning were both part of "natural law in the spiritual world." [152]

Moody's own view of evolution was, "It is a great deal easier to believe that man was made after the image of God than to believe, as some young men and women are being taught now, that he is the offspring of a monkey." [153] But his Biblical literalism was not as bitterly defensive as that of later fundamentalists. On the subject of the higher criticism he spoke less in anger than in sorrow: "What is the use of talking about two Isaiah's when most people don't know there's one?" [154] He admitted that there was much in the Bible that seemed mysterious, perhaps even inconsistent, but that was one of the proofs of its supernatural authority to him. When someone asked him what he did with a particularly difficult passage he said:

"I don't do anything with it."
"How do you understand it?"
"I don't understand it."
"How do you explain it?"
"I don't explain it."
"What do you do with it?"
"I don't do anything with it."
"You don't believe it, do you?"
"Oh, yes, I believe it." [155]

While he was willing to have some of the men who believed in theistic evolution and the higher criticism attend the Northfield Conferences and was hurt when his more conservative friends called them infidels, he believed that such scholarly research should be confined to the seminary classroom. George Adam Smith recorded a revealing conversation he had with

[152] For the ease with which Drummond reconciled evangelism and evolution, see his address "Dealing with Doubt" which he gave at the Northfield Student Conference in 1887, *A College of Colleges,* pp. 35 ff.

[153] Gamaliel Bradford, *Moody,* p. 64.

[154] Quoted in A. L. Drummond, *American Protestantism* (Edinburgh, 1949), p. 345.

[155] W. R. Moody, *Moody* (1900), p. 495.

Moody on the subject of Biblical criticism in 1899: "He was frankly hostile," said Smith. "What's the use of criticism?" he asked. "It's creating division in the Church. It's restraining revivals. It's paralyzing preaching." Moody proposed what he thought would be a practical solution to the problem: "Couldn't we agree to stop the critical controversy and go on with the Lord's work together. . . . Couldn't they [the Biblical scholars] agree to a truce for ten years, bring out no fresh views, just let us get on with the practical work of the Kingdom?" [156] Like most revivalists, when faced with a difficult problem that seemed to stand in the way of evangelism, he preferred to ignore it as though it did not exist.

Moody's attitude toward the social gospel movement was marked by the same unwillingness to let fresh views alter his own conception of the real "practical work of the Kingdom." To begin with, the social gospel doctrine of the fatherhood of God and the brotherhood of man was contrary to Moody's theology. "I want to say very emphatically that I have no sympathy with the doctrine of universal brotherhood and universal fatherhood. . . . Show me a man that will lie and steal and get drunk and ruin a woman—do you tell me that he is my brother? Not a bit of it. He must be born again into the household of faith before he becomes my brother in Christ." [157] One or two of Moody's more liberal biographers portrayed him in later years as sympathetic to the social gospel because, they said, he preached a religion of service and social betterment. They pointed to his efforts on behalf of the YMCA, YWCA, temperance, the orphans of England, city missions, and the inmates of prisons. In his work among the poor of Chicago he often gave coal, food, and clothing to the needy, rescued erring sons of his parishioners from the hands of the law, and found jobs for deserving young men. But his charity was always secondary to his soul winning.[158] The essence of his attitude toward the

156 George Adam Smith, introduction to Henry F. Drummond, *D. L. Moody* (New York, 1900), pp. 24, 25, 28, 30, 32.

157 From an unidentified clipping in the Moodyana Collection, Moody Bible Institute, Chicago.

158 In 1876, Moody said, "When I was at work for the City Relief Society before the [Chicago] fire I used to go to a poor sinner with the Bible in one hand and a loaf of bread in the other. Dr. Chalmers used to forbid his missionaries giving away money or supplies. He said those things ought to come

social problems of his day was contained in his statement, "A heart that is right with God and man seldom constitutes a social problem and by seeking first the kingdom of God and His righteousness nine-tenths of social betterment is effected by the convert himself and the other tenth by Christian sympathy." [159] Insofar as he had a philosophy of charity it was the same Gospel of Wealth proclaimed by Andrew Carnegie. Aid should be given to help the deserving man to help himself, but not any more aid than would get him started. "There is a good deal that we think is charity," Moody said, "that is really doing a great deal of mischief" because it encouraged people to expect handouts instead of working for a living.[160]

One of Moody's most prominent supporters in Scotland, James C. White, later Lord Overtoun, provided a striking example of the prevailing outlook of the philanthropic Christian businessmen who admired, and were admired by, Moody. Overtoun was a partner in a large chemical firm in Shawfield near Glasgow. Having been converted in the British awakening of 1859–60 he eagerly welcomed all of Moody's visits and sat on his platform nightly throughout the Glasgow revivals of 1874, 1882, and 1892. He was a leading contributor to all the charitable causes which Moody supported, but was particularly interested in home missionary work among the poor and in foreign missions to the heathen of Africa. In 1899, the workers at Overtoun's chemical plant went on strike against low wages, a twelve-hour day (with no time off for meals), a seven-day week, unsanitary working conditions, and a complete absence of safeguards against the occupational hazards and disease prevalent in chemical manufacturing. Overtoun told newspaper reporters that "he had no personal knowledge of the matters in question as, owing to the heavy demands of his religious and public activities . . . he had not for many years taken any part in the

by other hands, and I thought he was all wrong. My idea was that I could open a poor man's heart by giving him a load of wood or a ton of coal when the winter was coming on, but I soon found he wasn't any more interested in the Gospel on that account." W. H. Daniels, *Moody, His Words* (New York, 1877), pp. 431–32.

159 W. R. Moody, *Moody* (1930), p. 170.

160 Gamaliel Bradford, *Moody,* p. 87. Like Carnegie, Moody told the poor, "There is many a man that will help you if you will show a disposition to help yourself." Moody, *"To All People,"* p. 489.

management of Shawfields works. . . ." [161] The Armours and McCormicks, who were Overtoun's equivalents in the United States, took the same attitude toward "Christian sympathy" for the poor and "social betterment" for the laboring class. To them labor was a commodity; only individuals were subjects for charity. Business was one thing, soul winning another. Social gospelers were dangerous or radical because they tried to mix the two. Moody was a force for righteousness because he kept them separate.

Moody's approach to political reform followed the same lines. "The nation is now crying 'reform'" he said in 1877. "I don't know how long they are going to continue that cry; they have kept it up ever since I remember; but there will be no true reform until Christ gets into our politics. Men are all naturally bad and cannot reform until the Reformer gets into their hearts." [162] Like Finney, Moody believed that it was a Christian's duty to cast his ballot for honest men, but he never had any doubts that the best man was always the candidate of the Republican party. In 1896 he became so frightened by the oratorical skill and charm of William Jennings Bryan, who certainly was the embodiment of pietism in politics, that, according to Moody's son, "he redoubled his own personal efforts in behalf of McKinley." [163] On the other hand, Moody admired the talents of self-made men like Richard Croker, the boss of Tammany, and once asked Croker to use his influence against a bill that would have permitted the theaters to open in New York on Sundays.[164]

Some of Moody's lay supporters, men such as William E. Dodge, John Wanamaker, and John H. Converse, were active in sporadic attempts to obtain municipal reforms in their cities, but their interest in overthrowing boss rule was primarily to install the type of "good government" which would lower taxes and cease threatening business interests with adverse regu-

[161] See Donald Carswell, *Brother Scots* (London, 1927), p. 209. Overtoun did, however, hasten to correct some of the evils when J. Keir Hardie published the facts in the *Labour Leader*.

[162] W. H. Daniels, *Moody, His Words* (New York, 1877), pp. 185–86.

[163] Paul Moody, *My Father*, p. 47. W. G. Blaikie claimed that in 1880 Moody told him that "universal suffrage" was "among the perils of the country, the result of which no man could foretell." W. G. Blaikie, "Transatlantic Notes," *Catholic Presbyterian* (London), IV (October, 1880), 307.

[164] Paul Moody, *My Father*, p. 220.

lations. The political activities of such evangelical businessmen, like their religious and social activities, were motivated predominantly by their desire to place in office honest men with "good business principles" and not by any attempt to alter the conditions which produced dishonest politicians. The Christian League, which John Wanamaker helped to found in 1894 to reform the Republican party in Philadelphia, was inspired primarily by the Rev. Charles H. Parkhurst's crusade against Tammany's protection of prostitution and gambling.[165]

The confusion in Moody's outlook between his overly optimistic faith in the evangelization of the world through human agency and his overly pessimistic doctrine that the world was getting worse and worse was never resolved. When Lord Overtoun asked him to return to Scotland for a fourth visit in 1899, Moody began by saying, "The work in my own country has never been so promising" and then went on to point out that "Destructive theology on the one side and the no less evil spirit of extreme intolerance on the other side have wrought wide dissension in many communities." He then described the growing "spirit of bitterness" in theological debates and the "depleted churches." [166] Apparently he could not be happy unless he were involved in overcoming such obstacles. To him the Christian life was all warfare.

When he had the heart attack which eventually took his life, Moody was in the midst of a revival meeting in Kansas City. Instead of leaving behind him a universal, nonsectarian church made up of all true evangelical believers, as he had hoped, he left only a growing schism which his successors rapidly made unbridgeable.

That evangelical orthodoxy and the revivalism it supported was about to lose its hold upon the more promising members of the younger generation at the turn of the century was indicated in an article entitled "The Passing of the Revivalist" which appeared in the *Arena* in January, 1899. It was written by the Rev. David C. Utter of Denver, Colorado, who began by stating that "The old-fashioned revival is a thing of the past. The

[165] See L. A. Loetscher, "Presbyterians and Political Reform in Philadelphia from 1870–1917," *Journal of Presbyterian History,* XXIII (March, June, 1945), 12. See also H. A. Gibbons, *Wanamaker, passim,* and Richard Lowitt, *W. E. Dodge, passim.*

[166] W. R. Moody, *Moody* (1900), p. 496.

people of our country who are still young will have none of it." His reason for believing this was that revivalists not only rejected biological evolution, but that they refused to believe in "the slow but very real improvement of human society through the ages." They were, like Moody, too pessimistic about the question of social reform and too otherworldly in their reliance upon a supernatural conversion experience. Utter, like the believers in Bushnell's Christian nurture, held that "ninety-nine persons" out of every hundred "grow up in virtuous ways from infancy" and "enter the higher life without any conversion or change of heart." Religion, as Utter defined it, was simply a man's resolution to "devote his life and all his powers to the uplifting and bettering of humanity." [167]

Utter was a Unitarian and the *Arena* was a muck-raking journal, but the views expressed in this article were obviously more representative of the trend in American social and religious thought than Moody's. For Moody to demand committal to a theological outlook which flew in the face of irrefutable scientific and scholarly evidence, for him to disparage all efforts at social reform despite their stark necessity, could hardly help but alienate the intelligent youth of the day. Yet the more the old theology was attacked and the more the old social traditions altered, the more Moody was convinced that human nature was wicked and that only supernatural assistance could redeem society. Moody, like Finney, believed that through revivalism divine power could be harnessed to human goals. But he was disillusioned to find that after the initial enthusiasm for his revivals in the perplexed 1870's, churchgoers and nonchurchgoers alike quickly adapted themselves to urban-industrial society and regained their confidence in the gradual working out of God's kingdom on earth. Some wanted to control and direct their destiny and environment; others wanted to leave the development to the slow but sure processes of evolution. Some took up political action, some social service, and some merely advocated self-help or charity. But most Americans continued to believe, in some way, in the perfectibility of man and of society.

[167] David C. Utter, "The Passing of the Revivalist," *Arena,* XXI (January, 1899), 107 ff.

However, if Utter was right in claiming that Moody's theology seemed outmoded to the enlightened members of the younger generation, he was wrong in assuming that revivalism was a thing of the past. Even without the support of the enlightened and the reformers, the revival tradition still had a wide appeal among members of the older generations, and among those less sophisticated young people fresh from the farm who continued to pour into the cities. Many who thought they had outgrown the evangelical outlook were quick to return to it whenever their self-confidence faltered. The third great awakening was just reaching its crucial turning point at the turn of the century, and there were many who thought the evangelical churches could still provide its leadership. Moreover, Utter underestimated the ability of the professional evangelists to adapt their message and methods to the changing times. Even before Moody died revivalists were practising their trade in such a way as to make the old-time religion seem new.

CHAPTER 6

"The Golden Rule . . . Up to a Certain Point"

The two most remarkable evangelists in the profession at Moody's death were Samuel Porter Jones and Benjamin Fay Mills. The former was called "the Moody of the South"; the latter was hailed in 1895, while Moody was still alive, as "the foremost evangelist of the day." Both of them owed a great deal to Moody indirectly, but neither was ever closely associated with him. In fact, admirers asserted that Jones and Mills were noteworthy primarily because they were leaders of "the new evangelism." Washington Gladden described Mills as "a new type of evangelist" whose conception of the gospel message was "certainly unlike the conception which has been current" among revivalists. The Rev. P. S. Henson, a prominent Baptist pastor in Chicago, claimed in 1886 that Jones's revival preaching in Chicago was "doing a work that Moody never did and yet which mightily needs to be done." [1]

What was thought to be novel about these men was their emphasis on the social aspects of Christianity. Instead of preaching that the conversion of individuals was the be-all and end-all of religion, Jones and Mills emphasized the duties which Christian living entailed in relation to others in the church, in

[1] *The Great Awakening in Columbus, Ohio, Under the Labors of Rev. B. Fay Mills and His Associates,* ed. Henry Stauffer (Columbus, Ohio, 1895), pp. 5, 12; Chicago *Tribune,* March 7, 1886, p. 10.

the community, and in the nation. Salvation in their revivals was the beginning of a new effort in holy activity, not merely the conclusion of a search for personal absolution and security. In its activistic aspects their message resembled Finney's, but to their contemporaries they were preachers of a new "social" gospel.

And yet for all this, Jones and Mills were totally different in personality, style, and message. That two such dissimilar men could both be viewed as part of the social gospel movement was indicative of its inherent ambivalence. Moreover, their careers ultimately demonstrated the general incompatibility of professional evangelism and the social gospel. In the revivals of "Sam" Jones, the reform aspects were specious and repressive. In the revivals of B. Fay Mills, the soul-winning aspects eventually atrophied from disuse. The progress of these two men, both of whom reached the peaks of their careers in the 1890's, illustrated the basic inability, or unwillingness, of most evangelical Protestants in America to meet squarely the challenge of the new urban-industrial society. Because of this failure evangelists and evangelistic churches lost, as David Utter predicted, the respect and support of the next two generations. And even "liberal Protestantism," which was more friendly toward science and social reform and cooler toward revivalism, failed to capture the real spirit of the third awakening.

Samuel Porter Jones was born in Chambers County, Alabama, in 1847.[2] His grandfather and four of his uncles were Methodist preachers, and his grandmother had read the Bible from cover to cover thirty-seven times "on her knees." His father, John J. Jones, felt the urge to follow his brothers into the ministry but decided that he could make a more secure living as a lawyer and businessman. In 1856 Sam's mother died and for three years he and his two brothers and sister lived with their pious grandparents. Then his father remarried and settled in Cartersville, Georgia, where the children came to live in

2 For biographical details of Jones see Laura M. Jones (assisted by the Rev. Walt Holcomb), *The Life and Sayings of Sam P. Jones* (Atlanta, 1906); Samuel P. Jones, *Sam Jones' Own Book with an Autobiographical Sketch* (Cincinnati, 1887); Walt Holcomb, *Sam Jones* (Nashville, 1947). I have supplemented these accounts with the Jones Papers in the possession of the Rev. Walt Holcomb, Atlanta, Georgia, and by conversations with Mr. Holcomb and his wife, the youngest daughter of Sam Jones.

1858. During the Civil War John Jones served as a captain in Lee's Army of Virginia. Sam was too young to fight.

After the war Sam concluded his desultory education by graduating from Euharle High School in June, 1867. At the graduation ceremony he delivered a valedictory address which reflected the outlook of the generation which came of age in the ashes of the Southern Confederacy. He lamented "Our country ruined, our schools expunged, and our names extirpated from the list of humans through the instrumentality of merciless conquerors"; but he did not despair. "If we will only rely on that all gracious being who shields the weak from the oppressor, we will have nothing to fear. He will fill our hearts with hope, courage, and confidence." After quoting Longfellow's "Psalm of Life," he declared to the assembled parents, "Fathers, just say you will give us a Collegiate Education and we will prove to you that there is Washingtons, Websters, and Clays who will spring as it were from the very dust of humiliation." [3]

But the young orator did not get a collegiate education. His father intended to give him one, but Sam's health broke down, and he decided instead to read law at home. In 1868, after only one year of legal study, he was admitted to the Georgia bar and began what seemed a promising career. But he took to drink. His friends later claimed that he was driven to it in order to seek relief from "nervous dyspepsia." Whatever the cause, it soon destroyed his law practice. By 1872 the only job he was able to get was that of furnace stoker in a factory near Cartersville where he shovelled coal for twelve hours a day. In spite of the pleas of his wife and the births of two children he could not give up drinking.

Then, dramatically, in August, 1872, he promised his dying father never to touch another drop. A week later, in the agony of keeping his vow, he was converted under the revival preaching of his grandfather, Samuel G. Jones. When the old man called for the anxious to come forward, Sam walked down the aisle of the little country church and said, "Grandfather, I take this step today. I give myself, my heart, and life, what is left of it, all to God and His cause." Immediately he felt a call to

[3] A copy of this valedictory in Jones's handwriting is among the Jones Papers in the possession of the Rev. Walt Holcomb, Atlanta, Georgia.

the ministry, to spread the word of what salvation had done for him, and, perhaps, unconsciously, to sublimate his desire for liquor by constantly exhorting others to give it up. His grandfather encouraged him, and a week after his conversion Sam Jones preached his first sermon. In November, 1872, he was admitted to the North Georgia Conference of the Methodist Episcopal Church, South, as an itinerant preacher.

The North Georgia Conference assigned Jones to a rural circuit which had five churches scattered in four different counties. It soon became apparent that Jones was no ordinary circuit preacher. His success in conducting revival meetings in his own churches led to his being asked by nearby pastors to help them with their annual revivals. His fame grew steadily in northern Georgia as he was shifted, according to Methodist custom, from one circuit to another. By 1880 he was spending only 50 per cent of his time preaching in his own circuit. The rest of the time he was conducting revivals for other pastors in nearby towns. In December, 1880, the North Georgia Conference decided to free his talent from the restraints of pastoral work and made him the fund-raising agent for the Methodist Orphan Home in Decatur, Georgia. The orphanage had a debt of $20,000 and Jones was given permission to preach anywhere in the United States where he thought he could raise money for the institution.

He started preaching in various Methodist churches in small towns such as Winterville, Athens, Harlem, and Thomson, Georgia. Then he moved into the bigger churches in the cities of Macon, Savannah, Augusta, and Atlanta. The pastors admitted him to their pulpits for one night and at the conclusion of his sermon the collection was taken for the orphanage. Since it was known in advance that attendance would require contributions, it required an attractive speaker to draw a crowd, and Jones quickly developed a style which aimed to please.

Jones was not required, however, to devote his entire time to fund-raising for the orphanage. When he could, he was expected to help Methodist ministers conduct revival meetings, and there was no objection to his helping in a "union" revival in which several denominations took part as long as the Methodists were among them. His popularity soon brought him invitations to speak out of his home state. In 1883 he conducted a two-week series of meetings for the Methodist churches of Louisville, Kentucky, which received some attention from the secular press. The Louisville *Commercial* called his meetings the most exciting since the revival conducted in that city by Major D. W. Whittle and P. P. Bliss (two of Moody's associates) in 1875. Jones was described by the daily papers as "an eccentric speaker," "somewhat peculiar in his manner," but commendable for "his originality, his zeal and his courage." The newspapers were particularly impressed by a meeting he held for men only in the Louisville Masonic Temple at which he delivered a blistering attack on the sins of profanity, Sabbath breaking, gambling, licentiousness, and intemperance. Though the Louisville papers gave only a few brief paragraphs to the revival, they noted one striking novelty which distinguished it from previous revivals: "The speaker was frequently interrupted by loud applause." [4] The people of the post-war South were eager to be told of their sins and exhorted to righteousness.

Jones's first attempt at a large-scale, city-wide revival took place in Memphis, Tennessee, in 1884, where thirteen pastors of five different denominations united to sponsor him. "He is an original character," said the Memphis *Avalanche,* "and preaches in a way peculiarly his own. At one moment he raises a smile at his quaint and homely illustrations or his incisive way of presenting a truth, and the next he melts to tears by his tender pathos or carries his congregation by the vehement way in which he denounces sin or urges his hearers to a better life." At a meeting for men only, "Hundreds of men wept like whipped children and when they were called for prayer the whole audience went down on their knees." It was claimed that "incalculable" good would result from the meetings, even though the audiences were made up of "the best people of the city—men and women who have been for years the working elements in the churches." Four hundred "public professions of faith" were reported and one hundred had joined the churches by the end of the meetings.[5]

[4] Louisville *Commercial,* January 31, 1883, p. 4; February 1, p. 4, February 3, p. 4. Louisville *Courier-Journal,* February 5, 1883, p. 6.

[5] Memphis *Avalanche,* January 19, 1884, p. 4; January 22, p. 4, January 26, p. 4.

The reports of the Memphis meetings brought Jones invitations to Chattanooga, Jackson, and Knoxville, Tennessee, to Waco, Texas, and to T. DeWitt Talmage's tabernacle in Brooklyn. "He has loomed into importance as an evangelist and revivalist," said one newspaper in 1884, "until he stands now second only to Talmage and Moody."[6] But the campaign which first put Jones at the top of the profession was his Nashville revival in 1885. In this city of 50,000, it became obvious that Jones was taking revivalism on a new tack. He was turning it into a combination of popular entertainment and civic reform.

Over some vehement opposition from the more staid pastors, the Nashville ministerial association voted to invite him to "the Athens of the South" and to erect a tent for 5000 in which to hold the meetings. Jones had previously spoken on one occasion in the city and the Nashville *Union,* deprecating his imminent return, denounced his "coarseness, vulgarity, slang and positive misrepresentations." The newspaper's editor insisted that "Our people are past the age of being ridiculed or abused into religion." That Jones should be "invited to come again," said the editor, "amazes us beyond expression."

But when he arrived the people of Nashville packed his revival tent three times a day for four weeks, while the evangelist berated them, amused them, and cajoled them into coming forward to sit on the "mourners' " benches and there pledge themselves to lead Christian lives. At the conclusion of the meetings the *Union* editorialized on a new note: "This strange preacher walked into our city and attacked the vices and immoralities of social life and the evil practices of church members like a frontiersman would fight a forest fire that threatened his fences and barns. . . . As a teacher of life's virtues, as an example of moral courage, he will long be remembered. . . . Mr. Jones is displaying sound judgment and great courage and at the same time a truly Christian spirit in telling people plainly and bluntly of their shortcomings." Some claimed that Jones made 10,000 converts during this month in Nashville. It also made Jones's reputation as "the Moody of the South."[7]

[6] Quoted in L. M. Jones, *Life and Sayings,* p. 107.

[7] See *ibid.,* pp. 133 ff., for an account of the Nashville revival with quotations from the Nashville *Union.*

Sam Jones was a man of medium height, slight build, and often subject to illness and spells of exhaustion. But he possessed a fiery spirit and a passion for preaching which drove him to constant activity. His deepset eyes flashed righteous indignation at one moment and twinkling amusement the next. While waiting to speak he nervously jiggled his gold watch chain or pulled at the pointed ends of his drooping black moustache. But once under way he proceeded casually and wholly at ease. His dark hair was combed straight across his brow so that the forelock continually fell forward, and as he spoke he frequently ran his fingers through his hair to push it back. Sometimes he walked around to the front of the pulpit and spoke leaning back upon it with his elbows resting on its front edge. At other times he gestured vigorously with his arms and occasionally, in hot weather, shed his coat and spoke in his shirtsleeves. "Among his many gestures," said one reporter, "the one which appears the most effective is when he holds his hand out at half arm with index finger pointing toward his audience and says, 'Listen! Listen!' " Sometimes he would point straight into the audience and say, "You, old feller!" and every eye would turn to see who had been singled out as the erring sinner.[8]

Jones was in earnest about the importance of his mission and his sarcastic ridicule was often violent in its intensity, but he tempered his zeal with a folksy sense of humor delivered in a slow Southern drawl and with a poker face that seemed incongruous in a religious service. "Fun," he said, "is the next best thing to religion," and it was often hard to tell whether he was more intent upon the former or the latter. "We have been clamoring for forty years for a learned ministry," said Jones, "and we have got it today and the church is deader than it ever has been in history. Half of the literary preachers in this town are A.B.'s, Ph.D.'s, D.D.'s, LL.D.'s, and A.S.S.'s." The tenor of Finney's sermons had been carefully reasoned argument, and of Moody's, sentimental pathos. Jones's sermons were characterized by wit, invective, homespun philosophy, and satirical humor: "If anyone thinks he can't stand the truth rubbed in a little thicker and faster than he ever had it before, he'd better get out of here." Contemporary observers often compared Jones to the professional humorists then in vogue on the lecture

[8] Boston *Herald,* January 24, 1897, p. 33.

platforms, men like Mark Twain, Josh Billings, and Artemus Ward. But Jones considered himself more than a mere entertainer. He saw himself as the leader of a great crusade to save the nation from the worldliness and sin which were turning the churches into "religious crocheting societies" and the social life of the cities into Babylonian debauchery.

Jones opened his revival in Nashville in May, 1885, with a sermon that resembled Moody's opening sermon in Brooklyn about Gideon's Army "taking the land." But instead of using a Biblical analogy, Jones referred to an incident in the Civil War in which the Confederate General, Cockrell, acting on orders from General Hood, stormed and captured the fort at Locust Grove against desperate odds. "Brethren of Nashville," Jones said, after giving a stirring account of the battle, "at this hour, as adjutant-general of the Lord Jesus Christ, I point my finger at the citadel of sin in Nashville and tell you that my Lord and Saviour presents you all His love and He asks at your hands this fort that is desolating so many hearts. . . . And I want every man and woman here today that wants to join the warfare against sin, whether you are in the church or not, if you would be on the right side and try to win the city to Christ, I want everyone that would see the city presented to God to stand up." According to the newspapers, "Nearly the whole congregation rose." Apparently no one in 1885 thought it blasphemous or egocentric for Jones to call himself the "adjutant-general of the Lord Jesus Christ" as many had when Finney used the term sixty years earlier.

As Jones saw it, the primary purpose of a revival was to "draw the line" on the various moral issues of the day and then to demand that all who claimed to be Christians "take a stand" and get "on the right side" in the warfare. In Jones's sermons the issues all became very clear and simple. The enemies of Christianity were those who indulged in, or condoned, dancing, card-playing, gambling, circuses, swearing, theater-going, billiards, baseball, low-cut dresses, society balls, novel reading, social climbing, prostitution, and above all else, drinking alcoholic beverages. The forces of righteousness were those "born-again" church members who read the Bible regularly, who actively engaged in soul winning, who were respectable, honest citizens, who contributed generously to all religious enterprises, who prayed frequently, and who were never in debt. Every revival which Jones conducted, from Nashville in 1885 to Oklahoma City in 1906, was first and foremost an effort to enlist the religious forces of the city into an army of righteousness for a concerted crusade against sin. The changes which this approach brought to mass evangelism were significant both theologically and socially.

Revival preachers had always dramatized the Christian life as a warfare against the forces of evil, but they usually insisted that men must first save themselves, or be saved by God, before they could march out to save the world. Jones considered the mere fact of enlistment in his army of civic crusaders tantamount to conversion. Conversion, as he defined it, was not so much a change in belief nor the acquisition of grace through faith, but rather a change in moral conduct, a resolution, as he put it, to "Quit your meanness" and fight for decency. "Conversion scripturally means simply two things," he explained: "1. I have quit the wrong. 2. I have taken hold of the right." Like Finney, Jones believed that man had the common sense, the will power, the free will, and the moral strength to act rightly if, under the stimulus of the preacher, he would only exert himself. But he simplified Finney's theology considerably. In his sermon, "Religion, A Reasonable Service," Jones said, "It's astonishing how we know right from wrong and wrong from right. . . . Just as certainly as any railroad leads into or out of this city, just so certainly a man who will quit wrong and take to doing right will find his way to God." [9] He preached so constantly on the theme that "heaven is just the other side of where a man has done his best" that in one volume of his sermons the publisher felt it necessary to add a footnote early in the book stating, "Mr. Jones would insist that divine grace is a circumstance not to be left out." [10] But the fact was that Jones did leave it out most of the time.

[9] S. P. Jones, *Sam Jones' Own Book,* p. 144. In explaining Jones's social and theological views I have quoted from a variety of sources, including newspapers, Jones's published sermons, and the Jones Papers, without any particular regard to chronology. There is no evidence that Jones's views changed on any of these matters after 1880, and in each of his revivals he merely repeated the same sermons over and over with only slight variations in style.

[10] S. P. Jones, *Sam Jones' Own Book,* p. 56.

In explaining the difference between his theology and that of Moody, Jones said, "Mr. Moody lingers about Calvary more than I do. I linger more about Sinai." [11] Moody emphasized the blood and Jones the law. Although Jones fully believed that conversion required belief in the substitutionary atonement, he seemed at times to be denouncing Moody for overemphasizing it. "I get disgusted," he said, "with some little fellows who are always talking that they preach Christ and nothing but Christ to sinners. I would as soon preach Socrates to an unconverted sinner as to preach Christ. He's got just about as much use for one as the other. The law of God is a great moral force which moves the world and the law is what ought to be preached first, that conviction may follow." [12]

Jones's reaction from the pre-Civil War emphasis upon individual crisis conversion or, as it was called in the South, "heart religion," was vigorous. "The mere believing that Christ died to save sinners doesn't amount to much," he said. "When you come into heaven your entering depends upon what you've been doing down here; there's nothing said about the blood of Christ." [13] He wanted deeds, not words, as the test of salvation. The process of conversion, which Finney talked of in terms of God's moral government, Jones talked of as a commercial transaction. God's law was "a business contract binding on you" and also upon God. "It is his business to save you." "You do what God tells you to do, and then if God doesn't do what he said he would do, you have an issue that will bankrupt heaven in a minute." [14]

11 Boston *Herald,* January 5, 1897, p. 1.

12 L. M. Jones, *Life and Sayings,* p. 451. This contrast between Jones and Moody exemplified the perennial, seesaw-like alternation in the emphasis of revival preaching, as in Christian theology itself, between hope and despair, between grace and the law, between salvation by works and salvation by faith. Finney had emphasized the law and good works. Moody emphasized repentance and faith. Sam Jones followed Finney. So in the early twentieth century did Billy Sunday. But in 1950 the revival emphasis of Billy Graham was back again to that of Moody. American churchgoers have responded with fervor to either appeal provided the presentation was powerful enough and their mood was right.

13 Baltimore *American,* May 8, 1886, p. 2.

14 S. P. Jones, *Sam Jones' Own Book,* pp. 197–98, 160. Or as he put it in another sermon, "It is my business to preach reformation; God's business to preach regeneration." "You convert yourself, and when you convert yourself, God regenerates you." Pp. 505, 508–9.

Many of Jones's auditors were shocked less by this contractual theology than by his view that a man could and should join a church *before* he was regenerated. According to Jones, part of the process of taking "the Lord's side" was to "take the side with the Lord's people." Jones illustrated this by the story of the man who heard his preacher say, "If a man will do before he gets religion just as he thinks he would do after he gets it, he will get it." Well, said Jones, "this fellow was a sensible man, and he took it in in all of its bearings." That very day the man joined the church. When he came home and told his wife, she asked incredulously, "Have you got religion?" The man answered, "No." "Well, what in the world did you join the Church for without religion?" "Well, the preacher said if I would do before religion as I thought I would do after I got it, I would get it; and I know I would join if I had it, and I am going to do before I get it just what I think I would do after I get it." His wife shook her head, "Well, well, well, that beats anything I ever heard." The man then began to read the Bible regularly, to conduct family prayers, to attend the Wednesday night prayer meetings, to lead in prayer at the church, just as though he had "got religion," all to the shocked indignation of his wife. But, said Jones, "he just plowed his furrow along that way for about two weeks and got the biggest case of religion that any man ever heard of." [15] So it all amounted to the same thing in the end.

Like Finney, Jones found that the religious life in his section of the country had become formal and stereotyped. People were waiting to "get religion" through the miraculous interposition of the Holy Ghost and they thought of revivals as occasions when God sent his power from on high to turn them from their wicked ways. "A good many men are looking for some mysterious transformation, some sudden, unexpected, serious, radical transformation," said Jones, echoing Finney's complaint. But Jones pointed out to his audiences that he had not been transformed by any sudden influx of the Spirit but simply by resolving to give up drinking and become a preacher. Conversion had not changed him from infidelity to faith: "If a man believes anything after he gets religion that he didn't believe before he got it, I have never had any religion. I never saw

[15] *Ibid.*, pp. 210–11.

the day in my intelligent life . . . that I didn't believe what I believe tonight. . . . I was as well satisfied up to twenty-four years of age that Jesus died to save sinners, and that I was a sinner and that he was able to save unto the uttermost as I am tonight. I believed in Jesus Christ twenty-four years and lived just as if I didn't believe a word of it. But for thirteen years I have believed it, and I have lived the best I could, God being my helper." [16]

As in western New York in the 1820's, most people in the post-Civil War South believed in the fundamental truths of the gospel. What Jones wanted was to have them live up to the moral aspects of those beliefs and to stop waiting for a cataclysmic crisis experience. "I never ask a man what sort of experience he had to begin with, but 'Brother, are you loyal to God now? Do you love the right? Do you hate the wrong?' " To those who believed that they must wait for the spirit to move them, that they must have a feeling or an emotional excitation of some sort before they could believe that they had "got religion," Jones said, "Feeling is the result of religious exercise, just as perspiration is the result of physical exercise. . . . You stir around and begin to right the wrongs you have done in this city. . . . You will have the feeling." He ridiculed those old Methodists who claimed that religion was a change of heart. " 'O, I believe in heart religion' you hear folks say. 'That's my sort of religion.' Well, I believe in finger religion as strongly as heart religion. . . . If I couldn't have it in but one place I want it in this hand here and make it go out and do something for somebody. Your heart religion isn't worth a thing in the world by itself. . . ." The decline in heart religion in the post-Civil War South was a major reformation. In the wake of Jones's preaching only Negroes and "poor whites" continued to indulge in religious emotionalism, at least, in the cities. He not only made heart religion seem useless, he made it seem inadequate and immature. "I'm sorry for you if you have only heart religion," he said.[17] In effect, Jones transformed country-bred pietists into urban civic reformers while Moody rebuked urban meliorists for lacking rural piety.

16 *Ibid.*, pp. 134–35.
17 *Ibid.*, pp. 134, 144, 126, 217–18.

Because Jones talked so much about the sins of the world and about saving society he was considered by many to be a vigorous advocate of social reform. To him the means of grace included more than joining a church and reading the Bible and praying. To be a Christian a man had to "Take hold of the right" in all those issues "that will help humanity and bless the world." As he once told a reporter, "I am not so much for getting people to believe as to follow Christ and imitate Him." He called this "practical religion" or "positive religion" or "muscular Christianity." "I like a broad, useful, aggressive Christianity—a Christianity with a musket and a cartridge belt," he said. "Satan won this country by fighting and we must win it back from him in the same way." [18]

But it invariably turned out that by fighting Satan and helping humanity he simply meant to encourage paternalistic charity on the one hand and on the other to impose the moral code of rural Georgia upon every individual in the country whether he wanted it or not. When he spoke of "the good old practical religion" and "doing your duty" he meant that men should give up the things of this world and endeavor to make everyone else give them up too. "Here is a man who has been drinking all his life. He is going to a saloon. He decides to quit. What must he do to be converted? He must turn from liquor and join a temperance society, which is the antipodes of the saloon." [19] It would be negative religion for a man to be concerned only with reforming his own sins. Positive religion meant joining the prohibition movement, and Jones's revival meetings often seemed like little more than prohibition rallies. Here Jones differed from Finney as well as Moody, both of whom tried to keep the churches out of politics.

This attempt to bring the forces of the churches behind legislative action on social questions had some precedent in Lyman Beecher's campaigns in New England against duelling, lotteries, and delivering the mail on Sundays, but Jones's civic reform revivalism was a startling reversal of the position the southern churches had taken in pre-Civil War days. When the issue of slavery was first raised in the national conventions and

[18] *Ibid.*, p. 123; L. M. Jones, *Life and Sayings*, pp. 189, 270; Chicago *Tribune*, March 6, 1886, p. 7.

[19] L. M. Jones, *Life and Sayings*, p. 464.

missionary board meetings of the various denominations after 1830, the southerners took the stand that slavery was a civil institution and that the churches were not to meddle in secular affairs. Consequently the South's ministers had exhibited the same attitude toward temperance, gambling, and Sabbatarian reforms prior to 1880. They forbade their members to gamble, go to theaters, and get drunk, but they did not advocate laws against these vices. After the Civil War, however, this attitude steadily lost ground.

By 1882 an article appeared in a southern Methodist journal which bluntly claimed that "so far from continuing to hold the doctrine that the Church must abstain from all teaching on civil questions, the true doctrine is that wherever a moral question has been adversely acted upon by the State, the necessity for fearless, outspoken truth becomes the more urgent upon the part of the Church." [20] The writer of this article, the Rev. David C. Kelley, said that it was the duty of the church to take an active part in settling the questions of sabbath desecration, intemperance, and gambling. Four years later the southern Methodist church officially declared that the sale and manufacture of alcoholic beverages was a sin. From this it was only a short step to advocating church support for the legal prohibition of the manufacture and sale of alcoholic beverages. And once the churches took this stand they tacitly admitted that the northern churches had been perfectly justified in making a political attack upon slavery as a moral question. By 1887 the South firmly believed that "The minister who stands silent with his finger in his mouth while the battle for moral reforms that involve the Church [rages], incurs the secret contempt of even the vicious elements of whom he is the ally." [21]

[20] *Quarterly Review* quoted in Hunter D. Farish, *The Circuit Rider Dismounts* (Richmond, Virginia, 1938), p. 97. Farish's book is an excellent discussion of the changing temper of Southern Methodism after the Civil War.

[21] See Farish, *Circuit Rider Dismounts,* pp. 314, 320, 103. The Southern revivalist "Sam" Small, who was converted by Jones and who for thirteen years was Jones's assistant evangelist, often compared the prohibition movement (in a backhanded way) to the antislavery crusade: "Nearly twenty-five years ago misguided men in the South fired the first shot upon Fort Sumter that awakened this entire nation and led to reform and led to liberties and led to the release of the slaves from bondage . . . but today, in a holier and grander cause, by the approving smile of God, old Georgia has fired a gun upon the Sumter of sin and intemperance in this country that will arouse this whole nation." Quoted in S. P. Jones, *Sam Jones' Own Book,* pp. 533.

Several explanations have been offered for this about-face. Some claim that the South had a guilt-complex over the failure of the Lost Cause which its ministers had assured them was ordained of God; defeat was taken as a sign of divine displeasure and so, after 1865, the South put on sackcloth and ashes and resolved to be more religious, more pure in its moral life, than any other part of the country even if this meant giving up some of the old pleasures.[22] Others take a more cynical view that the Prohibition movement, at least, was simply a movement to keep the freed slaves under control and that many of the whites who supported it had no intention of giving up alcohol themselves.[23] The fact that the early prohibition laws in southern counties and states permitted private citizens to import alcohol for their own consumption lends some strength to this contention. It has also been said that the southern churches, particularly the Methodist and Baptist, which remained separated from their northern brethren, felt themselves in competition with them to prove their righteousness. The northerners had called them sinners over slavery in the years immediately after the war and continued to taunt them for their hesitancy in joining in the moral crusades against alcohol, gambling, theaters, cards, and dancing.[24] Some contend that the prohibition crusade, particularly in its political aspects, was a diversion to add spice to the political dullness of the one-party system. And finally, it may be assumed that the South, like the North, was unconsciously pushed by science and secularism into a more worldly concern for humanity in order to compete for the allegiance of the populace and to compensate for a dwindling sense of contact with a personal God.

More significant, however, than these unverifiable assumptions in explaining the southern churches' interest in moral reform was the rise of "the New South." With the development of industry and the growth of its cities the South began to face some of the same problems the North faced: the flocking

[22] W. J. Cash, *The Mind of the South* (New York, 1941), pp. 132–33.

[23] See Martha B. Bruere, *Does Prohibition Work?* (New York, 1928), pp. 112–144, and F. C. Iglehart, *King Alcohol Dethroned* (Westerville, Ohio, 1917), p. 257. D. L. Moody disagreed with Jones's views on prohibition, but he excused him on the ground of the South's peculiar problem: "Sam Jones is a Prohibitionist, and as he lives in the South I don't much blame him." Boston *Herald,* January 5, 1897, p. 1.

[24] See Farish, *Circuit Rider Dismounts,* pp. 97–103.

of poor workers into slum areas and factory towns dislocated old customs and mores; poverty and social unrest produced increases in crime and alcoholism, disregard of the Sabbath, and a search for new amusements and excitement. In the cities anonymity decreased social control while loneliness and frustration weakened self-restraint.[25]

After 1880 the South's hostility to Yankee progress and materialism gave way to enthusiasm for the economic rejuvenation which industrialization would bring to the region. But the ministers who lauded the enterprise and community spirit of the new textile, transportation, and manufacturing magnates looked with distrust upon the new proletarian class. The southern factory worker, while much less obstreperous than his counterpart in the North, nevertheless might someday, it was feared, prove susceptible to the radicalism which socialists, anarchists, and union agitators fomented. Southern pulpits soon began to repeat northern bromides about intemperance as a cause of poverty and working-class discontent: saloons were called centers of anarchist and socialist plotting, alcohol maddened the unemployed or the disgruntled; poverty was increased by the money the worker spent on drink; political demagogues bought votes with rum and whiskey; and foreigners brought their continental Sunday with its beer gardens and dancing into communities where worship and prayer were the only permissible activities on the Lord's Day. An article printed in a Methodist journal in Baltimore, and widely quoted in other southern religious journals in 1880, pointed out that "There is a foreign population among us who have imported into this country their infidel and socialistic ideas, and are seeking to engraft them upon our institutions and social customs. . . . There is nothing we should guard with more jealous care than the observance of the Sabbath. Let that be ignored and the very foundations of public morality and private virtue will be undermined." And a few years later southern religious journals were warning their readers that "The socialist, under the garb and guise of the working-man, is influencing the men of toil who want rest and recreation after the labors of the week; and into greedy ears he is pouring the glowing promises of much

25 See Liston Pope, *Millhands and Preachers* (New Haven, Connecticut, 1942), *passim.*

better times for the laborer when the capitalist shall have been robbed and the Churches shall have been destroyed. We must pay more attention to home missions, especially in our large cities. . . ." [26]

The South had few foreigners and fewer socialists in the decades when Sam Jones helped to push the churches into a more active part in purifying the cities by his revivals, but as it came to emulate the North in its religiosity and its economic system, so the South came to consider that the problems of Christians, patriots, and capitalists were the same everywhere. What was to stop an anarchist from throwing a bomb in the center of Nashville as well as in Chicago? Who could tell when the coal miners near Birmingham, Alabama, might decide to imitate the Molly Maguires of eastern Pennsylvania? And everyone knew that infidelity would have spread its fatal seeds among southern colleges had not the ministers led an attack upon atheistic professors and nipped the heresies in the bud. Rural preachers and churchgoers in the South had always feared the cities and insisted upon a narrow moral code in regard to recreational activities. With the rise of industrialism and the growing gap between rich and poor in crowded manufacturing centers, the urban clergy joined their country cousins in a crusade to make the South safe against all attempts to "engraft" new ways "upon our institutions and social customs." Progress and prohibition must go hand in hand if the New South was to preserve the old traditions.

Consequently Sam Jones was hailed in the 1880's as "a social force" for community improvement in one southern city after another. While Moody was praised for preaching humility and submissiveness to the poor, Jones was praised for telling respectable churchgoers to enact laws to restrain the unconverted. "Right demands," said Jones of the liquor trade, "that we put this traffic out of the reach of the people." [27] A few church leaders complained at first, "Brother Jones, you ought to preach a little more to us about Christ and not raise so much noise about other things," or "Brother Jones," you "are not preaching anything but reformation." But such men were old-fashioned. The great majority of southern churchmen were in full accord

26 Quoted in Farish, *Circuit Rider Dismounts,* pp. 101–2, notes.
27 Baltimore *American,* May 7, 1886, p. 4.

with Jones's assertion that "We want preachers to be aggressive and determined" and that the purpose of muscular Christianity was to "raise the devil."[28] Jones made such an impression in Nashville in 1885 that he was invited to address the state legislature which was in session. He told the legislators about the evils of the liquor traffic and also offered them some suggestions on how to reform the prison system.

Before he left the city the Nashville *Christian Advocate* spread its endorsement of him to its one million subscribers throughout the South. His preaching in Nashville, said the *Advocate,* "has been attended by unprecedented crowds, and with the most extraordinary results. Drunkards have renounced their liquor-drinking; gamblers have given up their evil occupation; church members, convicted of complicity with sin, have broken off from wrong courses; thousands of persons of all ages, sexes, and grades of society have publicly announced their purpose to give up their sins and lead better lives." Jones wrote home to his wife that the revival was "glorious" and that he was receiving numerous invitations to conduct revivals: "Preachers and Laymen from many states are here after me."[29]

Throughout the remaining twenty-one years of his life Jones was overwhelmed with more invitations than he could accept in the largest cities in the nation. In the fall of 1885, he was invited to St. Louis and St. Joseph; in 1886 he conducted meetings in Cincinnati, Chicago, Baltimore, Indianapolis, Toronto, St. Paul, and Omaha; in 1887 he preached in Kansas City and Boston; in 1889 in Los Angeles, Sacramento, San Francisco; in 1890–91 in Chattanooga, Little Rock, Wilmington. In 1893 he gave up his connection with the Decatur Orphanage to devote his full time to professional evangelism. Although he passed the peak of his career by the middle of the 1890's, he continued to return year after year to the cities of his earlier triumph. He conducted eighteen revivals in Nashville alone. And between visits to larger cities he preached in almost every city with a population of over 10,000 in the South. Jones frankly stated his reasons for preferring to conduct his revivals in the South: "I find the people further South are more easily moved. They

28 L. M. Jones, *Life and Sayings,* pp. 187, 189, 150.

29 *Ibid.,* pp. 154–55; Jones to his wife, May 26, 1885, in the Jones Papers owned by the Rev. Walt Holcomb, Atlanta, Georgia.

haven't got the intellectual difficulties that curse the other portions of the country." [30]

Jones was not particularly interested in the technical machinery of professional revivalism. In general he followed the theory and methods laid down by Finney and Moody, whose careers were familiar to him. He usually sought and obtained the united support of the majority of evangelical ministers before he would consent to come to any city, but outside the South he often met opposition because of his "lack of dignity" in the pulpit. In several cities almost no advance preparation was made for his revivals. His invitation to St. Louis came from only one pastor, though others cooperated after he arrived. He came to Boston at the request of the Methodist preachers and though many Baptists cooperated with him the Congregationalists declined to do so. In Chicago his support came from the South Side ministerial association and lacked the city-wide backing that Moody had obtained. But in the cities of the South he could count upon almost unanimous support from the Methodists, Baptists, Presbyterians, and Disciples who made up almost 90 per cent of the churchgoing population. The Episcopalians usually did not cooperate with him but their opposition was not very loud.

Like Moody, and in keeping with the general religious spirit of his age, Jones went out of his way to play down denominational differences. "Theology," he said, "is a good thing. It is a good thing to stuff with sawdust, like the skin of a fish, and put in a museum as a relic of antiquity." "If I had a creed I would sell it to a museum." "Orthodoxies are what has ruined this world." Like almost all professional revivalists he asked, "Wouldn't it be a good idea to have . . . a Church universal?" Such a church would of course be based upon the fundamentals but it would ostensibly have no creed. "It is not faith in a creed that saves. The Methodist creed cannot be swallowed by a great many intelligent men. The Presbyterian creed has never gone down some very good, wise men. The Catholic creed does not suit others." The creed a man professed "is an accident" which usually depended upon the family into

30 L. M. Jones, *Life and Sayings,* p. 238.

which he is born. But at bottom, "it's faith in a person, and not in a creed, that saves the soul." [31]

The fact that Jones, like Moody, was praised so highly for this tolerant, almost indifferent, approach to religious doctrine indicated the extent to which theology had ceased to play a part in American religion. In 1892 Jones claimed that the Christians of the United States were divided into three groups: Roman Catholic, Protestant, and "non-conformist." He was on the whole more tolerant toward the first than the last of these. Among the "non-conformists" he listed the "Second Adventists, Christian Scientists, extreme holiness cranks." It was his view that a third party was as improper in religion as in politics. According to Jones, America was not a place for non-conformists.[32]

Jones sometimes conducted his revivals in church buildings, but in order to maintain a nonsectarian approach and to reach larger crowds he preferred to use tents, auditoriums, skating rinks, or armories. The renovated skating rink used in Chicago held 7000 and the total attendance was estimated at 260,000 over the five weeks. In other cities the tents or auditoriums seldom held over 5000 and total attendance figures were usually in the neighborhood of 150,000. In some Southern towns he spoke in tobacco or cotton warehouses, or "bush arbors," and in several places special wooden tabernacles were built for him. But on the whole his revivals were not as vast in scale or cost as Moody's early meetings. The executive and finance committees for Jones's revivals seldom included businessmen who were nationally known though they contained men such as J. V. Farwell, Jr., Fleming Revell, George Harvey, and A. H. Borden in Chicago; Joshua Levering in Baltimore; Lamar Collier in Atlanta; John W. Thomas, Jr., in Nashville, and George A. Baker in St. Louis. The expenses for Jones's meetings were kept low by the fact that he seldom stayed more than five weeks in any

[31] S. P. Jones, *Sam Jones' Own Book*, pp. 346, 450, 348–49, 361.

[32] This statement was contained in a letter which Jones wrote to the Atlanta *Journal* on April 9, 1892. Jones's letters to the *Journal* were in the nature of weekly columns which he was paid for writing. He wrote these letters from 1892 to 1906. The majority of them are contained in several scrapbooks which are part of the Jones Papers in the possession of the Rev. Walt Holcomb, Atlanta, Georgia. Unfortunately the clippings are not always dated in these scrapbooks.

city and usually only three. There were the usual expenses for advertising and for the rent and renovation of the "tabernacle," but even in Chicago, where he preached for five weeks, the total expenses came to only $6000, including $2400 for rent, $1000 for publicity and printing, and $400 for "repairs."[33] Unlike Moody, Jones did not request or require that this money be raised privately; collections were taken at each of the meetings and these usually proved sufficient.

Jones considered it part of his task to help stimulate the collections for expenses so as not to leave the cooperating churches with a deficit. On the opening night of his second revival in St. Louis in 1895, he spoke at the Music Hall and announced to the crowd, "The rent of this hall, with the concession made to religious meetings, is $2000. The audience that comes here night after night and on Sunday afternoons must pay that $2000 or this gentleman talking to you will pay it. You can take your choice. If you don't pay, I will." At this a voice from the crowd yelled, "We won't let you Brother Jones, not a cent." Jones answered, "I never yet had a crowd that would not do the clean thing. The people will do right. I believe the people can be trusted." On the next night Jones remarked that the first night's collection had been very low. Too many were putting pennies and nickels into the plate. "Now I have read in the Bible all about 'tabernacles' but nothing about tabernickels. Again, the Lord says in Revelations that he despises a 'Nicolaitan.' As for those who contribute pennies, did not Paul say, 'Alexander the coppersmith did me much evil'?"[34]

As in Moody's revivals, ushers and choir singers were usually trained beforehand, but forty ushers and a choir of 400 were about the maximum for any of Jones's meetings. Soon after his success in Nashville, Jones acquired a soloist named E. O. Excell who accompanied him as Ira Sankey accompanied Moody. And like Sankey, Excell was soon involved in publishing hymnbooks to be used in Jones's meetings. But Jones went beyond Moody in acquiring several other helpers who made up his entourage. He hired a private secretary to help him with his correspondence, a stenographic reporter to take down his sermons for publication, a choir leader who assisted Excell, an

33 Chicago *Tribune,* April 5, 1886, p. 12.
34 St. Louis *Globe-Democrat,* March 4, 1895, p. 2; March 5, p. 2.

assistant evangelist who divided the meetings with Jones, and for a time he even hired an assistant who worked especially among young people. Later evangelists expanded this core of assistants into much larger teams of "specialists."

Jones's meetings followed the well-established pattern. Afternoon and evening meetings at the auditorium were supplemented by noon prayer meetings and sometimes by a sunrise "Inspiration Meeting" at 6 A.M. Special evenings were set aside for men only, women only, businessmen, young people, mothers, "commercial travelers." Jones spoke in factories, shops, office buildings, schools, and temperance rallies in addition to his sermons at the tabernacles. In some places the cooperating churches discontinued all their activities during the revival except their Sunday morning and evening services in order that all religious attention might focus on the revival.

Recognizing, as Moody did, the importance of publicity for his meetings, Jones gave reporters special seats on his tabernacle platforms. In general the newspapers were cordial and cooperative and found his slang and his attacks on civic immorality good headline material. One typical headline read:

JONES OF GEORGIA ENTERTAINS:
THE FAMOUS EVANGELIST CAUTERIZES
HIS CONGREGATIONS:
Says He Is Going to Stir up the Wickedness
Of Memphis If They Tear His Clothes Off
And Run Him Out of Town—Promises to
Make Things Lively.[35]

In San Francisco, however, William Randolph Hearst's *Examiner* reported Jones's sermons in dialect and spread the impression that he was a clown and his revival a farce. After a few days of this ridicule Jones turned upon the Hearst reporters and denounced them from the platform: "You little sap-headed reporters, with eyes so close together that you can see through a keyhole with both of them, are sent here at night to take down my sermons; now if you can't report them as I deliver them, you stay away from here. You seem to think your mission is to make my sermons funnier and more sensational, and in your ridiculous attempts you are slandering me and the cause. Now, bud, if you are doing the best that you can, your paper had better

[35] Memphis *Appeal-Avalanche,* February 8, 1893, p. 5.

put you on a job that is small enough for your caliber and let them send a man here that is big enough for the occasion." [36]

As in all revivals the climax was the call for converts. Jones usually waited four or five days before he made his first call. Occasionally he used inquiry rooms, though he himself did not attempt to have personal conversations with the inquirers as Moody and Finney did. That was left up to the cooperating clergymen. More often Jones simply cleared the front rows of the tabernacle and held an "after-meeting" service. One call for "mourners" was described in the St. Louis *Globe-Democrat:* Jones had just given an hour and one-half sermon entitled "Escape for Thy Life" to an audience of men only. At its conclusion he asked all those to rise who would say, "By the grace of God I will lead a better life and serve God and do right." Almost one-third of the 6000 men present stood up. "And now while we sing a hymn a minute," said Jones, "every man and boy that says here is my hand to serve God and do right, stay a few minutes and give me your hand and let us settle it here this afternoon. While we stand and sing, come and give me your hand." Excell led the choir in "That Old-Time Religion" as Jones held out his right hand. "The vast audience seemed to surge toward the man who had so profoundly moved it. Men almost fell over each other in their determination to grasp the evangelist's hand . . . down the aisles the stream of men continued to come. . . . They came boldly, with gladness and relief in their eyes, with the air of men who had found something good and were anxious not to lose it. Mr. Jones' hands, right and left, were shaken and squeezed and tugged and his eyes flashed as with a holy fire. He kept up an unremittant 'God Bless you.'" According to the reporter, this "extraordinary reception" continued for thirty-five minutes until "fully 2000 of the 6000 men who had heard the sermon had come forward to give the pledge to lead a better life." [37] On such occasions there was no after-meeting. But in most instances only fifty to one hundred came forward to shake Jones's hand and take one of the front seats. Jones gave them a brief exhortation to live up to their pledge and then the pastors and personal workers of the cooperating churches circulated among them answering

[36] L. M. Jones, *Life and Sayings,* p. 278.
[37] St. Louis *Globe-Democrat,* March 11, 1895, p. 2.

questions and persuading them to sign decision cards. The conversion experience had come a long way from the agonized writhings of Finney's early meetings to the handshake and "God bless you" of Jones.

Jones had no qualms about publicizing the estimated numbers of his converts and was perfectly sincere in considering a resolve to lead a better life adequate proof of conversion. He told a reporter in Chicago in 1886 that he had converted "not less than 50,000" since he had begun preaching. And in an autobiographical sketch printed in 1887 he said that "over the past twenty-four months of my ministry . . . not less than twenty thousand souls have been brought to Christ." By the end of his career, in 1906, the estimate had risen to 500,000 conversions out of a total audience of twenty-five million. Estimates on individual campaigns offered by Jones or his assistants averaged about 2000 each:

Memphis (1884)	1000	Chicago (1886)	1500 to 3000
Chattanooga (1884)	1000	Baltimore (1886)	1200 to 2500
St. Joseph (1885)	2220	San Francisco (1889)	1200
Birmingham (1885)	1800	Memphis (1893)	2500
St. Louis (1885)	1600	Boston (1897)	2500
Cincinnati (1885)	2000		

It is probable that Jones deserved some credit for the rapid growth of the Methodist church in the South in the last quarter of the century, though not so much as he and his eulogists claimed. The southern Methodists had lost 113,000 white members and 129,000 Negro members between 1860 and 1866. Though the denomination grew steadily after 1866, the growth was less rapid in the urban than in the rural areas prior to 1880. Then, simultaneously with the growing popularity of Jones, urban Methodism picked up momentum in the 1880's.[38] Unlike the country people who flocked into the northern cities, those in the South tended to bring their religious zeal with them. Jones and his fellow evangelists doubtless recruited many of them for the urban churches although a large proportion preferred the less formal "holiness" and "Adventist" sects which Jones so heartily disliked. It is also likely that Jones's new emphasis on civic reform helped to bring back into the

[38] See Farish, *Circuit Rider Dismounts,* p. 30, 67–69. Farish credits revivalism for this Methodist resurgence but does not mention Sam Jones.

fold many church members who had dropped away during the war either from disappointment over the churches' unsuccessful espousal of the Confederacy or simply because they were tired of the old "heart religion." Jones put a new purpose and spirit into religious activity which made support of the church in the interest of the community welfare seem more vital.

However, neither Jones nor any of the many other white evangelists in the South at the time had any influence on the Negroes, who steadily drifted out of the white churches and into their own independent denominations. Jones, like all professional revivalists in the South, followed the practice of segregating his audiences. Usually the revival meetings were limited to whites only. When Negroes were admitted they sat in "Jim Crow" sections where they were smiled at patronizingly. Even Moody followed this practice on his southern tours. Sankey noted in Meridian, Mississippi, "We have one side of Tab. for Blacks. D. L. has them sing alone, some times 'just to show the white people how to sing.'"[39] When Negroes were not admitted to the regular meetings, evangelists like Jones and Moody sometimes made a gesture in their direction by holding one or two special meetings during the revival "For Colored Only."[40]

Jones took the stock paternalistic attitude toward the Negro. He saw no reason for them to have social equality, the right to vote, the right to enter the public schools, nor to enter any professional or white-collar career. In one of his weekly columns in the Atlanta *Journal* in 1900, he commented on Georgia's adoption of the white primary system which effectively disenfranchised the Negro. According to Jones "the negro is to blame largely for this state of things, for if the negro had realized that the best white people of the south were his best friends and he had quit ganging with the liquor crowd and let Yankee-Doodle alone he would have been much better off today. For the good negroes there is room in the hearts of the best

[39] *The Ira D. Sankey Centenary: Proceedings of the Centenary Celebration of the Birth of Ira D. Sankey Together with Some Hitherto Unpublished Sankey Correspondence* (Lawrence County Historical Society, New Castle, Pennsylvania, 1941), p. 55.

[40] Sankey records that when Moody scheduled a meeting for Negroes only in Chattanooga the Negroes boycotted the meeting. Ira D. Sankey, *My Life and the Story of the Gospel Hymns* (Philadelphia, 1907), p. 88.

southern people. . . . Separate seats in street cars and separate coaches on trains for white and black teach us that socially they can't mix and wherever there is mixing of the races, at the polls or in the parlor, it's the lowest down whites and the meanest negroes doing the mixing." As for educating the Negroes to a better way of life, "the best negroes I know in Georgia today were never in a school house." [41] He had no sympathy with those who were "blubbering over the death of the miscegenationist, Fred Douglass, a nigger with a white wife." [42] And when asked by a reporter in California about the relevance of Christianity to racial equality, he answered, "No, I do not think Christianity requires that the white race should meet the negro on terms of social equality." [43]

It was claimed for Jones, as for Moody, that "He will get hold of the masses," but he had no more respect for the poor whites in the South than he did for the Negroes. In fact, he generally associated the two groups together and thus helped to exacerbate the bitterness between them. "I hardly ever mention circuses; they are too low-down for me. Down South all trashy niggers and low-down white folks go to circuses." And "If there is anyone I want to see go to heaven it is poor white folks and niggers." [44] When he was asked in 1894 whether he believed that the churches were doing all they could to reach the poor, he answered, "If the church does not reach the poor it is more the fault of the poor than of the rich church members. Frequently the rich feel more kindly toward the poor than the poor do toward the rich." [45]

Because he spoke more frequently and vividly on contemporary social, political, and economic problems than most of his fellow revivalists, Jones provided a clearer index to the outlook

[41] This letter in its published form, dated June 1, 1900, is among the clippings in one of the scrapbooks in the Jones Papers in the possession of the Rev. Walt Holcomb, Atlanta, Georgia.

[42] Nashville *American,* March 1, 1895. Pagination deleted from clipping in scrapbook in Jones Papers owned by the Rev. Walt Holcomb, Atlanta, Georgia.

[43] San Francisco *Examiner,* March 24, 1889, p. 2.

[44] *Sam P. Jones' Sermons with a Biography by Theodore M. Smith* (Philadelphia, 1886), pp. 97, 51. This was probably a pirated edition of Jones's sermons taken from verbatim reports; words like "nigger" were edited out of the authorized editions.

[45] Clipping from an unidentified newspaper dated February 11, 1894, in one of the scrapbooks among the Jones Papers in the possession of the Rev. Walt Holcomb, Atlanta, Georgia.

both of the profession and of the audiences which supported it. On the whole the attitude taken by revivalists toward these problems were remarkably similar, and even though Moody thought Jones vulgar and differed from some of the theological aspects of his message, he was always friendly and cooperative toward him whenever their paths crossed. Jones, like Moody, clearly spoke for and identified himself with the middle class. "The backbone and sinew of any city or community is the middle class," he said, "the honest, industrious toiling thousands to whom the government must look in every emergency for support and for the maintenance of law and order. . . . The luxuries of the rich and [the] mean squalor of the poor furnish but a poor soil out of which manhood is grown . . . among the middle class we find the purest moral atmosphere." As far as Jones was concerned, heaven was to be populated exclusively by the middle class: "Society at the bottom and at the top has gotten beyond the reach of God on the one side and humanity on the other and these two extremes will meet at last where the devil will run his willipus-wolipus over the whole business and millionaires and paupers together will join Dives in his prayer, 'Oh, for a drop of water to cool my parched tongue.' "[46]

Like Moody, Jones also gave full vent to the Protestant ethic which nineteenth-century Americans honored as the success myth. "Give me a fellow with enterprise and vim and push and go," said Jones. That was the kind of boy who made good. On the occasion of Paderewski's fifth tour of the United States in 1902, Jones pointed out to the young men of the country that the great pianist, who had achieved success through "work, perseverance, suffering," now made $150,000 on one tour. "It is now almost impossible to estimate Paderewski's wealth." Jones then described what a young man must do, "If you would succeed and be a gentleman." His precepts included, "shun idleness," because "an idle boy is the devil's saddle horse"; "avoid all games of chance" because "they destroy your taste for honest toil just as yellow-back novels destroy all taste for useful knowledge"; be "careful of your company" and "stick to

[46] Letters to the Atlanta *Journal* dated November 4, 1892, and May 31, 1901, in the scrapbooks, Jones Papers, owned by the Rev. Walt Holcomb, Atlanta, Georgia.

the Bible." "Don't be skeptical, agnostical, or jasackical in religion." Playing the stock market was also taboo: "A dollar earned by sweat and toil is worth a million won on puts and calls." If a young man would merely "observe these things" he would surely "succeed in [his] calling as Paderewski has in his." [47]

In Jones's ethic, as in that of most evangelists, to be in debt was as dishonest as to be a thief. "These bankruptcy and homestead laws have been the curse of this country in all ages of it. . . . I want to see the day come when you can sell a man's shirt off his back to pay his debts." [48] At a time when the farmers of the South and Midwest were banding together in revolt against a system which left them perpetually in debt, Jones told them it was a matter of character and not of economics. "If the sheriff comes on you and takes your house and your stock and your all, let him take them, and then walk out with your wife and children bareheaded and barefooted so that you can say, 'We are homeless and breadless, but my integrity is as unstained as the character of God.' " [49]

He pitied the boy who was born rich and the girl whose parents encouraged her to enter the gay whirl of society life. He said he did not intend to leave his sons one dollar: "If they are of any account they won't need it; and if they are no good, money would be a curse to them." [50] Daughters would be better off if put to work as soon as possible in a textile mill or sweatshop: "Those poor girls go to sewing hard every day working on a machine and those rich girls go to keeping up with the fashion. Now watch them three years from that time and the fashionable girl looks sallow and pale and bloodless and nearly dead on her feet, and there [at her machine] is the red, rosy, healthy, vigorous girl. It will kill a girl quicker to keep up with the fashion than if she sews all day for a living." [51] Like William Graham Sumner and a great many middle-class followers of Herbert Spencer, Jones had no difficulty in equating the

[47] Jones letter to the Atlanta *Journal,* March 17, 1902, in the scrapbooks in the Jones Papers, owned by the Rev. Walt Holcomb, Atlanta, Georgia.

[48] St. Louis *Globe-Democrat,* November 24, 1885, p. 10.

[49] *Sam P. Jones' Sermons* (Philadelphia, 1886), *op. cit.,* p. 65.

ping of an interview Jones had with a reporter in New York on February

[50] Chicago *Tribune,* March 9, 1886, p. 3.

[51] *Sam P. Jones' Sermons* (Philadelphia, 1886), *op. cit.,* p. 255.

theory of survival of the fittest with the will of God: "God projected this world on the root-hog-or-die-poor principle. If the hog, or man either, don't root, let him die." [52]

The mixture of Christianity and chauvinism which became increasingly popular in revival preaching after 1890 was perfectly evident in Jones's statements. He asserted that "we have the most advanced civilization in the world today" and that "God has given us the greatest country the sun shines on." [53] This he attributed primarily to the supremacy of the Anglo-Saxon race, which had proved itself superior to all others. "If there were 150,000 more Chinese in this State than white," he said in California in 1889, "and if they all had the privileges of the ballot, you could then realize the fearful menace to civilization which the domination of an inferior race presents to the South." According to the reporter, Jones then went on to say, "He thought a party which would unite the better class of Southern people with the better class of Northern people on a platform which should demand the supremacy of the native-born white population of the South against Negro rule and the supremacy of the native born population of the North against the foreigner greatly to be desired." He told the reporter, "I am a Know-Nothing in politics, but I do not see how such a movement can be explained to the people and brought about. The country is being weakened by the influx of a lower and alien element. I greatly desire to see this country become and remain American, and am a firm believer in the superiority of the stock from the British Isles." [54] Later evangelists were to find a riper climate of opinion in the 1920's in which to "explain" these theories to the public.

In politics Jones was the mauve decade's equivalent of a Dixiecrat. He had no use for Greenbackers or Populists. To Jones all third party movements were led by "demagogues" who advocated "class legislation" which would be harmful to the in-

[52] Quoted in an unidentified clipping in one of the scrapbooks in the Jones Papers owned by the Rev. Walt Holcomb, Atlanta, Georgia.

[53] Letters to the Atlanta *Journal,* dated July 20, 1898, and May 31, 1901, in the scrapbooks in the Jones Papers owned by the Rev. Walt Holcomb, Atlanta, Georgia.

[54] San Francisco *Examiner,* March 24, 1889, p. 2. Jones did not state these views in his sermons, but he evidently had no qualms about expressing them to reporters for publication.

dustrious middle-class citizen. Though he claimed to be a Democrat, he frequently asserted his distaste for Bryan and he praised McKinley as "one of the grandest types of real American manhood."[55] He lumped "radical" political orators like Bryan and Tom Watson with labor agitators as undesirable citizens. "Political orators and labor agitators are largely responsible for the condition of things in the political and industrial fields of our country. . . . The labor agitator profits by strikes and friction in the labor world. The political orator profits by friction in the political world. . . . If we could get rid of our politicians and labor agitators . . . then the men in this country could go to work, and work and frugality would soon solve the problems and settle the questions."[56]

During his revival in Chicago, two months before the Haymarket Riot, Jones did not mention the grievances which were currently causing bloody outbreaks in the city over the lockout at the McCormick Harvester Factory. But he went out of his way to abuse the parades and picnics by which the workingmen tried to raise enthusiasm for their cause. "It is said Chicago has more of the Communistic element in it than any other city in America. . . . Look at your workingmen going out to some celebration. Look on the flag and see the inscription, 'Our Children Cry for Bread.' . . . A more Communistic power [slogan?] was never put on a flag than that. Those same men went to the grove and drank up that day 1400 kegs of beer. (Laughter) If you will put your beer-gardens and barrooms out of this city and put these millions into bread and meat you will have the fattest and plumpest children and the most prosperous city on the face of the earth. (Applause) But an old devil walking around and toting a flag and saying his children cry for bread—why if you were to stick a knife in his belly four gallons of beer would run out. (Great laughter)."[57]

[55] Toledo *Blade,* March 9, 1899. Jones said of the election of 1896: "I didn't vote the Democratic ticket this year. They voted into the mud. . . ." Boston *Herald,* January 13, 1897, p. 6. It does not appear that he ever voted for the Democratic Party after his conversion. He got around this difficulty in the South by claiming that the Prohibition Party was the only honest party and that it had the answer to all the nation's problems. See below.

[56] Unidentified clipping in the Jones Papers owned by the Rev. Walt Holcomb, Atlanta, Georgia.

[57] Chicago *Tribune,* March 15, 1886, p. 3.

Shortly after the Haymarket Riot, Jones explained to an audience in Baltimore, "When you come down to bed-rock, all this communism and Anarchism are based upon the liquor traffic. Where did the Chicago Anarchists hold their secret conclaves? In the back part of barrooms." He warned the industrious middle class, "Do you know what communism is? . . . It is the 50,000 poor men who have been debauched by whiskey who say they have spent the money which you have been accumulating and they are now calling upon you to divide." Year in and year out Jones hammered into his audiences the argument that prohibition would put an end to all the nation's economic problems. "What would the discussion between labor and capital amount to if the $1,200,000,000 wasted on drink could be emptied into the pantries and upon the tables of all our homes? If whiskey was banished from our land no more children would cry for bread. . . ." [58] And his audiences agreed.

Yet despite this obvious conservatism, Jones was considered a liberalizing force in American church life by many evangelicals. He was continually praised for his frequent references to current events and for putting less emphasis upon theology and more on moral reform. "Ever since the days of the 'Swing trial,' " said the Rev. H. W. Thomas in 1886, "Chicago has suffered from hyper-orthodoxy in which to be orthodox seemed more important than to be religious, and the new departure of Brother Jones in this respect will be a relief." The Rev. Mr. Thomas was pleased because Jones had said in Chicago, "We are all the children of a great good Father," and since "the Fatherhood of God" was one of the phrases used by the social gospelers, Thomas thought Jones qualified as something of a liberal. The Rev. P. S. Henson, who said that Jones was doing work that Moody never did, supported him because "there are great public questions touching public morals and public decency, touching Sabbath breaking, rum-drinking and rum-selling, gambling, licentiousness, fraudulent dealing . . . that need

[58] Baltimore *American,* May 5, 1886, p. 3; May 10, p. 4. Unidentified clipping of an interview Jones had with a reporter in New York on February 11, 1894, in one of the scrapbooks in the Jones Papers owned by the Rev. Walt Holcomb, Atlanta, Georgia.

[to] be treated with just such sledgehammers as he knows how to wield." And the Rev. David Swing, whose trial for heresy in 1875 led to his resignation from the Presbyterian church and his founding a nondenominational institutional church in Chicago to reach the downtown poor, praised Jones as "a most powerful exponent and advocate of the religion of action" and called his revival "the most intellectual one Chicago has yet enjoyed." In Jones's revivals, said Swing, the conversions "will be placed upon a basis of solid sense rather than upon mere hymn singing and transient sentiment." [59]

Inasmuch as the leading figures in bringing Jones to Chicago were Moody's friends Revell and Farwell, it would not be correct to see this praise of Jones as a rebuke to Moody. And yet it was obvious that in many cities in the North and South the mood of the churches after 1885 was turning away from a religion of personal conversion based upon preaching "the blood." In part this change was a reaction from the sanctimonious religiosity which bulked so large in the work of Moody and his imitators. In part it was a reaction from the narrowing fundamentalism which under the pressure of the higher critics and theistic evolutionists was beginning to lash out at "liberals" and to put them on trial for heresy wherever possible. But in addition there was a general feeling among many middle-class churchgoers that something ought to be done to try to remedy the social and economic system of the country. Swing called Jones "a valuable Christian moral force" who "is anxious to have us get to Heaven both on earth and beyond." In the sense that Jones was more concerned with the things of this world than those of the next, perhaps this was true. But the true religious reformers of this period, the social gospelers like Washington Gladden and Walter Rauschenbusch, had an optimistic faith in man and in progress toward the millennium which was entirely lacking in Jones. Jones had little to say about millennialism, but he did believe that "Today this nineteenth century is wicked, far more wicked and far more outrageous in its flagrant sins than the century

[59] These various opinions are quoted in the Chicago *Tribune,* March 7, 1886, p. 10; and L. M. Jones, *Life and Sayings,* p. 211.

behind us . . ."[60] Jones's approach to reform was not liberal and constructive but authoritarian and repressive. In spite of his talk about civic reform and social sins, he really thought of sin as an individual matter which became a social problem only when a great many individuals refused to restrain themselves. Jones may have sounded radical compared to Moody but the measure of his conservatism became crystal clear when he was put face to face with a genuine reformer.

Such a showdown occurred in Jones's Toledo revival in 1899. In this campaign he was invited to bring religion to a city which had recently elected as its mayor a man who actually claimed to live and to administer the law according to the Golden Rule. It happened, with one of those quaint ironies of history, that the name of the Golden Rule mayor was the same as that of the evangelist, Samuel Jones. The battle of Mayor Sam Jones, popularly known as "Golden Rule" Jones, against evangelist Sam Jones was one of the classic events of modern revivalism. It demonstrated so neatly the utter incompatibility between professional revivalism and progressive reform that in retrospect the whole affair seemed like a carefully contrived practical joke.

Samuel Milton Jones, who had been elected mayor of Toledo in 1897, was born in Wales in 1846. His father brought the family to America in 1849 and became a tenant farmer in Lewis County, New York. Young Jones never had more than thirty months of regular schooling in his life and at the age of fourteen he left his father's farm to take a job in a sawmill. In 1865 he joined the rush to the oil fields of Titusville, Pennsylvania, and managed to make enough money to invest $10,000 in the formation of the Ohio Oil Company of Lima. In 1887 this company was bought out by John D. Rockefeller's Standard Oil Company but Jones continued to invest in oil and to tinker with oil drilling machinery. In 1894 he opened a factory in Toledo to manufacture a new type of sucker rod which he had invented and perfected himself. (A sucker rod was a metal pipe twenty-five to thirty feet long which was essential in pumping oil out of the wells.) Though the Acme Sucker Rod Company did not make him as rich as Rockefeller, it made him a very wealthy man, wealthy enough to try some experiments in fac-

60 S. P. Jones, *Sam Jones' Own Book,* p. 181.

tory management which brought him the nickname of "Golden Rule" Jones.[61]

Samuel M. Jones had imbibed a profound respect for religion from his Welsh mother. While living in Lima, Ohio, from 1887 to 1892, he had been a prominent member of the Methodist Church, president of the YMCA, and a contributor to many charities and reform movements, particularly those for prohibition. Shortly after he moved to Toledo in 1892, he came under the influence of the Rev. George D. Herron, a social gospel minister whose flaming oratory aroused many Midwesterners in this period on behalf of a program of Christian socialism to bring about the Kingdom of God on earth. In a book entitled *The New Redemption,* written in 1893, Herron wrote, "He who builds a mercantile establishment upon the basis of the Golden Rule is a greater and wiser philanthropist than he who founds hospitals for the poor out of the gains of selfishness." [62] Jones, who was shocked by the sight of men begging for jobs in the depression of 1893, decided to put Herron's ideas into practice in his factory.

As he told his employees, "I believe that God is *our Father;* that is, that all spring from one divine source. If you believe this, then it follows that you must admit the idea of Brotherhood; if you admit the idea of Brotherhood, you must admit the idea of Equality. . . ." [63] Golden Rule Jones had no use for Marxian socialism which denied the idea of brotherhood by setting one class against another. He held that all men ought to act as if they were members of one family. All did not have equal brains, strength, or talents, but all should try to help one another without rewards or favoritism to the few. The system of laissez-faire capitalism, based upon an ethic of selfishness and competition, did not seem to him compatible

[61] For much of the autobiographical data on Jones as well as for the background of Toledo politics in the 1890's I am indebted to an unpublished doctoral dissertation by Harvey S. Ford, "The Life and Times of Golden Rule Jones" (University of Michigan, 1953). See also Brand Whitlock, *Forty Years of It* (New York, 1916); Allan Nevins, "A Biographical Introduction" to *The Letters and Journals of Brand Whitlock,* ed. Allan Nevins (New York, 1936), and the article on Jones in *National Cyclopedia of American Biography,* Vol. X (New York, 1909), p. 414.

[62] Quoted in Ford, "Golden Rule Jones," p. 55.

[63] Samuel Milton Jones, *Letters of Labor and Love* (Indianapolis, 1905), p. 32.

with the Golden Rule or with the ethics of the Sermon on the Mount.

To show that he could practice what he preached and still run his business successfully, Jones announced in 1895 that the Acme Sucker Rod Factory would henceforth be run according to the Golden Rule. He asked his workers to treat him as he was going to treat them. Then he inaugurated a system of employee relations which was fifty years ahead of its time. He began by cutting the work day from ten hours to eight hours and raising the minimum wages to $2 a day. He gave every worker a Christmas bonus of 5 per cent of his yearly salary on the ground that they had a right to share in the profits of the company over and above their regular wages. He established an employee insurance plan to which the company donated 1 per cent and the workers 1 per cent of their wages. He purchased a plot of ground next to his factory which he called Golden Rule Park and made a children's playground at one end and held weekly band concerts at the other. He brought popular speakers on political and economic subjects from all over the country to address his employees in the park or in a hall in the factory. He set up an employee restaurant at which hot meals were served for fifteen cents though they cost him twenty-one cents. An annual company picnic endeavored to break down the barrier between the front office and the shop. A company band was organized for those with musical talent. Jones was one of the first employers in the United States to give his employees shares of stock in the company and to grant summer vacations with pay to factory hands. He even abolished the use of supervisory bosses and time-keepers and left every employee free to work on his own responsibility.[64]

In 1899 he reported, "After nearly four years, I am pleased to say that the Golden Rule works. It is perfectly practicable and worthy of a trial. But my experience has shown me that it is a *social,* not an industrial rule, and no *one* can truly live

[64] See Ford, "Golden Rule Jones," pp. 55–65. Jones once explained his popularity with his workers by saying, "Most employers keep about eight out of every ten dollars which their employees earn for them. I keep only about seven, and so they call me 'Golden Rule' Jones." Nevins, "A Biographical Introduction," I, xxxiv.

the Golden Rule until all live it."[65] Nevertheless the factory continued to thrive. In order to give his theories a wider public application Jones entered politics in 1897. As a good businessman he had always voted Republican, and he had supported McKinley against Bryan in 1896. In 1897 his Golden Rule outlook did not prevent him from joining the political machine controlled in Ohio by Mark Hanna and James Foraker. The machine gave him the nomination in 1897 for mayor of Toledo and Jones campaigned on a platform of "good government."

Toledo was a city of about 100,000 at the time and roughly one-quarter of its population was foreign-born, predominantly German. The Democrats, attempting to appeal to the Germans and the workers against Jones, portrayed him as a Sunday school puritan. If Jones became mayor, said the Democrats, he would close all the saloons and enforce strict Sabbatarian observances. Jones, however, considered the prohibition issue secondary. Although himself a teetotaler, he had no intention of leading a crusade against the saloons and stated that he would simply follow public sentiment in regard to them. He campaigned for cheaper street car fares. Nevertheless prohibition became one of the central issues of the campaign. The wets insisted that a vote for Jones was a vote for prohibition and many of the dries supported him for this reason. When he was elected by the narrow majority of 518 out of 21,000 votes, he wired to his friend, the Rev. Washington Gladden, that he had won "in spite of six hundred saloons, the street car companies, and the devil." Gladden replied, "Hallelujah!"

To redeem one aspect of his "good government" pledge, Jones tried to repress the gamblers and bookies in the city and to close the "wine rooms" which were headquarters for prostitution. But he put little pressure on saloons which he considered merely an "evidence of wrong social conditions." "The popular conception of 'good government' " he said sadly, "seems to be confined to the thought of restraining saloons, gambling houses and brothels, but I think I have a larger conception . . .

[65] Quoted in the *National Cyclopedia of Biography,* Vol. X (New York, 1909), p. 414, in the article on Jones.

what I understand by 'good government' . . . is expressed in the word Brotherhood." [66] And brotherhood in terms of municipal government meant to him that the public welfare should come before the profits of the utility companies even if this meant public ownership of the water, fuel, lighting, and transportation system. But the question of morals kept intruding itself into his administration because of the existing state and city "blue laws."

Ohio had enacted a law in 1883 which prohibited any saloon from being open or any liquor from being sold on Sunday. A Toledo city ordinance of 1864 required in addition that saloons be closed at 11 P.M. on weekdays and prohibited stage plays, concerts, or the conducting of any business on Sundays. Jones refused to enforce the state law for Sunday closing of the saloons on the ground that not more than 25 per cent of the people in Toledo favored such a move and that the saloon was simply a social club for the poor at which they could gather on Sunday, their only day off. Moreover, he supported the City Council's action in repealing the ordinance requiring saloons to close at 11 P.M. on weekdays and forbidding concerts and plays on Sundays. He devoted his efforts as mayor to reforming the police department and to extending the municipal control of public utilities. By the end of his two-year term he had antagonized not only those religious voters who had thought him a prohibitionist, but also those businessmen who disliked the idea of public ownership. The ministers of the city formed a committee which waited upon him and demanded that he enforce the state blue laws. When he refused they denounced him from their pulpits. The businessmen of the city were upset because Jones not only wanted the city to continue to control the water and fuel system, but he also wanted it to take over the street railway and illuminating gas systems as well. To them this was socialism.

In December, 1898, the Ministerial Association of Toledo, consisting of some sixty Protestant ministers, invited evangelist Sam P. Jones to conduct a city-wide religious revival to be held the following March. Since evangelist Jones was well known for his prohibition and "civic reform" sentiments, and since the date for the next mayoral election was April 3, it seemed

[66] Quoted in Ford, "Golden Rule Jones," p. 147.

only too obvious that the ministers were going into politics. Several pastors self-consciously told a reporter after their meeting that "The coming of Evangelist Jones is intended to have no bearing whatever on the candidacy of Mayor Jones for re-election." But upon further questioning by the reporter "It was admitted, however, that the administration of city affairs would be very likely to get a general overhauling at the hands of the noted preacher." One of the city's newspapers ran an editorial called "Two Sam Joneses" which took notice of the ministerial association's dissatisfaction with the mayor and predicted "there ought to be a hot time in the old town" during the next election campaign.[67]

While the pastors were setting up committees and making general preparations in the weeks preceding the revival, the local Democrats and Republicans were holding their nominating conventions for city offices. The Democrats nominated for mayor a man named Dowling who promised to campaign against the "hazardous experiments" in public ownership advocated by "Golden Rule" Jones. Jones fully expected the Republicans to renominate him, but to his dismay the party politicians chose a man named Charles E. Russell, who repudiated Jones's policies and promised to campaign on a platform calling for a "business administration." While Mayor Jones was still debating whether to admit defeat or to try to enter the race as a third party candidate, evangelist Jones arrived in town to start the revival. The first meeting was held at the city Armory at 2:30 on Sunday, March 5.

As mayor of Toledo, Samuel M. Jones was asked to say a few opening words to introduce Samuel P. Jones. Since it looked as though the mayor would not be running in the campaign the tension over the revival had dropped. The mayor spoke to the crowd at the Armory saying that he was pleased to see "that a great many Toledoans were interested in the welfare of men's souls" and that he himself believed that "nothing else but the love of Christ at the heart of society" would save the world. "Things are awfully wrong now, but they are going to be right. He taught us to pray, 'Thy kingdom come.' Why then should it not come?" The mayor concluded by

67 Toledo *Blade*, December 19, 1898, p. 3, January 30, 1899, p. 2; Toledo *Bee*, January 31, 1899, p. 4.

saying it gave him "great pleasure to introduce to you Reverend Sam P. Jones, and there are other Joneses." He received a round of applause.[68]

Evangelist Jones spoke on the text, "I have fought the good fight," and said, "The first thing to be done in Toledo is to separate the crowd . . . we must make the issue square and draw the line. . . . You can't tell who is a church member without asking the preacher. . . . I'm here for a fight and I'm going to say things to start it. If you can say worse things about me than I can about you, just lam in, Bud. I despise a dull time." But the evangelist did not say anything that day about civic corruption or the saloons. For the first week he devoted himself to amusing and scolding the audiences: "The Sweet Bye and Bye is all right but I hit 'em in the Naughty Now and Now." "A man asked me if a white man differed from a negro in his instincts. I said, no, he differs in his outstincts." "Some of you sing, 'Must Jesus bear the cross alone, And all the world go free? No, there's a cross for everyone, And an Easter bonnet for me.' "

The nearest his sermons got to the election campaign were some asides about "Any town that can put up with 700 saloons is the nastiest place next to hell." And "God will bless no city that desecrates the Sabbath." He let it be known that he was neither a Democrat nor a Republican: "I'm a prohibitionist from snout to tail."

On March 9, Mayor Jones, having decided that he had sufficient popular support to give him a fighting chance at re-election, entered the mayoralty race as an Independent. To do this he had to present a petition signed by a large number of backers. The local papers (one Democratic and one Republican) noted gleefully that among the signers of his petition were "Joe Casper, the pool room king," a gambler named Bright, and Chief of Police Raitz who had once been caught taking a drink while on duty and who would have been fired had not Mayor Jones decided to give him another chance. This was too much for evangelist Jones. He told the noon prayer meeting for businessmen on March 11, "You have got three men running for mayor. . . . Just look at the gang that

[68] All quotations that follow on the Toledo revival are taken, unless otherwise noted, from the Toledo *Blade* or the Toledo *Bee* for March–April, 1899.

is following each . . . and I will tell you what kind of man he is. . . . You elect Sam P. Jones mayor of this city and I will shut up your saloons on the clock and close up your assignation houses . . . and I would hire a chief of police that would not go into a saloon and take a drop of whisky any more than he would go into a duck pond and drown himself."

But this was mild compared to the blast the revivalist let loose on March 12 at a meeting for 6000 men at the Armory. The headlines in the Republican paper, the Toledo *Blade,* read, "EVANGELIST'S HOT SHOT; JONES BATTERIES TURNED ON MUNICIPAL AUTHORITIES; DECLARES IF THE DEVIL WERE MAYOR HE WOULD NOT CHANGE A THING." The headlines in the Democratic Toledo *Bee* read, "SAM P. JONES RIPS UP TOLEDO'S ADMINISTRATION; HE PREFERS RULE OF HATE TO THE RULE OF LOVE THAT KEEPS THE SALOONS OPEN." Among the evangelist's remarks were these: "You have an apostle in this town who can do everything by love. My, my! If love would have regulated the laws of this town it would have taken wings and flown off long ago. Is it love that runs 700 saloons wide open seven days a week, 400 bawdy houses every night, and 150 gambling dens that carry your young and old men down to hell?" Toledoans should "make men live up to the official oaths of their office and do their duty." He denounced foreigners who desecrated the Sabbath as well as the officials who let them: "For every decent German or reputable Irishman I have the hand[shake] but for a whitewashed Dutchman or an anarchistic Irishman I fix my foot. If you don't like this country go back. . . . Let us have an American sabbath and be decent." He concluded, "You say I'm fooling with politics. I'm not. I'm naming no names, but I am running my engine on the track and if anything gets in the way it's going to be run over."

The next morning evangelist Jones spoke at a special meeting of the cooperating pastors and laymen who met together to put the churches formally into the election campaign. "Don't compromise," said Jones, "with a little mayor who stands a block to the law. You must not mix politics with religion but you are justified in mixing religion with politics. I used to be a preacher on the poorest circuit in Georgia and had many trials, but I preached the truth and now I am the best paid preacher on the continent." This apparent *non sequitur* seemed to indicate that mixing religion with politics would lead to handsome rewards, but of course the issue had to be one which respectable middle-class citizens would support. One of the pastors at this meeting moved that a committee of ministers try to obtain a pledge from each of the three candidates promising that if elected he would "enforce the law against the saloonists, gambling, and houses of ill fame." Another minister said "the time was ripe to take some action" for "the law and order element." The motion was passed and a committee appointed, though one minister pointed out that he had already spoken to Mayor Jones on this matter and knew he would not commit himself. Everyone recognized that the only possible outcome of the committee's action would be to hurt the mayor.

The Republican candidate, Russell, who had hitherto said nothing about saloons, now issued a ringing statement that if elected he would use all the authority vested in the mayor's office to enforce the law against "the impudent assertions of the brewers, saloons, gamblers, and brothels," Russell called upon "every good citizen" "to take off his coat and work for the home and fireside." The Democratic candidate, Dowling, hedged on the question. As expected, Mayor Jones told the ministerial committee, "It would not be consistent for me to sign a paper pledging myself to make Toledo anything more than what its citizens desire it to be." He also said, "I do not believe that the extirpating method to which [the Rev.] Mr. Jones pins his faith is either the Christian or the scientific method. . . . I believe the only way in which the saloon will finally disappear will be through the growth of the loving spirit in mankind which will provide an opportunity for people to live decently human lives. . . ." [69]

But evangelist Jones would have none of that. For the remainder of his stay in Toledo, a stay which was extended from March 19 to March 22 at the request of the ministers, he continued to "draw the line" and "fire hot shots" at the mayor in the name of decency, respectability, and Christian manhood. "When a man takes the oath of office to do the duties of that

[69] Samuel Milton Jones, *The New Right* (New York, 1899), p. 106.

office, draws his salary and does not do it, he is a perjured scoundrel in the sight of God and honest men. (Applause) If you have a law on your statute book you don't enforce, you have communism inaugurated. If you have a state law you can't enforce, you have anarchy in your midst."

The city's two newspapers gave the evangelist's remarks front page headlines and tried editorially to prove that their respective candidates would do just as the ministers wished. The *Blade* said of Russell: "The moral element in this city" will back him. The *Bee* claimed that Russell was a hypocrite and that Dowling and the Democrats were the real advocates of reform: "Russell is trying to sneak in under the *Bee's* white flag of purity." If Mayor Jones's policies were continued for another two years, said the *Bee,* "Capital will immediately put Toledo on the list of municipalities to keep away from. . . . Capital isn't investing in towns that are run by theorists. . . . The Golden Rule and the Declaration of Independence have nothing to do with it. Our credit is at stake. . . . Think this over. It affects your pocketbook." The *Blade* ran a series of cartoons on its front page depicting Jones as a tool of the saloonkeepers and declared editorially, "The socialism of Mayor Jones breeds anarchy."

Throughout the month of March the city's ministers (with a few notable exceptions) denounced Jones from their pulpits and called for a civic clean-up. The Rev. G. A. Burgess, a Congregationalist and a prime mover in bringing the evangelist to the city, quoted statistics in his Sunday morning sermon on March 19 to show that the private ownership of public utilities was cheaper than public ownership. "But the financial question is not the leading question," said Burgess; "Moral legislation" was. Mayor Jones's failure to enforce the laws against the saloons was "anarchy." "Ministers almost to a man feel betrayed and outraged. They feel that the one great thing to be settled first is, Shall Toledo obey the law?"

Mayor Jones tried to counter these attacks by insisting that the moral question was a red herring. "It is a false issue raised to divert the public mind from the main question . . . the prize they are playing for is nothing less than one of the most gigantic schemes of franchise-grabbing ever concocted." [70] As

[70] *Ibid.,* p. 99.

the mayor saw it, the ministers were the dupes of "the corporate interests," particularly the city traction company which had been out to defeat Jones from the start in order to prevent his taking over the street railways from which they were making exorbitant profits. The vested interests, he claimed, had seized upon the revival and the prohibition question to cover up their real objectives which were to maintain their monopolistic utility franchises through which they bilked the public.

As the mayor stated his platform it included the following planks: "Public ownership of all public utilities"; "No grant of new or extension of existing franchises" by the city to private interests; "The abolition of the private system of doing city work"; "A minimum wage of $1.50 per day for eight hours of common labor," and "Organized labor to be employed on all public work." [71] But in campaigning for this program Jones spoke not in terms of socialism or even of social reform, but in terms of Christianity and brotherhood. As his chief lieutenant and successor, Brand Whitlock, wrote, "He was like an evangelist in a way, and his meetings were in the broad sense religious." [72] He literally believed that the Golden Rule was a feasible solution to the prevailing social problems and he believed that the average voter could be trusted to vote for his program if its aims were made clear.

Sam P. Jones, the professional evangelist, had a less exalted view of the application of Christian ethics to civic and social reform. His culminating blow for righteousness came at the final meeting of the revival on March 22. There were various reports of the exact words he used. Brand Whitlock quoted him as saying, "I am for the Golden Rule myself, up to a certain point, and then I want to take the shotgun and the club." [73] According to the mayor the evangelist said, "I believe in the Golden Rule, too, up *to a certain extent,* but then I want to take up the hickory club and the shotgun." [74] The headline of the Toledo *Bee* read, "Jones' Farewell . . . Says Shotgun Is Better Than the Golden Rule in Politics." The version re-

[71] *Ibid.,* p. 91.
[72] Whitlock, *Forty Years of It,* p. 128.
[73] *Ibid.,* p. 114.
[74] S. M. Jones, *The New Right,* p. 107.

corded by the *Bee's* reporter had Jones saying, "I have nothing to do with politics, but I have to do with a theory that will land your town in ruin. . . . I see a mad dog coming over my fence and my wife and children are there. Do I say, 'I believe in the Golden Rule for that dog?' The mad dog in this town is the saloon and the shameless houses. . . . I say the way to meet a mad dog is with a shotgun." And he concluded, "O, brethren of God's ministry, how you can clean up these fellows if you go to work."

Whatever his last words were, it was clear that evangelist Jones had no use for Mayor Jones, nor for his political platform. According to the evangelist's official biographer, the final sermon "was one of the most powerful that the evangelist had preached, and its effect upon his audience was unmistakable. Mr. Jones won a great victory for municipal reform in Toledo, and changed the moral atmosphere of the city." [75]

During the remaining week of the election campaign the Anti-Saloon League organized rallies endorsing Russell; the ministers continued to deliver sermons demanding law enforcement; and the two newspapers printed cartoons and editorials lampooning the mayor's crack-pot ideas. But on election day Mayor Jones carried every ward in the city except one, and won by a landslide. The votes were: for Jones, 17,782; for Russell, 4,472; for Dowling, 3,293. According to the Toledo *Blade* the mayor's "personal popularity" made the voters "overlook his visionary theories." "The socialistic theories of Mr. Jones, dangerous as they appear to the great mass of thinking men, appeal to a class of voters who have nothing to lose and everything to gain." The mayor put it somewhat differently: "The people have kept their minds on the one great question—Shall we have the Golden Rule of all the people or the rule of cash by a few people?" There was no comment from the ministers, but their subsequent endorsement of other professional evangelists indicated that the outcome of the election had in no way affected their faith in revivalism to solve the "moral questions" of the day. Evangelist Jones continued to tour the country bringing his method of civic reform to other

[75] L. M. Jones, *Life and Sayings,* p. 283. The Rev. Walt Holcomb informs me that he did most of the writing of this biography and not the evangelist's wife. Mr. Holcomb was the evangelist's assistant in many campaigns.

corrupt cities. The people of Toledo continued to vote Mayor Jones into office at election after election until he finally died in office in 1904. Then they voted for his friends.

The Toledo revival epitomized Sam P. Jones's career and indicated the path which professional evangelism was to take in the twentieth century. In some cities, particularly in the South, he was successful in persuading the citizens to outlaw saloons and drive out the other enemies of evangelical purity. By the end of the nineteenth century, revivalists were devoting as much effort to this kind of "municipal reform" as they were to the salvation of souls. To some extent the two had always gone together. Revivalism had always been, at least indirectly, a means of maintaining certain socially accepted standards of behavior,[76] but Jones and his twentieth century imitators began to emphasize social conformity for its own sake. For those too "low down" to accept the puritanical code of rural Georgia by means of conversion, Jones and his successors proposed to use not the shotgun and the club but the more powerful weapons of social pressure and legally enforced blue laws. As a result, revivals rapidly lost their last elements of religious worship and became increasingly theatrical and demagogic.

Jones admitted, for example, that his jokes and his slang were consciously employed to attract and amuse the crowd. "You needn't bother about my eccentricities. I only put them on to get you here." "I'm trying to put my style and grammar down on a level with you." It was Finney's argument for getting results carried to its logical extreme. "I am ready to change myself," said Jones, "if any fellow gives me a method to catch more fish." [77] But it is worth remembering that the professional revivalists were not alone in this attempt to reach the people by making religion more attractive. Many distinguished pastors in this era were just as eager for crowds and headlines and thought it their duty to outshine the secular

[76] The Rev. Calvin Colton offered the following justification for modern revivalism in 1832: "Society, the world, must be melted down in a common crucible, or else the moral elements will still remain heterogeneous, a dissociate, and discordant. In theory, a genuine revival, as I would define it, is exactly and in all respects calculated for the universal amalgamation and purification of society." *History and Character of American Revivals of Religion* (2d. ed.; London, 1832), p. 34.

[77] L. M. Jones, *Life and Sayings*, pp. 229–30.

amusements which competed with their church services. Henry Ward Beecher, Joseph Cook, T. DeWitt Talmage, Lyman Abbott, P. S. Henson, Newell D. Hillis, F. W. Gunsaulus, Russell H. Conwell, Charles H. Parkhurst were among those who turned their pulpits into platforms for public forums and their sermons into oratorical displays. Like Jones, all of these men found that writing books, publishing magazines, writing weekly newspaper columns, and lecturing on chautauqua or lyceum circuits was a profitable as well as an opportune method of spreading their message and their fame. Jones spent every summer after 1885 touring chautauqua circuits. He received $200 to $500 each for lectures entitled "Character and Characters," "Manhood and Money," "The Ravages of Rum," "The Battle of Life and How to Win It," "Get There and Stay There," "Sawciety," "The World As It Is and the World As It Ought to Be." That Jones competed successfully as a lecturer with men such as Mark Twain, Bill Nye, William Jennings Bryan, Robert G. Ingersoll, and James Whitcomb Riley, as well as with his ministerial colleagues clearly indicated his talent as an entertainer.[78]

When Jones said that he was the best paid preacher on the continent in 1899 it was not simply an idle boast. His income from 1881 to 1906 averaged $30,000 a year. During his thirty years as a professional evangelist, he estimated in 1906, "I have made over $750,000 with my tongue." [79] Far from resenting this, the ministers and laymen who invited Jones to their city to conduct a revival accepted it as indubitable evidence of his importance, financial success being the commonly acknowledged sign of value for anything in the gilded age, even for preachers. And inasmuch as the laborer was worthy of his hire, the finance committees at his revivals went out of their way to assure him a suitable compensation for his work for them. He received not only the collections taken at the last two days of the meetings, but outside private subscriptions as well. In

[78] Copies of the broadsides and advertising leaflets issued by the chautauqua bureaus for which he worked are among the Jones Papers owned by the Rev. Walt Holcomb, Atlanta, Georgia.

[79] L. M. Jones, *Life and Sayings*, pp. 330–32. Several of Jones's account books containing lists of where he spoke and how much he received from each chautaqua engagement are among the Jones Papers owned by the Rev. Walt Holcomb, Atlanta, Georgia.

order to stimulate the giving toward the "free will offering" at the final meetings, the chairman of the finance committee would take the platform before Jones arrived and hold what amounted to an auction for contributions. He would call first for all those in the audience who would give or pledge $100 for the evangelist to stand or to raise their hands, then for all who would give $50, then $25, $10, $5, $2, and $1. Pledge cards and envelopes were passed out by the ushers to those who stood up. Like Jacob Knapp, Jones let it be known in one town what he had received in previous cities. Asked in San Francisco if he had been well remunerated on his tour of the West Coast, he answered, "I have not. I was paid $2000 in Los Angeles, but it cost me about $1000 to bring my family out here and my expenses since I arrived have been necessarily large. . . ." His average remuneration for a three- or four-week revival ranged from $1500 to $4000. Usually about $1000 of this came from tabernacle collections. The rest was realized by private subscriptions. Sometimes Jones paid his assistants' salaries and expenses out of this, but more often these were included in the general expenses of the revival.[80]

But Jones was not in the profession for profit. He sincerely believed that "positive Christianity" would solve all the nation's problems and that prohibition was the great need of the day. As a rallying cry for mass commitment to evangelicalism, prohibition proved to be an almost perfect tool. At a time when the whole country was uneasy over the maladjustments of industrialism and urbanism, prohibition offered a simple and speedy cure for everything from political corruption to labor agitation. As a moral and religious question it gave the revivalist the appearance of being a social reformer in the name of Christianity. Even many progressive reformers, who were far more concerned about prevailing problems than Jones, nevertheless accepted prohibition as one of the steps in the path of progress. In addition, the prohibition movement was free from theological, denominational, geographical, and political partisanship. Men of all faiths and parties could agree on this where they could agree on nothing else. Jones tossed

[80] For statements of Jones's remuneration see San Francisco *Examiner,* March 24, 1889, p. 2; April 1, p. 2; Baltimore *American,* May 29, 1886; Chicago *Tribune,* April 5, 1886, p. 1.

off the bitter struggle between Bryan and McKinley in 1896 by saying, "One of them based his campaign on the platform of gold-buggery while the other was for gold-diggery, but neither one opened his mouth much on the subject of the liquor traffic during the entire campaign."[81] Although the prohibition movement was sometimes portrayed as a rural versus urban movement, professional revivalists never had any difficulty in marshalling enthusiastic support for it in their city campaigns. After many of Jones's revivals church and lay leaders organized Law and Order Leagues to mobilize public action for prohibition and the enforcement of old blue laws.[82] In the cities of the South the activities of these Leagues, led by the leading members of the community, were of great importance in effecting statewide prohibition amendments.

But there were many, even in the churches, who doubted the value of prohibition as the panacea for the nation's ills and who felt that Jones's type of revivalism would be more detrimental than helpful to the churches in their fight for the allegiance of the younger generation. One of these was B. Fay Mills, who in the early 1890's searched for a way to reconcile the emotional prohibition crusades of his professional colleague, Sam P. Jones, with the social gospel attitude taken by his friends Golden Rule Jones and Washington Gladden. Mills wondered whether modern revivalism could be made an effective method for advancing the brotherhood of man and for building the New Jerusalem on earth. The new system of city-wide mass evangelism which Moody had perfected could reach a vast audience, but in the end Mills found that the function and tradition of revivalism were not broad enough to support the message he wanted to preach. As a professional evangelist he

[81] Toledo *Blade,* March 7, 1899. Pagination deleted from clipping in the scrapbook in the Jones Papers owned by the Rev. Walt Holcomb, Atlanta, Georgia.

[82] In some Southern cities Jones encouraged these Law and Order Leagues to take the law in their own hands against illegal saloons: "You are lying around here waiting for the officers to do it," he told one crowd, "when any twenty of you can get in a hack and drive around to these fellows and tell them to clean out and get out of business or you will not guarantee the consequences —it will straighten things out." *Popular Lectures of Sam Jones,* ed. Walt Holcomb (New York, 1909), p. 94. It was only a short step from this kind of muscular Christianity to the vigilante activities of the Ku Klux Klan in the 1920's.

was expected to preach individual repentance and to obtain new or reconsecrated church members. Since prohibition was basically thought of as a question of personal morality, that too could be incorporated into revivalism. But it proved impossible to preach both individual repentance and social responsibility from a revival platform. Neither the preachers nor the church members wanted or expected it. When he tried to do so, conservative churchmen assailed him for undermining orthodoxy and the average pastor was merely confused. Yet during his brief career in the profession Mills made some striking contributions to its technique as well as to its message.

Mills was short and "boyish in appearance" with "light blue eyes full of tenderness, of medium build, light brown hair." One reporter said he was "a smooth-faced, unassuming sort of person and by the majority [in the audience] was supposed to be the organist or some attendant" until he entered the pulpit and began to speak. His delivery was called "attractive by its very simplicity. There are no great flights of eloquence, no sudden outbursts of passion"; nor did he show any "careful preparation." His sermons were "off-hand, spontaneous, not a note being used to assist his memory." [83]

His father, Thornton A. Mills, was one of the few students at Lane Seminary in 1834 who did not adopt antislavery views. He became a prominent Presbyterian minister and at one time was elected moderator of the Old School Presbyterian General Assembly. B. Fay Mills was born in 1857 in Rahway, New Jersey, and educated at Phillips Academy, Hamilton College, and Lake Forest College. He was ordained by a Congregational Council in Cannon Falls, Minnesota, in 1878. After serving pastorates in Cannon Falls, Greenwich, New York, and Rutland, Vermont, he decided to become a revivalist in 1887. His first revivals were in small towns like Montclair and Morristown, New Jersey; Andover and Newburyport, Massachusetts; Decatur, Jacksonville, and Springfield, Illinois. Although prior to 1891 he conducted meetings in larger cities—Brooklyn, Wilmington, New York, Boston, Philadelphia, and Indianapolis—these were not city-wide revivals but localized affairs in which only ten or twelve churches joined.

[83] Cincinnati *Enquirer,* January 22, 1892, p. 8; St. Paul *Daily Pioneer Press,* May 11, 1893, p. 1.

In 1891 he evolved his District Combination Plan of evangelism and tried it out in Cleveland with the support of forty-five churches. One participating minister remarked that "the mechanical features of the preparations seemed at times unpleasantly obtrusive," but the total of seven thousand conversions obtained in seven weeks set the stamp of approval on this new system. Mills soon found himself in such demand that he was booked for revival engagements a year or more in advance. During the next five years he rose to the top of the profession as a result of successful city-wide campaigns in Cincinnati, Omaha, St. Paul, Minneapolis, Providence, Columbus, and Portland (Oregon).

The revival system which he called the Mills District Combination Plan of Evangelism owed something to the method Moody had used in London, Baltimore, and St. Louis, but its technical efficiency was far advanced over Moody's crude mechanics. Compared with the simple arrangements used by Sam Jones it was complicated in the extreme. Both Jones and Moody had left the preparation for their revivals up to the local pastors, offering no more than a few suggestions and stipulations as to the place of meeting and the training of choirs, ushers, and personal workers. The bulk of the work and planning depended upon the imagination and skill of the volunteer workers, and these often proved highly inadequate. Mills, however, left nothing to chance. His plan was so intricately detailed that he printed a booklet entitled "Suggestions to Committees in Charge of Special Meetings Conducted by the Rev. B. Fay Mills," which contained step-by-step instructions for advance preparation and the conduct of the revival.

Many of these suggestions were commands rather than advice. "It must be understood," wrote Mills, "that during the meetings they [the meetings] are to form the work of the Church and no ordinary church plans or customary order must be allowed to interfere with the carrying out of the plans of your committees." [84] Pastors were obliged to arrange their

[84] For the details which follow see *Mills' Meeting Memorial Volume,* ed. J. J. Francis and C. B. Morrell (Cincinnati, 1892). See also H. A. Blodgett, *Times of Refreshing: the Story of the Mills Revival in St. Paul, Minnesota* (St. Paul, 1893); J. D. Lowden, *The Story of a Revival* (Elizabeth, New Jersey, 1892). There is a good biographical sketch of Mills by Luther A. Weigle in the *Dictionary of American Biography* (New York, 1934).

schedules "so that no appointment can by any possibility conflict with the meetings," and all church services by the cooperating churches had to be cancelled for the duration of the meetings—even Sunday morning worship services. This was a complete reversal of Moody's policy that revivals should supplement the regular church work. Mills considered the churches' programs secondary to his work.

The District Plan required the division of the city into four or five sections, each of which was to have a centrally located building for revival meetings and a complete set of committees. Just as Moody had evangelized London in four sections, so Mills conducted his city-wide revivals piecemeal. Six committees were to be organized by the churches in each of the districts: finance, advertising, music, devotional, canvassing, and ushers. The chairmen of these district committees constituted the central committee, and they had charge of hiring a large meeting hall in the center of the city, into which Mills moved for a final week or two of meetings after preaching in each of the districts. This federated method had the advantage of bringing the revival into closer touch with the cooperating churches and enabled a greater number of persons to be actively engaged in the work. It had the disadvantage of duplicated effort and expense. It usually happened that those who attended the central meeting which wound up the campaign were the same persons who had attended the various district meetings in the preceding weeks.

Mills's instructions were very explicit in regard to the committee work. Member of the finance committees had to be made up predominantly of "businessmen." These committees were responsible for raising the funds in each of their districts for the revival, and Mills suggested three methods for doing this: collections could be taken at each meeting; "private subscriptions" could be solicited "before the meetings commence"; or an "assessment of the churches concerned in proportion to size and financial strength" could be made. In any case Mills made it clear that he assumed no responsibility for the financing. "The churches combining in the movement must agree to bear the incidental expenses of the series of meetings."

The expenses of a Mills revival varied from $3000 to $5000, and with twenty-five to eighty churches cooperating, this sum was not great when apportioned among them. Most cities followed this scheme, and each cooperating church was held responsible for a contribution fixed by the finance committee. These assessments ranged from $25 to $300, depending upon the number of churches cooperating and the resources of each. Most of the money collected went for rent, advertising, and printing. Mills stated in his booklet, "If you wish to include the travelling expenses and hotel bills of my musical associate and myself, I have no objection." But he emphatically prohibited the finance committee from making any "subscription or collection for us as we can consent to receive no salary." Like most evangelists, Mills preferred to rely on "such free will offerings as individuals desire to make to the Lord" for his services.

The booklet did not say precisely how these free will offerings were to be made, but Mills had a system for this too. "If you desire to consult me further upon this matter, I can tell you concerning the most delicate plans that have been devised in other places; but we desire to be very careful lest the work should suffer in any way from the manner of collecting money for our support." The usual method was by means of Offering Envelopes given out by the finance committees at the meetings or through the churches. The offerings were then mailed or handed directly to the evangelist by the contributors. This proved so efficient and satisfactory to all parties that no record is available concerning the amounts received by Mills in any of his revivals. He never complained when they were small or boasted when they were large.

The advertising committee, for which Mills recommended at least one layman, printed posters and handbills and issued tickets for the special meetings for men, women, children, mothers, and so on. This committee was to "see that reporters attend all services" and that "complete reports are printed in every issue [of the local papers] even if you have to write them or hire a man to do it for you." This committee was also responsible for conducting the "Midweek Sabbath," which became a feature of Mills' meetings. On one Wednesday in each revival all the stores and offices in the city were personally asked to close up for the day in order to direct attention to the revival. In Cincinnati three thousand business establishments cooperated. In St. Paul five hundred closed.

The music committee recruited and trained choirs of 100 to 150 for the district meetings and 500 to 600 for the central meeting. The Sankey hymnbook was suggested by Mills because "by special arrangement with the publisher" these books were loaned free to the choirs provided a stand was set up at each meeting hall for the sale of the hymnbooks to the crowds at "not under 30 cents" each. The committee on canvassing was to organize church members into teams to call upon "everyone in the city" in order to deliver invitations to attend the meetings, an idea borrowed from Finney. The devotional committee arranged two daily prayer meetings, one at 8:30 A.M. for men and one at 2:30 P.M. for women.

Mills was particularly concerned with the work of the ushers committee. Unlike Moody and Jones he used his ushers as personal workers. He called them his "assistant evangelists" because in addition to showing the people to their seats, they also talked and prayed with inquirers who came forward after the sermon. Mills met with his ushers before each meeting for instructions and prayer and specified that only mature Christians, preferably Sunday School workers, be chosen for these positions. The ushers also had the task of passing out and collecting the decision cards which were an important part of Mills's system.

Mills did not originate the use of decision cards, but he made more consistent and systematic use of them than any previous evangelist. The card which was handed to all inquirers stated:

> I have an honest desire henceforth to lead a Christian life.
>
> Name____________________________
> Residence________________________
> Church or pastor preferred____________
> Date_____________________________

Mills's business-like mind was not content with the haphazard tabulations of Moody and Jones. He wanted an exact count of the decisions and a complete record of the results of his work. The statistics for each of his revivals were not rounded off to the nearest thousand or hundred but could be tabulated to the last integer. What was more, the decision cards were carefully divided among the cooperating ministers so that each of them could hold in his hands the concrete dividends for his efforts. A convert who failed to specify what church or pastor he preferred was assigned to one of the cooperating churches on the basis of the proximity of his residence to the church. This avoided some of the squabbling over the spoils, and Mills at one time had a special follow-up assistant who visited all persons who failed to specify a church preference.

But in spite of the obvious advantages of the decision card system in following up the influence of a revival, the drawbacks to it were significant. All professional evangelists adopted the card system after 1895, and their respective reputations came to rest more and more upon their statistical record and less upon their preaching ability or personal character. The pressure to inflate and boast about convert statistics was great, and the card system was soon being flagrantly abused.

Mills claimed that in his twelve years as an evangelist he spoke to five million persons and converted two hundred thousand of them. But the statistics for his campaigns revealed a high percentage of cards which were obviously not bona fide conversion in the accepted sense of the term. For example, many of them were cards signed by active church members who at Mills' urging reconsecrated themselves to Christian living. Later evangelists overcame this confusion by having a separate space on the card to be checked "Reconsecration," but Mills's cards made no such distinction. Another misleading factor was that many of the cards were signed by Sunday School children who attended Mills's Saturday afternoon children's meetings. These were not true conversions in most cases. Still another discrepancy between the total cards signed and the total conversions was the fact that many cards were later found to contain fictitious names and addresses. Five per cent of the cards in Mills's Cincinnati campaign were in this category.[85]

But these were not the only problems. In St. Paul 10 per cent of the cards were found to contain addresses from "out of town" and hence were never followed up by any of the churches which supported Mills.[86] Nor could the cooperating ministers

[85] Cincinnati *Enquirer,* March 9, 1892, p. 8.
[86] St. Paul *Daily Pioneer Press,* May 31, 1893, p. 4.

follow up the average of 10 to 15 per cent of the cards which contained preferences for churches not affiliated with the revival. Some cooperating ministers might have been pleased that others profited from their labors and expense, but it would be a broad-minded evangelical who could rejoice over the large number of cards which were handed over to Catholic, Unitarian, Universalist, Jewish, Quaker, Swedenborgian, or Christian Science churches as designated by some of Mills's converts. The Roman Catholic Archbishop, John Ireland, sustained none of the cost or labor of the St. Paul revival; yet he received more cards than any of the cooperating ministers. How valuable to Catholicism these 500 cards were or whether Ireland ever followed them up is unknown, but it was significant of the watering down of evangelical doctrine in revivalism after 1890 and the new emphasis upon morality and "decency" that persons who considered themselves converted by a professional evangelist saw nothing incongruous about expressing their desire to join a Catholic or Unitarian or Christian Science church.

Equally unsatisfactory on the whole were those cards which contained no statement of church or pastoral preference. Often as many as 20 per cent were left blank in this regard. It was more than likely that these "converts" were impressed by Mills and his revival but not really interested in connecting themselves with the less-exciting services of the average minister.

Mills was sufficiently successful and honest to be perfectly frank in publishing these detailed analyses of his cards. Lesser revivalists, however, tended to publish nothing but their card totals and to call them all "converts." Mills' popularity, however, did not depend simply upon his technical efficiency and mechanical innovations. His reputation as "a new type of evangelist" stemmed more from his message than from his methods. For Mills was one of the first and perhaps the only professional revivalist ever to break with the emphasis upon individual reform and to preach primarily a doctrine of social responsibility and social action.

During the first five or six years of his revival career, Mills preached a simple evangelical message which concentrated attention upon the need for personal repentance and conversion. Occasionally he attacked card playing, gambling, intemperance, and dancing, but for the most part he emphasized the sins of "pride, vanity, dissatisfaction, impatience." He told the unfortunate that "there never came any sorrow into your homes that God did not send it to you." [87] His early sermons entitled "Faith," "The Gift of God," "The Conversion of Jacob," "Entire Consecration," "The Master Calleth for Thee," and "The Choice of Life" were simply statements of the orthodox fundamentals of revivalism with a heavy emphasis on moralizing and the homely application of Biblical stories. Mills was characterized by the newspapers as a winning or "persuasive" speaker. His tone, unlike that of Moody or Jones, was gentle, pleading, and urgent without being strident or aggressive. Ministers praised him for the "deep solemnity and entire absence of excitement" in his meetings. He "constantly holds out the possibility of being a Christian simply because it is right, and forsaking sin simply because it is wrong." He told no jokes and indulged in few rhetorical flourishes or pathetic stories. There was "no excited waving of the arms, no sensationally acted scenes." [88]

In 1893 Mills, like Golden Rule Jones, came under the influence of George D. Herron and was converted to the concept of social Christianity. From that time on Mills began to inject social gospel doctrines into his preaching. In a book of sermons entitled *God's World,* which he published in 1894, he talked of the brotherhood of all men under the fatherhood of God, of Christ's coming to save the world rather than individuals, and of the optimistic future in which all social and economic problems would be solved. Christ preached that if a man "performed his duty to his fellow-men he would be all right in the sight of God." All men must recognize "that God is the Father of us all. Universal brotherhood implies universal Fatherhood and a man will never be right with any other man until he comes to see in him a brother . . . and in a certain sense the brother of the Lord Jesus Christ with all the possibilities that dwelt in Christ." [89]

A year later he was delivering revival sermons on "Christianity and Socialism," "The Church and the Kingdom," and

[87] *Mills Meeting Memorial Volume, op. cit.,* p. 123.

[88] *Ibid.,* pp. 94, 2; St. Louis *Globe-Democrat,* April 8, 1897; St. Paul *Daily Pioneer Press,* May 11, 1893, p. 1.

[89] B. Fay Mills, *God's World* (New York, 1894), pp. 31, 229–30, 279.

"The Kingdom of Heaven on Earth." Previously he had seldom spoken of the millennium. Now he came out strongly in favor of the postmillennial view, held by all social gospelers, that "God's kingdom may come on the earth 'as it is in heaven.'" In the light of this new conception of the gospel, he explained, "I would not say quite so much come to Jesus as come with Jesus." [90] Superficially this resembled Sam P. Jones's call to imitate Christ rather than to believe in him. But Jones never caught the real spirit of the social gospel. He never saw, as Mills did, that socialism was more than a greedy attempt of the working class to divide among themselves the money accumulated by the industrious middle class. Mills realized how much of the appeal of socialism in the 1890's lay in its concept of human brotherhood and in its ethic of cooperation rather than competition.

In his sermon on "Christianity and Socialism" Mills expressly repudiated the individualistic religion of most revivalists which had become so inextricably interwoven with a defense of laissez-faire capitalism and the status quo. "There have indeed been some pure minds," he said, "who have had a conception of Christianity as strictly individualistic, and who have looked at the aims and power of the spirit of Christ only in its relationship to individuals." But most professed Christians who took this view, he went on, thought socialism and Christianity to be "entirely distinct from one another." Such an outlook could be held in 1895 only by "the ignorant, reactionary, or pietistic Christian." As Mills expressed it: "Almost all the Christians who are now worthy of the name have come to see that the aim of Christ was not simply to produce a pure individual in a personal sense, but to produce the right individual for the sake of a righteous society; and I am sure that by far the larger proportion of the true hearted followers of the humble Nazarene would join me in saying that if I had to choose between being a Socialist in the spirit of Christ, but without His name, or being an unsocial Christian, I would be more loyal to Him in the former choice than in the latter." [91]

[90] *The Great Awakening in Columbus Ohio Under the Labors of Rev. B. Fay Mills, op. cit.*, pp. 44, 47.

[91] *Ibid.*, pp. 61–62.

Once Mills had joined the social gospel movement he went all the way. He quoted John R. Commons, William H. Fremantle, Thomas Kirkup, Washington Gladden, George Herron, and "the French Socialists of 1850" in his attacks upon the prevailing economic order. Quoting F. W. Sprague on the contrast between capitalism and socialism, he said, "Society will no longer tolerate its old dogmas respecting private property, freedom of contract, and free competition; its conception of the State as a mere political institution, or labor as a mere commodity, its necessary conclusion that money is of more consequence than men, that might makes right, that men being unequal must take the consequences of inequality, that some may justly live in idleness and luxury while others toil and starve, that the social grist of vice is necessary and natural. . . . These dogmas . . . have at length become so offensive to the prevailing sense of right as to be no longer tolerable." "To all of which," added Mills, "I say 'Amen.' "[92]

Unlike Moody and Jones, Mills was convinced that the world was "growing better" and that progress would be as rapid as it was inevitable, for "God intended the establishment of a terrestrial, spiritual, universal, everlasting kingdom upon the earth through human agency." The duty of the Christian and of the churches was not simply to save drunkards, prohibit the liquor traffic, and cut out cards, dancing, and theaters, but it was "the business of the Church . . . to see that there is better care for the poor . . . to be concerned about the physical welfare of all cities and citizens, better pavement, cheaper heat and light and transportation and communication, pure water and more of it. . . ." Like Golden Rule Jones he thought that more was to be gained from municipal ownership of utilities and the refusal of "valuable franchises" to private companies than from enforcing out-of-date blue laws.[93]

Nor did Mills limit his statements to mere generalizations. He specifically attacked the Pullman Company, the president of the Brooklyn street car company, and Jay Gould for injustice to striking workers. He excoriated the trustees of Trinity Church in New York because "it has some of the filthiest and

92 *Ibid.*, pp. 64–65.
93 *Ibid.*, pp. 59, 55.

vilest and most degraded and most disease-bringing tenement houses in the city of New York; and it takes the revenues it gets from these places, where they are murdering people body and soul, in order to establish missions in the name of Almighty God." He denounced churches which left the city and moved into the suburbs "for no other reason than that the people around them were so wicked" or because they found they could sell their downtown property for a profit. He ridiculed the then current heresy trials in the Presbyterian Church over evolution and the higher criticism and accused the Methodist Church of electing its bishops "by methods that would disgrace the lowest politician in the country." He refused to spare businessmen who contributed to churches and charities or who built colleges and hospitals. "Some of them are built by money that is the price of blood and by methods that have been born in the darkest pits of hell. The most conspicuous Christian university of this continent, bidding fair to be the greatest Christian school of the world, was built by money drawn from various sources but most of it money that was gained by the commission of almost every crime that is possible to the hands and heart of man. The largest and most extensive industrial institute of modern times was built by money that was gained by such nefarious traffic in the necessities of life as fairly caused men to die of hunger on account of it!" [94]

This sort of challenge to the churches and to their leading laymen was new in modern revivalism. It was this which caused Gladden to praise Mills as the exponent of a "new evangelism" and which led the ministers of Columbus, Ohio, who joined Gladden in backing a Mills revival in their city in 1895, to declare that "his work in this city proves that at least one man can preach both a personal and a social gospel with equal earnestness and power." The cooperating ministers of Columbus published a book describing Mills' revival there, and one of them wrote a description of the "New Era in Evangelism" which he thought Mills had inaugurated. "The Mills meeting in this city has shown clearly that the old-time revival, with its intense fervor and power has developed into" a movement

[94] *Ibid.*, pp. 58–59, 66–67. Presumably Mills referred to Chicago University, built on Rockefeller money, and the Armour Institute.

"for personal and social righteousness and rebuking of all persons and institutions that dare to array themselves against God and the true interests of men." According to this minister, "The new evangelism differs from the old mainly in the fact that to the conviction of personal sins and effort to save men from them is added conviction and sorrow for social sins and a practical effort to improve the material, political, and social environment in which the individual lives. . . ." [95]

As part of his effort to spread the new message, Mills included in the Columbus revival a Christian Convention which was attended by 170 ministers from all over Ohio. At this convention papers were read and discussed on such topics as "Evils in Material Conditions," "Educational Defects," "Business Sins," "Political Sins," "The Christianization of Business," "The Regeneration of Politics," "The Salvation of Society," and "The Moral Influence of the Public School." It was a far cry from the Christian Conventions which Moody had held, and was still holding, in connection with his revivals where the topics for discussion were "How To Reach the Masses," "How To Conduct Prayer Meetings," and "How To Deal with Anxious Inquirers." The usual result of Moody's meetings was a growth in Bible classes and tract distribution. Mills's meeting in Columbus produced a Civic Federation made up of the ministers of all denominations, including Jews and Roman Catholics, which under the leadership of Washington Gladden was designed "to promote the common welfare" of the city.

Mills demonstrated that there was a large reserve of social consciousness among religious people which could be tapped for constructive reform efforts. But somehow the churches were unable to mobilize this force effectively. The leadership of men like Mills and Gladden might bring a sense of Christian social responsibility temporarily to the surface, but it required a sustained effort on the part of the ordinary pastors and lay leaders to keep it alive. This effort proved impossible. The average pastor found the social and economic problems of the day too complex for his limited knowledge and felt awkward when he tried to talk about them in his pulpit. Many parishioners might sympathize with the social gospel point of

[95] *Ibid.*, pp. 12, 147.

view in a general way, but when the wealthier laymen, who acted as trustees, sustained the church deficits, and generally directed church affairs, contemplated the possible results of encouraging socialism and labor unions, they were not likely to give their ministers much support. The result was that in spite of Gladden's chairmanship, the Columbus Civic Federation could come up with no better program to promote the common welfare than to agree to devote one Sunday to sermons on "The Enforcement of the Law" in the hope of persuading the mayor to "close the gambling places" as legally required. What Mills had hoped would be the start of a profound reorientation in the life of Columbus—a reorientation that would change the whole environment and bring about a new social order—eventually fell into the well-established channels. The churches felt more at home with clearcut "moral questions" like prohibition or gambling. The division between religion and business, between the church and politics, was too deep and long-standing to be bridged by a few revival sermons on the brotherhood of man and the coming of the kingdom. Revivalism by tradition and by its ephemeral nature was not an effective means for obtaining social gospel ends.

It was ironic that a revival message as different as Mills's was from Jones's could end up in the same type of action among churchgoers. Jones's Law and Order Leagues and Mills's Civic Federation proved to be the same because the churches preferred the easy way out. They persuaded themselves that prohibition was the Christian solution to all problems. As a result the political reformers, the sociologists, the scientists, and the teachers became the leaders of the progressive generation by default. R. H. Tawney's words, used in a different context, were applicable to the Protestant Church in America in the 1890's: ". . . the social doctrines advanced from the pulpit offered, in their traditional form, little guidance. Their practical ineffectiveness prepared the way for their theoretical abandonment. They were abandoned because, on the whole, they deserved to be abandoned. The social teaching of the Church had ceased to count, because the Church itself had ceased to think." Although church membership continued to grow, the Church itself "was neglected because it had become negligible."[96] Thinking men turned their efforts elsewhere.

Shortly after his meetings in Columbus, Mills found himself under attack from conservative ministers for his castigation of the churches and their wealthy lay leaders. The editor of the Methodist *Christian Advocate* in New York, the Rev. J. M. Buckley, became a particularly bitter antagonist and in a number of articles extending over the next two years he helped to hound Mills out of the evangelical churches. In April, 1896, Buckley found "indubitable evidence of a new departure" in Mills's preaching "calculated to excite alarm." His source for this was the sermons preached in Columbus. In an open letter he condemned Mills's attacks upon the Presbyterian heresy trials, upon the Methodist methods of electing bishops, and upon a "benefactor" of the church to whom "you apply the coarse and profane expression, 'cursed robber.' " By September, 1897, Buckley was accusing Mills of "beguiling unstable souls" away from orthodoxy. As a young man Mills had been "thoroughly orthodox," said Buckley, but now "he was surrendering the biblical and particularly the Christian way of preaching the Gospel for what might be called the ethical. . . ." Washington Gladden and the liberal ministers of Columbus might praise this new social revivalism, but to Buckley it was infidelity, and the majority of the nation's evangelical ministers agreed with him.[97]

In the fall of 1897 Mills admitted in answer to these attacks that he had indeed shifted his emphasis, but he denied that he was a Unitarian as some accused him of being. "I have for several years been gradually modifying my theories. I never in my evangelistic work preached the old school theology which has always seemed to me unnatural and immoral." He claimed to be more in harmony with the views of Horace Bushnell and F. D. Maurice. (Buckley commented on this that these were

[96] R. H. Tawney, *Religion and the Rise of Capitalism* (New York, 1926), pp. 185–86.

[97] *Christian Advocate* (Methodist, New York), April 23, 1896, p. 265; July 23, p. 490; September 23, 1897, p. 618. See also the *Congregationalist* (Boston), July 8, 1897, p. 41; September 9, p. 342, September 23, p. 425, October 14, p. 517. It is revealing that the "ethical" aspects of Mills's preaching were so vehemently denounced while the "social reform" aspects of Sam P. Jones's preaching were so highly praised by conservative evangelicals.

"perhaps as vague names as he could give from the point of view of theology.") Mills went on: "I have been led to accept most of the conclusions and hypotheses of what might be called modern thought concerning the unity of the universe, the development of the world, and the progressive character of revelation. I would not dogmatize either in affirmation or denial concerning the Scriptures, the supernatural character and work of Jesus, or the mysteries of the world to come." [98] But Mills still considered himself both a good Congregationalist and a good Presbyterian (he had been Presbyterianized in 1895 when he took a short pastorate in the Fourth Presbyterian Church in Albany).

Nevertheless, the doors of evangelicalism began to close in his face. In October, 1897, he undertook a series of revival meetings in Boston under the sponsorship of Edward Everett Hale, Horace S. Sears, Edwin D. Mead, E. A. Horton, and William M. McInness. Although ministers of all denominations were asked to join in sponsoring the meetings which were held in the Music Hall, it was clear that the Unitarians were his principal backers, and the evangelicals held aloof. Mills spoke at the Music Hall and the Hollis Street Theater in Boston every Sunday for the next two years. His talks were entitled "The Application of Modern Religious Thought to Modern Practical Problems," and several of them were published in a volume which he called *Twentieth Century Religion*. Then, in 1899, he abandoned evangelism entirely and left Boston for Oakland, California. Here he became pastor of the First Unitarian Church, thereby entitling all his opponents to say, "I told you so," and casting new suspicion on the theological vagaries of the social gospel.

Mills was quite explicit about his reasons for leaving the revival profession. "I left my evangelistic work first because I despaired of the possibility of a genuine, widespread awakening and inspiration of the church; second because of a social vision by which I came to conceive of Christ as the Saviour of the social organization rather than of individuals, and third because of the universal viewpoint which came to me through my study of the great books of all ages and nations through which the Bible ceased to be to me the exclusively inspired

[98] The *Congregationalist,* September 9, 1897, p. 350.

Word of God."[99] Thus ended the revival career of the one man who tried to combine professional soul-winning and the social gospel.

A strange postscript was written to Mills's life in 1915 when he decided to renounce his Unitarianism and return to the Presbyterian Church. Though he did not give up his faith in religion as "that fine sense of soul which connects the individual with the Universal Purpose," he now recognized, he said, that this did not "constitute a genuine gospel" because it took "no account of the depravity and helplessness of the ordinary human nature." The outbreak of World War I in 1914 (and by implication the failure of the social gospel movement) "convinced me that this is not an earth whose regeneration may be expected day after tomorrow according to my optimistic prophecies, but a lost world . . . helpless and hopeless save through some demonstration in history of an essential redemption and salvation."[100]

There was a tolerance and a breadth in Mills's thought which marked him off from the general run of professional evangelists. He tried after his reinstatement into Presbyterianism in 1915 to return to revival work, but he was not successful. He died the following year while ministers all over America were hailing Billy Sunday as a new type of evangelist with a new message.

Sam Jones and B. Fay Mills each caught something of the spirit of the progressive movement which began in the 1890's. It was a movement of protest and hope: protest against change by conservatives and hope for better things by liberals. It received part of its impetus from the moral fervor of the Christian faith and part from the materialistic meliorism of Spencer's social Darwinism. Like most aspects of American social thought, it combined faith in God with faith in man. But the evangelical participants in it put too much faith in reforming the individual first while the social gospelers put too much faith in changing man's environment. Both groups believed in enacting their panaceas into law, but the evangelicals wanted laws to restrict the evil tendencies encouraged by drink, gam-

[99] B. Fay Mills, "My Practical Evolution," The *Advance* (Chicago) LXVII (June 24, 1915), 1251–52.

[100] *Ibid.*, p. 1252.

bling, theater and dancing, while the social gospelers wanted laws to restrict the evil tendencies of monopolies, political machines, and fraudulent business practices. Basically the evangelicals wanted only such reforms as would conserve the old ways. The social gospelers were willing to modify the system to meet new needs.

Professional evangelism was now openly aligned with the conservative elements in religion, politics, and business, although the false panacea of prohibition sometimes blurred this fact. Evangelists tried to end the growing cleavage between the churches and those outside the churches by utilizing revivalism to elicit or compel conformity to an increasingly narrow pattern of thought and action. But they succeeded only in confirming prejudices and social antagonisms. What was more important for their profession, they found themselves unable to reconcile the schism within Protestantism which became known as the conflict of fundamentalism versus modernism. The spiritual impetus of the third great awakening slipped through the hands of the churchmen as they locked in battle with each other.

CHAPTER 7

"The American Type of Christianity" and "This Godless Social Service Nonsense"

Modern revivalism entered a new phase at the turn of the century. For the first time since Finney's day, a significant body of opposition to revivals developed within the evangelical churches. This opposition came from three sources: the social gospelers on the left, the moderates (those tending toward modernism) in the middle, and the more thoughtful conservatives on the right. Summed up in a sentence, the conservatives had some misgivings about mass revival techniques but continued to believe that soul-winning was the primary goal and function of the churches; the social gospelers thought social reform was primary, and the moderates thought that both were of equal importance.

The incipient social gospelers who had praised and cooperated with Moody in the 1870's began to see by the 1890's that mass evangelism in the name of the Christian fundamentals was not only failing to solve the problems faced by the churches and the nation but that it had begun to have a positively harmful effect. Its narrow theology alienated the intelligent; its inadequate social message irritated those who wanted real reforms; its increasingly secular, mechanical, and commercial techniques shocked the devout. Instead of uniting the moral and spiritual fervor of the churches behind a crusade for a better world, revivalists were squandering it upon expensive and fruitless church rallies. The failure of B. Fay Mills convinced social gospel leaders like Washington Gladden that revivalism could not be coordinated with their aims. After 1900 the social gospel movement concentrated upon the formation of social service departments within their denominations and worked toward the unification of Protestant social effort under the auspices of the Federal Council of Churches. Social gospelers did not deny the importance of saving men's souls, but they believed that first they must change men's environment.

The thoughtful theological conservatives cared little about environment. They directed their criticism of modern revivalism primarily against its methods and results rather than against its theology or its purpose. The Rev. George F. Pentecost, for example, a forceful Baptist minister, had given up his Boston pastorate in 1878 at Moody's urging in order to devote himself to itinerant evangelism. But in 1900 he abandoned the profession in dissatisfaction and annoyance and issued a call for a new approach to revivalism. "In my humble judgment," he said, "the day of the ignorant, unfurnished, and vulgar sensational evangelism is vanished." "The future evangelist will be the associate and helper of the pastor or pastors . . . and not the 'boss of the whole show.'" Instead of grandiose city-wide campaigns carried on in "halls and public buildings," the work of "the new revival . . . will be carried on by individual churches or small combinations of churches of the same denominations." Conversions, said Pentecost, should be obtained by patient and serious pastoral consultation and not in "after meetings" where "indiscriminate 'workers' with a few texts of Scripture" seek to "railroad inquirers" into a hasty and shallow decision to accept Christ.[1]

An even more powerful dissent from the prevailing practices of modern revivalism on the part of thoughtful conservatism came from the Rev. George E. Horr, editor of the national Baptist weekly, *The Watchman,* and later President of Newton Theological Institute. "We believe," Horr wrote editorially in 1899, "that Mr. Moody himself admits that the day for great hippodrome religious services in which the idea of a church

[1] Quoted in the *Watchman* (Baptist, Boston), September 6, 1900, p. 9.

is lost in an atmosphere of a mass meeting has been rapidly passing away." Moody's "method of evangelism . . . however much we may dislike to make the confession . . . has not grown in effectiveness." Horr had made some statistical investigations of the results of Moody's revivals and concluded: "The statistics appear to show that in Eastern Massachusetts, for example, the addition to the evangelical churches for five-year periods after the Great Tabernacle meetings in Boston were not so large as for five-year periods before. And most pastors have observed that the quality of the material brought into the churches under these influences is not so high as that gained by the devoted work of the local church by its own methods among its own clientage." Not only were hippodrome revivals unsuccessful in adding valuable new church members, said Horr, but "in the instances in which they have been apparently most blessed they have been followed by a disheartening period of spiritual indifference" among the regular church members. Horr and others like him talked of evangelists who "have proved themselves sordid, self-seeking, and unworthy in character"; of churches which "have suffered from the injudicious methods and coarse preaching of certain evangelists"; of "drastic presentations of the truth [which] have alienated many"; of revivals "manufactured by machinery"; and of "whole communities [which] have been burned over by some evangelists so that they are not fertile to the gospel seed." [2]

In between the conservative critics, like Pentecost and Horr, and the radical critics, like Mills and Gladden, lay the growing ranks of moderates and "liberals" who also expressed doubts about the virtues of old-fashioned mass revivalism. These evangelicals had imbibed sufficient amounts of the higher criticism and of theistic evolution to resent the "orthodox" theology of professional evangelism which had finally been frozen into the rigid "five points of fundamentalism" by the Niagara Bible Conference in 1895. In this formulation of evangelicalism the loosely phrased "essentials" of the gospel were codified into the dogma of the literal infallibility of the Bible, the virgin birth, the substitutionary atonement, the resurrection, and the im-

[2] *Ibid.*, January 20, 1898, p. 8; October 26, 1899, pp. 9–10; November 30, p. 10; December 21, p. 7; January 4, 1900, p. 12.

minent, bodily, premillennial second coming of Christ.[3] The modernists preferred to think that revelation was progressive and that an immanent God was working out his will in history through the evolutionary process. But while they disliked the narrowness of fundamentalism and the commercialized sensationalism of revivalism, few of them were ready to abandon the view that soul-winning was the central purpose of the ministry. Nor were they willing to go so far as the social gospelers toward putting the churches actively behind the progressive movement for political and economic reforms. What the moderates wanted was a revivalism which would be both intellectually respectable and emotionally fervent, which would show some awareness of the need for social reform and yet would not substitute socialism for regenerating individuals. They felt that a more practical application of the Christian message was needed, but they did not want the churches to take any stand on the controversial issues of capital and labor. In short, they wanted to have their cake and eat it too.

In the arguments over the need for a "new evangelism" which filled the religious journals at the turn of the century, several alternatives were proposed. The conservative group represented by Pentecost and Horr tended to favor what they called "personal evangelism" and "pastoral evangelism." By this they meant simply that if every pastor would preach like an evangelist and if every Christian would try to convert his friends and neighbors, soul-winning could proceed apace without resorting to the "mass" revival techniques which inevitably became vulgar and commercial. The social gospel leaders, however, talked in terms of an "ethical revival" such as B. Fay Mills had advocated but without the use of Mills's mass evangelistic machinery. The most forceful exponent of this viewpoint was Josiah Strong.

Strong first became famous as the Secretary of the Home Mission Society of the Congregational Church in 1885 when his book, *Our Country,* issued a stirring plea for more home mission work in the slums of the great cities. Since then he had been secretary of the Evangelical Alliance, cofounder of

[3] See Norman F. Furniss, *The Fundamentalist Controversy, 1918–1931* (New Haven, 1954), p. 13; and S. G. Cole, *History of Fundamentalism* (New York, 1931), p. 34.

the Open and Institutional Church League, president of the American Institute of Sociology, associate editor of *The Kingdom,* and founder of the League for Social Service and the American Institute for Social Service. He was later to play an influential role in the founding of the Federal Council of Churches in 1908. Strong spelled out his attitude toward revivalism in a book called *The Next Great Awakening,* which was published in 1902. In it he began by asserting that the old-fashioned revivalism was no longer effective and that the revivalism of the twentieth century needed a new message and a new method. The new message, he said, must be based upon the hitherto neglected truth that the great theme of the preaching of Jesus was the Kingdom of God. When Jesus spoke of seeking the kingdom he did not mean either seeking to enter heaven or seeking to become a member of the visible church, but seeking to effect the social ideals of Christianity "on earth as it is in heaven." "The kingdom of God is Utopia made rational and destined to be made actual." In order to guide men toward this utopia, Jesus set forth certain principles which Strong called "Jesus' social legislation." These consisted of "the law of service, the law of sacrifice, and the law of love," which together worked for social justice, for more adequate distribution of property, and for the universal brotherhood of man. If the church is to live up to its mission, "she will seek to save *men* rather than *souls,* and she will endeavor to discharge her mission to society as well as to the individual. She will discover that it is much wiser to clean up the 'mud puddle' so that the jewels will no longer get lost, than it is to devote all of her time to recovering a small portion of the lost jewels." Strong frankly declared that this would mean transforming the selfish and competitive principles upon which modern capitalism was based, acknowledging the rights of organized labor, and rearranging "the distribution of political power" so as to disconnect it from "the centralization of industrial power." In the next great awakening, as Strong visualized it, the supernatural power of divine grace would not express itself through spectacular mass meetings under the leadership of some sensational revivalist. It would express itself through a great upsurge of Christian endeavor for the reformation of American social, political, and economic life. It would be led by dedicated, well-informed churchmen of all ranks, and inspired by the social teachings of Jesus. Where possible the reformation would be accomplished by loving persuasion and voluntary cooperation; where necessary, by local, state, and national legislation.[4]

Strong's approach was vigorously denounced by the defenders of old-fashioned revivalism. The tradition, though under attack, still had a devoted following among a great many evangelical church leaders who considered Strong's views little better than infidelity and socialism. One of the leading defenders of mass revivalism was Moody's friend, the Rev. Amzi Clarence Dixon, an influential Baptist pastor of Brooklyn and Boston who in 1906 became pastor of the Moody Church in Chicago and in 1909-1910 helped to edit the series of volumes called *The Fundamentals,* which launched the fundamentalist movement in earnest against both modernism and the social gospel. Dixon published a book in 1905 called *Evangelism Old and New,* which gave a direct rebuttal to Strong, and on several occasions Dixon lectured to ministerial groups using a chapter from this book entitled "Evangelism, True and False." True evangelism he defined as preaching "the new birth," "repentance and faith," and "winning souls to Christ." False evangelism he called that "which depends upon change of environment to produce change of character." Quoting the story of the philanthropic landlord who razed his slum tenements and erected model apartment houses only to find that "his tenants were using his bathtubs for coalbins," Dixon remarked: "It cost him something to learn that swine cannot be made into sheep by change of environment." "False evangelism," which encouraged this sort of reform, Dixon claimed, was nothing but "socialistic evangelism." It was the baneful counterpart of the new "bloodless evangelism" or "academic evangelism," which "insists upon intellectual training, moral culture, and humanitarian activity." He said that this academic evangelism was "turning many of our colleges and institutions into hot-beds of infidelity or refrigerators of indifference" because it had adopted "the pagan carpenter theory of naturalistic evolution instead of the Biblical teaching of creation by fiat of God." Dixon be-

[4] See Josiah Strong, *The Next Great Awakening* (New York, 1902), pp. 35, 55, 83, 115, 108–9, 162–63.

lieved that there could be no reconciliation between science and religion any more than between socialism and free enterprise. It was the duty of the church to convert individuals and to keep out of politics. The only true revivals in the past were those led by "believers in the inspiration and infallible authority of the Word of God" who, like Moody, sought to save souls and not to change environment. So it would be in the future, or the church would be false to its mission.[5]

Caught between the anti-intellectualism of Dixon's revivalism and the anti-orthodoxy of Strong's, the moderate evangelicals were inevitably headed for schism. The compromise approach of the more thoughtful conservatives like Pentecost and Horr was too colorless and inadequate to be a viable alternative. As the pressure of the progressive movement and the evidence of scholarship gradually pushed more and more clergymen into the liberal camp, many searched desperately for some way to maintain the old traditions of the faith. That the schism implicit in the controversy over revivalism was postponed until the 1920's can be attributed primarily to the overwhelming sense of optimism which characterized the temper of the times. Even A. C. Dixon, though a premillennialist committed to the idea that the world would see bitter days before Christ's return, stated in the introduction to *Evangelism, Old and New,* "In spite of much worldliness, many apostasies, and the spirit of grasping greed which to a large extent prevails in the commercial world, the day-dawn of a world-wide revival begins to appear. Let us continue to pray, while we work for its coming." Dixon, like Moody, occasionally forgot his premillennialism and talked of "the evangelization of the world in this generation." [6] In the glow of this universal optimism a way was found to reconcile the irreconcilable views of Strong and Dixon. By substituting prohibition, "social service," and Americanism for the theology of evangelicalism, modern revivalists managed

[5] See A. C. Dixon, *Evangelism Old and New* (New York, 1905), pp. 43 ff.; and *Watchman,* February 22, 1906, pp. 10–11.

[6] "As we read the record of this world-wide missionary work by all denominations, we have a widening vision of the gospel's power and every lover of his race who knows the record of these facts can but exclaim, 'Glory to God in the highest and on earth, peace and good will among men' while he stands on the mountain-top of vision praying for the evangelization of the world." Dixon, *Evangelism Old and New,* p. 209.

to soar to new heights of popularity in the very shadow of the volcanic clouds of disruption.

The most forceful and eloquent proponent of this nationalistic school of evangelicalism was the Rev. Warren A. Candler, a bishop of the Methodist Episcopal Church, South. In a book called *Great Revivals and the Great Republic,* published in 1904, Candler put into concrete form the religious atmosphere in which modern revivalism flourished from 1900 to 1920. And he did it by relying almost as heavily as Strong upon the prevailing concepts of divine immanence, Christian perfectionism, social Darwinism, and America's manifest destiny as leader of the Anglo-Saxon race. Although he was both theologically and politically as conservative as Dixon, Candler was also as convinced as Strong that history was on the side of Christianity and of the English-speaking peoples who were its chosen carriers. Candler emphasized the orthodox view of Dixon that reform would come only through the personal regeneration of sinful men, but his whole tone embodied the optimistic liberalism of Strong that God was working out his purpose through man's individual and social perfection and that if men would just put their minds to it they could conquer all their difficulties.

This book was also important because, despite implicit, and occasionally explicit, statements to the contrary, many moderates believed that Candler was not necessarily opposed to human efforts at social reform so long as they were piously undertaken. Candler seemed to leave the door open for those vague interpretations of the term "social service" which, to a large extent, shared the credit with nationalistic Christianity as a means of temporarily glossing over the differences between liberal and conservative evangelicals. Because Candler's book was in so many ways representative of the prevailing evangelical outlook which underlay the revivalism of this period, it is worth looking at in more detail.

Warren Candler was not only a Methodist bishop; he was a former editor of his church's official journal, the Nashville *Christian Advocate,* a former president of Emory College, a friend and admirer of Sam P. Jones, a zealous prohibitionist, and the brother of Asa G. Candler, the Coca-Cola magnate. In his book he purported to speak simply as a historian of religion. "This volume is a study of American history," he stated in his preface, a study based on the premise that "the forms and forces of national life take their rise in the religion of the people." Candler was convinced that "the fruitful periods of a nation's history are those during which religion is flourishing, and periods of religious declension are marked by the withering of all social and political activity." He concluded his preface with the statement that "a careful and unprejudiced consideration of the facts presented will lead to the conclusion that a revivalistic religion—the prevalent form of Christianity in American Churches—is at once the salvation of our own country and the hope of other lands." [7]

Since it was the essential theme of the book that "revivalistic religion" always had been and always would be the divinely appointed means of settling national and international problems, Candler proceeded to give a few examples of the ways in which God had been working out his plan for the triumph of Anglo-Saxon ideals. Utilizing some ideas of the British historian, William E. H. Lecky, and some of his own, Candler drew a parallel between the "fearful peril" from which the revivalism of John Wesley and George Whitefield saved England and the very similar peril from which Moody and Sankey had recently saved the United States. England in the eighteenth century faced the same grave problem of "rising industrialism" with "workingmen agglomerated in the town" and becoming "nomadic in habit and irritable in temper," subject to the "fearful temptations" and "feverish excitement" of the cities. The rich grew richer and the poor, poorer, "and all the bonds of sympathy between class and class were weakened." Meanwhile, across the channel in France under Louis XVI "were heard the mutterings of mass discontent" incited by "poisonous infidelity and perilous radicalism" to the point where "a hatred for all

[7] W. A. Candler, *Great Revivals and the Great Republic* (Nashville, Tennessee, 1904), pp. 3, 7. He also tended to agree with those "who have ventured to affirm that as goes the United States so will go the world"; p. 297. The long-standing relationship between revivalism and nationalism has been noted above in connection with millennialism. The tendency of American ministers to extol patriotism as a Christian virtue was hardly new in 1904 (for example, see the quotations in Charles C. Cole, *Social Ideas of the Northern Evangelists 1826–1860* [New York, 1954], pp. 159–164.) But there was a distinctly harsher and more strident tone in the Americanism expressed by revivalists in the twentieth century which was symptomatic of the declining prestige of "the old time" religion.

constituted authority" and "an insatiable appetite for change" were eventually to erupt in "the frenzy" of a "direful revolution." Imperceptibly, "the influence of French infidelity" and "the new and popular theories of liberty" infiltrated the minds of the British lower classes and might well have aroused them to rebellion too. But, fortunately, "the heavenly visitation" known as the evangelical revival prevented this. "Instead of an era of destructive revolution there was inaugurated . . . nothing short of a moral revolution" which "opened a new spring of moral and religious energy among the poor, and at the same time gave a powerful impulse to the philanthropy of the rich." The benevolent charities of the wealthy employers and the new concept of brotherly love instilled in the poor by Wesley and Whitefield "healed the breach" between the classes, "solidified the nation, and saved the day." Thus when the French Revolution did break forth, the workingmen of England were so imbued with religion that they "recoiled with horror from the antichristian tenets that were associated with [it]." [8]

Most of this Candler quoted from Lecky. It was in contemplating the long range effects of the Wesleyan revival that he added his own views. The new vigor and the spiritual unity of Britain after 1750 "raised the enfeebled England of Walpole's time to the puissant power which eventually overcame the French, thus giving North America to be the home of an Anglo-Saxon civilization and assuring the predominance of Anglo-Saxon influence in India and 'the Far East.'" It led Napoleon, out of hatred of Britain, to sell the Louisiana Territory to the United States, and "its purchase eventually brought on the conflict of the Anglo-Saxon and the Latin civilizations for the possession of Texas—a conflict . . . completing the evacuation of North America by the Latin forces antagonistic to the evangelical Christianity and Saxon civilization." [9]

[8] *Ibid.*, pp. 139–43.

[9] *Ibid.*, pp. 150–51. Though Candler made no acknowledgment of the fact, he may have taken some of these ideas from a paper by J. M. T. Johnson on "The Significance of the Louisiana Purchase to American Protestantism," which was described in the *Watchman*, May 28, 1903, p. 13. It was curious that Candler made no reference to the Spanish-American War, which most evangelicals considered the final evacuation of Latin forces from North America. The justifications of Anglo-Saxon–Protestant–democratic imperialism which were crystallized in American popular thought by this war were, however, perfectly evident throughout Candler's book.

The destiny of Britain and the United States was further linked by the spread of Methodism to America which "broke the shock of the Revolutionary War" in 1776 and later saved the new nation from "flying away from the center of Anglo-Saxon unity to follow the movements of revolutionary France" under the "liberal" influence of Thomas Jefferson.[10] Having survived the evils of deism and Jeffersonian democracy by means of the Great Awakening of 1800 and the revivals of Nettleton and Finney, and having passed safely through the Civil War and the "race problem" as a result of the Prayer Meeting Revival of 1858, "the Great Republic" was faced in 1875 with a new test of its stability: the conflict between rich and poor, between capital and labor, had come to the United States. But God raised up Moody and Sankey "to reach the masses," and "the results . . . attributed to the Wesleyan revival in England in the eighteenth century we have seen following also the revival in the days of the Moody and Sankey meetings in America in the nineteenth century." "What they accomplished in the way of soothing the irritations of the social system, and of postponing, if not preventing, the worst industrial disorder, can scarcely be over-estimated." For "neither time nor place forestalls the operations of the fundamental principles of wealth and the sensitiveness of poverty, casting down the animosities of class against class, and establishing the noblest brotherhood of souls."[11] Candler used the words "brotherhood of souls" and not "the brotherhood of man" advisedly. He wanted no one to mistake him for an advocate of the social gospel.

This became abundantly clear in his final chapter, entitled "The Next Great Awakening," which, it turned out, was the *raison d'être* for the book. Great as the influence of Methodism and Moody had been in America, Candler concluded, "perfect success has not been realized" in obviating "the perilous conflict of the irritable industrialism of the days that were to come." But this was in no way the fault of revivalistic religion. "The partial failure is easily explained by the fact that disturbances

[10] Candler, *Great Revivals,* pp. 159, 165. Candler has an amusing passage comparing the parlous state of the nation in the days when Jefferson was "the idol of the masses" and the halcyon days of William McKinley, "a fervent Methodist"; pp. 278–80.

[11] *Ibid.,* pp. 290, 276–77.

between labor and capital have been most frequent in those industries in which the laborers have been brought from the unevangelized masses of Continental Europe, and the capital has been supplied by men who feared not God nor regarded man." [12] But there was more to the problem than unevangelized labor and godless tycoons, said Candler.

There were, in fact, a whole host of perils facing the United States in the year 1904 which had prevented the complete success of Moody's work and which necessitated a new great awakening. In addition to "selfish wealth" and "angry want" there were "the fires of socialism"; "the peril of immigration"; the "great menace of Romanism"; the heresies of "Mormonism," "spiritualism," and "Christian Science"; the problem of "intemperance"; and the encroaching "doctrines of modern materialism" fostered by the "current hypotheses of science," the "prevalent theories in philosophy," and the "academic cant" of a "microscopic [higher] criticism." Candler here gathered together all the prevailing evils which had been blamed for the decline of religion since 1875 and called for a new great awakening to meet them. For "there is no peril menacing the Great Republic today that . . . has not been met and overcome by revival . . . during the past." And, he concluded, "the hope of mankind is in the keeping of the Anglo-Saxon nations, led by the United States; and evangelical Christianity, with Methodism in the forefront, is the hope of these nations." [13]

Unlike Strong's appeal for a revival of social conscience and self-sacrificing service, Candler demanded that the next great awakening be a call to arms, a massive campaign of Christian warfare designed to drive the enemies of evangelical religion to unconditional surrender. Candler maintained that "moral forces are always aggressive" and "intolerant of opposition." A religion which admitted any merit in other religions "confesses thereby its unfitness." Survival of the fittest among religious faiths was even more voracious than among biological species, races, or nations, for religions must be in a state of perpetual war, each against all, until the strongest attained "universal dominion" and exterminated the rest. "The world must soon be all Christian or all anti-Christian" and "the earth must in-

[12] *Ibid.*, p. 275.
[13] *Ibid.*, pp. 291, 293, 300, 303, 320, 286.

evitably become more uniform in religion and moral government." American "revivalistic religion" was to provide the cutting edge for this fight to the finish with all other religious faiths. "If the movement of Providence over the Anglo-Saxon nations is not to terminate . . . , they must continue to be lifted and strengthened by greater and greater revivals of religion till their mission is fulfilled." And, quoting Carlyle, he called for "the great man, with his free, direct, force out of God's own hand" to lead the way.[14]

The leader, or leaders, of this great revival, would be "aided by all the modern devices of transportation and communication," but they would still preach the same old "fundamental truths" of religion, for in order to fulfill its mission revivalism had to speak with authority and only the old-time religion could "speak with authority to all classes, from the highest to the lowest, and subdue the men of all races with an unearthly imperialism." The reason that a humble, uneducated man like Moody could reduce to impotence the teachings of "Mr. Tyndall and Mr. Spencer and Mr. Huxley" was that "he preached not 'advanced thought' but the authoritative truths of an ancient revelation." "The doctrines of justification by faith, the new birth, the witness of the Spirit, and Christian perfection . . . only need to be really believed and fervently preached to renew the world in righteousness and true holiness." [15]

The social gospel message which Strong advocated was, according to Candler, not only not "authoritative" it was detrimental. "A languid liberalism bears no fruits." "Liberalism has never produced a revival of religion." "The outworn terms of a fatalistic theology [Calvinism] have been substituted by the scientific terminology of 'heredity,' 'environment,' and such like" which destroy men's urge to forge to the top. Social gospel ministers relied on the cold facts of sociological analysis and bureaucratic programs of social reform instead of upon the warm glow of evangelical charity. The next great awakening, Candler said, "will convert the rich men," and "they will be turned to their needy brothers." It will "feed the hungry,

[14] *Ibid.*, pp. 283, 307, 324. Candler may have rejected Spencer's agnosticism, but it was all too apparent that he had been profoundly influenced by his social Darwinian concept of survival of the fittest in races, nations, and social systems.

[15] *Ibid.*, pp. 300–301, 320.

clothe the naked, and seek the outcast and forlorn," but it "will make more of their spiritual wants" than of their "physical needs." All contemporary efforts to promote a revival which would encourage progressive social legislation were on the wrong track. "The next great awakening will be a revival of religion—not a political reform nor a philanthropic scheme of social amelioration." [16]

One key to the contrast between Candler's defense of mass revivalism and Strong's attack upon it was their respective attitudes toward Moody. While Candler insisted that Moody preached the same old doctrines of evangelical orthodoxy which had been successful in every preceding age, Strong insisted that the revivals of every era differed markedly in their doctrinal emphasis. "Be it observed," wrote Strong, "Moody did not repeat the message of Finney, nor did Finney repeat that of Wesley, nor Wesley that of the Puritans . . . though the substance was the same the form and method were new because the times were new. The men who today expect to reproduce Moody's results by reproducing his message and his methods will fail. . . ." For religion, like biological forms, "needs to change the form of its expression from time to time in order to adjust itself to changed conditions." [17]

But the more important key to their dispute was Strong's insistence that the churches must "seek to save men rather than souls." Candler was not only convinced that saving souls was sufficient; he insisted that it was certain to culminate in the conversion of the world. He remarked significantly that Moody was orthodox in all his doctrines "with the single exception of his views as to the millennium." [18] For Candler refused to believe that the world was a wrecked vessel from which only a few could be saved. His parenthetical and hastily covered criticism of Moody was one of the main reasons why Candler's views provided the basis upon which moderates and conservatives could join hands in revivalism. Premillennialism was no more fashionable among middle-class churchgoers in 1904 than Moody had found it to be in 1875, and Candler accurately reflected the main stream of contemporary evangelical thought

[16] *Ibid.*, pp. 314, 316, 320, 323–24, 313.
[17] Strong, *Next Great Awakening*, pp. 47–8, 16.
[18] Candler, *Great Revivals*, p. 271.

in his implicit warning to revivalists to steer clear of the pessimistic doctrine of the imminent second coming. To him this was as fatalistic and stultifying as Calvinism or the theory of heredity and environment. Although twentieth century revivalists, almost without exception, inconsistently continued to hold Moody's premillennial view despite their optimistic faith in America's manifest destiny to convert the world, they never would have obtained the support they needed for urban mass evangelism had they insisted too strenuously on preaching about it. In their efforts to straddle the positions of Strong and Candler, evangelists reluctantly and almost unwittingly became a part of the progressive movement for human betterment. Not until after 1920, when the schism within evangelicalism was too wide to be bridged even for the sake of soul-winning, did premillennialism become prominent in revival preaching. By then the evangelization of the world did not seem so simple a matter.

The aspect of Candler's argument which revealed most profoundly the transformation taking place in modern revivalism was his eagerness to associate "revivalistic religion" with Anglo-Saxon racism and American jingosim. Here he again approached the views of Josiah Strong and many other moderate evangelicals who, following the Spanish-American War, had defended the movement toward American imperialism on the grounds of Anglo-Saxon destiny.[19] Strong, however, thought of Christianity as a check upon the evils of survival of the fittest, a force for preserving the weak and elevating the poor. Candler tended to make racism an argument for conformity by conversion. Candler was magnanimously willing to include as Anglo-Saxons "not only the people directly descended from the Angles and the Saxons, but those also who, by collateral descent or by political association with them, have been conformed to their type and identified with their destiny. . . ."[20]

[19] Strong had been talking about Anglo-Saxon destiny since 1885, when his book *Our Country* had made such a sensational impact upon the country. His later books, *Expansion* (New York, 1900) and *The New Era* (New York, 1903), carried on this theme but, as noted below, without the intolerant animus which marked the attitude of Candler and professional revivalists in general. For Strong's place in the development of Anglo-Saxon racism in the United States see John Higham, *Strangers in the Land* (New Brunswick, New Jersey, 1956), pp. 39, 122, 138.

[20] Candler, *Great Revivals,* p. 296.

But the implications of this were the very opposite of tolerant.
Candler not only failed to come to grips with the fundamental paradox of mass evangelism in regard to this question of mass conformity, but he aggravated the paradox. The regeneration of the human heart was, by definition, an individual, not a communal, affair. Yet revivalists had always tried to do in bulk what their doctrines maintained could be done only individually. All revivalists recognized and utilized the fact that crowd psychology reinforced the impact of their message. But most of them failed to see that in utilizing this fact they more often pitted the individual against the crowd than against the fundamental tenets of Christianity. In most revival meetings the great bulk of the congregation were already committed to the moral and ethical tenets of the revivalist, even if not to his theology. Sam Jones frankly accepted the fact that he had the force of the community behind him in championing the local mores, and he wielded it as a bludgeon against those who dared to stand out against him. But Jones had merely asked men to conform to the social standards of their local community. Candler made religion a matter of loyalty to a set of vague Anglo-Saxon and American ideals. The attitude which he took toward the perils facing the nation was similar to that expressed by Moody in his fear of communism and labor agitators. He was unwilling to accept these perils as inevitable problems and differences stemming from economic maladjustment, immigration, and freedom of thought and religion which could be settled by mutual toleration, compromise, and social reform. To him the animus behind the perils of labor unions, Catholicism, Darwinism, and Mormonism was unchristian, unpatriotic, and contrary to the best interests of the future of all mankind. The professional evangelists who reiterated these concepts for the next twenty years virtually reduced modern revivalism to ritualistic mass commitments to a social conformity defined in terms of "*the* American way of life."

During the first two decades of the century the high-flown appeal to nationalism, as expressed by Candler, helped to overarch the smoldering theological schism within evangelicalism and the conflict between liberals and conservatives in other areas as well. To many moderates, caught between their faith in the old doctrines and their commitment to progress, Candler's outlook provided a useful transitional framework. In the name of the national welfare it transcended questions of dogma in religion and politics and helped to give an impetus to change in spite of its claim to uphold the old-time religion. Conservatives who might have fought modernists for departing from the fundamentals instead cooperated with them in evangelistic campaigns designed to advance American and evangelical destiny by converting "the dangerous classes." On the other hand, moderates, who might have become more liberal, had the urgency of soul-winning kept before them as a primary goal, or were led to believe that prohibition was the answer to all social problems. Candler consciously proclaimed that his message was a means of "solidifying the nation" in a time of crisis. But by solidifying a majority of the conservatives and moderates behind a crusade to Americanize rich and poor, labor and capital, foreigner and native-born, he only put off the day of reckoning. History was not, in the long run, on his side. Although the intolerance implicit in his nationalism was to bear bitter fruit in the 1920's, modernism won the day in theology. The conservatives helped to blunt the edge of progressivism by their revivals, but they also let time work for the modernists by failing to force the theological issue when they still had a majority on the side of the fundamentals. And in the hazy atmosphere of revival oratory all sorts of plans for "social service" were concocted and temporarily supported which marked at least nominal departures from the old conception of charity. Many a conservative who attacked "selfish wealth" and "godless tycoons" was indirectly sustaining the progressive attempt to regulate free enterprise, just as many moderates who preached that labor should rely on Christian love rather than strikes helped to sustain the public hostility toward trade unions and distrust of the unevangelized masses.

Candler was by no means the originator of this concept of "Christian Americanization," though he gave it a new twist. Since Moody's day the home missionary movement had been instilled with it. City missionaries, inspired by a complex mixture of love and hate, of affection and disdain, of hope and fear, worked tirelessly from 1880 onward to bring the message of evangelical truth and the American success myth to the downhearted and downtrodden urban slum dwellers. But their labors made little headway against the constant influx of new immigrants and their children. "There is only one thing which can fuse into a homogeneous mass our diverse nationalities," said one Baptist home mission agent in 1899, "and that is a common worship and a common religious faith." The foreign-born and their children, said another, "must be Christianized and Americanized or [they] will destroy our political, industrial, and religious life and push us to the wall in the struggle for existence." "The seeds of revolution, if not of ruin, lie in these heterogeneous elements. They are at war with our true prosperity and the very genius of our institutions. . . . the very blood of many of them is anti-republican, anti-protestant, anti-religious." The only solution to the peril the immigrants presented was to "give them Puritan customs and habits. Christianize them for the good of the country." The Chicago correspondent of the *Watchman* opened a discussion of the state of religion in that city in 1903 with the statement, "Our hardest problems are all connected with the conversion of our great foreign population to the American type of Christianity." [21]

Professional evangelists steadfastly claimed that their revivals were helping the home missionaries to Americanize the masses, and in spite of all the evidence to the contrary, modern revivalism continued to be supported in the twentieth century because it was thought to be advancing this cause. The process by which modern revivalism was transformed from the pious soul-winning of D. L. Moody to the barn-storming, 100 per cent Americanism of Billy Sunday can be traced in the careers of the men who led the profession during the early years of the century: Reuben A. Torrey, J. Wilbur Chapman, Milan B. Williams, Burke Culpepper, Rodney Smith, and William E. Biederwolf. Although these men did not promulgate so blatantly the Anglo-Saxon racism and jingoism of Candler, they all believed it. And they fully shared his conviction that na-

[21] S. B. Thing, "Evangelistic Work in New England," *Watchman,* June 22, 1899, p. 14; L. A. Freeman, "Gospel Work Among the Foreign Born," *ibid.*, July 16, 1903, p. 23; Samuel Zane Batten quoted in *ibid.,* May 23, 1903, p. 13; "L.T." in *ibid.,* July 9, 1903, p. 20.

tional solidarity and future national greatness depended entirely upon the progress of revivalistic religion.

These six evangelists represented both sides of the revival tradition in America, that of the untutored but fervent exhorter which descended from the itinerants of the first great awakening through Myrick, Knapp, Swan, and Jones; and that of the educated but evangelistic clergymen which descended from Jonathan Edwards and George Whitefield through Nettleton, Beecher, and Mills. Torrey, Chapman, and Biederwolf were college graduates with formal seminary training and sufficient theological knowledge to entitle them to the doctor of divinity degrees they were awarded. Williams, Culpepper, and Smith had almost no education and no formal theological training, but they had the call and the gift of speech which made them genuine folk preachers.

Although these six men differed widely in personality and style, they all shared a common faith in the old-time religion and a common opposition to science, modernism, and progressivism. And all but one of them had some connection with the organization known as the Interdenominational Association of Evangelists. This association of professional evangelists was started at the Winona Lake Bible Conference in Indiana in 1904. With its formation itinerant evangelism achieved a formal unity as a profession which it had hitherto lacked. Like all such professional associations, the I.A.E. served the dual function of providing national cohesion and a measure of standardization in the trade. At its yearly conventions in Winona Lake, trade secrets and new techniques were discussed and the problems facing the profession received attention if not remedies. The I.A.E. never coordinated its work with that of the various denominations, nor was it ever able to exert such influence over its members as did the American Bar Association or the American Medical Association, whose members had to be licensed by law. But it did serve to provide some stability and self-regulation within the growing profession, and most of the evangelists who attained or hoped to attain fame became members of it.[22]

[22] See Vincent H. Gaddis, *The Story of Winona Lake* (Berne, Indiana, 1949), p. 63; the *Congregationalist,* September 30, 1915, p. 447; *Watchman,* September 15, 1910, p. 28. No records of the association seem to have been kept, and al-

In the prolonged defense of evangelical Americanism against all that was modern, Reuben A. Torrey devoted himself primarily to attacks upon science and the higher critics, and in doing so he paid the penalty for being too uncompromisingly "old-fashioned." Although he claimed to be Moody's direct heir in mass evangelism, it sometimes appeared that he was more intent upon saving "the fundamentals" than upon saving souls. He embodied A. C. Dixon's approach to revivalism rather than the more ambiguous approach of Candler. Typical of the headlines during his revivals was one in the Philadelphia *North American* on March 8, 1906: "HELL IS ABSOLUTELY CERTAIN, DR. TORREY WARNS HIS HEARERS." The two slogans which he adopted as the keynotes of his work were "Get Right with God" and "Pray Through." [23]

Torrey was the son of a New York banker. He graduated from Yale College in 1875 and Yale Seminary in 1878. After a four-year pastorate in Garretsville, Ohio, he studied theology in Germany (at Leipzig and Erlangen) for a year, but instead of imbibing the higher criticism for which German universities were noted, he conceived a passionate hatred for it and remained a confirmed literalist all his life. In 1883 he became pastor of the Open Door Church in Minneapolis and from 1886 to 1889 was superintendent of the Minneapolis City Missionary Society. He had met Moody in 1878 in New Haven, and eleven years later, Moody asked him to be the first superintendent of his Bible Institute in Chicago. Torrey remained at this post until 1908, and in addition he served as pastor of the Moody Church from 1894 to 1906.

When Moody was stricken with his fatal heart attack during the revival in Kansas City in November, 1899, Torrey rushed out to take over the meetings for him. For two years after Moody's death Torrey debated whether or not to take up re-

---

though it reached a peak of one thousand members at one time, it never included all the members of the profession. Biederwolf, Chapman, and Sunday were elected to office in it. It apparently became defunct in the 1930's, when mass evangelism reached its lowest ebb.

[23] For general information on Torrey see F. G. Beardsley, *A History of American Revivals* (New York, 1912), pp. 311 ff.; F. G. Beardsley, *Heralds of Salvation* (New York, 1939), pp. 178 ff.; Grover C. Loud, *Evangelized America* (New York, 1928), pp. 251 ff.; and G. T. B. Davis, *Torrey and Alexander: The Story of a World-Wide Revival* (New York, 1905).

vivalism as a profession. When he received an invitation to conduct a series of meetings in Australia in 1901, he took this as a sign that he was definitely called to carry on Moody's work. He hired as his soloist and chorister for the trip a former student of the Moody Bible Institute, Charles M. Alexander, who was soon being praised as the twentieth century Ira D. Sankey. Their tour of Australia lasted six months, and then Torrey, unconsciously yielding to the prevailing impulse toward evangelical imperialism, decided to make his revivalism worldwide. He proceeded to spread revivalistic religion through mission stations in China, Japan, Tasmania, New Zealand, India, and finally ended up in the British Isles.

The reports of the "Torrey-Alexander round-the-world tour" were given wide coverage in the religious journals of Britain and America as an example of aggressive Christian enterprise to save the world for Christianity and progress. In Australia they reportedly won 20,000 converts. The total for the complete four-year trip was 102,000. The great bulk of these were garnered during the three years Torrey and Alexander spent in the British Isles, where many of the same persons who had supported Moody's various tours invited them from city to city. In most British cities the results of Torrey's meetings surpassed those of Moody, at least statistically. In seven cities Torrey's converts numbered as follows: Birmingham, 7700; Manchester, 4000; Cardiff, 3750; Bolton, 3600; Belfast, 4000; Dublin, 3000; London, 17,000.

The climax of the world tour was a five-month campaign in London in which Torrey spoke in Royal Albert Hall and in a specially built tabernacle in South London. His executive committee was headed by Lord Kinnaird and W. G. Bradshaw, deputy chairman of the London City and Midland Bank. They raised $85,000 for the expenses.[24] The *Saturday Review* of London published a scathing report of the meetings entitled "The Manufacture of Revivals," which said: "When the evangelists came to London they announced themselves . . . in the spirit of an American syndicate competing for the electrification of the Underground Railway. . . ." According to this article the audiences at the Albert Hall were composed neither

24 G. T. B. Davis, "Moody's and Sankey's Successors," *Ladies Home Journal,* November, 1905, p. 77.

of "the fashionable" nor "of the poor uneducated," but were "mostly the rank and file of the various dissenting bodies," "the respectable thousands who are interested in the more elementary aspects of religious emotion and who consider themselves as having been saved long before the arrival of Torrey and Alexander." [25]

Torrey was accused, as Moody had been, of making money out of his revivals, but though he complained of disappointingly small "honoraria" in his letters, he actually received no money at all for his work in Britain. As superintendent of the Moody Bible Institute he received a salary of $5000 a year throughout the tour, and he agreed to turn over to the Institute any compensation which was given to him for his revival preaching. If the one hundred pounds given to him by Lord Overtoun for his work in Scotland and the seventy-five pounds given to him by the committee in Belfast were typical, the Institute may well have lost money by this bargain.[26]

Nevertheless, the jibes against the commercialism and machinery of his revivals bothered Torrey. Writing from Liverpool in 1904, he confided to A. P. Fitt, secretary of the Bible Institute: "Many of the evangelists are being ruined by commercialism that has entered in evangelistic work. A good deal of commercialism has been creeping into our work, and more and more machinery and, I fear, less dependence upon God. I am going to have a talk with Alexander about it. . . ." Torrey's sincerity in this regard was obvious. "I want to eliminate the financial element from my work as much as possible and am disposed to accept no set figure from anyone, but take what the Lord shall send me from time to time." [27]

Upon his return to the United States in December, 1905, Torrey received a mixed reception which betokened the passing of the old evangelical unity that had made Moody's path so triumphant. Those who yearned for a new great awakening in terms of the "true evangelism" or "old-fashioned revivalism"

[25] "The Manufacture of Revivals," *Saturday Review* (London), April 8, 1905, pp. 444–45.

[26] Letters from Torrey to Fitt, Belfast, May 2, 1903; Liverpool, November 19, 1904; Liverpool, November 29, 1904, in the Moodyana Collection, Moody Bible Institute, Chicago.

[27] Torrey to Fitt, Liverpool, November 29, 1904, Moodyana Collection, Moody Bible Institute, Chicago.

were enthusiastic in their welcome of "Moody's and Sankey's successors." But those who had adopted "the new theology" and preferred an "ethical revival" based on "the social teachings of Jesus" were cautious and critical. The great majority of evangelical ministers who hovered between these two outlooks were generally well-disposed to cooperate with a revivalist who had made such an impressive statistical record abroad and who promised to bring new members into their churches. Torrey soon received and accepted invitations to lead city-wide campaigns in Toronto, Philadelphia, Atlanta, Ottawa, San Francisco, Omaha, Cleveland, Nashville, and Chicago. From 1905 to 1911, when he retired from evangelism to become Dean of the Los Angeles Bible Institute, Torrey conducted revival meetings in most of the large cities of the country.

As in Moody's revivals, well-to-do laymen were prominent in persuading the churches to extend invitations to invite Torrey to their city. In Chicago, Henry P. Crowell, President of the Quaker Oats Company and a trustee of the Moody Bible Institute, organized "The Laymen's Evangelistic Council of Chicago" to lead the Torrey revival there in 1907. Crowell had printed at the top of the stationery used by this Council the explanatory note, "A Business Men's Movement." In Atlanta, the leading layman in the revival was Asa G. Candler. The Nashville campaign in 1906 "originated with two or three businessmen" who organized a laymen's committee which shouldered "the finances and the entire business management of" the revival.[28] Probably the most successful of Torrey's campaigns was that in Philadelphia in the spring of 1906. John Wanamaker and John H. Converse, President of the Baldwin Locomotive Works, were among its chief supporters.[29] The meetings lasted 62 days and were held in three different armories at a cost of $38,365. The publicity, committee work, and

[28] There is an interesting letter from H. A. Myers to A. P. Fitt, dated Nashville, July 27, 1907, in the Moodyana Collection at the Moody Bible Institute, which describes in detail the manner in which the laymen of Nashville originated and directed the whole Torrey revival. The ministers were asked to, and did, add their cooperation, but the laymen's committee, said Myers, "had practically the entire charge of everything connected with the Torrey-Alexander Meetings except the actual conduct of the services."

[29] For details of this revival see L. A. Loetscher, "Presbyterian Revivals Since 1875," *Pennsylvania Magazine of History and Biography,* LXVIII (January, 1944), 76 ff.; and *The Record of Christian Work,* XXV (November, 1906), 998.

inquiry room procedure were similar to Moody's system. The Philadelphia revival committee claimed that 7000 converts were made, although only 3615 signed decision cards.

An article in *Current Literature* in February, 1906, summarized some of the attacks being made upon Torrey by American church leaders under the heading, "The New Attitude Toward Evangelism." [30] What was new about it was that in the 1890's the conservative evangelicals had attacked "the new evangelism" of B. Fay Mills, but now the liberal evangelicals were attacking what claimed to be "the old-time religion." In November, 1905, the Rev. Charles S. MacFarland, then pastor of a Congregational Church in Malden, Massachusetts, attacked Torrey's work on the basis of two summers spent investigating the impact of Torrey's tour of Britain. "Leading men both conservative and liberal in their thought," said MacFarland, "expressed themselves in every case in terms of varying degrees of doubtfulness or of explicit statement that on the whole the effect has been harmful." The objections cited most often to MacFarland were Torrey's denunciations of liberals as "infidels," his use of "large machinery," and the "widespread advertising" which gave the movement a commercial aspect.[31] A month after MacFarland's attack, S. Parkes Cadman, Reuen Thomas, and H. C. Meserve, all prominent Congregationalists, joined MacFarland in recommending that members of their denomination dissociate themselves from all Torrey revivals. Cadman charged Torrey with "clinging to obsolete traditions which have been discarded by the sane, reverent, and constructive scholarship of Christianity" and with preaching a literal, narrow-minded view of the gospel which was "not Protestantism." [32] The editor of the *Outlook* and various ministers from other denominations declared that Torrey's "literalism, conventionalism, and emotionalism" were "not the marks of Christian religion" and that his revivals were characterized by "brass band work, big 'statistics,' and everything on the score of Bigness." [33]

[30] "The New Attitude Toward Evangelism," *Current Literature,* XL (February, 1906), 163 ff.

[31] *The Congregationalist* (Boston), November 11, 1905, p. 678.

[32] *Ibid.,* December 9, 1905, p. 882; January 27, 1906, p. 134.

[33] *Outlook,* LXXI (December 2, 1905), 806–8.

The editors of more conservative religious journals like the *Presbyterian,* the *Missionary Review of the World,* and the *Watchman* sprang at once to Torrey's defense. Although the *Watchman* had previously criticized Moody's methods it had by no means abandoned the cause of the old-time religion, and the editor who replaced Horr in 1904, E. F. Merriam, had no sympathy with those who attacked revivalism from liberal grounds. In an editorial entitled "Get Out of God's Way" he revealed the growing bitterness and combativeness of the conservatives as they closed ranks against the liberals: "There is an immense amount of private opposition" to Torrey and Alexander, it said, among "pastors holding to the new theology." And it warned, "Those that are working for the advancement of the cause of Jesus Christ and for the glory of His name are on His side. No Christian is justified in criticizing or opposing their work no matter how much they may differ in method or belief." [34]

A large part of Torrey's difficulties lay in his unprepossessing personality. A stocky, square-cut man, with a bald head, carefully trimmed white sideburns, and a pointed beard, Torrey had the air of a pontific professor in the pulpit. He dressed in a well-tailored sack coat with a white bow-tie and a high, starched wing-collar. On the street he usually wore a high hat, and he always talked as though he had one on. With typical pompous gravity he once told a reporter, "I cannot say that I fully advocate the old-time style of revival where emotion was the chief instrument. . . . I always think of myself as a lawyer when I get up to speak and of the audience as a jury" [35]—by which, presumably, he meant that he spoke argumentatively, which was true. He told A. P. Fitt that he thought the students at the Moody Bible Institute should be excused from their classes to attend his revival meetings in Chicago because "the evening meetings would be practically a lecture and the noon meetings certainly will be lectures on Apologetics." [36] He had absolutely none of Moody's humor and gruff humanity, and he completely lacked Moody's persuasive personal appeal.

[34] *Watchman,* February 15, 1906, p. 7.

[35] Philadelphia *North-American,* February 1, 1906, p. 1.

[36] Torrey to Fitt, Philadelphia, September 15, 1907, Moodyana Collection, Moody Bible Institute, Chicago.

He could be patronizing, vehement, or assertive, but he never acquired what among the profession was called the "winsome" style or "the wooing note."

Nor was Torrey's pulpit delivery particularly appealing. "In the main he stood with his hands folded before him, merely turning his head and his body to face the different portions of the audience." Occasionally, toward the end of a sermon, he let himself go: "In exhortation he shakes both fists with the strenuousness of President Roosevelt. In entreaty he stretches out both strong arms in invitation." He was at his most passionate when lecturing on Hell. A reporter described him during such a sermon as speaking "with shining beads streaming down his face, which was red as fire with his intense effort, with tight-clenched fists which like sure hammers drove home his fiery darts and in trumpet tones that fall on the vast assemblage like prophetic warnings." Evidently his intensity did not sway the whole audience that night, however, for in the midst of his fiery description of hell as "the insane asylum of the universe," someone in the audience let out a "titter of laughter." Torrey became apoplectically indignant: "This is no subject for laughter," he roared. The incident typified his inability to carry his audiences with him even on those topics which were most dear to his heart.[37]

Nevertheless, large numbers of church members and churchgoers filled his meetings in city after city from 1905 to 1911. They came for several reasons. One was to hear the old doctrinal message preached in its simple, fundamental purity without qualification: "Dr. Torrey is . . . thoroughly loyal to the Scriptures," wrote one admirer. "He maintains that the Bible means exactly what it says and what it says is true." Or as Torrey himself said, "In ninety-nine out of a hundred cases the meaning that the plain man gets out of the Bible is the correct one." He preached dependence on the blood of Christ and the necessity of immediate conversion in the good old evangelical tradition: "You are either on the road to heaven or on the road to hell, and you should know which one it is. There is no deceiving God. . . . It is not enough to say 'I guess I'm saved.' You must know it!" It was not exactly "heart reli-

37 Philadelphia *North American,* February 1, 1906, p. 1; March 8, p. 1; Atlanta *Constitution,* May 7, 1906, p. 1.

gion" as Torrey preached it, but it was emphatic and authoritative.[38]

Those who were confused by the abstruseness of the new theology's doctrine of "immanence" and who distrusted the radicalism of the social gospel were thrilled and reassured when a "learned" and "educated" man like the distinguished-looking Dr. Torrey denounced the Darwinians, the liberals, and the higher critics. "I claim to be a scholarly preacher," he said, ". . . and yet I believe the old-fashioned Bible doctrine regarding hell."[39] He ridiculed what he took to be the evolutionary hypothesis by holding up his elegant gold pocket watch before the crowd and saying, "If I should tell you that the atoms embraced in this timepiece danced together until they formed a watch, I should be expounding a belief fully as rational and logical as the philosophy of evolution." And "there is not one single instance of scientifically observed and recorded transmutation of species." These dogmatic assertions were enthusiastically applauded by his audiences. Newspapers apparently took Torrey at his word, and the headlines after this sermon in Philadelphia read: "DARWINIAN THEORY TORN TO SHREDS BY TORREY AT REVIVAL: PROVING THERE'S A GOD, EVANGELIST ASSAILS SCIENTISTS. NO MISSING LINK." His tone with the higher critics was simply sarcasm: "There never was any lower criticism than the alleged 'higher criticism.'"[40]

A third reason why people went to hear Torrey was that he preached the same old social morality with which they were so familiar. He attacked card playing, theater-going, gambling, and dancing as works of the devil: in dancing "there is a contact between the sexes that is permitted nowhere else in decent society. I have never seen a decent dance."[41] He attacked wealthy society women who "evade the responsibilities of motherhood," and he said that some of the rich needed a true revival more than the poor. Though he did not emphasize prohibition, he devoted at least one sermon in each revival

[38] *Watchman,* February 8, 1906, p. 21; Philadelphia *North American,* February 3, 1906, p. 8.

[39] R. A. Torrey, *Soul Winning Sermons* (New York, 1925), p. 290.

[40] Philadelphia *North American,* February 8, 1906, p. 1; Atlanta *Constitution,* May 7, 1906, p. 1.

[41] Philadelphia *North American,* February 9, 1906, p. 1.

to the evils of drink. He claimed that his belief in the Second Coming, to which he also devoted one sermon, entitled him to be called an optimist, because it at least gave him some hope amid the encircling gloom: "In the Return of our Lord is the perfect solution, and the only solution, of the political and commercial problems that now vex us."[42] For this reason he had no use for the radical political theories being put into effect in Wisconsin by the followers of Robert LaFollette: "If any state in the Union needs a revival," he said in 1906, "that State is Wisconsin." Nor did he have any use for new religious sects which offered a more optimistic view of the universe such as Christian Science, "Millennial Dawnism," "Occultism," Theosophy, or Baha'ism, all of which he denounced from the pulpit as heresies or paganisms of the worst sort. "Mrs. Eddy," he told a Philadelphia audience, is a "false Christ."[43]

Yet in spite of this message, so comforting to those who felt threatened by the changing times, Torrey would never have been a successful revivalist had it not been for his singing partner, Charles McCallom Alexander. Though only eleven years younger than Torrey, Alexander's methods of evangelism were as different from his as the mid-Victorian era was from the Jazz Age. Alexander was a product of the professional chorister training offered by Moody at the Chicago Bible Institute. He brought to Torrey's meetings the efficiency, the heartiness, and the bounce which characterized the drummer's approach to soul-winning. Torrey, although superintendent of the Moody Institute, had been trained far differently at Yale. The difference between the two men was patent to every observer: "What Dr. Torrey lacks in personal magnetism is possessed by Mr. Alexander in bountiful measure."[44]

Alexander was born in a village called Meadow, Tennessee, in 1867, and attended the small college at Maryville, Tennessee. In 1887 he left college without graduating in order to become chorister for a Quaker evangelist named John Kittrell. Alexander was tall, slim, genial, with a pleasant singing voice, a mild Southern drawl, and a folksy manner which revival audiences warmed to at once. After a short stint with Kittrell,

[42] R. A. Torrey, *The Return of the Lord Jesus* (Los Angeles, 1914), p. 7.
[43] Philadelphia *North American*, February 10, 1906, p. 4; March 28, p. 3.
[44] *Ibid.*, February 11, 1906, Sec. 3, p. 1.

he went to the Moody Bible Institute and became for a time musical director of the Moody Church. He assisted Moody in his 1893 Chicago World's Fair revival and then joined the colorful evangelist, Milan B. Williams. For seven years he and Williams toured the small towns and cities of the Midwest until Torrey asked him to come to Australia with him in 1901.

Alexander preferred to be known to his friends and to his audiences simply as "Charlie." Unlike Sankey he did not start his solos with prayer nor assume a pious solemnity before the crowd. Instead of an organ accompaniment he preferred the trills and cadenzas of a piano. Instead of prayers he told jokes and stories. He did his utmost to break down the last barriers of dignity and formality in revival meetings. His attempts to mold the crowd into a jovial friendly unit during the half-hour song service preceding Torrey's sermon resembled more nearly the techniques of a master of ceremonies at a Rotary convention than those of a choir director and soloist at a religious service. It was a remarkable innovation in revivalism when "Charlie" warmed up a crowd by having the choir of six hundred to a thousand voices sing a rousing hymn like "O Lord Send the Power Just Now" and then turned to the audience and asked them to sing a chorus just to see if they could sing louder than the choir. After a short competition between the crowd and the choir, he would have the men in the audience compete with the women, and then those in the balcony compete with those on the main floor. "Sweeping his hand toward the galleries he called for one volunteer, just one, who would sing the refrain alone." When a man stood up in Philadelphia and sang the chorus through "nervously," Alexander smiled jovially and said, "Good, my friend. How long have you been a Christian?" "Twelve years." "Good, sing it again." The man did. Alexander turned to the audience, "I got a blessing from that man's singing. He put his heart into it. I want you all to do the same." If the audience sang listlessly, he would stop them in the midst of a hymn and scold, "We don't allow visitors in these services. If you can't be one of us, you have no business here, and to be one of us you have to sing. Everybody in this audience has got to sing." Because he said this with a smile and seemed so earnestly interested in making them have a good time, the audiences always responded warmly. "From the beginning of a service Mr. Alexander dominates an audience," said one reporter, but it was the domination of a cheerleader, not of a schoolmaster. "To Mr. Alexander," it was generally agreed, "is due the credit for arousing the revival spirit in so far as it has been manifested in these services." Critics of Torrey commonly said that the people went to the meetings to hear the singing rather than to hear Torrey.[45]

Torrey was not entirely pleased with Alexander's methods. He particularly frowned upon his penchant for publicity and money-making. In a letter to Fitt from Belfast in 1903, Torrey lamented the fact that Alexander was "financing" a newspaperman named Williamson to act as his publicity agent. Alexander, like most revival choristers, could not resist publishing his own collections of songs for use at his revival meetings. Torrey complained that although Alexander gave a portion of his income from the sale of these hymnbooks to the Moody Bible Institute, he kept the "lion-share" for himself.[46]

On the whole, the hymnbooks used in the Torrey-Alexander meetings differed little from those in Sankey's volumes except for a more superficial piety and more syncopated rhythm. Among the more popular of them were "What a Wonderful Savior," "I'm a Subject of the King of Kings," "Throw Out the Lifeline," "When We All Get to Heaven," "What a Friend We Have in Jesus," "God Will Take Care of You," "Are You Coming Home Tonight?" and "Tell Mother I'll Be There." The message which predominated was one of reassurance, as in the popular "Jesus Is A Friend of Mine":

Why should I charge my soul with care?
The wealth in every mine
Belongs to Christ, God's Son and Heir,
And He's a friend of mine.

And when He comes in bright array,
And leads the conquering line,
It will be glory then to say,
That He's a friend of mine.[47]

[45] *Ibid.*, February 5, 1906, p. 1; February 11, Sec. 3, p. 1.

[46] Torrey to Fitt, Belfast, May 25, 1903; Liverpool, January 2, 1905. In 1904 Alexander married Helen Cadbury, daughter of Richard Cadbury, the wealthy English cocoa and chocolate manufacturer, but this did not curtail his eagerness for publishing and selling hymn books.

[47] *Alexander's Hymns* No. 3, ed. Charles M. Alexander (London, Marshall Bros. Ltd., n.d.), No. 143.

Alexander boasted that he had paid $30,000 for the copyrights to some of his hymns, but the bickering between him and other choristers and hymn writers, like D. B. Towner, Charles H. Gabriel, and E. O. Excell, over copyrights and plagiarism became so heated that Torrey eventually decided to dispense with his dynamic young partner. Torrey commented to A. P. Fitt in 1908 upon the publication of Alexander's latest compilation, "I wish Charlie had a little more conscience"; several of the hymns in his new book were, Torrey said, "practically pirated." [48]

When Alexander split with Torrey in 1908, he immediately joined forces with the man whom Moody referred to in 1895 as "the greatest evangelist in the country," John Wilbur Chapman. Chapman, who had worked with B. Fay Mills as well as with Moody, was as modern in revival techniques as Alexander was in singing techniques. Together they soon eclipsed Torrey as leaders of the profession and held the limelight until William A. Sunday took it from them. Torrey retired from evangelism in 1911 in order to become dean of the Los Angeles Bible Institute.[49]

Chapman had been educated for the ministry at Oberlin, Lake Forest, and Lane Seminary.[50] While at Lake Forest in 1878 he went to Chicago to attend one of Moody's revival meetings and, in the inquiry room afterward, Moody personally converted him from a nominal to a born-again Christian. He was licensed to preach by the Presbytery of Whitewater, Ohio, in 1881 at the age of twenty-two. During the next ten years he served pastorates in Liberty, Indiana; Schuylerville, New York; Albany, New York; and Philadelphia. His Philadelphia pastorate from 1890 to 1892 was in John Wanamaker's Bethany Presbyterian Church. He resigned this position to take up revival work for three years, during which he aided Moody and

[48] Torrey to Fitt, September 23, 1908, Moodyana Collection, Moody Bible Institute, Chicago. See also the correspondence between Alexander and Fitt in this same collection.

[49] For Moody's comment on Chapman see *The Family Call* (Philadelphia) November 23, 1896, p. 8. Torrey, who helped A. C. Dixon to edit *The Fundamentals* in 1910, continued to be a leading figure in the fight against modernism until his death in 1928.

[50] For biographical details see Ford C. Ottman, *John Wilbur Chapman* (New York, 1920); and J. K. MacLean, *Chapman and Alexander: the Story of Their Lives and Work* (New York, 1915).

B. Fay Mills and conducted revivals of his own. Among the moderate-sized cities in which he preached were Montreal, Canada; Saginaw, Michigan; Burlington, Vermont; Saratoga, New York; Ottawa, Illinois; Bloomington and Fort Wayne, Indiana. One of his assistants in these years was William A. Sunday.

In 1896 he helped to found the Winona Lake Bible Conference and that same year became vice-president of the Moody Bible Institute. He returned to Bethany Church as pastor for four years from 1895 to 1899 and then moved to the more fashionable Fourth Avenue Presbyterian Church in New York City. In 1901 the wealthy Presbyterian lay leader John H. Converse persuaded the Presbyterian General Assembly to make Chapman the secretary of a new committee on evangelism, a task which occupied most of his time for the next four years. Chapman's attempt to organize evangelistic meetings to aid weak Presbyterian churches in "the great home mission sections and in rural communities where the need was imperative" did not prove particularly successful even though Converse was willing to foot all the bills.[51] Chapman continued to serve on this committee until his death in 1918, but he devoted most of his efforts after 1905 to promoting a new method of urban mass evangelism which he called the Chapman Simultaneous Evangelistic Campaign. He had given up his New York pastorate in 1903.

Chapman developed this new simultaneous method out of his experience with Moody and Mills. It consisted of dividing a city into a number of districts each of which was to conduct a revival simultaneously with every other district. In order to do this Chapman organized a "brigade" of coevangelists and singers who went with him from city to city. While Chapman and Alexander conducted revival meetings in a large centrally located auditorium, pairs of evangelists and choristers conducted their revivals in churches, theatres, and halls throughout the other districts and even in the outlying suburbs. A plan similar to this had been tried by Moody in Chicago in 1893, and in 1896 Chapman had directed a group of fifteen evangelists in a similar experiment in Philadelphia. But the first attempt

[51] See Ottman, *Chapman*, pp. 121 ff.

to employ the simultaneous method in all its details took place in 1904 when Chapman took seventeen evangelists to Pittsburgh, divided the city into nine districts, organized church members into committees in each district, procured nine meeting places, and taking the largest central one for himself, conducted a revival that constituted a radically new departure in modern revivalism.

Chapman used Mills's system of committees, publicity, choirs, ushers, prayer meetings, and canvassing, but the fact that the whole city was galvanized into action at once seemed much more efficient to most ministers than Mills's piecemeal District Combination Plan. Chapman continued to work out the intricacies of the system, and after 1908 when Alexander joined him, he was ready to try the largest cities in the country. In March, 1908, two years after Torrey's revival in Philadelphia, Chapman divided that city into forty-two districts, and with John H. Converse and John Wanamaker again leading the executive committee, he and twenty-one pairs of evangelists and choristers conducted meetings for three weeks in one half of the city; then they all shifted simultaneously into the other twenty-one districts for three more weeks. Chapman and Alexander held services in Bethany Church during the first half of the revival and in Russell H. Conwell's Baptist Temple during the second half. Over four hundred churches of almost every denomination cooperated in this revival, including the Quakers, led by Rufus M. Jones, the Lutherans, headed by Rev. E. H. Delk, the Episcopalians, led by Bishop Alexander Mackay-Smith, and the Moravians, under Bishop C. L. Moench. Even the Mennonite and Schwenkfelder churches took part. The total cost of the campaign was slightly over $30,000. The total attendance was estimated at 35,000 nightly for the six weeks, or a total of 1,470,000. Moody had reached only 1,050,000 in Philadelphia in 1875–1876 in ten weeks at a cost of $50,000. Moody converted perhaps 3500; it was estimated at first that Chapman converted 8000, though later inquiries indicated that this was exaggerated. John H. Converse praised the new system not only because it united all faiths but because "it is planned and conducted on business principles." The slogan adopted by Chapman as the keynote of the campaign, a slogan which appeared on posters, billboards, lapel buttons, banners, and all the stationery used throughout was "The King's Business." [52]

In February, 1909, Chapman collected a corps of thirty evangelists and thirty choristers for the most successful campaign of his career. He divided the city of Boston into twenty-seven districts and tried to awaken the whole metropolis in one three-week swoop. Chapman and Alexander conducted the central meetings in Tremont Temple. Chapman's brother, E. G. Chapman, "a businessman of rare ability, sagaciousness, suavity, and effectiveness," who acted as "Advance Agent" and "Business Manager" for the complicated revival, had worked for a year in advance in order to organize the committees, direct the advertising, and raise an advance guaranty fund of $10,000 to cover initial expenses. The total expenses came to almost twice that. The Rev. Arcturus Z. Conrad of Park Street Church was chairman of the executive committee. Two prominent businessmen, G. E. Briggs and Allen G. Emery, headed the finance committee. A total of 166 churches cooperated.[53]

Some idea of the complexity and variety of this revival can be gathered from the types of meetings involved. Two preaching services were held daily in most of the twenty-seven districts and Tremont Temple. At 4:15 every afternoon a special talk for children was also held in Tremont Temple. Every Sunday-afternoon meeting was for men only, and scattered through the campaign there were special meetings for mothers, "Old Folks," young people, and parents. Special days were advertised as Good Cheer Day, Flower Day, a Day of Rejoicing, and Education Day. On Flower Day everyone who attended was asked to bring a flower; these were collected at all of the district meetings and then distributed the next day to hospitals, sanitariums, and rest homes. Education Day was devoted to reaching grammar school children and teachers. The Day of Rejoicing required each person to bring a small gift of food or clothing to the meetings; these gifts were later distributed to the poor. Special efforts were made "to reach the

[52] See Loetscher, "Presbyterian Revivals," pp. 81 ff.; and Philadelphia *North American*, April 16, 1908, Sec. 2, p. 1.

[53] See A. Z. Conrad, *Boston's Awakening* (Boston, 1909); and weekly accounts in the *Watchman*.

hopeless people in the lower sections of the city," and in Boston, as in all his other campaigns, Chapman conducted meetings specifically designed for drunkards, actors, university students, businessmen, office workers, shop girls, and fallen women. All of these not only kept the churchgoers busy and interested, but they provided good copy for the local newspapers.

A total of 990 services were held in Boston between January 26 and February 17 by Chapman and his brigade. The essence of the new method was to saturate the city with religion. Nightly attendance for the simultaneous meetings was estimated at 20,000, and the total attendance (including, of course, repeaters) was 720,000. In addition, four final services were held at Mechanics Hall by Chapman and Alexander after the district meetings had closed, adding 44,000 to the attendance total. Although no one was able to get an accurate count of the total decisions, the daily average for all meetings was estimated at 300, which would have totaled close to 7000 for the twenty-three days, excluding the Mechanics Hall meetings. The money for the campaign was raised by private subscription and by collections taken at the meetings. The twenty-seven coevangelists and Chapman were paid by means of free will offerings taken during the final three days of the meetings in each district. The twenty-seven choristers received regular salaries, which were considered part of the expenses of the campaign. Some of the evangelists and singers who worked with Chapman in this or other campaigns were W. E. Biederwolf, Leander W. Munhall, William Bell Riley, William J. Dawson, James M. Gray, Thomas C. Needham, Henry W. Stough, Daniel S. Toy, A. W. Spooner, George T. B. Davis, Henry Ostrom, John Elliott, James O. Buswell, Charles T. Schaeffer, Albany Smith, Ernest and Everett Naftzger, F. M. Lamb, Laurence Greenwood, and Homer A. Rodeheaver. Almost all of these were members of the Interdenominal Association of Evangelists, of which Chapman became vice-president in 1910.

There were some criticisms of Chapman's new technique even from those ministers who cooperated with his campaigns. "Some of us may not always find the somewhat overbusinesslike activity altogether worshipful," said one. Many "were fairly frightened at the complexity of the machinery and its man-made look." A few thought Alexander's method of conducting the musical aspect of the meetings overshadowed the preaching and detracted from the religious quality of the services. Some disliked the fact that Chapman and his coworkers dispensed with inquiry rooms and held only "after-meetings." It was even hinted that Chapman's practice of making a general rather than a specific call for persons to come forward after his sermons produced "misleading" statistics regarding the number of converts. The *Watchman* regretted that in giving "the invitation" Chapman's "method is to include Christians and unconverted of various classes in the hope that by drawing a net full of a multitude of all sorts of fishes some new and valuable specimens may be caught." [54]

But on the whole most cooperating ministers, among whom were the great bulk of the evangelicals both liberal and conservative during the years 1904–1909, believed that the simultaneous system "was surely 'God-given' and Dr. Chapman is correct in saying he believes this movement was born in Heaven." Chapman was particularly praised for being "absolutely safe and sane" as well as for his "purity of speech and honest methods." The more enthusiastic called his technique "an advance on Evangelistic prophecy," and predicted that "this 'interdenominational simultaneous movement' is destined to be the most potent form of extensive evangelism in the next decade." In 1906 a Syracuse minister claimed after Chapman's revival in that city, "There is no doubt in our minds that the simultaneous meeting solves the problem of city evangelism" for "Syracuse lives in an atmosphere of real Christianity today." [55]

A large part of Chapman's popularity was due to his ability to straddle the more divisive religious questions of the day and yet give the appearance of being "a man of fearless and fervid spirit." On the question of fundamentalism, for example, where Torrey was so aggressively dogmatic, Chapman offered this statement of his principles to a magazine on the eve of his Boston campaign: "While every evangelist associated with

[54] For these criticisms by cooperating pastors see the *Watchman*, February 28, 1907, p. 12; February 6, 1908, p. 32; February 25, 1909, p. 6.

[55] *Ibid.*, February 22, 1906, p. 21; February 28, 1907, p. 12; February 6, 1908, p. 32; February 26, 1909, p. 6; January 27, 1910, p. 28.

me, so far as I know, holds to the old evangelical statement of truth, yet we all realize that truth has a modern application. This is the age of social service and it is the time when the church must be called upon to bear the burden of those who are oppressed. Selfishness, greed, avarice, and all kindred sins we rebuke without fear or favor. We preach no selfish salvation, but present a Saviour who, when we are saved ourselves, inspires us to save others. We seek not so much to keep men out of hell as to keep hell out of them. . . . But of course we insist upon the acceptance of Christ as a personal Saviour." [56] The term "social service" might be taken to imply that Chapman was a liberal, and his attacks upon "selfishness" and "greed" might seem to make him at least sympathetic with the social gospel, but taken as a whole his statement and practice were conservative in the extreme. Like Candler, all that he or his associates (or his converts for that matter) were committed to was soul-winning, inculcating personal morality, and encouraging almsgiving.

For example, in his sermon on "The Perils of Riches and Poverty" Chapman stated, "I do not seek to criticize the rich men of this or any other city who get their money honestly. . . . I do denounce the rich who are so unchristianlike as to pile up fortunes for their own selfish ends while hundreds of men, women, and children are in need. . . . How many of them are charitable enough to give money to help others? Thank God there are many charitable men in Philadelphia." [57] Social service to Chapman meant what Warren Candler called the "philanthropy of the rich." Chapman set an example for the rich of Philadelphia in a highly publicized exhibition: "Introducing a new sort of evangelism into the present simultaneous revival," said the Philadelphia *North American,* "Dr. J. Wilbur Chapman, Charles M. Alexander, and Mrs. Alexander headed a slumming expedition through the downtown district in an automobile yesterday afternoon, entered eighteen desolate homes and scattered one hundred dollars in provisions and toys among needy families. . . . It was one of the most novel features of the campaign." [58]

[56] *New England Magazine* (Boston), February, 1909, p. 756.
[57] Philadelphia *North American,* March 26, 1908, p. 1.
[58] *Ibid.,* April 9, 1908, p. 1.

Chapman's friend and biographer noted frankly that Chapman "repudiated uncompromisingly the spurious but popular Gospel that prescribes material remedies for social ills." [59] Like all conservative revivalists Chapman opposed legislative remedies for current economic problems: "Talk about the difficulties between capital and labor—I believe there would be no such things if the spirit of Jesus controlled both sides." [60] Though he, like Moody, was praised for his efforts to reach the poor and combat "the contagion of sin in the ever-condensing thickness of modern society," his only message for the poor was, "If you tell me yours is a home of poverty and Jesus abides with you, then I know that you do not mind poverty." [61]

His attitude toward the higher criticism was demonstrated by his demand in 1909 that all missionaries who doubted the inerrancy of Scriptures should be recalled from abroad at once. And when war broke out in Europe in 1914 he declared, according to his biographer, that "the moral collapse of the German people was the bitter fruit of destructive Biblical criticism." [62] Yet because he urged interdenominational harmony and seldom took issue squarely with theological problems, he was able to win the support of many who considered themselves moderately liberal. Men like S. Parkes Cadman, who denounced Torrey, eagerly took part in Chapman's campaigns because they saw no conflict with liberalism. Other ministers, however, endorsed Chapman because they thought his revivals helped to silence advocates of the new theology. A Los Angeles pastor noted happily that after Chapman's revival "a reaction from the liberal tendencies of doctrines" had taken place in the city.[63]

According to one editor of Chapman's sermons, he was "timid and shrinking" by nature and this was what produced "the wooing note," the "pathos," the "great tenderness of sympathy" in his sermons. Chapman was a short, oval-headed man

[59] Ottman, *Chapman*, p. 314. Ottman quotes Chapman as believing "that social wrong is only the symbol of spiritual wrong and that spiritual remedies will alone heal what is ultimately a spiritual malady."

[60] J. W. Chapman, *Evangelistic Sermons* (New York, 1922), p. 22.

[61] *Ibid.*, p. 13. For praise of Chapman as a man who urged "the Church's responsibility to meet the social sins and moral abuses of this generation," see Ottman, *Chapman*, p. 315.

[62] Ottman, *Chapman*, pp. 203, 274.

[63] *Watchman*, March 22, 1906, p. 11.

with thin lips, sparse dark hair, and a pair of pince-nez perched on his pinched little nose. He was one of the few professional evangelists who rarely employed aggressive, fiery pulpit techniques. Though he was not as shy and retiring as some people thought, he preferred to be known as a man who brought "spiritual dignity and grace" to revivalism. His tone was usually pleading and friendly. He assumed that his audiences believed in the orthodox evangelical doctrines and the middle-class virtues. His call to conversion commonly took the form of asking all those to stand who were willing to "get in line with every decent man who is trying to make this city better." [64] His sermons consisted of numerous sentimental stories strung upon some theme which had as its climax an appeal to the best in man, or to the love of home, mother, or country. One auditor counted seventeen such stories in one half-hour address. Unlike Torrey he did not deal much with the controversial subject of the Second Coming, but he occasionally told his audiences, "Your resistance of God's love is dangerous. Today may be your last day." And he noted sadly, "If we are honest, we are obliged to say that the old days were more to be desired than those in which we live at present." [65]

But there was more to Chapman's campaigns than simply benign or genial cajoling. He, like Candler, thought revivalism should try to soothe the antagonism of greedy gain and angry want. He opposed the perils of socialism, intemperance, immigration, and indirectly at least, "Romanism." In all his campaigns he had assistants whose principal task was to visit shops and factories and talk to the workingmen who might fall prey to union agitators. His factory assistant in Philadelphia, Laurence Greenwood, told the assembled workers at the A. M. Collins Manufacturing Company in 1908, "Religion was made to order for the laboring man. And I want to tell you that it is a far better investment than membership in a union." [66]

That many of his supporters saw Chapman's campaigns as counterattacks upon the influx of un-Americanized immigrants was evident in the Rev. A. Z. Conrad's book describing the

64 See Loud, *Evangelized America,* p. 276.

65 Chapman, *Evangelistic Sermons,* p. 143; J. W. Chapman, *When Home Is Heaven* (New York, 1917), Introduction.

66 Philadelphia *North American,* March 20, 1908, p. 1.

Boston campaign. Conrad went out of his way to point out how desperately Boston needed such a revival. It was a city, he said, in which 70 per cent of the inhabitants were foreign-born or the children of foreign-born. "Boston has become almost a foreign city," he lamented. Though he did not directly assert that converting Irish and Italians would in effect be converting Roman Catholics to evangelistic religion, he did point out that the evangelical churches of Boston had only 120,000 members out of a population of one million, and he implied that all the rest of the population was fair game for evangelism.[67] A Baptist minister of Fall River was even more blunt in offering the reason why Chapman had been invited to that city in 1907: "The significance of such a movement appears only as it is understood that Fall River is one of the most foreign of our New England cities and that it is the center of a very strong Roman Catholic influence. Such a movement, uniting the Protestant forces, will serve to counteract the discouraging tendency of such an overwhelming Catholic influence." [68]

Chapman's work against intemperance was at times as vigorous as that of Sam P. Jones. He regularly delivered a sermon on "The Perils of the Saloon" in which he said, "There is nothing so hellish this side of hell as the saloons in our large cities." Unlike Moody, he firmly believed in legislating prohibition. "Don't you think that the government should take some action against this 'crime of crimes'? Just think how quick the saloon would be rooted out if those people at Washington would start something." Like Jones he was ready to draw the line and make prohibition a test of true religion: "You are either a Christian, against whiskey, or you are not a Christian, for whiskey." [69] He hired Mr. and Mrs. William Asher, who specialized in converting drunkards, to conduct meetings in saloons and in front of saloons in each of his revivals, and he persuaded Evangeline Booth to speak at his meetings against the evils of rum.

There was good evidence that the principal purpose of his campaign in Philadelphia was to promote the local option movement which culminated in an election during the revival.

67 A. Z. Conrad, *Boston's Awakening,* pp. 13–14.

68 *Watchman,* July 4, 1907, p. 18.

69 Philadelphia *North American,* March 28, 1908, p. 1; April 13, p. 1.

An editorial in the Philadelphia *North American* on April 11, the day of the primary election, explained the connection: Philadelphia, like the rest of Pennsylvania, was controlled by the Republican boss, Boise Penrose. The issue was whether or not Penrose could get his slate nominated on April 11 in the Republican primary. Since nomination to the Republican ticket was tantamount to election, the matter was an intraparty fight. The election day editorial read: "The voters face two paramount issues—local option and Penrose. Until a few months ago the Penrose issue seemed of overshadowing importance. But the local option tide has risen so rapidly during the last one hundred days that by comparison it has dwarfed —or more strictly speaking, has absorbed—the Penrose issue." [70] Penrose had come out against local option in spite of the fact that Chapman had led his noon prayer meeting in a prayer for Penrose two weeks before the primary. To elect the Penrose ticket was therefore not only to support boss rule but also to oppose local option, and local option was the first step toward statewide prohibition. The *North American* was owned by Rodman Wanamaker and edited by E. A. Van Valkenberg, an ardent supporter of all evangelists and a vigorous good government crusader like John Wanamaker. It did its best to boost Chapman, prohibition (via local option), and civic reform. But the result of the primary was the usual victory for the Penrose machine.

It was hoped, nevertheless, that the revival campaign would strengthen the Law and Order Society in existence in Philadelphia. As Chapman said, "The purpose of such an evangelistic campaign is to quicken the public conscience, to uplift the moral atmosphere." If he could not defeat the saloon and the bosses, at least he could denounce cards, theater-going, and dancing: "You can't be a Christian and dance; you can't attend the theaters and be a Christian." [71] Like Sam Jones's "positive Christianity," Chapman's moral uplift revivals were largely negative in character.

After 1909 Chapman's Simultaneous Campaign technique slowly went out of favor. A series of failures followed the Bos-

[70] *Ibid.*, April 11, 1908, p. 8.

[71] *Ibid.*, April 16, 1908, special section; April 18, 1916, p. 6; Loetscher, "Presbyterian Revivals," p. 85.

ton revival. Ford C. Ottman, one of Chapman's evangelistic colaborers, stated that the revivals in Bangor, Portland, Dayton, and Columbus in 1910 were not successful.[72] The thoroughly sympathetic *Christian Workers' Magazine* reported that the Chapman-Alexander meetings in Chicago in 1910 "have not realized all that was hoped for them." In particular the district meetings "did not largely attract the people and disappointment was felt. . . . We can only hope that the reaction may not be too serious."[73] The blame was laid upon Chapman's coworkers rather than on Chapman himself, but it was perfectly evident that Chapman's method had palled upon the devotees of revivalism. From 1909 to 1914 Chapman and Alexander spent a considerable part of their time on worldwide revival tours. They spent eight months in 1909 touring Australia, Korea, Manila, Hongkong, Canton, Shanghai, Tokyo, and Yokohama, visiting many of the same missionary areas that Torrey and Alexander had visited in 1901–2. In 1911 they toured Wales and Ireland. In 1912–13 they returned to Australia and also visited New Zealand, Tasmania, and Ceylon. In 1913–14 they toured England and Scotland. Although religious journals continued to give coverage to this international revivalism, the secular press lost interest. Other revivalists undertook the same worldwide tours; they were no longer news. By 1910 the stops were as clearly routed as a theatrical circuit and the backers were always the same.

The churchgoing public in America, however, was becoming as fickle toward its platform artists as the theater-going public. Chapman continued to conduct revival meetings until 1918, but by 1912 he had to yield the center of the stage to Billy Sunday, just as Torrey had earlier had to yield to him.[74] Sunday's revivalism marked, among other things, the peak of the profession's theatricality, but in this he drew less upon his experience with Chapman than upon the tradition established by Sam Jones and carried on by Milan B. Williams, Rodney "Gypsy" Smith, and Burke Culpepper. These men represented the more colorful wing of the profession and capitalized upon

[72] Ottman, *Chapman,* p. 206.

[73] The *Christian Workers Magazine,* XI (February, 1911), p. 443.

[74] It was significant of the high repute of Chapman and indirectly of professional evangelism in these years that he was chosen moderator of the Presbyterian General Assembly for the year 1917–18.

the fact that they were not "high-brow" preachers like Torrey and Chapman but simple men of the people. They did their bit not only toward making revivalism more secular but in making it a homogenizing force for evangelical righteousness.

Milan B. Williams entered revivalism in 1889 after a career as a YMCA secretary.[75] During his revivals in the 1890's he was assisted at times by both Charles Alexander and Billy Sunday. Like Jones, he emphasized civic reform particularly against mayors and police chiefs who failed to enforce local prohibition laws. He wanted, like Jones, to get rid of "sectarianism" and unite the citizenry for "the purification of our towns." In places where saloons were allowed to run illegally he told his audiences, "You have got about the lowest down crowd of pups this side of hell" in office. "I preached one time in a mining town in Virginia" and "on a certain afternoon I preached to men. The tent was crowded to its utmost capacity. I stripped off my coat and cuffs and laid in for a couple of hours' preaching. I took up everybody from the officials right on through and laid open the sins of that community as best I could." When the meeting was over the people went out "to talk and discuss and some to leave the 'dis' off." [76]

Williams boasted, "We organized our civic federation in Belle Plain [Iowa] and started out against seven or eight illegal saloons. . . . We closed them up and gave them twenty-four hours to get out of town." He urged his congregations to join the fight for local decency the way a frontier sheriff would organize a posse, except that he said, "You can conquer in the name of Christ and home and native land." "I hear you have one [man] in this town that even slaps his old mother around," he said in Waterloo, Iowa. "Is it true?" A voice from the crowd answered, "Yes." "Well, you ought to get a rope and make a noose in it and you ought to put that noose around that fellow's heel, or something, I don't much care what. Then just swing him up once or twice to see how it feels. . . . Citizens sometimes have to take things of that kind in their own hands and dispose of them very summarily."

[75] For a short sketch of Williams' early career see *The Institute Tie* (Chicago), October 30, 1892.

[76] This and the illustrations below from Williams' sermons are taken from his book *If Any Man Will* (Chicago, 1897), which consists of verbatim reports of the sermons he gave during a revival in Waterloo, Iowa, in 1896 or 1897.

Williams's theology was like that of Jones: "The true theology of conversion is to quit sin and serve God." As a country preacher he enjoyed poking fun at big city preachers: "The metropolitan pulpit is responsible for a great deal of the devilment and infidelity today. Some little fellow who did first-rate in a country pulpit is called or sent to New York or Chicago. Next we hear of him he is reading a paper at some ministerial meeting about the fallibility of scripture or against the atonement, trying to get a little cheap notoriety. A good man in the country, but couldn't be trusted in the big city."

The theatrical in Williams led to jokes which were introduced simply to raise a laugh, like the one about "a Hebrew who went into a restaurant" and ordered "haluf a dozen" bad oysters and ate them. Then he ordered "haluf a dozen" good oysters and ate them. When the waiter asked for an explanation, the Hebrew answered, "Vell . . . you see it vas like dot; I have a tapevurm; und I fed him de bad oysters because dey is sheeper; den ven he got full, I ead de goote vons for myselluf." [77]

After 1901 Williams mixed revival preaching with the more lucrative profession of lecturing on "Sex Problems As Related to Health and Disease, Morality and Religion, Heredity and Environment, Both in the Individual and Society at Large." The relationship between sex and religion veered off into the question of the perils of immigration and the virtues of the Anglo-Saxons: "Our reckless greed for emigrants has hurt us morally beyond repair. Italy, sending her two hundred thousand a year to our shores, has brought other evils besides the Comorra, the Mafia, and the Black Hand. Sexual immorality, nameable and unmentionable, has come from her shores. China and Japan have flooded the country with their prostitutes who have brought the most dangerous types of venereal disease; while

[77] Williams, *If Any Man Will,* p. 54. The strain of antisemitism which crept into the sermons of some revivalists at the turn of the century was not typical of the profession. Most revivalists accepted the view that the Jews were a chosen race whose separateness was part of God's divine plan. Just prior to the Second Coming all Jews would, according to premillennialist prophecy, be converted to Christianity "in a day." Hence the fate of the Jews was integrally connected with the fate of Christian fundamentalism, and in the 1930's evangelists like Billy Sunday denounced Adolf Hitler for precisely this reason. For Sunday's view see, W. G. McLoughlin, Jr., *Billy Sunday Was His Real Name* (Chicago, 1955), pp. 290–91.

Russian Jews have given our officials more trouble than any other class by their persistence in importing and selling women for immoral purposes." "But," he pointed out, "scan England and America, the home of orthodox and aggressive Christianity and see if our customs are not better than those of other nations. . . ."[78]

In 1897 Williams dedicated a volume of his sermons to J. B. Culpepper, the father of Burke Culpepper. J. B. Culpepper was a Methodist circuit-rider in Georgia, and he trained his son Burke to preach at the age of eight.[79] Burke was called "the Boy Preacher" until 1899, when at the age of nineteen he was licensed to preach by the Methodist Episcopal Church, South. Like Williams, Burke Culpepper was an admirer and imitator of Sam Jones. After Jones's death in 1906 the newspapers began to call Culpepper "the Sam Jones of today." After 1912, when Billy Sunday was the central figure of the profession, Culpepper was called "the Billy Sunday of the South." He preached in every state in the union before his death in 1948, but most of his revivals took place in the South.

Because of the way he raced up and down the platform and even into the aisles of the church while he exhorted, the newspapers called him "an unbridled cyclone." He was an uncompromising fundamentalist, premillennialist, and prohibitionist. "Can you imagine the Virgin Mary smoking, drinking and playing cards?" he would ask. "God pity the little wart who says the Bible has no part in our public schools." "I'd rather give my children tablets of bi-chloride of mercury than to have them go to school to some of these state universities." A born showman and actor, Culpepper made his revivals a blend of vaudeville, stump speaking, and the old-time religion at its most frothy. He even acted out the story of Christ's trial and crucifixion, playing all the parts himself, to the delight of his audiences.

More popular in northern churches than Culpepper in these years was Rodney "Gypsy" Smith. Smith had two assets in addition to his dramatic talent: he was in fact a converted gypsy

[78] M. B. Williams, *Sex Problems* (7th ed.; New York, 1910), pp. 93–94. This book was published by Fleming H. Revell.

[79] James Culpepper, *Burke Culpepper* (Louisville, 1952).

and he was an Englishman.[80] His father and two uncles were active evangelists in the British Isles in the 1870's and were billed as "The Three Gypsy Brothers" or "The Converted Gypsies." Smith was converted at the age of sixteen (according to one story, shortly after having heard Ira Sankey sing), and from 1877 to 1882 he worked with William Booth, preaching on street corners and mission halls for the Salvation Army. In 1882 he was drummed out of the Army by Booth for accepting a present of a gold watch from some of his admiring converts. He made his first trip to America in 1889, but did not make any particular impression as an evangelist until his Boston revival in 1906.

Here under the auspices of the Boston Evangelical Alliance and the personal sponsorship of A. Z. Conrad, Smith conducted fifty meetings at Tremont Temple which were attended by 116,500 persons. Cards were signed by 2290 persons, 850 of them children. The *Watchman* called him "England's greatest evangelist" and claimed that "not since the Moody and Sankey meetings of 1877 has Boston witnessed such great evangelistic services."[81] He remained a perennial favorite in evangelical circles for the next thirty years. By 1936 he had conducted thirty-three separate revival tours in the United States.

Unlike Williams and Culpepper, Smith was admired for his heart-warming tenderness and eloquence. "His language is the pure Anglo-Saxon of John Bunyan and John Bright. There is nothing in his address to offend good taste." As one observer put it, "He has such a nice way of flaying his victims. . . ." He was pre-eminently "winsome" and in turn could be sentimental, eloquent, or "manly." When calling for persons to come forward after his sermons he would say, "Listen to the wooings of the Divine Spirit, his drawing on your heart strings, and respond to his voice." Then he would warn, "You who will not be saved today may perish tomorrow." He was without any formal education, and some ministers complained that "now and then his exegesis seemed a little far-fetched," but this could be forgiven a man who "fearlessly held up the worthlessness of a mere

80 See Rodney Smith, *Forty Years An Evangelist* (New York, 1923); Harold Murray, *Sixty Years An Evangelist* (London, 1937); E. F. Bayliss, *The Gipsy Smith Missions in America* (Boston, 1907).

81 *Watchman,* November 29, 1906, p. 12.

fashionable profession" of faith and preached the purest evangelical orthodoxy.

Smith opposed the liquor traffic and stood firmly on the fundamentals, but he was never fanatical or violent in the pulpit. At his most vehement he would say, "Before the judgment seat you will be charged with murder—deliberate murder—the breaking of your mother's heart" if you do not give up your sins and turn to Christ. He pleaded and coaxed more in the vein of Chapman than of Sam Jones. His preaching appealed to those evangelicals who disliked the machinery of Chapman and the vulgarity of Williams and Culpepper. His English accent also helped to add a little tone to his meetings. On several occasions, however, he got caught up in the tide of moral uplift and led torchlight parades into the slum districts of the cities in order to attract the poor and the wicked to a revival service held in a theater or auditorium in the red-light district. He was in favor of reform by conversion and prohibition, but like Chapman, he was willing to call this "social service" if that suited his audiences better than the term Christian charity.

All the successful evangelists of the first quarter of the twentieth century, and there were hundreds of them, adapted themselves to the progressive movement by utilizing the prohibition theme, the social service theme, the Americanization theme, or elements of all three. But prior to Billy Sunday's triumphant expression of these pious ambiguities, the most successful exponent of them was William E. Biederwolf. Biederwolf was a graduate of Princeton College and Princeton Graduate School, where he obtained an M.A. in 1892. Having decided to enter the ministry, he received a B.D. from Princeton Seminary in 1895.[82] He spent the 1895–1896 revival season as a member of

[82] For biographical data see Ray E. Garrett, *William Edward Biederwolf* (Grand Rapids, Michigan, 1948). Garrett's book is uncritically eulogistic.

Some mention should be made here of William J. Dawson, the English evangelist who enjoyed a brief but highly popular vogue in the first decade of the century. He was a liberal in theology but believed that "the time has clearly come for liberal theology to justify itself in the eyes of the people." In his autobiography he explained his brief and frustrating experience as a professional revivalist by saying, "My general purpose may be described as an effort to reconcile culture with the simpler forms of religious and social zeal," a purpose toward which he was inspired by taking part in one of Gypsy Smith's torchlight parades into the slums. For several years Dawson was one of Chap-

B. Fay Mills's staff and then went abroad to study theology at the University of Berlin and at the Sorbonne. Like Torrey, he rejected the higher criticism and became an ardent fundamentalist. Upon his return to the United States he served as pastor of a Presbyterian Church in Logansport, Indiana, and then, in 1900, took up evangelism.

For several years he aided Chapman, first on Converse's evangelistic committee for the Presbyterian Church and later as a coevangelist in the Simultaneous Campaigns. In 1906 he branched out on his own, hiring as his chorister first Paul Gilbert, then Homer A. Rodeheaver, and finally, after 1910, W. M. Weeden. From 1906 to 1910 he conducted tent and tabernacle meetings in small towns and cities like Xenia, Streator, Lorraine, and Piqua, Ohio; Freeport and Monmouth, Illinois; and Hannibal, Missouri.

According to his biographer, "Dr. Biederwolf went into all of his own revivals with a chip on his shoulder; that is, he was out to hunt down and fight the devil. . . . Wherever he went he gave himself unreservedly to the task of the conflict between the forces of righteousness and the forces of evil." In other words, he made civic reform and prohibition the principal motifs of his campaigns. His most popular sermons were those on "Sowing and Reaping," "The White Life," and "The Square Man." One of his favorite devices for arousing public attention and enthusism for his revivals was to organize "Civico-Religio-Industrial Parades." Led by uniformed veterans of the G.A.R. and Spanish-American War, these parades included members of the cooperating churches, Sunday school children, the local fire department, the city officials, the members of the various fraternal lodges, delegations from local shops and factories, and the revival choir, all singing hymns and carrying banners to promote an atmosphere of fervent town spirit as they marched to the tabernacle with Biederwolf at their head to hear one of his rousing sermons. An editorial in the Piqua *Daily Call* said

---

man's brigade of evangelists and then conducted revivals on his own both in England and the United States. But his attempt, like Mills's, "to win assent by sweet reasonableness" in revivalism appealed to only a very limited audience. See W. J. Dawson, *The Autobiography of a Mind* (New York, 1925); and W. J. Dawson, *The Evangelistic Note* (New York, 1905).

after his five week campaign in that city, "The city admires Dr. Biederwolf for his fearless attack on wickedness in high places as well as low, and they love him for his tender appeals to live the better life." By 1910 he was described as "an evangelist of many years experience" with "exceptional preparation for his work" who was "recognized as the peer of Gypsy Smith, Chapman, Torrey, and W. A. Sunday." [83]

Biederwolf never attained the popularity of Sunday, but he held city-wide campaigns after 1910 in cities the size of Fall River, Massachusetts; Watertown, New York; Allentown, Pennsylvania; and Charlotte, South Carolina. In 1910 he was elected President of the Interdenominational Association of Evangelists. By 1915 he was receiving $15,000 a year from the free-will offerings at his campaigns. In 1913 the Federal Council of Churches appointed him secretary of its new commission on evangelism. From 1914 to 1917 he was executive director of this commission which defined two of its principal objectives as being: "To place renewed emphasis on the fundamentals of the Gospel," and "To elevate the standard and to safeguard the work of a sane and thorough type of evangelism." [84] The work of this commission in many respects duplicated that of the Interdenominational Association of Evangelists, though the convention in Winona Lake continued to supply a useful opportunity for social and business intercourse among the members of the profession until the mid-1930's.

Like most evangelists of his day, Biederwolf believed that the fundamentals of the Gospel and the fundamentals of Americanism went hand in hand. He devoted a great deal of his revival efforts to shop meetings in order to sway laboring men from the anti-American tendencies of labor agitators. He attacked the saloon as though it were a foreign importation, and thought that foreigners were the foremost opponents of teaching Biblical literalism in the public schools: "My father was foreign-born," he said in 1915, "but I say if a European don't like the laws of this country, let him stay at home. . . . If atheists and infidels and Jews and other rebels don't like our public schools

[83] Quoted in Garrett, *Biederwolf,* p. 29; *Watchman,* December 29, 1910, p. 21.

[84] Charles E. Schaeffer, *A Brief History of the Department of Evangelism of the Federal Council of Churches* (New York, 1951).

where the word of God is read, let 'em take their kids and hike out." [85] The saloon and socialism went together: "The flag of the saloon is a dirty red flag." "The open licensed saloon came out of hell and the whole nation is ready to celebrate its return to where it belongs." Anyone not ready to inaugurate national prohibition was implicitly not a member of the nation and probably a communist to boot.

Biederwolf considered the premillennial theory of the Second Coming part of the Christian fundamentals and in later years wrote several books on the subject, but in his heyday he seldom stressed the doctrine. Instead, like his colleagues, he advocated "social service" and soul-winning.

In 1911–12 Biederwolf played a prominent part in the famous Men and Religion Forward Movement which was designed to arouse the whole nation to a great spiritual effort to solve the social and religious problems of the day. Organized by a group of laymen led by Fred B. Smith, and with the cooperation of prominent ministers and evangelists of all shades and denominations, the movement took a year to plan and another year to execute. Some saw it as predominantly a nationwide soul-winning campaign, others as the culmination of twenty-five years of social gospel activity.[86] The main effort of the movement was directed toward holding a week of open forums, conferences, and public religious meetings in nearly seventy of the largest cities in the nation for the purpose of increasing "the permanent contribution of the Church to the best life of the Continent, socially, politically, commercially, and physically and to emphasize the modern message of the Church in social service and usefulness." Such diverse figures as William Jennings Bryan, Washington Gladden, Gypsy Smith, Jane Addams, Newell D. Hillis, and Henry Wallace took part in the closing conference of the movement in Carnegie Hall. By putting its emphasis upon "social service," the movement managed

[85] Quoted in *The Truth Seeker* (New York), May 8, 1915, p. 295. See also William E. Biederwolf, *Evangelism, Its Justification, Its Operation, and Its Value* (New York, 1921), p. 18.

[86] For various interpretations of this movement see C. H. Hopkins, *The Rise of the Social Gospel in American Protestantism 1865–1915* (New Haven, 1940), pp. 296–98; G. G. Atkins, *Religion in Our Times* (New York, 1932), p. 160; Charles R. Stelzle, *A Son of the Bowery* (New York, 1926), pp. 154 ff.; F. G. Beardsley, *A History of American Revivals* (New York, 1912), p. 335 ff.

to please everyone, but its good intentions were productive of few permanent results.

With the election of Woodrow Wilson and the legislative reforms of 1912–15, the social gospel movement reached its zenith, and the fervor it had generated went into a gradual decline, though it left a residue of liberal ideas among many ministers.[87] The mounting frenzy of the prohibition movement, the hardening lines of the fundamentalist-modernist controversy, the outbreak of war in Europe, and the general belief that reform had conquered the main evils and gone far enough toward changing the old system—all contributed to this decline. Nor were the professional revivalists without their influence upon it. Since 1890 the liberals and conservatives of evangelical Protestantism had been running like men in a three-legged race. Tied together by mutual interest in evangelism, charity, and prohibition, the progress of evangelicalism was hobbled by the attempt of the liberals to move further toward social action while the conservatives strained to keep the churches out of the temporal spheres of economics and politics. The professional evangelists, striving for unity and cooperation in order to promote their campaigns, did their best to blur the issues while leaning their weight toward the conservative position. The big and small businessmen whose financial contributions were essential to city-wide evangelism as well as to denominational social action had reluctantly yielded a bit to the desire for economic reform and regulation under the goading of conscience, the attack of the progressives, and the leadership of the conservative reformer, Theodore Roosevelt. But they drew back when political power passed out of their hands in 1912. The social gospelers, overconfident of their popular support, foolishly sought to push their advantage and began to bite the hand that fed them.

The Rev. Charles Stelzle, for one, thought that as secretary of the Presbyterian Church's department of Church and Labor, it was his duty to protest "in the name of the Church against the unnecessary slaughter of workingmen in the Pittsburgh rolling mills." He was indignant when "a former Moderator of the General Assembly" pointed out to him that by attacking the

87 See Paul A. Carter, *The Decline and Revival of the Social Gospel* (Ithaca, New York, 1956).

steel industry which was heavily studded with prominent Presbyterian laymen, he "was 'killing the goose that lays the golden egg.'" When Stelzle persisted in his course, the General Assembly specifically warned him that "the Department of Social Service should be conducted with more emphasis upon the evangelistic element." The budget of Stelzle's department was cut so drastically in 1913 that he resigned. His departure from the post was applauded by the editor of the *Presbyterian* who remarked, "Mr. Stelzle started out in the service of the Gospel, but his drift and development has been into and along sociology." If he "continues in his present line he will pass into Socialism." [88]

A similar reaction took place in the evangelical denominations in the South. In 1915 the editor of the Texas *Christian Advocate* criticized the misconstruction which he said was being put upon the purposes for which the Methodist-Episcopal Church had created its commission of social service. "The General Conference did not contemplate in this action that the church should throw itself indiscriminately into the work of all conceptions of social reform and make these fads take the place of preaching the old-fashioned Gospel as a means to personal and social salvation." Misguided ministers were plunging "into the effort to make the church a factor in determining the questions at variance between labor and capital." They failed to see that there was a distinct difference between "social service" and "socialism." The latter "strives to equalize wealth upon a basis that is impractical and revolutionary" and "antagonistic to the present order of things." But true "social service has nothing to do with politics directly or with economics as such." Its object is "to put into men and women a desire for righteousness and an ambition to develop into the best manhood and womanhood possible. When this is accomplished, then the proper re-adjustment of their conditions will take on shape normally and beneficially." [89]

Even the Federal Council of Churches, which from its founding had been a social gospel stronghold, had to yield to conservative pressure after 1912. It created a commission on evangelism to balance its commission on social service. And it modi-

[88] Stelzle, *Son of the Bowery*, pp. 168 ff.
[89] Quoted in *Zion's Herald* (Methodist, Boston), January 13, 1915, p. 45.

fied its strong stand on economic questions voiced in the Social Creed of the Churches in 1908 by adding planks which made prohibition and the divorce rate matters of equal weight with "the equitable division of the product of industry" and the improvement of the conditions of labor. After 1912 the Council's budget for the promotion of prohibition was almost twice as large as that for the promotion of all the other aspects of its social creed combined.[90]

It was no accident that Billy Sunday rose to fame on the crest of this reaction against the social gospel. "Some people," he said, "are trying to make a religion out of social service with Jesus Christ left out. That is why your Men and Religion Forward Movement was a lamentable failure. They made the Christian religion a side issue." The *Watchman-Examiner* and other conservative journals which had laughed at or ignored Sunday before 1912 now began to quote him more frequently: "Billy Sunday believes in social service," said the *Watchman-Examiner* approvingly in 1914, "but he sees the danger of magnifying it and ignoring Christ and his salvation. He says, 'We've had enough of this godless social service nonsense.' "[91]

It was part of Billy Sunday's genius that from 1908 to 1918 he was able to appear to be both a leader of the old-time religion and a spokesman for twentieth century religion. But there was never any doubt that his heart lay with the "Old Side" in this final phase of the third great awakening.

90 See John A. Hutchinson, *We Are Not Divided* (New York, 1941), pp. 46–47, 55, 102–3. The budget of the commission on social service never went over $25,000 a year between 1912 and 1920, but the Council's temperance commission spent "over $150,000" between 1916 and 1920. *Ibid.*, pp. 101, 148.

91 *Watchman-Examiner,* August 13, 1914, p. 1066. A review of Winston Churchill's social gospel novel, *The Inside of the Cup,* in this same journal was also an interesting commentary upon this reaction: The reviewer stated that the action of Churchill's crusading hero, who left his pastorate to engage in social reform work when his wealthy trustees refused to let him speak on the problems of capital and labor, was reminiscent of "B. Fay Mills' departure from general and successful Gospel evangelism to crass humanitarianism." December 4, 1913, p. 442.

CHAPTER 8

"Christianity and Patriotism Are Synonymous"

One hundred years of modern revivalism reached a giddy climax in the career of William A. (Billy) Sunday. Under his aegis, professional evangelism attained the ultimate limits of secularization and tribalism. Theology assumed a secondary role. By what might be called a kind of reverse english, the Christian Americanization of the foreigner led to Americanized Christianity for the native-born. Revivals became unabashedly dramatic performances where audiences laughed at, cried over, cheered and applauded the histrionics of a master showman who personified the ideals of "American Christianity." And the conversion process was reduced to a decision to be "decent" and patriotic. To his critics Sunday and his revivals represented nothing but the last sputterings of the old-time religion and the frustrated hysteria of those who were out of step with the times. But there was more to Sunday than that.

His revivalism was a climactic manifestation of the profound confusion and uneasiness among a wide segment of the American people which had been broiling for over thirty years. In his sermons and public statements he gave vivid and colorful expression to many of the feelings and opinions of that large group of moderate, average, middle-class citizens (churchgoers, occasional churchgoers, and lip-service Protestants) who were deeply concerned about the issues of the day but who found both the liberal and the reactionary approaches to these issues unsatisfactory. For the first ten years of his career, from 1896 to 1906, Sunday was the idol of the small town inhabitants of the corn belt. For the next ten or twelve years he was the idol of the city cousins of these rural evangelicals. To both audiences his revivalism represented a nostalgia for the nineteenth century and a fear of the twentieth.

In the nineteenth century the independent farmers, small businessmen, salaried clerks, and white-collar workers (from whose ranks came the audiences which applauded Sunday) had been the acknowledged backbone of the country and had felt secure in their position and outlook. But in the twentieth century they began to think that they were the forgotten men, caught between the overwhelming power of big business and big labor and faced with a collapse of their whole scheme of social, political, and economic values.[1] A good example of the attitude of this group (who always thought of themselves as "the people") was an editorial entitled "Commercial Feudalism" published in the *Watchman* in 1908: "On the one side . . . the people are becoming the serfs of large employers, and on the other the subjects of labor unions. In either case, freedom, independence, and the chance for the formation of the highest character is lost; and the people are being reduced to a state of feudalism with two classes of overlords instead of one. . . . The combinations of capital seek to reduce him to the position of a working serf and the combinations of labor would reduce him to a simple member of a labor union."[2]

That Sunday was recognized as a significant force in America by reason of his relationship to "the people" was demonstrated not only by his astonishing popular success as an evangelist but also by the deference paid to him both by the average man and by persons of prestige and power. In 1914 he was ranked eighth in a nation-wide poll conducted by the *American Magazine* on the question, "Who is the greatest man in the United States?"[3] Between 1915 and 1918 Theodore Roosevelt, William Jennings Bryan, and Woodrow Wilson felt it necessary to

1 There is no doubt that modern revivalism from at least 1890 onward was stimulated by the anxiety over what Richard Hofstadter has described as "the status revolution." See his chapter on this subject in *The Age of Reform* (New York, 1955).

2 *Watchman* (Baptist, Boston), December 31, 1908, p. 5.

3 *American Magazine,* LXXVIII (October, 1914), p. 63.

express publicly their regard for Sunday and his work. State and local politicians were always prominent on his revival platforms. For years the leading businessmen of the nation gave their time and money to promote his campaigns, while newspapers and magazines of all sorts devoted millions of words to describing his every word and deed. Although Sunday's part in the progressive movement diverted rather than advanced its central aims, he was nevertheless an authentic voice of that movement, and he could not be ignored.[4]

The problem in examining Sunday's career is to discover just what segment of the progressive movement he did represent and precisely what he, and those perplexed and inarticulate persons he stood for, thought and felt about the changing pattern of American life. Sunday claimed to support "progressive orthodoxy" in religion, "Christian social service" in reform, and Theodore Roosevelt in politics, and this seemed to satisfy most of his supporters. But in his role as spokesman for evangelical moderatism, Sunday purposely made his platform so broad and vague that from 1906 to 1918 he was also hailed as a leader by many liberals and by many conservatives both in the churches and in politics. John D. Rockefeller, Jr., characterized Sunday very neatly when he said in 1917, "Mr. Sunday is a rallying center around whom all people interested in good things may gather." [5] Because Sunday sincerely and honestly strove to defend what "the people" considered the good old American tradition of individualism, he became the champion of all those who hoped nostalgically for a simple solution to contemporary problems in terms of this tradition. For this reason John Leland, the President of the Cadillac Motor Company, called Sunday in 1918 "this great plumed knight clothed in the armor of God." [6]

William Ashley Sunday was born on November 19, 1862, in a two-room log house one mile south of Ames, Iowa.[7] His father, William Sunday, was a brick mason who had enlisted in the

[4] Hofstadter notes in this same regard that "such men as George W. Perkins and Frank Munsey" (both of whom were supporters of Sunday's revivals) "may perhaps be accused of joining the Progressive movement primarily to blunt its edge." *Age of Reform,* p. 144.

[5] Boston *Herald,* January 19, 1917, p. 1.

[6] *Ibid.,* January 12, 1917, p. 5.

[7] For biographical information on Sunday see W. G. McLoughlin, Jr., *Billy Sunday Was His Real Name* (Chicago, 1955); Theodore T. Frankenberg, *The*

Union Army four months before Sunday's birth; he died on December 23, 1862, without ever having seen his third son. Sunday's mother married again in 1868, and two more children were added to the family. In 1874, when his step-father disappeared, Sunday and his older brother, Edward, were sent by their mother to a soldier's orphans' home in Glenwood, Iowa. Two years later he returned to work on his grandfather's farm near Ames.

According to his mother, Sunday was "a good boy" who "would go after things pell mell." He "always had an extra supply of energy," and he "liked to play games where he could show his strength, for he was a strong little lad." He was also exceedingly sentimental and quick-tempered. Shortly after his return from the orphan home in 1876, he quarreled with his grandfather and ran away to the neighboring village of Nevada, Iowa. From the age of fifteen he was on his own in the world.

In Nevada he held various jobs, as hotel porter, stable boy, and janitor, while working his way through high school. However, he left high school without graduating in order to obtain the more coveted honor of becoming a member of the Fire Brigade of Marshalltown, Iowa. In Marshalltown he also took a part-time job as assistant to an undertaker and furniture-maker, and he played baseball for the township team. When this team won the State Championship in 1883, largely through his efforts, Sunday accepted an offer to join the Chicago White-stockings to make a career of baseball. For eight years he played right field for various teams in the National League and broke several records for base-stealing and speed at rounding the bases. Between seasons he worked as a fireman on the Chicago and Northwestern Railroad.

After 1883 Sunday made his home in Chicago, and it was here that he had the conversion experience which eventually led him into evangelism. As he told it, the experience began one afternoon in 1886 after he had been having a few drinks with some of his teammates in a downtown Chicago saloon. Outside the saloon they stopped to listen to a group of gospel singers from the Pacific Garden Mission. They were, he said, "singing

Spectacular Career of Rev. Billy Sunday (Columbus, Ohio); Elijah P. Brown, *The Real Billy Sunday* (Dayton, Ohio, 1914); and William T. Ellis, *Billy Sunday, The Man and His Message* (Philadelphia, 1936). The Ellis book contains Sunday's brief "Autobiography."

the Gospel hymns that I heard my mother sing in the log cabin in Iowa." When the singers invited the ballplayers to attend a service at the mission hall, Sunday accepted. "I went to the mission that evening and liked what I heard. I went back again and again," and finally, through the motherly persuasion of Mrs. George Clark, the wife of the founder of the mission, "one night I went forward and publicly accepted Christ as my Saviour."

The conversion does not seem to have been particularly emotional. Sunday's mother had been a spasmodically devout Methodist, and his religious training in the orphans' home had been strict and pious, but he had never shown any interest in religion. After his conversion he gave up drinking, betting, and going to the theater, and he refused to play baseball on Sunday, but he did not give up his career. From some of Sunday's remarks it seems that his courtship of the girl he was soon to marry played a large part in his conversion. Helen A. Thompson was the daughter of a Chicago dairyman and ice cream manufacturer. The family were strict Presbyterians, and Mr. Thompson did not like his daughter's being courted by a nonchurchgoing baseball player. Soon after Sunday's conversion he joined the Jefferson Park Presbyterian Church to which the Thompsons belonged. Two years later, having worked his way up to the post of Sunday school superintendent, he succeeded in winning the father's consent to marry Helen. But he continued to play baseball.

In the winter of 1887–1888 Sunday took a course in rhetoric at Evanston Academy, the preparatory school associated with Northwestern University. The next two winters he took Bible lessons at the Chicago YMCA and worked at the Y's central branch, where he often heard Moody speak but never became intimate with him. Here he also came to know J. V. Farwell and Cyrus H. McCormick (Jr.). In 1891 he was offered a full-time position as assistant secretary of the religious department of the Chicago YMCA. He felt that he "was called definitely to enter Christian work" and gave up a baseball contract that would have earned him $500 a month for the season for a job that paid only $83 a month all year round. "They didn't call me a grafter then," he was fond of saying in later years. During his three years with the YMCA his salary never rose above

$1500 a year, and it was often many months in arrears. With two young children and with obligations to help his invalid brother at home, Sunday was hardpressed to make ends meet, and when he was offered a job as J. Wilbur Chapman's assistant at $40 a week in 1893, he took it.

As Chapman's advance man, Sunday obtained a valuable apprenticeship in the revival profession by organizing local committees, choosing meeting places, training ushers, arranging for publicity, organizing prayer meetings, and generally laying the groundwork for Chapman's campaigns for three years. Occasionally, when Chapman's arrival was delayed, Sunday conducted some preliminary meetings himself. He also acted as an usher, spoke at overflow meetings, helped to take up the collections, and undertook personal work with inquirers at the after-meetings. Once or twice during these years when Chapman had no revivals scheduled, Sunday assisted Milan B. Williams and Charles Alexander with their revivals in the Midwest. When Chapman temporarily gave up revivalism to return to Bethany Church as pastor in December, 1895, Sunday was forced to start work on his own. Again it was a matter of earning a living rather than of following a call to save souls which brought the decision.

Chapman gave him a recommendation to the pastors of Garner, Iowa, who were looking for an evangelist to conduct their annual revival meetings, and on January 3, 1896, backed by three churches, Sunday began his first independent campaign in this town of 1300. Through his work with Williams and Chapman he had imbibed the styles and manners of both the learned and the folk traditions in evangelism. His lack of education and his personal temperament inclined him toward the folk tradition. His ambition and his respect for the ministry led him to imitate Chapman. At this time he was thirty-four years old, five feet eight inches tall, had a slim athletic build, and a likable but not particularly handsome face. He wore his light, balding hair parted in the middle. His blue eyes were friendly and sparkling, but neither hypnotic, like Finney's, nor dynamic, like Moody's. Generous and warm-hearted, he still had a quick temper, but it cooled equally quickly. Outside observers seemed most impressed by his charming smile and his ingenuous, boyish good nature. "His manner is magnetic and his smile so winsome," said one journalist early in his career, "that the heart of a misanthrope would go out toward him. When he reaches out to shake hands, and give that firm, hearty, grip, it is time to surrender." [8]

When Sunday started his career he was too conscious of his social and intellectual shortcomings to try to meet the Presbyterian standards for ordination. He had had no formal theological training, and his first sermons were borrowed wholesale from Chapman and interspersed with illustrations from Moody, Williams, and Jones. In his early attempts to imitate Chapman, Sunday dressed in a wing collar, bow tie, and cutaway coat. He tried to make up in dignity for what he lacked in education. But he spoke more in the style of Moody than of Chapman: "People like Sunday's preaching," said a newspaper account in 1896. "He preaches plain, practical sermons and seems to get hold of the people in a way that few can. His sermons and manner are similar to those of Mr. Moody. . . . No one can say they signed [decision cards] while under excitement, for Mr. Sunday appeals to their good sense and judgment only." [9]

But by 1900 he gave up attempting to be dignified. Chapman's style simply did not fit his personality. He found that he had more in common with the folksy humor of Sam Jones, the slangy vernacular of M. B. Williams, and the rough aggressiveness of Moody than with his urbane and serious mentor. As one Iowa newspaper described him in 1903, "He is not conventional. . . . He is not namby-pamby. . . . He does not mince words. . . . He is not dull. . . . He is not afraid to wave his hands and shout." [10] Another paper described him as "young, talented, well-educated, eloquent, humorous, with powers of ridicule and denunciation developed to perfection with a fearlessness and bravery seldom equalled," and "a delivery that is most surprising and almost bewildering in its rapidity, with its boundless energy and enthusiasm. . . . He is an up-to-date man. . . . He is in no old rut." [11] Like Finney, he recognized that the revivalist could and should take liberties which the regular pastors could not.

[8] Quoted in Brown, *The Real Billy Sunday,* p. 86.
[9] Sigourney *News* (Iowa), January 30, 1896, p. 3.
[10] Jefferson *Bee* (Iowa), December 17, 1903, p. 1.
[11] Audubon *Republican* (Iowa), January 30, 1902, p. 1.

Sunday's style in the years after 1900 and for the rest of his career was compounded of two basic ingredients: slangy humor and florid rhetoric. He knew that his audiences admired the eloquence of orators like William Jennings Bryan and Robert G. Ingersoll. He also knew that they liked a man who was "of the people" and who was not ashamed to admit it. Though he lived in Chicago from 1883 to 1910, he always associated himself with the rural background of his childhood: "I was bred and born not in Old Kentucky but old Iowa. I am a rube of the rubes. I am a graduate of the University of Poverty. I have blacked my boots with stove blacking, greased my hair with goose grease. I never knew what an undergarment or a night dress was until I was eighteen years old. I have dried my face and wiped my proboscis on a flour sack towel. I have helped grub up stumps that stood in the way of the plowshare of advancing civilization. My autobiography can be summed up in one line from Gray's 'Elegy in a Country Churchyard': 'The short and simple annals of the poor.' "[12] Yet some of his sermons led to the following descriptions by local reporters in 1904: Sunday is "the most spectacular and forceful preacher in the nation today"; his sermons are "prose poems and pictures," studded with "rhetorical gems"; one of them contained a "sparkling, particolored, pulsing vivid description of Eden with Adam and Eve—a wonderful picture painted with riotous voluptuousness of color in words—a poem equal to any of Ossian in strength and the only prose poem ever heard equal to the finest passages of Robert G. Ingersoll—one of the most beautiful oratorical flights in the English language—a sustained and amazing rhetorical flight such as is heard only once in a generation—this rolled over the immense audience which perhaps expected horse play!"[13]

The audiences expected horseplay because Sunday was not above giving them horseplay. One headline in 1904 read: "EVANGELIST DOES GREAT VAUDEVILLE STUNTS IN TABERNACLE PULPIT." Another, a year later, compared him to the newest form of popular entertainment with which Sunday had constantly to compete for his crowds: "TABERNACLE KINETOSCOPE: REV. WILLIAM SUN-

[12] Jefferson *Bee*, December 17, 1903, p. 1.
[13] *Daily Gate City* (Keokuk, Iowa), January 30, 1902, p. 5.

DAY FLASHES A SERIES OF MOVING PICTURES IN THE PULPIT."[14] The way Sunday acted out scenes on the tabernacle platform was as good as a Keystone Comedy or "The Perils of Pauline." "Those who went to hear him last night to be entertained got the worth of their money," said one account. "There is an accuracy in his mimicry that is seldom seen since Clara Morris left the stage."[15]

In addition to dramatizing his sermons, Sunday adopted another sensational trick which he had picked up from M. B. Williams. "Sunday grew so lurid that he shed first his collar, then his coat, and as he closed his sermon, proceeded to put on his raiment with the nonchalance of a man talking to an intimate friend in his boudoir."[16] After 1905 Sunday was frequently pictured in cartoons preaching in his shirtsleeves with perspiration pouring off his brow as he "lambasted the devil" with "hot shots at sin." He also gave up his wing collar and frock coat and dressed "like a businessman."

Because of his success as an evangelist in the small towns of the Midwest, Sunday decided in 1903 to present himself for ordination to the Presbytery of Chicago. He had reason to believe that his ability to win souls would make up for his lack of education. He did not have Moody's talent for carrying all before him, and it embarrassed Sunday to have to explain to those ministers who called for his services that he was not ordained. The stigma of his baseball background, his sensational style, and the innate feelings of inferiority which plagued him all his life also goaded him into making this move. The examination of the presbytery was not exacting. The members of the examining board were, as he had hoped, disposed to overlook his lack of training. As one member of the board said, "God has used him to win more souls to Christ than all of us combined, and must have ordained him long before we ever thought of it." After a few perfunctory questions, most of which Sunday could not answer, it was moved to pass him anyway, and Sunday duly became an ordained Presbyterian minister.[17] He

14 *Ibid.*, October 2, 1904, p. 1; Burlington *Hawk-Eye* (Iowa), November 12, 1905, p. 4.

15 Centerville *Daily Citizen* (Iowa), October 1, 1904, p. 1; *Daily Gate City*, October 2, 1904, p. 1.

16 Centerville *Daily Citizen*, February 2, 1905, p. 1.

17 Brown, *The Real Billy Sunday*, p. 200; Ellis, *Billy Sunday*, pp. 487–88.

never held a pastorate, and he performed only one marriage ceremony in his life, but his ministerial status was of inestimable help to him. His self-confidence was further bolstered by the receipt of the degree of Doctor of Divinity in 1912 from a small denominational college. It was easier for him to denounce the foibles of D.D.'s when he was one himself.

Sunday's theology had been formulated for him by the workers in the Pacific Garden Mission and by the Bible Class teachers at the Chicago YMCA. It was the same simple evangelicalism that Moody had preached, and from the day of his conversion in 1886 to the day of his death in 1935, Sunday never swerved from the creed of the five points of fundamentalism. The substance of his doctrine was summed up by him in ten words: "With Christ you are saved, without him you are lost." Because of Adam's sin and man's innate propensity for evil, everyone was doomed to hell who did not repent of his sins and accept Christ's substitutionary atonement on faith. Moody had devoted considerable time in his sermons to the informal exegesis of such terms as "Grace," "Repentance," "The Blood," and "Assurance." But Sunday reduced theology to the simple choice of heaven or hell: "You are going to live forever in heaven or you are going to live forever in hell. There's no other place—just the two. It is for you to decide. It's up to you, and you must decide now."[18]

Sometimes, like Moody, he stooped to conquer by telling skeptics that accepting Christ could be considered simply "insurance against hell" and that they ought to get converted "just in case" there was such a place. At other times, he said, "If I positively knew that death was nothing but an eternal sleep, I'd live my life as I am living it for the peace and joy and decency that comes to me now. So it sums up that all God wants is for a man to be decent." It was this approach to salvation which led liberals and Unitarians like Lyman Abbott and John Haynes Holmes to say that at heart Sunday preached simply a religion of morality and ethics even though he called himself a fundamentalist.[19] Sunday described the substitutionary atonement

[18] Boston *Herald,* December 9, 1916, p. 3.

[19] *New York Times,* May 10, 1915, p. 12; Boston *Herald,* December 15, 1916, p. 14. For statements by Abbott and Holmes see The *Outlook,* CXVI (May 16, 1917), p. 98; and the *New York Times,* April 19, 1915, p. 11.

by saying that God had "paid a price" for men's souls by crucifying Christ. To refuse to believe in Christ was "withholding from God what he paid for on the cross," and hence "When you refuse you are not giving God a square deal." [20] He dispensed with inquiry rooms in his meetings, his wife said, "because he made it so simple that there was no need for inquiry rooms." [21] All that a man had to do to obtain forgiveness for sins, the approbation of his fellowmen, and the personal "peace of soul" which came from "accepting Christ" was to "hit the sawdust trail." To hit the trail was to walk down the sawdust-covered aisles of Sunday's tabernacles after his sermon, shake his hand, and sign a decision card. Having signed the card, the penitent was handed a booklet which stated. ". . . by this act of coming forward . . . you are NOW a child of God" and "you have NOW eternal life." [22] This was the theology which Sunday called "the old-time religion of our fathers," and he insisted that unless all Americans accepted this version of Christianity and returned to "the old-fashioned gospel," the nation was doomed.

The pietistic aspect of Sunday's revivalism was evident from the outset of his career. Although he tried to conciliate everyone within a respectable range of moderatism, he declared open war upon what he considered the extremes of lukewarm ecclesiasticism and liberal theology. He denounced all those "time-serving," "hypocritical," "hireling ministers," who gave up the old faith in order to please their liberal parishioners or to get in line with some higher critic. "They've been crying peace. There is no peace. Some people won't come to hear me because they are afraid to hear the truth. They want deodorized, disinfected sermons. They are afraid to be stuck over the edge of the pit and get a smell of the brimstone." In 1903 he said, "Infidelity is rampant and rank unbelief is preached from many a pulpit," and he called for a return to a converted ministry: "There are lots of preachers who don't know Jesus. They know about him, but they don't know him. Experience will do more

20 Ellis, *Billy Sunday,* p. 432.

21 Mrs. Helen A. Sunday to the author in a personal interview, August 23, 1951.

22 This booklet is quoted in Ellis, *Billy Sunday,* p. 312.

than forty million theories." Like Moody, he disowned the theory of the universal brotherhood of man: The doctrine of "the Fatherhood of God and the Brotherhood of Man is the worst rot that ever was dug out of hell and every minister who preaches it is a liar." [23]

He had absolutely no use for the "bastard theory of evolution" nor for any minister who tried to reconcile it with the Bible by the sophism that "evolution is God's way of doing things." When the Rev. Dr. Wallace, a modernist who co-operated with Sunday's Toledo revival in 1911, remonstrated with him privately for being so intolerant on this subject, Sunday went up to where Wallace sat on his platform the next day, shook his fist in Wallace's face, and yelled so the audience could hear, "Stand up there, you bastard evolutionist! Stand up with the atheists and the infidels and the whoremongers and the adulterers and go to hell!" [24] Sunday, like many of his followers, found security and certainty in a world of doubt by relying upon the literal infallibility of the Bible. But this did not mean that he, or they, lacked the American faith in mechanical progress or respect for science. "If by evolution you mean progress," he told a group of two hundred Boston Unitarians, "I go with you. But if by evolution you mean that I came from a monkey, good night!" [25] It was not until the 1920's that Sunday repudiated intellectuals and intellectualism entirely and declared, "Science and religion can never be reconciled." [26]

Sunday's popularity in the years before 1920 was based less upon these negative, backward-looking aspects of his theology than upon his ability to blend this "old-time religion" with the new social consciousness of the progressive movement. "It is as a reformer that Mr. Sunday has warmed the hearts of all who desire better things," said the Rev. W. M. Randles of Wilkes-Barre.[27] Taking his cue from Sam P. Jones and M. B. Williams, Sunday was quick to jump on the bandwagon of civic reform

[23] Jefferson *Bee,* December 24, 1903, p. 5; Ellis, *Billy Sunday,* pp. 196–98; the *Congregationalist* (Boston), May 28, 1913, p. 728.

[24] Quoted by Washington Gladden in "The Trouble with Billy Sunday: Some Grounds for Opposition," the *Congregationalist,* May 29, 1913, p. 728.

[25] Boston *Herald,* November 14, 1916, p. 5.

[26] *New York Times,* December 21, 1925, p. 15.

[27] The *Congregationalist,* April 24, 1913, p. 566.

and moral uplift which lumbered along by fits and starts from 1890 to 1915. As Sunday saw it, a crusade against sin was *ipso facto* a crusade for social reform. Saving souls led to a transformation of society. By 1901 he was advertising his revivals as "civic clean-ups" and "moral reform" movements which would make any town he came to a better place to live in, to bring up children in, to do business in. The headline after his first night in Ottumwa, Iowa, in 1908, read: "W. A SUNDAY USHERS IN 'BIG CLEAN-UP.' Fiery Evangelist in Opening Sermon Tells of Good He Will Accomplish in Ridding Ottumwa of Crime."[28] Sunday delivered two sermons early in each campaign attacking what he called the "social sins" of dancing, card playing, gambling, theater-going and commercial dishonesty. "His caustic criticism of society and the social evils has gained for him in the first two weeks the largest crowds ever seen here except at a genuine circus," said one report in 1901 with unconscious irony.[29]

Far more popular and dramatic, however, than these attacks were his sermons against the saloon. In discussing "the liquor problem" Sunday also touched upon such questions as "the [free] silver bugbear," "municipal reform," "revision of the tariff," and "political corruption." But he always ended by dismissing these as secondary problems growing out of "the damnable liquor traffic." This enabled him, like Sam Jones, to show his awareness of these other problems and express a vague general sympathy for combatting them, but it never required him to face the issues squarely. "A man said, 'I will tell you what is the matter with the country; it's over-production.' You lie; it's under consumption. . . . We have been dumping into the whiskey hole the money that ought to have been spent for flour, beef, and calico, and we haven't the hole filled up yet." Like so many supporters of prohibition in his day, Sunday was convinced that financial panics, depressions, and poverty in general would disappear if the money wasted on alcohol were spent on more useful goods. This would automatically increase production and employment. Prohibition would also solve the problem of capital and labor, for if workingmen spent less

28 Ottumwa *Daily Courier* (Iowa), November 7, 1908, p. 1.
29 Centerville *Daily Citizen,* February 2, 1905, p. 1.

money on booze they would have more money for staples and would not be constantly demanding higher wages and foment-ing trouble when they did not get them. Thus while launching what in his eyes was primarily a moral crusade against personal sin, Sunday posed as a man who was greatly concerned with the fundamental economic and political problems of the times.

In almost every one of his revivals Sunday rallied the forces of prohibition by organizing petitions for anti-saloon referen-dums or by arousing enthusiasm for a referendum about to come up for a vote. Sunday did not, like Finney, try to make temperance an appendage of revivals. In fact, he often seemed to make revivalism an appendage of the prohibition move-ment. In cities where local ordinances against saloons were not being enforced, he helped to organize Law and Order Leagues to put pressure upon the city officials. The Civic Federation which grew directly out of his campaign in Burling-ton, Iowa, in 1905, exerted sufficient pressure upon the mayor of that city to make him enforce the laws for closing the saloons at ten P.M. and all day Sunday and also to prevent gambling in saloons. This did not abolish saloons in Burlington, but it won Sunday immense prestige when newspapers throughout the state of Iowa headlined: "BURLINGTON IS DRY: BILLY SUNDAY HAS MADE GRAVEYARD OUT OF ONCE FAST TOWN." The Burlington *Hawk-Eye* stated that "under the masterful leadership of William A. Sunday" there had been "a veritable revolution in public opinion" in that city regard-ing the saloon. This, said the *Hawk-Eye,* was "a splendid fruit-age of the great religious awakening in Burlington."[30] The prohibitionists in many cities in the years thereafter credited Sunday's revivals with materially promoting the success of their efforts.

As in the case of Sam P. Jones's Toledo revival, however, more perspicacious observers noted that local politicians fre-quently used the muddle-headed emotional fervor of Sunday's "civic reform" movements to hide their nefarious political shenanigans. The Rev. Joseph Fort Newton, describing Sun-day's invitation to Dixon, Illinois in 1903, said, "It was odd

[30] See Des Moines *Register and Leader,* December 2, 1905; Dubuque *Daily Times,* December 27, 1905; and Burlington *Hawk-Eye,* December 20, 1905, p. 7.

to see a putrid political gang so anxious for the people to get a dose of 'old-time religion'; but it would divert attention from the game they were playing. . . ."[31] Sunday, in all innocence, allowed himself to become a pawn in such games. When questioned, he always indignantly declared, "I never allow politics to enter my work." But Brand Whitlock, when he was mayor of Toledo in 1911, said that Sunday was brought to the city by the same combination of naïve religious reformers and astute local business interests and their political henchmen which had brought Sam P. Jones to Toledo to fight Golden Rule Jones. Their purpose, said Whitlock, was "to divert attention" from their own illegal and greedy practices "by pointing out a smaller evil."[32] Sometimes the "smaller evil" included not only saloons but also houses of prostitution. Sunday's moral reform efforts included ringing statements against "bawdy-house keepers" and "white slavers" who ought to be "shot at sunrise" for the protection of American womanhood. His dramatic sermon, given to men only, called "Chickens Come Home To Roost," was a grim exposé of the prevalency of venereal disease and its horrible consequences.

Sunday's early fame as a reformer was matched by the astounding record he achieved as a soul-winner between 1896 and 1906. During this decade he conducted exactly one hundred separate crusades, 90 per cent of them in cities of less than 10,000. Extant figures for his converts in 30 of these cities indicate that they averaged a total of 20 per cent of the population, and it was reported that a high percentage of these joined a church. In some towns the local newspapers listed the name of each person who went forward during the meetings to shake Sunday's hand. Under the solicitous scrutiny of parents and friends, "the converts were applauded with the clapping of hands as they made their way forward and there were few dry eyes in the audience as the news was whispered about that this one or that one had come out."[33] Under these circumstances

[31] Joseph F. Newton, *River of Years* (Philadelphia, 1946), p. 99.

[32] Brand Whitlock, *Forty Years of It* (New York, 1914), pp. 186, 257.

[33] Jefferson *Bee*, January 7, 1904, p. 1. For an analysis of Sunday's impact upon these small towns in the Midwest see McLoughlin, *Billy Sunday*, pp. 198–99, 207.

the local pastors had little difficulty in following up the converts and bringing them into the churches.

As Sunday advanced to larger cities the number of trail-hitters in each campaign grew steadily until it finally reached a peak of 98,264 for one ten-week campaign in New York City. But the proportion of converts to the population of the larger cities steadily decreased. In cities of 30,000 to 50,000 he converted about 15 per cent of the population; in cities of 100,000 to 500,000 it dropped to 9 per cent; in cities of 500,000 or a million it was only about 4 per cent. Nevertheless, 4 per cent of 500,000 was a very sizable figure, and it far outdistanced the totals attained by Chapman, Torrey, Moody, Jones, or Finney. The *New York Times* was fully justified in describing Sunday in its obituary notice as "the greatest high pressure and mass conversion Christian evangel that America or the world has known." [34]

Sunday claimed that during his career he preached to one hundred million persons in the days before radio and public address systems, and that he converted one million of them. Making due allowance for the fact that many of his auditors were repeaters and that all who "hit the trail" were not necessarily converts, the boast may not have been too far wrong. A total of 593,004 persons came forward to shake his hand in his twenty most successful revivals, and he held almost 300 revivals during the course of his forty-year career.

BILLY SUNDAY'S TWENTY MOST SUCCESSFUL REVIVALS

City	Date	Trail-hitters	Free-will Offering
Columbus, Ohio	1912–13	18,137	$ 20,929.58
Wilkes-Barre, Pa.	1913	16,584	23,527.66
Pittsburgh, Pa.	1914	25,797	46,000.00
Scranton, Pa.	1914	16,999	22,398.00
Philadelphia, Pa.	1915	41,724	53,246.80
Paterson, N. J.	1915	18,200	25,000.00
Omaha, Nebraska	1915	17,500	20,000.00
Syracuse, N. Y.	1915	21,155	24,124.00
Trenton, N. J.	1916	19,640	32,358.00
Baltimore, Md.	1916	23,085	40,780.00
Kansas City, Mo.	1916	25,646	32,000.00
Detroit, Michigan	1916	27,109	46,102.00

[34] *New York Times,* November 7, 1935, p. 1.

Boston, Mass.	1916–17	64,484	$ 53,585.00
Buffalo, N. Y.	1917	38,853	42,204.74
New York, N. Y.	1917	98,264	120,490.26
Los Angeles, Calif.	1917	18,824	18,000.00
Washington, D.C.	1918	16,838	16,332.00
Chicago, Illinois	1918	49,165	56,000.00
Norfolk, Virginia	1920	20,000	33,149.28
Cincinnati, Ohio	1921	15,000	30,568.00
TOTALS		593,004	$756,795.32 [35]

Sunday's success was due not only to his personality, his well-organized revival machine, and the skill with which he unconsciously gave vent to the frustrated feelings of the embattled middle class. He succeeded in large part because he seemed able to fulfill a very pressing need in American Protestantism, a need evidenced by decreasing church attendance, increasing church deficits, and a general decline of clerical influence and authority. Sunday thought of himself as, among other things, an efficiency expert for the churches, and he designed his campaigns to appeal to those urban ministers who felt that they were fighting a losing battle against the effects of secularism.

Ray Stannard Baker wrote a book in 1910 called *The Spiritual Unrest* in which he described the anxiety of these ministers and the desperation with which they were "trying various constructive measures for *getting back to the common people*." He pointed out that neither the institutional church system, the slum mission movement, the Emmanual Movement, nor the evangelistic campaigns of Torrey, Chapman, Gypsy Smith, and other urban evangelists had "prevented the steady decline of church influence, nor have they changed as yet the tone of disheartenment with which many Protestant leaders look upon the situation." He quoted the words of Charles Stelzle, one of the leading clerical prophets of gloom: "The church today seems to have arrived at one of the most crucial periods of her history." [36]

Stelzle compiled figures in 1912 to show that while the

[35] These statistics are taken from various newspapers, usually from the leading paper in each city. Since no two newspapers ever gave the same totals even for the same revival, and since Sunday kept no official record, the accuracy of these figures is open to question, but their general import is clear.

[36] Ray S. Baker, *The Spiritual Unrest* (New York, 1910), pp. 55, 88, 90. Baker noted parenthetically that some church leaders in the Midwest were already turning to Sunday for help (p. 262).

Protestant church membership in the United States from 1880 to 1890 had grown almost twice as fast as the population, in the decade from 1900 to 1910 it had barely kept up with the population growth.[37] These figures were even more alarming when analyzed in terms of the city churches. Twenty of the largest cities of the country which were to turn to Sunday for aid in these years showed an average increase in church membership between 1890 and 1916 of only 2.5 per cent, while the churches of the nation as a whole increased by over twice that amount in the same period. Furthermore, in one-third of these 20 cities the proportion of Protestant church members had actually declined.[38] Some blamed this entirely upon the increasing proportion of Catholic and Jewish immigrants, but in most American cities a sizeable part of the urban population was made up of native-born Americans with evangelical backgrounds who had trekked from the countryside into the city to make their way up in the world. The churches could not even reach these obvious sources for membership. In spite of the increasing size of the urban population the Protestant churches in city after city moved uptown or out into the suburbs, half following and half leading their well-to-do church members in the exodus. "Within recent years," said Stelzle in 1910, "forty Protestant churches moved out of the district below Twentieth Street in New York city while 300,000 people moved in." The same had happened in other cities. Obviously, Stelzle announced, "the church has sounded a dismal retreat in the face of the greatest opportunity which has ever come to her."[39]

But this often-discussed "problem of the downtown church" was not, as Baker and Stelzle implied, simply a failure of proselyting nerve. It was also a question of money. Between the years 1906 and 1916 the total debt on church property in the United States increased 53 per cent, and in the cities with populations of 50,000 to 100,000 it increased 84 per cent. Even if a minister persuaded his trustees not to move the church uptown or out to the suburbs, even if he succeeded by various

37 Charles Stelzle, *American Social and Religious Conditions* (New York, 1912), p. 192.

38 For a chart giving these statistics see McLoughlin, *Billy Sunday,* p. 191.

39 Quoted in R. S. Baker, *Spiritual Unrest,* p. 55.

methods in bringing the downtown working class people into his church, he found it almost impossible to raise the money to pay for the increased operational costs. Suburban or uptown churches which tried to do their duty toward "the masses" by supporting a downtown mission or institutional chapel found that the cost of maintaining two establishments in the face of decreasing interest in missionary activity among middle-class church members raised the costs for the few zealous Christians to prohibitive heights. The average conscientious minister was left in a quandary. Frustrated in his desire to spread the gospel and help the poor, unable to exert any real spiritual influence over those who were technically members of his church, he flirted for a time with the social gospel ideas only to find himself denounced by his wealthy trustees for leaning toward socialism. As a result the only possible solution seemed to be to rely upon the old system of mass evangelism and hope that somehow it could be made workable. Hence the continued support, year after year, for the revival campaigns of a constant procession of professional evangelists. In each case the ministers tried to believe that these revivals would do some good and then had to admit, after they had passed, that their problems were no nearer solution. In 1910, a year after Chapman's most spectacular and well-organized simultaneous campaign in Boston, the Rev. C. M. Gallup addressed the Massachusetts Ministers' Association on "Our Problem Today" and said, "The prevailing forms of evangelism are not as effective as they used to be." Few evangelists could do "more than scratch the surface of the life of the cities." Yet one of Gallup's proposals for reaching the "great masses of people apathetic to the church" was to find a man like Charles Finney who could be both "scholarly and evangelistic." "For such a leader the church is waiting." [40] Five years later the ministers of Boston eagerly invited Billy Sunday to their city.

There was some hesitancy at first on the part of urban ministers, particularly in the East, to put themselves in the hands of a man who was called "the baseball evangelist" and whose sensationalism went far beyond anything yet seen in modern revivalism. But the adjustment was only a matter of time.

[40] Clarence M. Gallup, "The Realism of Jesus and Our Problem Today," *Watchman-Examiner* (Baptist, Boston), December 29, 1910, p. 9.

Magazines like the Baptist *Watchman-Examiner,* which in 1907 described Sunday as a preacher who "outrages every accepted canon of religious worship," declared in 1914 that he was "sent of God." The Rev. A. E. Isaac of Columbus, Ohio, typified many urban ministers when he wrote in 1913, "Three years ago when asked what I thought of Billy Sunday, I said I had little use for him and believed that he was only a cheap sensationalist." Then he heard Sunday speak and decided to investigate him further. "I was thoroughly convinced that God was working through him for the salvation of souls."[41] When Sunday came to Columbus in 1912 and brought 18,137 persons down the aisles as converts, Isaac was firmly convinced that Sunday was the leader the church needed. A member of the ministerial association of Syracuse explained that the ministers who invited Sunday to that city in 1915 "were anxious, over-anxious, for anyone who could reach and win the great outside multitude and bring them into the churches." "They wanted and needed, and they still need, a great increase in financial resources," and "one of the reiterated arguments of the managers of Mr. Sunday's campaign has been this promise of increased pew holders and financial prosperity."[42]

Ministers whose church membership had increased as a result of a Sunday campaign wrote glowing reports of their newfound prosperity which were widely published in religious journals. One such minister claimed that Sunday's revival in his city "brought his church an addition of 305 members . . . a beautiful $20,000 home . . . increase of $600 in salary . . . two weeks added to his vacation." Others told of new churches being erected, of enlarged Bible classes, and of old mortgages paid off, all because of the new zeal imparted by Sunday's preaching.[43] It was no wonder that some discouraged ministers, explaining their support for a man whose views they did not agree with, used the terms that the Rev. Pearse Pinch had used speaking to a reporter for the *American Magazine:* "Why, my dear sir, the man has trampled all over me and my theology. He has kicked my teachings up and down that platform like a

[41] *Watchman-Examiner,* April 10, 1913, p. 12.

[42] Frederick W. Betts, *Billy Sunday: The Man and Method* (Boston, 1916), pp. 9, 10, 11.

[43] See *Watchman-Examiner,* September 7, 1916, p. 1136; The *Congregationalist,* April 24, 1913, p. 564.

football. He has outraged every ideal I have had regarding my sacred profession. But what does that count against the results he has accomplished? My congregation will be increased by hundreds." [44]

Statistically the evidence was certainly overwhelming that Sunday's revivals "produced results"; or, as one minister put it, "He can deliver the goods." Year in and year out in city after city Sunday's revival organization produced a constant stream of individuals who walked down the sawdust-covered aisles of his tabernacles to shake his hand. There was a great deal of admiration for the man and the system that could guarantee these results. Most ministers apparently agreed with Moody that it did not matter how you got a man to Christ as long as you got him there.

Though Sunday's revival techniques were principally refinements of those of his predecessors in the profession, he carried modern revivalism to a new peak of mechanical efficiency. He claimed to base his ideas upon those of Finney and often quoted Finney's *Lectures on Revivals* in defense of his new measures, but he more frequently compared his techniques with those used by big business. "I am not only a preacher but [a] businessman," he said in one of his sermons. "I endeavor [to] bring: 1. System [and] organization; 2. Business principles; 3. Common sense" into revival work.[45] According to the *New York Times*, "Sunday and his helpers made it clear that they were going after souls as a successful commercial corporation goes after sales." [46] One professor of economics ranked the efficiency of Sunday's

[44] Lindsay Denison, "The Rev. Billy Sunday and His War on the Devil," *American Magazine*, LXIV (September, 1907), 454–55. From a slightly different angle the Rev. George A. Coe of Union Theological Seminary offered the following explanation of why Sunday's revivals found support among liberals as well as among moderates and conservatives. "Another contributing factor is the fact that so many ministers are at their wits' end with regard to religion as an effective community force. Said one of them, 'I do not accept Sunday's theology, and the families of my church will not accept his standards of Christian living, but this city needs to be stirred up.' The motive here is not shallow, for the medicine is bitter. . . ." "Why Do Ministers Want Billy Sunday?" The *Congregationalist*, September 16, 1915, pp. 378 ff.

[45] Quoted from the outline of Sunday's "Sermon to Businessmen," among the Sunday papers, Winona Lake, Indiana. Since the death of the evangelist's widow, some of the papers have been transferred to the Winona Lake Christian Assembly, Inc., Winona Lake, Indiana.

[46] *New York Times*, April 10, 1917, p. 22.

organization with that of the Standard Oil Company, the United States Steel Company, and the National Cash Register Company.[47]

The heart of Sunday's revival corporation was "the Sunday Party," a corps of more than twenty experts, each of whom specialized in some particular aspect of revivalism and to whom he delegated authority to direct that aspect of the revival's activities. He had started this organization in 1900 by hiring a chorister to conduct the choirs and sing solos. That same year his wife began to accompany him and to act as his business manager. In 1904 he hired an advance agent to pave the way for him, and to act as night watchman and custodian of the wooden tabernacles which were built for him in each city. By 1906 he found it necessary to hire a research assistant to help him in gathering material for new sermons, and then he thought it would be advantageous to employ a person who would help the churches which cooperated with him to organize Bible classes. From then on the party grew by leaps and bounds. He hired a soloist to assist his chorister and a pianist to assist the soloist. He acquired a publicity manager to feed news stories to the press, and a private secretary to handle his mail. Other assistants became the director of men's work, the director of businesswomen's work, the director of students' work, and the reservation secretary. He even hired a personal masseur, a cook, a housekeeper, and a man to supervise the building of the tabernacles. Most of the directors had assistant directors. The aggregate of salaries for this staff became so large by 1908 that Sunday stipulated that the local committees should include one-third to one-half their pay as part of the local expense of the campaign.

One of the most important members of this staff was Homer Alvin Rodeheaver, choir leader, soloist, trombonist, and expert master of ceremonies. "Rody" joined the Sunday Party in 1910 after five years as chorister for W. E. Biederwolf. Though he was not a graduate of the Moody Bible Institute, Rodeheaver used all the up-to-date techniques developed by Alexander. He was the first gospel singer to make a name for himself on phonograph records, and he not only went into the hymnbook

[47] See Homer A. Rodeheaver, *Twenty Years with Billy Sunday* (Winona Lake, 1936), p. 119.

publishing business, but he began his own record manufacturing company as a sideline. As Sunday's chorister for twenty years, Rodeheaver's suave, polished geniality provided a valuable complement to Sunday's slangy virility. One admiring observer wrote, "Rody is one of the greatest adjuncts a revivalist ever had. His musical ability, his sense of humor, his southern accent, his ability to catch the feeling of the crowd, and his sympathetic smile . . . make him as appealing a figure on the platform as Bryan was in the freshness of his career."[48] Like Alexander, Rodeheaver encouraged audience participation in a half-hour song service preceding each sermon and introduced many new and lively tunes to revivalism, a few of which he wrote himself. Among the most popular songs of the Sunday revivals were "Brighten the Corner," "If Your Heart Keeps Right," "Since Jesus Came into My Heart," "I Walk with the King, Hallelujah," "The Old Fashioned Meetings," "The World Is Bright, the World Is Good," "Everyone Ought To Love Jesus," and "De Brewer's Big Horses." The last was a temperance song sung in Negro dialect.

Rodeheaver always instructed his huge choirs of 2000 voices to "go at it like selling goods," and the two pianists who accompanied the singing "hustled along with a swing" in which, said a reporter, "there is just a hint of syncopation."[49] On the whole there was little to differentiate the musical aspects of Sunday's meetings from those of his immediate predecessors, and many of the Sankey hymns were still popular with the crowds. A more optimistic tone perhaps, less emphasis on doctrinal hymns, and a larger number of temperance or militant Christian songs merely added to the increasingly secular aspect of revivalism.

Next to Rodeheaver the most important member of the Sunday Party was the advance man. This post was held in turn by I. E. Honeywell, L. K. Peacock, John W. Welch, E. H. Emett, James E. Walker, Albert Peterson, Harry D. Clarke, and Willis G. Haymaker. The advance man was the key figure in scheduling and preparing for a revival. He often made the initial contact with those laymen and ministers who were open to the idea of having Sunday come to their city. He helped them to

48 Boston *Herald,* November 19, 1916, editorial section, p. 1.
49 Providence *News,* September 23, 1918, p. 4.

swing the other ministers and business leaders into line and made the preliminary arrangements for the tabernacle site, the renting of a house in which the Sunday Party stayed, the publicity, the raising of the "guarantee fund" to pay for the initial expenses, and the setting up of the local committees to handle the various phases of the revival work.[50] The invitation to Sunday was often tendered two or three years before he could fit a city into his schedule. The preliminary work for a campaign in a large city began six months to a year before the opening of a revival.

Sunday's revivals lasted from six to ten weeks, depending upon the size of the city, and they cost from $30,000 to $200,000, excluding the free-will offering for Sunday. As in Moody's campaigns, the chief expense was always for the tabernacles, but unlike Moody, Sunday advised his local committees to incorporate themselves according to the laws of the state in order that no individual would be held responsible should the meetings go bankrupt—a contingency which never arose. The audited expense account for Sunday's revival in Philadelphia illustrated the allocation of the expense money:

Repayment of sundry loans	$17,155.00
Expenses of visiting speakers	6,014.20
Tabernacle construction	24,750.35
Tabernacle maintenance	6,024.94
Office expenses (rent, clerk-hire, telephone, stationery, postage, supplies)	8,859.98
Traveling expenses and a proportion of the salaries of the Sunday Party	7,187.50
Rent and maintenance of the house-headquarters for the Sunday Party	4,372.84
Committee expenses	6,819.33
Paid out to various charitable institutions from tabernacle collections	16,224.71
Total expenditures	$97,408.85

All but $12,000 of the receipts to pay these expenses came from tabernacle collections, but prior to the campaign $50,000 in pledges was raised in order to provide a basis upon which to

[50] For an example of the advance man's use of high-pressure techniques in rounding up support among reluctant ministers see the *Congregationalist*, May 22, 1913, p. 696.

raise the $17,155 in loans from which the initial expenditures were made.[51]

Sunday received far better support from the nation's leading businessmen than any revivalist since Moody. Among his more important backers were John Wanamaker, A. J. Drexel-Biddle, John D. Rockefeller, Jr., S. S. Kresge, Elbert H. Gary, Frank Munsey, George W. Perkins, Louis F. Swift, Henry Clay Frick, J. Ogden Armour, Henry A. Stimson, Josephus Daniels, and John M. Studebaker. Nor did Sunday ever have much trouble in rounding up ministerial support for his revivals. Except for the most liberal social gospelers there was scarcely a distinguished evangelical clergyman in the country who did not go out of his way to associate himself with one or another of Sunday's campaigns.[52]

The number of church members who volunteered to do the menial chores of Sunday's campaigns was estimated at 50,000 in New York and 20,000 to 30,000 in other large cities. These included as many as 8000 who volunteered for choir singing, 2000 ushers, 700 secretaries (to help fill out decision cards), 5000 personal workers (to deal with anxious inquirers after the sermons), 200 doorkeepers, 1000 women to help organize the businesswomen of the city, 1000 women to hold meetings in hospitals, hotels, business places, 500 women to manage the noon lunches for businesswomen, 500 women to care for children under four at the tabernacle nursery, and 5000 to 10,000 persons willing to organize "cottage prayer meetings" twice each week in their homes.

All of this preparatory work led up to the opening meeting of the campaign, which always took place on a Sunday morning. One of Sunday's prime stipulations was that all the co-operating churches must agree to shut their churches for the duration of the campaign. This helped to fill the 15,000 to 20,000 seats in the tabernacles three times each Sunday and twice each weekday. But closing the churches was not in itself enough to assure continuous crowds. For this a delegation system was carefully developed by Sunday and his team of experts. Each member of the Sunday party was expected to extend the

[51] From the official *Report of the Executive Committee in Charge of Sunday Campaign* (Philadelphia, 1915).

[52] For the opposition of Washington Gladden see "The Trouble About Billy Sunday," *loc. cit.*, p. 728.

revival's impact to a certain segment of the population: Sunday himself held "parlor meetings" in the homes of the wealthy; the director of men's work held meetings in shops and factories to reach the workingmen; the director of business-women's work held meetings in office buildings, department stores, telephone exchanges, laundries and hotels; the directors of students' and children's work met with the Boy and Girl Scouts, the Sunday school classes, the high school students, college Christian associations, YMCA's, YWCA's, and church young people's groups. Each of Sunday's directors made arrangements for those he contacted to come in groups to the tabernacle, where on certain nights large blocks of seats were reserved for them. Every campaign had a businesswomen's night, a Bible class night, a businessmen's night, a students' night, and children's meetings on Saturday afternoons. In addition, contact was made with all local clubs, lodges, civic groups, church societies, veterans' organizations, and fraternal orders. Sunday received permission to speak at the local high schools and colleges in almost every city. A special reservation secretary was ready to grant a block of seats to any group whatever which called up in advance and requested them. Every night in the campaign there were from twenty to fifty delegations on hand, some of them as large as 2000 to 3000, all in reserved seats. Members of the cooperating churches usually reserved seats in groups in order to be sure of finding space, for the general public was admitted only at the last minute to fill such seats around the perimeter of the tabernacle as were left after the delegations were seated. Saturday nights were "out-of-towners" nights, and there were evenings devoted to "old folks," city employees, and to those whose ancestry was Scandinavian, German, Scottish, and Welsh.

The delegation system not only served to reach all the various strata of the cities but it also gave variety and publicity to the meetings. Furthermore, it provided a core of persons with a common outlook upon which Sunday could play in making his appeals for conversion. Often, when giving his "invitation," Sunday would mention some of the delegations by name and say, "Come on, you Masons," "Come on Epworth Leaguers, Christian Endeavorers, everybody. What'll you do?" or "Come on, Swedes; the Swedes have never been cowards yet. So come on." He would wave a green lantern when railroad employees were present and call, "Come on, Boston and Maine," or "Come on, Erie." He waved a Scottish flag on Scotch-Night and cried, "Come on, Scotchmen. Show some of the grit of Wallace and Bruce." By calling on the group by name he hoped to appeal to its collective pride so that if one or two went forward the whole delegation would feel impelled to follow.

A large measure of Sunday's success in producing trail-hitters was due to the manner in which his magnetic personality expressed itself through his sermons. All of them were dramatic and vivid. Even without the use of a microphone and loudspeaker he could make twenty thousand persons follow his address and keep their eyes fastened on him from beginning to end. He did this in part with his voice, a peculiarly rasping and hoarse voice but one which was capable of a wide range of expression. "Seldom does he lower his voice for effect," wrote one reporter, "but often he lingers on a word or a syllable, his tone rising in pitch almost to a falsetto and resulting in a wail that penetrates to the air outside the building. It is weird, but effective." He spoke at the rate of three hundred words per minute, but his sentences were short and simple, and he acted out every word he uttered so that those who did not hear it could see it. Like any experienced showman he knew how to draw laughter or applause, how to wait for it, and when to repeat a line or vary it slightly a second time in order to wring the full response from it.

The drama of the performance was heightened by his pounding the pulpit, standing on a chair, swinging a chair over his head, sliding, jumping, falling, staggering, whirling, and even doing handsprings on the 30 foot platform. At the conclusion of his more dramatic sermons he would jump on top of the pulpit and vigorously wave an American flag. "Just watching these movements is apt to be exciting for the spectator." Heywood Broun, the drama critic of the New York *Tribune,* compared Sunday to the ebullient George M. Cohan and concluded, "George Cohan has neither the punch nor the pace of Billy Sunday. . . . It is true that Cohan waved the flag first, but Billy Sunday has waved it harder. . . . It is in language that the superiority of Sunday is most evident. . . . All in all we believe that Sunday has more of the dramatic instinct than Cohan." [53]

Sunday, like Sam P. Jones, claimed to preach a masculine, aggressive, muscular Christianity. No one, "not even Mr. Roosevelt himself," said one writer, "has insisted so much on his personal, militant masculinity." Sunday told his audiences that he admired "the man who has real, rich, red blood in his veins instead of pink tea and ice water." After pointing out that "I'm still pretty handy with my dukes" he would declare that Jesus "was no dough-faced, lick-spittle proposition. Jesus was the greatest scrapper that ever lived." The conclusion was patent: "Let me tell you, the manliest man is the man who will acknowledge Jesus Christ." [54]

The drama and excitement of Sunday's technique was matched by the amount of laughter and cheering which took place. Sunday, like Jones, spent many of his summers (the off-season for revival work) touring the chautauqua circuits. There came to be little difference between his speeches to the secular, fee-paying chautauqua customers and the sermons he delivered to the religious revival congregations. He made a conscious effort to dissociate his meetings from the sentimentalism which characterized Moody's: "I don't appeal to your handkerchiefs," he said. "I haven't told you of any deathbed scenes, but I try to show you that religion is the most reasonable thing in the world." [55] Jokes, slang, mimicry, and hyphenated catalogs of expletives made up a large part of his repertoire. Telling of the death of Commodore Vanderbilt, Sunday said a man asked at the time, "How much did he leave?" "He left it all. Naked you came into this world and naked you will crawl out of it." He ridiculed hypocritical churchgoers by saying, "You listen to the sermon, pick up the hymn book, and sing, 'Jesus paid it all' when you have debts that are outlawed. He doesn't pay them. He doesn't pay for that hat or that set of false teeth you are wearing. You get up and sing, 'I am standing on the solid rock'—you are probably standing on a pair of shoes you haven't

[53] Quoted in "Dramatizing Billy Sunday," *Literary Digest,* LI (October 2, 1915), 713.

[54] Ellis, *Billy Sunday,* pp. 204, 205; *The Life and Labors of Rev. William A. (Billy) Sunday* (Herman-Poole Co., Decatur, Illinois, 1908), p. 19.

[55] *Life and Labors of Rev. William A. (Billy) Sunday,* pp. 151, 306–7.

paid for yet." He rattled off his denunciations of "those ossified, petrified, mildewed, dyed-in-the-wool, stamped-in-the-cork, blown-in-the-bottle, horizontal, perpendicular Presbyterians" and the "red-nosed, buttermilk-eyed, beetle-browed, peanut-brained, stall-fed, old saloon keeper" and received with a broad grin the applause he expected at the end of his breath.

He paraphrased Bible stories to the great delight of his audiences: David "decided to go out and tell Goliath where to head in. So Saul said, 'You'd better take my armor and sword.' David put them on, but he felt like a fellow with a hand-me-down suit about four times too big for him, so he took them off and went down to the brook and picked up a half dozen stones. He put one of them in his sling, threw it, and socked Goliath in the coco between the lamps, and he went down for the count." In another sermon, after quoting the description of Christ's transfiguration, "And as he prayed the fashion of his countenance was altered," Sunday turned to the audience and said, "Ladies, do you want to look pretty? If some of you women would spend less on dope and cold cream and get down on your knees and pray, God would make you prettier." [56]

To the fastidious this was sheer blasphemy. The president of Princeton University refused to permit Sunday to speak on the campus because of these breaches in taste. Speaking for President Hibben, Dean West of the Princeton Graduate School said, "No decent person can read these quotations without shame; in the name of decency and of the purity and sanctity of our Christian faith, Princeton University positively refuses to approve of Mr. Sunday's performance as suitable for the edification of our students." But Princeton was almost the only college campus in the nation where he was not asked to speak. President W. H. P. Faunce of Brown University said of him, "God bless any man who, by any method, can reach the hearts of men." The administrators of Pennsylvania University said, "He has a special message which deeply stirs many who are in need of moral stimulation and the powerful incentive of religion." [57]

[56] Ellis, *Billy Sunday,* pp. 252, 282.

[57] Dean West was quoted in the *Truth Seeker* (New York), April 24, 1915, p. 261; Faunce in the Providence *Journal,* September 28, 1918, p. 2. For the view of the Pennsylvania administrators see *Old Penn Weekly* XII (March 28, 1915), 789.

Sunday justified his slang with the explanation, "I want to reach the people so I use the people's language." Many church leaders seemed to think that this was the language of the masses whom they wanted so much to reach. A leading banker in Columbus admitted, for example, that though Sunday's sermons "seemed coarse and vulgar to me," they undoubtedly "gave him a hold upon the imaginations and consciences of the masses which a more refined and scholarly preacher could not obtain." Bishop Joseph F. Berry, senior bishop of the Methodist-Episcopal Church (North) said that Sunday would reach "the man in the street—the man whom the average preacher cannot persuade to enter his sanctuary." And John D. Rockefeller, Jr., gave as his reason for supporting Sunday, "Our churches do not lay hold of the masses of the people. If he can reach them there is just one place for me, and that is at his back." [58]

But as in the case of all preceding professional evangelists who achieved national fame, Sunday's audiences were "conspicuously middle class. . . . Simple, common-sense, practical, domestic America." A Philadelphia minister reported happily, "There was nothing in the meetings to attract undesirable citizens." The Rev. W. N. Walker of Scranton, describing the trail-hitters, said, "Only a small percentage belong to the jetsam and flotsam of society. The great majority live in comfortable homes. They have always been valuable members of society." Even after Sunday's famous "booze sermon" it was remarked that those who came forward to renounce liquor and to follow Christ "were not 'down-and-outers'; they were not booze-soaked men; they were not feeble-minded old men or sobbing little boys. They were fine, bright men, most of them between twenty-five and forty." Such men would, of course, have been valuable additions to the churches, but unfortunately almost all of them were church members already.[59]

A year after the Philadelphia revival of 1915, which Sunday considered his most successful campaign, a local minister who had cooperated with it reported that only 12,000 of the 41,000 trail-hitters joined a church and that only 5000 of these "were confessions for the first time." Moreover, he continued,

[58] *Watchman-Examiner,* January 22, 1914, p. 18; *Zion's Herald,* January 20, 1915, p. 69; *New York Times,* May 20, 1916, p. 10.

[59] See *New Republic,* March 20, 1915, p. 173; *Zion's Herald,* July 3, 1918, p. 846; *Watchman-Examiner,* May 14, 1914, p. 151; and January 21, 1915, p. 4.

"I gather from many pastors that most of the 7000 who were revived have slipped back into the world. Many of the 5000 did not 'stick' and those who are still in the churches are of a wandering disposition and not very loyal to their pastors."[60] Six months after the New York revival, which Sunday considered his second most successful campaign, one of its most avid supporters declared, "The Billy Sunday meetings in New York were a failure when counted in terms of the additions to the church life."[61] A statistical survey of the cooperating New York churches disclosed that "none of the churches received large accessions of new members, the largest numbers uniting with the churches of which the committee had been able to learn are as follows: Fort Washington Presbyterian Church, forty-eight; another church, nineteen; still another, twenty-five." The Chicago correspondent of *Zion's Herald* reported after Sunday closed there, ". . . that there is general disappointment over this campaign is an open secret . . . for such vast expenditure and such large publicity and blowing of trumpets, the results are entirely unjustifiable."[62]

Sunday obviously was not able to make the impression upon the big cities that he had made in the rural Midwest in terms of new church members. Even in those urban churches where a large number of accessions was reported as a result of a Sunday revival, statistical analysis covering the five years before the revival and the five years afterward show that the immediate increase was usually counterbalanced by a precipitous decline thereafter. Wanamaker's Bethany Presbyterian Church in Philadelphia, for example, had 3549 members the year before Sunday's revival, 3796 members at the end of the revival year, and only 1945 members five years later. Cortland Myers' Tremont Temple in Boston had 2507 members the year before the revival, 3046 the year after, and only 2783 five years later. The First Methodist church of the Rev. H. I. Rasmus in Spokane reported 1500 members the year before Sunday came, 1800 the

[60] *Watchman-Examiner,* June 15, 1916, p. 177.

[61] Curtis Lee Laws in the *Watchman-Examiner,* January 3, 1918, p. 3. Ten years after Sunday's New York revival the Rev. Charles L. Goodell, Secretary of the Commission on Evangelism of the Federal Council of Churches, reported, "only 200 church members could be traced to the Sunday meetings." *Literary Digest,* XCV (October 8, 1927), p. 32.

[62] *Watchman-Examiner,* December 20, 1917, p. 1648; *Zion's Herald,* July 3, 1918, p. 846.

year after the revival, and 701 members five years later. The Rev. T. M. Maguire's Ruggles Street Baptist Church in Boston gained 201 members the year of Sunday's revival but five years later had 632 fewer members than it had the year before Sunday came to Boston.[63]

There were, of course, churches which benefited from Sunday's work and which did not suffer any relapse afterward. Joseph Vance's First Presbyterian Church in Detroit grew steadily from 1222 members five years before the revival to 1936 five years after. James L. Gordon's First Congregational Church in Washington, D.C., grew from 1125 members in 1912 to 1419 by 1922. Maitland Alexander's Presbyterian Church in Pittsburgh gained 401 members the year of Sunday's revival and gained 460 in the next five years, but except for the revival year the general rate of growth was the same for the years following the revival as for the five years preceding it. A. Z. Conrad's Park Street Church in Boston neither increased nor decreased its steady rate of growth through the five years on either side of the revival or during the year of the revival.

It would probably be as unfair to blame Sunday for the decreases in membership of a particular church as it would be inaccurate to praise him for the increases. In general the downtown churches which profited from his campaigns were already among the more vigorous and important churches in the city. If they took advantage of the revival and continued to gain afterward, their aggressive pastors deserved as much of the credit as Sunday. If a church declined it was not necessarily a sign of relapse from the revival, for countless other causes could contribute to it, such as the death or removal of a popular pastor, a move uptown, or a general shift in the city's population or commercial activity which changed the neighborhood in which the church was situated.[64] About the only significant conclusion that can be drawn from statistical analysis of Sunday's big city revivals from 1906 to 1918 is that they did not seriously

[63] These statistics and those below are taken from the official yearly reports of the denominations concerned.

[64] It is worth noting, however, that Dr. F. H. Laflamme, field secretary of the New York Church Federation of evangelical churches, said in 1928 that after investigating the persons who joined a church after hitting the trail at one of Sunday's meetings, "We find that, taking it on a six-months basis, eighty per cent of Mr. Sunday's conversions relapse. . . ." Quoted in Grover C. Loud, *Evangelized America,* p. 364.

alter the over-all picture one way or the other. The downtown churches continued in a precarious position; the suburban churches continued to grow in membership though not in attendance figures; and the masses, the lower classes, continued to be indifferent, if not hostile, to the regular evangelical churches.

Sunday himself seemed to have no particular illusions about his ability to reach the masses. "I am a halfway house," he said, "between the brownstone church and the Salvation Army. They are both needed and so is the halfway house."[65] The brownstone church symbolized the churches of the well-to-do; the Salvation Army, the church of the poor. Sunday reached those in between. Occasionally delegations of members of the AF of L unions or the foremen and superintendents of some shop might attend Sunday's meetings, but the real "masses," the blue-collar factory hands or manual laborers who were paid by the hour and who in most cases, scarcely spoke or understood English, never turned up. And if they had, they would scarcely have appreciated Sunday's approach to their problems.

Sunday's principal concern, however, was not with the lower classes but with those whom he considered the lifeblood of the country, the country-bred, evangelically oriented, native-born Americans who through piety and hard work would rise to the top. His revivals were the union picnics and Tammany rallies of the white-collar workers. His sermons were the banners which proclaimed the middle-class slogans of "Thrift, Sobriety, Piety, and Hard Work," "Decency and Morality," "Individualism and Opportunity," "Stability and Order." But Sunday faced a difficult, if not impossible, task in preaching his nineteenth-century small-town standards to the social climbing urban dwellers of the twentieth century. In preaching to the younger generation he seemed embarrassed by his old-fashioned views of social behavior and adopted a tone of mock indignation which blunted their force: "Let me tell you, sister, when I see you smoking a cigarette, I don't want to know anything about you. I've got your number." Or, "When a girl comes into church with skirts six inches above her shoe-tops a man cannot keep his mind on prayer meeting." Or, "A young man

[65] Ellis, *Billy Sunday*, p. 201.

would not come to see a girl of mine in the parlor unless I had a hole cut in the ceiling with a Gatling gun trained through it." [66]

Sunday's orthodox fundamentalism, which he euphemistically called "progressive orthodoxy" or "positive Christianity," also had to yield somewhat to modern tendencies, although his audiences always applauded when he stated that he believed the Bible was the word of God from cover to cover. Hell and heaven, he explained, need not be taken literally: "It doesn't make any difference whether the gold in the streets in heaven is literal or not. . . . God said 'streets of gold' in order to convey to us the highest ideals our minds could conceive of beauty." The devil was not so much a person as the temptation to do wrong: "If there is no devil why do you cuss instead of pray? Why do you lie, instead of telling the truth?" And even divine miracles were no longer possible. God did not strike individuals dead for opposing revivals as he had in Finney's day because God obeyed natural law: "God doesn't throw the universe out of gear to stop and punish one sinner." In a desperate effort to make the Bible seem reasonable to young men who had studied or were studying social Darwinism and evolutionary biology in high schools and colleges, he defended the miracle of the Virgin Birth in terms of parthenogenesis: "In the lower orders of animal life a sexless existence is noted, among the bees for example. If there, why is it thought impossible that a virgin should conceive of the Holy Ghost and give us God's son?" [67]

But the most serious departure from the old ways in Sunday's preaching was the apparent nonchalance with which he equated salvation with decency, patriotism, and manliness, and the way he played down the necessity for any personal crisis experience. "What I want and preach is the fact that a man can be converted without any fuss." [68] Like Moody, he discountenanced any exhibition of excitement or hysteria during his meetings. Persons who shouted "Hallelujah" or "Amen" were

[66] Boston *Herald,* November 13, 1916, pp. 3, 4; Providence *News,* September 23, 1918, p. 4.

[67] See Ellis, *Billy Sunday,* pp. 182, 399; Boston *Herald,* December 22, 1916, p. 4; *Illinois State Register,* March 1, 1909, p. 3.

[68] Ellis, *Billy Sunday,* p. 151.

at first told, "Two can't windjam at once, brother; let me do it." If they persisted, the ushers were instructed to throw them out. Sunday wanted a well-ordered mass response and not any individual communions with the Holy Spirit. He did not deny that the Holy Spirit could transform a drunken bum to a stalwart saint in the twinkling of an eye, but unlike Moody and Finney, he did not think this required anguished prayer and contrition in an inquiry room. It could be done with a simple shake of the hand and a firm resolution to do better.

Sunday fell into this Pelagianism because it was not the drunken bums at whom his services were aimed. Like all professional revivalists his primary intention was to make the average, respectable citizen give up his bad habits, profess his belief in the fundamentals, and pledge himself to join a church. In Sunday's eyes this was not difficult, because the average man was not such a bad fellow at heart. "Multitudes of men live good, honest, upright, moral lives. They will not have much to change to become a Christian." As Sunday saw religion, it was merely "a question of whether you are interested in decency." "A man will be a Christian if he is decent and if he is not a Christian he forfeits any claim to decency." Sunday's invitations to come forward after his sermons were often so loosely phrased as to lack any real religious content. "Do you believe it's right and manly to be a Christian? Then come on down. If you don't, stay where you are." Or, "I want the inspiration of taking the hand of every fellow who says 'I'm with you for Jesus Christ and for truth.' Come on. You've been mighty fine tonight." Or, "Come on down and take my hand against booze, for Jesus Christ, for your flag." [69]

It was not surprising that observers saw more smiles than tears among the trail-hitters. After all, said Sunday, "God made this world for us to have a good time in." [70] His faith in the innate goodness of most men may have been inconsistent with his view that "this sin-soaked world is going to hell so fast it is breaking the speed limit" and his doctrine that "there can

[69] *Life and Labors of Rev. William A. (Billy) Sunday,* pp. 33, 324; Boston *Herald,* November 29, 1916, p. 8; December 11, p. 12; January 17, 1917, p. 2. *Watchman-Examiner,* May 17, 1917, pp. 629–30.

[70] Boston *Herald,* January 19, 1917, p. 9.

be no millennium til Jesus comes," but it jibed perfectly with his patriotic belief in the American dream.[71]

"We are citizens of the greatest country in the world and we will admit it," he said. The discovery of America ranked in his mind with the birth of Christ as one of the four greatest events in history.[72] He was convinced that America was still the land of opportunity for any man with push, tact, and character. His sermons, like Moody's, were filled with the platitudes of Poor Richard and the success myth, slightly modified by evangelical trappings. "Christianity is your character and character is your capital." Like Russell H. Conwell, he maintained that "following Christ you may find a gold mine of ability that you never dreamed of possessing." "It pays to serve God." "I never saw a Christian hitting the ties and panhandling; I never saw a Christian that was a hobo. . . . They that trust in the Lord do not want for anything." In his sermons "The Forces That Win," "Hot Cakes off the Griddle," and "How To Be a Man," Sunday denied that large scale industrialism and business nepotism made it any more difficult for a young man to rise from office boy to corporation president in the twentieth century than it had been in the nineteenth. "Anyone who says this a rich man's country lies. It's a hellish life. Everybody has a show." "Everybody can win out if you make up your mind to do it." [73] The vociferousness of these protests seemed to indicate that he and his audiences were trying to prove by loud reiteration what they had begun to doubt in their hearts.

The core of Sunday's appeal to the middle class was his two-pronged attack upon big business and radical labor in the name of the old principles of free enterprise and rugged individualism. Taken by themselves, some of his statements against malefactors of great wealth were as forceful as any made by a true

[71] *New York Times,* April 5, 1915, p. 4; and Boston *Herald,* December 14, 1916, p. 4. His sermon on the Second Coming, which he delivered once in each campaign, presented the orthodox fundamentalist view: "Many think the millennium will come gradually by everybody getting better but the Bible doesn't teach any such thing. It says the world will grow worse. Lawlessness will grow worse." Boston *Herald,* December 14, 1916, p. 4.

[72] See reproduction of Sunday's sermon notes opposite p. 31 in Rodeheaver, *Twenty Years with Billy Sunday.*

[73] *Life and Labors of Rev. William A. (Billy) Sunday,* pp. 352, 69; Boston *Herald,* January 17, 1917, p. 9; Washington *Evening Post,* January 12, 1918, p. 2; Boston *Herald,* November 18, 1916, p. 4.

progressive, a muckraker, or a social gospeler. In his sermon entitled "Positive and Negative Religion," he said:

We have produced in America . . . men whose private lives are good but whose public lives are very bad. For instance, we have produced men who, while they will not shoot a man with a pistol, will sit in New York city and by a vote on the board of directors' meeting set in motion forces which ultimately may take a man's life out in the Pacific slope. . . .

This seemed a direct slap at his wealthy backers, like Rockefeller and Frick, who heedlessly cut wages and then employed strike-breakers against their protesting workers. The sermon went even further:

Men who would not pick the pockets of one man with the fingers of their hand will without hesitation pick the pockets of 80,000,000 people with the fingers of their monopoly or commercial advantage. Men in whose hands the virtue of your wife or daughter would be as safe as in your own but who will drive hundreds of cases of virtue over the line into vice by the pressure of starvation wages which they pay.

He even seemed to advocate child labor laws when he condemned "men who will gladly draw their check for $10,000 and give it to a child's hospital and see nothing ridiculous in the fact that the $10,000 for the child's hospital came out of $200,000 made from a system of child labor which crushes more children in one year than the hospital will heal in ten." [74]

And in a sermon entitled "Jekyll and Hyde" he made a statement against slum housing and oppressive labor conditions which was worthy of B. Fay Mills at his most radical. For once he placed the blame for the crime bred in such conditions upon society rather than upon the individual:

I believe if society permits any considerable proportion of people to live in foul, unlighted rooms where from eight to ten people live, cook, eat and sleep, working year in and year out from fourteen to fifteen hours every day; I believe if society allows deserving men to stagger along with less than a living wage; if society permits the shoulders of widowed motherhood to be forced down under the industrial burdens and throws the unripe strength of children into the hopper of corporate greed to be ground up into dividends, that society must share the responsibility if these people become criminals, thieves, thugs, cut-throats, drunkards, and prostitutes.[75]

[74] Boston *Herald,* December 9, 1916, p. 3.
[75] *Ibid.,* January 12, 1917, p. 5.

Here he spoke for the troubled conscience of his audience. Like the progressives, he appealed to the personal responsibility of each citizen in a democracy and stirred up guilt feelings inculcated by the evangelical doctrine of the providential punishment of nations for the sins of individuals. To many it was self-evident that the middle class was as responsible for its plight as labor or capital, for did not democratic countries always get the kind of government they deserved? [76]

Sunday's muckraking statements received headline attention in the era of the progressive movement and led some progressives and social gospelers to think that Sunday's revival might be a help to their cause. But out of an average of 125 sermons which Sunday delivered in every campaign, such statements could be counted upon the fingers of one hand. On the whole Sunday and his audience were more interested in finding scapegoats for their ills than in holding themselves responsible.

Furthermore, if these statements were taken in the context of the whole sermon, their force was considerably diminished. While Sunday seemed in these remarks about big business to discern the fact that personal morality was not sufficient to exonerate a man from a lack of social conscience, he refused to draw the obvious conclusion either that these big businessmen were immoral in a more profound sense than his ethical code recognized or else that there was a social ethic which required the public regulation of the right of free enterprise in the name of the general welfare. In the same sermon in which he apparently held society responsible for the drunkards, criminals, and prostitutes who came out of the slums, he remarked, "I don't like to see you trying to put it all on environment and take away the responsibility from the individual who's got a rotten heart. A man is not supposed to be the victim of his environment." He was speaking to a Boston audience, and he made the allusion specific: "If you are right in your heart you will be right whether you live in the North End, Beacon Street, Commonwealth Avenue, or the Fenway." [77] In one sermon he deplored the increasing "concentration of wealth" and stated

[76] For the evangelical motivation in progressivism see Hofstadter, *Age of Reform,* pp. 203–4; and W. G. McLoughlin, Jr., "Professional Evangelism: The Social Significance of Religious Revivals Since 1865," unpublished doctoral dissertation, Harvard College Library, 1953, pp. 604–5.

[77] Boston *Herald,* January 12, 1917, p. 5.

dramatically that "twelve men practically control the wealth of the United States today. Twelve men can put the United States out of business." But instead of continuing with an attack upon this dangerous state of affairs he went on: "I marvel that some of our institutions get along with all the cranky laws we have. With the laws of states and the government and the prices of commodities, I don't see how any railroad can turn a wheel. Never was there a time when we had more cranky, asinine laws on our statute books." [78] Since this sermon was delivered in 1916, after the passage of the Federal Trade Commission Act and the Clayton Act, it constituted an argument against the regulation of the power of the twelve men who controlled the country, rather than a plea for limiting their power. The members of his audience, most of whom either cherished the hope that they might someday be captains of industry or were already small entrepreneurs who associated themselves with capital rather than labor, disliked the thought of government regulation as much as Sunday did. Like him, they believed that free enterprise had made America great and that tampering with the laws of supply and demand might wreck it.

In the end, therefore, Sunday offered his auditors no solution to their dilemmas except more revivalistic religion. It was not social reform that was needed: "We've got to get back to the old-time truths . . . and back to the spirit of our forefathers" as expressed in the sermons of Finney, Wesley, Whitefield, the Puritans, and Martin Luther.[79] Whether this outlook was optimistic or pessimistic depended upon how quickly a man thought the world could be converted so that it would return to its old ways. In his heyday Sunday, like Warren Candler and A. C. Dixon, seemed confident that the American type of revivalistic religion was about to sweep the world. "I want to say that the warfare against sin and the devil is not hopeless. Not only will the tide turn (thank God the tide is already turning), it is already started and it is coming in. . . . Perdition will not always pour her black river of filth and of damnation and of misery and of sorrow into our hearts, our homes, our

[78] *Ibid.,* December 14, 1916, p. 5.
[79] *Ibid.,* November 20, 1916, p. 5.

communities, and our nation." [80] In a sermon in 1916 he flatly asserted, "I am not a pessimist. I am an optimist of the optimists. I believe a brighter day never dawned for the church of Christ." As an optimist he said, "There is no prejudice between man and man, between masses and classes, between capital and labor, which cannot be driven from the world by the principles of Jesus Christ in men." [81] This was Finney's old pietistic and perfectionist reliance upon God's power and not on man's efforts. Soul-winning, not social reform and "godless social service," was the one answer to all questions: "The only thing that pleases Jesus is winning souls." "All human schemes of reconstruction must be subsidiary to the Second Coming." "You can't legislate men out of the slough of despond." And, "The trouble with the church, the YMCA, and the Young People's societies is that they have taken up sociology and settlement work but are not winning souls to Christ." [82]

Yet Sunday's audience did not have the same zeal for soul-winning that Moody's and Finney's audiences had. He steamed them up to "do something" about the plight they were in, but few of his converts joined the Billy Sunday Businessmen's Clubs or the Virginia Asher Businesswomen's Clubs to devote their spare time to evangelistic work among their friends or among the downtrodden.[83] Most of his trail-hitters were ready, however, to take part in the activities of the Anti-Saloon League, and Sunday departed from the pietistic tradition to the extent of countenancing prohibition activity as something more than an appendage to revivals. This was one reform which he believed could legislate men out of the slough of despond. Unlike the antislavery crusade, prohibition was not a divisive force within Protestantism, but it was a divisive force between Protes-

[80] From Sunday's sermon, "The Fir Tree," copyrighted in 1917 and printed privately by him on newsprint for distribution in advance to the press. Copies are among the Sunday Papers, Winona Lake, Indiana.

[81] Boston *Herald,* November 13, 1916, p. 5. *New York Times,* April 16, 1917, p. 11.

[82] *Life and Labors of Rev. William A. (Billy) Sunday,* p. 302; Sermon notes for "The Second Coming," in Sunday Papers, Winona Lake, Indiana; Boston *Herald,* November 16, 1916, p. 4; Pittsburgh *Press,* January 4, 1914, Edit. Sec., p. 8.

[83] Virginia Asher, formerly one of Chapman's assistants, was for many years Sunday's director of businesswomen's work. For the activities of these clubs see McLoughlin, *Billy Sunday,* pp. 217 ff.

tantism and many of those outside the churches. In supporting prohibition many of Sunday's supporters found occasion also to vent their spleen against such un-American scapegoats as unassimilated foreigners, whiskey politicians, saloon-keepers, and booze-soaked labor agitators. The sin of intemperance cast a wide net.

But the most divisive social question within Protestantism was "the labor problem," and here Sunday followed Finney by trying to subordinate the issue to revivalism. In his early years Sunday's tendency to use his revivals for prohibition rallies aroused criticism from persons who thought that by doing so he unwittingly diverted attention from the corrupt actions of local politicians. After he attained national fame and his revivals received the backing of leading businessmen, several prominent friends of the labor movement accused him of being a tool of big business. It was said that the nation's industrial leaders invited him to their cities for the specific purpose of distracting attention from labor unrest by stirring up enthusiasm for religion and prohibition. George Creel, a newspaperman, civic reformer, and later chairman of Woodrow Wilson's wartime Committee on Public Information, made such a charge in his eyewitness account of the purpose and results of Sunday's revivals in Denver and Colorado Springs in 1914. At the time Sunday was invited to hold these revivals the mining interests of Colorado were engaged in a vicious struggle with the United States Mine Workers' Union. The workers were evicted from the company towns, and on April 20, 1914, a pitched battle had taken place between the strikers and the National Guard in which thirteen of the strikers' wives and children lost their lives. This "Ludlow Massacre" raised a national furor and touched off a Congressional investigation of the strike in which the responsibility of the mine operators for fomenting the trouble was fully demonstrated. Sunday's revivals in Colorado took place in the months of May, June, August, and September, 1914. While he did not say one word about the strike or the massacre during these four months, he did lead a vigorous crusade for statewide prohibition which resulted in the state's voting dry that fall for the first time in its history, much to everyone's surprise.

Creel summed up the matter in an article for *Harper's Weekly* called "Salvation Circus":

The men who invited "Billy" Sunday to come to Colorado, who raised the money for his revivals, were the men whose lawlessness had precipitated the strike and whose arrogance was responsible for the policy of extermination adopted towards the strikers by the operators. . . . As a result of his revivals, the industrial issue fell from sight. Prohibition became the one great overwhelming importance. The operators gave unstintedly to the "dry" campaign and sent the word down the line that every controlled vote must be cast for the "dry" candidates. . . . Carlson, the Prohibitionist idol, was elected [governor]. No sooner had he taken office than the fact became apparent that he was a "coal company man." The operators chuckled. They had "put one over," thanks to the aid of Billy Sunday. They had used the prohibition mania to sneak in their governor and their legislators. . . . Carlson rammed a bill through the legislature providing for a special judge to try strike cases. He appointed a [former] coal company attorney. Every union leader was indicted on trumped up charges. Carlson sent the attorney-general to prosecute them assisted by the high-priced attorneys of the coal companies. . . . Man after man was found guilty of murder and sentenced to the penitentiary for life. That was how Billy Sunday brought God to Colorado.[84]

Creel did not blame Sunday personally. Sunday was, he thought, merely a dupe of unscrupulous vested interests. But, Creel said, "There is no doubt that Sunday is being maneuvered from industrial centre to industrial centre as the result of a very shrewd plan." Other progressive and radical reformers, like John Reed, Upton Sinclair, Scott Nearing, and Rabbi Stephen S. Wise, made similar charges concerning Sunday's revivals in Paterson, Philadelphia, and the mining towns of West Virginia.[85] Eugene Debs called Sunday "a vulgar harlequin, a ranting mountebank, who, in the pay of the plutocracy, prostitutes religion to perpetuate hell on earth."[86] Carl Sandburg, writing for *The Masses* in 1915, issued a blast in his prose-poem "To Billy Sunday."

[84] George Creel, "Salvation Circus," *Harper's Weekly,* LX (June 19, 1915), 580. For a more detailed analysis of Sunday's part in the Colorado strike which on the whole substantiates Creel's statement see McLoughlin, *Billy Sunday,* pp. 242–50.

[85] See John Reed, "Back of Billy Sunday," *Metropolitan Magazine,* May 1915, pp. 10 ff.; Lightner Witmer, *The Nearing Case* (New York, 1915); Upton Sinclair, *The Profits of Religion* (Pasadena, California, 1918); *New York Times,* May 2, 1917, p. 7; and May 15, 1922, p. 36.

[86] *The Melting Pot* (St. Louis), Vol. III (April, 1915), pp. 5–6.

> You, Billy Sunday, put a smut on every human blossom. . . .
>
> You tell $6 a week department store girls all they need is Jesus, you take a steel trust wop, dead without having lived, gray and shrunken at forty years of age, and you tell him to look at Jesus on the cross and he will be all right. . . .[87]

Even the writer of the "Topic of the Times" column in the *New York Times* wrote in 1916 that Sunday was supported by the well-to-do "as a police measure—as a means of keeping the lower classes quiet." [88]

Creel was probably right in saying that Sunday did not consciously engage in antilabor activities, but Sunday and his team of experts firmly believed that salvation and prohibition would be more useful to the workingman than trade unions. The Rev. Isaac Ward, whom Sunday hired as director of men's work, expressed what was probably the prevailing view within the Sunday Party. Speaking of the meetings which he and his assistant conducted in the shop's and factories as part of Sunday's campaigns, Ward said, "We never touch labor problems. We teach only that old-time gospel of the cross. It's amazing how men who have never gone inside a church are ready to respond to that old gospel. It's the only solution to the problem of capital and labor. The great gospel of Jesus Christ finding the way into the hearts of men makes man love man, makes capital appreciate labor and labor appreciate capital. Labor agitation disappears in some places because of the meetings in the plants and factories. That is its moral and economic value. In some places strike agitation has been eliminated altogether." [89]

The point of view of the businessmen who supported Sunday was fairly typified by Alba B. Johnson who succeeded John H. Converse as president of the Baldwin Locomotive Works in Philadelphia. Johnson told John Reed, "You know the widespread social unrest is largely due to the workingman's envy of those who make a little more money than he does. Now Billy Sunday makes people look to the salvation of their own souls, and when a man is looking after his own soul's good he forgets his selfish desire to become rich. Instead of agitating

[87] *The Masses,* Vol. VI (May, 1915), p. 15.
[88] *New York Times,* May 20, 1916, p. 10.
[89] Boston *Herald,* November 14, 1916, p. 3.

for a raise in wages he turns and helps some poorer brother who's down and out." [90]

Sunday's ministerial supporters were interested in the prohibition aspects of his campaigns not only for their effect upon strikes but also for their influence in Americanizing the foreign-born. The editor of the *Watchman-Examiner* voiced the continuing evangelical concern with this problem in 1914 when he offered the following analysis of the reasons for the defeat of a Prohibition referendum in Texas: "In the district where the foreigners predominate the saloon vote was almost solid. It will take a great Anglo-Saxon majority to overcome this foreign influence. . . . Broadly speaking, the lower elements of all the foreign peoples among us will be controlled by the liquor interests." This, concluded the editor, was "a tremendous argument for home missions." [91] It was also an argument for promoting Sunday's revivals, for Sunday never missed an opportunity to denounce "the continental Sabbath" and the European "beer garden." "Look at the brewers," he exclaimed. "What are their names? No Americans, thank God!" (Sunday's own name two generations back had been Sonntag, but it was harder to Americanize the name Schlitz.) Foreigners brewed the beer, foreigners drank it, and intoxicated foreigners committed over two-thirds of the crimes in the country. "Sixty-nine per cent of our criminals," said Sunday, "are either foreign-born or of foreign parents." "America has become the backyard in which Europe is dumping its paupers and criminals." Sunday accepted unquestioningly the biased propaganda of the Immigration Restriction League and the Dillingham Immigration Committee's report. He passed on to his audiences the belief that there was a stereotype of the 100 per cent pure American which could not only be defined scientifically and statistically but could also be discerned just by looking at a man: "You walk in the streets of New York or Philadelphia or Chicago and not one out of every three faces will have the strains of pure Americanism." Like Warren Candler, the only foreigner Sunday was willing to accept as an American was one "who wants to come here and assimilate our ways and conditions." Which

[90] John Reed, "Back of Billy Sunday," *loc. cit.*, p. 12.
[91] *Watchman-Examiner,* August 13, 1914, p. 1072.

meant that he must become a teetotaler, a Bible-believing Protestant, and a "decent," middle-class citizen.[92]

Sunday's xenophobia and intolerance of diversity, like that of most Americans, increased rapidly after the United States entered World War I in 1917. It seemed logical then for Sunday to assert what had been implicit in revival preaching since the turn of the century: "I think that Christianity and Patriotism are synonymous terms and hell and traitors are synonymous." Sunday began to call himself "God's recruiting officer," but instead of voluntary enlistment he favored impressment in the army of Americanism by force of public opinion. When Attorney-General A. Mitchell Palmer began his wholesale imprisonment and deportation of alien "radicals" in 1919, Sunday applauded the move: "If they don't like the way we do things, let them get out of here and leave. We don't propose to adjust this country to suit a lot of anarchists." In fact, Sunday did not propose to adjust the country to anybody. By the middle of the twenties he was blandly telling his cheering crowds, "America is not a country for a dissenter to live in." [93]

Having tied Christianity to the coat-tails of the national destiny and to the war to make the world safe for democracy, Sunday and his professional colleagues continued to preach their special brand of American Christianity in the reactionary period which followed 1918. Revivalism played its part in the "red scare," the immigration restriction laws, the renascence of the Ku Klux Klan, and the general antiliberal tone of the 1920's. Sunday's meetings in this decade, and particularly during Alfred E. Smith's campaign for the Presidency in 1928, took on the air of a "konclave" of the KKK. On one or two occasions bands of hooded Klansmen paraded into Sunday's tabernacles in full regalia to applaud his messages. In most cities, however, the Klan members came dressed in their ordinary business suits and white collars.[94]

[92] Boston *Herald,* November 20, 1916, p. 5; and December 4, p. 4.

[93] Providence *News,* October 2, 1918, p. 12; Sunday's sermon "The Fir Tree" in the Sunday Papers, Winona Lake, Indiana; and Sunday's typewritten sermon notes for "The Ten Commandments," also among the Sunday Papers.

[94] In spite of attempts to hold the Populists to blame for the rise of the Ku Klux Klan (see for example Hofstadter, *Age of Reform,* p. 81 and *passim)* and to see the movement as primarily a rural one, there is good evidence that at least in its early stages it was led by respectable business and professional men and pillars of the churches in the cities as well as in rural areas. See H. P. Fry,

Yet in spite of the basically conservative and often reactionary outlook of revivalists, the profession did not continue to thrive in the twenties. This was in part because revivals were, by definition, crusades for uplift, and Americans were tired of crusades. It was partly because revivalism had already achieved its most popular goals, such as prohibition, immigration restriction, and the general acceptance of the shibboleths that McKinleyism was normalcy and that America was only for 100 per cent Americans. And it was partly because in those respects in which modern revivalism was most vitally concerned to make good—where it was, by its own standards, bound to stand or fall—it failed completely. It failed to reach the masses; it failed to halt the spread of secularism; it failed to rejuvenate the spirit of the churches, to reestablish the influence of the clergy, to defeat the heresies of modernism, to evangelize the world, and to stem the tide of science worship. And it failed most miserably in its attempts to reenthrone in the minds of Americans the nineteenth-century small-town code of beliefs and behavior which was the basis of fundamentalism.

Moreover, professional evangelism in the first two decades of the century had deprived the revival tradition of its last shreds of authority and respect by the flamboyant, high-pressure attempts to "get results" at any cost. Evangelists like Sunday, Chapman, Torrey, and Smith, for all their sincerity and devotion to the cause of soul-winning, made revivalism a laughing stock for the generation which came of age in the twenties. The national comedy which took place in Dayton, Tennessee, in 1925 symbolized the disrespect into which the old-time religion had fallen. Sunday may have suspected this when he declined to come to Dayton to assist his old friend Bryan in making this last stand for fundamentalism.[95]

The Modern Ku Klux Klan (Boston, 1922), p. 17; W. J. Cash, *The Mind of the South* (New York, 1941), p. 336; J. M. Mecklin, *The Ku Klux Klan* (New York, 1924), p. 100; Paul M. Angle, *Bloody Williamson* (New York, 1952), pp. 134 ff.; L. Mellett, "Klan and Church in Indiana," *Atlantic,* CXXXII (November, 1923), 586; "Platforms of the People and the Mind of the Klan," *Outlook,* CXXXVII (June 25, 1924), 306–9; "Why They Join the Klan," *New Republic,* XXXVI (November 21, 1923), 321–22. The best analysis of nativism in the 1920's and its relationship to fundamentalism is in John Higham, *Strangers in the Land* (New Brunswick, New Jersey, 1955), see esp. pp. 234–299.

[95] See *New York Times,* July 4, 1925, p. 2.

Sunday continued to find support for his campaigns in "the Bible Belt" during the 1920's, but his attacks on bootlegging, his denunciations of evolution, his jibes at the "anti-Christian, Agnostic, Naturalistic, Modernism represented by Fosdick" found little support outside the Southern states. His attacks upon radicals, "pinkos," "bolsheviki," and foreign entanglements found more sympathetic listeners, and he did his best to keep the country from cooperating with the League of Nations or the World Court, but he could not maintain his national popularity. No matter how much he might lament over the lost generation's "drift into the Boom-Boom, Whoopee, Jazz, Bootlegging, Joy-riding current," and no matter how often he insisted "America needs a tidal wave of the Old-Time Religion," his days were numbered. He held his last city-wide campaign in the little town of Mount Holly, New Jersey, in 1930. In the remaining five years of his life he preached in various one-church revival services for a faithful following of stubborn fundamentalists, but he was never again front page news. Unable to account for the failure of "the gospel truths" to win the victory he had predicted so confidently, Sunday renounced his optimism for a profound pessimism after 1930. Only the cataclysmic Second Coming of Christ, he began to assert, could possibly redeem the nation and lead the world to peace and prosperity. Using some vague calculations about "the times of the Gentiles" which were to last for 2520 years and claiming that this "last dispensation" began in 586 B.C., Sunday came to the conclusion that the year 1935 might well see the end of the world as predicted in Revelations.[96]

Most of the religious and lay leaders of evangelical Protestantism had repudiated Sunday long before he reached this extreme. Some of those who had hailed him in 1912 as a new prophet and who had praised tabernacle revivalism as the most efficient of all evangelistic techniques were already revising their opinions as early as 1916. Bishop Joseph F. Berry, who had been one of the prominent figures in bringing Sunday to Philadelphia and who lauded Sunday's work in speeches and articles for several years, issued an attack against tabernacle evangelism in 1916 which, while not aimed specifically at Sun-

96 See Sunday's typed sermon notes for "The Coming Dictator," which he wrote in 1933 or 1934. Sunday Papers, Winona Lake, Indiana.

day, could hardly help but undermine his prestige. Berry's article, "Criticisms of Present Day Evangelism," stated the six most common objections to tabernacle evangelists of the Billy Sunday type: (1) the "two weeks of vitriolic attack upon ministers and church members" by the evangelist at the start of almost all such campaigns; (2) the exaltation of the role of the revivalist and the lack of recognition given to the supporting pastors; (3) "the present 'shake-my-hand' method" of dealing with inquirers which was "superficial and perilous"; (4) the overemphasis upon statistics and their misleading character; (5) the "vulgar display" of gifts presented to the revivalists by visiting delegations at each service; (6) the high pressure methods used to obtain a large free-will offering for the revivalist at the conclusion of the meetings.[97]

Sunday was as guilty of all these charges as the rest of the profession. But the most damaging argument against his work in the mind of the general public was that he was making money out of soul-winning. It was generally known that his free-will offerings had totaled over a million dollars by 1918, and while the laborer was worthy of his hire, it seemed incongruous to have millionaires engaged in the revival business. It made winning souls seem like a means to wealth instead of a task undertaken for the glory of God. Moreover, there was evidence that Sunday's supporters and the members of his Party often went to great lengths to assure a large remuneration for him. Instead of merely taking a collection for him at the last day of the campaign, it became the practice to solicit outside subscriptions for several weeks before the closing. In Columbus a group of prominent laymen "took charge of the collection the last day for Mr. Sunday. . . . They telephoned to some of the leading businessmen and gave them an opportunity to subscribe in advance." As a result of their efforts Sunday received $20,-929 for his eight-weeks' work.[98] Other cities felt constrained to equal or surpass the record set by Columbus. In Denver, in 1914, a cooperating Episcopal minister, Dean H. Martyn Hart, asked the audience at the tabernacle shortly before the drive

97 Joseph F. Berry, "Criticisms of Present Day Evangelism," *Zion's Herald,* January 19 1916, p. 74. For another attack by Berry on the profession see *ibid.,* February 28, 1917, p. 268.

98 *Watchman-Examiner,* April 10, 1913, p. 12.

for subscriptions for Sunday's "free-will offering" started, "Surely Denver does not want to fall behind other cities?" Hart said a goal of $24,000 had been set for Denver. Its attainment was promoted in precisely the same manner as a charity fund drive.[99] Philip Loeb of Montclair, New Jersey, complained in 1915 that Sunday's offering was nothing but "organized begging." [100] A Congregational minister in Paterson reported that toward the end of the revival there a member of Sunday's Party presented the cooperating ministers with a 28-page list of influential citizens in the Paterson area who were to be approached by their pastors to give money for the offering.[101] The Rev. Hamilton Schuyler of Trenton said that the methods used to raise the offering in his city were nothing short of "polite blackmail." [102]

These charges led John D. Rockefeller, Jr., to investigate Sunday's methods, but he exonerated him of any blame.[103] Sunday tried to still the criticism by donating his entire free-will offering of $120,000 in New York to the Red Cross, YMCA, and YWCA. And in Chicago he donated his free-will offering of $56,000 to the Pacific Garden Mission. But his general attitude was that it was nobody's business how much money he got or what he did with it. Once he made the inept comment: "In spite of all these high figures you kick about what I get, what I'm paid for my work makes it only about $2 a soul, and I get less proportionately for the number I convert than any other living evangelist." [104]

It was not only Sunday's commercialism, however, which brought professional evangelism into disrepute. The vulgarity, sensationalism, and unscrupulous methods of the host of minor revivalists who imitated him contributed just as much to the debacle. Charles Stelzle estimated that in 1911 there were 650 active professional evangelists in the country and over 1300 more engaged in part-time revival work.[105] Almost all of them did their best to imitate Sunday's style and methods. Some of

[99] *Rocky Mountain News,* October 24, 1914, p. 1.
[100] *New York Times,* April 28, 1915, p. 12.
[101] *Ibid.,* May 10, 1916, p. 24.
[102] *Ibid.,* March 2, 1917, p. 9.
[103] New York *World,* June 18, 1917, p. 16.
[104] Quoted in Frankenberg, *Spectacular Career of Rev. Billy Sunday,* p. 213.
[105] Charles Stelzle, "The Evangelist in Present Day America," *Current History,* XXXV (November, 1931), 225.

them went far beyond him. Bishop Berry said in 1916, "Advance agents of evangelistic parties are running to and fro in the land seeking to make engagements for their chiefs, in some cases actually offering liberal commissions to pastors who will assist them to get into their communities. How far is that removed from attempted bribery?"[106] Pretentious evangelists placed advertisements in religious journals praising their own effectiveness and offering to talk terms with any town which needed a good spiritual shakeup. They called themselves by nicknames and added little tags to distinguish themselves. By 1915 there were five called "The Singing Evangelist," three called "The Boy Evangelist," five called "The Gypsy Evangelist," and dozens of others with such self-adopted titles as "The Railroad Evangelist," "The Businessman's Evangelist," "The Cowboy Evangelist," and "The Labor Evangelist." The trade had become so crowded that cutthroat competition, sensational advertising, and spectacular gimmicks were regularly resorted to. One evangelist called himself a "thriller." Another claimed that he could convert 34 per cent of the population in any town he visited. One evangelist advertised his two harp players as an exceptional feature. An evangelist named Henry W. Stough, who at one time was an official of the Interdenominational Association of Evangelists, attracted attention to himself by "exposing" crooked dealings in the cities he visited. His crusading zeal brought him a suit for libel in 1915 when, in his misguided efforts to clean up the town of Hazleton, Pennsylvania, he gratuitously denounced four influential city officials and businessmen by name as "riff-raff," "plug-uglies," and political "bosses."[107]

It was in order to put some check upon the irresponsible antics of such foolish or unscrupulous revivalists that the Federal Council of Churches set up its Commission on Evangelism in 1912. Joseph F. Berry was vice-chairman, William H. Roberts, chairman, and William E. Biederwolf, secretary. Most of the work fell to Biederwolf, who prepared a series of test questions which he said all ministerial groups should apply to any man whom they were considering for an evangelistic campaign.

106 *Zion's Herald,* January 19, 1916, p. 74.

107 For Stough see Philadelphia *Public Ledger,* June 25, 1915, p. 6; June 29, p. 1; and June 30, p. 10.

The questions were: "Does he give proper attention to his financial obligations? What and where was his education? What and where were his pastorates? What was his success as a pastor? What was the largest meeting he ever addressed and what was the success of his efforts?" [108] The commission also recommended the use of a standardized decision card which would clearly differentiate those trail-hitters who were already church members, those who had formerly been members, children, and first decisions. The only plan that Biederwolf offered regarding the financial remuneration of evangelists was that some way be found to pay them a fixed salary rather than to let them depend upon free-will offerings.[109] But these proposals were too vague to be helpful, and the Federal Council had no more power to enforce them upon the profession than did the I.A.E.

The truth of the matter was that the ordinary ministers and laymen were as much to blame for the evils of the situation as the professional evangelists. Blinded by the eulogies and statistics about the profession which were published in religious journals, they were overeager to find some simple solution to the complex problems facing their churches. Instead of employing an evangelist to "supplement the regular activities of the church," said one critic, the ministers had employed them as a "substitute." [110] The evangelist could hardly be blamed for talking disparagingly about the incompetence of the regular ministry when the ministers themselves confessed as much. Sunday felt perfectly justified when he bluntly told the cooperating ministers at the outset of each campaign: "You brought me here. I did not ask to come. . . . You must do what you are told. . . ." [111] The worst fears of Finney's critics in the 1830's were realized by 1915. The ministers were no longer considered competent to save souls. Efficiency experts had to be hired to do their work for them. But since there

108 Charles E. Schaeffer, *A Brief History of the Department of Evangelism of the Federal Council of Churches,* pp. 5–6.

109 See W. E. Biederwolf, *The Evangelistic Situation* (Chicago, 1917); and W. E. Biederwolf, *Evangelism, Its Justification, Its Operation and Its Value* (New York, 1921) for this and other proposals to reform the profession as well as for a defense of it.

110 *Watchman-Examiner,* November 11, 1915, p. 1446.

111 Pittsburgh *Press,* December 29, 1913, p. 1.

were not enough Billy Sundays to bring efficiency to every community, less efficient and less honest practitioners sprang up to cater to the market.

Typical of the ruinous results of rushing headlong into a campaign under the leadership of inferior men was the sad experience described by a minister of Cincinnati in 1917. An attempt had been made to invite Billy Sunday, but he had turned down the request because it had come from too small a percentage of the evangelical churches. "Some of the ministers on Walnut Hills—and these too representing some of our strongest churches—closed up without much serious forethought with Dr. [Henry W.] Stough." There were about fourteen churches cooperating, and "they built a tabernacle seating 7000" for the revivalist. The campaign lasted six weeks and was "the most colossal failure" and "one of the greatest religious trajedies [*sic*] ever seen in Cincinnati." The tabernacle was never "more than a third or at the most half full." "Reports that two or three hundred responded at times [to calls for conversion] meant nothing as they only showed the number who went up after all appeal for a changed life ended in a desire for Christians to reconsecrate themselves. . . ." "The awful deadness in the whole situation" brought a "look of dispare [*sic*] on the faces of the clergy" who had been "prematurely drawn into it. The collections have not met the running expences [*sic*]" and "the men who have underwritten the amount are of course broken-hearted or 'mad as hornets' over the experience." It was significant that the Walnut Hills ministers could think of no way to remedy this tragedy except by sending a "Macedonian cry" to Sunday to reconsider his decision and come rescue them.[112]

Such disappointments, multiplied in scores of other cities, brought about the repudiation not only of tabernacle evangelism but of professional mass revivalism in general by almost all denominations and ministerial associations. Bishop Berry was perhaps a little premature when he stated in 1918, "Vocational evangelism is dead," for Charles Stelzle reported that probably half of the 650 members of the profession (as of 1911) were still

112 Letter from the Rev. F. N. Riale to Mrs. William A. Sunday, dated Cincinnati, Ohio, February 8, 1917. The letter is in the Sunday Papers, Winona Lake, Indiana.

finding occasional employment in some churches in 1931.[113] But there was no doubt that the one hundred year tradition of modern revivalism subsided into a relatively unimportant and unsung role in the evangelical churches for thirty years after 1920.

The decline of the revival tradition coincided with the passing of America's third great awakening. By 1915 the manifold crises in American social, theological, and intellectual life which, since the 1870's, had stimulated revivalism had been resolved for the great majority of Americans. For better or for worse most churchgoers had accepted modernism as the new orthodoxy and the nation at large had come to terms with urban industrialism. The awakening had started, as had the two previous awakenings, in the churches. It began as a conflict between scientific scholarship and revealed religion. But it soon was engaged in dealing with the whole host of social. political, and economic problems which conservatives saw as perils; and liberals as challenges. The evangelicals, lacking the education and sophistication to grapple realistically with the complexities of the new era, turned to their traditional wellsprings of faith. But in their fearfulness of change they made the mistake of associating faith with a literal Bible and an untenable theological framework. Worsted in one encounter after another, their faith shrivelled and hardened into imprecations, incantations and rituals of purification. The revivalists, who in the past had seemed like prophets, now seemed more like witch-doctors. The best of them could only offer the old remedies of charity, self-denial, and personal regeneration. The worst of them betrayed their calling by engaging in flamboyant crusades against various scapegoats. The call for a new evangelism had been answered simply by jazzing up the old-fashioned revivalism. By 1900 the awakening had passed out of the hands of the revivalists and into the hands of the social gospelers and progressive political reformers. And because it did not, after that, take the form of previous revivals, it was ignored, repudiated, or patronized by the majority of evangelicals who called it nothing but an "ethical revival." Yet for all its shortcomings, the social gospel and progressive movement

[113] *Zion's Herald,* December 25, 1918, p. 1641; Charles Stelzle, "The Evangelist in Present Day America," *Current History,* XXXV (November, 1931), p. 225.

(they were really one movement in which the secular and sacred were inextricably mixed) constituted a wave of nationwide spiritual fervor just as spontaneous and deeply felt as the movements associated with George Whitefield and Charles Finney—perhaps more so, since its influence spread far beyond the churches.

No doubt the premises of this awakening and the increasingly secular trend of the times would, in any case, have led many of its converts into politics, teaching, sociological research, labor relations, and journalism rather than into the ministry. But in spite of that they need not have been lost to the churches. The evangelical leaders missed a golden opportunity to maintain their position of influence and respect by their refusal to accept social reform as a legitimate sphere for religious activity or even for religious concern. Had they met the challenge of secularism as the social gospelers urged, by raising the intellectual and spiritual level of the churches to a new plane and by recognizing that laissez-faire individualism was even less defensible in religion than in economics, they might have won back the waning allegiance of the younger generation. Instead, they attacked the social gospelers for infidelity and denounced men like "Golden Rule" Jones for socialism while at the same time they hastened the secularization of religion by their own enthusiastic support of revival campaigns which were combinations of vaudeville theatrics, patriotic rallies, and prohibition crusades.

Even when, after 1915, the majority of the urban ministers (those who controlled the denominational machinery) repudiated fundamentalism and acknowledged the claims of science, scholarship, and, to a smaller extent, social reform, it was a pyrrhic victory. In effect they simply acknowledged their ignorance of the modern world and accepted the role of handmaidens to science. As their spokesman, Harry Emerson Fosdick, declared in 1935, "We have at times gotten so low down that we talked as though the highest compliment that could be paid to Almighty God was that a few scientists believed in him." [114]

[114] Harry Emerson Fosdick in the *Christian Century,* December 4, 1935, quoted in Herbert W. Schneider, *Religion in 20th Century America* (Cambridge, Mass., 1952), pp. 107–8.

As for modern revivalism, it seemed ruined beyond repair. In so far as it did continue to exist, it did so in the rural areas of the South and Midwest and as part of the annual camp meetings and Bible conferences where fundamentalism continued to hold its ground. It flourished also among the holiness and Pentecostal sects, the churches of the unsophisticated, the uneducated, and the disinherited. But it ceased to hold the respect or attention of the major evangelical denominations. The I.A.E. withered away in the 1930's as its members took up full-time pastorates or some other form of Christian work. For a generation professors of sociology and church history looked upon mass revivalism as an obsolescent form of religious activity. The concept of Horace Bushnell, that children could be educated into Christianity without ever knowing that they were unsaved, came into its own. Even among the Methodists and Baptists church membership became simply a graduation exercise from the Sunday school or Young People's group. Neither the ministers nor church members thought a crisis conversion experience, even of the shake-my-hand variety, was necessary.

In spite of Stelzle's gloomy prediction of 1912, however, evangelical church membership did continue to hold its own with population growth, especially when World War I and immigration restriction cut off the heavy influx of non-Protestants. Lay leaders like John D. Rockefeller, Jr., decided that Fosdick was right and Billy Sunday wrong and rallied around the new banner of modernism. What was even more traitorous to the old-time religion, Rockefeller, and many like him, decided that the great crusade for prohibition had been a mistake and advocated repeal of the Eighteenth Amendment.

Although church membership continued to grow, it was not until the mid-1930's that more than one-half the population belonged to some church. American churchmen could never be content until everyone belonged. Even before tabernacle evangelism went into eclipse, the search for a new evangelism began again. It was found quickly enough, but it failed to produce a fourth awakening. That had to wait until after World War II when the nation faced a new and vastly different crisis than it had ever faced before.

CHAPTER 9

"Specialists in the Engineering of Mass Consent"

Charles L. Goodell, speaking as Secretary of the Commission on Evangelism of the Federal Council of Churches, said in 1921, "This has been the greatest year in evangelism which America has ever seen . . . not by any feverish campaign or by a few remarkable personalities, but by a steady and constant emphasis on pastoral and personal evangelism." A year earlier, Cortland Myers, long a supporter of mass evangelism, wrote an article entitled "The New Evangelism," in which he said, "Old methods of evangelism . . . must give place on the whole to something better; that is, face-to-face work, whether by pastor or Sunday school teacher or ordinary church members." In 1922 the Federated Council of Churches of Pittsburgh concluded after a series of ministerial conferences that mass evangelism of the type represented by Billy Sunday, Gypsy Smith, and other "imported" revivalists was "too high-priced, too much commercialized, obsolete, false in stimulation and ineffective" and should be discarded for visitation evangelism. As one Pittsburgh pastor remarked after experiencing two of Gypsy Smith's campaigns and one of Sunday's, "Professional evangelism must be adjudged a failure and relegated to the limbo of outgrown methods." [1]

Even secular newspapers, using the newly popular language

[1] *Watchman-Examiner* (Baptist, New York), August 18, 1921, p. 1054 and April 8, 1920, p. 162; *Literary Digest,* LXXII (March 4, 1922), 33; Pittsburgh *Christian Outlook,* XVII (November, 1921), 3.

of psychology, attacked the "surrender to collective hysteria" produced by the "old-time evangelist's methods, his deliberate attempt in the name of the Lord to produce a mob psychosis." An article in the New York *Herald Tribune* stated in 1927 that mass evangelism was not only "ephemeral as a moral agency, but its effect both on the individual and on society" was "harmful." And "In any event the great dignity of the 'visitation' method seems quite as pronounced as its greater effectiveness." [2] By 1930, two-thirds of the city church federations in the United States were using visitation evangelism in some form as their main evangelistic activity.[3]

Visitation evangelism was not a new idea in the twenties. The practice of evangelizing by doorbell-ringing had been part of Moody's system in the 1870's and had been tried on various scales repeatedly since that time. For three years, from 1913 to 1916, the ministers of Indianapolis, having decided not to invite Billy Sunday to their city, conducted a protracted city-wide visitation campaign based on house-to-house evangelism by groups of church members. They claimed to have added 20,000 new members to their churches. In 1914 the Church Federation of St. Louis inaugurated a "one-to-win-one" campaign of combined personal and pastoral evangelism which was given wide publicity in a book by the Rev. Elmer T. Clark called *The New Evangelism.* Clark claimed that 10,000 new church members had been obtained by the work of lay visitors during Lent. "One denomination alone received over two thousand" new members on Easter Sunday. The plan included a religious census of the city to determine where nonchurch-members lived, a course of instruction in soul-winning for church members who volunteered to act as lay evangelists, and then systematic visitation by these laymen and laywomen who attempted to persuade the nonmembers to sign a pledge to join one of the cooperating churches. The pastors followed up the lay workers by writing or visiting those persons from whom pledges had been obtained. Clark said that twenty-five other cities were making plans to utilize this system in 1915.[4]

[2] Quoted in "Abjuring the Sawdust Trail," *Literary Digest,* XCV (October 8, 1927), 33.

[3] H. Paul Douglass, *Protestant Cooperation in American Cities* (New York, 1930), p. 336.

[4] See J. R. Brown, *Methods in Evangelism* (New York, 1926), *passim,* for dis-

The avowed success of these visitation campaigns, their low cost compared to tabernacle evangelism, their lack of sensationalism, and their emphasis upon the work of local pastors and church people rather than upon outside specialists led many cities to try them. Their popularity increased as that of professional mass evangelism decreased. It was not long before this form of evangelism acquired a number of professional "experts" who, for a fixed fee, would manage the technical aspects of the campaign and direct it to a guaranteed success. Under the leadership of the Rev. Guy H. Black and the Rev. A. Earl Kernahan, city-wide visitation evangelism became subject to many of the same abuses and criticisms as city-wide mass evangelism. Kernahan, who gave up a pastorate in Somerville, Massachusetts, to devote himself to this work, opened an office of Directed Survey and Visitation Campaigns in Washington, D.C., in 1923. Through the usual publicity methods and the publication of numerous books and articles on the subject, Kernahan quickly established a reputation as a new type of efficiency expert for the churches. When the ministerial association of a city voted to employ him and his staff, he first sent his specialist in "directed surveys" to conduct a religious census and work up a long list of "Prospect Cards" upon which the campaign was based. Then another expert arrived to train the laymen and laywomen of the cooperating churches in home visitation techniques and to ask them to sign a "Visitation Committee Agreement Card" on which they specified the precise hours they would work during the weeks of the campaign. If sufficient church members did not volunteer, professional "paid visitors" could be hired from Kernahan's office. A budget was drawn up, and the cooperating churches were required to donate in proportion to their means to meet the expenses.[5]

Kernahan found it most effective to concentrate the visitation effort within a one- or two-week period after the "survey" was completed and the "visitors" were trained. During this period the visitors met each night for dinner at one of the co-

---

cussion of the Indianapolis system and others similar to it. See Elmer T. Clark, *The New Evangelism* (Nashville, 1915) for the St. Louis system. Clark gave credit to the Rev. L. E. Todd for originating many aspects of the St. Louis system.

[5] See A. E. Kernahan, *Christian Citizenship and Visitation Evangelism* (New York, 1929), and A. E. Kernahan, *Visitation Evangelism, Its Methods and Results* (New York, 1925).

operating churches, where they heard pep talks, sang inspiriting hymns, exchanged notes on techniques, were given formal instructions, and then went out in pairs to make their visits. Each pair of home visitors was given eight or ten "prospect cards" and was instructed to write upon each one the results of their visit. Those prospects who were persuaded to join a church were asked to sign a "Record of Decision Card" and to name a specific day on which they would present themselves for membership. Across the top of the prospect card of such "converts" the visitors wrote "Won." On those cards which were not "won" the visitors had to state the reason why.

When the visitors reported for supper at the church the following night, the professional director of the campaign looked over the cards turned in from the previous night's work. He reassigned or took for himself the difficult cases for a second visit. Then he spoke to the assembled workers to suggest solutions to any peculiar or recurrent problems which they had encountered. He also asked those who had been particularly successful to report their experiences in order to encourage the downhearted. When all the prospects had been visited, the campaign ended. The visitors were then held responsible for following up their "won" prospects to see that they came to church and eventually joined.

Kernahan made astonishing claims for the success of his campaigns. Out of 370,750 prospects whom he had lined up in various campaigns between 1923 and 1929, 185,867 had been won, he said. His reliance upon statistics was as great as that of professional mass evangelists, but because he, or the visitors he trained, dealt with each individual face to face, it appeared that his statistics were more reliable. Among his campaign claims were the following:

City	*Date*	*Prospects*	*Decisions*
Omaha	1924	3000	1248
Des Moines	1924	2300	1220
Sioux City	1924	1400	760
Des Moines (2d visit)	1925	1565	1104
Burlington, Iowa	1925	1308	625
Baltimore	1926	6400	3040
New York	1927	2304	1017
Pittsburgh	1928	11,140	6469
New York (2d visit)	1928	17,810	10,042
Boston	1928	5301	3491

Kernahan claimed that 96 per cent of those who had joined a church as a result of his campaigns were still active members six months later.

However, as in the case of mass evangelism, these statistics were misleading. Kernahan admitted that 20 per cent of his "decisions" were obtained from persons who had been church members before but who had become lax in their attendance or had moved into the neighborhood recently and not yet established new church connections. More important, he implied that every decision became a church member, but this was not necessarily the case. In a Kernahan-directed campaign on Long Island, New York, visits were made to 9191 prospects, decisions were obtained from 868, but only 540 of these subsequently joined a church.[6]

The inexpensiveness of visitation evangelism was also exaggerated. A Kernahan campaign might cost from $3000 to $15,000 depending upon its scope, but there were no public collections taken, as there were at tabernacle campaigns, to cover this. The money came directly out of the regular budgets of the cooperating churches.

The two major complaints against visitation evangelism were that it did not reach the masses and that its approach to soul-winning was no more spiritual than that of city-wide tabernacle campaigns. Kernahan readily acknowledged that his system did not try to reach the whole city on all its social levels. The religious census, or directed survey, automatically excluded as prospects all persons not of Protestant background. The visitation system worked best (and was used predominantly) in small cities, uptown areas, or suburbs where respectable middle-class church members visited the apartments or homes of respectable middle-class neighbors. The tenement dwellers in downtown slum districts were left to the Salvation Army and the mission halls. The adoption of the visitation system was a virtual acceptance of the fact that the regular Protestant churches were exclusively middle-class institutions and had abandoned any hope of reaching the workingman.

The superficial, commercial, and secular aspects of visitation campaigns were equally obvious. If the professional mass evangelist went after souls like a big manufacturing corporation, the

[6] "Abjuring the Sawdust Trail," *loc. cit.*, p. 32.

professional visitation evangelist went after them like a Fuller Brush salesman or an insurance agent. "The workers should be instructed," said Kernahan in the tone of a sales manager, "to be direct, courteous, and persistent. The moment they meet a person at the door they should announce their errand. . . . Then after getting into the home (always get in; if a person does not invite you in, say, 'We'll only take a few moments of your time, may we please come in and go over the matter with you?'). . . ."[7] Tabernacle evangelists were usually ordained, and most of them had at least attended a Bible College, but Kernahan said that to be a home visitor a man "does not need to have an extensive religious background or training and experience. He does not need to be educated. . . ." Kernahan allowed about two hours to train laymen in the art of selling Christianity from door to door.

It was simply a matter of learning the four basic types of appeal: the appeal to conscience or to "Christian Citizenship"; the appeal to the Christian home; the appeal for Christian service; and the exhortation to be prepared for the hereafter. The visitors were instructed to ask each prospect whether he would live in a community where there were no churches, no public schools, no system of jurisprudence, no opportunity to send his children to Sunday school. When the prospect answered "No," the visitor was to "impress him with the fact that he was demanding a certain kind of social environment which is in a real sense Christian. . . . I would ask him if he did not think it perfectly fair to put his life into the Church if he desired the continuance of the kind of an environment which he now demanded"; after all, these institutions "have been fostered and nurtured in the heart of the Christian Church." This was the same appeal to "play fair," to "get in the game," to "take a stand for all that is decent," which lay at the heart of Billy Sunday's preaching. And like Sunday, Kernahan had nothing but scorn and abuse for the man who would not conform to this ideal of decency: "A man who fails to conform under conditions just stated is a religious slacker," he bluntly told the volunteer visitors.[8]

[7] Kernahan, *Visitation Evangelism, Its Methods,* p. 57.

Kernahan claimed as an advantage of his system that it did not depend upon the narrow tenets of fundamentalism. "Too often the professional evangelist," he said, ". . . is reactionary in his theological outlook" and his converts "are won to a certain theological interpretation of the Bible which is mechanical and out of date." [9] But in visitation evangelism no religious message was necessary at all until the prospect went to join the church of his choice, and then it was up to the pastor. A "decision" made in response to the appeals of a home visitor was not to any spiritual commitment or theological viewpoint but merely to the fact that religion, or more precisely, church membership, was in some vague way useful to the community. As one Baptist minister described the new evangelism of the 1920's, "We should call upon persons not to be saved but to become Christians," and each man was left to define Christianity as he chose. Or, as Kernahan said in 1925, "The thing that people are most interested in now is what does Christianity do for life?" He rightly apprehended the postwar religious climate when he noted, "We have come to a period in Christian history when people are not at all interested in dogmatism." [10]

In this new age of enlightenment "the old-time religion" was considered the emotional outlet of the primitive, the hick, the unsophisticated. Not even the George F. Babbitts could tolerate fundamentalism. Babbitt "admitted that he was too much the scholar and poet to imitate the evangelist, Mike Monday," but he was convinced that "it was respectable and beneficial to one's business to be seen going to services; that the church kept the Worst Elements from being still worse; and that the pastor's sermons, however dull they might seem at the time of taking, yet . . . 'did a fellow good—kept him in touch with Higher Things.' " [11] In this religious atmosphere even Kernahan's watered-down revivalism in terms of Christian citizenship was hard to maintain. The churches soon tired of his high-pressure techniques. Although two-thirds of them used some

[8] Kernahan, *Christian Citizenship,* pp. 60–64, 72, 126.

[9] Kernahan, *Visitation Evangelism, Its Methods,* pp. 30–31.

[10] *Ibid.,* pp. 40, 113, 112; *Watchman-Examiner,* July 7, 1921, p. 852.

[11] Sinclair Lewis, *Babbitt* (New York, 1922), pp. 207–8. See also R. S. and H. M. Lynd, *Middletown* (New York, 1925), for a description of the religion of the average American in the 1920's.

form of visitation evangelism after 1930, they abandoned the elaborate city-wide campaigns in which Kernahan specialized. The Institute of Social and Religious Research reported in 1930:

Great difficulties are often met in the financing of visitation evangelism, in securing the sufficient cooperation, and in pushing lay participants to the point of actual results. The numbers reached are often sadly small relative to the vast population of areas it is attempted to cover. In view of somewhat disillusioning experiences along these lines, federations are becoming somewhat wary of accepting direct charge of visitation campaigns with the accompanying financial responsibilities.[12]

Between 1930 and 1950 the majority of urban and suburban Protestant churches did their visitation by themselves or occasionally joined in a visitation program with one or two nearby churches to round up new people in the neighborhood or to bring lapsed members back. But the practice of city-wide revivalism, of whatever variety, fell into disuse, and few thought it would ever again play a major part in the church life of the nation. Willard L. Sperry, Dean of Harvard Divinity School, writing for a British audience in *Religion in America,* said in 1946, "We are tired of religious revivals as we have known them in the last half century. . . . Among all but the most backward churches it is now agreed that education ought to be, and probably is, the best way of interesting our people in religion and of identifying them with one or another of our many denominations. Our efforts therefore have been turned from the religious revival to religious education." According to Sperry, Horace Bushnell's principles of "Christian nurture" had triumphed. "At the present moment the more sober and less ecstatic types of church expect their children to grow up into the Christian life and thus into church membership as a result of their training in church schools." [13]

Even in the South and rural West, where fundamentalism was still strong, the major denominations gave up revivalism after 1930. The fundamentalist church leaders were as convinced as the modernists that the tradition had outlived its usefulness. Certainly some of the worst exemplars of the profession had been active among fundamentalist churches and

12 Douglass, *Protestant Cooperation,* p. 337.
13 W. L. Sperry, *Religion in America* (New York, 1946), pp. 161–62, 171.

the crass exhibitionism and commercialism of second-rate evangelists had shocked even the staunchest believers in the old-time religion. After the great depression set in, the scarcity of money everywhere curtailed the efforts of those who still might have supported city-wide evangelistic campaigns.[14]

Many people expected that the depression following the crash in 1929 would produce a return to religion in some spectacular way, but they were mistaken. With the possible exception of the "Prayer Meeting Revival" of 1857–1858 there has been no significant correlation between periods of depression and periods of revival in the United States. The American attitude had been at once so optimistic as to expect depressions to be merely temporary readjustments and so fatalistic as to believe that the law of supply and demand had to correct itself. In the 1930's the optimistic belief in self-reliance remained, but the fatalistic aspect disappeared. An editorial in the *Christian Century* noted in 1935 that among all classes of people "the idea prevails that our economic system is a man-made system. And being man-made it can be remade." Although Americans disagreed as to how to remake it, they were nevertheless certain that the depression "is not an 'act of God' like an earthquake, but it is due to the failure of human intelligence or the blind power of entrenched privilege, or both. It is therefore not something about which one need get 'religious.'"[15] In 1936 a National Preaching Mission sponsored by the Federal Council of Churches failed miserably. A year later Samuel C. Kincheloe, Associate Professor of the Sociology of Religion at Chicago Theological Seminary, published a "Research Memo on Religion in the Depression" for the Social Science Council. In it he pointed out that while "many looked

[14] Charles Stelzle sent out questionnaires to 100 of the most prominent professional evangelists in 1935 inquiring about the state of their trade. He found that "very few have had engagements even for a few weeks during the year. . . . Almost all of the larger cities are closed to them. However, even the agricultural areas which formerly regarded camp meetings or evangelistic services as an annual necessity are shutting out the itinerant preacher." "The Passing of the Evangelist," *The Presbyterian Tribune,* June 27, 1935, pp. 9–10. For a brief discussion of the breakdown of the revival tradition in the South in these years see H. M. Miller, "Religion in the South," *Christendom* VII (Summer, 1942), 309–312, 317–18.

[15] *Christian Century,* September 18, 1935, pp. 1168–70. Quoted in Samuel C. Kincheloe, *Research Memo on Religion in the Depression* (New York, 1937), pp. 93–94.

for the depression to bring revivalism back," there was "general agreement that there is little or no evidence that this has transpired." He dismissed in a footnote the fact that in "rural parishes of the South" there were some ministers who believed that the depression was "God-sent." It was Kincheloe's hypothesis that secularization was so far advanced in America that no pervasive revival of religious interest was possible.[16] Instead of turning to God for help, even churchgoing people turned to the New Deal "brain trust" in Washington. What Kincheloe missed, as Sperry did, was the fact that there was a revival of religion going on among those citizens who had not become secularized but who, for that very reason, were not frequenters of the churches of the respectable denominations which Kincheloe and Sperry looked upon as the only significant repositories of American religious life.[17]

Sperry spoke patronizingly of the "backward" and "ecstatic" churches as though they were the last lingering remnants of American illiteracy and underprivilege which would soon be raised to the level of "modern liberal Protestantism." But if American church membership, particularly Protestant membership, continued to grow in the years between the wars, it was largely because of these backward churches and ecstatic new denominations. They sprang up and flourished on every side and carried on, almost sub rosa, the old evangelical pietistic tradition until it flowered again in the ashes of Sperry's liberalism.[18]

The revivalistic activity of the new sects was not the beginning of a new awakening so much as the continuation of a longstanding revolt against the loss of piety in the regular denominations. As a pietistic revolt this activity could perhaps be logically traced back to the perfectionists and adventists of the second great awakening. But in its contemporary form it had its beginnings in the 1870's when the first "prophetic

[16] Kincheloe, *Research Memo,* pp. 45 ff., 95. See also the Lynds, *Middletown in Transition,* pp. 301 ff., for a similar view of American secularism in the 1930's.

[17] Kincheloe did note that "members of the minor 'fundamentalist groups'" seemed to have increased substantially during the depression, but he felt that "their rate of growth has been fairly constant during the period since 1925" and let it go at that. *Ibid.,* p. 8.

[18] See for example R. S. and H. M. Lynd, *Middletown in Transition* (New York, 1937), p. 297, regarding the growth of holiness churches.

conferences" protested against the declining interest in Biblical prophecy, perfectionism (or holiness), and adventism among the major denominations. At first the protest was within the denominations, but by 1900 the dissidents were splitting off to form new sects with titles emphasizing their "holiness" or "Pentecostal" fervor. These groups were closely associated with the fundamentalist wings of the major denominations but, like the Separatists of seventeenth-century England, they wanted a "reformation without tarrying for any" while the fundamentalists, like the Puritans, hoped to reform the denominations from within (reform them *back* to true Christian principles).

By the 1930's, however, most of the fundamentalists were themselves separated in spirit if not in fact from their denominations. Many pastors and congregations which had been Baptist, Methodist, Presbyterian, or Disciples disaffiliated and either adopted the status of independent churches or took up a holiness title of their own invention. Many other congregations remained nominally within their denominations but had closer ties with the new sects than with the old. Although Sperry and Kincheloe did not realize it, America had by the mid-1930's two national Protestant religions. The first was liberal Protestantism, a blend of Kernahan's Christian citizenship and Babbitt's vague desire to keep in touch with "higher things" which pervaded most of the evangelical churches. The second was pietistic fundamentalism. The differences between these two national religions was not only theological but social, economic, and intellectual. Most liberal Protestants and most social scientists, noting that the pietistic sects were popular among the poorer and more socially backward segments of the population, assumed that pietism was simply an immature form of liberal Protestantism. Increased educational facilities, social welfare legislation, and a higher standard of living, they contended, would elevate these benighted people to the point where they would join the mainstream of American life and thought, and leave their primitive religious notions behind. But the cleavage between the two wings of Protestantism was deeper and wider than that, not only in regard to social and economic privilege, but in terms of religious commitment. To its adherents, pietistic fundamentalism was a way of life, not a

Sunday morning ritual. And in the years between 1875 and 1945 they evolved an institutional framework and a cultural milieu which provided them with a means of perpetuating their ideological separateness.

The religious tenets of this second wing of Protestantism were essentially those of all pietistic movements since the Reformation, even though in certain respects they were closely integrated with a nationalistic commitment to American democracy and free enterprise capitalism. These tenets consisted of an extremely literalistic reliance upon the Bible, a puritannical morality, a pessimistic or escapist outlook on world history, and a perfectionist view of the meaning of salvation. The range of emotionalism, social withdrawal, Biblicism, millennialism, and mysticism within the group was wide. There was a tendency on the part of the older denominations, especially those which had themselves been lower-class sects at one time, to tar them all with the brush of the most ecstatic types and call them "Holy Rollers" or "the radical fringe." But these people preferred the terms "Evangelical" or "Holiness" or "Pentecostal" and most of them deplored the extremists who indulged in "snake handling" or emotional orgies. The vast majority of these fundamentalists were respectable, pious folk who expressed their fervor by intensively devout praying, hymn singing, Bible reading, and soul-winning.

In the days before the Scopes trial fundamentalism was associated primarily with the rural areas of the nation, and H. L. Mencken solidified this notion in the public mind by referring aciduously to "the Bible belt" as though it were roughly equivalent to the corn, cotton, and soy bean belts. But even as Mencken's phrase set the stereotype the pattern of fundamentalism was changing. Actually it had never been confined to any one region though it had been predominantly rural. In 1925, contrary to general belief, its leadership and dynamic force came from its urban adherents. On the whole the heart of this form of evangelical pietism lay in that group of upper-lower class and lower-middle class people in the nation's metropolitan centers whom sociologists and social workers referred to as "the marginal group." Although fundamentalism had its paupers and its millionaires, the majority of its members lived on the fringe between the middle and lower classes and constituted what might be called "the unsuccessful middle class." Insecure, frustrated, feeling inferior and different, most of them were struggling not so much to get into a higher social bracket as to keep from sinking into a lower one. Most of these pietists were former tenant farmers, "hill billies," poor whites, small town folk who had drifted into the cities to work in mills and factories as farming became less and less profitable and the lure of steady employment seemed to offer some hope of improvement. Having taken jobs in factories and mills, few of them were able to work their way out of the company towns or into the more respectable areas of the cities and suburbs. For solace and a sense of belonging they sought to recreate in various store-front churches and gospel tabernacles in the cities the simple, enthusiastic, friendly religion which had been part of their community life in the country. As such it constituted not a halfway house to the more liberal churches but the focal point of a culture within a culture.

At the upper end of the financial scale in this pietistic group were a few who by good fortune or hard work had made a rapid financial rise but who failed to find, or refused to seek, acceptance or happiness among the more solidly established old middle class. Because they could not, or would not, shuck off their ingrained frame of values and morals, they utilized their new-found wealth to promote the religion which gave meaning to their lives, thereby assuming positions of leadership in the holiness and Pentecostal denominations, or among the die-hard fundamentalists of the established denominations.

Estimates of the number of persons associated with this second wing of Protestantism were based primarily on guesswork, as these people were not given to statistics and did not like those who were. It probably would not be too far wrong to claim, however, that some twenty million persons were among those pietists who were thoroughly alienated from liberal Protestantism by 1945. Perhaps ten per cent of these were extremists, predominantly rural and Negro. Probably about half were still associated, in name at least, with one of the major denominations. About six million were members of the new holiness and pentecostal sects, and about two million were members of independent, "Bible-believing," store-front churches and tabernacles.[19]

In an article entitled "Those 'Store-Front' Churches," Ralph M. Riggs, Home Missions Secretary of the Assemblies of God churches, described the genesis of a typical independent holiness church in the 1930's. As so often happened, this one grew out of a free lance revival campaign.

"In April, 1935," said Riggs, "Ralph Byrd came to Atlanta, Georgia, and rented an old vacant building for a three-week revival. He then fasted and prayed for three days and felt definitely led of the Lord to remain in Atlanta and establish a church. He obtained a tent and began a tent meeting which lasted five months without a single night off. Great crowds attended and many souls were saved. While this meeting was still in progress he found an old dilapidated tabernacle which had been used as a wrestling arena and contracted to purchase it for $2950 believing [trusting?] God for the money. When it was repaired and renovated and it came too cold to continue on in the tent, they moved and their crowd followed them. It was not at all uncommon to have 1000 people in attendance. With this remarkable success as an example, other like-minded ministers were inspired and undertook to found other churches in various parts of the city." Within a few years there were seven such independent, "Bible-believing," "Christ-preaching," churches in Atlanta.[20]

Riggs characteristically explained the reason for the burgeoning of independent, nondenominational churches like Byrd's on the ground that "the staid, orthodox church is not evangelistic enough. The spontaneous springing into existence of these warm, informal, evangelistic centers seems to be the protest of the Holy Spirit against what might be called the complacent piety of 'regular' churches. . . . There are many who will go into an ordinary store building or assembly hall who would not enter a regular church." Writing in 1945, Riggs noted, "The movement has grown faster than it has produced mature teachers and most fanaticism is the result of the

[19] See Marcus Bach, *Report to Protestants* (New York, 1948), for an interesting account of this aspect of Protestantism. I have doubled his estimate of ten million members (p. 262). See also "The Third Force in Christendom," *Life,* June 9, 1958, pp. 113 ff.

[20] *United Evangelical Action* (Cincinnati), IV (August 1, 1945), 4–5.

lack of teaching . . . fanaticism is reprehensible and repelling. Wherever it exists it is a distinct liability and drawback . . . [perhaps] the devil has attached these discredits to the movement in order to drive away seeking souls." The attempt to maintain a religion true to the old fundamentals without fanaticism indicated the semirespectability of these churches and clearly marked them off from the snake-handling cults. When Byrd later moved his congregation from the wrestling arena to a $51,000 church edifice, he took the first step away from the enthusiastic pietism of its rural origin. However, the ostensible motive behind this step was not to become more like the regular churches but to outshine them in fervor. The pietists might put on the façade of respectability, but they maintained their fundamentalist outlook and their militant antagonism toward the deadness and formality of the "regular" churches.

Byrd's work in Atlanta typified another aspect of this movement. It demonstrated what happened to the professional evangelists who were so numerous in Sunday's day. Having thrown in their lot with the fundamentalists, the revivalists could no longer obtain the cooperation of the regular denominations needed for their trade. After the debacle of the 1920's, most of the members of the Interdenominational Association of Evangelists and the graduates of the various Bible institutes and colleges founded or preached in independent churches and tabernacles in cities all over the nation. The Clinton H. Churchill Evangelistic Tabernacle in Buffalo was founded by a convert of Sunday's in 1921; the Chicago Gospel Tabernacle was founded by Paul Rader of the Moody Bible Institute in 1922; Aimee Semple MacPherson gave up her barnstorming tent revivals to open Angelus Temple in Los Angeles in 1923. Similar to these were Katherine Kuhlman's Denver Revival Tabernacle, E. J. Rolling's Detroit Metropolitan Tabernacle, T. H. Elsner's Philadelphia Gospel Tabernacle, Karl Wittman's Tabernacle in Toledo, Dewitt Johnston's People's Gospel Tabernacle in Fort Wayne, Luke Rader's River Lake Gospel Tabernacle in Minneapolis, and Harry D. Clarke's Billy Sunday Memorial Tabernacle in Sioux City. These and others like them formed a regular circuit for those older evangelists and choristers who still retained the urge to itinerate and for younger men who felt the call. Almost all these tabernacles maintained a radio station, or at least a radio program, a weekly journal, a summer Bible camp, and some kind of home or foreign missionary activity. They found an immediate and enthusiastic response and built up large and devoted congregations which were willing to contribute, often to tithe, faithfully and generously in exchange for the services rendered. Among these people the tradition of modern revivalism was perpetuated.

In conjunction with these tabernacles which supplied the regular Sunday services, midweek prayer meetings, and various entertainment and social occasions for the marginal middle class, there arose a host of Bible Schools and Bible Colleges designed to provide the type of "Christian education" which these people believed was no longer available in state, independent, and denominational colleges. Typical of these was the one founded in 1927 by Bob Jones, Sr., one of the popular evangelists of Sunday's time. He called it Bob Jones College and placed Mrs. Sunday on the board of trustees; later he gave her and her husband honorary degrees for their aid in raising funds. In addition to providing a fundamentalist oriented general education, Bob Jones College trained men and women for missionary activity and church work of all sorts. Among similar institutions were the Moody Bible Institute, the Los Angeles Bible Institute, William Jennings Bryan College, Northeastern Bible Institute, Southeastern Bible College, Piedmont Bible College, Detroit Bible Institute, Houghton College, Providence-Barrington Bible College, and Wheaton College in Illinois. In addition to patronizing these schools, the fundamentalists in some cities founded "Christian High Schools" to compete with the "godless" public high schools. These middle-class American pietists wanted not only a high school but a college education for their children.

Throughout the 1930's the independent churches and tabernacles, the holiness and pentecostal sects, and the various interdenominational fundamentalist groups within the ranks of the older denominations went through countless amalgamations and divisions. Although they agreed on the five points of fundamentalism, there were still questions of emphasis, of polity, and of social outlook which kept them apart. Like all pietistic movements, this rebellion against the regular, national, "established" church system was individualistic and independent in the extreme. Each congregation was a world unto itself, and each pastor was the sole shepherd of his flock. United on the fundamentals, they were often divided on every other ground. Politically they ranged from complete withdrawal from all political activity to the most rampant type of fascist totalitarianism. Socially they ranged from a kind of communistic brotherhood of all believers to the most exclusive type of racism. But these extremes were principally among the poorest and least educated.

Among the more commonly shared ideas of the more stable elements in the movement were a strident nationalism, a xenophobic isolationism, an assertive individualism, and a latent authoritarianism. As confirmed premillennialists they were pessimistic about any type of reform save that of converting individuals; yet their perfectionism was so strong that they believed that converted, soul winning individuals might save the world. The insecurity of their social and economic position bred a sense of inferiority which manifested itself on the one hand in rejection of all the worldly pleasures or vices which characterized the social life of the well-to-do, and on the other hand, in self-righteous assertions of their own special position of divine favor. Generally speaking, their puritanical morality contained the essence of the Protestant ethic with its stress upon those traits of hard work, thrift, and sobriety which led back into the world many who started out in withdrawal from it.

Although their newspapers, sermons, Bible conferences, and radio broadcasts were numerous and polemical, their voices were at first like those frustrated builders of the Tower of Babel. Their leading spokesmen in the 1930's were almost entirely negative and hypercritical. When not attacking the modernists, the social gospelers, and the radicals, they attacked each other for failure to maintain certain nebulous standards of doctrinal piety. Some of the more virulent spokesmen devoted most of their efforts to attacking the Roman Catholic Church. Others, like Gerald L. K. Smith, Gerald B. Winrod, J. Frank

Norris, Bob Shuler, Luke and Paul Rader, William Bell Riley, and Mordecai Ham, injected antisemitic and anti-Negro demagogy into their preaching and journalism.[21]

The coming of World War II, however, brought a change in the inchoate pietistic movement, as it did throughout American life. The years 1929–1939 had been traumatic ones for the average American. The most crippling depression since the start of the Industrial Revolution severely jolted the belief in perpetual progress. The war of Japanese imperialism in Asia; the defeat of democracy in Italy and Germany by despots without principles who nevertheless had the support of the people; the betrayal of whatever good might have come out of the Russian Revolution by the ruthless Stalin; the inability of the League of Nations, the disarmament pacts, and isolationism to maintain the peace and security of the world or of the United States, shattered one after another of the hopes and refuges of the idealistic American mind. The horrors of the war itself and the perplexities of a divided world in which America had, willy nilly, to assume the leading role in international power politics, climaxed the series of historical shocks which formed the background of America's fourth great awakening. The resurgence of neo-fundamentalism was merely one aspect of a theological and intellectual reorientation which affected the whole of American life more profoundly than any that preceded it.

One aspect of the theological reorientation in Protestantism had begun almost as soon as modernism became established (just as Bushnell had proclaimed certain aspects of modernism at the moment evangelicalism defeated Calvinism, and just as the Methodists had proclaimed Arminianism while neo-Calvinism was winning the first great awakening). The new theology called itself "neo-orthodoxy" and received its inspiration from European theologians for whom World War I was the debacle of the liberal ideal of progress. Under the leadership of Reinhold Niebuhr and Paul Tillich, American liberal Protestants began a critical re-examination of their theology at the end of the 1920's which took them "beyond modernism." Niebuhr's opening remark in *Reflections on the End of an Era,*

21 See Ralph Lord Roy, *Apostles of Discord* (Boston, 1953); and Paul Carter, *The Decline and Revival of the Social Gospel* (Ithaca, New York, 1956).

in 1931, set the tone of the new school: "In my opinion, adequate spiritual guidance can come only through more radical political orientation and more conservative religious convictions than are comprehended in the culture of our era." The aim was to dispel the shibboleth that Christianity must stand or fall with the advance of laissez-faire capitalism and at the same time to reject the facile belief in a benevolent God working out his benign purpose in history. But the abstruse theology of neo-orthodoxy was difficult to propagate and not until the 1940's were more than a handful of American ministers ready to come to grips with its challenge. Meanwhile, the politically liberal outlook of Niebuhr and his colleagues suffered the consequences of a too close association with the socialistic wing of the Age of Roosevelt. The urgencies of the depression stimulated the re-examination of modernism, and they also pushed Americans into the rapid assimilation of social controls over economic life which had barely been started in the progressive movement. World War II heightened government regulation and centralization, and in the bitter aftermath of a fruitless victory, the Age of Roosevelt passed into the Age of Reaction. Anxiety over failures to achieve a peaceful world was coupled with anxiety within American society over economic prosperity and social insecurity. Never before had the contrast between materialistic well-being and spiritual emptiness created so stark and widespread a sense of failure. After three hundred years Americans had conquered the New World wilderness only to find that they were now required to face the same age-old, insoluble problems of human destiny which they had avoided by their flight from the Old World. Their attempt to make America a utopian model for the world to follow now seemed to have been merely the creation of a fool's paradise. By combining the ideals of the Protestant ethic, perfectionist millennialism, and enlightened reason, they had succeeded in building a land of peace and plenty only to find that while other nations admired it for its power and wealth they did not find either its philosophy or its ideals applicable to their situation. This frustration was made more bitter by the fact that Americans were themselves not happy in the city they had built upon a hill.

As in the past, the difficulties of re-assessing and reformulating the values of American culture necessitated a new appraisal of the underlying Christian ethos. In this awakening Roman Catholics and Jews in America for the first time shared in the crisis. The neo-Thomism of Catholic intellectuals, the *Peace of Soul* sermons of Monsignor Fulton J. Sheen, the renascence of Jewish orthodoxy, the *Peace of Mind* philosophy of Rabbi Joshua L. Liebman, the neo-orthodoxy of Reinhold Niebuhr, the positive thinking of Norman Vincent Peale, and the existentialism of the agnostics, were all part of the same awakening. And so, too, was the return to popularity of the old-time religion which, in the preaching of Billy Graham and the neo-fundamentalism of the pietistic sects, brought an ecclesiastical conflict that generated what many thought was a genuine return to the days of Moody, Finney, and Whitefield. In order to understand Graham's part in the awakening it is necessary to relate his work to the attempts at consolidation which were undertaken among the second wing of Protestantism during the early 1940's. There were three significant organizations which, during the prosperous war years, sought to bring order and unity to the fundamentalist come-outers. They were the American Council of Christian Churches, founded by Carl McIntire in 1941; the National Association of Evangelicals for United Action, founded in 1942; and Youth for Christ International, started in 1943.[22] The McIntire group and the National Association of Evangelicals (NAE) both had as their main purpose the uniting of those independent churches and denominations which were out of sympathy with modernism into a rival federation to the Federal Council of Churches (since 1950 the National Council of Churches). McIntire gathered some of the more rabid fundamentalist groups into his American Council, but his association with various racists and his intolerance toward other fundamentalists who did not agree with him prevented his attaining the support of the more reasonable opponents of modernism. The American Council of Churches never spoke for more than 1,500,000 members.[23]

[22] See F. E. Mayer, *The Religious Bodies of America* (St. Louis, Missouri, 1956), pp. 496–98.

[23] See Roy, *Apostles of Discord*, pp. 196–198, 393–98.

The National Association of Evangelicals, however, was more successful. It was led by such capable ministerial administrators as Harold J. Ockenga (the first president of NAE), J. Elwin Wright, Donald Grey Barnhouse, Paul S. Rees, R. T. Davis, W. H. Houghton, Rutherford L. Decker, John W. Bradbury, Stephen W. Paine, L. R. Marston, Carl F. H. Henry, William Ward Ayer, Torrey M. Johnson, Howard W. Ferrin, Bob Jones, Sr., Charles E. Fuller, V. Raymond Edman, Charles Templeton, and Robert P. Shuler. These men were prominent leaders of the Bible colleges, fundamentalist journals, and prosperous urban tabernacles or independent churches. They were the social and intellectual elite of the marginal middle class, and they commanded wide respect and large funds from their followers. Within ten years of its founding the NAE claimed to speak for ten million church members of thirty different fundamentalist denominations or churches.[24] When a new wave of religious revivalism swept the nation in the 1950's, the NAE rightly claimed much of the credit for stimulating and directing it. In some respects the work of the NAE was reminiscent of Finney's attempt to organize a revival movement among the rural-born in the Eastern cities directed against the prevailing theological and ecclesiastical system of his day. But in the context of its times Finney's movement looked forward while the NAE looked backward.

According to J. Elwin Wright, the Chairman of the NAE's Commission on International Relations, the NAE was founded "on the conviction that the time had come when groups which could not conscientiously accept the leadership of existing interdenominational agencies must find some means of cooperation and expression." [25] Out of some 260 Protestant denomina-

[24] *Ibid.,* pp. 183–185, 391–92. Among the groups associated with the NAE by 1953 were Assemblies of God, Church of God, Evangelical Free Church of America, Free Methodist Church of North America, Grace Gospel Evangelistic Association, International Church of the Foursquare Gospel, International Pentecostal Assemblies, National Association of Free Will Baptists, Open Bible Standard Churches, Pentecostal Holiness Church, Primitive Methodist Church of the U.S.A., and Wesleyan Methodist Church of America. *Ibid.,* pp. 391–2.

[25] *United Evangelical Action,* April 15, 1946, p. 12. The constitution of the NAE stated as one reason for the organization that "in many areas of Christian endeavor the organizations which now purport to be the representatives of Protestant Christianity have departed from the faith of Jesus Christ. . . ." which was a direct slap at the liberal Protestantism of the Federal Council of Churches. Quoted in Mayer, *Religious Bodies,* p. 498.

tions in the United States, he pointed out, only twenty-five were associated with the Federal Council of Churches. Although the Federal Council spoke for thirty million of the nation's Protestant church members, the NAE believed that their organization would soon be able to speak for most of the remaining twenty-five million as well as for many formally associated with the denominations in the FCC. Despite the open rivalry of McIntire's ACCC, the NAE did not consider his movement a serious threat. Many in the NAE were surprised to find how easy their task was.

The time was ripe for this consolidation among the moderate fundamentalists. The "ultra-fundamentalists," represented by McIntire, had been discredited by twenty years of bluster and bombast. Modernism was undergoing a sharp reorientation under the influence of the neo-orthodox movement. The social gospelers (among whom were many of Niebuhr's followers), having achieved many of their goals through the New Deal, were facing a ground swell of theological and political conservatism which reached a climax during the furor over McCarthyism and the presidential election of 1952. But most important, the steady growth of a network of fundamentalist schools, publishing houses, journals, radio stations, Bible conferences, missionary alliances, and interchurch evangelistic activities of all sorts over the years had at last provided the institutional basis upon which a united, militant, and prosperous new fundamentalist crusade could be constructed. By 1951 the reactivation of the British Evangelical Alliance, under the prodding support of the NAE, led to the founding of the World Evangelical Fellowship which, as a counterpart of the World Council of Churches, made neofundamentalism international.

Because it was an ecumenical movement, because it tried to tone down some of the fanaticism of earlier fundamentalism, because it had no qualms about using the most up-to-date techniques of publicity and bureaucracy, the NAE appealed to the more respectable of the fundamentalists and repelled the more rigid and unsophisticated of them. On the whole, the NAE did not gain much support among the lower-class pietistic groups which still insisted upon complete autonomy for each congregation and which maintained a large measure of emotionalism and extreme theological legalism. Nor did all these groups associate with McIntire's ACCC. All such ecumenical organizations, they said, were bound to result in compromise with the world and a decrease in spiritual purity and independence. The unsophisticated wanted to be in the world but not of the world. The NAE wanted to be both.

The NAE was of two minds in its approach to ecumenicalism. It was so at odds with modernism, the social gospel, neo-orthodoxy, and all that the Federal Council of Churches had stood for since 1908 that its principal purpose seemed to some of its leaders to be to destroy the existing denominational and interdenominational organizations of the regular churches and incorporate the fragments into the NAE system. Many of the pronouncements of NAE leaders seemed to call for true believers to come out from among the heretics in open schism. Donald G. Barnhouse, writing in *United Evangelical Action,* the semiofficial organ of the NAE, said in 1945, "There is a wreck coming and . . . it is our business to save as many as possible out of the wreck . . . we who are born again have a tremendously important role here. . . . The existence of a select company of true sons of God constitutes the salt of the earth which keeps the whole mess from rotting. We are of more value to the United States than atomic bomb plants and bomber factories tho' the world will not admit it." [26] The editor of the same magazine, James deForest Murch, consistently attacked the Federal Council of Churches and noted with glee every schism which wracked the major denominations.[27] "The very heart of this movement," said Murch of the NAE, is "evangelism," and the type of evangelism seemed to be directed, like Finney's in the cities of the East, not so much toward saving those outside the churches as stealing sheep from or fomenting discord within the folds of nonfundamentalists.

But there was another and more influential group within the NAE which preferred a different approach. The leader of this wing was Harold J. Ockenga, pastor of Park Street Church, who was the Lyman Beecher of the new evangelical assimilation. He preferred to reform the old denominations from with-

[26] *United Evangelical Action,* November 1, 1945, p. 12.

[27] For the denominational schisms of the post-World War II period and their connection with the neofundamentalist movement see Roy, *Apostles of Discord,* esp. chap. xiv.

in, to capitalize upon the demoralization of the modernists and upon the trend toward the right in theology in order to recapture control of the ecclesiastical machinery which the fundamentalists had lost in the 1920's. The group which Ockenga represented hoped to swing whole denominations out of the orbit of the Federal Council of Churches and into the NAE. They were not willing to wait for the wreck of the old order and meanwhile to condone nibbling away at the edges of the old denominations. In the interests of a larger hope they bent every effort toward conciliation rather than schism, trying to entice wavering churchmen over to their side by persuasion rather than criticism. In doing this they stressed the term "evangelicalism" rather than "fundamentalism." It was claimed that evangelicalism was, after all, the essence of Christianity from which modernism had departed. And it was true that there were some in the NAE who did preach a more scholarly and open-minded evangelical orthodoxy than that of the 1920's. But the animating spirit of the new movement stemmed essentially from a dogmatic re-assertion of the same old five points of the Niagara Bible Conference with all the narrowness they implied. Nevertheless, in an effort to blur this fact the label of fundamentalism was persistently pushed off upon the McIntire group or upon the lower class "backward" and "ecstatic" churches which NAE spokesmen habitually referred to as "cults."

Compared to these "fanatics" the NAE did seem to many uncertain church people like a moderate organization based on a "conservative theology" which might prove a viable alternative to a defunct modernism and an unfathomable neo-orthodoxy. How far from being moderate either in theology or politics the NAE was, however, could easily have been discerned in the pages of its journal. An editorial in *United Evangelical Action* stated in 1954, "We are proud to walk in the steps of that grand company of so-called 'fundamentalists' who two generations ago blazed a trail for loyalty to Christ and the Bible in a forest of doubt and unbelief." [28] Other editorials and articles in the magazine denounced the left wing activities and leadership of the Federal Council of Churches, the infiltration of "reds" into the churches, the "revolution-

[28] *United Evangelical Action,* February 15, 1955, p. 13.

ary" activities of New Dealism, the "godless" public school system, the communist fifth column in the national government, the atheistic and heathen-dominated UNESCO, the subversive agitation of certain labor unions, "the subtle machinations of World Jewry" behind the United Nations, the racial miscegenation which would result from the enactment of a National Fair Employment Practices Commission Act, and the dangerous tendencies of the Roman Catholic hierarchy leading toward the overthrow of democracy. The magazine also praised the Bricker Amendment, Congressional investigations of communism in the colleges, churches and government, and the American Legion's "Back-to-God" movement.[29] In 1950 the magazine applauded the NAE convention for endorsing "free enterprise," and after the first year of President Eisenhower's administration the editor gave thanks for the "trend toward conservatism" and the "decided turn toward the Right in American politics." [30] The NAE's committal to "the American type of Christianity" was strong from the beginning. As the chairman of the association's Commission on Social Action, Carl F. H. Henry wrote in 1955, "It is not Capitalism therefore which is the guardian of Christianity, but Christianity which alone can safeguard free enterprise from perversion.[31]

The third fundamentalist organization which sought to reorganize evangelical Protestantism was Youth for Christ International. It was started in 1943 by the Rev. Roger Malsbary, a pastor of the Christian and Missionary Alliance Church in Indianapolis.[32] Backed by some "Christian businessmen" in

[29] *Ibid.* For attacks on the United Nations and UNESCO see August 1, 1945, p. 13; October 15, p. 12, January 1, 1954, p. 3. For articles attacking godless public schools and communist infiltration in government and churches, see August 15, 1945, p. 3; November 1, p. 21; January 21, 1949, p. 11; February 1, 1954, pp. 7, 13, 16; May 1, p. 13, August 1, p. 3. For attacks on New Deal liberalism see September 1, 1945, p. 12. For anti-Catholicism see October 15, 1947, p. 9; April 15, 1954, p. 13; and various advertisements for books exposing the evils of nunneries and monasteries. For attacks on the FEPC and World Jewry see October 1, 1949, p. 11. For praise of the Bricker Amendment see February 15, 1954, p. 31. Though these articles were not official pronouncements of the NAE (which disclaims responsibilities for Murch's editorials) there seems little doubt that the tone of the magazine was representative of the general viewpoint of the organization's membership.

[30] *Ibid.,* April 26, 1950; January 1, 1954, p. 11.

[31] *Ibid.,* May 1, 1955, pp. 7 ff.

[32] *Ibid.,* August 1, 1945, p. 18. See also Mel Larsen, *Youth for Christ* (Grand Rapids, 1947), pp. 19, 30 ff. It may be unfair to give Malsbary credit for orig-

Danville and Indianapolis, he began to hold Saturday night rallies for young people and members of the armed forces. Other fundamentalist pastors throughout the United States and Canada who had been trying similar experiments in their cities met with Malsbary at the first Youth for Christ conference at the Winona Lake Bible Conference in July, 1944. Youth for Christ rallies were given wide publicity by the Hearst newspapers at the specific direction of William Randolph Hearst. By the end of 1944 there were four hundred cities conducting weekly Youth for Christ rallies. At that time the Rev. Torrey M. Johnson, pastor of the Midwest Bible Church in Cicero, Illinois, became unofficial president of Youth for Christ and decided to make it into a more closely knit and aggressive organization. The upsurge of juvenile delinquency brought about by wartime dislocations in family life helped Johnson get the backing of the Christian War Veterans of America and of leading evangelical businessmen who were convinced that "Christ is the answer to juvenile delinquency." In July, 1945, Youth for Christ International was officially formed with Johnson as president, Richard Harvey, vice-president, and George Wilson, Treasurer.[33]

The NAE, in which Johnson was an active figure, gave Youth for Christ its full support and frankly saw it as an ally in winning young people away from the youth groups of the older denominations like the Epworth League and the Christian Endeavor Society.[34] Because of this, and because Youth for Christ organized its rallies upon the most flamboyant lines, hiring large auditoriums or stadiums, plastering the city with posters, bringing jazzy musical groups into their programs, and instilling the whole movement with the aura of an adolescent crusade for fundamentalism, the pastors of the regular churches

---

inating the movement, for as Larsen points out the idea had roots which went back before World War I. But Malsbary seems to have been the most important figure in initiating the present organization of the group. Among others who were prominent in organizing Youth for Christ organizations in the early 1940's were Jack Wyrtzen, Percy Crawford, Oscar Gillian, Ed. Darling, Charles Templeton and Torrey Johnson. Although Wyrtzen's activity antedated Malsbary's, he never officially joined the Youth for Christ group.

33 For the details of the formation of the organization see Larsen, *Youth for Christ,* pp. 82 ff. For support of it by the Hearst press see *ibid.,* p. 72.

34 *United Evangelical Action,* August 15, 1945, p. 9; August 15, 1947.

denounced it as divisive, emotional, and spiritually shallow.[35] *The Christian Century*'s editor called Youth for Christ "a streamlined expression of a traditionally conservative type of revivalism" which was "little concerned with the social or ethical bearing of the Christian faith."[36] Nevertheless, the movement flourished in postwar years, and in 1946 Johnson introduced it into the British Isles with the full support of the fundamentalist pastors and laymen there.

The resurgent activity of the fundamentalists coincided with the second influx into America's cities of rural folk seeking wartime jobs during the early 1940's, and this conjunction produced a new burst of evangelistic activity. In the very year that Dean Sperry was writing about the death of the revival tradition in America, J. Elwin Wright said, "For the first time since the days of Chapman and Alexander and Billy Sunday and other great evangelists of the early twentieth century, we are faced with the challenging situation of having many more calls for evangelistic campaigns than there are competent evangelists to go around." He attributed this to the confusion and dislocations of wartime life, to the "increase of wealth among the workers," to the declining morals resulting from women taking jobs in war industry, and to the uncertainty caused by the war and the discovery of the atomic bomb. "Only God can help us," he said characteristically, "in this time of vast change."[37]

After the war a new source of confusion developed among American pietists in the fear over the increased power of the "atheistic" Soviet Union, and a wave of hysteria began over the infiltration of communism into all aspects of American life.

[35] The seven-point doctrinal platform of Youth for Christ included as No. 1, "We believe the Bible to be the inspired, the infallible authoritative Word of God," and as No. 3, "We believe in the deity of our Lord Jesus Christ, in His virgin birth, in His sinless life, in His Miracles, in His vicarious and atoning death through His shed blood, in His bodily resurrection, in His ascension to the right hand of the Father, and in His personal return and glory." The rallies were so fervent in their patriotic Americanism that some accused the group of being fascistic, antisemitic, and anti-Negro. In 1945 the organization published an official denial of these accusations. Youth for Christ has always considered itself a potent force for anti-Communism. Larsen, *Youth for Christ*, pp. 88–89, 91.

[36] *Christian Century* (Chicago) November 14, 1945, p. 1244. This editorial denied, however, that Youth for Christ was fascistic or antisemitic.

[37] *United Evangelical Action*, October 15, 1945, p. 12.

Harold Ockenga, speaking to the annual Youth for Christ convention in the Billy Sunday Memorial Tabernacle at Winona Lake in 1949 said, "When situations such as have developed recently in the Judith Coplon case reveal the intrigue and unusual anti-God feeling so prevalent around our country, it's time for a revival." The NAE journal went on to report that "Ockenga felt that the revival will not come from the organized church burdened with machinery but through an interdenominational group with the true spirit of ecumenicity." [38] Somehow the fundamentalists self-righteously assumed that as the saving remnant who had kept themselves pure from the social gospel and New Deal "leftism" during the thirties, they were to lead a great revival for the salvation of the American way of life which the liberals, religious and political, had betrayed. The liberals, suffering from their own pangs of guilt, attacked by the neo-orthodox as well as by the fundamentalists for shallow optimism, acknowledged their past errors and began to think that perhaps a revival of religion was the only way out. To atone for their sins, and perhaps to rebuild the bridges they had burned, they turned to give a helping hand to those who spoke with such assurance of their orthodoxy and divine authority.

Billy Graham was a product of this realignment in Protestantism and of the postwar tension which transformed the nation's outlook from liberalism to conservatism. His roots were deep in the fundamentalist hinterland of the thirties. His flowering came with the re-emergence of the old fundamentalism under the more respectable title of "Evangelical Christianity." Speaking at the NAE annual convention in the afterglow of his first nationally acclaimed city-wide revival, Graham told his neo-fundamentalist auditors in April, 1950, "that he was proud to be a member of the National Association of Evangelicals and that he believed it to be raised up of God as the medium through which Bible-believing, Christ-honoring Christians might present a united front against the enemies of the evangelical faith and for constructive action." [39]

The key to much of Graham's subsequent career lay in a speech he delivered to the NAE convention two years later.

[38] *Ibid.*, August 1, 1949, p. 8.
[39] *Ibid.*, May 1, 1950, p. 3.

In it he began by saying that he agreed with Harold Ockenga that in the face of imminent national doom a new form of Christian unity was necessary: "I do not believe in organizational unity, nor do I believe in an ecumenical movement, but I believe in a spiritual ecumenical movement" of all "born-again believers." "A great change is taking place in this country," he went on; "Torrey Johnson said to me not long ago that in the city of Chicago there is very little real, old-fashioned, dyed-in-the-wool 'Modernism' left. I have found that absolutely true as I've travelled around. There's a reason that the Modernist is almost in a complete retreat. All his ideals and his intellectual props have been knocked out from under him, and he is standing almost in a vacuum now. He's moving toward neo-orthodoxy, but we're praying that he will go beyond neo-orthodoxy to the orthodox position." [40] But Graham wanted to do more than pray for the passing of modernism. *"It is time for action,"* he called. "It's time for an offensive in Revival." "We have defended ourselves long enough. Great books of Apologetics have been written, and today our position is being accepted more and more by the Church at large. I think now is the hour to take the flag and attack the enemy and move into the camps of the devil." Graham here qualified the enemy as being "not our brethren" but "the flesh, the world, and the devil," but the implication was clear enough. It was Harry Emerson Fosdick's address "Shall the Fundamentalists Win?" in reverse.

Graham's speech to the NAE convention in 1952 also reflected the sharp political tensions of the day when he noted, "In the coming election campaign there's going to be the Jewish bloc, there's going to be the Roman Catholic bloc, there's going to be the labor bloc, there's going to be the Irish bloc. They will put on tremendous pressure. They will vote as blocs. Some of them will almost hold the balance of power." Having sounded this alarming note, Graham then sought to rally the righteous: "Why should not Evangelicals across America be conditioned and cultured and instructed until we, too,

[40] This address is printed in full in Charles T. Cook, *The Billy Graham Story* (London, 1954), pp. 90 ff. Although Graham said here that he believed that the Modernist "can be loved back into the fold of orthodoxy" and that he would have "fellowship with any born-again believer," the militant note was far stronger than the irenic.

can make our voice known?" It was time for the born-again Christian bloc to assert itself. During the ensuing years Graham did his best to see that this bloc was "conditioned, cultured, and instructed" toward "the true orthodox position."

William Franklin Graham was born near Charlotte, North Carolina, on November 7, 1918.[41] His father owned a two-hundred-acre dairy farm which, except for a few years in the depths of the depression, was sufficiently prosperous to provide more than adequately for his family of six. The Grahams were members of the Associate Reformed Presbyterian Church (General Synod) which had split off from the Associate Reformed Church in 1822 because it believed the church was becoming too liberal. In this new church the standards of the Westminster Confession were rigidly adhered to and only the Psalms were sung.

As a boy Graham had to attend church regularly and was whipped with a leather belt by his father when he failed to pay close attention to the sermon. His father had always wanted to be a preacher himself, and his mother devoutly prayed that her firstborn son would someday get the calling. Having memorized the entire Shorter Catechism, Graham became a member of his family's church at the age of twelve. No conversion experience was required, though it was assumed that he would have one some day. Three years later, when prohibition was repealed, Graham's father bought a case of beer and forced the young boy to drink it until he got sick in order to implant in him a distaste for liquor. It did.

In 1934 Graham's parents persuaded him and two of his young friends, Grady Wilson and T. W. Wilson, to attend a local tent revival conducted by the itinerant evangelist Mordecai F. Ham. Ham was closely associated with J. Frank Norris, Harvey R. Springer, and several other fundamentalist racists in promoting antisemitism and anti-Negro views.[42] But among the rural fundamentalists of the South, Ham was noted primarily for his powerful hell-fire and damnation preaching. Over the objections of the local clergy, Graham's father and a

[41] For biographical information on Graham see Cook, *Billy Graham Story; America's Hour of Decision* (Wheaton, Illinois, 1951); Stanley High, *Billy Graham* (New York, 1956). The chronology in High's book is not, however, always accurate.

[42] See Roy, *Apostles of Discord*, p. 355.

group of other prominent laymen had invited Ham to conduct this revival in Charlotte.[43] Graham and his schoolmates attended the tent meetings for two weeks, and finally, under the promptings of a family friend who was acting as a personal worker in the revival, they went forward at the conclusion of one of the sermons and publicly "accepted Christ." The decision had no immediate effect upon Graham. He was already a regular churchgoer who did not indulge in any of the sins of card-playing, dancing, theater-going, or drinking, which the evangelist attacked. He continued to be a somewhat intractable high school student who preferred dating and driving the family car at reckless speeds to studying or praying. During the summer of 1935 he became a highly successful Fuller Brush salesman. But like Billy Sunday he had a great fondness for baseball and after graduating from high school in 1936 he spent the summer as a semiprofessional player on a local team. Then, in the fall he heeded the prayers and admonitions of his parents and enrolled in Bob Jones College, located at that time in Cleveland, Tennessee.

He still had little interest in religion, however, and although the courses were simple and evangelically oriented, he was asked to leave after one semester. Graham then transferred to the Florida Bible Institute near Tampa, Florida, which was associated with William Bell Riley's World Christian Fundamentals Association.[44] Under the persuasive influence of the dean of the institute and the continued prayers of his mother, Graham gradually worked his way toward a decision for the ministry. The decision was made one night while he walked alone on a golf course trying to console himself because a girl friend had rebuked his lack of religious purpose. "Somewhere around midnight . . . I knelt alongside the 18th green, bowing my knees and my heart and said, 'All right, Lord, if you want me, you have got me.' "[45] Shortly thereafter he was asked, as the Bible Institute's students often were, to conduct revival services at a small church near the college. It was a Baptist church, and halfway through the revival it became

[43] Armin Geswein, "How Billy Graham Was Converted," *Christian Life* (Chicago), September, 1957. Special Reprint edition; no pagination.

[44] Roy, *Apostles of Discord,* p. 379 note.

[45] Cook, *Graham,* p. 29; High, *Graham,* pp. 75–77.

known that Graham had never been immersed. In order to still objections, Graham agreed to be baptized by immersion at the end of the meetings. When the two-week campaign closed, Graham kept his promise and was baptized along with his converts. A few weeks later he sought and received ordination as a Southern Baptist minister from the St. John's Baptist Association of Northern Florida. No theological examination was necessary. The fundamentalist ministers of the association believed that his revival conversions were proof of his calling and ability. That was in 1939.

A year later Graham graduated from the Florida Bible Institute, but the school did not award degrees, and Graham was eager for more education. In the fall of 1940 he enrolled as a sophomore at Wheaton College, another fundamentalist Bible school, twenty-five miles south of Chicago. Graham chose to major in the "Bible-centered" department of anthropology (where he learned that the theory of evolution was false) and in 1943 received a Bachelor of Arts degree.[46] Two months after graduation he married a girl whom he had met at Wheaton, the daughter of a prominent Presbyterian missionary to China. For a time Graham toyed with the idea of joining the Army as a chaplain, but instead he took a pastorate in a Baptist church in Western Springs, Illinois, near Wheaton. His salary was $45 a week. The congregation of thirty-five Bible-believing Christians met in the basement of an unfinished church. Graham set about trying to raise funds to complete the building.

Then an opportunity came from Torrey M. Johnson, also a Wheaton graduate, who asked Graham to conduct a Sunday night radio broadcast over a local Chicago station. Johnson, busy helping the NAE and organizing Youth for Christ, wanted Graham to take over a program which he had started. Graham's church was to put up the $150 a week necessary to sustain this "radio ministry." Graham accepted and hired George Beverly Shea to assist him as soloist on the program. Shea, a graduate of Houghton Bible College in New York, was also

[46] Graham has since been awarded four honorary doctorates by different Bible Schools, a D.D. from King's College, Delaware, in 1948, a Doctor of Humanities from Bob Jones College in 1949, an LL.D. from Houghton College in 1950, and an LL.D. from Wheaton College in 1956. See *America's Hour of Decision,* p. 31.

working as a soloist and announcer from the Moody Bible Institute's radio station. The Graham-Shea program, called "Songs in the Night," became a local success, and the contributions from Chicago listeners helped Graham's church to meet the expenses for it.

Graham found evangelistic preaching more congenial than pastoral work, and when Torrey Johnson asked him to become the first "field representative" for Youth for Christ in 1945, at a salary of $75 a week, he accepted. He had been working with Johnson in the Youth for Christ movement since the fall of 1944.[47] As field representative he traveled throughout the United States, Canada, and the British Isles for three years, organizing Youth for Christ groups in cities which did not have them and conducting rally services for groups already in existence. Meanwhile his wife and daughter returned to Montreat, North Carolina, to live with her parents until Graham saved enough money to build a home of his own in Montreat. In 1948, Youth for Christ became more aggressively evangelistic, and Graham became the spearhead for city-wide revival services designed to win more persons over to the "spiritual ecumenicalism" of born-again believers.

In his three years of work for Youth for Christ, Graham managed to meet most of the leading figures in the fundamentalist camp and readily associated himself with the program of the NAE, whose magazine featured his activities regularly. Graham also gained valuable experience in organizing large-scale rallies and in speaking nightly to crowds of 3000 to 5000 in theaters, auditoriums, and football stadiums. As a field representative, he did not go alone but as a member of a team of young evangelists who shared his background and outlook. One of the members of this team was Cliff Barrows, who met Graham at a Youth for Christ rally in Asheville, North Carolina, in 1945 and who became his chief lieutenant as chorister, trombonist, and master of ceremonies. Barrows was a graduate of Bob Jones College. His wife, Billie, became the pianist for Graham's Youth for Christ team.

The slogan adopted as the motto of Youth for Christ was "Geared to the times, but anchored to the Rock." The Rock was Biblical fundamentalism. The timeliness was in evangel-

47 See Larsen, *Youth for Christ*, pp. 84, 104.

istic techniques. "We used every modern means," said Graham of his work with Youth for Christ, "to catch the ear of unconverted young people and then punched them straight between the eyes with the gospel." [48]

His career took a new turn in 1947 when William Bell Riley died after having persuaded Graham to take his place as president of the Northwestern Schools in Minneapolis. Riley had founded Northwestern Bible School in 1902 as part of his First Baptist Church. A leader in the fundamentalist crisis of the 1920's, Riley had raised money to expand the school's facilities and later added a theological seminary and a fundamentalist liberal arts college. In the neofundamentalist resurgence in the 1940's, Riley had been trying to raise a million dollars for a new set of buildings, and he saw in the dynamic young Graham a man who might complete the task. He also hoped that Graham might get Northwestern Schools accredited by the Association of American Universities. Graham accepted the presidency on two conditions: that he could continue his work as an evangelist and that he be permitted to retain his post as first vice-president of Youth for Christ.

Graham made one of his Youth for Christ associates, George Wilson, business manager of the schools. He appointed his childhood friend T. W. Wilson as assistant-president. He made Jerry Beavan, a teacher of theology on Riley's staff, the registrar of the schools. These three men managed the schools while Graham continued his itinerant evangelism. For three years Graham conducted most of his work as president by telephone, appearing in Minneapolis for little more than two months each year. But his growing popularity helped to raise the funds for the school. Finally, in 1951, Graham resigned the presidency (though he accepted the position as president of the school's board of trustees) in order to allow a full-time president to take charge. When he resigned he took George Wilson and Beavan with him to assist in running his revival organization.

In the fall of 1947 Graham had started holding city-wide evangelistic crusades which were only indirectly part of his work

[48] *Revival in Our Time: The Story of the Billy Graham Evangelistic Campaigns,* Special edition for Youth for Christ International (Wheaton, Illinois, 1950), p. 3.

with Youth for Christ. He had added to his team Grady Wilson as "associate evangelist" and George Beverly Shea as soloist. Graham and his team of five conducted revivals in Grand Rapids, Michigan, and Charlotte, North Carolina, in 1947; in Des Moines, Iowa, Augusta, Georgia, and Modesto, California, in 1948; in Miami, Florida, Baltimore, Maryland, and Altoona, Pennsylvania, in 1949. Although in Charlotte and Augusta his revivals were supported by the local ministerial associations, for the most part these campaigns did not have the cooperation of the majority of the regular churches, and Graham did not require that they should. Sponsorship by the local Youth for Christ group, a Christian laymen's group, and a majority of the fundamentalist churches was enough. These campaigns lasted from ten days to three weeks, and convert totals ranged from five hundred to fourteen hundred. They were no different from those of dozens of other fundamentalist revivals which were being held over the nation in the postwar years by a new crop of professional mass evangelists, among them Jack Shuler, Bob Jones, Jr., Merv Rosell, Hyman Appelbaum, Charles Templeton, Oral Roberts, Alan Redpath, Tom Rees, and Bryan Green. Local newspapers gave them brief coverage. Fundamentalist journals tried to say a word about all such revivals. But nationally there was no awareness before 1950 that mass revivalism had returned as a significant part of American church life.

The turning point in this situation came in October, 1949, when Graham's tent revival in Los Angeles suddenly received a flurry of national publicity. Some attributed this to the aging William Randolph Hearst, who was said to have telegraphed to all his editors in November, 1949, "Puff Graham." [49] Others attributed it to the news value attached to Graham's conversion of certain minor celebrities in Los Angeles whose names were news even though Graham's was not.

Graham had been invited to Los Angeles by the Christian Businessmen's Committee of Los Angeles for their annual three-week evangelistic tent campaign. The Los Angeles Youth for Christ organization added its support, and a few dozen of the local fundamentalist churches contributed volunteers for the choir, ushers, and personal workers. A tent for five thou-

[49] High, *Graham,* p. 148.

sand was erected in a vacant lot on the edge of the city, and publicity in the newspapers advertised what was to be a twenty-three-day revival: "Visit the Canvas Cathedral with the Steeple of Light," said the ads. "Billy Graham" in the "Big Tent," "All Star Supporting Party," "Great Chorus Choir," "Tidal Wave Interest," "Dynamic Preaching," "Heavenly Music—6000 Free Seats."[50] For the first three weeks the newspapers paid little attention to the campaign, but it attracted one hundred thousand auditors (including repeaters), and its backers decided to extend it for another week. The advertisements read, "Held Over Until October 23," "4th Great Week by Popular Demand," "Los Angeles' Greatest Revival Since Billy Sunday." Two other revivalists came to help Graham—Merv Rosell and Jack Shuler. The revival was extended for a fifth week, then a sixth, and finally ended after eight weeks. Of the three thousand persons who walked down the sawdust aisles of Graham's tent, the three most important were Stuart Hamblen, Louis Zamperini, and James Arthur Vaus. It was the conversion of these men which brought all the publicity.

Hamblen, the son of a Texas minister, conducted a folksy, cowboy-tinted television show called "Stuart Hamblen and His Lucky Stars" on a local station. Hamblen was also a member of the Star's Christian Fellowship Group, an organization of minor Hollywood celebrities who met together for prayer meetings and Bible study. The group had not been able to get Hamblen to make a clearcut "decision for Christ." Through his devout wife they persuaded him to attend several of Graham's meetings. Hamblen finally gave in and made a public profession of his faith in the tent and over his television program.[51] To prove his sincerity he sold his stable of race horses and began to compose religious-western songs. The announcement of his conversions had a great effect upon his local television audience.

Zamperini had been a former Olympic track star in the 1930's and a temporary hero in World War II. After the war he found it difficult to adjust to civilian life and turned to drink. His wife had been attending Graham's meetings seek-

[50] Los Angeles *Times,* October 1, 1949, Sec. 2, p. 2.
[51] *United Evangelical Action,* December 1, 1949, p. 3.

ing consolation. She was converted and persuaded Zamperini to attend. After attending several meetings he went forward, and his conversion was given wide publicity.

Vaus was unknown, but because of an alleged connection with the notorious racketeer Mickey Cohen, his conversion also received headlines. Vaus had formerly been a student for the ministry but had taken up wire-tapping and was involved in criminal investigations in Los Angeles. After his conversion he confessed that he had perjured himself at a recent grand jury investigation and gave himself up to the police.

These three conversions were all sincere and apparently permanent. Zamperini went into full-time religious activity as director of a Christian camp for boys, and Vaus returned to his original career as a minister. To those searching for signs of a new "work of grace," these seemed a full measure of proof. "We had gone to Los Angeles unheralded," Graham said. "When we left we knew that the Spirit of God had moved on that California city as never before. We believed also that there He gave proof that He would bless and use our ministry. . . ."[52] At the conclusion of the revival, squibs were published about the "Rising Young Evangelist" in nationally circulated magazines like *Time, Life,* and *Newsweek.* Graham's rise to fame, however, was not established by this one campaign. It took another two years of gradually increasing publicity and the mounting anxiety over the Korean War and "the Cold War" to make professional mass revivalism once again a topic of national interest.

From Los Angeles Graham and his team were invited to Park Street Church in Boston by Harold Ockenga, who showed none of the reluctance of Lyman Beecher to welcome the assistance of a sensational western revivalist in his campaign against the prevailing theological order. The one-week revival in Boston expanded to eighteen days, closing with a rally in Boston Garden and a decision by various pastors in New England to support a series of meetings by Graham in the largest New England cities. The campaign took place in March and April, 1950, after Graham concluded a crusade in Columbia, South Carolina. The leading lay supporter of Graham in New

[52] High, *Graham,* p. 150.

England was Allen Emery, Jr., the son of the man who had been chairman of Billy Sunday's Boston revival in 1916.[53] In July, 1950, Graham went to Portland, Oregon, to hold a revival in a specially constructed tabernacle. Out of the Portland meetings developed two new aspects of Graham's evangelism: a weekly nationwide radio broadcast and a series of documentary and fictional motion pictures in which Graham's revival sermons were the principal feature. Up to this time the only new technique which Graham had added to those of Billy Sunday was his use of a lapel microphone and a loudspeaker system in order to make his voice heard even when he whispered. Now Graham went into entirely new realms.

The decision to enter the motion picture field was made by the Billy Graham team shortly before the opening of the Portland crusade. In order "to preserve the story of what God did" in Portland, Graham made an agreement with Richard Ross, president of Great Commission Films of Hollywood, to make a documentary color film of the revival from start to finish. Ross, who had specialized in making religious films for distribution to church groups, called the Portland movie "Mid-Century Crusade." It was made available on a rental basis to church and civic groups, or if preferred, it was shown by an agent of the Graham team who took a collection from the audience to sustain the expenses. The principal use of the film, however, was to help arouse interest in preparation for a Graham revival. Cities which invited his services were free to use the film for publicity and inspirational purposes. The venture proved so useful to Graham that similar films were made by Ross of six later crusades, and in addition three full-length fictional films were produced dramatizing evangelism and sudden conversion centering around Graham's work. The "film ministry" of the Graham team became so elaborate that he eventually organized a company called the Billy Graham Evangelistic Films, Inc. (later called World Wide Pictures), in order to provide a staff and administrative system to manage it.

The radio ministry had a different origin. It was pushed upon Graham by the Walter F. Bennett Advertising Agency

[53] In other cities Graham also received support from the same persons who had supported Sunday, Chapman, and Gypsy Smith. In New York, for example, Cleveland Dodge, of the Phelps-Dodge Corporation, and Mrs. Cornelius Vanderbilt Whitney lent their support.

of Chicago, which had handled other religious programs over the major networks. After Graham's New England success Bennett hounded Graham for two months to get him to sign a thirteen-week contract for a nationwide half-hour broadcast with the American Broadcasting Company. Graham was tempted by the idea but did not know how to raise the $92,000 necessary to purchase the radio time. Then in Portland Graham decided to take the question to God in prayer, "Perhaps He did want me on the air." He knelt in his hotel suite with Bennett and prayed, he said, "the kind of prayer I have never prayed before or since." [54] Then he went before his tabernacle congregation and told them of Bennett's proposition and asked them to contribute toward the initial $25,000 to get the program under way. Bennett had assured him that once the program was on the air contributions from listeners would meet the rest of the costs. Graham told Bennett that if $25,000 was contributed to him by midnight the night of his prayer he would consider it a sign from God to sign the contract. Members of the tabernacle crowd donated or pledged $23,500 and the remainder came from other sources just before midnight. Graham declared it "a miracle" and signed.

Ross, the film director, was hired by Graham to produce the program, and on November 5, 1950, "The Hour of Decision" went on the air for the first time. The program consisted primarily of a sermon by Graham, usually originating from the scene of his current revival, but there were also solos by "Bev" Shea, choir singing directed by Cliff Barrows, Scripture reading by Grady Wilson, and "crusade reporting" by Jerry Beavan. Guest visitors who gave their "Christian testimony" added variety to the show, and Graham kept it timely by including in his sermons references to contemporary political, international, and social news. He was always introduced as "a man with God's message for these crisis days." The program was an immediate success and gradually expanded its coverage from an initial 250 stations to nearly 1000, with an estimated twenty million listeners weekly by 1958.

His popularity in this field eventually led him to try a national television program in 1952–53. But Graham's delivery in a studio lacked the spontaneity and fire that made his re-

[54] High, *Graham,* p. 163.

vival meetings so successful. Moreover, the show interfered with his traveling from place to place to conduct his campaigns. After the first attempt and some talk about finding a commercial sponsor, Graham gave up television except when it could be fitted into his crusades.

The financial management of the large sums required for these undertakings necessitated some sort of business organization. In October, 1950, George Wilson, who was at that time still business manager of the Northwestern schools, suggested to Graham the formation of a nonprofit corporation of which the Graham team would be the principal trustees and members of the board of directors. The Billy Graham Evangelistic Association, Inc., was formed according to the laws of Minnesota shortly thereafter, and an office was opened across the street from Northwestern Schools. Graham was president of the corporation; Grady Wilson, vice-president, George Wilson, secretary-treasurer, and Cliff Barrows and Graham's wife were members of the board.[55] By 1956 this corporation was operating on a budget of two million dollars a year with offices not only in Minneapolis but in London, Winnipeg, and Washington, D.C.

The major part of the funds for the budget came from solicitations made over the "Hour of Decision" broadcast. At the close of each program the audience was invited to "send your free-will gifts and offerings for the support of this program to Billy Graham, Minneapolis, Minnesota. That's all the address you need, just Billy Graham, Minneapolis, Minnesota." They were also reminded that such donations were tax deductible, and whenever funds ran low Graham made plaintive calls for help. By giving away free gifts to all those who wrote in, a mailing list of over one million names was built up for regular solicitation from the central office. In addition, money was solicited for the corporation from those who attended each revival. Normally all Sunday collections during a Graham revival as well as any surplus after payment of expenses were earmarked for the Minneapolis headquarters. In the city of Nashville alone, $93,000 was collected for the Graham corporation, a sum larger than the entire cost of the Nashville campaign.[56] By 1954 the official journal of the NAE was hailing Graham's lead-

[55] *Ibid.*, p. 165.
[56] *Ibid.*, pp. 156–59.

ership of the new era in mass evangelism with the words, "We are in big business." [57] Financially, at least, Graham's revivalism was far bigger business than that of any preceding professional evangelist.

In the four years following the Portland crusade, Graham conducted city-wide meetings in Minneapolis, Atlanta, Fort Worth, Shreveport, Memphis, Seattle, Hollywood, Greensboro, Washington, Houston, Jackson, Pittsburgh, Albuquerque, Chattanooga, St. Louis, Dallas, Syracuse, Detroit, and Asheville. In each of these he continued to model his technique directly upon that of Billy Sunday. He expanded his team, the exact counterpart of the Sunday Party, from five to thirteen in these years, and later it reached as high as thirty-five. The man he chose as his advance agent, Willis G. Haymaker, had been on various occasions advance agent for Billy Sunday, Gypsy Smith, and Bob Jones, Sr. But the majority of his team was composed of young men like himself, in their early thirties, trained in Bible schools, thoroughly fundamentalist in theology, and completely modern in techniques. Barrows, his chorister, consciously modeled himself upon Charles Alexander and Homer Rodeheaver, but he was also an expert at manipulating Graham's electrical loud-speaking equipment and in announcing the "Hour of Decision" broadcasts. Jerry Beavan not only directed the publicity for local crusades via newspapers, posters, handbills, stickers, and mailings, but he arranged for "saturation" spot radio advertising, local television broadcasts, and luminous automobile bumper cards and made weekly reports of the team's activities over the "Hour of Decision." [58] Graham proved himself in step with the times by conducting services at drive-in theaters for "shut-ins" who could not otherwise attend his meetings, and in Memphis he preached a sermon in an airplane which circled over the city as his message was broadcast to those on the ground. His most sensational innovation was to conduct mammoth services under klieg lights in the largest football and baseball stadiums in the country.

[57] *United Evangelical Action,* November 15, 1954, p. 13.

[58] Beavan's official title was Executive Secretary and Director of Public Relations of the Graham Team, but he actually did most of the advance work and probably ranked next to Barrows as the most important member of the team.

To fill his tabernacles, auditoriums, and stadiums, Graham carried Sunday's delegation technique to new levels of perfection. Chartered trains, planes, and buses were arranged months in advance, and local pastors and church groups from miles around were made to feel part of the campaigns by being given special reserved seats week after week for their members. Graham never aimed his revivals solely at a city proper. He called them "The Greater Nashville Crusade" or "The Greater Memphis Crusade" to indicate that his use of radio and television as well as his delegation system would reach metropolitan areas over a fifty-mile radius. In each crusade a system of "Prayer Partners" was organized which, in addition to agreeing to pray for the success of the revival, received weekly or biweekly mailings from crusade headquarters or from Minneapolis urging them to attend and to bring their friends.

In five cities Graham had special tabernacles constructed for him, but their cost increased the campaign expenses by $60,000 to $100,000. As in Sunday's campaigns, an advance guarantee sum was pledged by private subscription and paid back from collections taken at the tabernacle. In his early years Graham's campaigns were self-supporting, as Sunday's and Moody's had been, but when he reached the largest cities after 1953 the costs had to be subsidized by donations from elsewhere. About one-quarter of the $470,000 needed for his London revival in 1954 came from donors in the United States. Only about one-third of the $2,500,000 needed for New York was raised from tabernacle collections, although the average nightly collection was over $7000. The balance came from individuals, corporations, foundations, and from collections taken in earlier crusades. The people of Richmond, Virginia, gave $25,000 and the people of Louisville, Kentucky, gave $22,000 to help the revival campaign in New York City.[59] Part of the money raised in New York, however, was given to support the revival in San Francisco. Money was raised in Nashville and New Orleans for Graham's evangelistic tour of Europe in 1955, and part of the collections taken at his London crusade in 1954 went to sup-

[59] For the audited account of the London crusade see the *British Weekly*, October 7, 1954, p. 3. See also Curtis Mitchell, *God in the Garden* (New York, 1957), p. 169.

port his crusade in Glasgow a year later.[60] Graham's local committees, like Sunday's, were incorporated and their accounts audited and published at the end of each campaign. But the amount of financial juggling that went on between the local committee, outside donors, the "Hour of Decision," and the Billy Graham Evangelistic Association, Inc., was only dimly perceivable in these statistics. No dishonesty was involved, but the accounting was so vague as to leave questions as to who had contributed to what and how it was spent.

According to one account of the New York crusade, the expenses were met by $812,938.87 taken in collections at the meetings and by $2,004,532.17 raised by professional and private fund-raising efforts. The expenditures included $1,054,439. for Graham's coast-to-coast television broadcasts each Saturday night, $622,960.83 for rent of Madison Square Garden and other buildings, $133,706.07 for room, board, and other expenses of the Graham team, and $60,000 for the filming of "Miracle in Manhattan," a documentary motion picture of the crusade. Out of a surplus of $217,218 in income over and above all expenses, the local committee gave $150,000 to the Billy Graham Evangelistic Association, even though $233,481 had already been raised for that organization in New York by collections at the meetings. In view of this large sum given to the association, it might well be argued that the Graham team was simply juggling money from one pocket to another when it claimed that the salaries of Graham and the team were not included as part of the expenses of their revival crusades.[61]

[60] High, *Graham,* p. 156; New Orleans *Times-Picayune,* November 1, 1954, p. 6; *British Weekly* (London), April 29, 1954, p. 8.

[61] For a description of the financial arrangements of the New York crusade see Noel Houston, "Billy Graham," *Holiday,* XXIII (March, 1958), 80 ff. A mimeographed statement of the New York Crusade expenses obtained from the Protestant Council of the City of New York gives slightly different figures. See also the audited account of the Nashville crusade printed in High, *Graham,* pp. 156–59, which is not at all clear as to where the "Gifts" came from which sustained over one-third of the expenses, or which members of the team received payment as salaries, or how the money for the Hour of Decision was collected, or who decided to give $38,000 for Graham's European crusade out of the collections, or how the counseling and follow-up were paid for, or why collections were continued until $13,000 surplus was run up for the Association in Minneapolis.

From 1948 to the beginning of 1952 Graham had followed Sunday's method of obtaining his own remuneration. "Love-offerings" were taken for him at the conclusion of each campaign. He donated the $12,000 given to him in Los Angeles to evangelistic work, but he and Cliff Barrows kept the $16,000 received for their six weeks in Atlanta. Realizing that he might be tainted with the charge of commercialism and self-aggrandizement, which helped to bring professional evangelists of Sunday's era into disrepute, Graham evolved a method of obviating this after 1952. He had his evangelistic association put him on salary at $15,000 a year, and thereafter he received no free-will offerings. As his popularity grew, however, his income was supplemented by payment for magazine articles and by royalties from his books. His volume *Peace with God* sold over 500,000 copies and *The Secret of Happiness* sold over 200,000. Six other books by him sold in smaller but sizable numbers between 1953 and 1958. Royalties on these at standard publishing rates could be conservatively estimated to have added well over $100,000 to his income. He also received $7200 a year for his daily newspaper column, "My Answer" (which in 1957 was being syndicated in 110 newspapers) and royalties from his sermons on RCA records. Graham has been generous in his tithing, however, and most of his income beyond his salary has been donated to the Billy Graham Evangelistic Association or earmarked for religious and charitable gifts. Like Finney, Moody, and Sunday, he has lived comfortably without being covetous, and most of his luxuries have been gifts from admiring friends.[62]

Prior to 1951 Graham did not require that his invitation to a city be tendered by a majority of the Protestant clergy of that city. Until he modified his style, his theology, his politics, and his sensationalism, he found it difficult to win the support of the nonfundamentalist ministers, but like all his outstanding predecessors, he learned to be more cautious and diplomatic. Success and diplomacy went hand in hand. The year 1952 marked the turning point in Graham's career. It was in that year that he received his first major setback when his premature attempt to storm New York had to be canceled because so many

62 See Noel Houston, "Billy Graham," *loc. cit.*, for an account of Graham's income.

ministers there distrusted and opposed him.[63] The election returns of that year may also have influenced the change in his style and message. The strident political overtones of his sermons gradually softened; his fundamentalism became blurred; his sensationalism decreased. Even his style of dressing altered. He gave up wearing flowery, hand-painted neckties and pastel-colored suits with wide-lapels and a Hollywood drape and adopted instead conservative foulard ties and subtly textured grey and brown suits tailored in London and New York. Observers everywhere began to remark that Graham seemed to be showing signs of "maturity" and that the rough edges of his personality and presentation were wearing off. As his address to the NAE convention that year indicated, he had by no means given up his belief in aggressive, dogmatic evangelism, but it was significant that he felt, even in calling his brethren to arms, that he must emphasize "fellowship with all born-again believers" and a distaste for interdenominational feuds.

The changes paid handsome dividends in terms of growing respectability and popularity both nationally and internationally. Between 1953 and 1958 he visited some of the largest and most cosmopolitan cities of the world and was received socially in the best circles from London to Delhi. Queen Victoria had criticized Moody, but Queen Elizabeth II invited Graham to conduct a special service for her. In 1954 Graham held city-wide revivals in London, Nashville, and New Orleans; in 1955, in Glasgow and Toronto; in 1956 in Richmond, Oklahoma City, and Louisville; in 1957 he finally reached New York; in 1958 he went to San Francisco, and in 1959 he was scheduled to hold meetings in Melbourne and Sydney. In addition he held one- to three-day meetings in many of the major cities of Europe, India, Southeast Asia, and the Caribbean. As he rose to fame he strove desperately to maintain a sense of Christian humility. Few who met him, regardless of their opinion of his revivalism, disliked him. There was an ingenuous charm about his boyish earnestness which set him apart from most of his colleagues in the profession.

By 1955 Graham acknowledged, "I said a lot of things five years or so ago out of immaturity which I wouldn't say to-

[63] See *New York Times,* December 17, 1954, p. 28; and *Christian Century,* September 21, 1955, p. 1076.

day." [64] Some of these things were theological, some political, and some were simply matters of style and taste. Theologically Graham had preached an extreme form of Biblical literalism in his early sermons, even claiming to be able to specify the dimensions of hell and heaven. Heaven, he said, "is 1600 miles long, 1600 miles wide, and 1600 miles high." [65] Politically he made veiled attacks upon the New Deal–Fair Deal policies of the Democratic Party, speaking of "diplomatic betrayal" in foreign affairs and "our debt-ridden inflationary economy with its fifteen-year record of deficit finance and with its staggering national debt." [66] Like Billy Sunday, he told Biblical stories in a slangy vernacular, describing the prophet Amos as a "hill-billy preacher" and saying that the unfaithful of Noah's day thought of him as "an old crazy fellow" with "a screw loose somewhere." In an official biography written in 1951 with Graham's "full cooperation and consent," the biographer, Vincent C. Hogren, said of Graham, "He has no traffic with modernism, higher criticism, social gospel, or broad Bible interpretations." [67] Graham in those days thought of himself as a hill-billy preacher like the prophet Amos, and he was proud of it.

After 1952, however, he was more cautious in his expressions. He began to deplore "fumbling fundamentalists" and "ultrafundamentalists" who were intolerant, narrow-minded, and "sectarian." He began to embrace the figurative rather than the literal approach to the Bible.[68] He said a few kind words about the social gospel movement,[69] and he insisted that he was not a fundamentalist in the ordinary meaning of the term but an "evangelical" or, preferably, a "Christian." "There are so many shades of fundamentalism," he wrote in 1956, "and so many shades of liberalism, it is increasingly difficult to point to a man and say he is a 'liberal' or he is a 'fundamentalist' without qualifying explanations. If by *fundamentalist* you mean 'narrow,' 'bigoted,' 'prejudiced,' 'extremist,' 'emotional,' 'snake-handler,' 'without social conscience,'—then I am definitely not a

64 High, *Graham,* p. 86.
65 *Time,* October 25, 1954, p. 58.
66 *America's Hour of Decision,* pp. 143–44.
67 Vincent C. Hogren, "Billy Graham's Own Hours of Decision," printed in *America's Hour of Decision,* p. 35.
68 See High, *Graham,* p. 64.
69 William F. Graham, *Peace with God* (New York, 1953), p. 190.

fundamentalist. However, if by *fundamentalist* you mean a person who accepts the authority of the Scriptures, the virgin birth of Christ, the atoning death of Christ, His bodily resurrection, His second coming and personal salvation by faith through grace, then I am a fundamentalist. However, I much prefer being called a 'Christian.' "[70] This sounded like the protests of Finney and his friends at the New Lebanon Convention that they were not as extreme in their new views or measures as the easterners feared them to be.

That the NAE approved of Graham's attempt to proclaim a new middle way between fundamentalist bigotry and modernist heresy was evident in the blessing bestowed upon his speaking at Union Theological Seminary in 1954. Ultra-Fundamentalists, and some of Graham's earlier supporters considered it a betrayal of principle for Graham to consent to have fraternal relations with this stronghold of the latest form of infidelity. The neo-orthodox were by no stretch of the evangelical imagination "born-again believers." The Luther Myricks of 1954 felt that by speaking at Union Graham, like Finney, had succumbed to "popularity" and "come down on a level" with those whom he had set out to reform. But the editor of *United Evangelical Action* thought that much good might come from his speaking at Union "provided there is no compromise of the evangelical Christian faith."[71]

There were some associated with the neo-orthodoxy of Union Theological Seminary who were at first sympathetic toward Graham. However, as time passed it became evident that there could be no rapprochement on Graham's terms. By 1957 many neo-orthodox ministers looked upon his crusades as part of a carefully engineered maneuver by the resurgent fundamentalists to infiltrate the regular denominations and regain the control which they had lost so ignominiously in the 1920's. The fact that the Rev. Paul S. Rees, the president of the NAE in 1954, was appointed by Graham as an "associate evangelist" on his team that same year seemed to confirm this suspicion.[72]

[70] *Look,* February 7, 1956, p. 49.

[71] *United Evangelical Action,* April 15, 1954, p. 11.

[72] As Graham's assistant, Rees preached to cooperating ministers in each crusade on the theme that too many Protestants were "church conscious rather than Christ conscious." *New York Times,* May 21, 1957, p. 72. In 1958 the

In an editorial entitled "Fundamentalist Revival" in June, 1957, the *Christian Century* called Graham's rising popularity among regular churchmen "a portentous development." "The narrow and divisive creed which the churches rejected a generation ago is staging a comeback. Through skillful manipulation of means and persons, including a well-publicized association with the President of the United States, fundamentalistic forces are now in position to exploit the churches." [73] This fear, which Graham's friends labeled "sour grapes," was based on the fact that Graham had, by 1957, won endorsement for his New York City crusade not simply from the fundamentalist churches but from the Protestant Council of Churches in New York, which had been predominantly modernist and sympathetic with the National Council of Churches. In addition, the general secretary of the National Council of Churches was actively serving on Graham's New York committee.

Although it was reported that only 40 per cent of the Protestant Council of New York was eager to support Graham, the fact that another 20 per cent lent their tacit approval over the objections of the remaining 40 per cent seemed to the *Christian Century* to indicate that the fundamentalists were outmaneuvering the regular clergy.[74] Ministers of a more liberal bent who cooperated with Graham's New York campaign complained that he "places key church personalities in positions of 'prestige' while others of the fundamentalist variety run the show." The key personalities, usually moderately evangelical modernists, "have become mere figureheads used for the convenience of the Billy Graham Team. If you go down the line among the leaders of the crusade you will find a fundamentalist in practically every position of power. Once the churches promise to cooperate with the crusade they find it necessary to rubber-stamp every effort of the Billy Graham Team." [75]

NAE officially sponsored a nationwide "All-night prayer meeting" on April 16 to center attention upon Graham's coming revival in San Francisco, and this further confirmed the close relationship between this organization and Graham.

73 *Christian Century,* June 19, 1957, p. 749.

74 This was not mentioned in the *Christian Century* editorial but it was implicit. See *Christian Life,* February 19, 1956, p. 145, for the estimate of support within the Protestant Council.

75 Letter of the Rev. George C. Bonnell published in the *Christian Century,* August 7, 1957, p. 933.

The reason for opposition to Graham by the leaders of neo-orthodoxy were clear enough. They had seen the shortcomings in liberal Protestantism long before Graham arrived on the scene. And while they rejected modernism's optimism and its theology of immanence, they by no means wanted to turn back the clock to the old-time religion. The neo-orthodox not only accepted the higher criticism and the truth of the theory of evolution which Graham rejected, they also held a far broader social ethic in their interpretation of Christianity than Graham. In fact, the rejection of modernism had been for many of them based on the recognition that under modernist leadership the social gospel outlook was bound to fail, as indeed it had failed after 1912. Having painstakingly provided a new underpinning for the social ethic of Christianity in the 1930's, the neo-orthodox followers of Reinhold Niebuhr had no intention of letting it fall prey to the reactionary social philosophy of the fundamentalists or the neofundamentalists, either in or out of the NAE.

It was significant of this clash that while members of the NAE considered neo-orthodoxy a more subtle and insidious form of modernism, they considered Norman Vincent Peale "a born-again Christian." [76] Apparently the political conservatism of Peale overrode the objections to his Pelagian "positive thinking," while the political liberalism of the followers of Niebuhr overrode endorsement of their conservative theology. If it was clear that liberal Protestantism was the old school and neo-orthodoxy the new school in this awakening it was not clear whether neo-fundamentalism had anything at all to contribute except confusion.

Niebuhr persistently attacked Graham, not so much for his "evangelical" theology as for his failure to give it a social application. Graham, he said, was not merely oversimplifying theology, he was preaching a form of "Christian pietism . . . quite irrelevant to the political life of man." Graham "reduces faith to a simple panacea for all the ills of the world," and his "pietistic fundamentalism combines the naïveté of literalism with the simplicity of the old liberalism. It solves all problems of life by asking bad people to become good and to prove it by loving one another." This naïveté, said Niebuhr, was the result

[76] *United Evangelical Action,* March 1, 1955, p. 13.

of Graham's "perfectionist illusions" which assumed that salvation in a revival meeting not only offered a man forgiveness for sin but in fact freed him from all future temptation, or at least, gave him divine help to overcome such temptation.[77] Conversion, as Graham frequently said, produced "a radical transformation in human nature," and since it was the sinfulness of human nature which was at the root of all the world's problems, evangelism was the key to world peace and happiness. Graham often seemed to be saying that the conversion of a few key persons in civic or political life would go far to settle national and world problems. Speaking on "Organized Labor and the Church" in a Labor Day sermon, Graham mentioned "the ills, divisions, strifes, troubles and difficulties that beset the nation" and then went on to remark, "Wouldn't it be great if, as we celebrate Labor Day, our labor leaders would lead the laboring man of America in repentance and faith in Jesus Christ?" During his New York City campaign he remarked, "What if a teen-ager who had received Christ was elected mayor or borough President and put into practice the Christian principles by which he lives daily? What a revolution!" [78]

Niebuhr proposed that instead of following this visionary perfectionist approach to contemporary problems, Graham should follow the example of Charles Finney under whose inspiration "the abolition of slavery was made central to the religious experience of repentance and conversion." [79] Graham, he said, should make his converts feel that their Christian duty entailed actively working toward the abolition of segregation and racial discrimination even though this could only be done by "finding proximate solutions," not perfect ones. But Graham was more like Finney than Niebuhr realized. He, too, preferred to make all social reforms an appendage of revivalism and to subordinate all other activities to soul-winning. He, too, held out the promise of utopia through supernatural eradica-

[77] Reinhold Niebuhr, "After Comment Deluge," *Christian Century,* September 4, 1957, p. 4; and "Literalism, Individualism, and Billy Graham," *ibid.,* May 23, 1956, p. 641.

[78] W. F. Graham, "Organized Labor and the Church" (The "Sermon of the Month" for September, 1952, published by the Billy Graham Evangelistic Association, Minneapolis, Minnesota); *Newsweek,* July 22, 1957, p. 57.

[79] Reinhold Niebuhr, "A Proposal to Billy Graham," *Christian Century,* August 8, 1956, p. 921. See also Niebuhr's comment on Graham in *Life,* July 1, 1957, p. 92.

tion of personal sins. "The one great answer to our racial problem in America," Graham said in New York, "is for men and women to be converted to Christ." Although Graham chastised the churches in his book *Peace with God* for failing to be "the pace-setter" in overcoming racial discrimination, all his own revival meetings in the South prior to the Supreme Court's decision in 1954 had been conducted on the basis of segregated seating for Negroes.[80]

In calling Graham's message politically irrelevant, Niebuhr failed to see that in a less direct way Graham was preaching a social message that was very much relevant to the issues of the day. But it was diametrically opposed to the social and political views which Niebuhr considered implicit in Christianity. From the outset of his career Graham espoused the viewpoint of the ultra-conservatives in politics and economics. Not only did he attack in his sermons the "deficit spending" of the New Deal, but he consistently denounced "the twilight war" in Korea, the bungling United Nations ("they set the policies and we shed the blood and pay the bills"), the "give-away" foreign aid program, the firing of General MacArthur, the "betrayals" at Yalta and Potsdam, the evils of "big government" and "big labor," the "pinks and lavenders" in Washington, the "immorality in high places," the New Jersey Supreme Court's decision against the reading of the Bible in the public schools, "the infiltration of the left wing" into the schools and churches ("Communists are doing their deadly work in government, education, and even religion").[81]

Graham told his listeners on the "Hour of Decision" that one of the primary purposes of that weekly program was to "keep

[80] New York *Herald Tribune,* May 12, 1957, p. 24; Graham, *Peace with God,* p. 195. For segregation in Graham's early meetings see James L. McAllister, "Evangelical Faith and Billy Graham," *Social Action* (Congregational, New York), XIX (March, 1953), 22–23, 32. Graham's attitude toward the social obligations of the Christian was adequately summed up in his statement, "Jesus taught that we are to take regeneration in one hand and a cup of cold water in the other." Graham, *Peace with God,* p. 190.

[81] Most of these quotations are from the notes I have taken of the "Hour of Decision" broadcasts since 1951 or from reprints of these sermons published by the Billy Graham Evangelistic Association and distributed from time to time as "The Sermon of the Month." Similar quotations can be found in *Revival in Our Time,* and *America's Hour of Decision,* which contain some of Graham's early sermons. See also Ralph L. Roy, "Billy Graham's Crusade," the *New Leader,* August 1, 1955, pp. 6–8.

you abreast of fast-moving world events and try to interpret them for you in the light of Scripture."[82] Graham saw himself as a Christian news analyst and political prophet instructing and conditioning the growing "bloc" of evangelical, Bible-believing Christian voters. In July, 1953, the first edition of *Decision: Newsletter of the Billy Graham Evangelistic Association* was mailed to the one million or more persons on the Minneapolis mailing list. Graham said that the purpose of this newsletter was "to serve as a medium for presenting the current situation both nationally and internationally as it relates to the Christian position." Though he claimed to be neither a Democrat nor a Republican, he admitted that he had "strong feelings" about the outcome of the Presidential election of 1952.[83] His continual remarks about "the mess in Washington" and the need for "a new foreign policy" during the election year left no doubt as to which side he favored. On the eve of the election, according to the Pittsburgh *Press,* Graham "drew a startling parallel between President Truman and Adam" in regard to the commission of original sin.[84]

After the new administration took office, Graham's political attacks upon government policy subsided, and he became preoccupied almost entirely with the threat posed to American security by Communism. In various interviews with the press he seemed to go out of his way to defend the foreign policy of Secretary of State John Foster Dulles. When Mr. Dulles was criticized for defending the Portuguese possession of Goa, Graham had an interview with him and told reporters afterward that he thought the administration's policy had been "misinterpreted." "I don't think Mr. Dulles meant in the slightest to

82 W. F. Graham, "Hate Vs. Love" (Sermon of the Month for April, 1951, published by the Billy Graham Evangelistic Association, Minneapolis, Minnesota).

83 Officially Graham was registered as a Democrat, appropriately perhaps in the county of Buncombe, North Carolina.

84 Pittsburgh *Press,* September 7, 1952, Sec. 2, p. 25; and September 8, p. 7. The newspaper did not quote the sermon, but I have heard Graham use it on other occasions. In it he compares the decision of President Truman to send American troops to South Korea with the irrevocable consequences of Adam's original sin for all posterity. "Adam was the head of the human race, even as in this country our President is the head of our government. . . . When Mr. Truman went to war in Korea, you and I went to war in Korea, whether we liked it or not." Since most of Graham's listeners did not like the Korean War, the comparison was implicitly invidious.

endorse colonialism. I got the impression that the United States' policy is not to support colonialism in any way."[85] When Mr. Dulles was criticized for saying that the Eisenhower administration had several times saved the nation from the brink of war, Graham wrote an article for an evangelical magazine in which he said, "I believe that in spite of a few mistakes he [Dulles] has made that he has been one of the hardest working and most effective Secretaries of State in American history."[86] Graham had never come to the defense of Dean Acheson's mistakes in such a fashion.

Graham even acted as a semiofficial representative of the United States on his tours of Europe and Asia in the summer of 1954 and the spring of 1956. The Secretary of State endorsed his visit to Asia, Graham said, because Mr. Dulles felt "that particularly after the visit of Messrs. Khrushchev and Bulganin to India that America was in need of someone that would appeal to the masses of India." Graham said that he was going to India to "build some good will for the United States."[87] But whatever good will Graham may have aroused while he was in India was dissipated shortly after his departure by his suggestion that the United States could go far toward securing the friendship of Prime Minister Nehru by giving him a gift of a "stream-lined air-condition[ed] train or a new Cadillac, pure white." Gifts of this sort, he said, "would do more to demonstrate the friendliness of the Americans than all the millions of dollars given in economic aid."[88]

In spite of what some observers called Graham's "ability to grow" and his increasing maturity, his intellectual grasp of the complexities of modern life remained childishly simple and superstitious. His explanation for what he called the "paradoxical" increase in juvenile delinquency and crime while the nation was in the midst of a great religious revival in the 1950's was, "The Bible teaches us that we are engaged in a gigantic

[85] Associated Press dispatch in the New York *Herald Tribune,* January 15, 1956, p. 3.

[86] W. F. Graham, "Billy Graham's Diary," *Christian Life,* July, 1956, p. 14.

[87] *Ibid.;* and form letter from Billy Graham to the editor of the Newark *Evening News,* January 18, 1956, p. 20.

[88] *Christian Life,* April, 1956, p. 54. Graham defended this statement by saying that he merely thought American gifts to India ought to be more dramatic and not that he was suggesting that Prime Minister Nehru was open to influence by personal gifts.

spiritual warfare, and when God begins to move in a country, as he is now moving mightily in America, Satan also begins to move . . . the Bible teaches that there is a personal devil who has at his command great legions of demons and they become very activated at a time of spiritual revival."[89] This same demon-haunted attitude pervaded his thinking about communism: "My own theory about Communism is that it is masterminded by Satan. . . . I think that there is no other explanation for the tremendous gains of Communism in which they seem to outwit us at every turn unless they have supernatural power and wisdom and intelligence given to them."[90] This led Graham to take at times an almost fatalistic approach to American diplomacy and defense policies: "We can never lick communism with flesh and blood and guns and bullets. It's going to take the divine help of Almighty God." Graham believed that only through revivalism could America win God's help and stave off His judgment for national infidelity and wickedness. If everyone in America were to turn to Christ then "we would have divine intervention on our side."[91]

Graham's outlook on world history followed closely the nationalistic chauvinism of Warren Candler and Billy Sunday. Like them he linked together the fate of the world, the fate of democracy, and the fate of Christianity with the future of American revivalistic religion. The only difference was that the peril of communism was a far more compelling motivation for evangelism than the various perils his predecessors had used. "America is the key nation of the world," he said. "We were created for a spiritual mission among the nations." "America is truly the last bulwark of Christian Civilization. If America falls, Western culture will disintegrate." And "America cannot survive, she cannot fulfil her divine purpose, she cannot carry out her God-appointed mission without the spiritual emphasis which was hers from the outset."[92]

[89] *U. S. News and World Report,* September 27, 1957, p. 75.

[90] *Ibid.,* p. 78.

[91] From Graham's debate on the radio program "Town Meeting" on "Do We Need the Old-Time Religion?" Printed in *Town Meeting* (New York), January 2, 1951, p. 9.

[92] *Decision: Newsletter of the Billy Graham Evangelistic Association* (Minneapolis), March, 1956; W. F. Graham, "The Revival We Need" ("Sermon of the Month" published by the Billy Graham Evangelistic Association, Minneapolis,

From this it was only a step to conclude that free enterprise capitalism too had to be preserved if the world were to remain free and Christian. Graham frequently referred to "the dangers that face capitalistic America" and insisted that the nation must continue to be "devoted to the individualism that made America great." He claimed that free enterprise came to America with the Puritans and implied that the Bible itself proclaimed this economic system. In Greensboro, North Carolina, Graham told a revival audience that America must remain true to "the rugged individualism that Christ brought" and spoke of the Garden of Eden as a place where there were "no union dues, no labor leaders, no snakes, no disease." [93] In New York City Graham told one audience that the American way of life "is in growing danger" and urged them to "come back to Christ who gave us these freedoms which are threatened." [94] He advertised his "Christian movie" about Houston, Texas (entitled, *Oiltown, U.S.A.*), as "the story of the free enterprise of America—the story of the development and use of God-given natural resources by men who have built a great new empire." [95]

In discussing the possible future of America and its way of life, Graham was sometimes optimistic. "As a minister of the gospel I am an optimist. The world problems are big, but God is bigger." But more often he preached the premillennialism of the Second Coming with an intensity that was far removed from the sanguinary tone of Candler and Sunday. "I am deadly serious when I say that our country is falling apart at the seams," he declared. "The signs of the times" seemed to show infallibly that "we are living in the latter days. I sincerely believe that the coming of the Lord draweth nigh." [96]

But Graham's premillennialism was at times curiously secularized, first by his tendency to equate the impending possibility

---

Minnesota, 1956); form letter sent from Pusan, Korea to those on the association's mailing list, December, 1952, and signed "Billy Graham." Similar quotations have been made in his radio sermons, but in order to provide concrete references for authentication, I have quoted printed sources wherever possible.

[93] McAllister, "Evangelical Faith and Billy Graham," p. 23.

[94] Newark *Sunday News,* August 18, 1957, p. 2.

[95] From a circular advertising a London showing of the film in 1954.

[96] W. F. Graham, "Spiritual Inventory," "The Second Coming: A Glorious Truth," and "Revival or Disintegration" ("Sermons of the Month," published by the Billy Graham Evangelistic Association, Minneapolis, Minnesota, 1952, 1955).

of World War III with the divinely ordained end of the world, and second by his tendency to equate an inevitable conflict between the Satanic forces of Russia and the Christian forces of the United States with the battle of Armageddon. In Finney's day the psychological tension necessary for successful revivalism was generated by playing upon the average man's fear of his soul's burning in eternal hellfire. In the 1950's Graham generated tension by horrific pictures of hell on earth through nuclear warfare and the conquest of the United States by atheistic Communists. "Fear," said Graham, "is a legitimate motive" in evangelism, and the fear of communism was a more potent stimulus to conversion among Graham's contemporaries than the fear of hell.[97] Graham claimed that his purpose in preaching a message of fear was in part to arouse thoughtless nonbelievers to the dangers of delaying the question of salvation and in part to arouse the American people to the ideological threat posed to their existence which could only be met by a tidal wave of old-fashioned revival. Only a morally sound nation could meet the threat of communism at home and abroad. Only a born-again Christian could be at peace with God come what may. Just as Sam P. Jones and Billy Sunday made revivalism a crusade against the liquor traffic, Graham made revivalism a crusade against communism. And just as Finney declared slavery a sin so Graham declared communism a sin.

In sermon after sermon Graham explicitly stated in his call for converts, "Only as millions of Americans turn to Jesus Christ at this hour and accept him as Savior can this nation possibly be spared the onslaught of demon-possessed communism."[98] In a sermon entitled "Satan's Religion" Graham offered five ways in which "you can most effectively combat Communism." The first was "by old-fashioned Americanism"; the second, "by a conservative and Evangelical Christianity"; third, "by prayer. It is inconceivable that Communism could penetrate the barrier of a praying nation. . . ."; fourth, "by a genuine spiritual revival. Revivals . . . would purge America of the rats and termites that are subversively endeavoring to

[97] Quoted in an interview with Phyllis Battelle, "Billy Graham, Huge Humble Man of God," Hartford *Times,* August 27, 1957, p. 7.

[98] W. F. Graham, "Satan's Religion" ("Sermon of the Month," published by the Billy Graham Evangelistic Association, Minneapolis, Minnesota, 1953).

weaken the defense of this nation from within that it may fall prey to the international revolution of the Communist plot"; fifth, "by personal Christianity. . . . The greatest and most effective weapon against Communism today is a born again Christian."[99]

The pressure for conformity to 100 per cent Americanism under this type of preaching and in the midst of the hysterical red-scare of the early 1950's was far greater even than under Sunday's preaching during the Ku Kluxism of the 1920's. The scapegoats in the 1920's were foreigners, labor agitators, and Roman Catholics. In the 1950's the scapegoats were any and all nonconformists. The mood engendered by Graham's preaching was reflected in the letter which an ardent born-again Christian printed in *United Evangelical Action* in January, 1954, which said, "I can't say for sure that there is a difference between non-conformists, liberals, and Communists except that the Communist is rather inclined to be honest in his atheism and materialism."[100] It was not surprising that Graham consistently told reporters that he had no comment on the activities of Senator Joseph McCarthy nor that in one of his sermons he went out of his way to praise Congressmen who served on "investigating committees" to root out an un-Americanism: "I thank God," he said, "for men who in the fact of public denouncement and ridicule, go loyally on in their work of exposing the pinks, the lavenders, and the reds who have sought refuge beneath the wings of the American eagle, and from that vantage point, try in every subtle, under-cover way to bring comfort, aid, and help to the greatest enemy we have ever known, communism."[101] Like Billy Sunday, Graham made Christianity and patriotism synonymous: "If you would be a true patriot, then become a Christian. If you would be a loyal American, then become a loyal Christian."[102] Newspaper

[99] W. F. Graham, "Christianity and Communism" ("Sermon of the Month," published by the Billy Graham Evangelistic Association, Minneapolis, Minnesota, 1951).

[100] *United Evangelical Action,* January 1, 1954, p. 22, a letter signed by R. L. Wendt, Raleigh, North Carolina.

[101] W. F. Graham, "Labor, Christ, and the Cross" ("Sermon of the Month," published by the Billy Graham Evangelistic Association, Minneapolis, Minnesota, 1953).

[102] W. F. Graham, "Spiritual Inventory" ("Sermon of the Month," published by the Billy Graham Evangelistic Association, Minneapolis, Minnesota, 1955).

headlines describing Graham's sermons in San Francisco in June, 1958, read, "CHRIST OR REDS, GRAHAM WARNS."

Far from soothing national tensions and anxieties, Graham purposely sought to exacerbate them. He constantly predicted that World War III was just around the corner: "Two years and its all going to be over," he said in 1950. A year later, when the Iranian government nationalized its oil industry, "it was noticed," said Graham, "that the would-be burglars were waving red flags and speaking with a northern accent." As a result he prophesied that "the last tremendous battle predicted in the Bible, called Armageddon," would soon take place in the Middle East. When the Soviet Union launched its first earth satellite in 1957, Graham told his radio audience that "it is not only quite possible but very probable" that Russia would soon deliver an ultimatum to the United States to surrender or be destroyed.[103] The sense of overwhelming horror and frustration which these possibilities conjured up in the minds of Graham and his listeners made revivalism not only seem frantic but oftentimes pure escapism. Graham unwittingly acknowledged this when he stated in 1954: "The human mind cannot cope with the problems that we are wrestling with today. And when our intellectual leaders begin to admit that they don't know the answer, and that fact reaches the masses on the street, then they are going to turn somewhere. They will turn to all sorts of escapisms. Some will turn to alcohol. Others will turn to religion in the want of security and peace—something to hold on to." [104]

When he was on this tack Graham spoke of religion as a consolation, a solace which "will provide you with peace of mind, peace of soul, and peace of conscience." "Take courage . . . God is always with His people through thick and through thin." "The suffering of this present time is not to be compared to the glory that is ours yonder." "He can meet every need, lift every burden, solve every problem. . . . Let Him deliver you from the perils of present trouble. Let Him

[103] *America's Hour of Decision, op. cit.,* p. 119; W. F. Graham, "Position vs. Penalty" ("Sermon of the Month," published by the Billy Graham Evangelistic Association, Minneapolis, Minnesota, 1951). The references to the Soviet earth satellite are from my notes of the "Hour of Decision Broadcast" of November 10, 1957.

[104] Quoted in *U.S. News and World Report,* August 27, 1958, p. 87.

deliver you from the fear of the future." Sometimes he seemed to arouse his audiences to a state of incipient neurosis in order that he might offer salvation as a tranquilizer: "The glorious gospel of Jesus Christ" is the "miracle drug that can heal the ills of the world." [105] The Graham team often spoke of itself as though it were literally a business corporation organized to market this drug. "I'm selling the greatest product in the world," said Graham, "why shouldn't it be promoted as well as soap." [106] As one critic put it, Graham asked the question "Why not try God?" the same way that commercial advertisers asked, "Why not try Delovely soap?" [107] To many churchmen this use of the language and methods of sales promotion was the most reprehensible aspect of Graham's revivalism.[108] The *Christian Century* referred to Graham's team of experts and his connection with the Walter F. Bennett Advertising Agency as the use of "canny, experienced engineers of human decision." In each of Graham's revivals these engineers "have laid the tracks, contracted for the passengers," and directed "the traffic which arrives on schedule" into a new statistic for conversions. The crusades were "railroaded to success." Sounding very much like Horace Bushnell or the editors of the *Biblical Repository and Theological Review* of the 1830's, the editors of the *Christian Century* stated in 1957: "Our objections are to the Graham procedure which does its mechanical best to 'succeed' whether or not the Holy Spirit is in attendance. At this strange new juncture of Madison Avenue and the Bible Belt the Holy Spirit is not overworked; he is overlooked." This was "trumped up" revivalism instead of "a rhapsody of sudden grace." In modern theological terminology, it was a "manufactured kairos." [109]

[105] W. F. Graham, "Three Minutes to Twelve," "Teach Us to Pray," "Why Christians Suffer," "Peace Vs. Chaos" ("Sermons of the Month" published by the Billy Graham Evangelistic Association, Minneapolis, Minnesota, 1951, 1953.)

[106] *London Observer,* April 24, 1955; see also *This Week Magazine* (New York), April 21, 1957, p. 12.

[107] Malcolm Boyd, "Crossroads in Mass Evangelism," *Christian Century,* March 20, 1957, p. 359.

[108] Graham even seemed to imply that world peace could be bought for cash: "If everyone in the world would give a ten per cent of his salary tithe, as the Bible says we should, we could convert the whole world. Then we can have not only individual peace, but world peace as well." Phyllis Battelle, "Billy Graham, Huge Humble Man of God," Hartford *Times,* August 27, 1957, p. 7.

[109] *Christian Century,* May 15, 1957, p. 614.

In modern psychological terminology Graham's team was a group of "specialists in the engineering of mass consent."[110]

As in the past, however, the old refrain, "But he gets results," conveniently overruled all these objections in the minds of most ministers. Urban pastors, still trying to reach the masses, were even willing to overlook differences in theology. "Ministers have been discouraged and frustrated," said Graham in explanation of his invitation to New York city in 1957. "In talking with many of them we found almost a sense of desperation. Ministers who could not agree with us theologically . . . are willing to cooperate simply because there seems to be nothing else in sight for them to reach the conscience of this city."[111] Graham's team fully satisfied the American penchant for statistics in demonstrating their results. Nightly figures were released not only on the number of decisions made at the meetings but also the number of decisions made as a result of television, radio, movie, and telephone ministries of the team. It was reported, for example, that two hundred persons were saved from suicide during the New York campaign as a result of Graham's nightly television program with its telephone counseling supplement. The Minneapolis office kept a room full of filing cabinets with "decisions for Christ" received by mail and could also provide the statistical total of the Graham team's ministry for any given year. The figure averaged over 100,000 converts annually for the years 1950–58.

Graham claimed to have improved upon Billy Sunday's revival methods by means of a more complete "follow-up" technique conducted by a specialist who belonged to an association called The Navigators. The Navigators were a group of young Bible college graduates who had conducted follow-up work for the Youth for Christ organizations. Their work with Graham consisted of maintaining a follow-up office in each city for six months or more after a crusade in order to put pressure upon the cooperating ministers to visit those converts whose names and addresses were recorded on the decision cards. The principal work of the office consisted in mailing out form letters to the converts and the ministers and in tabulating the reply postcards. This added greatly to the cost of the campaigns, but

110 Malcolm Boyd, "Crossroads in Mass Evangelism," *loc. cit.*, p. 359.
111 *Time*, February 11, 1957, p. 56.

most ministers felt it was worth it, even though the work of visiting the converts was still up to them.

Analysis of Graham's meetings and their results, however, indicated that essentially the same weaknesses that had always plagued mass evangelism still remained. In the first place the crowds were made up overwhelmingly of persons already in church or attending church regularly. The repetitive delegation system promoted this, and most reporters noted that the same persons returned night after night carrying their Bibles and hymn books. Unlike Moody and Sunday, Graham and his team urged the audiences to return night after night. The general public was led to believe that when Graham filled a stadium or baseball park with 75,000 to 100,000 persons most of them were nonchurchgoers. But for weeks before any such event Graham would tell his supporters that it was their duty to pack these meetings in order to make a great "Protestant witness" or to avoid the shame that would fall upon the churches if the stadium should not be full. In a letter sent to encourage prayer partners' attendance at the Yankee Stadium rally in New York, Graham urged, "Whatever the effort and sacrifice I hope you will be there. We need you. . . . We would not want to have empty seats." It seemed that Graham was more interested in filling the stadium than in reaching the people of New York with an evangelistic message, for he arranged that the nationwide television broadcast of the Yankee Stadium meeting should be "blacked out" in the New York metropolitan area.[112]

As for the type of people who attended, one report of the crowd at the Yankee Stadium said, "It was the simple, staid, sure, saved of the retrogressive churches who held the field. . . . The Church did not meet the world at the stadium. The church met itself—its most comfortable, confident self. Convinced Christians convinced convinced Christians" and felt proud that the vice-president of the United States was there to bring them greetings from the President, who regretted that work prevented his attendance.[113]

Graham and his follow-up experts admitted that on the average 60 per cent of all decisions made at his revivals were made by persons already church members. In some cities, like Co-

112 *New York Times,* July 21, 1957, p. 48.
113 *Christian Century,* August 7, 1957, p. 933.

lumbia, South Carolina, the figure was over 75 per cent. After his Greensboro, North Carolina, crusade, a research team investigating Graham's results by interviewing ministers and decision-card signers reported, "Every 'convert' interviewed had previously had connections of some sort with the churches." [114] It was also admitted by the Graham team that a large percentage of the decisions made in each campaign were by children, and it may be fairly assumed that these children were brought or sent by churchgoing parents and were themselves members of a Sunday school or young people's group who would have joined the churches anyway. In New York 22,000 out of 55,342 decisions made in Madison Square Garden were made by persons under twenty-one. In Columbia, South Carolina, almost 1500 out of 5050 decisions were by children.[115]

An official analysis of the statistics of the follow-up of Graham's crusade in Toronto made six months afterward by a member of the local committee indicated that 75 per cent of those making decisions were already churchgoers. A total of 8161 decisions were recorded during the revival. Of these 531 were made by children, and 654 were made at a "dedication service." The 8161 decision cards were sent out to the cooperating pastors, and an analysis was made of 4960 of these cards on the basis of pastoral follow-up:

Church attendance:	
Already attending	3572
Now attending	339
Intend to begin attending	281
Do not intend to attend	178
Not checked by minister	590
	4960
Membership:	
Already members	2246
Now members	102
Intend to become members	800
Do not intend to join	242
Not checked by minister	1570
	4960 [116]

114 *Revival in Our Time,* p. 45; J. L. McAllister, "Evangelical Faith and Billy Graham," p. 20.

115 Curtis Mitchell, *God in the Garden,* p. 1; *Revival in Our Time,* p. 46.

116 These statistics were furnished by the Minneapolis office of the Billy Graham Evangelistic Association.

The net result after six months appears to have been 102 new members and 339 new attenders out of 8161 decisions. Yet Graham habitually referred to the decisions in each campaign as persons who "give their lives to Christ" as if they were all a statistical and qualitative gain for Christianity. Although there were often two or three churches in each campaign which reported gains of forty or fifty new members, these were invariably the most prominent, evangelical churches in these cities. There were far more cooperating churches which made no gain whatsoever.

The more important question is what percentage of those who make decisions at the revivals for the first time are still active church members some time later. Analyses have been made for both the London and Glasgow campaigns eight months to one year afterward. In fact, two analyses were made of the London results, one by the London *Evening Standard,* a secular newspaper, the other by the *British Weekly,* an interdenominational "Christian" paper. Graham had claimed 38,447 decisions in London as a result of his twelve-week crusade in the spring of 1954. The *Evening Standard* interviewed twenty ministers of the Church of England in London who received a total of 336 cards among them. They reported that 226 of these cards were signed by persons already members or regular churchgoers of their churches. Of the 110 nonchurchgoers, only thirty-five were still attending church eight months after Graham's departure. The *Evening Standard* concluded that if this sample was accurate, only 4000 out of Graham's 38,447 decisions represented a worthwhile gain to the churches as a result of the $470,000 expended.[117]

When this analysis was published, the *British Weekly,* which had strongly supported Graham's campaign, conducted its own investigation. It polled 1500 cooperating pastors and received answers from 520. Of these, 144 indicated that they had received no converts and 42 replies were discarded as inadequate. The remaining 334 replies indicated that the churches concerned had received a total of 3222 decision cards; 1657 of these, or 51.43 per cent, were signed by persons already church members or regular churchgoers. Of the remaining 1565 "more

[117] The *Evening Standard* poll is quoted in the *British Weekly* (London), February 10, 1955, p. 1; see also *Christian Century,* June 26, 1957, p. 782.

than half" had "some connexion with churches or church organizations." Ten months after the revival 1002 or 64.03 per cent of these "outsiders" were reported as attending regularly. There was no indication as to how many actually had joined a church. The London correspondent of the *Christian Century,* Cecil Northcott, considered the analysis of the *Evening Standard* more nearly correct and maintained that Graham did not reach "the unchurched, the non-religious." Stanley High, senior editor of the *Reader's Digest,* preferred to believe the analysis of the *British Weekly.*[118] It was still too early for a significant poll, but the Rev. Donald Soper, the foremost spokesman of British Methodism, expressed an opinion which substantiated Northcott. He said six months after Graham's revival in London that Graham "has caused no religious revival. His audiences have been almost exclusively church people or near-church people. He has not touched the outsider." [119] A Gallup poll conducted in England in April, 1957, three years after the revival, revealed that the average Englishman agreed with Soper. Fifty-two per cent of those polled, said Gallup, stated that not only was there no revival in Britain but that religious influences were actually decreasing.[120]

The analysis of Graham's Glasgow crusade of March–April, 1955, was made by Dr. John Highet, Lecturer in Sociology at the University of Glasgow. Highet conducted three censuses of the church membership and church attendance in Glasgow, one the year before the Graham crusade, one a month after the crusade, and one a year later. Highet found that in the seven Protestant denominations which contained 98 per cent of the Protestant church members of the city, the membership decreased from 203,430 in 1954 to 202,035 in 1955 and then increased to 207,232 in 1956. The church attendance, however, increased from 56,503 in 1954 to 67,078 in 1955 and then de-

118 See Shaun Herron, "What's Left of Harringay?" *British Weekly,* February 10, 1955, p. 1. A breakdown of the 3222 decision cards tabulated by Herron indicated that 60 per cent of them were signed by children between the ages of 10 and 19. For the interchange between Northcott and High see *Christian Century,* August 7, 1957, p. 228. See also Northcott's, "Four Years After Billy Graham," *British Weekly,* May 29, 1958, p. 1 in which he still maintained that the *Evening Standard's* estimate was correct. The statistics of the *Evening Standard* poll are contained in this article.

119 *Christian Century,* October 12, 1955, p. 1179.

120 *Time,* April 29, 1957, p. 44.

creased to 62,224 in 1956.[121] Graham had claimed 52,253 decisions for Christ as a result of his six weeks in Glasgow. At best it could be claimed that 7 per cent of this total, or 3802 persons, joined the churches and 11 per cent, or 5721 persons, were added at least temporarily to the church attenders. Inasmuch as Graham's revival was only one part of a large-scale campaign being waged by the Church of Scotland (known as the "Tell Scotland" campaign) from 1954 onward in an attempt to reach the unchurched, it was probably not fair to the Scottish churches to give Graham the entire credit for these increases. Whether the attendance continued to decrease or the membership to rise in the succeeding years would be a better test of the Scottish evangelistic effort than of Graham's temporary stimulation.

The first survey of the results of Graham's New York crusade in May–August, 1957, was conducted by the *New York Times* four months after the meetings closed. In 159 replies to questionaires sent to 504 Protestant ministers in the New York area, the *Times'* survey indicated that 64 per cent of all decision cards referred to cooperating churches contained the names of their own members. Of the 36 per cent who were not already members "many . . . went to another church or dropped out of sight." The general conclusions drawn by the *Times'* correspondent was that Graham's impact upon the city as a result of a crusade which cost $2,500,000 was slight and "fleeting." At most it gave the regular churches "a spiritual shot in the arm" and let Roman Catholics know that Protestantism was still alive in the city. As in past revivals, the *Times* had to report that "he made the least impact on mission churches in the underprivileged areas." [122]

No adequate evaluation of Graham's career is yet possible. That many Americans both in and out of the churches saw him as a man with a message for the crisis days was obvious. That his success was part of a general reorientation in American liberal theology and liberal politics also seemed clear. But that he had significantly altered the pattern or the results of pro-

121 *British Weekly*, London, August 22, 1957, p. 1.

122 *New York Times*, January 26, 1958, pp. 1, 64. For a contrary interpretation of the results by a member of Graham's team see "Whither the Converts" in *Christianity Today*, June 23, 1958, p. 34.

fessional mass evangelism did not seem likely. As a rallying center for many persons in a state of confusion, he was a typical revival figure. There was nothing new in his revival techniques except for the use of electronic devices. Nor was his message new, although for obvious reasons it emphasized more heavily than any previous revivalist's the note of worldwide catastrophe associated with the Second Coming of Christ.

But success and popularity over the years tended to blunt the distinctively pietistic features of Graham's theology. By the time he was popular enough to win the endorsement of the clergy of New York City, it turned out that he had lost a good deal of his following among the old-line fundamentalists. It was significant that when a nationally syndicated magazine asked him in 1955 to answer the question, What is America's greatest moral danger? he answered as any liberal Protestant might, "Vacations from decency." [123] Perhaps even more significant, was the disclosure by the *New York Times* that the church which received the largest number of decision cards from the crusade in New York was the Marble Collegiate Church of Norman Vincent Peale. There had always been a strain of positive thinking in Graham's preaching, but it came out much more clearly after 1955. In a sermon entitled "Partners with God," which he gave repeatedly to laymen's groups, Graham emphasized the fact that if a man went "in business with God" by becoming a good steward and tithing his income, he could double or triple his income. "You cannot get around it, the Scripture promises material and spiritual benefits to the man who gives to God." The titles of many of his sermons seemed taken from Peale's repertoire: "The Life That Wins," "What God Can Do for You," "The Cure for Discouragement," "The Cause and Cure for Uncertainty," "Victorious Christian Living." The message of these sermons, like that in Peale's, is that with reliance upon God a converted man can attain anything from self-confidence to a profitable business.

Graham claimed that his message presented American youth with a hard challenge of self-sacrifice and self-discipline in offering them Christianity, but in a nation in which 80 per cent of the adults were church members, where 51 per cent attended church regularly, and where almost everyone agreed that

[123] *This Week Magazine,* March 13, 1955, p. 8.

Christianity and "old-fashioned Americanism" went together, there was hardly any sacrifice involved in doing likewise. Nor did Graham make the process of conversion any more profound than past revivalists. For example, he told his radio and television audiences that they could receive Christ while they were driving along in their automobiles or sitting at a bar in a tavern. Of course Graham tried to insist that true Christians did not smoke, drink, play cards, swear, or go to the movies. And he preferred that all his converts devote their full time to prayer, Bible-reading, and soul-winning, but Graham's publicity managers and most of his ministerial supporters were willing to settle for regular church attendance, and that is what most of his converts settled for. Graham's supporters in the NAE tried to pretend that Graham's converts were going to revitalize Peale's church, and they rejoiced when some church members who attended the crusades complained that their ministers did not preach like Billy Graham.[124] But there was no indication that the popularity of Peale's neo-modernism was losing out to Graham's neo-fundamentalism. Niebuhr called Graham's message "A bland form of pietism" and even suggested that "this new evangelism is much blander than the old." [125] But on the whole Graham's preaching did not seem very different from that of previous modern revivalists.

The improved efficiency and thoroughness of the media of mass communications made Graham's rise to fame more rapid than that of former professional evangelists but for that same reason interest in his work might pall more quickly. By the middle of 1958 newspaper reports of his meetings had lost their tone of respect. Frequently they seemed to display boredom over the repetitious statistics and superlatives issued by Graham's publicity director. Only by globe-trotting to distant parts of the world was Graham able to inject continued news

[124] See "How One Church Got Steamed Up" and "Churches Come to Life" in the Special Reprint of *Christian Life,* September, 1957. The first article headlined the fact that Peale's church was "gaining new vision" as a result of the Graham crusade. The second reported that as a result of the New York crusade, "Liberal pastors are facing greater problems. Members who have been born again are going back to their churches and are not satisfied with the preaching they hear. They want Bible truth. And if they don't get it in their own church they will go where they can find it." Neither article offered any concrete proof for these assertions.

[125] *Life,* July 1, 1957, p. 92.

value into his exploits. Finney, Moody, Sam Jones, and Billy Sunday had maintained their popularity for only about ten years. Graham's decline might be gradual, as were those of Finney, Jones, and Moody, or it might be precipitous, like that of Sunday. Much would depend upon the methods and personalities of the host of imitators who sprang up on all sides. More would depend upon the adjustment made by the American people to the events of the 1960's. But whether America's fourth great awakening went beyond modernism or merely continued the trend toward secularism, the professional evangelist was not likely to provide the key to it or to stand long as a symbol of it.

EPILOGUE

"Diligent in Business"

The essential characteristic of modern revivalism since 1825 has been its effort to adjust the theological, ethical, and institutional structure of Protestantism to the changes in American culture. The evangelical theology which it helped to hammer out in popular form was admirably adapted to the American doctrines of self-reliant individualism, progress, and perfectibility. The ethic which the revivalist preached was in complete harmony with the American belief in enlightened self-interest coupled with voluntary cooperative efforts for charity. And the manner in which the profession fitted itself into the institutional structure of the churches accomplished the difficult task of creating a national religion without destroying either the technical separation of church and state or the independent self-government of the individual denominations. Modern revivalism may have antagonized a few of the staid conservatives and rationalistic liberals, but among the great bulk of American pietistic and moderate evangelicals it was a unifying force. In the name of saving souls it sublimated those sectarian bickerings which might otherwise have dissipated the energies and resources of Protestantism. By so doing it played a significant part in stabilizing the centrifugal forces of pietistic separatism.

While the professional revivalists have never been great theologians or leaders of public opinion, they have always been extremely sensitive to the changing currents of their times. If they have not been prime movers, they have often been catalytic agents of change. The revivalist has been a significant figure in American history precisely because he has always been so eloquent, persuasive, and colorful an embodiment of his times. Finney, Moody, Sam Jones, Sunday, Graham, and the rest, each sensed intuitively the profound feelings of hope and fear, of idealism and of guilt, which sought reassurance and help in critical and confused periods of national development. And with a strong, sure voice, each of them gave vivid expression to those symbols and ideals which have been the basis of the American dream.

But these achievements have not been obtained without a sacrifice. For all their pietistic fervor, modern revivalists have been a primary factor in the increasing secularization of American Protestantism. This has resulted in part from the kind of men who have been the leaders of the profession and in part from the limitations within which they worked. Revivalists have had to attract the attention of the masses without at the same time losing the support and respect of the clergy. They have had to preach in a simple, dramatic style and yet remain dogmatic and orthodox. They have had to shape their message to suit all denominations and to appeal to all social classes, all levels of age, education, and intelligence. In trying to follow the maxim of the apostle and be all things to all men in order that they might win some to Christ, they inevitably diluted and confused a message which, if it was to have any force, had to be concise, direct, and clear-cut. They thought they had solved this problem by reducing Christianity to a hard core of universally acknowledged fundamentals, but in the course of explaining these truths they either reduced Christianity to banalities or inflated it to vagaries.

This was evident not only in the revivalist's explanations of what a man must do to be saved and what salvation meant to the individual, but also in the manner in which the meaning of personal salvation was related to the social and historical values of the believer. Any person who sat through the usual series of sermons delivered during a revival campaign could virtually choose his own path to heaven. For example, at one moment the revivalist would proclaim that man had the power to change his own heart and in the next he would insist that only God can regenerate wicked human nature. At one moment he talked about the means of working up a revival (or selling his product) and in the next he declared "It is all God's doing and it is marvelous in our eyes." The poor man heard in one sermon that "It is harder for a rich man to enter into heaven than for a camel to pass through the eye of a needle," and was made to feel content with his lot because "Whom the Lord loveth he chasteneth." However, if the poor man were ambitious to get ahead, he was instructed in another sermon that by becoming a Christian he was certain to attain success. The rich man was told that while money was a curse, it was also a sign of God's approval; he was praised for working hard to make money so long as he gave some of it away to save souls, but he need not give away so much that it would hurt his business or deprive his family. The middle-class man was told that while he must not be too preoccupied with material things he was nevertheless the backbone of the country and he would please God by being diligent in his business and serving as a pillar in his church. Nonbelievers were urged to accept Christ on faith, or out of common sense, or out of fear of hell, or for the rewards of heaven (and earth). Church members were exhorted to attain perfection but warned that no one can be perfect; they were told that they were assured of going to heaven once they were saved but that they might backslide at any time. Born-again believers were told to be meek, to be aggressive, to endure scorn, to exterminate sin. The road of the believer was described as one of peace, joy, and security but also as a path of thorns and persecution. Everyone was urged to work for the millennium, but the millennium was sometimes portrayed as a cataclysmic miracle, sometimes as the moral or social reformation of the United States of America, and sometimes as the evangelization of the world in this generation.

In short, the revivalist utilized so many arguments that his theology became more like a grab-bag of rationalizations than a challenge to Christian commitment. While this helps to explain the wide appeal of revivalistic preaching, it is also one reason why its influence has been so fleeting. The regular pious church members who attended revival meetings were enthralled by the revivalist's vivid and dramatic presentation of ideas to which they were already committed and they did not notice his inconsistencies or contradictions. The unchurched auditor who went forward and was converted at a revival meeting accepted at his own evaluation the colorful vagaries of the revivalist. But he soon discovered upon entering a church that the theology of the local minister was cold, dull, and rigid by comparison. Only those pastors who were themselves colorful and vague managed to recruit many loyal new members from a mass revivalistic campaign. But ironically, these men, the Beechers, the Talmages, the Hillises, the Peales, did not really need any help from the evangelist. Their churches were already full.

The social message of the revivalist has been even less effective. It is fruitless to search for connections between modern revivalism and social reform movements. Of course modern revivalists have never been mystics advocating a monastic withdrawal from the world or praising the virtues of a contemplative life. Their Calvinistic heritage has prevented that, and besides, their whole purpose has been to find a rapprochement between Christian universals and the cultural relatives of American life. But the individualistic approach of evangelical Protestantism which the revivalists have preached since Finney's day reduced sin to such simple, personal proportions that for all his harping upon the essential depravity of human nature the revivalist managed to avoid facing up to the most difficult and perverse aspects of man's relationships to man. If some of the churches in America have supported movements for abolition, prohibition, social welfare legislation, government regulation of big business, desegregation, or any other efforts at social reform, this has been primarily because the laity insisted upon transforming Christian ideals into practical action and not because revivalistic theology required or even suggested it. Finney opposed abolition, Moody opposed prohibition, Sunday opposed social welfare legislation, and Graham opposed desegregation (at least until the Supreme Court decision) because the logic of their theology disparaged and even deplored collective efforts at reform. Since all sin was personal, all reform must be personal. Regeneration, not legislation, changed the human heart, and until that was changed all else was useless.

There was a hard core of truth in this approach, of course, or evangelicalism and revivalism would never have had such a wide and steady appeal. But in the exaggerated form in which it was preached by most professional evangelists it was as misleading as the rationalistic utopianism against which it railed. It was escapist because it ignored the social complexity of evil. It was shallowly optimistic because it assumed that evangelization was the simple cure for all contemporary problems. But a large part of the popularity of revival preaching lay in these very characteristics. Revivalists were not essentially at war with the American belief in progress and the perfectibility of man. They merely gave it a pietistic twist. Finney and B. Fay Mills were post-millennialists who thought that Christianity and science were working hand in hand toward a perfect world order. But even those revivalists who rejected theistic evolution and the gradual construction of the kingdom of God on earth by human effort uniformly gave thanks for the mechanical advances of science and believed that Protestantism, capitalism, and democracy had leavened the loaf of human destiny so that only a final effort to evangelize the world was needed to bring about Christ's return and the millennium. Revivalists thought in grandiose terms, and constantly felt that a tidal wave of religion was about to sweep over the United States, that the American (or Anglo-Saxon) form of democracy was about to sweep over the world, and that within a generation the gospel would be preached to all the heathen in such a form that they would at once accept it. "All things are possible with God" was the optimistic slogan of the revival message, and the revival techniques were designed to harness God's magnetic powers to human ends. No revivalist doubted that he knew what God wanted and how God wanted it done. And none doubted that God and he were working together toward the same goal.

As a consequence the revivalist compromised with American secularism on its own terms. Americanism and Christianity became synonyms. For all his efforts to check materialism and self-interest by urging the ascetic ideals of pietism and of "disinterested benevolence for the glory of God," the revivalist consistently endorsed the mores of this world and of his own country. The very nature of the revival profession with its high-pressure mass techniques distorted the essence of pietism. In the end the revivalist contributed more toward making men conform than reform.

All this does not mean that every revivalist was exactly the same as his predecessor. There were differences in their personalities, their styles, and in the theological and social emphases of their messages. Finney's emphasis on God's moral law, Moody's on the atoning blood of a burden-bearing Christ, Sunday's on muscular Christianity, and Graham's on the need for repentance, all suited the particular spirit of their times. And in the same way their personalities suited their times: Finney, the argumentative frontier lawyer; Moody, the aggressive, enterprising drummer; Sunday, the slangy sport, and Graham, the clean-cut college boy, each typified essential qualities at the heart of the generation to which they spoke. But while each new revivalist gave a slightly different emphasis to the evangelical ideology, none of them was able after 1865 to reconcile the old-time religion with the fundamental changes in American social and intellectual thought. Their improvisations on the old pietistic theme grew stale by repetition. Like the writers of popular songs, the revivalists captured the prevailing mood and catered to it by simply reworking familiar ideas. Their success was superficial and evanescent because they had no fresh insights to offer to meet the deeper currents and problems of their age. Finney alone looked forward. His successors all looked back. They had neither the ability nor the desire to break out of the pattern which he had set. At best they were perfectionists in a nation of pragmatists. At worst they were chauvinists catering to the Americans' insatiable demand for self-assurance.

Hence the traditions and technical developments of the profession have followed an unbroken line from Finney's laws of the mind to Graham's engineering of mass consent. Because of the diligence with which they pursued their business, revivalists have frequently pushed the virtues of pietistic evangelicalism into their opposites. In this regard American Protestantism has paid dearly for the unity, stability, and occasional stimulation which modern revivalism has brought it. For when the evangelical church leaders adopted Finney's new theories and measures they did so out of a sincere desire to revitalize the church life. They wanted to overcome those recurrent periods of formality and lukewarmness which have always plagued religion. They wanted to see church members constantly aglow with devout humility and fervent spiritual fellowship. They longed to put down forever the dangers of materialism, spiritual complacency, calculated philanthropy, formalized ritual, and to keep Christians consecrated in all aspects of their daily life and worship. In their efforts to emphasize the heart rather than the head, experience rather than book learning, the emotions (or religious affections) rather than reason, they turned to revival experts for help.

But all too often the professional revivalist turned heart religion into anti-intellectualism, humility into self-righteousness, emotion into irrationality, and piety into religiosity or hypocritical posturing. He even made the process of conversion as ritualistic as the formalities of the lukewarm religion he attacked. His revival machinery was better calculated to grind out impressive statistics than to arouse pietistic ardor. Organization and publicity produced an artificial enthusiasm, costly to generate but more costly not to. The revivalist was caught in a treadmill whose exhausting speed he set himself. The churches which periodically endorsed him and put themselves in his more efficient hands suffered his fate, and emerged from each round of feverish activity exhausted. The temporary boost to church morale was generally followed by apathy and backsliding instead of by increased zeal and dedication.

In the long run the task was impossible. A perpetual state of revivalistic fervor was too much for normal flesh and blood. Periodic galvanizations had a depressing rather than a stimulating effect. The evangelicalism which catered to this form of spirit-lifting resembled the immaturity of those who resort too often to alcohol or drugs for a pick up. And it had the same habit-forming effect.

On the whole the rate of church-membership growth in America has probably not been greatly influenced by revivalism. The spurts have been cancelled out by the declensions and the over-all rate of growth has remained fairly constant. But even if revivalists could be credited for the fact that America today has proportionately more church members, more church wealth, and more church activity than any other nation in the world, it would not be an enviable achievement. For in spite of, or perhaps because of, this quantitative religiosity, America has also acquired a reputation as the most materialistic and secularistic nation in the world.

Revivalism will continue to play a part in American life as long as Christianity remains a living religion. And, given the American penchant for organization and bigness, modern revivalism will undoubtedly continue to provide the most spectacular form of its expression. But it is unlikely that professional mass evangelism will help to keep Christianity alive or that any professional revivalist will ever play a major role in a future great awakening. There is a fundamental anomaly inherent in the professionalization of the revival spirit. Revivals are not articles for manufacture and retail. As pietists have asserted since the beginning of Christendom, the virtues of religion cannot be organized. But its vices can.

Note on the Sources

Since revivalism is by its nature concerned with experience, not theory, and since revivalists are by temperament and tradition concerned with the spoken rather than the written word, the sources for a study of revivalism are often random and elusive. The sermon notes of D. L. Moody, W. A. Sunday, and Samuel P. Jones (preserved by Mrs. Mary R. Moody, Mrs. Helen A. Sunday, and the Rev. Walt Holcomb) proved to be too sketchy to give an adequate impression of the force and color of their sermons. Revisions and marginal notes, however, frequently provided illuminating insights into the workings of the minds of these evangelists. Correspondence preserved in the same hands, supplemented by the Finney Papers at Oberlin College, the Lewis Tappan Papers in the Library of Congress, the Moodyana Collection at the Moody Bible Institute, the Wanamaker files in the Wanamaker Store in Philadelphia, and the Moody Papers in the possession of Mrs. Emma Moody Powell, proved more helpful in reconstructing the personalities and viewpoints of the leading revival figures and the social and religious climate in which they worked.

Occasionally these manuscript letters contained rewarding first-hand accounts of revivals and of the ecclesiastical maneuvering which attended them. Less reliable, but nevertheless crucial, material was provided by memoirs and published correspondence. Finney's *Memoirs,* Beecher's *Autobiography,* the *Letters of the Rev. Dr. Beecher and Rev. Mr. Nettleton,* Sprague's *Annals of the American Pulpit,* and a host of reminiscent ramblings by revivalists and their friends (the most important of which are mentioned in the footnotes) contain statements by participants in the early phases of modern revivalism which add depth (and contradiction) to the picture. Such publications are generally lacking for the post-Civil War revivalists, who had neither a sense of history nor the desire to write it.

Volumes of sermons by the more important professional revivalists must be read with due allowance for editorial polish and the misguided omission of those controversial, personal, or local references which provided the dynamic give-and-take between the preacher and his auditors. In a few cases their sermons were taken down almost verbatim for publication, and occasional pirated editions reveal the vitality missing from "authorized" versions. Among these verbatim volumes are almost all of Finney's collections of sermons including his *Lectures on Revivals, Sam P. Jones' Sermons with a Biography by Theodore M. Smith* (Philadelphia, 1886), Moody's *"To All People,"* Moody's *Glad Tidings,* Moody's *The Great Redemption* and *Moody's Latest Sermons* (Providence, 1894). Also verbatim are the unpublished copies of Sunday's sermons which he had printed on newsprint for distribution to the press (some of these are among the Sunday Papers, Winona Lake, Indiana) and the pamphlet "Sermon-of-the-Month" series published by the Billy Graham Evangelistic Association, Minneapolis, Minnesota. For the period after 1870 the daily newspapers proved to be the most fruitful sources of material, though due allowance must be made for journalistic haste, extravagance, and misplaced emphasis. Verbatim sermon reports of every sermon preached during a three-, six-, or ten-week revival campaign are often available in local newspapers for the major revival figures. Since Sunday published no collection of his sermons, these newspaper reports are the principal source of material for his words.

Newspapers are particularly valuable for descriptions of the mechanics of revivalism. They abound in details concerning the preparation, names of participants, financial statements (both official and unofficial), conversion and attendance figures, church cooperation (and opposition), follow-up results, and behind-the-scenes wire-pulling. For much of the colorful detail and incident of revival meetings the historian is indebted to the observant eye and facile pen of the contemporary local journalist. (It is lamentable that the increasing use of national press services has reduced the value of local newspaper accounts of revivals, for the press service limits itself to vague generalities and avoids controversial details. It is even more lamentable that so few libraries have kept files of those "yellow" journals and tabloids which give the most complete coverage of such social ephemera as revival campaigns.) After 1900 popular weekly and monthly magazines occasionally provide revealing feature stories or interviews, but on the whole these are bland fare designed to offend no subscriber.

Much more useful than the secular magazines are the denominational journals which are forced (or eager) to come to terms with the theological and ecclesiastical implications of each new wave of revivalism and each new revival personality. The intelligent and vigorous interplay between Charles Hodge's *Biblical Repertory and Theological Review* in Princeton, Nathaniel W. Taylor's *Christian Spectator* in New Haven, Lyman Beecher's *Spirit of the Pilgrims* in Boston, Leonard Woods and Charles Pigeon's *Literary and Theological Review* in Andover, and Finney's *New York Evangelist* and *Oberlin Evangelist* give invaluable scope and depth to the controversial nature of revival methods and theology from 1825 to 1850. The less profound but no less controversial pages of the post-Civil War religious press are indispensable to an understanding of the changing nature of American religious thought and practice. Particularly useful have been the pages of the *Watchman* (later *Watchman-Examiner), Zion's Herald,* the *Presbyterian,* the *Congregationalist,* the *Christian Advocate,* the *Liberal Christian,* the *Pilot,* the *Advance,* the *Christian Century, United Evangelical Action;* and in Great Britain, the *Christian* and the *British Weekly.* Free-thought journals like the *Melting Pot,* the *Truth Seeker,* and the *Iconoclast,* as well as progressive or liberal political journals like the *Arena, Metropolitan,* the *Masses,* the *New Republic,* the *Progressive,* the *Reporter,* and the *Nation,* often contain critical material not available elsewhere.

Unfortunately the ancient and honorable practice of pamphleteering has almost died out, but in Finney's day and to a lesser extent in the era of Moody and Sunday, a number of fugitive writings of this sort provided polemical but revealing accounts of a highly inflammatory sort about the less redeeming features of the revival profession. The more important of these are mentioned in the footnotes.

Since 1900, recordings and motion pictures have provided a new kind of historical material for the scholar. Unfortunately, few libraries or learned societies have made any attempt to collect these as a social record of the times. Commercial recordings of revival hymns and sermon excerpts are as ephemeral as pamphlets, and from my limited experience with the difficulty of assembling film for a television broadcast on modern revivalism I discovered how little care has been taken to preserve even such obvious historical sources as newsreel films. A few hundred feet of film is available, however, on Sunday and Aimee Semple MacPherson; the Billy Graham Evangelistic Films Company (now World Wide Pictures) has preserved the flavor of Graham's crusades; and Oral Roberts maintains documentary films of his meetings.

I have, with few exceptions, found the relatives, friends, and former associates of revivalists, from Moody to Graham, extremely generous of their time in discussing their personal recollections and contemporary opinions of revivalism. I have gratefully acknowledged my debt to these persons in the preface of this volume and in the bibliographic note to *Billy Sunday Was His Real Name.*

In the area of secondary sources there is a wide range of material which varies considerably in helpfulness. Discussions of evangelistic methods, homiletics, and the role of evangelism in the churches are too numerous to mention but are basic to an understanding of changing attitudes by interested and experienced church and lay leaders. Almost every revivalist has had his eulogistic biography, and the more prominent revivalists have had dozens of accounts written (usually by contemporaries) about them and their work. (See, for example, Wilbur M. Smith's *An Annotated Bibliography of D. L. Moody,* Chicago, 1948.) George F. Wright's biography of Finney is primarily a study of his theology from the viewpoint of the 1890's; although Robert S. Fletcher's *History of Oberlin College* provides an excellent account of Finney's relationship with Oberlin and Gilbert H. Barnes's *The Anti-Slavery Impulse 1830–1844* discusses Finney's relationship to abolition, a full length biography of Finney is greatly to be desired. A biography of Lyman Beecher has long been needed. The two biographies of Moody by his son, W. R. Moody, are the best available, but he, too, should be historically re-evaluated. There are no adequate biographies of Samuel P. Jones, B. Fay Mills, Reuben A. Torrey or any of the host of lesser figures. My study of Billy Sunday examines the place of his revivalism in the temper of the times. The popularized biographies of Billy Graham by Stanley High, Charles T. Cook, and others do not pretend to be either objective or scholarly.

Valuable historical monographs have touched peripherally upon revivalism and revivalists, and I have expressed my indebtedness to them in my footnotes. But little has been done directly with revivalists or revivalism since 1825 by historians. Sidney E. Mead's *Nathaniel W. Taylor* deftly lays bare the roots of modern revivalism in New England; Whitney R. Cross's *The Burned-over District* is a first-rate study of this tumultuous region. Timothy L. Smith's *Revivalism and Social Reform in Mid-Nineteenth Century America* carefully analyzes religious life and thought in the 1850's, and Charles C. Cole, Jr.'s, *The Social Ideas of the Northern Evangelists 1826–1860* assembles a large number of comments by an odd assortment of ministers (the majority of whom were not professional revivalists) on the social issues of the pre-Civil War period. Bernard A. Weisberger's *They Gathered at the River* provides the best running account of revivalism from Jonathan Edwards to Billy Sunday, but it leaves the fundamental questions unanswered.

No student of American intellectual history can afford to neglect giving careful consideration to the numerous books and articles of Reinhold Niebuhr and H. Richard Niebuhr which have provided so many thought-provoking insights into all aspects of American religious development. I have drawn indirectly upon them in more ways than I have been able to acknowledge in my footnotes.

A final word about statistics. Although I have utilized such statistics as are available on church membership in the United States Census reports and in the various denominational yearbooks, it is unlikely (except in the broadest perspective) that sufficiently accurate figures are, or ever will be, available on which to base a rigorous statistical analysis of the impact of modern revivalism either upon the nation at large or upon any segment of it. This is in part due to the unreliability and incompleteness of the statistics and in part to the numerous imponderable variables which the statistics do not take into account.

Index

Abbott, Lyman, 220, 230, 274, 327, 409
Abolition, 82, 107 ff., 139, 142, 146, 169; *see also* Antislavery movements
Advance man, 422, 495
Advertising in revivalism, 87, 98, 137, 156, 185, 219, 222, 232, 303, 308, 333-34, 369-70, 376, 383, 480, 489, 492 ff., 513 ff.
After-meetings services, 304, 348, 382, 410; *see also* Inquiry rooms; Invitation to come forward
Agnosticism, denounced by revivalists, 181, 446
Aiken, Samuel C., 33, 34, 51
Aitken, W. H. M. Hay, 184, 196
Alexander, Charles McCallom, 367, 374-77, 381, 383, 389, 405, 421, 481
American Colonization Society, 108
American Council of Christian Churches, 474, 476, 477
Americanism, 267, 355 ff., 361-64, 390-91, 393, 395-96, 400, 443 ff., 471, 508 ff., 527, 528
Amusements, denounced by revivalists; *see* Moral reform—outlook of revivalists
Anarchism, 312, 321, 444
Andover Theological Seminary, 89, 125, 164
Anglican Church, 8-9, 182, 183, 196, 203
Anglo-Saxon racism, 310, 354 ff., 361, 443; *see also* Americanism
"Animal feelings," 86-91; *see also* Emotionalism in revivals
Anti-Catholicism, 31, 38, 131, 137, 181, 184, 189, 197, 210, 267 n., 268, 358, 362, 385-86, 444, 471-72, 479, 483
Anti-ecclesiasticism (anticlericalism), 45 ff., 58-59, 83-84, 88, 100, 122, 127, 131-32, 135, 144, 154, 176, 181-82, 194, 205-10, 273, 388-89, 390, 410; *see also* Pietism
Anti-intellectualism, 66-67, 76-77, 80, 88, 119-20, 122, 131, 353, 358, 373, 411, 529; *see also* Evolution; Pietism; Science
Anti-Negro; *see* Negroes and revivalism
Anti-Saloon League, 325, 439; *see also* Prohibition
Anti-Semitism, 390-91, 395, 472, 479
Antinomian perfectionism, 104-5, 118, 132
Antislavery movements, 82, 108 ff., 139, 142, 144, 162, 171; *see also* Negroes and revivalism; Slavery
Anxious meetings, 94-95; *see also* Inquiry rooms
Anxious seat, 56-57, 95 ff., 137, 148, 156, 160, 162, 182, 238, 244-45
Arminianism, 9, 12, 46, 74-75, 186, 211, 236, 246; *see also* Evangelicalism
Armour, George, 174, 225
Armour, J. Ogden, 424
Arnot, William, 212
Asher, William, 386
Asher, Mrs. William, 386, 439
Associate Reformed Presbyterian Church, 484
Atheism, denounced by revivalists, 130, 197, 210, 269, 395
Attacks on revivalism; *see* Opposition to revivals
Awakenings, 3-11, 523-30; *see also* First Great Awakening; Second Great Awakening; etc.

"Babbitt, George F.," 461, 465
Backsliding and backsliders; *see* Effects of revivalism
Bacon, Leonard, 60
Baha'ism, 374
Bainbridge, Cuthbert, 177, 181, 184
Baird, Samuel J., 37 n.
Baker, Daniel, 153, 162
Baker, Ray Stannard, 416-17
Baldwin, Mathias, 156
Baptism, 95-96, 138, 141, 154, 161, 300
Baptist Church, 12, 22, 57, 66, 88, 91, 136-44, 174, 181, 243, 266
Baptist Temple, 379
Barnes, Albert W., 45-49, 83
Barnhouse, Donald Grey, 475, 477
Barrows, Cliff, 487, 493, 494, 495, 498
Beavan, Jerry, 488, 493, 495
Beecher, Catharine, 60-61
Beecher, Edward, 63, 78
Beecher, Henry Ward, 30, 220, 241, 274, 327, 526
Beecher, Lyman, early career of, 30; on evangelical assimilation, 37-38, 44, 64, 100; and Finney, 35 ff., 44-45, 60 ff., 74-75, 77-78, 90, 100, 104; heresy, trail of, 14, 78; and Lane Seminary, 81-82; and Nettleton, 33, 35, 44-45; opposes professional evangelists, 146; social conservatism of, 35-36, 82, 100, 130-31; and the Tappan brothers, 53, 81-82; and N. W. Taylor, 31, 45-46, 67, 90; theology of, 31, 44-46, 74-75, 96-97, 105; and the Unitarians, 30, 39, 60, 63; mentioned, 11, 12, 13, 14, 40, 42, 44, 50, 64, 73, 120, 161, 180, 190, 207, 210, 294, 365, 477, 491
Beecherism, 13 n., 40, 67; *see* Beecher, Lyman; New Haven theology
Bellamy, Joseph, 19
Beman, Nathaniel S. S., 28, 35, 36, 37, 45, 49, 51, 83, 96, 139, 171
Bennett, James Gordon, 163
Bennett, Walter F., 492-93, 513
Berry, Bishop Joseph F., 429, 446-47, 449, 451
Bethany Presbyterian Church, 379
Bewley, Henry, 177, 184
"Bible Belt," 466, 513
Biblical Repertory and Theological Review, 46, 64, 65, 75, 147, 220
Biederwolf, William E., 364, 381, 393-96, 421, 449-50
Big Business and revivalism; *see* Business, revivalism as a
Billy Graham Evangelistic Association, Inc., 494, 496
Billy Graham Evangelistic Films, Inc., 492
Billy Sunday Businessmen's Clubs, 439
Bissell, Josiah, 54
Black, Guy H., 457
Blaikie, William G., 191-92
Bliss, James C., 52
Bliss, Peter Paul, 178, 234, 236, 286
Blue laws; *see* Moral reform outlook of revivalists; Prohibition; Sabbatarianism
Boardman, C. A., 60
Bob Jones College, 470, 485, 487
Bolsheviki, 446
Bonar, Andrew, 190
Bonar, Horatius, 190, 194, 200, 203, 205
Booth, Evangeline, 386
Booth, William, 184, 230 n., 391
Boston, revivals in, 60-78, 152, 155, 218, 223 ff., 263 ff., 305, 381, 491-92
Boyle, James, 132
British Evangelical Alliance, 476
British Evangelical Awakening of 1859-60, 183-84
British evangelists, 153, 159-60, 178, 183-84, 195-96, 198, 247, 489
British Isles, revivalism in, 152, 178-216, 183-84, 198, 202-3, 206, 263, 367, 479, 517-19
British Weekly, 517-18
Broadway Tabernacle, 83 n.
Brockway, J., 28-29
Brooks, Phillips, 219, 227 n.
Broun, Heywood, 426
Brown University, 428
Bryan, William Jennings, 278, 317, 327, 329, 396, 401, 407
Buckley, J. M., 343
Burch, Isaac H., 174
Burchard, Jedidiah, 26, 132, 133, 134, 144, 157
"Burned-over district" (western New York), 10, 20-23, 26 ff.

Bushnell, Horace, 149-52, 157, 280, 343, 454, 462, 472, 513
Business, revivalism as a, 166 ff., 216, 221 ff. (*see also* Professionalization of revivalism); revivalists' attitudes toward, 113-16, 252-57, 258, 363, 435-37, 509 (*see also* Protestant ethic); support for professional evangelism by, 94, 155-56, 163, 184, 215, 222-26, 230, 273, 301, 397, 402, 442-43 (*see also* Dodge; McCormick; Rockefeller; Stokes; Tappan; Wanamaker; *et al.*)
Byrd, Ralph, 468-69

Cadman, S. Parkes, 275, 370, 384
Calvinism, 8-11, 12, 13; breakdown of, 19 ff., 31 ff., 41, 44-47, 64, 65 ff., 98, 102, 120, 151, 161, 169
Camp meetings, 10, 12, 22-23, 79, 91, 92-94, 95, 99, 137, 238
Campbell, Alexander, 66
Campbellites, 22-23, 38, 66
Candler, Asa G., 354 ff., 369
Candler, Warren A., 354 ff., 366, 383, 385, 438, 443, 508
"Cannot-ism," 67 ff.
Carnegie, Andrew, 277
Catholic Church; *see* Anti-Catholicism; Roman Catholic Church
Causes of revivalism, 3-11, 54-57, 130-32, 168-69, 179-81, 184, 185-92, 196-97, 219 ff., 293 ff., 373, 400-402, 416 ff., 464 ff., 472 ff., 481 ff., 523-30
Chapin, Josiah, 60
Chapman, E. G., 380
Chapman, Wilbur J., 364, 377-78, 395, 404, 416, 481
Charteris, Archibald, 190, 192, 214
Chatham Street Chapel, 80, 94, 98, 110
Chicago, revivals in, 152-53, 155, 218, 223 ff., 263, 305
Children and revivals, 133, 149-52, 155-58, 232, 240
Choirs; *see* Music and musicians in revivalism
Choristers; *see* Music and musicians in revivalism
Christian, The, 181, 182, 185
Christian Century, The, 463, 502, 513, 518
Christian Lyre # 1, The, 99
Christian nurture, 149-52, 157, 280
Christian Science, 301, 336, 358, 374
Christian socialism; *see* Social gospel
Church membership; *see* Effects of revivalism
Churchill, Clinton H., 469
Circuit riders, 89, 285; *see also* Methodists
Civic federations, 341-42, 389; *see also* Law and Order Societies
Civil War, 106, 112 n., 162, 175, 238, 239, 283, 295, 357
Clark, Elmer T., 456-57
Clarke, Harry D., 422, 469
Cohan, George M., 426-27
Cohen, Mickey, 490
Commercialism in revivals, 137, 142-44, 221, 368, 376, 420 ff., 447-50, 460, 513 ff.
Concio ad Clerum (by N. W. Taylor), 45-46
Conference of Christian Workers, 183
Conformity; *see* Social conformity and social pressure in revivalism
Congregational Church, 8, 12, 13, 14, 15, 18, 19, 20, 22, 30, 33, 37, 45, 60, 62, 63, 77, 80, 93, 104, 122, 123, 128, 129, 135, 138, 146, 150, 171, 181, 243, 266, 300, 330, 344
Conrad, Arcturus Z., 380, 385, 392, 431
Consecration, 103-5, 112 n., 116, 117, 147-48, 249; *see also* Sanctification
Conservatism of revivalists; *see* Politics and revivalists; Social reform and revivalism
Converse, John H., 278, 369, 378-79, 442
Conversion, of the major evangelists, 16-17, 172, 284, 403-4, 484-85; psychology of, 68 ff., 85 ff., 113; social status of converts, 56, 266-67, 367-68, 429 ff.; statistics of, 57-58, 130, 145, 200 ff., 262-63, 334-35, 367, 370, 379, 392, 414-16, 429 ff., 458, 516 ff.; theological explanations of (*see* Theology of revivalism)
Covenant card; *see* Decision card
Cox, Samuel H., 50, 52, 59

Craig, George, 212
Creel, George, 440-41, 442
Criticism of revivals and revivalists; *see* Opposition to revivals
Croker, Richard, 278
Culpepper, Burke, 364, 391, 393
Cumberland Presbyterians, 22, 66
Cushman, R. W., 141
Cuyler, Theodore, 178, 218, 242

Dana, Daniel, 22 n.
Daniels, Josephus, 424
Darwinism, 10, 120, 151, 184, 213, 256, 274-75, 359, 362, 373, 411, 486, 503; *see also* Evolution; Social Darwinism
Davenport, James, 33, 91
Dawson, William J., 381, 393 n.
Debs, Eugene, 441
Debt, as a sin, 113-14, 309
Decision cards, 157, 264, 334 ff., 410, 450, 458 ff., 514
Decisions for Christ; *see* Conversion; Statistics of revivals; Trail-hitting
Decline of revival fervor, after 1831, 78, 144-49; after 1918, 10, 451 ff., 462 ff.
Deists, 9, 23, 24-25, 31, 38, 121, 138, 144, 269, 357
Delegation system, 424-26
Denominational rivalry; *see* Fundamentalism; Hopkinsianism; Modernism; Neofundamentalism; Nettleton; Schism; etc.
Denominational unity; *see* Evangelical unity
Devil, 18, 294, 373, 433, 508
Disciples of Christ, 300
Disestablishmentarianism, 186-88, 196, 213
Disinterested benevolence, 70, 102 ff., 106-7
District Combination Plan of revivalism, 331 ff.
Dixon, Amzi C., 352 ff., 366, 438
Dod, Albert B., 65, 84, 95, 96, 98, 145-46, 250 n., 278
Dodge, David L., 43 n., 46, 47, 50 ff., 218
Dodge, William E., 50 ff., 117 n., 177, 226, 229, 267 n., 278
Douglass, Frederick, 307
Drummond, Henry, 195, 216, 275
Duff, Alexander, 188-89
Duffield, George, 83
Dulles, John Foster, 506-7
Dutch Reformed Church, 9
Dwight, Timothy, 12, 19, 31, 96
Dwight, Timothy, Jr., 60

Earle, Absalom B., 153, 154-55
Economic aspects of revivalism; *see* Business; Financing of revivalism; Labor; Social reform
Economic reform and revivalism; *see* Social reform
Ecumenicalism; *see* Evangelical unity
Edinburgh, revivals in, 152, 185 ff., 200-201, 203-4, 205, 263 ff.
Edman, V. R., 475
Eddy, Mary Baker, 301, 358, 373
Edwards, Jonathan, 8, 11, 19, 31, 34, 35, 37, 74, 85, 90, 95, 105 n., 167, 365
Edwards, Justin, 44
Edwardseanism; *see* Calvinism; Hopkinsianism
Effects of revivalism, 3-11, 57-58, 144 ff., 167 n., 199 ff., 215-16, 262 ff., 270-71, 305-6, 334 ff., 349, 361, 367, 370, 414 ff., 429 ff., 452-54, 458 ff., 514 ff.
Ely, Ezra Stiles, 48, 49
Emancipator, The, 108
Emerson, Ralph W., 120
Emery, Allen G., 380
Emery, Allen G., Jr., 492
Emmons, Nathaniel, 19, 21, 74
Emotionalism in revivals, 28-29, 86 ff., 89-92, 93, 94, 127, 130-31, 137, 147, 193-94, 245, 250-52, 293, 433-34; *see also* Psychology of revivalism
Employer-employee relations; *see* Labor
Engels, Friedrich, 180
Episcopal Church, 243, 266, 300, 379
Evaluation of revivals, 3-11, 400, 523-30; *see also* Effects of revivalism
Evangelical Alliance, 37
Evangelical Union, 210, 212
Evangelical unity (evangelical assimilation), disrupted by revivals; promoted by revivals, 37-38, 54, 60, 107, 121, 135-36, 150, 154, 162,

169, 279, 300; *see also* Opposition to revivals; Schism
Evangelicalism, 6, 13, 37, 40, 54, 65, 67, 121, 125, 149, 161, 169, 186-87, 190, 197, 212, 215, 328, 349, 361, 393, 397, 446, 452, 529
Evangelists; *see* Finney; Graham; Moody; Sunday; *et al.*
Evolution, 10, 120, 151, 184, 197, 213, 256, 274-75, 352, 358, 359, 360, 373, 411, 433, 486, 503
Excell, E. O., 302, 377
Excitement in revivals; *see* Emotionalism in revivals
Exhorters, 23, 88, 91, 132; *see also* Itinerants
Expenses of revivalism; *see* Financing of revivalism
Experience religion, 72; *see also* "Heart religion"

Fairbairn, Patrick, 214
Faith-healing, 138
Farwell, John V., 174, 223, 225 n., 229, 267 n., 273, 313, 404
Fasting, 138
Faunce, W. H. P., 428
Federal Council of Churches, 10, 169, 348, 351, 395, 398-99, 449-50, 455, 463, 474, 476, 477-78
Ferrin, Howard W., 273
Field, Marshall, 273
Financing of revivalism, 26-27, 52, 80, 142 ff., 155, 184, 222, 224 ff., 301-2, 327-28, 332-33, 367 ff., 379 ff., 415-16, 423 ff., 447 ff., 457, 459, 462, 493 ff.; *see also* Remuneration of revivalists
Finney, Charles Grandison, and Beecher, 11-14, 30, 35 ff., 44 ff.; in Boston, 60-78; on business ethics, 113-16; on Calvinism, 18 ff., 23 ff., 42, 66 ff.; conversion of, 16; early years, 15-18; general estimate of, 11-15; on Hopkinsianism, 18 ff., 43-44, 65 ff., 102 ff.; on itinerant exhorters, 23, 132; later career of, 152, 163, 178; *Lectures on Revivals,* 65-66, 83 ff., 109, 420; *Memoirs,* 23, 25, 29, 41, 42, 53, 88, 112; on Methodists, 22-23, 88; on millennialism, 105-6, 111-12; and Moody, 166-70, 207-8, 211, 244, 246, 247-49, 280; and Nettleton, 33 ff.; and New Haven (or New School) theology, 11-14, 18, 20 ff., 44-47, 90, 104; new measures, 29, 34 ff., 42, 43, 46, 54-57, 85 ff., 130; in New York, 50 ff., 79 ff.; and Oberlin, 82, 110-11; perfectionism of, 103-5, 116, 148; on personal morality, 117-20; personality of, 16-17; in Philadelphia, 40, 42 ff.; on politics, 116-17; and Presbyterian Church, 41, 45 ff., 58-59, 78, 83-84, 100; professionalizes revivalism, 122, 127, 132; in Providence, 60; on psychology of conversion, 68 ff., 85 ff.; pulpit style of, 27 ff., 55-57, 88 ff.; results of, 144 ff.; in Rochester, 54 ff.; on science, 84 ff.; *Sermons on Various Subjects,* 65 ff., 83; on slavery, 108 ff.; on social reform, 100 ff., 107 ff., 113; and the Tappan brothers, 50, 53, 76, 79 ff., 108, 110, 112, 116; and N. W. Taylor, 11-14, 30, 35 ff., 45 ff.; on temperance, 54, 112; theology of, 18 ff., 35 ff., 40, 65 ff., 96, 97, 101-2, 149; on universalists and deists, 24-25; urban revivals of, 40 ff.; western revivals of, 27 ff.; and Westminster Confession, 23 ff., 66-68, 100; in Wilmington, 42; mentioned, 11, 127, 129, 144, 163, 165, 184, 190, 219, 267, 289, 290, 291, 355, 360, 406, 438, 453, 475, 504, 520, 528
Finneyism, 40, 51; *see also* Finney, theology of
First Great Awakening, 8-9, 12, 33, 122
Fitt, A. P., 368, 369 n., 371, 376-77
Foote, Horatio N., 26, 132
Formalization of revivalism, 13, 55, 96, 97, 121, 137 ff., 148, 153, 262, 400, 420 ff., 446 ff.
Fosdick, Harry Emerson, 446, 453, 483
Four-day meetings; *see* Protracted meetings
Fourth Great Awakening, 10, 472 ff., 521
Free Church of Scotland, 186 ff., 201 ff., 215
Free will; *see* Calvinism; New Haven theology; "New Heart" sermon; Westminster Confession of Faith

Free-will offering; *see* Remuneration of revivalists
Frick, Henry Clay, 424, 436
Frontier revivalism, 131-32; *see also* "Burned-over district"; Camp meetings; Exhorters
Frost, John, 30, 35
Fundamentalism, 10, 168, 176, 190, 212, 257, 346, 349-50, 361, 370, 372-73, 383, 384, 394, 397, 409, 433, 445, 453-54, 461, 462-63, 465 ff., 472, 476, 481 ff., 500-502
Fundamentals, The, 352, 377 n.

Gabriel, Charles H., 377
Gale, George, 18, 23-26, 29, 36, 40, 55
Garrison, William Lloyd, 108, 112 n.
Gary, Elbert H., 424
German Reformed Church, 9, 43, 48
Gilbert, E. W., 42-43
Gillett, Moses, 55
Gladden, Washington, 282, 313, 317, 329, 339, 340, 341, 343, 348, 396
Gladstone, William E., 199
Glasgow, revivals in, 195, 197, 201-2, 205, 208-9, 214, 263 ff., 518-19
God's World, 337
Gompers, Samuel, 270 n.
Goodell, Charles L., 455
Gospel Hymns, 234 ff.
Gospel singers; *see* Alexander; Music and musicians in revivalism; Rodeheaver; Sankey; Shea
Gould, Jay, 339
Gowan, A. G., 206
Graham, Sylvester, 118
Graham, William Franklin, Billy Graham Evangelistic Association, Inc., 494, 496; Billy Graham Team, 487, 495, 502; conversion of, 484-85; early career of, 484-89; finances of, 496-98; "Hour of Decision," 492-93, 495, 505; Los Angeles revival of, 489-91; opposition to, 501 ff.; revival methods of, 489 ff., 513 ff.; revival results of, 514 ff.; sermon styles of, 500; social and political views of, 503 ff., 521; theology of, 482-84, 500-501, 504, 507-8, 520; with Youth for Christ, 487-89; mentioned, 7, 10, 274 n., 291 n., 474, 528
Gray, James M., 381
Great Britain; *see* British Isles
Great Revivals and the Great Republic, 354-63
Greeley, Horace, 163
Green, Ashbel, 47, 48, 78
Green, Bryan, 489
Green, Samuel, 60
Greenwood, Laurence, 385
Griffin, Edward D., 78
Guaranty fund; *see* Financing of revivalism

Hall, Newman, 177, 206
Ham, Mordecai, 472, 484-85
Hamblen, Stuart, 490-91
Hamilton Seminary, 138, 140
Hammond, Edward Payson, 153, 155-57
Harvey, Joseph, 47
Hastings, Thomas, 99
Hawes, Joel, 44, 77, 78
Hawthorne, Nathaniel, 133
Haymaker, Willis G., 422, 495
Haymarket Riot, 269, 311-12
Hearst, William Randolph, 303, 480, 489
"Heart religion," 67; *see also* "New Heart" sermon
Heaven, 259, 433, 500
Hell, 16, 137, 140, 251, 372, 409, 433, 434, 500
Hellfire sermons, 89-90; *see also* Pulpit styles
Henry, Carl F. H., 475, 479
Henson, P. S., 282, 312, 327
Heresy, 14, 43, 45, 48, 49, 73-78, 81, 83, 150, 187-88, 190, 215-16, 298, 313, 340, 343
Herron, George D., 315, 339
Hewitt, Nathaniel, 47
Higher criticism, 181, 197, 275-76, 279, 358, 366, 373, 384, 394, 410-11, 503
Hillis, N. D., 327, 396, 526
Hitting the trail, 420, 425-26, 434-35; *see also* Effects of revivalism; Invitation to come forward; Statistics of revivals
Hodge, Charles, 75 n., 220, 274
Hogg, Quintin, 184

Holiness, 103-5, 116, 147-48, 249; *see also* Holiness Churches; Perfectionism
Holiness Churches, 464 ff.
Holmes, John Haynes, 409
Holton, Samuel S., 171
Home missions, 26, 123 ff., 158, 267, 272-74, 350, 363 ff., 378; *see also* Americanism; Immigrants and immigration
Hopkins, Samuel, 19, 31, 37, 70 n., 74, 102 ff., 252
Hopkinsianism, 15, 19 ff., 31, 32, 37, 44-45, 47, 77, 102, 146, 164
Horr, George E., 348-49
"Hour of Decision"; *see* Graham, William F.
Humor in revivals, 139-41, 241 ff., 287-88, 303, 320, 406-8
Humphrey, Heman, 44, 77, 146
Hurst, John F., 162
Hymns; *see* Music and musicians in revivalism
Hyper-Calvinism; *see* Calvinism
Hysteria in revivals, 28-29, 32, 90-92, 137-38, 245; *see also* Emotionalism in revivals; Psychology of revivalism

Immediate or instantaneous conversion, 96-98; *see also* "New Heart" sermon
Immigrants and immigration, 297, 310, 321, 358, 385, 390, 417, 443; *see also* Americanism; Home missions
Impact of revivalism; *see* Effects of revivalism
Industry and revivalism; *see* Business; Labor
Ingersoll, John, 132
Ingersoll, Robert, 407
Inquiry rooms, 98, 182, 193, 234, 244-46, 252, 259-62, 304, 369-70, 410, 434; *see also* Anxious meetings
Insanity and revivals, 91-92, 261-62
Institutionalization of revivalism, 122-65, 166, 183-84, 365, 381, 395, 420 ff., 445, 448, 450, 454, 489-502, 513 ff.; *see also* Professionalization of revivalism
Interdenominational aspects of revivalism, 37-38, 44, 64, 100, 135-36, 154, 184, 214, 219-21, 300; *see also* Evangelicalism
Interdemoninational Association of Evangelists, The, 365, 381, 395, 450, 454
Invitation to come forward, 56-57, 95 ff., 238, 304, 382, 385, 410, 434; *see also* Trail-hitting and Trail-hitters
Ireland, Archbishop John, 336
Itinerants (itinerant exhorts and evangelists), 22-23, 26, 88, 92-93, 122-65, 183-84, 196; *see also* Finney; Graham; Moody; Sunday; *et al.*

Jackson, Andrew, 100, 114, 117, 120, 131
Jeffrey, R. T., 214
Jesup, Morris K., 226
Jews, 267, 336, 341, 390, 417; *see also* Anti-Semitism
Jocelyn, Simeon, 99 n.
Johnson, Alba B., 442
Johnson, Torrey M., 475, 480, 483, 486, 487
Jones, Bob, Sr., 470, 475, 495
Jones, Rufus M., 379
Jones, Samuel Milton ("Golden Rule"), 314-26, 329, 339, 414, 453
Jones, Samuel Porter, Americanism of, 310, 362; compared to Finney, 291-92; compared to Moody, 282, 287, 288, 291, 300-301, 313; early career of, 283-87; general estimate of, 282-83, 345-46; on labor, 311-12; on Negroes, 306-7, 310; personality of, 288; on politics, 310-11; on prohibition, 318 ff., 328 ff., 311-12; on the Protestant ethic, 308-10; results of, 305-6; revival methods of, 300-305, 327-28; on social and moral reform, 289-99, 308, 314; style of, 288-89, 303, 326-27; theology of, 290-300; Toledo revival of, 314, 318-26; mentioned, 342, 354, 386, 387, 391, 406, 411, 412, 413, 414, 427, 510, 520

Kelley, David, 295
Kelman, John, 191, 192, 205
Kernahan, A. Earl, 457-61, 465
Kincheloe, Samuel C., 463-64, 465
Kinnaird, Arthur, 184, 194, 367

Kirk, E. N., 153, 171-72
Kittrell, John, 374
Knapp, Jacob, 136-37, 140-44, 152, 154, 157
Ku Klux Klan, 444
Kuhlman, Katherine, 469

Labor, attitude toward, by revivalists, 114-16, 189, 267-71, 274, 297, 309, 311-12, 338-40, 350, 355-58, 362, 384, 385, 395, 440 ff., 459, 504; *see also* Protestant ethic
Lane Seminary, 81-82, 111, 330
Law and Order Societies, 329, 342, 387
Lawrence, Amos A., 225, 227 n.
Lay Evangelism, 129, 184, 220
Leavitt, Joshua, 59, 76, 99, 108, 109, 147
Leckey, W. E. H., 355-56
Lectures on Revivals (Finney), 65-66, 83 ff., 100, 104, 105, 109, 145, 420
Lectures on Revivals (Sprague), 13, 78, 128 ff.
Leland, John, 402
Levering, Joshua, 301
Liberal Protestantism; *see* Modernism
Liebman, Joshua L., 474
Lincoln, Abraham, 112 n.
Literary and Theological Review, 14, 125
Littlejohn, Augustus, 26, 132, 133
Locke, John, 24, 67
Loeb, Philip, 448
London, revivals in, 152, 196, 202-3, 206, 263, 367, 517-18
Los Angeles, revivals in, 489-91
Los Angeles Bible Institute, 369, 420
Lowe, David, 185
Ludlow, S. B., 48-49, 59
Ludlow Massacre, 440
Lutheran Church, 379

McCarthyism, 511
McCormick, Cyrus, 174, 177, 225
McCormick, Cyrus, Jr., 273, 311, 404
McCosh, James, 219, 220
MacFarland, Charles S., 370
McGranahan, James, 234
McIntire, Carl, 474
Aimee Semple, 469
78, 81, 132, 163
oger, 479-80
0, 315

Mason, Lowell, 99
Masons, 138, 252
Masses, The, 441
Masses, reaching the, 179-80, 190, 191, 195, 199, 200, 203, 205-6, 267-71, 307, 341, 357, 363, 432 ff., 439, 459
Matheson, Hugh, 184, 196
Mechanics of revivalism; *see* Methods of revivalism
Membership; *see* Effects of revivalism
Men and Religion Forward Movement, 396
Mencken, H. L., 466
Merriam, E. F., 371
Merwin, Samuel, 60
Methodist Christian Advocate (Nashville), 299, 354
Methodist Christian Advocate (New York), 343
Methodists, 9, 12, 22-23, 57-88, 91, 97, 138, 158, 160, 174, 181, 219, 238, 243, 268, 283 ff., 295, 300, 305, 315, 354, 357, 358, 398
Methods of revivalism, 29 ff., 34 ff., 85-100, 124 ff., 148 ff., 194-95 ff., 221 ff., 300, 301-3, 331 ff., 378 ff., 420 ff., 492 ff.; *see also* Advertising; Delegation system; District Combination Plan; Financing; New Measures; Professionalization of; Pulpit styles; Simultaneous evangelistic campaigns; Tabernacle evangelism; Visitation evangelism
Meyer, F. B., 181
Mildmay Christian Conference, 177
Millennialism, 104-6, 111-12, 121, 169, 256 ff., 313, 355 n., 360-61, 385, 390 n., 396, 435, 446, 466, 471, 501, 509-10
Miller, William, 105-6
Mills, Benjamin Fay, compared to Moody, 329, 331-32, 339, 341; District Combination Plan of, 331 ff.; early career of, 330-37; general estimate of, 282-83, 329-30, 345-46, 349; leaves revivalism, 344-45, 399 n.; results of, 335-36; theology and social views of, 337 ff.; mentioned, 348, 365, 370, 377, 378, 394, 436
Ministry, changing concept of, 9, 87-88, 122-32, 149-52, 450-451

Missions; *see* Home missions
Mitchell, William, 125-29
Modernism, 10, 106, 150, 168, 257, 346, 363, 397, 410-11, 445-46, 453, 464-65, 472, 476, 483, 503, 509 ff., 525, 527
Moody Bible Institute, 272 ff., 366, 369, 371, 373-74, 376, 378, 421, 470, 487
Moody Church, 176, 229, 352, 366
Moody, Dwight Lyman, on Americanization, 267; in British Isles, 178 ff.; compared to Finney, 166-70, 207-8, 211, 246, 249, 250 n., 252, 253, 280; contemporary criticism of, 197-98; conversion of, 172; early life of, 170-78; Edinburgh revival of, 185 ff., 200 ff.; Engels on, 180; and evolution, 274-75, 213; expenses of revivals of, 184, 222, 224 ff.; general estimate of, 166-70, 180-81, 182; on higher criticism, 275-76, 279; later career of, 271-72; in London, 196-200, 202-3; methods of, 182, 194-95, 206-7, 217 ff., 221 ff., 230 ff., 259 ff., 271; Moody Bible Institute, 272-74; on Negroes, 306; personality of, 174-75, 230; and Plymouth Brethren, 177, 257-58; on politics, 278-79; premillennialism of, 167, 169, 256 ff.; on the Protestant ethic, 252 ff.; pulpit style of, 239 ff., 251 ff.; Queen Victoria on, 198; results of, 199 ff., 215-16, 262 ff., 270-71; and Sankey (*see* Sankey); G. B. Shaw on, 197; on social gospel, 276-77; on social reform, 257 ff., 269 ff., 276 ff.; on temperance, 232-33; theology of, 210 ff., 246 ff., 261 ff.; and YMCA, 174-78, 229; mentioned, 10, 90, 153, 155, 156, 160, 164-65, 288, 291, 313, 329, 331-32, 341, 348-49, 352, 353, 355, 357, 358-59, 360, 362, 366, 375, 377, 378, 379, 384, 386, 423, 427, 435, 456, 499, 520, 528
Moorehouse (or Moorhouse), Henry, 153, 159-60, 178, 183, 247
Moral reform outlook of revivalists, 31, 54, 100 ff., 106 ff., 112-20, 146, 170, 210, 252 ff., 259 ff., 271 ff., 286, 287, 289-99, 308, 314, 328-29, 336-37, 345-46, 373-74, 377 ff., 383-87, 397-99, 411-12, 414, 432-33, 435 ff., 453 ff., 521, 526-27; *see also* Prohibition
Moral suasion, 74-76
Morgan, J. P., 225, 226
Morgan, Richard Cope, 177, 181, 196, 225 n.
Mormonism, 139, 358, 362
Mourner's bench, 95, 287; *see also* Anxious seat
Munhall, Leander W., 381
Murch, James DeForest, 479-80
Music and musicians in revivalism, 99, 178, 192-93, 222, 229, 233-39, 302, 334, 367, 374-77, 381, 383, 389, 394, 405, 421-22, 481, 486, 487, 489, 493, 494, 498; *see also* Alexander; Barrows; Rodeheaver; Sankey; Shea
Myrick, Luther, 26, 30, 132, 133-36, 144, 501

Nash, Daniel, 26, 132
National Association of Evangelicals, 474-83, 486, 487, 501, 503
National Council of Churches, 502; *see also* Federal Council of Churches
Navigators, The, 514
Nearing, Scott, 441
Needham, George C., 153, 159-60
Negroes and revivalism, 100, 108 ff., 162, 170, 293, 306-7, 310, 467, 472, 504-5
Nehru, Jawaharlal, 507
Neo-Calvinism; *see* Calvinism
Neo-Edwardseanism; *see* Hopkinsianism
Neofundamentalism, 472 ff., 483, 500-501, 503
Neo-orthodoxy, 474, 476, 482, 483, 501, 503
Nettleton, Asahel, career of, 32-33; and Finney, 33 ff., 44-45, 50, 51; theology of, 32-33; mentioned, 30, 43, 46, 53, 78, 95, 99 n., 122, 126, 128 n., 135, 355, 365
New Divinity, 13, 54, 78, 81, 96, 121, 136, 147, 151; *see also* New Haven theology
New Divinity Tried, The, 64 ff.
New Evangelism, The, 456

"New Evangelism," 341, 350, 452, 455-56
New Haven theology (Beecherism, New Divinity, Taylorism), 10, 13, 14, 20 ff., 31-33, 38-39, 44-47, 48 n., 63, 67, 90, 104, 123
"New Heart" sermon, 65 ff., 84, 87, 91, 103, 140
New Lebanon Convention, 37 ff., 44, 45, 64, 77, 81, 96, 127
New Lights, 9
New measures in revivals, 29, 34 ff., 42, 43, 46, 54-57, 58, 80, 85-100, 124-25, 130, 136, 149, 154-65, 182, 194-95, 206-7, 217 ff., 221 ff., 230 ff., 259 ff., 271, 331 ff., 378 ff., 420 ff.; *see also* Methods of revivalism; Professionalization of revivalism
New School (Presbyterian and Congregational), 10, 65, 83, 104, 123, 138, 161, 168, 172, 186
New York City, revivals in, 50 ff., 79 ff., 152, 160, 163, 218, 223 ff., 263, 416, 424, 430
New York Evangelist, The, 52, 76, 109, 145, 147, 152
Newton, Joseph Fort, 413
Next Great Awakening, The, 351-52
Niagara Bible Conference, 349
Niebuhr, Reinhold, 472, 474, 503-4, 521
Norris, J. Frank, 471, 484
Northwestern Schools, 488
Norton, Herman G., 26, 52, 59
Noyes, John Humphrey, 104, 118

Oberlin College, 82-83, 104, 110-11, 118, 120, 152
Oberlin Evangelist, The, 106
Oberlin Perfectionism, 103-6, 147, 136
Ockenga, Harold J., 475, 477-78, 482, 483, 491
Old School (Presbyterian and Hopkinsian), 10, 15, 65, 98, 104, 122, 146, 147, 149, 152, 161, 330, 343
Oneida Evangelical Association, 26-27, 52
Oneida Perfectionism, 104, 118
[illegible]tion to revivals, 28-30, 33 ff., 51-
[illegible]50-62, 64-66, 73 ff., 93,
[illegible]44, 146-52, 194-98, 279-
[illegible]324, 347 ff., 367-70, 381-
[illegible]440-42, 446-48, 501 ff.
Ordination of evangelists, 31, 123-29, 408, 486
Ott, J. M. P., 220
Ottman, Ford C., 220
Our Country, 351
Overtoun, Lord; *see* White, James C.
Owen, Robert, 116

Pacific Garden Mission, 403-4, 409, 448
Paley, William, 120
Palmer, A. Mitchell, 444
Park, Edwards A., 89
Park Street Church, 63, 380, 477, 491
Parker, Joel, 52, 54, 57, 58
Parker, Theodore, 115
Parkhurst, C. H., 279, 327
Pastoral evangelism, 350, 455
Patriotism; *see* Americanism
Patterson, James, 40, 43
Peace with God, 498, 505
Peale, Norman Vincent, 474, 503, 520, 521, 526
Pelagianism, 107, 434, 503
Pennefeather, William, 177, 181
Penrose, Boies, 387
Pentecost, George F., 348
Pentecostal churches, 464 ff.
Perfectionism, 101, 103-4, 112 n., 116, 117, 132, 136, 147-48, 169, 171, 249, 439, 464-65, 503, 528
Perkins, Ephraim, 28
Perkins, Nathan, 47, 78
Personal evangelism; *see* Visitation evangelism
Personal reform; *see* Moral reform outlook of revivalists; Prohibition; Temperance
Personal workers, 98, 223, 334
Personality of major revivalists, 27 ff., 55-57, 88 ff., 137-44, 154-59, 193, 239 ff., 251 ff., 283, 288-89, 303 ff., 330, 337, 371, 385, 389, 391, 392, 406 ff., 426 ff., 500
Phelps, Anson, G., 50 ff., 218
Philadelphia, revivals in, 40, 42-52, 218, 223 ff., 263 ff., 369 ff., 416, 429, 430
Philadelphian, The, 48
Phillips, Philip, 178, 234
Pietism, 5, 6, 7, 8, 9, 13, 41, 59, 66, 76 n., 102, 117, 120, 131-32, 176,

207, 241, 257, 293, 410, 439, 464 ff., 481, 503
Pinch, Pearse, 419-420
Plan of Union, 15, 18, 37, 100, 123
Platt, Jonas, 50
Platt, Zephaniah, 50 ff.
Plymouth Brethren, 177, 257-58, 193 n.
Politics and revivalists, 3-4, 5, 13, 35-36, 43, 116-17, 130-32, 139, 278-79, 288-89, 294 ff., 299, 310-11, 319 ff., 329, 346, 444, 503 ff.
"Popery"; *see* Anti-Catholicism
Porter, Ebenezer, 35, 47
Porter, Noah, 78
Postmillennialism, 115-16, 167; *see also* Millennialism; Social gospel
Potter, Henry C., 220, 242
Prayer meetings, 98, 138, 192, 195, 231-32
Prayer Meeting Revival of 1857–58, 162-64, 173, 183, 463
Premillennialism, 105-6, 167, 169, 213, 256-59, 349, 353, 360-61, 374, 396, 434, 438-39, 446, 509 ff.; *see also* Millennialism
Presbygationalism; *see* Plan of Union
Presbyterian Church, 8, 9, 12, 13, 15, 16, 18, 20, 22, 23, 33, 37, 38, 41, 42 ff., 45, 52, 57, 58-59, 65, 66, 78, 81, 83-84, 88, 93, 98, 100, 104, 123, 129, 135-36, 144, 145, 161, 181, 183, 185 ff., 220, 265, 300, 313, 340, 344, 378
Presbyterian Quarterly and Princeton Review, 220, 246
Presbyterian schism of 1837, 10, 15, 65, 78, 112 n., 122, 125, 144, 161
Princeton College and Seminary, 18, 24, 46, 47, 65, 66, 75, 77, 83, 84, 129, 147, 149, 171, 220, 246, 393, 428
Professional evangelists; *see* Finney; Graham; Moody; Sunday; *et al.*
Professionalization of revivalism, 13, 120-21, 122-65, 166, 183-84, 217-33, 365, 381, 395, 420 ff., 445, 448 ff., 450, 454, 489-502
Progressive orthodoxy, 150
Progressive revelation, 101, 108
Progressivism, 363, 397, 402 n., 411, 437, 452
Prohibition, 138, 294, 295 ff., 318 ff., 323, 328 ff., 342, 363, 373-74, 386-87, 393, 396, 397, 412-13, 439-40, 453, 454
Prostitution, 156, 189, 210, 233, 414
Protestant ethic, 113 ff., 252, 267, 270, 308-10, 364, 435 ff., 471
Protracted meetings, 57, 92 ff., 124, 129-30, 137, 162
Providence, revivals in, 60, 152, 266, 331
Publicity in revivalism; *see* Advertising
Pulpit styles of major revivalists, 27 ff., 55-57, 88 ff., 137-44, 154-59, 193, 239 ff., 251 ff., 283, 288-89, 303 ff., 330 ff., 337, 371, 385, 389, 391, 392, 406 ff., 426 ff., 500
Puritanicalism; *see* Moral reform; Prohibition
Psychology of revivalism, 6, 68-73, 84 ff., 90-91, 113, 183, 245, 250-52, 261-62; *see also* Emotionalism in revivals

Quakers, 336, 379
Quarterly Christian Spectator, 127, 150

Racism; *see* Americanism; Anglo-Saxon racism; Negroes and revivalism
Radcliffe, Reginald, 184, 195
Rader, Luke, 469, 472
Rader, Paul, 469, 472
Rainy, Robert, 190
Rand, Asa, 64 ff., 73
Reed, John, 441
Rees, A. A., 181
Rees, Paul S., 475, 501
Reflections on the End of an Era, 472-73
Reform, and reformers, 3-4, 54, 82, 102-20, 130-32, 148, 162, 170, 310-11, 503 ff., 521; *see also* Moral reform outlook of revivalists; Prohibition; Social reform
Religion in America, 462
"Religious affections," 86 ff.
Remuneration of revivalists, 26-27, 80, 127, 142-44, 155, 228-30, 327-28, 333, 368, 395, 447-48, 450, 498
Results of revivalism; *see* Effects of revivalism
Revell, Fleming H., 174, 267 n., 301, 313

Revival hymns; *see* Music and musicians in revivalism
Revivals, analysis of (general), 3-11, 400, 445, 523-30; British revival of 1859–60, 183-84, 198; *see also* First Great Awakening; Second Great Awakening; etc.
Riggs, Ralph M., 468
Riley, William Bell, 381, 472, 485, 488
Ritualism, 189, 196
Roberts, Oral, 489
Rochester, Finney's revival in, 54 ff.
Rockefeller, John D., Jr., 402, 424, 429, 436, 448, 454
Rodeheaver, Homer A., 381, 394, 421-22, 495
Rollings, E. J., 469
Roman Catholic Church, 30, 220, 267, 300, 301, 336, 341, 358, 362, 382, 385-86, 417, 444, 479, 483; *see also* Anti-Catholicism
Roosevelt, Theodore, 371, 397, 401, 402, 427
Rosell, Mervin, 489
Ross, Richard, 492, 493

Sabbatarianism, 31, 270, 286, 297, 312, 318, 321
Sacramental meetings, 92
Sacred Songs and Solos, 234 ff.
Sacrilege, 234, 428; *see also* Vulgarity
Salvation; *see* Conversion
Salvation Army, 159, 230 n., 459
Sanctification, 103-5, 112 n., 116, 117, 147-48, 249
Sandburg, Carl, 441-42
Sankey, Ira David, 154, 178, 182, 192-93, 222, 228, 229, 233-39, 306, 391
Sawdust trail, 410; *see also* Trail-hitting
Schism, 10, 14-15, 59, 65, 66, 77-78, 97, 112 n., 122, 125, 144, 149, 161, 168-69, 187, 279, 346, 353; *see also* Fundamentalism; Modernism; Social gospel
Schuyler, Hamilton, 448
Science, 68-73, 84 ff., 101, 120-21, 167, 181, 189, 213-14, 219, 274-75, 352, [illegible] 373, 411; *see also* Evolution
[illegible] 66
[illegible] vals in, 185 ff.
[illegible] mon Sense Philosophy,

Second blessing; *see* Perfectionism
Second Coming of Christ; *see* Millennialism
Second Great Awakening, 9-11, 12, 22, 122, 131, 144 ff.
Secret of Happiness, The, 498
Sectarian rivalry, 38-39, 184, 243
Secularization of revivalism, 102 ff., 107, 181, 452-53
Segregation in revivalism; *see* Negroes and revivalism
Sentimentalism, 140, 154-55, 235-36, 239 ff., 250-51
Sermon styles; *see* Pulpit styles
Sermons on Various Subjects, 83
Shaftesbury, Seventh Earl of, 177, 179-80, 184, 199, 267
Shea, George Beverly, 486, 489, 493
Sheen, Bishop Fulton J., 474
Shorey, J. H., 232
Showmanship; *see* Advertising; Personality of major revivalists; Pulpit styles
Shuler, Bob, 472, 475
Shuler, Jack, 489
Simultaneous evangelistic campaigns, 378 ff., 394
Sin; *see* Moral reform outlook of revivalism
Sinclair, Upton, 441
Singing in revivals; *see* Music and musicians in revivalism
"Sinners Bound to Change Their Own Hearts," 65 ff.
Skinner, Thomas H., 43, 45, 49
Slang, 287, 389, 391, 406 ff., 427-29
Slavery, 82, 107 ff., 139, 162, 294-95; *see also* Negroes and revivalism
Slum meetings, 195, 393
Small, Sam, 295 n.
Smith, Alfred E., 444
Smith, Fred B., 396
Smith, Sir George Adam, 167 n., 202, 216, 275-76
Smith, Gerald L. K., 471
Smith, Nathaniel, 26, 30, 132
Smith, Rodney ("Gypsy"), 364, 391-93, 395, 396, 416, 455
Smith, William Robertson, 190, 215, 216
Social conformity and social pressure, in revivalism, 13, 95-96, 301, 326, 346, 361 ff., 443 ff., 511

Social Creed of the Churches, 399
Social Darwinism, 106, 257, 309-10, 345, 358, 360, 362, 433
Social gospel, 106, 114, 150, 168, 220, 276, 283, 312-13, 329, 337 ff., 342, 347 ff., 357, 359, 397-99, 437, 452, 476, 500
Social reform and revivalism, 3, 4, 5, 36, 53, 54, 100 ff., 107 ff., 113-16, 131-32, 170, 252 ff., 256 ff., 269 ff., 276 ff., 288-99, 306-26, 337 ff., 351 ff., 359, 383-87, 397-99, 411-12, 432-33, 435 ff., 453 ff., 504, 526-27; *see also* Social gospel
Social service, 353 ff., 363, 383, 393, 396, 398-99
Socialism, 180, 197, 297-98, 337-38, 353, 358, 385, 395, 398
"Society" attacked by revivalists, 57, 118-19, 308
Specialization of revivalism; *see* Professionalization
Spencer, Herbert, 257, 309, 345; *see also* Social Darwinism
Sperry, Willard E., 462, 464, 465
Spirit of the Pilgrims, The, 62 n., 64, 77, 130
Spiritual Unrest, The, 416
Sprague, F. W., 339
Sprague, William B., 50-53, 59, 79, 81
Spurgeon, Charles H., 177
Statistics of revivals, 57-58, 130, 145, 200 ff., 262-63, 334-35, 367, 370, 379, 392, 414-16, 429 ff., 458, 516 ff.; *see also* Effects of revivalism
Stebbins, George C., 234
Stelzle, Charles, 197-98, 416-17, 448, 451, 454
Stimson, Henry A., 424
Stoddard, Solomon, 7
Stokes, Anson Phelps, 226
Stone, Barton W., 66
Stoneites, 22, 38
Storefront churches, 468 ff.
Story, Joseph, 225, 227 n.
Stough, Henry W., 381, 449, 451
Stowe, Harriet Beecher, 96
Strong, Josiah, 350 ff., 358, 361
Stuart, Alexander Moody, 190
Stuart, George H., 156, 177, 178, 218, 225 n., 229, 242
Stuart, Moses, 35
Student Volunteer Movement, 272
Success myth; *see* Protestant ethic
Sunday, William Ashley, on Americanism, 443 ff.; conversion of, 403-4; decline of, 445 ff.; early career of, 403-9; on evolution, 411; general estimate of, 400-402; methods of, 420-26; personality of, 405-6; popularity of, 416 ff.; on prohibition, 413, 439-40; on the Protestant ethic, 435 ff.; pulpit style of, 406 ff., 426 ff.; results of, 414 ff., 429 ff.; on social and moral reform, 411-12, 432-33, 435 ff.; on the social gospel, 399, 411; theology of, 409 ff., 433; mentioned, 10, 86 n., 291 n., 345, 364, 377, 388, 389, 390 n., 391, 393, 395, 399, 455, 456, 481, 485, 492, 495, 508, 510, 520, 528
Sunday, Mrs. William A., 404
Sunday Party, the, 421 ff., 447
Swan, Jabez, 136-40, 142, 152
Swedenborgianism, 139, 336
Swing, David, 312-13
Systematic Theology, 104

Tabernacle evangelism, 154, 196, 223-28, 271, 301, 349, 424-25, 451
Talmage, T. DeWitt, 219, 242, 287, 327, 526
Tappan, Arthur, 50, 53, 108, 110, 116
Tappan, Lewis, 50, 53, 54, 58, 76, 79 ff., 108, 110, 112
Tawney, Richard H., quoted, 342
Taylor, Nathaniel W., theology of, 45-47, 63-64, 67, 77, 90, 104, 105, 127; mentioned, 11, 12, 13, 14, 31, 38; *see also* New Haven theology
Taylor, William, 153, 159-60, 196
Taylorism, 46, 67; *see also* New Haven theology
Temperance, 54, 112, 138, 139-40, 189, 210, 232-33, 253-54, 276, 284 ff., 294, 297, 358, 385; *see also* Prohibition
Templeton, Charles, 475, 489
Tennent, Gilbert, 126
Tenney, Caleb J., 44, 46, 78
Tents, 156, 287, 301
Theatrics; *see* Pulpit styles of major revivalists
Theistic evolution, 10, 151, 257; *see also* Evolution

Theology of revivalism, 3, 18 ff., 31-32, 35 ff., 40, 41, 65 ff., 84 ff., 96, 97, 101-2, 113, 149, 154-55, 210 ff., 246 ff., 260 ff., 290-300, 337 ff., 372-73, 409 ff., 433, 482-84, 500-501, 504, 507-8, 520
Third Great Awakening, 10, 168-69, 345-46, 347 ff., 451 ff.
Thomas, H. W., 312
Thomson, Andrew, 194
Thoreau, Henry D., 116
Tocqueville, Alexis de, 9
Toledo, revival in, 314, 318-26
Torrey, Reuben Archer, 273, 364, 366-67, 382, 384, 385, 388, 416
Towner, D. B., 377
Trade unions, 267-71, 311-12, 363, 440; *see also* Labor
Trail-hitting and trail-hitters, 415-16, 425-26, 434-35; *see also* Effects of revivalism
"Triangularism," 44, 48 n.; *see also* Hopkinsianism
Tyler, Bennet, 32, 46, 63, 78

"Ultraism," 130, 132, 146
Unemployment, 254-56; *see also* Labor
"Union meetings" for revivals, 154, 161, 285, 420 n.
Union Theological Seminary, 155, 501
Unions; *see* Trade unions
Unitarians, 9, 28, 30, 31, 38, 39, 41, 53, 61, 63, 81, 138, 150, 152, 160, 171, 172, 212, 220, 221, 264, 280, 336, 343, 344, 411
United Evangelical Action, 477-79, 501
United Presbyterians, 186 ff., 199 ff.
United States Christian Commission, 175
Unity of denominations promoted by revivals, 13, 135-36, 154, 161, 162, 169, 181, 184, 189-90, 191, 192, 193, 214, 219-21, 300
Universalists, 22-23, 24-25, 38, 138, 139, 142, 220, 336
Unpardonable sin, 154
Urban problems and revivalism, ... 296-98, 416 ff.
... of revivalism, 13, 40 ff., ... ff., 95, 166 ff.
... , 102-3, 107
... C., 279-81

Van Cott, Maggie, 153, 158-59
Van Valkenberg, E. A., 387
Vanderbilt, Cornelius, II, 225, 226
Varley, Henry, 153, 159-60, 183, 196
Vaus, J. Arthur, 490-91
Visitation evangelism, 264, 456-62
Volunteer, The, 64
Vulgarity, 141, 194, 219, 287, 308, 348; *see also* Pulpit styles of major revivalists; Slang

Walker, W. N., 429
Wallace, Robert, 187-88, 210
Wanamaker, John, 177, 218, 223, 224 n., 269 n., 275, 278-79, 369, 377, 379, 387, 424
Wanamaker, Rodman, 387
Ward, Isaac, 442
Wars and revivals, 6-7
Watchman-Examiner, 348, 382, 401, 443
Weld, Theodore, 41, 47, 51, 55, 78, 79, 82, 108, 111, 112, 132
Wesley, John, 103, 104 n., 126, 355-56, 360, 438
Westminster Confession of Faith, 18-19, 20, 23 ff., 38, 41, 48, 66, 68, 81, 123, 135, 186-87, 190, 192, 209-10, 212-13
Wheaton College (Illinois), 470, 486
Whelpley, Samuel, 44, 48 n.
White, James C. (Lord Overtoun), 184, 277-78, 279
Whitefield, George, 8, 126, 355-56, 365, 438, 453
Whitlock, Brand, 324, 414
Whitman, Walt, 120
Whittle, D. W., 286
Willard, Frances, 232-33
Williams, Milan B., 364, 375, 389-91, 393, 405, 406, 411
Wilmington, revivals in, 42, 51
Wilson, George (of Edinburgh), 204
Wilson, George (of Minneapolis), 480, 488, 494
Wilson, Grady, 484, 493, 494
Wilson, J. H., 192, 205
Wilson, James P., 43, 45, 48
Wilson, T. W., 484, 488
Wilson, Woodrow, 401, 440
Winona Lake Bible Conference, 365, 378, 480
Winrod, Gerald B., 471

Wise, Stephen W., 441
Wisner, Benjamin B., 62, 73-75
Wittman, Karl, 469
Woods, Leonard, 14 n., 35, 47, 77
Workingman and revivals; *see* Labor; Immigrants and immigration; Effects of revivalism
World Evangelical Fellowship, 476
World Wide Evangelism, 367, 388, 507
World Wide Films, Inc., 492
Wright, Benjamin, 16
Wright, Elwin J., 475, 481
Wyrtzen, Jack, 479 n.

Yale Seminary, 15, 31, 64, 104, 150
YMCA, 174-78, 222, 229, 271, 273, 276, 315, 404, 439

Zamperini, Louis, 490-91